EMPLOYMENT LAW IN CHINA

This book provides clear and concise explanations to over 200 questions on China's current employment laws. It helps readers answer the question: "What are my rights and what should I do?" in given practical situations.

Adopting a question-and-answer format, the book covers a wide range of topics including labor dispute procedures, employer obligations and immunities, employee entitlements, work injuries, wages, misconduct, and termination. In addition to employment law, the book also includes interdisciplinary material on trade secrets, non-competition, personal information protection, and administrative and criminal liabilities.

The book provides advice in the form of direct answers that set out the statutory principles, legal analysis, conclusion, and comments. It carefully selects and cites over one thousand court cases to illustrate employment law practice and the legal consequences of specific issues. It also distinguishes the different local regulations and judicial practices across provinces and cities.

This book is written for readers who are familiar with general concepts but may not have formal knowledge of the law. To this purpose, it will be a valuable resource for business owners, employees, and HR specialists. It will also appeal to legal scholars and professionals who provide corporate legal counsel.

Dong Wang is a barrister and solicitor in New Zealand. He is a former part-time employment arbitrator of the Shenzhen Employment Dispute Arbitration Committee, a member of the Guangdong Employment Law Society, and an expert witness on Chinese employment law for the Supreme Court of Queensland, Australia, with extensive theoretical and practical experience.

Peng Zhao is the director of Royal Law Firm, China. He has extensive practical experience in employment dispute cases, including the 2016 Linak case before the Supreme Court of China. He is also highly experienced as corporate legal counsel for business operations, covering commercial law, company law, and intellectual property law.

EMPLOYMENT LAW IN CHINA

A PRACTICAL GUIDE

DONG WANG AND PENG ZHAO

informa law
from Routledge

Cover image and design by Addison Zheng

First published 2025
by Informa Law from Routledge
4 Park Square, Milton Park, Abingdon, Oxon OX14 4RN

and by Informa Law from Routledge
605 Third Avenue, New York, NY 10158

Informa Law from Routledge is an imprint of the Taylor & Francis Group, an informa business

British Library Cataloguing-in-Publication Data
A catalogue record for this book is available from the British Library

Library of Congress Cataloging-in-Publication Data
Names: Wang, Dong, (Lawyer), author. | Zhao, Peng, (Lawyer), author.
Title: Employment law in China : a practical guide / Dong Wang and Peng Zhao.
Description: 1. | New York : Routledge, 2025. | Includes bibliographical references and index.
Identifiers: LCCN 2024053693 | ISBN 9781032951256 (paperback) |
ISBN 9781032951294 (hardback) | ISBN 9781003583301 (ebook)
Subjects: LCSH: Labor contract–China. | Labor laws and legislation–China. |
Confidential business information–Law and legislation–China.
Classification: LCC KNQ1279 .W36 2025 | DDC 344.5101–dc23/eng/20241205
LC record available at https://lccn.loc.gov/2024053693

ISBN: 9781032951294 (hbk)
ISBN: 9781032951256 (pbk)
ISBN: 9781003583301 (ebk)

DOI: 10.4324/9781003583301

Typeset in Times New Roman
by Deanta Global Publishing Services, Chennai, India

CONTENTS

Preface		ix
Glossary of Common Terms		xi
CHAPTER 1	EMPLOYMENT RELATIONS	1
	Introduction	1
1.1	Employment Relations: Principle and Classification	1
1.2	Difference between Employment and Contract Relations	13
1.3	Special Types of Workers and Work Relations	22
1.4	Labor Dispute Procedure	30
CHAPTER 2	EMPLOYMENT COMMENCEMENT	43
	Introduction	43
2.1	Employer Obligations at the Start	43
2.2	Double-Wage Damages and Employer Immunity	51
2.3	Calculation of Double-Wage Damages	62
2.4	Probation Period and Validity of Employment	81
CHAPTER 3	EMPLOYEE ENTITLEMENTS	96
	Introduction	96
3.1	Employee Leaves and Special Entitlements	96
3.2	Sick Leave and Female Employee Rights	115
3.3	Employers Handling Work Injuries	128
3.4	Employee Entitlements for Work Injuries	144
CHAPTER 4	PERFORMANCE OF EMPLOYMENT CONTRACT	157
	Introduction	157
4.1	Wage Entitlements, Calculation, and Payment	157
4.2	Employer Management and Disciplinary Actions	168
4.3	Strike, Equity Incentive, and Employer Misconduct	188
CHAPTER 5	EMPLOYMENT TERMINATION	207
	Introduction	207
5.1	Resignation, Retirement, and Party Demise	208
5.2	Employer-Initiated Employment Termination	228

5.3 Calculation of Termination Compensations 247
5.4 Other Issues for Employment Termination 258

CHAPTER 6 TRADE SECRETS AND NON-COMPETITION 272
Introduction 272
6.1 Trade Secret Protection 272
6.2 Non-Competition 302
6.3 Personal Information Protection 311

CHAPTER 7 SUMMARY AND PRACTICAL GUIDELINES 320
Introduction 320
7.1 Principles of Conduct in Employment Relationships 320
7.2 Collective Contracts and Individual Contracts 320
7.3 Distinguishing between Employment Relations and Contractor Relations 321
7.4 Selecting Different Types of Employment Contracts During Recruitment 322
7.5 Rights and Obligations under General Work Hours or Irregular Work Hours Employment Contracts 322
7.6 Rights and Obligations under Part-Time Employment Contracts 323
7.7 Rights and Obligations under Labor Dispatch Contracts 323
7.8 Judicial Procedures for Employment Disputes 324
7.9 Matters Related to Recruitment and Employee Onboarding 325
7.10 Purchase of Social Insurance 326
7.11 Signing Written Employment Contracts 326
7.12 Probationary Period for Employees 327
7.13 Invalidation of Employment Contract 328
7.14 Paid Annual Leave 329
7.15 Bereavement Leave 329
7.16 Special Protection for Female Employees 330
7.17 Maternity Leave and Paternity Leave 330
7.18 High-Temperature Allowance 331
7.19 Matters Related to Sick Leave 331
7.20 Recognition and Handling of Work Injuries 332
7.21 Work Injury Entitlements 333
7.22 Employee Wages 334
7.23 Employee Overtime Pay 336
7.24 Workplace Rights and Mental Damages 336
7.25 Lawful Disciplinary Actions 337
7.26 Employee-related Financial Compensation 338
7.27 Multiple Employers' Use of an Employee 340
7.28 Employee Position Transfer 340
7.29 Employee Collective Strike 341
7.30 Equity Incentive 342
7.31 Unjustified Wage Deduction and Arrear 342
7.32 Administrative and Criminal Penalties for Employers Violating Employment Law 343
7.33 Resignation and Forced Resignation of Employees 344

7.34 Employee Retirement 344
7.35 Employee Death and Employer Demise 345
7.36 Lawful Dismissal 346
7.37 Economic Redundancy 348
7.38 Termination for Major Change in Objective Condition 348
7.39 Termination of Employment for Employee's Incompetence 349
7.40 Termination of Employment Due to Employee's Gross Misconduct 349
7.41 Protection of Trade Secrets 350
7.42 Non-Competition Agreement 351
7.43 Personal Information Protection 352
7.44 Company Rules and Regulations and Contracts Management 353

Afterword 355
Index 357

PREFACE

This book aims to present practical issues in Chinese employment law through concise questions and answers, addressing the question "What are my rights and what should I do?" It is an innovative effort to select the most practical knowledge from a vast amount of information for readers. This book may be one of the most practical and cutting-edge Chinese employment law books available, offering insights into the forefront of practical issues.

Lawyers outside Mainland China: you will discover the practical value of this book. Originally drafted as a reference document for our law firm's employment lawyers, it covers the most common litigation and non-litigation employment law issues in China, including concise practical guidelines and over a thousand cases.

Professors and students at universities: you will also discover the educational value of this book. Unlike academic/case law legal textbooks, this book concisely integrates the basic principles, legal provisions, and judicial practices of Chinese employment law. It helps students directly and quickly grasp the know-how of Chinese employment law.

Investors in China or **foreigners working in China**: you may also unexpectedly discover the reference value of this book. Although it is a lawyer's toolkit, it clearly and concisely presents your employment law rights and offers suggestions on how to handle specific practical issues. This book simplifies the complexity of the law into clear and straightforward information.

Our firm conviction is that conciseness is the most pressing demand the public has for legal books.

It is both possible and necessary to provide synoptic answers to complex legal questions. My understanding as a lawyer and labor arbitrator from long-term practical work is that no matter how complex an employment law issue may be, the answer is always simple: what rights do I have and what is my best option? What people are most concerned about is actually having a simple answer to "What are my rights and what should I do?" and concise, if not terse, corresponding legal and case basis.

This book has three characteristics:

(1) Concise and to-the-point answers. The explosion of knowledge and limited human energy have dictated that modern readers should minimize redundant and interfering information when reading books. Each article in this book is composed of a concise answer, a brief explanation of legal principles or rules, and a concise legal analysis combined with judicial precedents and legal rules. The book provides direct answers to general practical questions. For questions

involving multiple variable factors, this book introduces a unique hierarchical and networked explanatory structure, connecting different articles through indexes. This facilitates readers to quickly grasp answers while also allowing them to delve into further details.

(2) A large number of court cases in support of the answers. Employment laws are the most contradictory and loophole-ridden legal department among all legal departments in China. Readers may be misled if they rely solely on legal rules to find a guide to action for a specific circumstance. The best way is to seek court decisions for answers and see how judges have ruled on the specific circumstance. Although China functions under a civil law system, its courts still strive for consistency in their decisions. The extensive case citations in this book greatly increase the breadth of practical issues and the reliability of the answers. More than 1,000 Chinese judicial precedents have been carefully selected from the nearly 10,000 precedents I have reviewed.

(3) Coverage of different local regulations and judicial practices in different provinces and cities. Because of the contradictory nature of Chinese employment law practice, the book aims to provide reliable practical answers to readers located in all parts of China, so the cases cited are from courts nationwide, and the differences in judicial practices are classified and compared. Therefore, the answers in the book contain a large number of explanations, such as "the High Court of Guangdong Province, Beijing Municipality, and Hebei Province support this view," but "the High Court of Sichuan Province and Shanghai City hold the opposite," to help readers to understand judicial practices in different regions. This is necessary to answer the question "What are my rights and what should I do?" for readers in different regions.

In addition to the content of the employment laws itself, this book also involves some interdisciplinary practices, such as the protection of trade secrets (intellectual property law), non-competition issues, personal information protection, and administrative and criminal liabilities for employers' violations of law. The book also endeavors to use demonstrative cases to explain the implementation of the law, such as how to calculate sick leave wages, economic compensation for employment termination, unused annual leave pay, etc., and has a detailed and systematic summary of some special topics based on practice, such as disciplinary punishment, position transfer, salary reduction, and classification of terminations of employment relationship. The book also compiles a "Glossary of Common Terms" in alphabetical order to facilitate readers to look up concise explanations of terms in the book.

This book highly condenses legal analyses, case laws, regional differences, and the forefront of labor dispute practice, all to answer the question in the hearts of readers, "What are my rights and what should I do?"

We hope this book will help you avoid risks in Chinese employment law and handle employment disputes. If you have any questions, please feel free to contact us via the email address provided below. We will respond as soon as possible.

Royal Law Firm (China)
Dong Wang, Founding Partner (wangdong@royalaw.com)
Peng Zhao, Director Partner (zhaopeng@royalaw.com)

GLOSSARY OF COMMON TERMS

Ability incompetence means that an employee is not competent in performing their job due to their work ability instead of health reasons. The employer may terminate the employee's employment contract, with economic compensation provided to the employee, if the employee remains incompetent after an employer-arranged training or position transfer.

Accumulative service years means the total service years of an employee for any employer, whether they are continuous or not. Accumulative service years are one of the factors in deciding an employee's entitled paid annual leave or paid sick leave.

Acquisition infringement of trade secret means the unauthorized transfer, replication, or possession of a trade secret by individuals who have access to or possess or have control over the trade secret without the permission of the right holder of the trade secret.

Assignment contract, also known as the employment contract that ends at task completion, means a temporary employment contract with no fixed term and which is terminated upon completion of specific tasks.

Burden of proof means the responsibility in judicial proceedings (including labor dispute judicial proceedings) for collecting and submitting evidence to prove specific facts claimed. The party bearing the burden of proof faces a higher risk of losing the case because if that party fails to submit sufficient evidence, the judiciary will not recognize the fact, which affects the direction of the case, as established.

Child labor means workers under the age of 16. Except for professional artists or athletes with parental consent, the use of child labor is illegal.

Civil servant relationship means the hiring relationship between government agencies and civil servants, governmental institutions and staff, social organizations and employees, and the military and civilian personnel. The difference between employment relationship and civil servant relationship is that they have different types of employer.

Collective employment contract means an employment contract signed between employees collectively, through a union or group, and the employer.

Contractor relationship means a civil contract relationship between entities such as enterprises and labor service providers, also known as an independent contractor relationship. In some judicial decisions, contractor relationships are also referred to as Guyong relationships (雇佣关系), which differ from the substantive nature of employment relationships in Taiwan and Hong Kong law.

Customer poaching means the act of an employee, whether current or departed, using the relationships and influence established with customers during their employment to divert those customers to a company or individual associated with the employee, resulting in the employer losing the customer.

Disciplinary action means a management measure taken by employers to punish employees who violate company rules and regulations or provisions of employment contracts, usually including warnings, demerits, or even termination of the employment relationship.

Disclosure infringement of trade secret means the unauthorized disclosure of a trade secret by a person who has access to or possesses the trade secret, causing the disclosure of the trade secret.

Dismissal or Employment termination means the termination or dissolution of the employment relationship.

Double-wage damages, also known as double-wage damages for the absence of a signed employment contract, means punitive damages stipulated in the Employment Contract Law for employers who unlawfully fail to sign a written employment contract with employees. The amount is usually the employee's wage during the period when the contract should have been signed but wasn't.

Due wages means the wages that employers are obligated to pay to their employees, including basic wages, bonuses, allowances, commissions, etc. In contrast to received wages, due wages are the wages before deductions for social insurance contributions, personal income tax, housing provident fund, and enterprise annuity.

Economic compensation means the compensation that an employer should pay to an employee according to the length of service when the employment relationship is terminated or dissolved in accordance with the statutory circumstances.

Economic redundancy means the act of an employer reducing the number of employees due to business difficulties. The implementation of economic redundancy by an employer must meet statutory substantive and procedural conditions; otherwise, it may constitute illegal dismissal.

Employee means personnel hired by an employer, also known as staff or worker.

Employer means the entities that employ workers within China, excluding government agencies, governmental institutions, social organizations, and natural persons.

Labor administrative authority means the government agencies responsible for supervising, inspecting, and managing employers' compliance with and enforcement of employment laws, including labor bureaus and their labor inspection agencies.

Employment arbitration means the quasi-judicial first-level adjudication procedure for labor disputes.

Employment arbitration committee means the quasi-judicial first-level adjudication institution for labor disputes.

Employment contract means the contract between an employer and an employee regarding the provision of labor and payment of remuneration.

Equal pay for equal work means the legal principle under the Employment Contract Law that employees in the same or similar positions should receive similar or equal wages.

Fine, also known as economic penalties, means a type of disciplinary action taken by employers against employees who violate company rules and regulations by deducting wages. The legality of fines is disputed in judicial practice, and places where fines are allowed must also comply with restrictions on the proportion of monthly fine deduction not exceeding a certain percentage of wages.

Forced resignation means an employee being compelled to resign due to specific lawful reasons (such as the employers' unjustifiable wage arrears). The employees who are forced to resign have the right to claim economic compensation from the employer.

General work hours and Irregular work hours refer to a work time system where standard working hours cannot be implemented due to industry characteristics, nature of work, natural conditions, or seasonal conditions. General work hours and irregular work hours typically use methods such as concentrated or rotational rest and flexible working hours to balance employees' work and rest, but the overall average working time should be consistent with standard work hours.

High temperature allowance means the allowance that employers are legally required to pay to employees during periods of high temperatures if the employer cannot ensure working conditions outdoors at 35 degrees Celsius or indoors at 33 degrees Celsius.

Host employer means the company that actually utilizes the labor of the employee(s) in a tripartite relationship of labor dispatch. The other two parties are the dispatch employer, namely, the labor dispatching agency, and the dispatched employee(s).

Identification of work injury means the administrative procedure in which social insurance institutions' inspectors examine the causes of employees' injuries or illnesses and their relevance to the work they engage in, determining whether the employees' injuries or illnesses constitute work-related injuries or occupational diseases. If it is determined to be a work injury (including occupational diseases), the employee is entitled to work injury treatment; otherwise, the employee can only request medical treatment.

Illegal termination, also known as unjustified dismissal or illegal termination of employment, means termination of the employment relationship by the employer without legal reasons or in violation of statutory procedures. The legal consequence of illegal termination is that the employer must compensate the unlawfully dismissed employee or reinstate the employee.

Internal retirement means the arrangement made by state-owned enterprises or institutions, based on institutional reforms or operational difficulties, where employees close to retirement age are retired early and receive a certain living allowance monthly.

Interruption of limitation of arbitration means the restart of the one-year limitation of labor arbitration due to certain legally prescribed events. These events may include employee complaint to relevant governmental or judicial authorities (such as a labor inspection agency), or claim of rights by one party against the other party (such as sending written letters urging payment of severance pay), or the other party's agreement to fulfill obligations (such as promising through email or letter to pay wages owed).

Jurisdiction means the right of a particular labor arbitration committee or court to adjudicate on a particular labor dispute issue (such as claims for economic compensation), excluding the jurisdiction of other institutions.

Juvenile worker means employee aged between 16 and 18 years. Juvenile workers receive special protection under the employment laws.

Labor capacity appraisal means the assessment, conducted by a labor capacity appraisal committee based on medical institutions' professional opinions, of an employee's ability to live independently or engage in labor activities after suffering from work-related injury or occupational disease, or non-work-related injury or illness.

Labor dispatch means a tripartite employment contract between a dispatch employer (labor dispatch company), a host employer (the company that actually employs the workers), and an employee or employees.

Labor dispute, also known as employment dispute, means a dispute related to or arising from employment relations, such as claims for unpaid wages or economic compensation. A labor dispute application must be submitted to the labor arbitration committee.

Limitation of arbitration means the time limit within which workers or employers must file a labor arbitration application. If the applicant exceeds this time limit, even if the claim is legitimate, the labor arbitration committee or court will strike it out. This limitation period is one year, and it starts from different points in time depending on the nature of the application. However, if there is an interruption or suspension of the limitation period, the limitation period may be restarted or extended.

Long-term unpaid leave means the arrangement where employees temporarily cease work and stop receiving wages while retaining their job positions, typically implemented by state-owned enterprises due to structural reforms or financial difficulties. During long-term unpaid leave, the employment relationship generally remains intact, and the employee's length of service continues to accumulate.

Major change in objective situation means significant changes in the operating environment of an employer that affect its business operations. Major change in objective situation is one of the legitimate reasons allowed by the employment laws for employers to terminate individual employment relationships or implement economic redundancies.

Medical care leave, also known as medical care leave for illness or non-work-related injury, means the period during which employees are entitled to rest and treatment for illnesses or non-work-related injuries, as prescribed by law. The length of the sick leave period depends on the employee's accumulative service years, continuous service years for the current employer, and the number of sick leave days already taken by the employee.

Medical incompetence means that an employee who has suffered from illness or non-work-related injury is not competent in performing their job. If the employee is not competent in performing their original job after their medical care leave and returning to work, and remains incompetent after an employer-arranged position transfer, the employer may terminate the employee's employment contract, but must pay economic compensation.

Medical treatment allowance means an additional allowance granted to employees whose employment ends due to illnesses or non-work-related injuries, with an amount not less than six months' wages. Employers must pay medical treatment allowances to employees under two conditions: the employer terminates the employment relationship due to the employee's medical incompetence (the inability to perform duties after medical care leave, provided that the employee remains incompetent for work after being position-transferred), and the employee's labor capacity appraisal is rated at level five to level ten.

Mental damages, also known as damages for mental harm, means the damages claimed by employees for mental suffering caused by factors related to employment relations. Mental damages are a concept under tort law and are generally not supported under the employment laws. However, in special circumstances, such as severe disability caused by work-related injuries or occupational diseases, it may be supported.

Minimum wage standard means locally prescribed minimum wage standards in each province and city. Employers are obligated to pay employees no less than this minimum wage standard for their completed standard working hours.

Non-competition means the trade restraint that employers sign agreements with employees who have access to the employers' trade secrets, stipulating that the employees shall not engage in competitive industries for a certain period of time after employment termination. The employer is obliged to pay the employee non-competition allowance during this period.

Non-competition allowance means the compensation paid by an employer to an employee who has agreed not to engage in competitive industries for a certain period after the employment termination.

Non-competition contractual damages means contractual damages that an employee should bear according to their non-competition agreements signed between the employer and the employee if the employee breaches the non-competition obligation.

Occupational disease means diseases specified in the "Classification and Catalogue of Occupational Diseases" that employees contract as a result of their occupational activities. After identification of work injury (i.e., determination of occupational disease, as work injury includes work-related injuries and occupational diseases), employees are entitled to work injury entitlements.

Occupational hazard means hazardous substances, such as dust, noise, and toxic chemicals, that endanger the health of employees and have caused or may cause occupational diseases.

Paid sick leave means the period during which an employee is entitled to rest and receive treatment with wage pay when they are sick. Wages in paid sick leave are typically 60% of the employee's normal wages, and the duration of the paid sick leave varies from 3 to 24 months depending on the employee's accumulative service years and service years for the current employer.

Paid work injury leave means the period during which employees with work-related injuries or occupational diseases have the right to cease work for treatment and rest. During paid work injury leave, employees receive the same salary and are entitled to corresponding allowances and compensations from social security funds and their employers.

Part-time employment contract means a flexible employment contract where employees' weekly working hours do not exceed 24 hours. This type of employee may serve multiple employers, and the contract can be orally agreed upon by both parties and terminated at any time without employers' liability of economic compensation.

Paternity leave means paid leave entitlement for male employees due to their wives' childbirth.

Payment in lieu means a third-day alternative wage pay for an employer not giving 30-day notice of termination. Under certain statutory circumstances, employers are required to provide a 30-day notice before terminating their employment contracts with employees. However, the employer can choose to pay 30 days' wages as an alternative to this advance notice. This 30-day alternative wage is called payment in lieu.

Permanent employment contract means an employment contract without an end date. Employers may enter into fixed-term employment contracts with a newly hired employee; however, they must sign permanent employment contracts with some employees due to service years for the employer or the number of times of signing fixed-term employment contracts.

Personal information means various information related to identifiable natural persons recorded by electronic or other means, including the individual's identity, contact information, qualifications, profession, personal characteristics, financial information, credit information, health and physiological information, and even actions taken by the individual. All information that can identify the person is considered personal information.

Personal information outbound transferring means the act of providing personal information to entities outside of China. Transferring personal information abroad requires filing or approval procedures with the Chinese government.

Piecework wage means a form of wage payment based on the quantity of work completed (such as the number of products completed on an assembly line or the number of newspapers delivered), reflecting the principle of "the more you work, the more you earn." differing from standard work hours wages that are paid based on hours worked.

Position transfer means the change of job positions by the employer for existing employees, constituting a change of condition of employment contract. Legal position transfers must be agreed upon by employees or meet specific conditions; otherwise, employees can refuse the transfer.

Probation period, also known as trial period, means the period during which an employer assesses the competence and suitability of a new employee. If the new employee fails to meet the hiring requirements, the employer has the right to terminate the employment relationship without providing severance pay.

Punitive damages, also known as punitive damages for illegal termination of employment, means the punitive compensation that an employer should pay for unlawfully dismissing an employee, calculated as twice the ordinary economic compensation.

Received wage means the actual wages paid by employers to employees. In contrast to due wages, received wages are the amount paid to employees after deductions for social insurance contributions, personal income tax, housing provident fund, and enterprise annuity.

Reinstatement means the right of an employee to request to resume their position when the employer unlawfully terminates the employee's employment contract. If the court deems reinstatement feasible, it shall order the employer to cooperate with the reinstatement; if not feasible, it may order the employer to pay punitive damages for the illegal termination of the employment relationship. Of course, the employee can also choose not to be reinstated and demand punitive damages straightaway.

Service years for current employer means continuous service years for which an employee has been working for their current employer. Service years for current employer is an important factor for determining the employee's entitlement to paid medical care leave or economic compensation in the case of termination.

Standard work hours means the work system where employees work 8 hours a day for 5 days a week, totaling 40 hours per week.

Supplementary damages means the responsibility of the employer to pay punitive damages ranging from 50% to 100% of the amount owed if the employer acted in unjustifiable deduction or arrears of wages or overtime wages, refusal to pay economic compensation, or paying wages under minimum wages, and refusal to pay the outstanding after being ordered to rectify by the labor administrative authority.

Suspension of limitation of arbitration means the temporary suspension of the remaining limitation period of labor arbitration due to specific events. The deadline for the limitation of labor arbitration is extended corresponding to the length of time of these specific events. These events refer to any legitimate reasons that prevent parties from filing labor arbitration applications, such as a force majeure event, a lockdown during an epidemic, or an employee's hospitalization due to illness.

The 2020 Supreme Court's Judicial Interpretation refers to the Interpretation of the Supreme People's Court on the Application of Law in the Trial of Labor Dispute Cases (I) (Judicial Interpretation [2020] No.26). This judicial interpretation is the integration by the Supreme Court of the past four judicial interpretations on the application of law in trial of labor dispute, including Judicial Interpretation (2001) No. 14, Judicial Interpretation (2006) NO. 6, Judicial Interpretation (2010) No. 12, and Judicial Interpretation (2013) No. 4, which are repealed.

Three protected periods means the pregnancy, maternity, and lactation periods, collectively, for female employees. Under the employment laws, female employers in these three protected periods are entitled to special protection rights.

Time-off in lieu means the compensatory arrangement where employees take rest during working hours for the time they worked overtime, either upon their request or as arranged by the employer.

Trade secret means proprietary business information and technical data owned by employers, not known to the public, safeguarded through confidentiality measures, and with commercial value. Employees, whether current or former, are prohibited from infringing upon their employer's trade secrets.

Training service agreement means the agreement between an employer and an employee stipulating that the employer will provide specialized training to the employee, and the employee commits to serve the employer for a certain period (service period) as the consideration of the training. If the employee violates the service period commitment, they shall be liable for contractual damages provided in the agreement.

Unjustified wage arrear means the circumstance in which an employer fails to make its employee's full or partial wage payment at statutory or agreed-upon wage payment time without justified reasons, while not explicitly refusing to pay the amount. Unjustified wage arrear is illegal. The consequences of unjustified wage arrear include that the employee may proceed a forced resignation and claim economic compensation against the employer.

Unjustified wage deduction means the circumstance in which an employer deducts or fails to pay the full amount of an employee's wages that should have been paid without justified reasons, with clear intention of refusing to pay. Unjustified wage deduction is illegal. The consequences of unjustified wage arrear include that the employee may proceed a forced resignation and claim economic compensation against the employer.

Unused annual leave pay means cash payment made by employers to employees for the remaining unused paid annual leave days that the latter are entitled to if they did not fully utilize them.

Wage or salary means remuneration for labor, including various basic wages, bonuses, and allowances paid on a predetermined payment cycle.

Wage reduction refers to the reduction of wages by the employer for existing employees, constituting a change in the conditions of the employment contract. Legal wage reductions must be agreed upon by employees or meet specific conditions; otherwise, it constitutes unjustified wage deduction.

Waiting-for-work means the arrangement made by state-owned enterprises due to institutional reforms or economic difficulties, where employees are temporarily suspended from work, provided with basic living expenses, and reinstated when there are vacancies. This is not a common situation in private organizations, which are the majority in China's economy.

Work hours system means various rules formed in employment relations due to the different characteristics of working hours. China's current work hours systems include full-time work system, part-time work system, irregular work hours system, and general work hours system.

Work injury entitlements means the allowances and compensations that employees should receive from social security institutions and employers when they suffer from work-related injuries or occupational diseases.

Work injury recurrence, also known as recurrence of old injuries, means the situation where an employee, who has previously suffered from a work-related injury or occupational disease, has recovered or stabilized after a period of treatment and recuperation but later experiences a recurrence of the same injury or illness. Work injury recurrence also includes the recurrence of old injuries for military personnel.

Work-related injury means injuries related to work reasons, work locations, and work hours. It is a form of employer's non-fault liability.

CHAPTER 1

Employment Relations

Introduction

When a person gets paid for a job in China, they naturally have a work relationship with an organization or a person. To clarify legally whether the work relationship is an employment relationship or not and what kind of employment relationship it belongs to is the foundation of the rights and obligations under the employment legal relationship and answering the question "What are my rights and what should I do?" when disputes arise. Following this, we will examine important practical issues such as different types of employment relationships and procedures for handling labor disputes.

The series of questions and answers in this chapter mainly involves the basic principles of employment relation, collective employment contract, the distinction between employment relation and contractor relation, common contractor relationships and special employment relationships, the types of employment relations, fixed-term employment contract, employment contract that ends at task completion (assignment contract), the characteristics of a casual employee, identification of general work hours and irregular work hours, volunteer worker and employment relationship, the protection of child labor, a family-member employee, employment relationship related to an employee over retirement age, the identification and invalidity of labor dispatch, labor outsourcing and representative offices for foreign enterprises, civil servant relationship, etc. This chapter also lists some special employment relations and common types of contractor relations.

For the procedures of labor dispute, this chapter outlines the dispute resolution process and analyzes the time limits for labor arbitration, the jurisdiction of the labor arbitration committees over dispute cases, and the remedies or pathways available for case appealing to the courts. These are all important matters closely related to employment relationships or disputes.

1.1 Employment Relations: Principle and Classification

1. What is the principle by which employer and employee treat each other?

Answer: Employment relations in China are regulated by the 2018 Labor Law and the 2012 Employment Contract Law. The application of the employment laws in China, like other sciences, follows specific sub-principles derived from general principles, which, in turn, are based on the fundamental principles of Chinese employment laws.

Article 1 of the Employment Contract Law stipulates that the fundamental purpose of formulating the law is to protect the legitimate rights and interests of employees and

DOI: 10.4324/9781003583301-1

to build and develop harmonious and stable employment relations.[1] For example, in the case of Li Zhong of Guangdong Provincial High Court's Shenzhen Alfat Electrical and Mechanical Co., Ltd. in 2009, the court found that the employer's illegal dismissal prevented the employee from receiving RMB 1 million of annual salaries and purchasing a property, and that since the damages of breach of contract were difficult to determine, the employer was obligated to bear the high contractual damages stipulated in the contract, in accordance with the principle of protecting the legitimate rights and interests of employees.[2]

In addition, according to the principle of harmonious employment relations in the Employment Contract Law, both employers and employees should treat each other in good faith and in a fair and reasonable manner.[3]

For the employers, employees are the foundation of the company's successful operation and the team members of the company's harmonious and friendly work environment. The employers should treat employees in good faith, understand the needs of employees, and strictly protect the rights of employees stipulated by law.

For employees, the employer they serve is part of the core elements of the economic prosperity and development of society and the source of their income and career development. Employees should abide by the company rules and regulations, especially abide by professional ethics, and protect the interests of the employer.

2. What are the types of employment relations under China's employment laws?

Answer: Under the employment laws, different types of employment relationships mean different rights and obligations and different legal consequences. According to the termination time of employment relations and the types of work arrangements, China's Employment Contract Law and judicial decisions stipulate or list the following six types of employment contracts.

The first is permanent employment contracts, in which no expiry time is provided for, are normally full-time contracts. Full-time employees typically work 40 hours per week (5 days and 8 hours per day), while casual employees work less than 24 hours per week.

The second is fixed-term employment contracts, which are contracts with a termination period. This is the most commonly used way to recruit new employees in China. Since the implementation of the Employment Contract Law in 2008, if a fixed-term employment contract is terminated, the employer shall pay economic compensation according to the post-2008 length of service of the employee (please refer to "167. How to distinguish the calculation of economic compensation and punitive damages for service years before and after 2008?"). A fixed-term employment relationship is typically full-time.

1 Article 1 of the Labor Law also stipulates the principle of protecting the legitimate rights and interests of workers.

2 Li Zhong v. Shenzhen Alpha Mechanical and Electrical Industry Co., Ltd., Guangdong Provincial People's High Court (2009) Yue Gao Fa Shen Jian Min Ti Zi No. 131. The court held, "Because of the manifest disparity between both sides, the court should highlight the principle of protecting or inclining to protect the legitimate rights and interests of workers, so as to achieve substantive fairness."

3 Civil Ruling of the Supreme People's Court of the People's Republic of China (2014) Min Shen Zi No. 735, Hu Song v. Beijing Nonggongshang Development and Trading Co., Ltd. The court held that the employee and the employer had reached a mediation agreement, but the employee changing their mind after receiving the compensation violated the principle of good faith. The court rejected the employee's claim.

The third is labor dispatch, that is, an employment relationship in which the dispatch employer (a human resources company) dispatches the employee to the host employer (that is, the employer that actually uses the employee's service) to engage in temporary, auxiliary, and alternative work. The characteristic of this kind of employment relationship is that the employment relationship (with the dispatch employer) is separated from the actual labor use relationship (with the host employer). Labor dispatch can only apply to employees on a full-time basis and in the form of a fixed-term employment contract.[4]

The fourth type of employment contract is called the employment contract that ends at task completion (hereafter referred to as assignment contracts). Assignment contracts have uncertain termination dates, but they are similar to fixed-term employment contracts in essence, because they come to an end when the task is completed.

The fifth is the system of irregular work hours and the system of general work hours. They apply when the standard work hours cannot be implemented because of the nature of the work, natural conditions, or seasonal conditions. General work hours and irregular work hours are both a kind of quasi-full-time work hours, that is, the total work hours of employees are similar to full-time work hours, but only a special arrangement for busy and idle periods is made.

The sixth is the casual employment contract. This is a flexible type of employment contract with work hours of not more than 4 hours a day, or not more than 24 hours a week. The two parties may have an oral contract and terminate the employment relationship at any time.

The above types of employment relations are not strictly distinguished according to one specific indicator. For example, if we strictly distinguish according to the work hour system, there will only be the standard work hours, casual and irregular work hours, and general work hours; permanent employment contracts, fixed-term contracts, labor dispatch, and assignment contracts may be classified into the standard work hours rather than separate categories. The purpose of our classification here is to facilitate the legal analysis and explanation of related employment rights and obligations and "What are my rights and what should I do?" in the practice of the employment laws.

3. Should I sign a collective contract or an individual contract when I join a company?

Answer: A collective contract is a contract that is signed by employers and trade unions or employees collectively. The contract's terms and conditions apply to all trade union members or the employees who participate in the collective contract. The purpose of collective contract system setting is to protect the rights of employees' collective bargaining and their employment rights. In contrast, the individual contract is an employment contract negotiated and signed by employee and employer individually.

Therefore, if you join an employer where there is a collective contract, you can join the trade union (or the employee organization concluding the collective contract) and sign the collective contract, and the conditions of your employment are basically the same as those of the collective contract. You also can choose to sign an individual contract with the employer to negotiate more favorable terms and conditions in your individual contract than those in the collective contract. At present, the most common employment contract in practice in China is still the individual contract.

4 Article 30 of the Regulations on the Implementation of the Employment Contract Law.

It should be noted that an employer must sign a written employment contract with any new employee within 30 days of the commencement of the employment. If the two parties are unable to agree on the employee's wage within the 30 days, the wage shall be subject to the collective contract if available. If no collective contract is in place, the principle of equal pay for equal work shall apply.[5]

Additionally, trade unions in China are not autonomous worker organizations in the general sense, but organizations under the control of the Chinese government. As stipulated in the Trade Union Law: "A mass organization of the working class voluntarily united by the workers under the leadership of the Chinese Communist Party, and it is a bridge and link between the Chinese Communist Party and the workers." Therefore, in judicial practice, labor disputes involving the rights of trade union members, the rights of trade union representatives to the employer, and the statutory obligations of trade unions to organize strikes are almost unseen.

4. What is the legal effect of signing a collective contract by employer and employees?

Answer: According to the Employment Contract Law in China, after employees negotiate collectively and sign a collective contract with their employer, the collective contract shall be registered with labor administrative agencies (normally the local labor bureau). If the agency does not raise an objection within 15 days, this collective contract becomes effective.[6]

Whether the collective contract is effective or not may be related to the determination of whether the employer has effectively signed employment contracts with their employees and the corresponding liability for double-wage damages in the absence of a written employment contract.[7] For example, in the case of He Zijian before Shenzhen Intermediate Court of Guangdong Province in 2021, the court held that although the employee had signed a collective contract with the employer, the collective contract had not come into effect because it had not been submitted to the labor administrative authority, and that the employer was deemed not to have signed an employment contract with the employee and should compensate double-wage damages.[8] In addition, there are also decisions, such as the 2016 case of Pan Yabao before Zhaoqing Intermediate Court and the 2020 case of Tian Fan before Beijing The Third Intermediate Court, which hold that even if a collective contract has been signed, it cannot be regarded as a signed employment contract and exempted from the responsibility of double-wage damages.[9]

---

5 Article 11 of the Employment Contract Law.

6 Articles 51 and 54 of the Employment Contract Law.

7 This is a special damage under the Employment Contract Law 2008, where an employer is liable to pay the same amount of wages as punishment for the duration in which no written employment contract was in place without legitimate reasons.

8 Siping Pengcheng Property Management Co., Ltd. v. Zhang Jinhua, the Siping Intermediate People's Court of Jilin Province (2016) Ji 03 Min Zhong No.1144; Shenzhen Lingqi Industrial Co., Ltd. v. He Zijian, Shenzhen Intermediate People's Court of Guangdong Province (2021) Yue 03 Min Zhong No. 16252; Bazhou Ditong Trenchless Engineering Co., Ltd. v. Hongjiang, People's Court of Korla City, Bayingolin Mongol Autonomous Prefecture, Xinjiang Civil Judgment (2015) Ku Min Chu Zi No. 1828.

9 Guangdong Tairi Elevator Co., Ltd. v. Pan Yabao, the Guangdong Zhaoqing Intermediate People's Court (2016) Yue 12 Min Zhong No. 287. The court held that even if the employer and the trade union have signed a collective employment contract, it should also sign individual employment contracts with the workers. Beijing Aozhiya Trading Co., Ltd. v. Tian Fan, the Third Intermediate People's Court of Beijing (2020) Jing 03 Min Zhong No. 11595.

The entry into force of a collective contract may also affect the terms and conditions of an employee's individual employment. Although Article 55 of the Employment Contract Law means that the wage level of an employee's individual employment contract shall not be lower than the wage level of the equal position in the collective contract, in judicial practice, some courts have made contradictory decisions based on the rules of Article 11 of the Employment Contract Law on the determination of wage amount.[10] In the case of Xu Xiaohong before Shenzhen Intermediate Court in 2014, the court also held that the wage growth ratio of individual contracts could not refer to the average wage growth ratio stipulated in collective contracts.[11] Therefore, the legal application and its legal consequences of Article 55 of the Employment Contract Law in judicial practice warrant further observation in the future.

The rule that individual contract conditions shall not be less favorable than collective contract conditions in China's employment laws is different from the rule of collective contract under common law. Common law countries such as New Zealand stipulate that "collective contract conditions shall not be applied automatically unless the employee joins the trade union," in order to protect the collective bargaining advantage of the trade union. Employees shall be formally entitled to the conditions stipulated in the collective contract only if they pay union dues to become members.

5. Is it legal for my employer to sign a fixed-term contract with me instead of a permanent employment contract?

Answer: The employment law in China encourages employers to sign permanent contracts with new recruits and employees (Article 12 of the Employment Contract Law). In the practice of the employment laws, however, the most common form of contract is a fixed-term contract between employers and their new employees, which is lawful.

But, the Employment Contract Law has different rules for employees to renew their contracts. If an employer has signed two consecutive fixed-term contracts with their employee after 2008, or the employee has consecutively worked for the employer for more than 10 years and both parties agree to continue the employment relationship, the employer must sign a permanent employment contract with the employee.

Courts around the country have different practices in treating the signing of the employment contract following two consecutive fixed-term contracts. For details, please see "56. Should a permanent employment contract be signed after two consecutive fixed-term employment contracts?" In addition, if a written employment contract has not been signed one year after the employment commences, it is deemed that both parties have a permanent employment contract in place.

---

10 Luo Rongheng v. Dujiangyan Branch of Chengdu Rural Commercial Bank Co., Ltd., the Sichuan High Court Civil Ruling (2018) Chuan Min Shen No. 4332. The court held, "Article 11 of the Employment Contract Law of the People's Republic of China stipulates that … that is to say, wages are determined first according to the employment contract, the collective contract is applicable only when there is no or unclear provision in the employment contract, and the principle of equal pay for equal work is implemented only when further there is no collective contract. Therefore, it is not necessary to consider the rule of individual contracts' conditions not being lower than that of collective contract."

11 Xu Xiaohong v. Wal-Mart SZITIC Department Store Co., Ltd. Shenzhen Zhongshan Branch, Wal-Mart SZITIC Department Store Co., Ltd, the Shenzhen Intermediate People's Court of Guangdong Province (2014) Shen Zhong Fa Lao Zhong Zi No. 4500.

If, according to the above situations, the employer is obligated to sign a permanent employment contract with the employee but does not do so, or both parties are deemed to have formed a permanent employment contract type of employment relationship, the employer may not terminate the employment relationship with the employee on the grounds of a fixed-term contract's expiry, otherwise it may constitute an illegal dismissal.

6. Is my employment contract on general work hours (or irregular work hours) considered valid?

Answer: Irregular and general work hours under the employment laws are set due to the characteristics of industries, position requirements, nature of works, natural conditions, or seasonal conditions, where standard hours cannot be applied. The general work hours system is due to the nature of the work or seasonal or natural conditions that make it impossible to arrange work evenly over a relatively longer period (such as a year), while the irregular work hours system is due to the nature of the work that makes it impossible to arrange work according to standard hours within a single workday (such as security night shifts).

Compared with the standard work hours, they can only balance staff's work and rest by means of intensive work, concentrated or rotational rest, and flexible work hours, but the overall average work hours in the two systems should be consistent with the standard work hours.[12]

Judging from the judicial decisions of courts around the country, the validity of the employment contract signed by an employer and their workers under the system of general work hours or irregular work hours mainly depends on the following factors: the characteristics of the job or industry, whether it has been examined and approved by the labor administrative authority, and the agreement or understanding of both parties on the work hour system.

Firstly, job or industry characteristics are the fundamental reasons why employers cannot implement the standard work hours but can only implement general work hours or irregular work hours. In practice, the most common positions that may be involved include senior managers, field workers, salesmen, loading and unloading personnel, firefighters, remote well station personnel, some transportation and on-duty personnel,[13] airport staff,[14] security guards, monitors, toll collectors, elevator workers, etc. Cleaners may also be deemed special positions.[15]

12 Article 5 of the Ministry of Labor's Regulations on Approval of Enterprises' Implementation of Irregular Work Hours and General Work Hours: "irregular work hour system and general work hours system apply week, month, season, and year as computation period of number of work hours, but its average daily or weekly number of work hours are basically the same as the standard work hours."

13 Article 2 of the Supplementary Official Reply of the Ministry of Labor on the Implementation of Irregular work hour system and General work hour system for Some Petroleum Workers in 1996.

14 Employment Dispute Application between Cheng Zheng and Nanjing Lukou International Airport Co., Ltd. Civil Ruling of Jiangsu Provincial People's High Court (2014) S.S.M.S.Z. No. 192.

15 Civil Judgment of Second Instance of Employment Contract Dispute between Zhu Yonggang and Shanghai Zhiyou Security Service Co., Ltd. Civil Judgment of Shanghai the Second Intermediate People's Court (2020) Hu 02 Min Zhong No. 3311. "As approved by the Human Resources and Social Security Bureau of Yangpu District, Shanghai, during the period from June 1, 2017 to May 31, 2019, the irregular work hour system will be implemented for the senior management and marketing personnel of Zhiyou Security Company; and the general workhour system based on quarterly cycle will be implemented for the security, monitoring, charging, elevator workers and cleaners."

Secondly, whether the two parties have clearly agreed on the general work hours or irregular work hours or whether they have knowledge of it is also an important factor. If the employer advocates one of these two special work hour systems and the employee agrees, or if the employment contract between the two parties clearly stipulates one special work hour system, the court will be more inclined to recognize the same. For example, in the case of Zhang Qiang before the Intermediate Court of Panjin City, Liaoning Province in 2022, the court held that Mr. Zhang Qiang had no objection to the signing of the document containing the irregular work hour system, so his objection in the lawsuit to the irregular work hour system was not established.[16]

Lastly, it is controversial in practice whether the general work hours and irregular work hours must be examined and approved by the labor administrative authority. At present, courts in different places have different practices on this issue. Some cases in courts, including those in Guangdong, Shandong, and Jiangsu Provincial High Courts, hold that these two work hour systems must be examined and approved by the labor administrative authority, and that the work hour system without examination and approval is not established[17]. In 2020, the Ministry of Human Resources and Social Security and the Supreme Court jointly issued a typical case number 13, which also approved this practice.[18] However, some courts, including the High Court of Beijing, Shanxi Province, Xinjiang Autonomous Region, the First Intermediate Court of Shanghai, and the First Intermediate Court of Tianjin, consider that the two parties can effectively agree on this work hour system without administrative approval.[19]

---

16 Judgment of Second Instance of Employment Dispute between Zhang Qiang and Kunlun Energy (Panjin) Co., Ltd. Civil Judgment of Intermediate People's Court of Panjin City, Liaoning Province (2022) Liao 11 Min Zhong No. 1135. "According to the signatures of the employees involved in the feedback form of the implementation plan of the wage assessment method, Mr. Zhang Qiang recognized the nature of his work and the wage system, so Zhang Qiang's claim that Kunlun Energy had never informed Zhang Qiang to implement the irregular workhour system could not be established."

17 Dai Li, Jidian Art Training (Shenzhen) Co., Ltd. Employment Dispute Civil Application for Retrial Review Civil Ruling Guangdong Provincial People's High Court (2021) Yue Min Shen No. 5132. "In this case, Dai Li and Jidian Company did not agree on the irregular workhour system in the full-time employment relationship between the two parties, nor was it approved by the labor administrative authority, nor did it conform to the industry characteristics of the irregular workhour system in the above provisions, so Dai Li's claim could not be established." Shandong Baixin Medical Products Co., Ltd., Lu Xiaoyi Employment Dispute Civil Application for Retrial Review Civil Ruling Shandong High Court Civil Ruling (2021) Lu Min Shen No. 7271. Civil Ruling on Employment Dispute Appeal and Application between Zhu Hualin and Changzhou Zhongheng New Materials Co., Ltd. Civil Ruling of Jiangsu High Court (2019) Sumin Shen No. 3698.

18 Notice of the Ministry of Human Resources and Social Security and the Supreme People's Court on Jointly Issuing the First Batch of Typical Cases of Labor and Civil Servant Disputes (Ministry of Human Resources and Social Security Letter [2020] 62). Case 13 of the typical case—Whether it is valid for the employer and the worker to agree on the implementation of the irregular work hour system. The court ruled that the irregular work hour system without administrative approval is invalid, and the employer should pay overtime wages for all non-normal work hours.

19 Liu Xiaojin, Xinjiang Bohai Cement Co., Ltd. Civil Ruling of Employment Dispute Civil Second Instance Civil Ruling of the High Court of Xinjiang Uygur Autonomous Region (2023) Xin Min Shen No. 114. Employment Dispute retrial between Li Jin and Taiyuan Branch of Beijing Dawang Food Co., Ltd. Civil Ruling of Shanxi Provincial People's High Court (2022) Jin Min Shen No. 328 (non-approval of irregular work hour system does not affect the validity). Civil Ruling on Employment Dispute Retrial Review and Trial Supervision between Cui Jiaping and Beijing Jingcheng Jiufang Hotel Management Co., Ltd. Civil Ruling of Beijing High Court (2019) Jing Min Shen No. 4495. Appeal Case of Labor Remuneration Dispute between ZGP and HM Company Civil Judgment of Shanghai the First Intermediate People's Court (2011) Hu Yi Zhong Min San (Min) Zhong Zi No. 1242. Rongbao (Tianjin) Security Service Co., Ltd., Wu Zhiqiang Employment Dispute Second Instance Civil Judgment Tianjin the First Intermediate People's Court Civil Judgment (2021) Jin 01 Min Zhong No. 1039.

Special attention should be paid to the fact that if the general work hours or irregular work hours cannot be effectively established, the relationship between employers and workers shall be deemed as the standard work hours, and employers will bear the risk of high overtime wages, because under the standard work hours, the worker's work hours outside the normal work hours (such as 9 to 5 from Monday to Friday) during the periods of concentrated work will be regarded as overtime. This is the major risk of the employer when the general work hours or irregular work hours cannot be established.

7. What are common special employment relationships in daily life?

Answer: In employment law practice, there are the following four types of special employment relations in daily life.

The first is the particular type caused by the subject qualification of the employer. The Employment Contract Law stipulates that legitimate employers include enterprises, individual economic organizations, private non-enterprise organizations, state organs, governmental institutions and social organizations.[20]

Among these, the state organs are relatively special employers in judicial practice. Although there are judgments in judicial practice pointing out that there are no obstacles to state organs being employers,[21] the courts around the country are generally inclined to strictly examine the employment contracts signed by the state organs and workers. Workers may not be recognized as employees of state organs because of the governmental recruitment requirements of pre-approval, hierarchical management problems, and the employee's role being not within the scope of the business of the state organ.[22] This is a defect of the employment laws in practice that fails to follow the principle of protecting the legitimate rights and interests of workers.

In addition, case law shows that property owners' committees do not have the standing of employer subject, and thus, an employment contract signed by the employee and the owners' committee is invalid.[23] However, residents' committees are legitimate and

---

20 Article 2 of the Employment Contract Law of the People's Republic of China.

21 Excellent Judgment Document of Beijing Court in 2018, Employment Dispute Appeal Case between Chen Maolin and Taiyanggong District Office of Chaoyang District People's Government of Beijing, Beijing the Third Intermediate Court (2016) Jing 03 Min Zhong No. 11997. The court held that "Taiyanggong Office is the dispatched organ of Chaoyang District People's Government of Beijing, and there is no law to restrict it as the subject of employment relations. Therefore, according to the above legal provisions, the Taiyanggong Office has the subject qualification of employment relations."

22 Fujian Nanping Intermediate Court (2015) Nan Min Zhong Zi No. 500, Nanping Public Security Bureau Traffic Police Detachment and Zheng Minghua Employment Dispute Second Instance Civil Judgment. The court held that according to Article 5 of "the Ministry of Personnel's Reply on the Implementation of relevant Issues of 'the Labor Law' on workers hired by State Organs and Institutions" (Renbanfahan [1995] No. 8), local state organs' establishment of employment relationships with workers must be examined and approved in advance by the relevant competent personnel administrative departments. Hence, in this case, although the Traffic Police Detachment signed the Temporary Employment contract with the worker, the parties did establish an employment relationship. Jin Shulan and Sanjian Resident Committee of Nanyang Town, Tinghu District, Yancheng City, and the People's Government of Nanyang Town, Tinghu District, Yancheng City Civil Judgment of the Second Instance of Employment Dispute Civil Judgment of Jiangsu Yancheng Intermediate People's Court (2020) Su 09 Min Zhong No. 2884. Feng Huiqing and Pingyin County Rose Town People's Government Employment Dispute Appeal Case Jinan Intermediate People's Court of Shandong Province Civil Judgment (2017) Lu 01 Min Zhong No. 5656. Civil Ruling on Employment Dispute Retrial Review and Trial Supervision by Wang Suzhen and the Office of Hui'an County Committee of the Communist Party of China, Fujian Provincial People's High Court (2020) Min Min Shen No. 375.

23 Dong Wanfeng, Wenhui Parking Service Department, Renhe District, Panzhihua City, etc. Civil Judgment of Second Instance of Employment Dispute Civil Judgment of Intermediate People's Court of

qualified employers, and an employment contract signed by one is valid.[24] If a representative office of a foreign company directly employs employees without labor dispatch, it shall constitute a contractor relationship with the employees.[25]

The second special case is where construction and mining enterprises contract projects (business) or management rights to individual personnel who are not eligible to be employers, or to a company that has no engineering qualification to handle the project; the enterprises may assume the responsibility of the employer for the workers recruited by the contractor, the personnel, or the company.[26] This rule is specifically applicable to employment treatment or work-related injury liability, not to the formation of employment relations between the employees and the enterprises.[27]

For example, company A contracts out a project to company B (or individual B) without engineering qualification for construction of the project, and B recruits employee C. As a result, B disappears after receiving the project payments, and employee C can claim compensation from company A for the loss of their wages. This kind of employer's responsibility does not mean that employer A and employee C have established an employment relationship, and the final identification of employment relations still needs to examine the substantive relationship and the cognitive agreement between the two parties.[28]

The third type is due to the special status of specific employees. Whether the company's directors, shareholders, partners, and other special personnel who have common interests with the employer can become employees of the company still needs to be judged according to the substantive relationship of subordination and non-independence and the perception of both parties. For example, in a company with a large number of shareholders, if the chairman is still controlled by the board of directors or shareholders and is responsible for it, their share of the company's equity is relatively small, and the chairman has signed an

Panzhihua City, Sichuan Province (2022) Chuan 04 Min Zhong No. 705. Employment Dispute Appeal between Wu Ping and the Owner Committee of Zhongshi Garden, Chengzhong District, Xining City Civil Ruling of Xining Intermediate People's Court of Qinghai Province (2016) Qing 01 Min Zhong No. 1438.

24 The Supreme People's Court released the outstanding cases of the national court system in 2022, Zhongxing Community Resident Committee, Zhongxing Town, Youxian District, Mianyang City v. Jiang Anyuan Employment Dispute Case, the court of Youxian District, Mianyang City, Sichuan Province (2021) Chuan 0704 Min Chu No. 2292.

25 Fu Jianwei v. New Hope Foundation (Hong Kong) Beijing Representative Office Employment Dispute Case Beijing Shunyi District People's Court Civil Ruling (2015) Shun Min Chu Zi No. 10413.

26 Article 4 of the Notice of the Ministry of Labor and Social Security on Matters Relating to the Establishment of Employment Relations in 2005 stipulates that if an employer, such as a construction or mining enterprise, contracts a project (business) or management right to an organization or natural person that is not qualified as an employer, the employer who is qualified as an employer shall bear the responsibility of the employer for the workers recruited by the organization or natural person.

27 Article 62 of the 2015 Summary of the Civil and Commercial Trial Work Conference of the National Court (the Summary of Eight People) stipulates that the people's court shall not support the employer's request to confirm the existence of an employment relationship between the employer and the worker recruited by the actual constructor if the employer contracts the construction project to the contractor, and the contractor subcontracts or subcontracts it to the actual constructor. Article 94 of the Employment Contract Law stipulates: Where an individual contractor employs workers in violation of the provisions of this Law and causes damage to workers, the contracting organization and the individual contractor shall bear joint and several liability for compensation.

28 Civil Judgment on Employment Dispute Retrial between Sun Qiuliang, Henan Wanli Construction and Installation Co., Ltd. Civil Judgment of Henan High Court (2016) Yu Min Zai No. 637. Wang Qingchen and Jinzhou Zhucheng Construction Co., Ltd. Civil Judgment of Employment Dispute Retrial Liaoning Provincial People's High Court Civil Judgment (2018) Liao Min Zai No. 175.

employment contract with the company, they may still have an employment relationship with the company.[29]

Another special type of employee is an in-school student worker. Current judicial practice shows that there are two possibilities. One is that if the student is engaged in work-study activities arranged by the school to help students learn practical skills in enterprises, this work-study does not constitute an employment relationship with the internship employer. However, if the school has not arranged for the student to practice for the employer, and the employer also manages the student as a normal employee, the two parties are likely to have formed an employment relationship. See "41. Is it legal for my employer not to pay me as a student intern worker?"

Another kind of special employee is a foreigner or stateless person who is employed without a work permit in China. This does not constitute an employment relationship but a contractor relationship.[30] However, the Ministry of Human Resources and Social Security has stipulated that Taiwan, Hong Kong, and Macao residents who have been employed on the Chinese mainland since July 28, 2018 are no longer required to apply for work permits, so Taiwan, Hong Kong, and Macao residents who are employed in the mainland without work permits still have employment relations with their employers.[31]

The fourth situation is the special type of employment. The relationship between families and domestic service workers does not constitute an employment relationship (but a contractor relationship, or a service contract relationship between the families and domestic service companies). The relationship between helpers/apprentices and individual craftsmen is a contractor relationship, and the relationship between rural contractual operators and employees is a contractor relationship.[32] In addition, if the work relationship established between an employee and their second employer does not constitute special circumstances (such as the re-employment of those who are on long-term unpaid leave in state-owned enterprises), the employee does not have the standing to conclude a new employment contract, and the second work relationship may not be an employment

29 Supreme People's Court (2020) Supreme Fa Min Zai No. 50, Civil Judgment on Employment Dispute Retrial between Sun Qixiang and Jilin Midas Light Alloy Co., Ltd. Judge Wang Fubo pointed out that "[t]he second paragraph of Article 44 of the Company Law of the People's Republic of China stipulates that ..., which clearly affirms in the form of law that directors and their company can form employment relationships, and that the appointment relationship and employment relationship are not absolutely exclusive and incompatible. (Author's note: Articles 68 and 173 of the 2023 Company Law.)"

30 Article 33 of the Interpretation of the Supreme People's Court on the Application of Law in the Trial of Labor Dispute Cases (I) (Judicial Interpretation [2020] No. 26). Retrial of Employment Dispute between MICHAELDENG and Zhongshan Shenbao Electrical Appliance Manufacturing Co., Ltd. Civil Judgment of Guangdong Provincial People's High Court (2008) Y.G.F.S.J.M.T.Z. No. 63, Sino-US Joint Venture Kawajian Carpet Wool Crafts Co., Ltd. and WANGETSERINGSHRESTHA Employment Dispute Appeal Case Civil Judgment of the High Court of Tibet Autonomous Region (2015) Zang Fa Min Yi Zhong Zi No. 49.

31 The Notice of the Ministry of Human Resources and Social Security on Matters Relating to the Employment of Hong Kong, Macao and Taiwan Residents in the Mainland (Mainland), which was implemented on August 23, 2018, stipulates that from July 28, 2018, people from Hong Kong, Macao, and Taiwan no longer need to apply for the Work Permit for People from Taiwan, Hong Kong and Macao in the Mainland (Mainland). Article 12 of 2023 Consultation Draft on the Interpretation of the Supreme People's Court on the Application of Law in the Trial of Labor Dispute Cases (II).

32 Article 2 of the Interpretation of the Supreme People's Court on the Application of Law in the Trial of Labor Dispute Cases (I) (Judicial Interpretation [2020] No. 26).

relationship.[33] However, some cases hold that even so, the substantive relationship between the employee and the second employer should be examined to determine whether the two parties constitute an employment relationship, rather than simply denying the standing of the employee.[34]

It should be noted that even if two parties involved in work do not constitute an employment relationship, for example, if an representative office directly employs an employee, or an employer employs an employee who is over the retirement age and receives pension insurance benefits, the treatment or compensation to the employee should still be handled in comparison with the corresponding treatment of employment relations, including maternity leave treatment.[35] The worker does not need to go through the employment arbitration procedure but should sue directly to the court.[36]

We believe that according to the fundamental principle of protecting workers in China's employment laws, the legislature should amend or even reconstruct the distinction between employment relations and contractor relations at the level of system design, and incorporate some work relations with the characteristics of contractor relations (such as direct employment of Chinese employees by representative offices of foreign companies without labor dispatch) into employment relations so as to change the current situation of insufficient protection of employees' employment rights and interests under such special circumstances.

33 The Supreme People's Court issued the outstanding cases of the national court system in 2020, Guan Jianying v. Hunan Jiama Business Co., Ltd, Employment Dispute Second Instance Civil Judgment, Hunan Loudi Intermediate Court (2019) Xiang 13 Min Zhong No. 2065. The court pointed out that: "in this case, the appellant Guan Jianying is a regular employee of Loudi Works Section of China Railway Guangzhou Bureau Group Co., Ltd., who paid "five insurance and one fund" for him. On March 6, 2018, he was hired by the appellant Gama Company, while he did not terminate his employment with Loudi Works Section of China Railway Guangzhou Bureau Group Co., Ltd. In the court hearing, the Appellant acknowledged that he had a full-time employment relationship with the former employer, and that he did not belong to the enterprise's personnel who are on long-term unpaid leave, the internal retirees who had not reached the statutory retirement age, or the personnel on waiting-for-work, and the enterprise's personnel who had stopped production and had a long vacation, so he did not have the subject standing to establish employment relations with other employers as stipulated by law."

34 Li Baoquan and Huludao Jiada Transportation Co., Ltd. Civil Judgment of Second Instance of Employment Dispute Civil Judgment of Intermediate People's Court of Huludao City, Liaoning Province (2021) Liao 14 Min Zhong No. 1387. "In this case, although Li Baoquan signed a permanent employment contract with Jinxi Petrochemical Bohai Group Company, it can be seen from the certificates issued by Jinxi Petrochemical Bohai Group Company submitted by both parties that Li Baoquan was in a state of waiting-for-work. In fact, during Li Baoquan's work in Jiada Transportation Company, the route and time of his departure were arranged by Jiada Transportation Company, and the labor provided by him was an integral part of the business of Jiada Transport Company, and the payment of labor remuneration to Li Baoquan by Jiada Transport Company was also periodic, so there was a de facto relationship between the two parties."

35 Urumqi Meixinyuan Property Service Co., Ltd. and Ma Donghua Employment Dispute Civil Judgment of Civil Retrial, Xinjiang High Court (2022) Xinmin Zai No. 229. The court held that "[t]herefore, although Ma Donghua can not establish employment relations with the property company because he has exceeded the statutory retirement age, it does not affect the identification of work injury." Lu Liping et al. And Zhuang Xuemei et al. Civil Ruling on Employment Dispute Retrial Review and Trial Supervision Civil Ruling of Sichuan Provincial People's High Court (2020) Chuan Min Shen No. 6364. "With regard to the application of the law, the Measures for One-off Compensation Measures for Casualties of Illegal Host Employers are formulated in accordance with the Regulations on Work Injury Insurance, with the aim of making up for the system vacancy in the Regulations on Work Injury Insurance for illegal employment, and its decisions are consistent with the Regulations on Work Injury Insurance. According to the interpretation of the legal system, the court of first instance defines the case in accordance with work-related injury. It is a correct interpretation of the law, not a new interpretation beyond the law."

36 Application for Employment Dispute between Guangzhou Representative Office of Hong Kong Wanlida Co., Ltd. and Ren Xiaojuan Civil Ruling of Guangdong High Court (2014) Yue Gao Fa Min Shen Zi No. 95.

8. What are common contractor relationships in daily life?

Answer: Whether a worker is an independent contractor should be judged comprehensively according to the essence of the relationship between the two parties and the subjective understanding of both parties.

In China, self-employed individuals are likely to be contractors, such as self-employed architects, scaffolders, welders, and self-employed electricians and plumbers. Of course, if these individual operators operate in the name of a company, they are likely to be considered as independent contractors in the form of a company. The relationship between sailors or crew members and a ship manager company can be considered as either an employment relationship or a contractor relationship, depending on the nature of their relationship and agreements between the parties (please see "12. How do I distinguish between an employment relationship and a contractor relationship?").[37]

At present, the relationship between the emerging Internet platform and service providers is a difficult point in judicial practice. The courts still mainly consider the relationship between the two parties in terms of personal, economic, and organizational subordination and the agreement between the two parties. For example, the work mode of flexible and loose management generally is considered as a contractor relationship. Businesses of snapping-up orders generally are of a contractor nature,[38] but services such as delivery of goods and meals with relatively strict management can also be employment relations.[39]

According to case law, real estate agents are generally not contractors, but employees of companies. [40] Film projectionists who are paid on a per-show basis may be contractors.[41] Whether the cleaner is an independent contractor depends on the specific circumstances. If the cleaner takes the work arranged by the employer as the main source of income and is

---

37 Provisions of the Supreme People's Court on Several Issues Concerning the Trial of Disputes Involving Seafarers (Judicial Interpretation [2020] No. 11).

38 Chifeng Yunsu Running Service Co., Ltd. v. Lu Employment Dispute Second Instance Civil Judgment, Inner Mongolia Chifeng Intermediate People's Court (2019) Nei 04 Min Zhong No. 4645. "For Internet platform employment, we should adhere to the identification of personality subordination, economic subordination and organizational subordination, and fully respect the parties' intention and freedom of contracting. In this case, Lu is engaged in casual work, has the autonomy on whether to provide services, provides his own means of transportation, works freely, Lu and Yunsu Running Company have weak subordination, especially the two parties have signed a cooperation agreement to clarify the rights and obligations of the two parties, the actors' intention is true and should be respected. The court of first instance's finding of employment relations between the two parties is inappropriate."

39 Business of snapping-up orders is a type of platform-based business in which workers compete for orders from an Internet platform operated by a company. Civil Judgment of Second Instance of Employment Dispute between Zhang Jiashou and Fuzhou Taijiang Chiwantong Network Technology Co., Ltd., Fujian Fuzhou Intermediate People's Court (2019) Min 01 Min Zhong No. 4093. "From the point of view of this agreement, Party B Zhang Jiashou's picking up and delivering goods is the task arranged by Party A, which is essentially different from the casual Meituan takeout rider's independent snapping-up order mode."

40 Nanning Branch of Guangxi Shihua Real Estate Agency Co., Ltd., Fang Kui Employment Dispute Civil Judgment of Second Instance, Nanning Intermediate People's Court of Guangxi Zhuang Autonomous Region, (2021) Gui 01 Min Zhong No. 984. Xiamen Yuanzhongyuan Real Estate Agency Co., Ltd., Luo Yiquan and other civil judgments of the second instance of Employment Disputes, Fujian Xiamen Intermediate People's Court (2021) Min 02 Min Zhong No. 1498.

41 Linquan Xinying Film Distribution and Projection Co., Ltd. and Yu Rulin applied for a civil ruling to revoke the special procedure of arbitration award, Anhui Fuyang Intermediate People's Court, (2018) Wan 12 Min Te No. 19. "From May 2010 to January 2019, Yu Rulin signed a work agreement with Xinying Film Distribution and Projection Co., Ltd. of Linquan County. The two parties agreed to calculate the remuneration according to the number of films shown. The two parties formed contractor relationship, not an employment relationship, which does not belong to an employment arbitration matter."

strictly managed by the employer, they are employees; but if the cleaner can freely arrange the cleaning time and manning, and provides services for more than one company, they are likely independent contractors.

Other contractor relations include circumstances where representative offices of foreign companies directly hire workers, individuals hire other individuals for services, individuals are contracted to certain work (such as breeding and planting), workers engage in daily labor services, and craftsmen hire assistant workers.[42] According to the 2020 judicial interpretation of the Supreme Court on employment disputes, housekeepers, helpers and apprentices, and helpers of rural contractors are also contractors.[43]

In a word, to determine whether a worker is a contractor or an employee is not always clear-cut. We should comprehensively consider the substantive factors of the relationship between the two parties, such as the degree of control and dependence of the worker, as well as the understanding and agreements of the nature of the relationship between the two parties.

1.2 Difference between Employment and Contract Relations

9. How can I distinguish between my casual employees and full-time employees?

Answer: Casual employment is a more flexible type of employment relative to full-time. The two parties need not sign a contract (of course, signing a contract does not breach the law), and this employment relationship can be terminated at any time.

According to the Employment Contract Law and judicial decisions, whether an employment relationship is a casual employment depends on the following factors: weekly work hours, bilateral agreement, payment method, and pay period.[44]

Work hours are the most important consideration. Although the Employment Contract Law also provides for a maximum 4 hours as daily work hours standard, the distinguishing indicator in judicial practice is whether the total weekly work hours exceed 24 hours. Most judicial decisions regard this total weekly work hours as the first important judgment factor. If the worker's weekly work hours occasionally exceed 24 hours, will it lead to the recognition of full-time employment relations? From the case of Cao Yazhen in Zhenhai District Court before Ningbo City in 2013, the court did take the number of work hours as an absolute, stringent indicator, but tended to combine other factors to determine the employment relations between the two parties.[45]

---

42 Civil Judgment of Second Instance of Employment Dispute between Guangxi Ruiluyuan Technology Co., Ltd. and Liu Deqiang, Guangxi Nanning Intermediate People's Court, (2021) Gui 01 Min Zhong No. 7300. "The common contractor relationship in life is to do small jobs, such as individual bosses, contract industrialized farming, agricultural planting, and rural residents providing labor services on daily basis. They are all typical contractor relationships."

43 Article 2 of the Interpretation of the Supreme People's Court on the Application of Law in the Trial of Labor Dispute Cases (I) (Judicial Interpretation [2020] No. 26).

44 Articles 68 and 72 of the Employment Contract Law (the weekly work hours shall not exceed 24 hours and the pay period shall not exceed 15 days); Beijing Boken Energy Conservation Technology Co., Ltd. v. Li Yansheng, Beijing the Third Intermediate People's Court (2022) Jing 03 Min Zhong No. 3895. The court held, "To distinguish employment relations from casual employment relations, the main factors to be considered include the time for workers to provide labor, the period for employers to pay remunerations, the basis for calculating labor remunerations and the provisions of employment contracts."

45 Ningbo Zhenhai Baoxin High Strength Nut Factory v. Cao Yazhen, the Ningbo Zhenhai District People's Court Civil Judgment (2013) Yong Zhen Min Chu Zi No. 428. The court held that "[t]he definition of casual employment in our country is to adopt the standard of daily work hours combined with weekly work hours,

The agreement and cognition of both sides are also important factors. The employment law in China does not prohibit the employer from signing a written contract with casual workers. If the written contract stipulates the work hours being casual, it can be regarded as the preliminary proof of the formation of a casual relationship between the two parties. The perception of both parties to the relationship, including the expression of intention or the understanding of the closeness of the relationship between the two parties, is also an important factor. Of course, even if both parties agree or recognize it being casual, but the substantive characteristics of the relationship point to a full-time nature, the relationship between the two parties is still a full-time employment relationship.[46]

Pay period and hourly rate are also important considerations, but they are not decisive. In 2014, the Intermediate Court of Shaoyang City, Hunan Province, pointed out in a case that although the monthly payment of wages did not conform to the provisions of the casual wage payment period not exceeding 15 days, the court mainly determined whether it was casual work hours based on the number of work hours. In the case of Xu Shu before Kunshan City Court of Jiangsu Province in 2014, the court held that even though the employee's remuneration period was not hourly but monthly, the casual employment relationship should still be recognized according to the employee's work hours.[47]

Therefore, whether the employment relationship between your employer and you is casual or full-time should be judged comprehensively by considering the aforementioned factors. If a casual relationship cannot be established, the corresponding legal consequence is that the relationship between the two parties is full-time employment.

10. Can casual employees request to be transferred to a permanent or other form of employment contract?

Answer: Casual employment relations is a flexible type of employment. The Employment Contract Law stipulates that an employer may conclude an oral agreement with a casual employee, and both parties may notify the other party to terminate the employment

that is, in general, no more than 4 hours a day and no more than 24 hours a week, but there is no absolute stipulation that the daily work hours exceed 4 hours and the weekly work hours exceed 24 hours should render a full-time employment relationship. This Court is in the view that the judgment of casual employment and full-time employment relations should be based on the employer's purpose of employment, the workload and work hours of workers."

46 Xiamen Haokang Housekeeping Service Co., Ltd. v. Yu Juan, the Nanjing Intermediate People's Court of Jiangsu Province (2020) Su 01 Min Zhong No. 1863. The court held that "although Yu Juan has signed a casual employment contract with Haokang Home Economics Company, Yu Juan has submitted evidence to prove that her average weekly work hours from August 5, 2018 to August 4, 2019 far exceed the statutory casual work hours of 24 hours a week, this does not conform to the characteristics of casual employment relations. Even if both parties agree on casual employment relationships when signing the contract, they have changed to full-time employment relationship in actual performance."

47 Wang Yanlian v. Shaoyang University, the Hunan Shaoyang Intermediate People's Court Civil Judgment (2014) Shao Zhong Min Yi Zhong Zi No. 46. Judging from Wang Yanlian's work hours. The court held that "[a]lthough Shaoyang University pays labor remuneration to Wang Yanlian on a monthly basis, which is inconsistent with the provisions of Article 72, paragraph 2, of the Employment Contract Law of the People's Republic of China that 'the longest wage pay period for casual employment shall not exceed 15 days', it does not affect the determination of the nature of casual employment in this case." Xu Shuzhi v. Kunshan Haysville Fitness and Beauty Co., Ltd. the Kunshan People's Court of Jiangsu Province (2014) Kunhua Min Chu Zi No. 00614. The court held that "[a]ccording to the Plaintiff, the wage is not calculated on an hourly basis, and the wage is paid on a monthly basis. This Court is in the view that the key to the legal definition of whether the form of employment between the employer and the worker is casual employment lies in the work hours."

relationship at any time.[48] This provision is totally different from the permanent employment contract, which emphasizes the protection of the continuation of the employee's employment contract or the fixed-term employment contract, which secures employment within a certain period.

Therefore, we believe that although the law and practice are not very clear, employers should not be obligated to sign permanent employment contracts with their casual employees.

At present, prevailing judicial cases advocate that employers have no legal obligation to sign permanent employment contracts with casual employees. For example, in the case of Shen Sijingui in 2017, the Qingyuan Intermediate Court of Guangdong Province pointed out that casual employment is a flexible type of employment, and the employer has no obligation to sign a permanent employment contract. Similar cases include the case of Xiao Xiang before Anshun Intermediate Court of Guizhou Province in 2016 and the case of Li Meiai before Shanwei Intermediate Court of Guangdong Province in 2019.[49] However, in the case of Panshuixian in 2023, the Second Intermediate Court of Beijing held that the law did not prohibit employers from signing permanent employment contracts with casual employees who meet statutory conditions such as service years.[50]

Interestingly, there are court decisions that hold that employers and casual workers can sign work assignment contracts. For example, the Intermediate People's Court of the 12th Division of Xinjiang Production and Construction Corps held this view in the case of Chen Hua in 2022. [51] However, we believe that the signing of a work assignment contract means that the employer cannot dismiss the employee before the completion of the work assignment, which conflicts with the rule that both parties to a casual employment

48 Articles 69 and 71 of the Employment Contract Law.

49 Shen Sijingui v. State-owned Longping Forest Farm, the Qingyuan Intermediate People's Court of Guangdong Province (2017) Yue 18 Min Zhong No. 2319. The court held that "[c]asual employment is a relatively flexible form of employment. Although it is included in the scope of the Employment Contract Law of the People's Republic of China, it gives either party the right to notify the other party to terminate employment at any time, and the employer does not need to pay economic compensation to the workers. The permanent employment contract refers to the employment contract in which the employer and the worker agree that there is no definite termination time. There are strict legal provisions for employers and workers to request the termination of permanent employment contracts, which is different from casual employment. Therefore, there is no legal grounds in support of the Appellant's claims that the Appellee has signed a permanent employment contract with him and must pay punitive damages for illegal termination of the contract." Xiao Xiang v. Pingba Power Supply Bureau, the Anshun Intermediate People's Court of Guizhou Province (2016) Qian 04 Min Zhong No. 240. The court held that "[t]he employment nature of both parties is casual, which does not fall under the situation that permanent contract should be signed." Li Meiai v. Guangdong Power Grid Co., Ltd., Shanwei Lufeng Power Supply Bureau, the Guangdong Shanwei Intermediate People's Court Civil Judgment (2019) Yue 15 Min Zhong No. 156. The court held that "[a]ccording to Article 71 of the Employment Contract Law of the People's Republic of China, 'Either party to casual employment may notify the other party to terminate employment at any time.' Therefore, casual employment does not fall under the situation that permanent employment contracts should be signed."

50 Yongzhou Municipal People's Government Liaison Office in Beijing v. Pan Shuixian, the Second Intermediate People's Court of Beijing (2023) Jing 02 Min Zhong No. 2097. The court held that "Employment Contract Law of the People's Republic of China … does not prohibit casual employees from signing permanent employment contracts with their employers. Since Pan Shuixian has worked in the Liaison Office in Beijing for more than ten years, he shall be entitled to sign a permanent employment contract with the Office."

51 Chen Hua v. Xinjiang Tejin Tourism Investment Management Co., Ltd., the Intermediate People's Court of the 12th Division of Xinjiang Production and Construction Corps (2022) Bing 11 Min Zhong No. 213. The court held that according to the stipulation that "employers and employees may sign assignment employment through mutual negotiation and agreement," the agreements in the employment contract do not violate the provisions of the law and do not contradict the form of casual employment stipulated in the Employment Law.

relationship can terminate it at any time, so it is not appropriate for the employer to sign a work assignment contract with casual workers. For the same reason, it is not appropriate for employers to sign fixed-term and labor dispatch contracts with casual workers. Article 30 of the Regulations on the Implementation of the Employment Contract Law stipulates that the form of casual employment is not applicable to labor dispatch contracts.

In addition, in the practice of the employment laws, there are also casual irregular work hours or general work hours.[52] We believe that both the irregular work hour system and the general work hour system have the employer's obligation to arrange relatively stable and expectable work for employees, which is essentially different from the part-time system, in which both parties can terminate the relationship at any time. These are the issues that the employment law in China needs to clarify and amend at the legislative level.

11. Can a volunteer be an employee?

Answer: In principle, pure volunteers are not considered as workers under the legal system of the employment laws. However, in practice, employers may grant subsidies or provide benefits such as allowances or reimbursement to volunteers, at which time the situation will be somewhat complicated. The court will examine the agreement between the two parties, whether there is remuneration, the name and amount of remuneration, and other factors to determine whether there is a situation of evading employment law obligations in the name of volunteers.

For example, in the case of Huang Yingying before Bijie Intermediate Court of Guizhou Province in 2021, the court held that although a kindergarten had signed a volunteer service agreement with Huang Yingying, the agreement stipulated such matters as remuneration and social insurance under the employment laws, and therefore the two parties were considered to have a substantive employment relationship.[53]

However, when the employer is a government department, the court tends to focus more on examining the name of volunteer, agreed by both parties, and less on essential matters such as whether the volunteer receives remuneration and social insurance. For example, in the case of Xiang Yonghong before the Chongqing High Court in 2018, although a subdistrict office employed volunteers and contributed their pension insurances, the court still denied an employment relationship on the basis of the agreed volunteer agreement between the two parties. The case of Hu Guoxing in Shanxi Provincial High Court in 2017 is similar.[54]

We believe that the law should be implemented in accordance with a unified standard. No matter who the employer is, it should strictly examine the personal dependence relationship between volunteers and the employer and the subjective understanding of the

52 Li Ting v. Luoyang Jiaxuan Real Estate Co., Ltd., the Intermediate People's Court of Luoyang City, Henan Province (2021) Yu 03 Min Zhong No. 210.

53 Dafang County Central Kindergarten, Huang Yingying Employment Dispute Civil Judgment of Second Instance Civil Judgment of Bijie Intermediate People's Court of Guizhou Province (2021) Qian 05 Min Zhong No. 5176.

54 Xiang Yonghong and Chongqing Wanzhou District Disabled Persons' Federation Chongqing Wanzhou District Gaosuntang Subdistrict Office Employment Dispute Appeal and Application for Retrial Civil Ruling Chongqing High Court Civil Ruling (2018) Yu Min Shen No. 2263. Hu Guoxing v. Yangquan Public Security Bureau Employment Dispute Civil Ruling of Shanxi Provincial People's High Court (2017) Jin Min Shen No. 154.

relationship between the two parties, considering remuneration, social insurances, work management, and other aspects, to determine whether the two parties are under employment relations. See 12. "How do I distinguish between an employment relationship and a contractor relationship?"

12. How do I distinguish between an employment relationship and a contractor relationship?

Answer: It is a complicated legal issue to judge whether a work relationship is an employment relationship or an independent contractor relationship (called a Guyong relationship [雇佣关系] in some judicial decisions). An employment relationship is a legal relationship based on employees' personal and economic dependence on the employer, and thus, the law grants special protection to the employees (such as the right to rest and vacation, and the prohibition on the employer from arbitrarily dismissing employees).

In judicial practice, courts nationwide generally determine whether an employment relationship exists based on the former Ministry of Labor's "Notice on Matters Relating to the Establishment of Employment Relations" (LaoSheBuFa [2005] No. 12), which stipulates the three necessary conditions that must be simultaneously met for the establishment of an employment relationship, including: (1) the employer and employee meet the subject qualifications stipulated by laws and regulations; (2) the company rules and regulations formulated by the employer according to law apply to the employee, and the employee is subject to the employer's work management, engaging in paid work arranged by the employer; (3) the work provided by the employee is part of the employer's business.

From the perspective of employment law practice, the last condition is flawed. For example, an employer engaged in accounting services is fully entitled to sign an employment contract with an employee, agreeing that the employee will be fully responsible for providing meals and cleaning services for the company on a full-time basis; the employee's work is not part of the accounting firm's business, yet the two parties undoubtedly form an employment relationship.

Therefore, we believe that the second condition should be summarized as: the determination of an employment relationship should examine the substance of the relationship between the two parties. The key to recognizing an employment relationship is that the employee is subordinate and dependent on the employer, rather than independently operating to provide services to the employer.

Whether the substantive nature of the relationship between the two parties has the characteristics of the employee's subordination and non-independence should be judged from two aspects. On the one hand, we should examine the following factors from the employee's perspective: first, it is crucial to determine whether the employee is engaged in independent business, which is the most important characteristic. We need to assess whether the employee is also providing similar services to other companies, and whether the employee has the right to autonomously arrange for someone else to replace them at work. Other factors include the type of work hours the employee has (the closer the work hours are to full-time, the stronger the personal dependence, and it is more likely to be recognized as an employment relationship), the duration of the relationship between the two parties (the more temporary the work, the more likely it is to be identified as a contractor relationship), whether the employee has a business entity and pays taxes independently (if so, it can generally be determined as a contractor relationship), whether the nature of the employee's work is part of the employer's business (the more the employee's work involves the employer's core business, such as accounting work in an accounting firm, the closer it is to an employment relationship), and whether the employee uses their own tools and bears their own work costs.

On the other hand, from the employer's perspective, the degree of control the company has over the employee, whether the company treats them differently from other employees, and whether the company deducts social insurance contribution and personal income taxes on their behalf should be considered.

For example, in the case of Cong Mingzi before the Supreme People's Court in 2016, Mr. Cong Mingzi delivered newspapers for a newspaper office, spent fuel on his own car, operated on a family basis, and was paid according to the number of pieces delivered. Although the office provided a work certificate, work clothes, and bank cards, and evaluated his performance, the Supreme People's Court considered that the relationship between the two parties was a contractor relationship.[55] In 2022, Shanxi High Court also pointed out that the personal, organizational, and economic dependence of a worker in the work relationship is the core criterion.[56]

In the 2022 case of Wang Maochun before Fuxin Intermediate Court of Liaoning Province in 2022, it is held that the nature of the relationship between the two parties should not only rely on the contractual agreement between the two parties, but also, the essence of the relationship should be examined.[57]

If the employee claims that an employment relationship exists with the employer, and the employer denies it, the employee should bear the burden of proof to demonstrate the existence of the employment relationship, including providing evidence of a signed employment contract, wage payments, provision of labor, and acceptance of management.

There are different legal consequences under a contractor relationship and employment relationship; an employee under the latter receives stronger legal protection. For details, please refer to 15. "What are the different legal consequences of my employment relationship or contractor relationship with a company?"

Despite the aforementioned rules, there are many special forms of employment relations and contractor relations due to the unique deep administrative involvement of China's

55 Civil Judgment on Employment Dispute Retrial by Cong Mingzi and the Supreme People's Procuratorate of the People's Republic of China, Supreme People's Court (2016) Supreme Fa Min Zai No. 148.

56 Song Zhijun, Shanxi Zhongxin Ganzhuang Coal Industry Co., Ltd. Employment Dispute Civil Trial Supervision Civil Ruling, Shanxi Provincial People's High Court (2022) Jin Min Shen No. 2684. "Subordination/dependence is the core standard, including personality subordination, organizational subordination and economic subordination. The biggest difference between contractor relations and employment relations is that in addition to providing labor, workers in employment relations should also be subject to the management of the employer, obey its arrangements, abide by its company rules and regulations, and become part of the employer."

57 Liaoning Fuxin Intermediate People's Court (2022) Liao 09 Min Zhong No. 772, Mingzhe Group Co., Ltd. Fuxin Branch, Wang Maochun Employment Dispute Civil Judgment of Second Instance. "Whether the work relationship between a worker and an employer constitutes employment relationship can not be dictated only by the written agreement of the parties, but also by judging whether the work relationship conforms to the characteristics of employment relations."

employment laws and the shortcomings of the legal framework for employment relations. Please refer to "7. What are common special employment relationships in daily life?" and "8. What are common contractor relationships in daily life?"

13. I am a cleaner with a regular work schedule. Am I an employee of this company or a contractor?

Answer: The fact that you do cleaning work for a company and have a fixed shift schedule does not in itself identify you as an employee of the company. It also depends on other factors of the arrangement. For a detailed analysis of legal factors, please refer to "12. How do I distinguish between an employment relationship and a contractor relationship?"

You are more likely to be considered an employee of the company if your social insurance is purchased at the company, your service contract is written as an employment relationship, your work arrangement is controlled by the company, and your cleaning work is a relatively fixed arrangement and you are considered part of the employees.

Conversely, if the following conditions exist, you are more likely to be identified as a contractor: the contract between the two parties clearly states that you are a contractor, you can arrange for others to work instead of you, you buy your own social insurance, you use your own tools to work for the company, the company basically does not care how you clean and will not apply company rules and regulations to you, and you can refuse additional cleaning tasks required by the company.

In short, there is no black and white test for whether you are an employee or a contractor, and it is sometimes difficult to distinguish between various factors. Your relationship with the company ultimately requires a combined consideration of all of these factors.

14. Are employees on call at home entitled to wage payment?

Answer: The so-called standby work is a state of being on call at home, waiting for work arrangements. Compared to employees working night shifts at the employer's workplace, this is a more flexible work arrangement. Whether wages should be paid for standby work first depends on whether there is an employment relationship between the two parties. If this relationship is essentially a contractor relationship, the company is not obligated, unless otherwise stipulated in their contract, to pay the worker wages for the standby period based on the principle of employee protection under the employment laws.

If both parties do indeed constitute an employment relationship, the key question then is to determine whether this standby constitutes work under the employment laws. Chinese employment laws do not explicitly answer this question. The criteria for determining whether being on standby at home qualifies as work or overtime, based on current court decisions, are generally consistent with whether being on duty constitutes work or overtime. It should involve a comprehensive consideration of factors such as the requirements for being on standby, the freedom of movement, whether the worker is allowed to sleep, etc. Please refer to "115. An employer pays night allowance under the minimum wage to an employee on night duty. Is it legal?"

There are many cases ruling that standby at home does not constitute work,[58] but there was also a case holding that an employee working through WeChat at home was work.[59] It mainly depends on the nature of this kind of standby. If such standby arrangements impose high constraints on employees (for example, prohibiting alcohol consumption and restricting outings to no more than half an hour), require a rapid response from employees (such as expecting them to arrive at the worksite within one hour of receiving a notification), and entail significant responsibilities, then this standby is likely to be considered as work (and if it occurs outside normal work hours, it may be deemed as overtime). In such cases, the employee during the standby period should be entitled to at least the local minimum wage.

15. What are the different legal consequences of my employment relationship or contractor relationship with a company?

Answer: The law provides different rules on the rights and obligations for employees under employment relations and contractors under contractor relations. For example, the former is entitled to the most basic mandatory protection of employment rights, while the latter is entitled to freedom of contract and bargaining as equal civil subjects.

If you are an employee, you are dependent on the employer, and your work is part of the business. The relationship between you and the employer is regulated by the employment laws, and when a dispute arises, you should bring the employment dispute to the Employment Dispute Arbitration Committee. The employer shall provide you with paid annual leave and sick leave (if you meet the prescribed conditions), paid public holidays, rest and work-breaks, etc. The employer shall pay you no less than the minimum wage for your hours worked. If the employer wants to terminate the employment relationship with you, it must meet strict legal conditions and procedures. Employers are also obligated to deduct your social insurance contribution and personal income tax on your behalf. When you are injured at work, no matter whether you are at fault or not, the employer and/or social insurance institution must bear the responsibility related to work-related injuries.

But if you are an independent contractor, the relationship between you and the company is an equal commercial relationship, regulated by commercial law and contract law. Disputes between the two parties are handled by the courts like other commercial disputes. The remuneration paid by the company to you should be executed according to the contract. The company has no obligations to you such as rest, vacation, and minimum wage. You usually need to pay personal income tax and social insurance by yourself.

58 Li Gang and China National Heavy Duty Truck Group Co., Ltd. Civil Ruling on Civil Application for Retrial Review of Labor Dispute Shandong High Court Civil Ruling (2022) Lu Min Shen No. 7277. The court held that the bus drivers of the employer could rest most of the time except for commuting, so the overtime wages of employees could not be calculated on the basis of normal work hours. Civil Ruling on the Labor Dispute between the retrial applicant Fushun Jiaxin Commodity Concrete Co., Ltd. and the respondent Yin Ke Liaoning Provincial People's High Court Civil Ruling (2016) Liao Min Shen No. 4522. In the judgment, the court upheld the mode of working for 24 hours and and then resting for 24 hours without additional overtime pay. Civil Ruling on Labor Dispute Appeal and Application for Retrial between Zhe Tao and Yulin Central Branch of Tian'an Property Insurance Co., Ltd. Civil Ruling of Shaanxi Provincial People's High Court (2020) Shan Min Shen No. 2332. The court held that the situation that employees could not turn off their mobile phones after work could not be regarded as overtime.

59 http://m.cyol.com/gb/articles/2023-05/03/content_jpbVlBtwP3.html. The article reported that the Third Beijing Intermediate People's Court ruled that work-related chat through WeChat after work was considered employee's overtime work.

When you are accidentally injured at work, the liabilities shall be borne according to the fault between you and the company.[60] The termination and dissolution of the cooperative relationship between the two parties depends on how the service contract is agreed and how the two parties perform the contract.

It should be noted that in some cases of employment-like contractor relationships, for example, for work-related injuries of a contractor who is over retirement age and has already received pension insurance, the courts may also order the employer to assume the obligation of compensation for work-related injuries.[61] This may reflect the defects in the construction of the legal framework of employment relations in China, because it cannot explain why contractors sometimes may be entitled to certain rights under the employment laws (such as work injury entitlements). In real life, there is no clear boundary between employees and contractors, and sometimes it is difficult to distinguish between them. To assess the nature of the relationship for a worker, it is necessary to examine the substantive characteristics of the relationship between the two parties and their perceptions and agreements. Please see "12. How do I distinguish between an employment relationship and a contractor relationship?"

16. What are the differences between employment relationships of an assignment contract, a casual contract, and a contractor relationship?

Answer: The two types of employment relations, assignment contract and casual contract, still have the dependent characteristics of employment relations, and differ significantly from contractor relations, which bear relative independence and equality between the parties.

An assignment contract with a period of time to complete a certain task is quite different from a contractor relationship. A typical assignment contract is an employment contract signed by an employer and an employee for a specific research and development (R&D) task, which stipulates that the contract will be terminated upon completion of the task. Usually, this contract is a full-time job. Although this has the same business purpose as a contractor relationship (for example, outsourcing the task to a freelancer), the former is characterized by the fact that the employee is engaged in work under the management and control of the employer, and the employee has the characteristics of economic and personal dependence on the employer. Freelancers (contractors) in the latter are independently engaged in R&D work and self-managed work arrangements, often provide services for multiple companies, operate independently, and are not dependent on the employer.

60 Article 1192 of the Civil Code states that "[i]n case of contractor relationship between individuals, if the contractor causes damage to others due to contractor services, the party receiving contractor services shall bear tort liability. After the party receiving the contractor service bears the tort liability, it may recover the compensation from the contractor who acted intentionally or in gross negligence. If contractor suffers damage due to the service, both parties shall bear corresponding liabilities according to the respective faults."

61 Dingsheng Environmental Engineering (Shenzhen) Co., Ltd., Zhou Lingzhi Work Injury Insurance Treatment Dispute Retrial Review and Trial Supervision Civil Ruling Guangdong Provincial People's High Court Civil Ruling (2020) Yue Min Shen No. 2754. "Based on the facts of this case, we find that the court of second instance rightfully found that Zhou Mouhong's death should be treated as a work-related injury as there was an employment contract relationship between the deceased Zhou Mouhong and Dingsheng Company (the deceased was a person who had received pension insurance and was over retirement age)."

Casual employment relationships are the weakest employment relation in terms of personal dependence and management control. Although some courts believe that this is the third form of relation independent of employment relations and contractor relations,[62] and that termination of casual relations does not necessitate economic compensation at the end of the relationship, the Employment Contract Law and prevailing cases all consider it a kind of employment relations, where the employer has a certain management of employees, the employee has a certain degree of dependence on the employer, and the employer is obligated to purchase work injury insurance for employees. This is different from the independent and equal operation of contractor relations.

1.3 Special Types of Workers and Work Relations

17. I am a worker who is 15 years old. Should my employer assume the liability for my work-related injury?

Answer: Yes, the employer is liable to compensation for your work-related injury.

Workers under the age of 16 are considered child laborers in China. Their labor skills and intellectual cognition are in the primary stage of development, so they are relatively immature, vulnerable, and fragile in physical and psychological aspects. The employment laws adopt the principle of special protection for minor workers under the age of 16.

The law prohibits employers from recruiting children under the age of 16, otherwise the employer may be subject to administrative fines or criminal penalties, including imprisonment for up to 3 years. Exceptionally, if an artistic or sports employer recruits professional artists or athletes under the age of 16, the employer must obtain the consent of their parents or other guardians.[63]

Although it is prohibited by law, there are still cases of illegal employment of child labor by employers in practice. According to the principles of the Labor Law, child workers under the age of 16 do not constitute the subject of legal employment relations, but only constitute contractor relations with employers. However, when a child worker is injured at work or suffers from an occupational disease, the employer shall bear no less than the liability for work-related injury compensation under employment relations.[64]

18. Is a family member of the boss hired by the company considered an employee?

Answer: When a family member of the boss or actual controller of the employer works for the employer, this is a special situation. Unlike the ordinary employment relationship between employee and employer, the relationship involves domestic affection and kinship. Whether the relationship is an employment depends on the closeness of the relationship

---

62 Jiamusi Tianhong Trading Co., Ltd., Sun Long Employment Dispute Civil Judgment of Second Instance Civil Judgment of Jiamusi Intermediate People's Court of Heilongjiang Province (2023) Hei 08 Min Zhong No. 49. The court held that casual flexible employment is the third form of relationship, independent of employment relationships and contractor relationships.

63 Article 13 of the Regulations of the State Council on the Prohibition of Child Labor in 2002.

64 Article 66 of the Regulations on Work Injury Insurance, 2010: "The employer shall not use child labor. If the employer uses child labor and causes the disability or death of the child labor, the employer shall pay one-off compensation to the child labor or their close relatives, and the compensation standard shall not be lower than the treatment of work injury insurance stipulated in these Regulations." Article 2 of the One-off Compensation Measures for Casualties of Illegal Host Employers.

between the boss and the employee, as well as the specific arrangements between the two parties and the nature of the work.

First of all, the closer the kinship, the lower the possibility of the establishment of employment relations. For example, when a work relationship involves husband and wife, parents and children, siblings, etc., the kinship and human relations between the two parties make it difficult to establish an employment relationship. Among these relationships, the closest civil legal relationship is between husband and wife,[65] making it nearly impossible to form an employment relationship between them. For example, in the case of Fu Bin before Shenyang Intermediate People's Court in 2022, the court held that the period during which the employee claimed unpaid wages was the period during which there was a husband–wife relationship between the employee and the investor of the employer. Therefore, there was no employment relationship between the two parties during the period, and the wages claims were not upheld.[66] Similarly, work relationships between father, son, and brothers are also not likely to be considered employment relationships, based on human ethics and morality.

Second, when assessing the work relationship between non-family members or ordinary relatives, it is also necessary to consider the work arrangement and nature of both parties. If this arrangement conforms to the core characteristics of employment relations, including economic, organizational, and personal subordination or dependence, and the family member is bound by the company rules and regulations to work as other employees are, the two parties are likely to constitute an employment relationship. However, if this arrangement is a kind of family business management and family mutual assistance, the family member (the worker) also participates in the management and operation, and can freely decide whether to come to the office, then the employer may have no management authority over the family member. In this case, an employment relationship is unlikely to be recognized.[67]

---

65 According to the provision of the Marital and Family book of the Civil Code, the income of both spouses during marriage is the common property of the couple, and the spouse is also the first heir.

66 Judgment of Second Instance of Employment Dispute between Fu Bin and Shenyang Tongtai Automobile Driver Training Center Civil Judgment of Shenyang Intermediate People's Court of Liaoning Province (2022) Liao 01 Min Zhong No. 9996.

67 Civil Judgment of Second Instance of Employment Dispute between Peng Guilian and Linghaobo Civil Judgment of Nanning Intermediate People's Court of Guangxi Zhuang Autonomous Region (2020) Gui 01 Min Zhong No. 2597. "Secondly, there is a special family relationship between Peng Guilian and Ling Haobo. Peng Guilian worked in the farm run by Ling Haobo, which originally based on the equal and mutual assistance relationship between family members. This is essentially different from the personal subordination of employment relations. Looking at the evidence submitted by Peng Guilian in this case, it is difficult to conclude that Ling Haobo has implemented employment management over her. During her work in the farm, Peng Guilian lived and ate in the farm most of the time, had free access to work and rest, did not need any attendance, and had strong independence and autonomy in her work. This is obviously different from the general employment relations. Therefore, the Court does not recognize the existence of employment relations between Peng Guilian and Ling Haobo." Employment Dispute between Zheng Chunrong and Dalian Xinmingsheng Automobile Repair Factory Civil Judgment of Dalian Intermediate People's Court of Liaoning Province (2016) Liao 02 Min Zhong No. 7248. "The Appellee was invested and founded by the Appellant's mother-in-law Sun Zhenyun. Alongside with the Appellant and her husband Wang Yusheng, Sun Zhenyun's three sons and daughters-in-law all work in the factory, and their work income is the main source of family income. As far as the business model and the way of providing labor stated by both parties are concerned, it is a fact that the Appellant provides labor to the appellee, but the relationship between the two parties is not between the employee and the employer; The Appellant's work in the Appellee's office is actually a business activity. The Appellee does not have the right to manage the personnel and business of the Appellant. Therefore, the relationship between the Appellant and the Appellee does not have the basic characteristics of an employment relationship. It is not improper for the

19. If my employer continues to employ me after I reach the retirement age, do we still maintain the employment relationship?

Answer: It is a very complicated legal issue when an employer continues to employ an employee who has reached the statutory retirement age. There are several possible situations, as follows.

In the first case, if the employee has started to receive basic pension insurance benefits (limited to the employee's pension insurance, excluding urban resident social pension insurance and the new-style rural pension insurance),[68] the employment relationship between the two parties will be automatically converted into a contractor relationship.

The second situation is that if the employee does not receive basic pension insurance benefits, due to the different practices of the courts in the place where the employer is located, there are two possibilities: direct conversion to contractor relations and continuation of employment relations. Whether the employer is at fault in the employee's failure to receive basic pension insurance benefits, and whether the employer actively notifies the termination of employment relations, may produce different results.

Different results have potentially significant impacts on both parties' rights and obligations. If the relationship between the two parties is recognized as a contractor relationship, the employee will not be able to obtain some employment rights under the employment laws, such as double-wage damages in the absence of a written employment contract, but it should be noted that the employee may still be entitled to some rights under the employment laws, such as some work injury entitlements, according to the Supreme Court's judicial interpretation or special provisions of the law.

Judging whether there is an employment relationship bears subtle differences between continuously hiring a current employee who reaches retirement age and hiring a new employee who is already over retirement age. Please also see "20. A company just hired a 62-year-old employee. Is it an employment relationship?"

20. A company just hired a 62-year-old employee. Is it an employment relationship?

Answer: The situation in which an employee who is over retirement age is hired is slightly different from the one in which a current employee who reaches retirement age continues the employment. Please see Section 1.3.3, "If my employer continues to employ me after I reach the retirement age, do we still maintain the employment relationship?" for the latter.

The employee's age has exceeded statutory retirement age. After the employer hires her and has signed the employment contract, the relationship between both sides depends on whether she has been receiving basic pension insurance benefits (not including urban resident social pension insurance and new-style rural pension insurance). If she already

court of first instance to determine that there is no employment relationship between the Appellant and the Appellee."

68 Article 7 of the Interpretation of the Supreme People's Court on Several Issues Concerning the Application of Law in the Trial of Employment Dispute Cases (III) (Judicial Interpretation (2010) No. 12) stipulates that "having received pension insurance benefits in accordance with the law" should be understood as having received pension insurance benefits for employees in accordance with the law, excluding urban resident social pension insurance and new-style rural pension insurance.

receives the basic pension insurance, even if she has signed an employment contract with the employer, the relationship between the two parties is a contractor relationship.[69]

If you exceed the statutory retirement age and have not received the pension insurance benefits, there are different judicial practices in different places. The first is that the court examines whether the employer is at fault for the employee's failure to receive the pension insurance benefits. If the employer is at fault, the relationship between the two parties is an employment relationship; otherwise, it is a contractor relationship.[70] The other is to directly identify the relationship between the two parties as a contractor relationship, regardless of whether the employer was wrong about the employee's inability to receive pension insurance benefits.[71]

If the relationship between the two parties is recognized as a contractor relationship, the worker will not be able to obtain some employment rights under the employment laws, such as double-wage damages in the absence of a written employment contract, but it should be noted that the employee may still be entitled to some employment law rights according to the Supreme Court's judicial interpretation or special provisions of the law, such as some work injury entitlements.

21. My company has signed a labor outsourcing agreement with a human resources company. Is this legal?

Answer: Whether it is legal for your company to conclude a labor outsourcing contract depends on whether your company implements the purpose of labor dispatch in the form

---

69 Article 32 of the Interpretation of the Supreme People's Court on the Application of Law in the Trial of Labor Dispute Cases (I) (Judicial Interpretation [2020] No. 26) and Article 44 (2) of the Employment Contract Law both stipulate that new employees and current employees who receive pension insurance benefits are under, or are converted to, contractor relationships.

70 Mou Dianqing and Shandong Chenghui Property Management Co., Ltd. Civil Ruling on Employment Dispute Civil Application for Retrial Review Civil Ruling of Shandong High Court (2022) Lu Min Shen No. 6437. "In this case, the Applicant was over 50 years old when she came to work for the Respondent and was over the statutory retirement age, and her failure to receive the basic pension insurance benefits was not due to the Respondent. Therefore, it was not improper for the first-instance decision to determine that the work relationship between the two parties was a contractor relationship." Wang Xiaohai, Heilongjiang Hongbo Human Resources Service Co., Ltd. and other civil applications for retrial of Employment Disputes Civil Ruling of Heilongjiang High Court (2022) Hei Min Shen No. 145. Employment Dispute Retrial between Xuzhou Hanli Ecological Agriculture and Livestock Development Co., Ltd. and Min Min Civil Ruling of Jiangsu Provincial People's High Court (2020) Sumin Shen No. 1478. Xuzhou Tongshan District Highway Management Station and Hu Yonglan Employment Dispute Appeal and Application Civil Ruling Jiangsu Provincial People's High Court Civil Ruling (2020) Sumin Shen No. 3168. The court held that the age of the employee should not be considered, but the nature of the relationship between the two parties should be considered. Tianjin Yuancheng Property Service Co., Ltd. and Zhang Fucai and other Employment Disputes and Civil Servant Disputes Retrial Tianjin High Court Civil Ruling (2020) Jin Min Shen No. 293. The court held that the recruitment of employees over the statutory retirement age is not an obstacle to employment relations.

71 Article 18 of the Answers of the Civil First Division of Sichuan Provincial People's High Court on Several Difficult Questions Concerning the Trial of Employment Dispute Cases stipulates that "when an employer employs a worker who has reached the statutory retirement age but has not yet received the basic pension insurance benefits or received the pension, the work relationship between the two parties shall be handled as a contractor relationship." Civil Ruling of the High Court of Inner Mongolia Autonomous Region (2021) Nei Min Shen No. 741 Civil Ruling of Zhang Tuanzhong, Zhang Yu and other civil applications for retrial of employment disputes. The court held that the employer that recruited an employee who had not yet received pension insurance benefits but was beyond the retirement age constituted a contractor relationship with the employee. Civil Ruling on Employment Dispute Retrial Review and Trial Supervision between Peng Dingjun and Beijing Xinkang Wanjia Food Science and Technology Co., Ltd. Civil Ruling of Beijing High Court (2020) Jing Min Shen No. 4872.

of labor outsourcing. Although labor outsourcing and labor dispatch are both human resources companies sending personnel to the recipient to provide services, there are significant differences in purpose and mode between them.

The purpose of labor outsourcing is a kind of project outsourcing, that is, part of the company's work or the whole project is handed over to the outsourcing service provider, and the remuneration is settled according to the whole project for the purpose of obtaining the work results. The purpose of labor dispatch is to use the dispatched employees and settle the remuneration according to the personnel.[72]

The process of labor outsourcing is that the company manages the project as a whole, and only puts forward the overall requirements for the outsourcing service provider, while the outsourcing service provider is responsible for the specific work process, and the staff are directly managed by the outsourcing services provider. Labor dispatched staff are directly managed by the company (that is, the host employer).

Therefore, if your company does outsource the project or part of the operation as a whole, the labor outsourcing agreement is valid. If the purpose is to use the employees of the outsourcing company and your company directly manages these employees, it is called labor outsourcing but is actually labor dispatch, and the labor outsourcing is considered as labor dispatch. If the labor dispatch is deemed invalid, your company needs to assume the responsibility of the direct employer of the dispatched employees.

22. I was assigned to work for a company by a human resources company. What is the relationship between me and the human resources company?

Answer: If you have been assigned to work for your current company by a human resources company, there are four possibilities for your relationship with the human resources company and your current company.

The first possibility is that you are an independent contractor and have no employment relationship with the human resources company and the current company you work for. This usually happens if the work you do for the company is only part of your own business, the company's control and management over you is more flexible, and your social

72 Suzhou Industrial Park Yingruide Human Resources Management Service Co., Ltd., Zhang Dongling, etc. Confirmed the Civil Judgment of the Second Instance of Employment Relations Disputes Civil Judgment of the Intermediate People's Court of Suzhou City, Jiangsu Province (2023) Su 05 Min Zhong No. 1257. "There are obvious differences between labor dispatch and labor outsourcing in terms of control and management. In labor dispatch, the host employer directly commands and manages the daily work of the dispatched workers, and the dispatched workers are managed by the company rules and regulations of the host employer; while in labor outsourcing, the host company does not participate in the command and management of the workers, and the contractor directly commands and manages the workers." Civil Ruling of Chongqing High Court (2019) Yu Min Shen No. 990 on the Application for Retrial of the Right to Health Dispute between Chen Shouquan and Yang Fei of Lazars Network Technology (Shanghai) Co., Ltd. "The main differences between labor dispatch and labor outsourcing are as follows: first, the core element of labor dispatch is the labor process, and the risks of whether the dispatched employees can achieve the expected work objectives and whether the work is successful or not are borne by the host employers; The core element of labor outsourcing is the work results. The contractor can obtain the corresponding outsourcing fees only when the work results conform to the contract agreement. The risk of success or failure of the labor results of the outsourced employees has nothing to do with the employer (the party contracting out the project). Second, the dispatched employees are directly managed by the host employer; in labor outsourcing, the outsourced employees are directly managed by the contractor. Third, the settlement method of labor dispatch is determined according to the number of dispatched employees, work hours, unit price, etc., and the contract object is generally 'person'; labor outsourcing is generally settled according to the pre-determined labor unit price and the workload completed by the contractor, and the contract object is generally 'matter'."

insurance and personal income tax are handled by yourself. The human resources company only charges a service fee for having introduced you to the work opportunity.

Therefore, you have an equal civil relationship with the company where you are working. You are not an employee of the company. You cannot ask the company for the right to pay no less than the minimum wage, annual leave, sick leave, parental leave, etc. The remuneration for your services can only be determined according to the contract between the two parties. Disputes between you can only be submitted to commercial arbitration institutions or courts.

The second possibility is that you are an employee of the company you work for. This situation usually occurs when you sign an employment contract with the company, and the human resources company only provides recruitment services for you or the company. In this case, the company you work for is responsible for your daily management, wage payment, and so on, and the human resources company will no longer participate in the management after the recruitment. Any dispute you have with the company has nothing to do with the human resources company.

The third possibility is that you belong to a part of this human resources company manpower pool. You sign an employment contract with this human resources company and are sent to this company (again to be called the host employer) for a temporary, alternative, and auxiliary job. This situation is called labor dispatch. Your social insurance contribution and individual income tax are deducted in the human resources company managing your dispatch. Usually, you should approach the human resources company, instead of the host employer, for your employment law rights such as wages that are late or below the minimum standard. However, if the host employer (that is, the company you work for) is at fault in the damages to your rights and interests under the employment laws, it should bear joint and several liability with the human resources company.[73] In addition, if the host employer causes losses to you, the labor dispatch employer shall also bear joint and several liability for the damages.[74]

The fourth possibility is that you have signed a labor dispatch contract with the human resources company, which stipulates that your employer is the labor dispatch company, but because the labor dispatch is invalid, your host employer is recognized as your direct employer. You can claim your employment law rights directly from the employer, such as wages, overtime wages, rest and vacation rights, instead of claiming rights only from the labor dispatch company according to the labor dispatch contract. The advantage of this is that the host company, which actually runs the business, may be more capable of compensating you and enforcing a related judgment than the human resources company. Moreover, because the labor dispatch company is at fault in invalidity of the labor

73 The joint and several liability of the employer stipulated in Article 92 of the Employment Contract Law should be interpreted in combination with the obligations of the host employer; that is, the host employer shall not be liable unless it is at fault. For example, Li Xinqi, Shandong Radio and Television Bureau Service Center and other civil applications for retrial of employment disputes, Shandong High Court (2022) Lu Min Shen No. 9836. "There is no legal basis for Li Xinqi's request that the service center of Shandong Radio and Television Bureau, as the host employer, together with the dispatch employer, jointly and severally assume the obligation to pay economic compensation. This is beyond the scope of the legal obligation of the employer stipulated in Article 62 of the Employment Contract Law, and it is not improper for the first instance decision not to support it."

74 Article 92 of the Employment Contract Law of the People's Republic of China stipulates that if the host employer causes damage to the dispatched workers, the labor dispatch employer shall bear joint and several liability for compensation with the host employer.

dispatch, it should bear joint and several liability for your claim together with the host employer.[75]

23. Can a labor dispatch company sign permanent employment contracts with its staff?

Answer: Article 58 of the Employment Contract Law stipulates that a labor dispatch company shall sign a fixed-term employment contract with an employee for more than two years, but it does not stipulate whether it is necessary to sign a permanent employment contract by mutual agreement or when the legal requirements are met (for example, after the parties have signed two fixed-term contracts).

Judging from judicial decisions, the requirement of dispatch employers to sign permanent contracts with their employees is unlikely to be upheld in most courts in provinces and cities in China.

These places either stipulate in the form of local judicial guidance that labor dispatch must have a fixed-term contract rather than a permanent employment contract, or interpret the article in the Employment Contract Law that labor dispatch should have a fixed-term employment contract with over two-year terms, to the same effect. These places include Liaoning Province, Shandong Province, Fujian Province, Tianjin City, and Shanghai City.[76]

However, a few individual court decisions hold that the law does not prohibit labor dispatch from having permanent contracts, such as the case of Bai Xuerong, Guilin Intermediate Court of Guangxi in 2016.[77] This is another fundamental system defect of labor dispatch law in China due to insufficient understanding of the law and its purposes.

24. We are a representative office of a foreign company. Can we hire employees directly in China?

Answer: The representative office of a foreign company must employ employees through labor dispatch, and may not directly sign employment contracts with their employees.

75 Civil Ruling on Employment Dispute Retrial Review and Trial Supervision of Shenhuabei Power Shengli Energy Co., Ltd. and Xilingol League Yingxin Mechanical and Electrical Equipment Co., Ltd. and Xilinhot Chenda Human Resources Service Co., Ltd. Civil Ruling of Inner Mongolia Autonomous Region High Court (2019) No. 4675.

76 Article 10 of Liaoning Province's Guiding Opinions on Several Issues Concerning the Trial of Labor and Civil Servant Dispute Cases (1) stipulates that if a worker requests a labor dispatch company to sign a permanent employment contract, it shall not be supported. Sun Aiying, Jinan Kaiderong Human Resources Co., Ltd. Civil Ruling on Application for Retrial of Employment Dispute Civil Ruling of Shandong High Court (2021) Lumin No. 10597. "The second paragraph of Article 58 of the Employment contract Law of the People's Republic of China stipulates that … There is no problem of signing a permanent employment contract between the labor dispatch employer and the employee." Fujian Human Resources Service Co., Ltd., Zhou Rixiong and other civil applications for retrial of employment disputes Civil Ruling of Fujian High Court (2021) Min Min Shen No. 919. Wang Chen, Tianjin North Human Resources Management Consulting Co., Ltd. Heping District Branch Employment Dispute Retrial Review and Trial Supervision Civil Ruling Tianjin High Court Civil Ruling (2020) Jin Min Shen No. 1784. Civil Ruling on Employment Contract Dispute Trial and Supervision of Shanghai Foreign Service (Group) Co., Ltd. and Opma Shipping Brokerage (Shanghai) Co., Ltd. Civil Ruling of Shanghai High Court (2020) Hu Min Shen No. 1346. "In this case, the employee and the dispatch employer signed three consecutive fixed-term employment contracts. The labor dispatch relationship was different from the ordinary employment mode, and Chen Lieda's claim that Foreign Service Company's automatic renewal of his fix-termed infringed on his rights and interests in signing a permanent employment contract has no legal basis."

77 Civil Judgment of Guilin Intermediate People's Court of Guangxi Zhuang Autonomous Region (2016) Gui 03 Min Zhong No. 1469, Employment Dispute Appeal Case between Bai Xuerong and Guilin Branch of China Mobile Communications Group Guangxi Co., Ltd. "The special provisions of the Employment contract Law stipulate that when signing a contract, a fixed-term employment contract of more than two years should be signed, and it does not prohibit the signing of a permanent employment contract."

Although the Employment Contract Law provides for labor dispatch with mandatory requirements of temporary, alternative, auxiliary roles and no more than 10% of dispatched personnel in host employers, the Interim Provisions on Labor Dispatch allow an exceptional exemption for representative offices of foreign companies.[78]

If the representative office of a foreign company directly employs Chinese employees without labor dispatch, it may be ordered to make corrections and be subject to administrative penalties. For example, a representative office of a foreign company in Beijing that violates this provision may be subject to an administrative penalty of RMB 10,000 to 30,000.[79]

25. I am a civil servant. Is there an employment relationship between me and the government?

Answer: The staff working in government departments are normally civil servants, and the relationship between civil servants and the government is a civil servant relationship. Civil servant disputes (also known as "personnel disputes") refer to disputes arising from resignation, dismissal, and performance of service contracts between government organs and civil servants, governmental institutions or social group organizations and their staff, or the military and their civilian personnel.[80] Compared with the massive number of cases of employment disputes, civil servant disputes are very rare because of the strong position of government departments, and there are few valuable reference cases.

According to the judicial interpretation of the Supreme Court on civil servant disputes in 2004, the procedure of civil servant disputes shall be handled in accordance with the employment laws, while substantive rights disputes shall be handled in accordance with the civil servant dispute law. If there is no provision in the civil servant dispute law, the employment laws shall apply.[81] It appears that courts around the country have different approaches to whether and how to apply the Employment Contract Law of 2008 to civil servant disputes, and we have not found any cases that elaborate or stipulate clear principles within courts at all levels.

One approach appears to be that the Employment Contract Law should be applied to civil servant dispute cases in substance, and that all claims under the employment laws, including double-wage damages, economic compensation, punitive damages for illegal termination of employment, etc., are actionable.[82] This is reflected in the decisions of the Shanghai High Court and the Guangdong High Court.

---

78 Article 25 of the Interim Provisions on Labor Dispatch stipulates that the use of dispatched workers by representative offices of foreign enterprises and representative offices of foreign financial institutions in China, as well as the use of international ocean-going seafarers by seafarer employers in the form of labor dispatch, shall not be restricted by temporary, auxiliary, and alternative roles and the proportion of dispatched workers.

79 Article 11 of the Administrative Provisions of the People's Government of Beijing Municipality on the Employment of Chinese Employees by Resident Representative Offices of Foreign Enterprises, 1998.

80 Article 2 of the Regulations on the Settlement of Civil Servant Disputes in 2011.

81 Reply of the Supreme People's Court on the Application of Law in Civil Servant Dispute Cases of Public Institutions (Fa Han [2004] No. 30). "The substantive handling of Civil Servant Disputes in public institutions by the people's courts shall be governed by the provisions of civil servant management laws, but if the content of employment rights of public institution staff is not stipulated in civil servant management laws, the relevant provisions of the Labor Law of the People's Republic of China shall apply."

82 Feng Xianjie v. Dongguan University of Technology Civil Servant Dispute Civil Ruling of Guangdong Provincial People's High Court (2014) Yue Gao Fa Min Shen Zi No. 1964. Liu v. Shanghai Satellite Engineering Institute Civil Servant Dispute Case Shanghai High Court Civil Judgment (2014) Hu Gao Min Yi (Min) Zai Ti Zi No. 1.

The second approach appears to think that the substantive rights and obligations of civil servant dispute cases should be governed by the regulations of government departments, rather than by the Employment Contract Law. For example, in the case of Li Yao in 2020, the Lusong District Court of Zhuzhou City, Hunan Province, denied that Li Yao had the right to claim double-wage damages in the absence of a written employment contract.[83] In some cases regarding the entitlement to a permanent contract, some courts have appeared to recognize only the rule of the 2002 Ministry Personnel's stipulation that 25 consecutive years of service, or 10 consecutive years of service and less than 10 years from retirement, is the prerequisite for entitlement to a permanent contract, rejecting the conditions under the Employment Contract Law, that is, having had 2 consecutive fixed-term contracts or 10 consecutive years of service.[84]

1.4 Labor Dispute Procedure

26. What avenues should be taken to handle employment disputes between employers and employees?

Answer: In the event of an employment dispute between an employee and an employer, the first step to be considered is to negotiate a resolution with the opposite party. This may be the most effective and least detrimental approach. Resolving the issue through negotiation and communication rather than initiating legal proceedings can help maintain trust between both parties and preserve the continuity of the employment relationship.

If the employee is unable to resolve the dispute through negotiation, the employee can file a complaint with the competent labor administrative authority. For instance, issues such as illegal agreements for extended probation periods, withholding of identification documents or deposit, unjustified deductions of wages or overtime wages, non-payment of economic compensation,[85] as well as matters involving collective contracts, economic redundancy, illegal child labor, and excessive overtime hours, can be addressed through the labor administrative authority.

Another common recourse is the judicial process for employment disputes. If either party cannot resolve the matter through negotiation, the party should file for labor arbitration with the labor dispute arbitration committee in the locality where the employer is located or where the employee works. If both parties file for labor arbitration in the two locations, the labor arbitration committee where the employee works has priority

83 Li Yao and Zhuzhou Lusong District Digital City Management Supervision and Command Center Civil Servant Dispute First Instance Civil Judgment Hunan Province Zhuzhou Lusong District People's Court Civil Judgment (2020) Xiang 0203 Min Chu No. 487. The court held that according to the judicial interpretation of the Supreme Court, the rule of double-wage damages in the Employment Contract Law was not applicable in civil servant disputes.

84 Yu Pingjun v. Zhoushan Radio and Television General Station Personnel Dispute Appeal Case Zhejiang Zhoushan Intermediate People's Court Civil Judgment (2016) Zhe 09 Min Zhong No. 590. The Ministry of Personnel's Opinions on the Trial Implementation of the Civil Servant Employment System in Public Institutions ([2002] No. 35) stipulates that if a person has worked in the employer for 25 years or has worked continuously in the employer for ten years and is less than ten years from the retirement age prescribed by the State, they shall submit a contract for employment until retirement. The employer shall sign a contract with the employee until the retirement of the employee.

85 Articles 83, 84, 85 of the Employment Contract Law.

jurisdiction. Please refer to "32. Which labor arbitration committee has the authority to handle labor dispute cases?" for more details.

If either party is dissatisfied with the arbitration decision, they can appeal to the county-level or district-level court to initiate civil litigation and request a court judgment.[86] However, compared with the absolute right of appeal for employees, employers can only appeal certain arbitration decisions that meet specific conditions, while those that do not meet the conditions cannot be appealed. Please refer to "33. Can my company appeal to the court after losing in labor arbitration?" for more details.

After the first-instance judgment by the court, both parties can still appeal to the intermediate court. The judgment of the intermediate court is final. Therefore, the maximum level of litigation for labor dispute cases involves arbitration at the first level and litigation at two levels of court, which is known as "one arbitration and two court trials" for employment disputes. But under the Chinese civil litigation legal system, both parties still have the opportunity to apply for a trial supervision procedure, that is, to apply for retrial of the judgment that has already taken effect. Provincial high courts and even the Supreme Court may review cases for retrial; but the chance of initiation and success of a civil retrial is de minimis.

If an employer provides its employee with a wage arrears note, according to Article 30 of the Employment Contract Law, the employee can apply directly to the court for a payment order without going through the prior procedure of labor arbitration. If the employer does not raise objections within 15 days, the employee can apply for court enforcement.[87]

27. Is there a time limitation for employees or employers to file an employment arbitration application?

Answer: An employee or employer's time limit to apply for labor arbitration regarding labor dispute matters is legally referred to as the limitation of labor arbitration. According to Article 27 of the Labor Dispute Mediation and Arbitration Law, the limitation of labor arbitration is generally one year, starting from the day the applicant knew or should have known that their right(s) was/were harmed. The legal consequence of expiry of the limitation of labor arbitration is that the labor arbitration claim may not be upheld by the labor arbitration committee or the court. This is similar to the statute of limitations in Chinese civil litigation, where although the applicant or plaintiff holds substantive legal rights, these rights may be extinguished in judicial procedures due to delays in taking action.

Therefore, a labor arbitration applicant typically faces two issues. The first is how to determine the duration of the limitation of labor arbitration, including the starting and ending points. The second is whether a labor arbitration committee or a court will proactively review the limitation of labor arbitration or if it must review it only after the respondent raises it as a time-bar defense (i.e., requesting the application of the limitation of labor arbitration to limit or dismiss the applicant's arbitration claim) (see "28. Does the labor arbitration committee or court proactively review the limitation of labor arbitration?").

---

86 There are four levels of courts in China: district/county courts, municipal intermediate courts, provincial high courts, and the Supreme Court.

87 Articles 227 and 228 of the Civil Procedure Act.

We will discuss the first issue based on the types of labor arbitration applicant and the types of arbitration claims, and then create a detailed table of "the limitations of arbitration and starting points for common labor dispute claims."

The scope of issues for which employers can file labor arbitration applications is relatively limited, including claims for employees to compensate for losses caused by them, or demands for departed employees to bear contractual damages for breaching training service agreements or non-competition agreements.

According to Article 27 of the Labor Dispute Mediation and Arbitration Law, the limitations of arbitration for labor arbitration applications raised by employees can be divided into two categories.

The first category pertains to general limitation of arbitration, for which arbitration claims must be filed within one year from the date when the employee knew or should have known that their rights were violated. These claims include those for economic compensation, punitive damages, and supplementary damages. For example, if an employee is unlawfully dismissed, they must request punitive damages for the illegal termination within one year from the date of dismissal. Otherwise, even if the labor arbitration committee determines that the dismissal was unlawful, the claim for punitive damages shall be struck out.

The second category is the special limitation of arbitration concerning claims related to unjustified labor remuneration arrear. Labor remuneration is considered a fundamental employment right of employees, and thus, its arbitration claims are specially protected in terms of limitations. According to the Article 27, these claims are not subject to the one-year limitation mentioned above in that they are considered as an integrated, indivisible claim; for example, wage arrears over ten years may be claimed without the one-year restriction. However, they must be filed within one year from the termination of the employment relationship. Labor remuneration includes wages, overtime pay, commission, as well as any other remuneration paid in a fixed cycle, such as position wages, allowances, or year-end bonus.

For example, Ms. Li started working at a company on January 1, 2010 and was unlawfully dismissed by the company on January 1, 2024. During this period, the company unlawfully deducted RMB 100 from her salary each month. The total amount unlawfully deducted over the years was RMB 16,800 (14 * 12 * 100). She later filed a labor arbitration claim with the labor arbitration committee, requesting punitive damages for illegal termination of employment as well as the unlawfully deducted wages.

According to the special rules for labor remuneration arbitration claims, Ms. Li's wages unlawfully deducted over 14 years are not subject to the 1-year arbitration limitation. This means that Ms. Li can claim the full amount of RMB 16,800 for the wages deducted over the 14 years, rather than just the wages deducted within 1 year. However, Ms. Li must file a claim for the RMB 16,800 unlawfully deducted wages with the labor arbitration committee within 1 year after the termination of the labor contract, which is by December 31, 2024; otherwise, the labor arbitration committee may reject her claim based on the defense of limitation of arbitration raised by the employer.

Please refer to Table 1.1 for the limitations of arbitration and starting points for common labor dispute claims. All the items in its "Labor Arbitration Claims" column, except for those marked as for the employer, are claims for the employee.

Table 1.1 Limitations of Arbitration for Claims

Labor arbitration claims	*Limitations of arbitration and starting dates*
Unjustified wages (including overtime wages and interests on equity incentive) deduction or arrear	One year, starting from the date of employment termination. Please refer to "137. What is the difference in limitation of arbitration between unjustified wage deduction and unjustified wage arrear?"
Wages in medical care period	One year, starting from the date of employment termination.
Economic compensation	One year, starting from the date of employment termination.
Punitive damages for illegal termination of employment	One year, starting from the date of employment termination.
Supplementary damages	One year, starting from the date when the labor administrative authority orders the employer to pay.
Double-wage damages	One year, starting from the date when the employment contract should have been signed.
High-temperature allowance and other benefits	One year, starting from the day when the allowance should have been paid, in a daily and monthly calculation. Please refer to the limitation part in "78. How do Labor Regulations stipulate the high-temperature allowance?"
Unused annual leave pay	One year from the last date when the annual leave can be taken (two years after the annual leave days are obtained); however, it will change to special limitation of arbitration, one year after termination of the employment contract, if the new draft of Supreme Court's Judicial Interpretation II comes into effect.[88] Please refer to "75. How should employers manage employees' accrued annual leave over the years?"
Reinstatement (claim to continue to implement employment)	One year, starting from the date when the employee receives the termination notice.
Wage loss due to illegal termination	One year, starting from the date when the employee receives the termination notice.
Application for work injury identification to labor capacity appraisal committee	One year, starting from the date of work injury or the result of the work injury being found.[89]
Work injury entitlements	One year, starting from the date of work injury or the result of the work injury being found.
Probation period damages	One year, starting from each day of illegal implementation of probation period or the date of employment termination. Please refer to "30. Is it too late for me to claim probation period damages to the employer?"
Non-competition contractual damages (by employer)	One year, starting from the date when the employer knew or should have known the employee's breach of non-competition obligation.

(*Continued*)

88 Article 5 of consultation draft on the Interpretation of the Supreme People's Court on the Application of Law in the Trial of Labor Dispute Cases (II).

89 Article 17 of the Regulations on Work Injury Insurance.

Table 1.1 (Continued)

Labor arbitration claims	*Limitations of arbitration and starting dates*
Non-competition allowance	One year, starting from each day the employer failed to pay the non-competition allowance.
Year-End or Quarter-End Bonus and other Fixed Cycle Payments	One year, starting from the date of employment termination.
Loss of unemployment insurance benefit	One year, starting from the date of employment termination.[90]
Funeral allowance	One year, starting from the death date of the employee.
Confirmation of employment relationship	There are two disputed judicial views. One considers it as lawsuit of confirmation, which bears no limitation of labor arbitration. The other insists on one-year limitation of arbitration. Please refer to "29. Is employees' claim of employment relationship confirmation subject to one-year limitation of labor arbitration?"
Damages caused by employee	One year, starting from the date when the employer knew or should have known the damages.

It is worth mentioning that this one-year limitation of arbitration for labor arbitration is not necessarily an absolute deadline. In some cases, if specific events occur, this deadline may change due to interruption or suspension of the statute of limitations. Please refer to "31. What are the interruption and suspension of the limitation of labor arbitration?"

28. Does the labor arbitration committee or court proactively review the limitation of labor arbitration?

Answer: Whether the limitation of labor arbitration will result in restricting or dismissing a labor arbitration claim depends not only on the start date and duration of labor arbitration (see "27. Is there a time limitation for employees or employers to file an employment arbitration application?") but also on whether the labor arbitration committee or court is obligated to proactively review the limitation of labor arbitration or if they can review it only after the respondent raises a defense of limitation of labor arbitration.

Under current law, labor arbitration committees cannot reject a labor arbitration application on the grounds that it exceeds the limitation of labor arbitration. In the past, labor arbitration committees would typically proactively review the limitation of arbitration when a labor arbitration application was filed, and declined to docket a labor arbitration application that had exceeded the limitation of arbitration. This practice differed from the principle under Chinese civil law, which states that if the defendant does not raise a defense of statute of limitation, the court must not actively review the limitation. However, following the issuance of the 2017 Rules for Handling Labor and Personnel Disputes Arbitration,[91] labor arbitration committees should no longer reject a labor arbitration application on the grounds that it exceeds the arbitration limitation period. Nonetheless,

90 Su Mingqin v. Guangzhou Jiabai Le Furniture Design Co., Ltd. Labor Contract Dispute Retrial Review and Judgment Supervision Civil Ruling Guangdong Provincial High People's Court Civil Ruling (2019) Yue Min Shen 10847. Li Ruifeng v. Beijing Zhonghang Airport Hotel Co., Ltd. Labor Dispute Case Beijing Higher People's Court Civil Ruling (2017) Jing Min Shen 489.

91 After the promulgation of the 2017 Rules for Handling Labor and Personnel Dispute Arbitration, Article 30 of the rules, which sets the conditions for docketing arbitration applications, has removed the requirement

there are still a few cases in practice where labor arbitration committees rejected filing cases on the grounds of exceeding the limitation of arbitration; that is, the committees proactively reviewed the limitation of arbitration without respondents' raising a defense of limitation of arbitration.[92]

Currently, courts are generally more inclined than labor arbitration committees not to proactively review the limitation of labor arbitration. However, there is a divergence of opinion on whether the limitation of arbitration is binding if the respondent did not raise a defense of limitation of arbitration during labor arbitration but does so during litigation. The prevailing practice in courts is not to recognize a time-bar defense that was not raised during the labor arbitration stage but is raised during the court stage, in accordance with existing civil litigation rules.[93] Still, there are a few cases where belated raising of a time-bar defense is permitted, reflecting the inertia in judicial practice and the lack of legal clarity.[94]

It should be noted that Article 2 of the 2023 Consultation Draft on the Interpretation of the Supreme People's Court on the Application of Law in the Trial of Labor Dispute Cases (II) states: "If the parties do not raise a defence of limitation of arbitration, the people's court should not explain and clarify the issue of the limitation of arbitration." Its Article 3 also provides that a defendant who did not raise the defense of limitation of arbitration in the labor arbitration stage loses the defense in the court stage. Although this rule is still at the consultation stage and has not been enacted or implemented, it will further strengthen the legal principles that the labor arbitration committee and courts should not proactively review the limitation of arbitration and that a defense of limitation of arbitration not raised during the labor arbitration stage will be forfeited at the court stage.

---

from the previous version of the rules that labor arbitration applications must be filed within the limitation of labor arbitration period.

92 Chen Jingbo v. Yanji Pharmaceutical Glass Co., Ltd. Labor Dispute Civil Application for Civil Retrial Ruling Supreme People's Court Civil Ruling (2022) Zui Gao Fa Min Shen No. 234. In this case, the employee was terminated by the employer in 2003 but only applied for labor arbitration in 2019. The labor arbitration committee did not apply the 2017 Rules for Handling Labor and Personnel Dispute Arbitration to docket the case. The first- and second-instance courts and the Supreme Court all held that it was not improper for the labor arbitration committee and the courts to proactively review the limitation of labor arbitration. The overly long period of inaction may be an additional factor.

93 Article 2 of the Regulations of the Supreme People's Court on Certain Issues Concerning the Application of the Statute of Limitations in Civil Cases (Judicial Interpretation [2020] No. 17): "If the parties do not raise a statute of limitations defence, the people's court should not explain and clarify the issue of the statute of limitations." Fujian Province Changle City Certain Textile Industrial Co., Ltd. v. Yang Labor Dispute Civil Retrial Ruling Fujian Province Higher People's Court Civil Ruling (2023) Min Min Shen No. 801. The court held: "If the parties did not raise a defence regarding the expiration of the limitation of arbitration during the arbitration stage, after the labor arbitration committee has made a substantive decision, the people's court may no longer apply the limitation of arbitration, regardless of whether the party raises a defence based on the expiration of the limitation of arbitration during the court stage." Guangzhou Kandi De Electronics Technology Co., Ltd. v. Tang Jinlong Labor Contract Dispute Retrial Case Guangdong Province Higher People's Court Civil Ruling (2021) Yue Min Shen No. 11129, 11130.

94 Xiong Shengfeng v. Zhongshan Experimental Middle School, Huazhou District, Weinan City Labor Dispute Civil Retrial Ruling Shaanxi Province Higher People's Court Civil Ruling (2024) Shan Min Shen No. 1687. In this case, the employee claimed for double-wage damages against the employer and argued that the employer did not raise a defense of limitation of arbitration during the labor arbitration stage, and so, that the court should not review the limitation of arbitration. However, the first-instance, second-instance, and retrial courts all reviewed the limitation of arbitration based on the defense of limitation of arbitration raised by the employer during the first-instance proceeding.

We illustrate the application of these two legal principles with a simple case. Mr. Zhang resigned on December 1, 2024, and his employer owes him RMB 40,000 in wages. He should have applied for labor arbitration by December 1, 2025, but he did not do so until January 1, 2026. According to the principles, the labor arbitration committee must docket this arbitration application (and cannot reject it as they would have in the past). If the employer does not raise a defense of limitation of arbitration (i.e., claims that Mr. Zhang's labor arbitration application has exceeded the arbitration limitation period) during labor arbitration, the labor arbitration committee must uphold the claim and order the employer to pay Mr. Zhang the RMB 40,000 of wages. If the employer appeals to the court and then raises the defense of limitation of arbitration, the court should disregard this defense and uphold the original labor arbitration decision.

29. Is employees' claim of employment relationship confirmation subject to 1-year limitation of labor arbitration?

Answer: The issue of whether an employee's claim to confirm the employment relationship is subject to the one-year arbitration time limit stipulated in Article 27 of the Labor Dispute Mediation and Arbitration Law is a contentious one in the judicial practice of courts nationwide.

Some decisions from the Beijing Higher People's Court, Guangdong Provincial High People's Court, Hebei Provincial High People's Court, Heilongjiang Provincial High People's Court, and Shanghai the First Intermediate People's Court state that, according to Article 1 of the 2020 Supreme People's Court Provisions on Several Issues Concerning the Application of the Statute of Limitations in Civil Cases, only rights of debts claims (such as claims for payment of debts) are subject to the statute of limitations, while claims for confirmation are not. Therefore, labor arbitration applications for confirming employment relationship are not subject to the one-year limitation of arbitration under the employment laws.[95]

Beijing Municipal High Court, Guangdong Provincial High Court, Hebei Provincial High Court, Heilongjiang Provincial High Court, and Shanghai the First Intermediate People's Court have some decisions that, according to the provisions of Article 1 of the 2020 Supreme People's Court's Provisions on Several Issues Concerning the Application

95 Beijing Higher People's Court Civil Judgment (2023) No. 821, Case of Labor Dispute between a Certain Building in Beijing and Mr. Zheng. Guangdong Provincial High People's Court Civil Ruling (2020) No. 2762, Review and Supervision Civil Ruling on Labor Relationship Confirmation Dispute between Guangdong Federal Furniture Group Co., Ltd. and Ms. Chen Dongmei. Heilongjiang Provincial High People's Court Civil Ruling (2017) No. 365, Case of Labor Dispute between Wang Qiliang and Harbin Dream Tianhu Business Hotel Co., Ltd. Huanghe Road Branch. Hebei Provincial High People's Court Civil Ruling (2019) No. 8374, Review and Supervision Civil Ruling on Labor Dispute between Du Jinye and Yanshan University. Shanghai No. 1 Intermediate People's Court Civil Judgment (2022) No. 13088, Second-instance Civil Judgment on Labor Contract Dispute between Shanghai Jiasen Machinery Co., Ltd. and Wu Yonghong. Guangxi Zhuang Autonomous Region Higher People's Court Civil Ruling (2022) No. 5881, Review and Supervision Civil Ruling on Labor Dispute Civil Application for Retrial between Yang Chunji and Liuzhou Longcheng Chemical Plant. Jilin Provincial High People's Court Civil Ruling (2021) No. 4520, Review and Supervision Civil Ruling on Labor Dispute Civil Application for Retrial between Zhang Yanli and China Railway Shenyang Bureau Group Co., Ltd. Jilin Passenger Transport Section (formerly Tonghua Branch of Shenyang Railway Bureau Passenger Transport Company). Gansu Provincial High People's Court Civil Ruling (2022) No. 762, Review and Supervision Civil Ruling on Labor Dispute Civil Application for Retrial between Jin Jiangyun and Gansu Ninth Construction Group Co., Ltd. Shanxi Provincial High People's Court Civil Ruling (2021) No. 3779, Labor Dispute Retrial Case between Yan Xusheng and Shanyin County No. 1 Middle School. Jiangxi Provincial High People's Court Civil Ruling (2016) No. 260, Labor Dispute Dispute Case between Chen Zhenxiang and Jinxian County Rural Credit Cooperatives.

of the Statute of Limitations in Civil Cases, only claims for debt (such as claims for payment of debts) are subject to the statute of limitations, while claims for confirmation are not subject to the statute of limitations. Therefore, applications for confirming labor relations arbitration are not subject to the one-year arbitration time limit under employment laws.

On the contrary, courts such as the Guangxi High Court, Gansu Provincial High Court, Jiangxi Provincial High Court, Jilin Provincial High Court, and Shanxi Provincial High Court consider that the arbitration claim for confirming labor relations by employees is an item explicitly provided for in Article 2 of the Labor Dispute Mediation and Arbitration Law, and thus should be subject to the one-year limitation of arbitration prescribed by the law, and this time limit should be calculated from the date of termination of the employment relationship between the two parties.[96]

The Shandong Provincial High Court and the Xinjiang High Court have two different approaches in different cases. On the one hand, they recognize that such requests belong to the category of confirmation lawsuits in civil law and are not subject to limitation of labor arbitration.[97] On the other hand, some judgments hold that if the purpose of the confirmation lawsuit is to realize substantive rights, then it should be subject to the one-year limitation of arbitration.[98]

The legal consequences of whether the employee's claim to confirm the employment relationship is subject to the one-year labor arbitration time limit are obvious. If the court determines that an employee's claim exceeds the arbitration time limit, the employee loses the opportunity for judicial confirmation of the employment relationship and related claims. Judicial authorities should obviously use this restriction of limitation of arbitration cautiously.

From a literal interpretation perspective, the Labor Dispute Mediation and Arbitration Law supports the one-year limitation of arbitration in this. This conflicts with the legal principle in civil law that confirmation actions are not subject to statute of limitations. The inconsistency between legal rules and judicial practice is regrettable and requires clarification and improvement through future legislations.

---

96 Yang Chunji v. Liuzhou Longcheng Chemical Plant Labor Dispute Civil Application for Retrial Review Civil Ruling, Guangxi Zhuang Autonomous Region Higher People's Court, Civil Ruling (2022) Gui Min Shen No. 5881. Zhang Yanli v. China Railway Shenyang Bureau Group Co., Ltd. Jilin Passenger Transport Section (formerly Shenyang Railway Bureau Passenger Transport Company Tonghua Branch) Labor Dispute Civil Application for Retrial Review Civil Ruling, Jilin Provincial Higher People's Court, Civil Ruling (2021) Ji Min Shen No. 4520. Jin Jiangyun v. Gansu Ninth Construction Group Co., Ltd. Labor Dispute Civil Application for Retrial Review Civil Ruling, Gansu Provincial Higher People's Court, Civil Ruling (2022) Gan Min Shen No. 762. Yan Xusheng v. Shanyin County No. 1 Middle School Labor Dispute Retrial Case, Shanxi Provincial Higher People's Court, Civil Ruling (2021) Jin Min Shen No. 3779. Chen Zhenxiang v. Jinxian County Rural Credit Cooperative Union Labor Dispute Case, Jiangxi Provincial Higher People's Court, Civil Ruling (2016) Gan Min Shen No. 260.

97 Shandong Huangjin Gypsum Mining Co., Ltd., Zhang Zongcheng Labor Dispute Civil Application for Retrial Review Civil Ruling, Shandong Provincial Higher People's Court, Civil Ruling (2022) Lu Min Shen No. 7213. China Telecom Corporation Limited Xinyuan Branch v. Wang Manling Labor Dispute Second Instance Civil Judgment, Xinjiang Uygur Autonomous Region Higher People's Court Yili Kazakh Autonomous Prefecture Branch Civil Judgment (2019) Xin 40 Min Zhong No. 1518.

98 Li Xinqi v. Shandong Provincial Radio and Television Bureau Organ Service Center, Labor Dispute Civil Application for Retrial Review Civil Ruling, Shandong Provincial Higher People's Court, Civil Ruling (2022) Lu Min Shen No. 9836. A v. Kashgar Industrial Development Co., Ltd., Labor Dispute Civil Trial Supervision Civil Ruling, Xinjiang Uygur Autonomous Region Higher People's Court, Civil Ruling (2024) Xin Min Shen No. 7.

30. Is it too late for me to claim probation period damages from the employer?

Answer: If an employer violates the statutory limit of the probation period to set a probation period with an employee and completes the illegal probation period, according to Article 83 of the Employment Contract Law, probation period damages refer to the damages the employer is liable for based on the period exceeding the statutory limitation and the employee's wages standard in their regular contract period (as opposed to the probation period). For specific calculations, please refer to "61. What legal consequences will an employer face for extending a newly hired employee's probation period?"

Like other arbitration claims, the probation period damages should also be subject to the one-year limitation of labor arbitration. However, because this claim is relatively rare in practice, there are few cases illustrating how the one-year limitation of arbitration is applied. From the cases at the provincial high court level, there are two approaches.

The first approach treats it similarly to labor remuneration, where the arbitration claim must be filed within one year from the termination of the employment relationship. This is the approach taken by the high courts in Jiangsu Province and Ningxia Hui Autonomous Region.[99] The second approach applies the one-year limitation of labor arbitration for normal arbitration claims, verifying each day and month according to the limitation of arbitration, and this is followed by the high courts in Guangdong Province, Shanxi Province, and Shanghai.[100]

Which approach to limitation of labor arbitration for probation period damages applies obviously affects the amount of the damage employees may obtain.

For example, Ms. Li started working for a company on January 1, 2024, and her wage in the regular contract period is RMB 4,000. The company illegally extended the statutory maximum probation period from six months to one year. Therefore, the company should pay probation damages at RMB 4,000 per month from July to December 2024 (for how to calculate probation period damages, please refer to "61. What legal consequences will an employer face for extending a newly hired employee's probation period?"). Ms. Li resigned in August 2025 and filed a labor arbitration claim against the company for probation period damages in March 2026. If the labor arbitration committee applies the first type of limitation of arbitration rule, then the total probation period damages would be RMB 24,000 (4,000 * 6) as a whole, which does not exceed the limitation of arbitration, because Ms. Li filed the labor arbitration claim within one year after the termination. However, if the labor arbitration committee applies the second type of limitation of arbitration rule, then every day in the illegally applied probation period (from July to December 2024) is outside the protection period of the limitation of arbitration (from July to December 2025). Therefore, Ms. Li would not be able to obtain probationary compensation.

---

99 Li Jing v. Nantong Helin Construction Engineering Co., Ltd. labor contract dispute retrial case Jiangsu High People's Court Civil Ruling (2019) Su Min Shen 7856. Li Qi v. Ningxia Xiaojuren Machine Tool Co., Ltd. labor dispute case Ningxia Hui Autonomous Region High People's Court Civil Ruling (2015) Ning Min Ti No. 3.

100 Luo Hui v. Longchuan County Chronic Disease Prevention and Treatment Institute labor dispute retrial review and adjudication supervision civil ruling Guangdong High People's Court Civil Ruling (2019) Yue Min Shen 9787. Sun Zhanlong v. Yangquan Beiguo Shopping Mall Co., Ltd. labor dispute retrial review and adjudication supervision civil ruling Shanxi High People's Court Civil Ruling (2019) Jin Min Shen 871. Lin Kaiming v. Shanghai Chenggui Computer Technology Co., Ltd. labor contract dispute appeal civil ruling Shanghai High People's Court Civil Ruling (2014) Hu Gao Min Yi (Min) Shen Zi No. 1289.

31. What are the interruption and suspension of the limitation of labor arbitration?

Answer: Article 27 of the Labor Dispute Mediation and Arbitration Law stipulates the rules of limitation of arbitration that ordinary labor dispute claims must be filed within the one-year limitation of arbitration and that labor remuneration claims must be filed within one year after employment termination. In principle, if an employee or employer raises a labor dispute claim after this one-year time limit, the labor arbitration committee or court will strike out the claim, meaning the applicant, employee or employer, shall lose the right to win the case.

The interruption and suspension of the limitation of labor arbitration mean that the deadline of this one-year time limit can be postponed under special circumstances. In other words, this one-year limitation of arbitration and the deadline for losing the right to win the case determined by the former are not absolutely and completely immutable. Article 27 also stipulates that this limitation of arbitration can be restarted or suspended due to statutory events of interruption or suspension of the limitation of arbitration, rendering the deadline to be reset or rolled over accordingly.

The interruption of the limitation of labor arbitration refers to the recalibration of the one-year limitation due to statutory events. For example, if Ms. Li terminated her employment relationship with the employer on December 31, 2023, her arbitration claim for economic compensation should be filed within one year from December 31, 2023, to December 30, 2024. If during this period, there is an interruption of the limitation of arbitration, for example, if Ms. Li lodged a complaint with the labor inspection agency on October 1, 2024 demanding that the employer pay economic compensation, then the limitation of arbitration for Ms. Li's claim is interrupted. Thus, the original deadline of limitation of arbitration, December 30, 2024, becomes ineffective, and Ms. Li has a new period to file an arbitration claim for the employer to pay economic compensation from October 1, 2024 to September 30, 2025.

The events of limitation interruption as stipulated by the aforementioned law include three scenarios: when an employee seeks relief from relevant governmental authorities (such as Ms. Li's complaint to the labor inspection agency), or when one party claims their rights against the other party (such as Ms. Li sending a written letter urging the employer to pay economic compensation), or when the other party agrees to fulfill their obligations (such as the employer promising through email or letter to pay the outstanding economic compensation).

In the third scenario, "the other party agrees to fulfill their obligations," the interruption of the limitation of arbitration (i.e., the recalibration of the one-year arbitration time limit) should commence from the date agreed upon for the fulfillment of obligations. Although the Labor Dispute Mediation and Arbitration Law and the 2020 judicial interpretation by the Supreme Court omitted this point,[101] it is reasonable for the employee (or employer) to expect the other party to fulfill their promise of payment. This waiting

101 Item 3 of article 1 of the now-expired Interpretation by the Supreme People's Court on Several Issues Concerning the Application of Law in the Trial of Labor Dispute Cases (II) (Judicial Interpretation [2006] No. 6) stipulated that if the employer promises to pay wages, economic compensation, or welfare benefits, the labor arbitration time limit shall be accounted from the date of the promise. However, this provision was not included in the subsequent "Labor Dispute Mediation and Arbitration Law" or the "Interpretation of the Supreme People's Court on the Application of Law in the Trial of Labor Dispute Cases (I)" (Judicial Interpretation [2020] No. 26).

period for payment clearly should not be counted toward the limitation of arbitration, as otherwise, parties could exploit the limitation of arbitration to evade their compensation obligations by deceptively promising a payment date exceeding one year. This outcome would be clearly unfair. Of course, if there is no specified payment date in the agreement, the arbitration time limit should commence from the date when the other party agrees to fulfill their obligations.

The suspension of the limitation of labor arbitration refers to the temporary pause of the remaining time countdown of the one-year limitation of labor arbitration due to the occurrence of specific events, and the deadline for labor arbitration shall be extended according to the duration of these specific events. For example, in the same case, if Ms. Li's limitation of arbitration for claiming economic compensation is for the entire year of 2024, and if Ms. Li experiences a statutory reason for limitation suspension, such as being hospitalized for a severe illness (for example, stroke paralysis) for four months starting from October 1, 2024, and she is discharged from the hospital on February 1, 2025, then the limitation of arbitration for Ms. Li to apply for economic compensation should be suspended from October 1, 2024, and extended by four months. Therefore, she has the right to file for labor arbitration until April 30, 2025.

The specific events leading to the suspension of the limitation for labor arbitration refer to force majeure or other legitimate reasons that prevent the employee or employer from filing a labor arbitration application. These specific events include any legitimate reasons that prevent the parties from filing for labor arbitration, including city lockdowns during a pandemic[102] or an employee's hospitalization due to illness. It is worth noting that if an employee is detained for suspected illegal activities, it may not necessarily constitute a legitimate reason for suspending the limitation of arbitration, because the exercise of their civil rights is not necessarily affected during the detention.[103]

32. Which labor arbitration committee has the authority to handle labor dispute cases?

Answer: According to Article 21 of the Labor Dispute Mediation and Arbitration Law, employment dispute cases are handled (jurisdiction) by the labor dispute arbitration committee in the place where the employment contract is performed or where the employer is located. If both parties apply for arbitration to the labor dispute arbitration committees in the two places, the committee where the employment contract is performed has prevailing jurisdiction.

The procedure for employment dispute resolution involves arbitration first and then litigations in courts.

Based on the aforementioned statutory provision, during the arbitration stage, if both the employer and the employee file for arbitration with the labor dispute arbitration committees in the place where the employment contract is performed and where the employer

102 Chang Yunzhong v. Beijing Rongyada International Human Resources Co., Ltd., et al., Beijing the Third Intermediate People's Court Judgment (2022) No. 13079. The court held that the employee failed to provide evidence to prove the inability to file a labor arbitration due to the epidemic.

103 Zhang Wenchao v. Shenyang Huakai Garden Engineering Co., Ltd. Labor Dispute Civil Second Instance Civil Judgment Liaoning Shenyang Intermediate People's Court Civil Judgment (2023) Liaoning 01 Civil Final No. 4075.

is located, regardless of which party files first, the committee where the employment contract is performed has prevailing jurisdiction.

However, during the court stage, if both the courts, the court in the place where the employment contract is performed and the court in the place where the employer is located, accept lawsuits from both parties, the court that first accepted the case has jurisdiction. This rule is based on Article 36 of the Supreme People's Court's Interpretation of the Application of the Civil Procedure Act of the People's Republic of China: "In litigation where two or more people's courts have jurisdiction, the court that first accepted the case shall not transfer the case to another court with jurisdiction."

It is important to note that even if the employer and the employee have agreed on the jurisdiction of disputes in the employment contract, such an agreement is not legally binding, and the above legal jurisdiction rules must be applied.[104] For example, in the 2020 case of Beijing Haitian Zhiyuan Labor Service Company, Judge Yang Lichu of the Supreme Court pointed out that "the legal relationship involved in employment dispute cases is the employment relationship between the employer and the employee, which has personal attributes and does not apply to the relevant provisions of jurisdiction by agreement. Therefore, the jurisdiction clause stipulated in the employment contract in this case is invalid."

33. Can my company appeal to the court after losing in labor arbitration?

Answer: Article 47 of the Labor Dispute Mediation and Arbitration Law in 2008 aims to alleviate the burden of litigation on employees. It implements final adjudication rules for certain small-amount employment dispute claims. This rule changes the previous practice, where both parties could appeal any arbitration decision to the court. It stipulates that employers do not have the right to appeal to the court for certain claims where the arbitration award amount is lower than 12 times the local minimum wage standard. However, the right of employees to appeal to the court is not affected (Article 48 of the Law).

These claims include: wages for normal work during statutory standard working hours, wages during paid work injury leave, payment in lieu of notice, work injury medical expenses, non-competition allowance, economic compensation for termination or dissolution of employment contracts, double-wage damages, probation damages for illegal probation periods, punitive damages for illegal termination of employment contracts, other employment remuneration, compensation, or damages.[105]

For example, in Ms. Li's employment dispute case with the employer, if the arbitration ruling requires the employer to pay Ms. Li a salary of RMB 23,000 and an economic compensation of RMB 30,000, and the local minimum monthly wage standard is RMB 2,000 (12 times the minimum monthly wage standard is RMB 24,000), the arbitration committee divides these two awards into separate rulings. The ruling containing the RMB 23,000 salary is a final adjudication (because the ruling amount, RMB 23,000, is lower than 12 times the minimum monthly wage standard, RMB 24,000), and the employer has

104 Cao Wen v. Beijing Haitian Zhiyuan Labor Service Co., Ltd. Labor Dispute Civil Adjudication Document. Supreme People's Court of the People's Republic of China. Civil Adjudication Document (2020) Supreme Court Civil Jurisdiction No. 28.

105 Article 10 of "Opinions of the Ministry of Human Resources and Social Security and the Supreme People's Court on Issues Concerning the Connection between Labor Dispute Arbitration and Litigation (Part I)."

no right to appeal to the court for this ruling, but Ms. Li's right to appeal to the court is not restricted. The ruling containing the RMB 30,000 economic compensation is a non-final adjudication (because the economic compensation of RMB 30,000 exceeds 12 times the minimum monthly wage standard of RMB 24,000), and both parties can appeal this arbitration ruling to the court.

CHAPTER 2

Employment Commencement

Introduction

Once an employment relationship is established between an employee and an employer, both parties enter the initial stage of the employment relationship. This chapter lists common disputes during the initial stage of the employment relationship and analyzes the rights and obligations of both parties during the probation period. Regarding the complex issues arising from the provision of double-wage damages for failure to sign an employment contract as established by the Employment Contract Law, this chapter provides detailed practical analysis and explanations.

The questions and answers in this chapter mainly involve the following issues: the consequence of the renege in forming an employment contract, types and contribution amounts of statutory employee's social insurance, the judgment of the starting point of the employment relationship, the establishment and maintenance of employees' personnel files, the obligation of the employer to sign an employment contract with their employees and the consequences of violating this obligation, handling of an employee refusing to sign an employment contract, the limitation of arbitration for an employee's request for double-wage damages, the legality of the employer's retention of deposits or certificates, and the consequences of not paying for trial work, the relationship between interns and employers, the legal length, rights, and obligations of the probation period, the extension of the probation period, the termination of the employment relationship during the probation period, invalid employment contract, and invalid labor dispatch.

Especially, this chapter delves into the intricate exemption scenarios associated with double-salary damages in China. It distinguishes among three situations and provides a detailed explanation of how to calculate the compensation amount for double-wage damages in conjunction with the one-year limitation of labor arbitration.

2.1 Employer Obligations at the Start

34. What types of social insurance should employers buy for employees?

Answer: Employers are obligated to purchase the "five insurances and one fund" for most of their employees. However, for part-time employees, employers are only required to purchase work injury insurance,[1] and for foreign employees, there is no mandatory

1 Opinions on Several Issues Concerning Part-time Employment (Lao She Bu Fa [2003] No. 12) Article 3(12).

DOI: 10.4324/9781003583301-2

requirement to purchase the housing provident fund. The term "five insurances and one fund" refers to the social insurance system established in China since 2006. It means that every employer is obligated to purchase basic pension, basic medical, unemployment, work injury, maternity insurance (the five insurances) and the housing provident fund (the one fund) for their employees.

The contribution base for the five social insurance programs is, in principle, the individual employees' previous month's wages, but it is subject to an upper limit of 60% and a lower limit of 300% of the local social average monthly salary from the previous year. Some provinces and municipalities may also use individual average monthly wages from the previous year as the base.[2] In China at present, the issue of the social insurance contribution base is an area of low legal compliance. Many enterprises contribute to social insurance for employees merely based on local minimum wage standards rather than individual employees' previous month's wages. Consequently, due to this non-compliance, employers may have to compensate for discrepancies in certain items of social insurance entitlements, such as one-off disability allowance, caused by insufficient social insurance contributions.[3]

Some types of social insurance, including pension, medical, and unemployment insurance, are contributed by both employers and employees. In the case of insufficient contribution, the employees' loss of the aforementioned discrepancies in social insurance entitlements should be borne by both parties according to the ratios of the contributions.

The purchase of social insurance involves the proportion of individual contributions of employers and employees. At present, there is no uniform regulation on the proportion of employer and employee contributions to the five insurances in the whole country, the proportion varies from place to place, and the proportion of contributions in the same place may also be adjusted at different times.

Taking Shenzhen, Guangdong Province in 2023 as an example, the contribution ratio for pension insurance is 14–15% for employers and 8% for employees, which is the result of years of decrease. The contribution ratio for medical insurance is 6.2% for employers and 2% for employees. However, the contribution ratios for second and third tiers of medical insurance are 0.45% for employers and 0.1% for employees. For unemployment insurance, the contribution ratios are 0.7% for employers and 0.3% for employees. Contribution ratios for work injury insurance range from 0.14% to 1.14% for employers only, depending on different roles in different industries. Contribution ratios for maternity insurance (including male employees) are 0.5% for employers only.

The housing provident fund is jointly contributed by employers and employees during the performance of the employee's employment contract. It is used to assist employees in purchasing property or investing in renovation of their residences. In practice, the compliance status of housing provident fund contributions is lower than that of social insurance,

2 The basic pension insurance policy for urban employees in Sichuan Province clearly stipulates that the basic pension insurance premium for an employee shall be based on the average monthly wage from the previous year, or the wage of the previous month, of the employee.

3 Gao Gaiping, Guangzhou Liwan District Social Insurance Fund Management Center Financial Administration (Finance) Retrial Review and Trial Supervision Administrative Ruling No. 2770 of Guangdong Provincial People's High Court Administrative Ruling (2019). In the case, the employer purchased insufficient work injury insurance for the employee, and the employee insisted that the Social Security Bureau pay the one-off disability allowance in full. The Guangdong Provincial High Court held that the request should be made to the employer rather than the Social Security Bureau, and therefore rejected the request in the retrial.

and it wasn't until around 2015 that the government began to promote mandatory contributions. According to the "Regulations on the Management of Housing Provident Fund," both employers and employees should contribute at least 5% of employees' individual average monthly salaries from the previous year.

In addition, enterprise annuity is a supplementary pension insurance voluntarily decided by employers and workers in accordance with the Measures for Enterprise Annuity. It is not a mandatory obligation of employers, and employees can only withdraw it if it is in place when they reach retirement age.[4] Some courts, such as those in Beijing, even hold that disputes regarding enterprise annuity are not considered employment disputes.[5]

35. What liability should an employer bear if it reneges on its wage commitment to an employee candidate?

Answer: The employment laws do not have a specific provision regarding the consequences if an employer reneges on its commitment after finalizing an employment contract. But from the civil law angle, this employer ought to assume the "contractual negligence liability" under Chinese civil law, namely, liability of one party who violates the basic principle of good faith and fair dealing and who ought to compensate the loss of the other.

For example, in the case of Li Ziyi before the Third Intermediate Court of Beijing in 2022, the court held that when recruiting employees, the employer had reached an oral agreement with the candidate on RMB 9,500 in the probation period and RMB 10,500 in the regular employment period, but while the candidate was enrolling, the employer changed their mind and reduced the wages to RMB 7,200 in the probation period and RMB 9,000 in the regular employment period, resulting in the failure of the employee to sign the employment contract and enrolment. The court ordered the employer to pay the employee discretionary damages of RMB 9,000 on the grounds that the employer had violated the principle of good faith.[6]

This is a rare case of contractual negligence liability in concluding an employment contract. From the legal point of view, employees can also choose to require the employer to fulfill the original commitment of the employment contract. Conversely, if the employee has reached the main conditions of the employment contract with the recruitment employer, but changes his mind and refuses to enter the role, he may also be liable for compensation for losses.

36. When does the employment relationship begin: at the actual start of work or the time specified in the employment contract?

Answer: To determine when the employment relationship between an employee and an employer begins, both the provisions in the employment contract and the actual

---

4 Liang Haiqing and Maoming Petrochemical Hospital Co., Ltd. and Maoming Branch of China Life Insurance Co., Ltd; Liu Wei v. Xi'an Xihang Group Aerospace Ground Equipment Co., Ltd. Civil Ruling of Shaanxi Provincial People's High Court (2017) No. 1296.

5 Civil Judgment of Second Instance on the Labor Dispute between Tan Zhao and China Shipbuilding Industry International Trading Co., Ltd. Civil Judgment of Beijing the Second Intermediate People's Court (2021) Jing 02 Min Zhong No. 11343.

6 Civil Judgment of the Second Instance of Labor Dispute between Beijing Dianqu Education Technology Co., Ltd. and Li Ziyi Civil Judgment of the Third Intermediate People's Court of Beijing (2022) Jing 03 Min Zhong No. 5622.

commencement of work should be considered. The commencement of employment relationships is not necessarily determined by the signing of the employment contract.[7]

There are three situations in determining the commencement of employment. The first situation is that the commencement of employment relationship is the date when the employee starts to work (either a probationary work or regular work), if there is no employment contract in place.

The second circumstance is that if the employee's actual work starts earlier than the starting date specified in the employment contract, the actual work starting time is the commencement of the employment relationship. However, if the employee actually started working to help set up or register the employer's business, the employment relationship should begin when the employer is incorporated.

The third situation is that the employee starts work after they sign the employment contract. In this case, the starting date of the employment relationship shall be the commencement date specified in the employment contract. In other words, even if the employee does not report to the employer and start working on the start date specified in the employment contract, as long as both parties acknowledge this suspension and the contract is subsequently fulfilled after the suspension, the commencement time of the employment relationship remains the start date specified in the employment contract.

If the two parties dispute the start time of the employment relationship, the court will combine the evidence of the case and either uphold the claim of the employee (because the employer has the obligation to keep the files of employment relationships)[8] or determine the start time of employment relationships according to the evidence, such as wage payment and social insurance purchase.

The identification of the beginning of the employment relationship has an important impact on judging whether employees have employment relationships with employers and whether employers have the obligation to pay wages, purchase social insurance for employees, and calculate the length of service of employees.

37. How should employers set up and maintain employees' employment files?

Answer: Employers are rightfully obligated to provide a certificate of dissolution or termination of an employment relationship if the employment is dissolved or terminated, and to process the transfer of the employee's personnel file and social insurance. Employers should also keep employment contracts and wage payment records for at least two years after employees leave their jobs.[9]

---

7 Cong Mingzi, the Civil Judgment of the Supreme People's Procuratorate of the People's Republic of China on the retrial of labor disputes, the Supreme People's Court (2016) Supreme Fa Min Zai No. 148. "It should be noted that the judgment of whether there is an employment relationship between a worker and an employer does not necessarily require the signing of an employment contract as the prerequisite."

8 Anyang Guoyou Real Estate Co., Ltd., Cui Yin Labor Dispute Retrial Review and Trial Supervision Civil Ruling Henan Provincial People's High Court Civil Ruling (2020) Yu Min Shen No. 1257. "Guoyou Company, as the employer, did not comply with the law according to the provisions of Article 6 of the Labor Dispute Mediation and Arbitration Law of the People's Republic of China. It failed to provide relevant evidence of when the employment relationships between the two parties were established, so it was not improper for the original judgment to determine that the employment relationships between the two parties began in July 2011 according to Cui Yin's claim."

9 Paragraph 3 of Article 50 of the Employment Contract Law (employment contracts are kept for two years) and Article 6 of the Provisional Regulations on Wage Payment (wage payment records must be kept for two years).

According to Articles 8 and 18 of the Provisions on Management of Employee's Personnel Files, after the employment relationship is established, the employer bears the responsibilities of collecting, keeping, and receiving employees' personnel files; after the employment relationship terminates, the employer is responsible for transferring employees' personnel files.

The purpose of the employee's personnel file is to record the employee's wage payment, leave entitlements, evaluation of employee performance, and all employee work information to help the employer manage the employee's affairs and maintain legal compliance.

38. An employee refused to sign an employment contract after joining our company. What should we do?

Answer: Your company should immediately terminate the employment relationship.

The Employment Contract Law stipulates that employers must sign a written employment contract with their employees within one month after the employee's entry. Otherwise, they should bear the responsibility of compensating double-wage damages.

According to the provisions of Articles 5 and 6 of the Regulations on Implementation of the Employment Contract Law, if the employee refuses to sign a written employment contract within the first month, the employer should notify the employee in writing to terminate the employment relationship. There is no need to pay economic compensation to the employee, but the employer should pay the employee's actual working hours' labor remuneration. If the employee refuses to sign the contract after the first month, the employer should also notify the employee to terminate the contract, but the employer should pay the employee economic compensation and double-wage damages for the corresponding period.

The purpose of the punitive double-wage damages stipulated by the Employment Contract Law is to punish employers who intentionally fail to sign employment contracts with their employees, leading to employees being unclear about their rights and their interests being damaged. However, if the employee intentionally refuses to sign a contract in order to obtain double-wage damages, the law and the courts will not support such behavior.

39. Is it legal for the employer to collect my deposit and retain my certificate?

Answer: It is illegal for the employer to do so. Article 9 of the Employment Contract Law stipulates that employers shall not collect deposits or retain employees' certificates (including professional qualification certificates). Article 84 stipulates that if the employer violates the provisions, it must return the deposit and certificate to the worker. The labor administrative authority may impose an administrative fine of not less than RMB 500 but not more than RMB 2,000 per person.

For example, in the case of Zhang Jiadong before Jiangsu Provincial High Court in 2019, the court ordered the employer to return the employee deposit of RMB 10,000 together with interest to the employee.[10] In the case of Yang Songlin before Fujian Provincial High

10 Xuzhou Public Transport Group Co., Ltd. and Zhang Jiadong, Xuzhou New Bus Co., Ltd. Labor Dispute Appeal, Application for Civil Ruling Jiangsu Provincial People's High Court Civil Ruling (2019) Sumin Shen 8121.

Court in 2020, the court ordered the employer to return the registered constructor certificate of the employee that had been detained by the employer.[11]

A special case is whether employees' investment in shares constitutes a deposit. Generally speaking, as long as the two parties have a clear agreement on share and dividends, the investment does not constitute a deposit.[12] However, if the payment is imposed by the employer, or the purpose of the deposit is covered up in the form of shares, the payment may be recognized as a deposit.[13] In judicial decisions, the boundary between deposit and investment in shares appears to be blurred. The courts generally consider the name of the payment (deposit or investment in shares) and the closeness between the payment and the bonus that bears characteristics of wage (the more directly the payment is linked to the bonus, the more likely it is to be identified as a deposit; and the more it is an equity dividend, different from a bonus, the more likely it is to be considered equity investment).[14]

Another special case is the deposit of vehicles in the taxi industry. Taxi drivers and taxi companies generally constitute employment relationships. But as to whether a large amount of deposit paid by the driver according to industry practice (usually over RMB 100,000 or even higher) constitutes a deposit stipulated under the employment laws, the prevailing opinion of courts around the country is that there is a contractor relationship between taxi drivers and employers in addition to the employment relationship. The deposit is a matter under the contractor relationship, so it does not relate to the employment dispute.[15] However, the Intermediate People's Court of Shaoguan City, Guangdong

---

11 Civil Ruling on Labor Dispute Retrial Review and Trial Supervision of Yang Songlin and Fujian Lvrong Construction Engineering Co., Ltd. Civil Ruling of Fujian High Court (2020) Min Min Shen No. 1858.

12 Mudanjiang Dongan District Meijia Photography Shop and Yang Xingang Labor Dispute Civil Judgment Mudanjiang Intermediate People's Court Civil Judgment (2019) Hei 10 Min Zhong No. 1147.

13 Gansu Pathfinder International Travel Service Co., Ltd. v. Yang Labor Dispute Appeal Civil Judgment of Lanzhou Intermediate People's Court of Gansu Province (2017) Gan 01 Min Zhong No. 1925. "The contract did not stipulate, but the employer required employees to pay RMB 50,000 to buy shares or dismiss, thus violating the rules of deposit."

14 Civil Judgment of Second Instance of Labor Dispute between Pan-China Innovation (Beijing) Monitoring Instrument Co., Ltd. and Sun Wence Civil Judgment of Beijing the First Intermediate People's Court (2022) Jing 01 Min Zhong No. 10829. The court held that although the risk deposit of RMB 160,000 agreed by both parties was related to profit distribution, it was still an illegal deposit. Beijing Luoman Xianghe Trading Co., Ltd. and Wang Hongyi Labor Dispute Second Instance Civil Judgment Beijing the Third Intermediate People's Court Civil Judgment (2022) Beijing 03 Minzhong No. 11433. "In this case, both parties are engaged in virtual equity incentives, and Sanhe Company collects RMB 150,000 of Wang Hongyi's 'capital stock'. The essence is to collect RMB 150,000 as a prerequisite for paying the reward to Wang Hongyi, which does not conform to the aforementioned provisions, so the principal of RMB 150,000 paid by Wang Hongyi should be refunded." Civil Ruling of the High Court of Guangxi Zhuang Autonomous Region (2019) Gui Min Shen No. 5083. "The Employee Investment/Shareholding Agreement is obviously different from the General Investment Share Agreement, and the precondition for Meng Feifei to participate in the above income dividend is to become the employees of the store. Once the employment relationship is dissolved or terminated, the right to profit or equity held by the partner or shareholder will be withdrawn, and the partner or shareholder must not make any claim for liquidation and compensation after employment termination, which excludes the main rights of partners or shareholders. Therefore, the amount of RMB 30,000 that is called investment in shares actually has the nature of guarantee for the existence of employment relationships."

15 Pu Xiaobo, Sichuan Guangyun Group Cangxi Co., Ltd. Labor Dispute Retrial Review and Trial Supervision Civil Ruling Sichuan High Court Civil Ruling (2018) Chuan Min Shen No. 4481. Civil Ruling on Labor Dispute Retrial Review and Trial Supervision of Jia Shenghu and Qingdao Haibo Passenger Taxi Co., Ltd. Civil Ruling of Shandong High Court (2018) Lu Minshen No. 4838. Labor Dispute Appeal between Luo Guozhu and Guangzhou Guangjun Tourist Automobile Enterprise Group Co., Ltd. Civil Judgment of Guangzhou Intermediate People's Court of Guangdong Province (2017) Yue 01 Min Zhong No. 1954 3.

Province, decided a case in which it held that the deposit was under employment relationship, and the taxi company should return the deposit.[16]

40. An employer arranged a no-pay trial work for a candidate. Is it legal?

Answer: It may be illegal for the employer to do so.

Current judicial decisions show that although trial work has the nature of testing the ability of the recruited personnel, because the work is under the control of the employer, and the work content is an integral part of the employer's business, or the trial work has the nature of a probation period, the recruited personnel and the employer have established an employment relationship during the trial period.[17]

Since the employer has established an employment relationship with the job applicant, it must pay him no less than the minimum wage for these two days of work. As for the employer's refusal to sign an employment contract with the applicant after the two days, it can be viewed that the employer considers that the probation period has shown that the candidate is not up to the hiring requirements, and the employer terminates the employment relationship with him. If the employer can prove that the applicant does not meet the hiring requirements, the termination is legal.

41. Is it legal for my employer not to pay me as a student intern worker?

Answer: Whether you are entitled to remuneration, first of all, depends on whether you and the employer have formed an employment relationship. It is a complex legal and factual matter whether the interns engaged in work for an employer constitute an employment relationship.

The relationship between students in a school work-study program and the employer is generally not an employment relationship.[18] A work-study program is an activity that is organized by schools and aims to help students learn practical skills in enterprises.[19]

---

16 Shaoguan Longzhiquan Taxi Co., Ltd. v. Yin Chenghui et al. Labor Dispute Retrial Case Guangdong Shaoguan Intermediate People's Court Civil Judgment (2017) Yue 02 Min Zai No. 32.

17 Guizhou Qianlangbang Real Estate Marketing Co., Ltd., Zhanglin Labor Dispute Second Instance Civil Judgment Guizhou Qiandongnan Miao and Dong Autonomous Prefecture Intermediate People's Court Civil Judgment (2020) Qian 26 Min Zhong No. 3425. "Trial Period also belongs to the probation period. The probation period is included in the period of employment relationship." The appeal case of labor dispute between Zhaoqing Mingcheng Holiday Hotel Management Co., Ltd. and Jiang Qicong, the civil judgment of Zhaoqing Intermediate People's Court of Guangdong Province (2015) Zhao Zhong Fa Min Yi Zhong Zi No. 33, Jieqiang Washing Department of Liuzhou City, Luo Zemin Labor Dispute Civil Judgment of Second Instance Liuzhou Intermediate People's Court of Guangxi Zhuang Autonomous Region Civil Judgment (2019) Gui 02 Min Zhong No. 2140.

18 Article 12 of the Opinions of the Ministry of Labor on Several Issues Concerning the Implementation of the Labor Law of the People's Republic of China: "Students who use their spare time to work and study are not regarded as employed, and if they have not established employment relationships, they may not sign employment contracts."

19 Article 4 of the Measures for the 2018 Administration of Work-study Programs for Students of Institutions of Higher Learning: "The term 'work-study programs' as mentioned in these Measures refers to the social practice activities in which students, under the organization of the school, use their spare time to obtain legal remuneration through labor and use it to improve their study and living conditions." Article 24: "An off-campus employer that employs a student on a work-study program shall submit an application to the school work-study program management service organization, and provide a copy of the legal person qualification certificate and relevant supporting documents. After examination and approval, the school work-study management service organization recommends students who are suitable for the work requirements to participate in work-study activities."

Current judicial decisions show that work-study programs that meet the two characteristics mentioned above are generally not recognized as employment relationships.[20]

However, if a student continues to work for the employer after the end of the work-study program (for example, the student has graduated or the internship arranged by the school has expired), it is likely to be recognized as an employment relationship.[21] Another controversial situation is when students who meet the legal working age regularly work for an employer under no school arrangements, and some court decisions have identified these as employment relationships,[22] while others identify them as interns' work-study relationships and deny employment relationships.[23]

Based on the current judicial decisions, the main factors to judge the existence of employment relationships for students include: the age of the student and whether there is any concealment of age and student status, whether the two parties have signed an employment contract, whether the student has completed their studies, the purpose and intention of both parties for employment, the nature of the employer (for example, if the internship organization is a state organ, it may be more difficult to identify employment relationships), and especially, the benefits of the student internship to the employer (for example, the student is used by the employer as a regular worker). Courts usually make a decision based on the above factors.

Second, if the employer and the student do not constitute an employment relationship and thus constitute a contractor relationship, but the two parties have agreed on remuneration, then the student can also request remuneration according to the agreement. Of course, the student cannot get the protection of the rights under the employment laws, such as minimum wage, double-wage damages in the absence of a written employment contract, and so on. However, some of the employment rights, such as work injury entitlements, are still available to these students.

Therefore, whether you are entitled to be paid depends on the specific circumstances. If you are a student in school, but work for a company that you reached out to on your own,

20 Labor Dispute between Zhou Yanru and Foshan Nanhai Taoyuan Golf Club Co., Ltd. Civil Judgment of Guangdong Foshan Intermediate People's Court (2016) Yue 06 Min Zhong No. 5035, Application for Labor Dispute between Wu Yiping and Chongqing Vocational College of Architectural Engineering Civil Ruling of Chongqing High Court (2013) Yu Gao Fa Min Shen Zi No. 00838.

21 Civil Judgment of Second Instance of Labor Dispute between Huang Ruoting and Shaoguan Style Real Estate Hotel Co., Ltd. Civil Judgment of Intermediate People's Court of Shaoguan City, Guangdong Province (2016) Yue 02 Min Zhong No. 5.

22 Labor Dispute Case between Jiangmen Jiashida Industrial Co., Ltd. and Yang Junzhuo Civil Judgment of Guangdong Jiangmen Intermediate People's Court (2017) Yue 07 Min Zhong No. 1686, Changsha Sanitary Products Co., Ltd. v. Dai Lanping and Other Labor Dispute Cases Civil Ruling of Hunan High Court (2017) Xiang Min Shen No. 2632, Bulletin of the Supreme People's Court No. 6, 2010 (Total No. 164), 2009 Jiangsu Nanjing Intermediate People's Court Guo v. Jiangsu Yifeng Pharmacy Chain Co., Ltd. Labor dispute: whether the worker is a student does not affect the validity of the employment contract. "As long as the students who have not graduated have reached the legal age of employment, they have the qualification of labor subject and are entitled to the right to work. If the employer knows that the worker is a student when concluding the contract, and both parties have signed the employment contract and performed it in accordance with the contract, the contract does not violate the provisions of laws and regulations, and there is no fraud or threat. Therefore, it should be regarded that the employment contract is legal and effective, and the employment relationship is established."

23 Yu Qian and Liaoyang Radio and Television Station Labor Dispute Retrial Review Civil Ruling Liaoning Provincial People's High Court Civil Ruling (2022) Liao Minshen No. 2635, Shenzhen Sisini Jewelry Design Studio, Hong Xiaoqing Labor Dispute Civil Judgment of Second Instance Civil Judgment of Shenzhen Intermediate People's Court of Guangdong Province (2019) Yue 03 Min Zhong No. 16676.

and the employer also treats you as a regular employee, you are likely to have formed an employment relationship with the employer, and then, the employer's refusal to pay you because you are a student in school violates the provisions of the employment laws. However, if you are a work-study student arranged by the school, and the school and the employer have a detailed internship agreement stipulating that the internship is not paid, the agreement should be valid unless there are special circumstances (for example, the nature of the student's formal replacement of workers far exceeds the nature of social practice for learning and improvement). Even if the two parties do not constitute an employment relationship, the agreed remuneration for labor services is still binding on the employer.

2.2 Double-Wage Damages and Employer Immunity

42. What is double-wage damages for the absence of a signed employment contract?

Answer: The penalty rule of double-wage damages in the absence of a written employment contract (commonly referred to as double-wage damages), established in the 2008 Employment Contract Law, is one of the most significant legislative revisions to the original Labor Law. Its purpose is to address the widespread problem at the time where employers failed to sign written employment contracts with their employees.

Double-wage damages refers to the punitive compensation that an employer must pay to an employee when they fail to sign a written employment contract as required by the Law. During the period when the contract is not signed but within the legally stipulated conditions (such as within the scope of arbitration time limits), the employer must pay the employee the same wage for that period as punitive compensation.

This definition, generalized on the basis of judicial practice, encompasses three key issues for calculating the amount of double-wage damages for which employers are liable.

The first issue is to define a written employment contract. Generally speaking, a written employment contract should meet the minimum requirement on contents and terms under the law, including information of both parties, rights and obligations of both parties, wages, and rest and vacation benefits.[24] Entry registration forms for staff management, employment registration forms for government management purposes, and equity incentive agreements for employee incentives are not considered written employment contracts.[25]

If the written agreement signed by both parties cannot fully meet all the provisions required by the Employment Contract Law, but its main content substantially reflects the rights and obligations of both parties, it can still be considered that both parties have signed a written employment contract.

24 Article 17 of the Employment Contract Law stipulates the necessary clauses for an employment contract.

25 Ningbo Beilun District Xiaogang Zhengdao Household Goods Firm, Zhang Qiuyun Labor Dispute Second Instance Civil Judgment Zhejiang Ningbo Intermediate People's Court Civil Judgment (2021) Zhe 02 Min Zhong No. 1106 (Entry Registration Form), Cao Wei v. Deng Wei, etc. Contractor Relationship Dispute Civil Second Instance Civil Judgment Shandong Dezhou Intermediate People's Court Civil Judgment (2022) Lu 14 Min Zhong No. 2267 (Employment Registration Form), Sparta (Yichang) Sports Culture Communication Co., Ltd., Civil Judgment of the Second Instance of Xiangwenjun Labor Dispute, Civil Judgment of Yichang Intermediate People's Court of Hubei Province (2020) E 05 Min Zhong No. 282 (Equity Incentive Agreement).

The second issue is the three situations where an employer must enter into a written employment contract with an employee. The legislation on double-wage damages has brought about complex issues in practice. Distinguishing between different situations of entering into written employment contracts helps in analyzing and clarifying the final liability of double-wage damages and determining the amount.

Statutory rules and judicial practices indicate three possible situations where employers must sign employment contracts with their employees: new employee joining their employer, current employee meeting conditions for permanent employment contract, and current employee's fixed-term employment expiring while the parties are willing to continue the employment. Please see "43. Under what circumstances should employers sign written employment contracts with their employees?"

Even if the law stipulates the obligation of employers in signing employment contracts, in certain exceptional circumstances, employers may not be liable for double-wage damages even if they failed to sign the employment contracts with their employees. This could be due to situations where employers are not at fault for not signing the employment contracts, or if employees are at fault or act maliciously, or if employees implicitly waive their rights to pursue the damages, or if the law or judicial practice allows exemption from the liability. In such cases, the employers naturally do not need to bear the responsibility for double-wage damages. Please refer to "44. What are the exemptions from the obligation to pay double-wage damages?" for specific details.

The third issue is the calculation of double-wage damages. Once it has been determined that there are no exemptions for the employer failing to sign an employment contract with the employee, the period for which double-wage damages should be awarded ("liable period") can be determined. Determining the liable period should be a two-step process. The first step is to identify the actionable period, during which the employer unlawfully failed to sign an employment contract with the employee and could be held legally accountable, based on legal provisions and judicial practice. Please refer to "51. How is the actionable period for double-wage damages determined?" for specific details. The second step is to further restrict the aforementioned actionable period using the one-year limitation of labor arbitration, resulting in the liable period. Please refer to "53. Is it too late for me to claim the double-wage damages?" for specific details.

It is important to note that the aforementioned liable period should be respectively determined in the aforementioned three different situations where employers are required to sign employment contracts with their employees (i.e., new employee joining their employer, current employee meeting conditions for permanent employment contracts, and current employee's fixed-term employment expiring while the parties are willing to continue the employment). This is because they have different rules for the starting and cut-off points of the actionable period.

Once the liable period is determined using the above method, it's necessary to ascertain the amount of wages corresponding to the liable period. According to the rules of double-wage damages under the Employment Contract Law, the employer must additionally pay the employee the same wages from the corresponding liable period as punitive compensation. For more details, please refer to "58. How is the wage standard for double-wage damages determined?"

For detailed calculations of double-wage damages in the three types of situations, please refer to "52. How are double-wage damages calculated for a newly joined employee?",

"54. How are double-wage damages calculated for not signing a permanent employment contract?", and "57. How are double-wage damages calculated for not signing a new contract after the expiration of a fixed-term employment contract?"

It should be noted that the double-wage damages are punitive damages for the employer's violation of the obligation to sign a written contract, not employment remuneration or wages.[26] Therefore, the double-wage damages cannot be included in the monthly wage base for calculating economic compensation or other employment compensation.

Double-wage damages is a newly established form of employment claim under the Employment Contract Law. Like many other employment legislative regulations, the rules regarding double-wage damages created by legislators have left behind numerous flaws and loopholes. These include circumstances where double-wage damages may be liable, rules for commencement and cut-off points of liable period of double-wage damages, the application rule of one-year limitation of arbitration, and the determination of the wage standard for double-wage damages. All of these lack clear legal rules, requiring subsequent legislations by the National People's Congress or judicial interpretations by the Supreme People's Court to clarify and achieve unified judicial trial rules nationwide.

43. Under what circumstances should employers sign written employment contracts with their employees?

Answer: Article 10 of the Employment Contract Law stipulates the basic principle that "where there is an employment relationship, there should be an employment contract." The legal consequences for the employer's failure to enter into a written employment contract with the employee are that unless there are exemptions or limitations, the employer should generally bear the liability to compensate double-wage damages for the corresponding period during which the contract should have been signed but was not.

In practice, the obligation of the employer to enter into a written employment contract with the employee can be distinguished into three situations.

The first situation is that employers must sign employment contracts with their newly hired employees within one month of commencement of work. This obligation is based on Article 82 of the Employment Contract Law. If the employer fails to reach an agreement with the new employee on signing a written employment contract within one month of their commencement of work, the employer should promptly terminate the employment relationship.[27] In other words, during the statutory grace period of one month for new employee commencement, there is no risk of double-wage damages for not signing an employment contract, but a contract must be signed after this one-month period. Please refer to "52. How are double-wage damages calculated for a newly joined employee?"

The second situation is that employers must sign permanent employment contracts with current employees who have continuously worked for ten years and requested permanent contracts from their employers, or who have completed two consecutive fixed-term

26 Civil Ruling of Henan High Court (2021) Yu Min Shen No. 9262, Civil Ruling of Civil Application for Retrial Examination of Labor Disputes by Ahai Xiaoguan Liangtang Restaurant and Zhao Huimin, Zhengdong New District, Zhengzhou City. "The employer's payment of double-wage damages to the employee is based on the legal consequences of the employer's failure to sign a written employment contract with the employee in accordance with the provisions of the Employment Contract Law, which is of the nature of punitive damages."

27 Article 5 of the Regulations on the Implementation of the Employment Contract Law stipulates that if an employee fails to sign an employment contract within one month of joining the company, the employer may terminate the employment relationship without the obligation to pay economic compensation.

employment contracts and requested a permanent employment contract from the employer. A special case is, according to Article 14 of the Employment Contract Law, if an employee has been employed for more than one year and the contract has not been signed by both parties, it is deemed that a permanent employment contract already exists. Article 7 of the Regulations on the Implementation of the Employment Contract Law stipulates that the employer should immediately sign a permanent employment contract with the employee. Please refer to "55. Under what circumstances must employers sign permanent employment contracts with employees?"

The third situation is that an employer may need to renew the employment contract with a current employee whose fixed-term employment contract expires while both parties continue the employment. This obligation is based on the basic principle of "where there is an employment relationship, there should be an employment contract" in Article 10 of the Employment Contract Law. Due to a relevant provision in judicial interpretations by the Supreme People's Court, there is currently a huge disparity among courts nationwide regarding whether the employer should bear the obligation to renew the contract and compensate double-wage damages in this situation; however, if the Consultation Draft on the Supreme Court's Judicial Interpretation (II) takes effect, this type of double-wage damages shall be calculated according to the type for a newly hired employee (the first situation). Please refer to "57. How are double-wage damages calculated for not signing a new contract after the expiration of a fixed-term employment contract?"

44. What are the exemptions from the obligation to pay double-wage damages?

Answer: Employers theoretically should compensate double-wage damages when they fail to sign a written employment contract when they should have done so as required by law. However, in certain exceptional circumstances, employers may be exempt from the obligation of double-wage damages. These exceptions may include situations where employers are not at fault for failing to sign the contracts, or where employees are at fault or act maliciously, or where employees implicitly waive their right to claim the double-wage damages, or where exemption is allowed by law or evolves from judicial practice.

There are six categories of exemptions, as follows.

The first category of possible exemptions occurs when both parties subsequently sign or retroactively sign an employment contract. If the employer fails to sign an employment contract with the employee in a timely manner but later signs a contract with the actual signing date (subsequent signing of employment contract) or an earlier date (retroactive signing of employment contract), most courts nationwide recognize that such subsequent or retroactive signing of employment contract exempts the employer from double-wage damages' liability. However, some individual courts hold that remedial measures cannot exempt the employer from the liability. Please see "45. Can subsequent or retroactive signing of an employment contract exempt the employer from double-wage damages?"

The second category of possible exemptions occurs when labor dispatch is deemed invalid, and the worker has formed a direct employment relationship with the host employer but does not have a direct employment contract. Currently, the practice of most courts is to consider that the worker and the host employer have clearly formed the conditions of an employment contract directly, even if there is no regular employment contract between them. Therefore, the employer does not need to bear double-wage liability due to the invalidity. However, there are individual cases where courts ordered double-wage damages to punish the host employer for malicious labor dispatch. Please see "47. Is a host employer liable for double-wage damages for invalid labor dispatch?"

The third category of possible exemptions occurs when after the expiration of a fixed-term employment contract, both parties continue to perform the labor relationship without signing a new employment contract. There is serious divergence among courts nationwide on whether the parties are deemed to have signed an employment contract in application of the 2020 Supreme Court's judicial interpretation. Some courts, such as the High Courts of Henan Province, Guizhou Province, Jiangxi Province, Tianjin Municipality, and Anhui Province, cite judicial interpretations of the Supreme People's Court and believe that this constitutes the signing of an employment contract, and do not support claims for double-wage damages. However, there are also contrary precedents in courts such as the High Courts of Guangxi Zhuang Autonomous Region, Xinjiang Uyghur Autonomous Region, and Chongqing. And even within the same court, such as the High Courts of Guangdong Province, Heilongjiang Province, Jilin Province, and Guangdong Province Shenzhen Intermediate People's Court, there are two completely opposite decisions. This exception also includes the issue of whether a permanent contract should be signed after two consecutive fixed-term contracts have expired but have not been signed. Please see "57. How are double-wage damages calculated for not signing a new contract after the expiration of a fixed-term employment contract?"

The fourth category of exemptions occurs when an employee intentionally lets someone else sign the employment contract, provided by the employer, on their behalf or impersonates someone else to establish an employment relationship with the employer, and then later claims that they did not sign the contract and demands double-wage damages from the employer. Another similar situation is when the employee who handles the employment contract signing for the employer deliberately does not sign a contract for themselves. Currently, courts across the country treat all the three situations similarly and rule that the employee violates the principle of good faith and should not be entitled to double-wage damages. Please see "48. Is employer liable if employee purposely has someone else to sign the employment contract and then claims double-wage damages?"

The fifth category of exemptions occurs when after the expiration of a fixed-term employment contract, both parties sign a simple amendment agreement to the fixed-term employment contract, stipulating several changes (or only a change of contract period) based on the original employment contract to form a new contract. Regarding claims for double-wage damages in this regard, if the fixed-term employment contract provides that the contract shall automatically renew upon expiration, courts generally consider that the amendment agreement or the auto-renewal clause has formed a clear and regular employment contract, and do not support claims for double-wage damages. Please see "49. Will an amendment agreement after the expiration of a fixed-term employment contract lead to double-wage damages?"

The sixth category comprises other exceptions and exemptions. These include situations where employees are on special leave (such as on maternity leave, on standby, or on long-term leave); employees belong to special categories, such as retired or on long-term unpaid leave; employers are in a special stage, such as the preparatory stage; or employers are affected by circumstances like city lockdowns and shutdowns due to pandemics. Additionally, in cases where full-time employees establish de facto employment relationships with a second employer without signing an employment contract, due to legal restrictions on dual or multiple employment relationships, courts currently do not support claims for double-wage damages against the second or third employer in such situations. Please refer to "50. What are the other exceptions in practice under which employers are exempt from double-wage damages?"

In addition to the exemptions for the employer, there is also a one-year limitation of arbitration for the employer's liability to compensate double-wage damages (please refer to "53. Is it too late for me to claim the double-wage damages?") as well as the limitations on actionable period (involving the commencement and cut-off points for the period allowed by law; please refer to "51. How is the actionable period for double-wage damages determined?").

45. Can subsequent or retroactive signing of an employment contract exempt the employer from double-wage damages?

Answer: If an employer has not signed an employment contract with their employee within the statutory time limit and requires the employee to sign an employment contract with a starting date as the date of entry, there may be two situations in practice: one is to sign the contract subsequently, meaning that the date on which the employee's signature is indicated reflects the actual signing date; the second is to retroactively sign the contract, meaning that the date indicated on the contract as the employee's signature date is not the actual signing date, but a date required by law after entry (e.g. within one month after the new employee starts).

"The Opinion on proxy-signing, subsequently signing, and retroactively signing employment contract," an article in the "New Compilation of the Supreme People's Court's Judicial Opinions—Civil Volume" by the Supreme People's Court's Civil First Division published in 2014, explains in detail the difference between subsequently and retroactively signing employment contracts and concludes that employers do not need to pay double-wage damages for subsequently signed employment contracts, but they do for retroactively signed contracts, because the latter involves intentionally circumventing legal rules.

However, from judicial decisions, since the aforementioned opinion is only the opinion of the Supreme People's Court's Civil First Division and not an official judicial interpretation of the Supreme People's Court, it seems that courts across the country have not strictly followed this opinion in handling disputes over subsequently and retroactively signed employment contracts.

Currently, most courts across the country recognize that subsequently or retroactively signing employment contracts exempts the employers from the liability of paying double-wage damages. These courts include those in Guangdong Province, Guangxi Autonomous Region, Hubei Province, Shanxi Province (山西省), Guizhou Province, Jiangsu Province, Huai'an City in Jiangsu Province, Beijing, and Xinjiang Uygur Autonomous Region, among others.[28] However, there are also a few local courts that believe that subsequently or retroactively signing employment contracts cannot exempt the employer from the

28 Zhu Fengnan v. Nanhai Yanbu Baocheng Property Management Co., Ltd. Labor Dispute, Guangdong Provincial High Court Civil Ruling (2019) YueMinShen No. 12918; Wan Yali v. Chunmiao School, Jianghan District, Wuhan City Labor Dispute, Hubei Provincial High Court Civil Ruling (2014) EMinShenZi No. 00023; Xie Yaoying v. Lianshui Jiadebao Wood Products Co., Ltd. Labor Dispute Second Instance Civil Judgment, Huai'an Intermediate People's Court, Jiangsu Province Civil Judgment (2023) Su08MinZhong No. 91. Xu

liability of double-wage damages. These regions include Qinghai Province, Lianyungang City in Jiangsu, Weihai and Jinan City in Shandong, Shenyang City in Liaoning Province, Fuzhou City in Fujian Province, and Huaihua City and Shaoyang City in Hunan Province, among others.[29] Please refer to "46. Are there any typical judicial decisions on subsequent or retroactive signing of employment contracts?"

46. Are there any typical judicial decisions on subsequent or retroactive signing of employment contracts?

Answer: Our case study shows that most courts, including those in Guangdong Province, Guangxi Autonomous Region, Hubei Province, Shanxi Province, Guizhou Province, Jiangxi Province, Jiangsu Province Huaian City, Beijing City, Xinjiang Uygur Autonomous Region, and Shandong Province, consider subsequent or retroactive signing of employment contracts as employees' waiver of the right to double-wage damages.

Guangxi Zhuang Autonomous Region High Court (2022) GuiMinShen No. 4316: Guangxi Huixin Long Hotel Management Co., Ltd. v. Huang Meichun Labor Dispute Case. In this case, the company required the employee to subsequently sign the employment contract before agreeing to the resignation, so the court held that this could not be considered as the employee waiving the right of double-wage damages. It seems that the court in this case considered the employee's voluntary subsequent signing of the contract as a valid waiver of double-wage damages.

Xinjiang Uygur Autonomous Region High Court Civil Ruling (2019) XinMinShen No. 1391: Dong Jiankun v. Xinjiang Jinli Special Security Service Co., Ltd. Labor Dispute Case. In this case, the employee subsequently signed the employment contract two months after joining, and the court stated that there was no evidence to show that the employee's subsequent signing was involuntary, so double-wage damages should not be supported.

Shanxi Provincial High Court Civil Ruling (2019) JinMinShen No. 1045: Xu and Tai v. Shanxi Quanlian Human Resources Co., Ltd. Labor Dispute Case. In this case, the court considered that the starting date specified in the employment contract subsequently signed by the employee was the actual date of employment, which deems that the employee waived their right to double-wage damages.

Guizhou Provincial High Court Civil Ruling (2018) QianMinShen No. 3262: Liu Jun v. Guizhou Qianwanji Technology Development Co., Ltd. Labor Dispute Case. In this case, the employee specified in the termination agreement that he had subsequently signed the employment contract, which the court held was an acknowledgment of the waiver of the right to double-wage damages.

Tingfang et al; Labor Dispute Second Instance Civil Judgment, Beijing the Second Intermediate People's Court Civil Judgment (2022) Jing 02 Min Zhong No. 12913.

29 Rushan City Chengqu Street Office Jingwei Kindergarten v. Wang Xinghua Labor Dispute Civil Retrial Civil Judgment, Shandong Weihai Intermediate People's Court Civil Judgment (2023) Lu 10 Min Zai No. 5; Gao Hongbo v. Jinan Huangtai Gas Stove Co., Ltd. Labor Dispute Second Instance Civil Judgment, Jinan Intermediate People's Court, Shandong Province Civil Judgment (2022) Lu 01 Min Zhong No. 6595; Hao Guidong v. Liaoning Qiangdun Fireproof Door Co., Ltd. Labor Dispute Case, Shenhe District People's Court, Shenyang City Civil Judgment (2016) Liao 0114 Min Chu No. 1281; Li Jin v. Fujian Tianniu Mountain Real Estate Development Co., Ltd. Labor Dispute Second Instance Civil Judgment, Fuzhou Intermediate People's Court, Fujian Province Civil Judgment (2016) Min 01 Min Zhong No. 4499 (this case seems to imply that the company still needs to bear the responsibility of double-wage damages even if it signs employment contracts retroactively); Hunan Huaicheng Property Management Co., Ltd. v. Li Li Labor Dispute Appeal Case, Huaihua Intermediate People's Court, Hunan Province Civil Judgment (2017) Xiang 12 Min Zhong No. 64.

Jiangsu Provincial High Court Civil Ruling (2019) SuMinShen No. 7706: Xu Shougen v. Yangzhong Jinpeng Kitchen Equipment Factory Labor Dispute Case. In this case, the court believed that the employee's subsequent signing of the employment contract was a waiver of the right to double-wage damages.

Shandong Provincial Higher People's Court Civil Ruling (2019) LuMinShen No. 900: Song Yuliang v. Laiyang Henrun Food Co., Ltd. Labor Dispute Case. The court held that according to the Opinion on proxy-signing, subsequently signing, and retroactively signing employment contract by the Supreme Court's Civil First Division, the company was not liable to double-wage damages in the case of subsequent signing.

Guangdong Provincial High Court Civil Ruling (2021) YueMinShen No. 1146: Kuang Xiaofei v. Hongshan Street Community Health Service Center, Huangpu District Labor Dispute Case. The court pointed out in this case that the subsequent signing of the employment contract represented the genuine intention of both parties, so the company was not liable to pay double-wage damages.

Hubei Provincial High Court Civil Ruling (2014) EMinShen No. 00022: Wu Chunhua v. Chunmiao School, Jianghan District, Wuhan Labor Dispute Application Case. The court held that subsequent signing of the employment contract represented the genuine intention of both parties, so the company was not liable to pay double-wage damages.

However, there are a few courts, including those in Qinghai Province, Lianyungang City in Jiangsu Province, Weihai and Jinan City in Shandong Province, Shenyang City in Liaoning Province, Fuzhou City in Fujian Province, and Huaihua City and Shaoyang City in Hunan Province, that have held the opposite. Please see the following cases.

Qinghai Provincial High Court Civil Ruling (2021) QingMinShen No. 906: Qinghai Guoheng Tendering Agency Co., Ltd. v. Wu Xuezhou labor dispute case. In this case, the court held that even if the subsequent signing of the employment contract was a fact, it did not change the fact that the employment contract was not signed in time. Therefore, the original judgment to award double-wage damages was deemed appropriate.

Jiangsu Province Lianyungang Intermediate Court Civil Judgment (2022) Su07MinZhong 1419: Lianyungang Jicong Network Technology Co., Ltd. v. Zhuang Xingchen, et al. labor dispute case. The court held that subsequent signing (actually retroactive signing) of the employment contract did not change the fact that the employment contract was not signed within the statutory period, so the company should compensate double-wage damages.

Hunan Province Shaoyang Intermediate Court Civil Judgment (2019) Xiang05MinZhong 192: Longhui County Jiulong Construction Co., Ltd. v. Li Haijun labor dispute case. In this case, the court held that although both parties subsequently signed the employment contract, they did not agree to waive the employee's right to double-wage damages, so the company would still be liable to pay double-wage damages.

47. Is a host employer liable for double-wage damages for invalid labor dispatch?

Answer: After labor dispatch is deemed invalid, the corresponding employee should have established a direct employment relationship with the host employer. However, typically, there is only a tripartite labor dispatch contract for the employee and the host employer signed with the dispatch employer, without an employment contract between the employee and the host employer, because the employee only signed an employment contract with the dispatch employer. So, whether the employee at this point may claim double-wage damages for not having an employment contract with the host employer is a rare question.

From judicial practice, currently, most courts conclude that the host employer does not constitute failure to sign an employment contract with the employee in this case, and therefore, the host employer is not obligated to pay double-wage damages. Courts holding this view include those in Jiangsu Province, Beijing City, and Changchun City of Jilin Province. These courts' precedents indicate that although the labor dispatch contract is invalid, since an employment contract, although between the employee and the dispatch employer, already exists, the liability to pay double-wage damages cannot be established.[30]

The underlying legal logic is probably that the legislative purpose of double-wage damages, the punitive compensation for failure to sign an employment contract, is to punish employers for not entering into a written agreement with employees regarding employment conditions (including wages, etc.) to the detriment of employees' rights. However, since the labor dispatch contract or the employment contract between the employee and the dispatch employer has already clearly stipulated these employment conditions, the host employer therefore does not need to bear the obligation of double-wage damages.

However, there are also isolated judgments that suggest that if the employer maliciously evades its legal obligations by using sham labor dispatch, rendering the labor dispatch invalid, the employer should still bear the responsibility of double-wage damages.[31]

48. Is the employer liable if the employee purposely has someone else sign the employment contract and then claims double-wage damages?

Answer: If the employment contract is not signed by the employee themselves, there are two possible scenarios: the first is when the employee intentionally allows someone else to sign the employment contract on their behalf; the second is when the employee impersonates someone else and establishes a labor relationship with the employer. Another similar situation is that the employee who handles staff signing employment contracts for the employer deliberately does not sign a contract for themselves. In principle, if an employee claims double-wage damages from the employer under these three circumstances, the employer is not liable.

In the first scenario, according to the principle of agency law in civil law, the act of arranging someone else to sign on behalf of the employee constitutes valid agency, and it should be deemed that the employee has signed the employment contract. The Supreme People's Court's Civil First Division's "The Opinion on proxy-signing, subsequently signing, and retroactively signing employment contract" also states that in this situation, the employer is not required to pay double-wage damages.[32]

---

30 Zhang Hai v. Changzhou Public Transportation Group Co., Ltd., Second Instance Civil Judgment on Labor Dispute, Changzhou Intermediate People's Court, Civil Judgment (2020) Su 04 Min Zhong 3389; Tang Geyin v. Changchun University, Jilin Province Jingyi Property Service Co., Ltd., Changchun Zezhong Property Service Co., Ltd., Second Instance Civil Judgment on Labor Dispute, Jilin Province Changchun Intermediate People's Court, Civil Judgment (2018) Ji 01 Min Zhong 1423; Liu Xinjun v. Beijing Construction Group Co., Ltd., Labor Dispute Appeal Case, Beijing the Second Intermediate People's Court, Civil Judgment (2014) Er Zhong Min Zhong Zi No. 11879.

31 Luo Yuling v. China Mobile Tietong Co., Ltd., Xiaogan Branch, Second Instance Civil Judgment on Labor Dispute, Xiaogan Intermediate People's Court, Civil Judgment (2019) E 09 Min Zhong 798. In this case, the employer used multiple companies for labor dispatch in a malicious attempt to evade its obligations. The court ruled that the employer, for failing to sign an employment contract with the employee, should bear the obligation to pay double-wage damages.

32 "The Opinions on proxy-signing, subsequently signing, and retroactively signing employment contract" in the 2014 "New Compilation of Supreme People's Court Judicial Opinions: Civil Volume." According to this

In the second scenario, the courts usually determine that the employee has engaged in fraudulent behavior, so the employer is not obligated to pay double-wage damages. For example, in the case of Wu Suoxia in 2015, where the employee signed an employment contract with the employer under someone else's name and later claimed double-wage damages. Judge Fang Zhe from the Tianjin High People's Court concluded that since the employee fraudulently established an employment relationship with the employer, rendering the employment contract invalid, the original judgment not supporting the claim for double-wage damages was correct.[33]

In the third scenario, the courts usually consider that the employer is not liable for double-wage damages due to the employee's fault or fraud. For example, in the 2018 case of Duan Hanqiao, the general manager of the company, who was responsible for signing labor contracts with employees, intentionally did not sign one for himself. The Hubei Provincial High Court considered that the employee had the main fault for not signing an employment contract for himself, and therefore rejected his request for double-wage damages.[34]

The legislative intent for setting double-wage damages is to ensure that employees have written contracts specifying labor conditions. If an employee dishonestly arranges for someone else to sign the contract on their behalf, or impersonates others to sign the contract, or acts dishonestly causing the employer to have reasonably believed that the employee had already signed an employment contract, and then claims double-wage damages, the court will not uphold such claim.

49. Will an amendment agreement after the expiration of a fixed-term employment contract lead to double-wage damages?

Answer: It is a common situation that after the expiration of an employee's fixed-term employment contract, both parties are willing to continue the employment relationship. At this time point, the employer may choose to simplify the procedure by only signing an amendment agreement or declaration with the employee to extend the term of the employment contract, with most or all other conditions remaining essentially unchanged.

Some employees may contest that this amendment agreement or declaration does not constitute a regular employment contract and therefore demand double-wage damages for the absence of a signed employment contract.

Currently, the courts handle such situations by recognizing that both parties have effectively signed subsequent employment contracts, and thus do not support employees' claims for double-wage damages. For example, in the case of Liang Shunchao and 11 others in 2020, employees signed an "Amendment Agreement of Employment Contract" with 2 companies, agreeing to change their employer while maintaining the original contract's terms. The Guangdong High People's Court held that the signing of this amendment

---

Opinion of the Civil First Division of the Supreme People's Court, if an employee intentionally lets someone else sign the contract on their behalf and later demands that the employer pay double-wage damages, the court will not support such a claim.

33 Wu Suoxia v. Hebei Haichuan Human Resources Service Co., Ltd., Yanshan County Haichuan Human Resources Co., Ltd. Tianjin Development Zone Branch, and Jiaxing Precision Injection Molding (Tianjin) Co., Ltd., Civil Retrial Order on Labor Dispute, Tianjin High People's Court, Civil Retrial Order (2015) Jin Gao Min Shen Zi No. 0701.

34 Duan Hanqiao v. Bovery Westley Filtration Technology (Hubei) Co., Ltd., Hubei Provincial Higher People's Court Civil Ruling (2018) E Min Shen No. 1182.

agreement constituted the signing of an employment contract and did not support the employees' claims for double-wage damages.[35]

The legislative intent of double-wage damages is to ensure that employees have written contracts to specify labor conditions. If the agreement to amend the employment contract can determine the employee's labor conditions, thereby effectively ensuring the binding nature of the original employment contract's terms on both parties, the court will not rigidly determine that both parties have not signed an employment contract and will not support the claim for double-wage damages.

In a similar scenario where both parties have explicitly agreed in a fixed-term employment contract that the contract will automatically renew upon expiration, the court typically considers this to be a lawful agreement and that it should be regarded as if the contract had been formally executed, and the employer is not obligated to bear the responsibility for double-wage damages.[36]

50. What are the other exceptions in practice under which employers are exempt from double-wage damages?

Answer: Although the Employment Contract Law stipulates that employers should bear the responsibility of double-wage damages for not signing employment contracts, there are still some exceptions where employers are exempted from this responsibility. Apart from exceptions such as retroactive and subsequent signing of employment contracts, invalid labor dispatch, failure to renew fixed-term labor contracts, fraudulent signing of contracts by employees, and amendment agreements of employment contracts, there are also other exceptions.

These other exceptions include situations where employees are on long-term leave such as maternity leave, on long-term unpaid leave, internally retired, or on waiting-for-work, or where employers are in the preparatory stage or lack legal capacity, or where employers are forced to cease operations due to external factors (such as city lockdowns during pandemics), or where employers hire employees who are full-time employees of other employers.

For example, in a case handled by the Xifeng District People's Court of Qingyang City, Gansu Province in 2021, it was deemed that there was no fault on the part of the employer when the employee took maternity leave before the completion of the three-month probation period, so the claim for double-wage damages was not supported.[37] Another example is the fourth case of the top ten typical labor dispute cases related to the COVID-19 pandemic released by Beijing in 2020. It was determined that due to the lockdown of the city

35 Wang Yalan v. Sichuan Tobacco Company Yibin City Branch, Labor Dispute Case, Sichuan High People's Court, Civil Ruling (2016) Chuan Min Shen 3198. Liang Shunchao v. Shenzhen Western Bus Co., Ltd., Retrial Review and Supervision of Civil Ruling on Labor Dispute, Guangdong High People's Court, Civil Ruling (2020) Yue Min Shen 6647–6657.

36 Qinhuangdao Bishui Huating Club Co., Ltd. v. Wang Cuilan, Hebei Provincial Higher People's Court Civil Ruling (2020) Ji Min Shen No. 6024.

37 In the case of Deng v. Gansu Lanyang Technology Co., Ltd., Civil Judgment of First Instance, Case No. Gan 1002 Minchu No. 1831, issued by the Xifeng District People's Court of Qingyang City, Gansu Province in 2021, both parties signed a recruitment resume form containing the main terms of the employment contract and agreed to sign a regular contract after a three-month probation period. The court found that: "Before the expiration of the three-month probation period, the plaintiff took maternity leave, and the parties did not sign a written employment contract after the probation period. This court cannot determine whose fault it was for not signing the written employment contract" and thus rejected the employee's claim for double-wage damages.

and lockout during the epidemic, the failure to sign the employment contract in a timely manner was caused by the external reason, and since the employer was not at fault, the liability for double-wage damages could also be exempted.[38]

In addition, the courts currently do not support the request for double-wage damages in cases where a full-time employee establishes a de facto employment relationship with a second employer without signing an employment contract, as the law discourages dual employment relationships.[39] For example, in the case of Zhong Jianwei handled by the Liaoning High Court in 2021, the court did not support the employee's claim for double-wage damages because the employment laws do not encourage dual employment relationships. However, if an employee on long-term unpaid leave (i.e., one who maintains the employment relationship with the original employer) does not deliberately conceal the fact of long-term unpaid leave when joining a new employer, the new employer may still bear the liability for double-wage damages if no employment contract is in place.[40]

It should be noted that if the employer is aware of the employee's fault but fails to terminate the employment relationship with the employee in accordance with the law, resulting in the failure to sign an employment contract, the employer may still bear the responsibility for double-wage damages. For example, in the case of Xie Xiaoyan handled by the Guangzhou Intermediate People's Court in 2023, it was determined that "even if Xie Xiaoyan was at fault, in the absence of an agreement between the two parties on signing the employment contract, if Ji Xiang Space Company did not exercise the right to terminate the employment relationship within the statutory period and chose to continue the employment, it should be deemed to have waived the right to terminate the employment relationship, so JiXiang Space Company should bear the legal consequence for not signing a written employment contract."[41]

2.3 Calculation of Double-Wage Damages

51. How is the actionable period for double-wage damages determined?

Answer: When an employee claims for double-wage damages against their employer, it is necessary to determine the liable period, which is the final period used to calculate the amount of double-wage damages.

The liable period should be determined in two steps. First, it is ascertained based on the law and judicial practice to identify the actionable period (the most common actionable period is typically 11 months, from the expiration of 1 month of the employee's joining

38 In 2020, the Beijing Municipal Human Resources and Social Security Bureau released the fourth of the top ten typical cases of labor dispute arbitration related to the COVID-19 pandemic in Beijing: the case of Chen v. a certain educational consulting company regarding the dispute over employment remuneration recovery—where no contract was signed and the employer had notified employees in advance, double-wage damages could be exempted.

39 Zhong Jianwei v. Liaoning Jiaheng Real Estate Media Co., Ltd., the Liaoning High People's Court (Case No. 2634 of 2021) concerning the application for retrial of a labor dispute.

40 Guangzhou Aifengzhe Electronic Technology Co., Ltd. v. Lu Wei, the Guangdong High People's Court (Case No. 10476 of 2019) concerning the retrial and review of a labor dispute. The court found that the employee, who was on long-term unpaid leave from the previous employer, did not conceal this fact when joining the new company. Therefore, the court held that the new employer should bear the liability of double-wage for failing to sign an employment contract.

41 Guangzhou Jixiang Space Decoration Design Engineering Co., Ltd. v. Xie Xiaoyan, the Guangzhou Intermediate People's Court (Case No. 9955 of 2023).

to 1 year). The actionable period is a timeframe with a starting point and a cut-off point, without considering the one-year limitation of arbitration. Second, it is determined by using the statutory one-year limitation of arbitration to review and limit the actionable period, ultimately establishing the liable period.

Therefore, understanding the starting point and cut-off point of the actionable period for different types of situations where employment contracts are not signed (including new employees not signing contracts after one month of joining, employees not signing permanent contracts when legally required, and employees continuing to work after fixed-term contracts expire without signing a new contract) is crucial.

For the first type (new employees not signing a contract after one month of joining), the actionable period starts from the day after the one-month period expires and ends at the date when one year expires. According to Article 14 of the Employment Contract Law, if it is not arranged for a new employee to sign an employment contract after one year of joining, it is deemed that they have signed a permanent contract. Therefore, the starting point of the actionable period for this type is the day immediately after one month of joining, and the cut-off point is the date when one year expires.[42]

For the second type (current employees who should sign permanent contracts but have not), the actionable period starts from the day the employer should have signed the permanent contract and lasts for 11 months or 1 year.

Specifically, for this type, there are two scenarios: employees who have not been asked to sign a permanent contract after signing two consecutive fixed-term contracts, and employees who have worked continuously for ten years and have requested a permanent contract. For the first scenario, currently, the starting point for determining the actionable period recognized by national court cases is the day after the expiration of the second fixed-term contract or one month after the expiration of the second fixed-term contract. The cut-off date is 1 year from the expiration date of the contract, which means the maximum actionable period is either 11 months or 12 months.[43] Only the cases from

---

42 According to Article 14 of the Economic redundancy, if an employer fails to sign a written employment contract with an employee after one year of the employment, it is deemed that a permanent employment contract has been signed between the employer and the employee. Although Article 7 of the Regulations on the Implementation of the Employment Contract Law stipulates that the employer should immediately subsequently sign a permanent contract with the employee, judicial practice indicates that even if the employer does not comply with this provision later on, double-wage damages for the subsequent period will not be pursued. In the case of Wu Xuegen v. Foshan Shunde Hanma Jewelry Co., Ltd., Guangdong Higher People's Court Civil Ruling (2017) Yue Min Shen 1202, the court held that although the Regulations on the Implementation of the Employment Contract Law stipulate that employers should immediately sign a written employment contract with the employee, "Wu Xuegen's employment with Hanma Company for one year is deemed to have signed a permanent employment contract. Wu Xuegen's claim for double-wage damages for the period from November 1, 2014, to November 24, 2015, based on the failure of signing an employment contract has no factual and legal basis, so the court does not support Wu Xuegen's claim."

43 Yu Jianhua v. Shandong Ying Tian Law Firm, Judicial Review and Supervision Civil Ruling of Labor Dispute Retrial, Shandong Provincial High People's Court (2018) Lu Min Shen 3237. The court found that after the expiration of two fixed-term employment contracts and the continuation of contract performance by both parties, the employer should have signed a permanent employment contract with the employee. The starting point for double-wage damages is the day after the expiration of the second fixed-term contract, and the cut-off date is one year after the expiration of the contract. Ma Hong v. Dingyan Town People's Government of Rugao City, Labor Dispute Appeal, Civil Ruling of Jiangsu Provincial High People's Court (2018) Su Min Shen 2945. In this case, the employee had signed two consecutive fixed-term employment contracts. The court hold that "if the employer violates the laws and administrative regulations by not signing a permanent employment contract with the employee, the employer should pay the employee double-wage damages. The starting point for calculation is from the day after the expiration of the employment contract until the day before signing the

the Chongqing High Court deny the one-year cut-off for accountability.[44] For the second scenario, currently, most local courts follow the rules of signing employment contracts for new employees. That is, the starting point for the actionable period is one month after the employee's request for contract signing, and the deadline is one year after the employee's request for permanent employment contract signing. The actionable period is a maximum of 11 months.[45]

It is worth noting that according to Article 4 of the Consultation Draft on the Interpretation of the Supreme People's Court on the Application of Law in the Trial of Labor Dispute Cases (II), this actionable period will change to 1 year, meaning that the implementation of the aforementioned Judicial Interpretation (II) shall end the judicial practice of the 11-month actionable period.

For the third type (current employees whose fixed-term contracts have expired and who continue working without signing a new contract), based on current judicial practice, the starting point for the actionable period is the day after the expiration of the fixed-term employment contract or one month after its expiration. The accountability cut-off point is one year after the expiration of the fixed-term contract. Thus, the maximum actionable period is either 11 or 12 months.

Specifically, there are two approaches to determining the starting point for the actionable period in various court decisions for this type of situation. The first approach is to set the starting point as the next day after the expiration date of the fixed-term contract, which follows the practice of the one-month grace period for new employees. This viewpoint is supported by the High Courts of Shandong Province and Fujian Province.[46] The second approach is to set the starting point as the next day after the expiration of the fixed-term contract. For example, in the 2022 case of Gong Jinping, Judge Sun Chengsong of Beijing

permanent employment contract, for a maximum of eleven months." Zhang Hongle v. Intermediate People's Court of Lanzhou City, Gansu Province, Labor Dispute Retrial Examination and Supervision Civil Ruling, Civil Ruling of Gansu Provincial High People's Court (2019) Gan Min Shen 2045. In this case, after signing two fixed-term contracts, the two parties did not sign a permanent contract. The court concluded that the liable period for double-wage damages for not signing a permanent employment contract should refer to the rules for new employees, starting from 1 month after expiration of the second fixed-term contract to 1 year after its expiration, totaling 11 months.

44 Wen Xuan v. China Metallurgical Construction Group Co., Ltd. Labor Dispute Retrial, Civil Judgment of Chongqing High People's Court (2019) Yu Min Zai 94. In this case, the employee signed fixed-term contracts consecutively twice. The court confirmed that the liable period for double-wage damages should start from the day after the expiration of the second fixed-term contract. However, it concluded that there is no cut-off for double-damages liability similar to the one-year cut-off for new employees.

45 Xuchang Wanli Transportation Group Co., Ltd. v. Ma Haixia, Labor Dispute, Civil Judgment of Henan Provincial High People's Court (2015) Yu Fa Min Ti Zi No. 00102. The court held that the starting point for paying double-wage damages to employees who have worked for ten years is the day when the contract should have been signed, and the deadline is one year after that date. Chen Yilong v. Beijing Huanan Building Co., Ltd. Labor Dispute Civil Ruling of Beijing High People's Court (2014) Gao Min Shen Zi No. 01185. The court held that since the employee had worked continuously for more than ten years and had requested to sign a permanent contract, "Failure to sign a written permanent employment contract is a type of not signing written employment contract, so the maximum period for paying double-wage damages is not more than eleven months." Xuxiaoming v. Guangzhou Wohua Fire Engineering Co., Ltd. Labor Dispute Civil Application for Retrial Review Civil Ruling of Guangdong Provincial High People's Court (2020) Yue Min Shen 4037.

46 Tian Dingli v. China National Heavy Duty Truck Group Jinan Power Co., Ltd. Labor Dispute Retrial Examination and Supervision Civil Ruling of Shandong Provincial High People's Court (2018) Lu Min Shen 4835. In this case, the court upheld that the original judgment followed the contract-signing rules for new employees to handle the renewal of fixed-term contracts, allowing for a one-month grace period. Wuyishan Xingcun Linzhi Kindergarten v. Jiang Xuanying Labor Dispute Retrial Examination and Supervision Civil Ruling of Fujian Provincial High People's Court (2019) Min Min Shen 539.

the Third Intermediate People's Court reasoned that "the employer should have anticipated the legal consequences of the expiration of the original employment contract and the continuation of employment, so there is no need to provide an additional one-month grace period. The day after the expiration of the original employment contract is the date on which the employer should have signed a new employment contract and bear the legal consequences of not doing so."[47] Currently, court decisions across various regions indicate that the cut-off date for accountability for this type is one year after the next day after the expiration of the fixed-term employment contract, which is similar to the accountability cut-off for new employees who have not signed employment contracts within one year of employment.

It is worth noting that Article 4 of the 2023 Consultation Draft on the Interpretation of the Supreme People's Court on the Application of Law in the Trial of Laobr Dispute Cases (II) clarifies this issue. It stipulates: If an employer should have signed a fixed-term contract with an employee but did not, the period for calculating double-wage damages starts from the day following one month after the date the employer should have signed the employment contract. This means that if both parties wish to continue the employment relationship after the expiration of the fixed-term employment contract, the employer should sign the contract within one month after the contract expires. Otherwise, the employer shall be liable for double-wage damages. This means the starting point for calculating the double-wage damages shall be regulated as the next date of the one-month expiration date of the fixed-term employment contract.

Once the actionable periods for the three types are determined using the aforementioned methods, the liable period for double-wage damages can be finally restricted and determined based on the one-year limitation of labor arbitration, thereby determining the amount of double-wage damages.

52. How are double-wage damages calculated for a newly joined employee?

Answer: Article 82 of the Employment Contract Law newly stipulates that an employer shall have the legal obligation to sign an employment contract with a new employee within one month after the employee's entry into the job. Otherwise, the employer shall compensate the employee double-wage damages. The failure of employers to sign written employment contracts with newly recruited employees was a common situation in practice before 2008, which is the punitive legislative purpose of the new provision of double-wage in the Employment Contract Law.

The calculation of double-wage damages requires determining the liable period and the employee's wage standard. The liable period should be determined in two steps. The first step is to determine the actionable period based on the law and judicial practice (the most common actionable period is the 11-month period from 1 month after the new employee's entry into the job to 1 year). The actionable period is a period with a starting point and a cut-off point without considering the limitation of arbitration. The second step is to use

47 Wang Zhongxin v. Beijing Fengtai Hospital Labor Dispute Retrial Civil Judgment Civil Judgment of Beijing High People's Court (2021) Jing Min Zai No. 87. The court's final ruling confirms the original judgment's determination, namely, that the starting point for double-wage damages in the case of expiration of a fixed-term contract (without meeting the conditions for a permanent contract) is the second day after the expiration. Beijing Wushengchang Automobile Sales Service Co., Ltd. v. Gong Jinping Labor Dispute Second Instance Civil Judgment of Beijing the Third Intermediate People's Court (2022) Jing 03 Min Zhong 6983.

the statutory one-year limitation of arbitration to restrict the actionable period, ultimately determining the liable period.

According to "51. How is the actionable period for double-wage damages determined?" and "53. Is it too late for me to claim the double-wage damages?", the liable period for double-wage damages for newly joined employees who have not signed employment contracts is a maximum of 11 months, starting from 1 month of joining to 1 year after joining.

After determining the liable period, the corresponding wage for that period should be determined. For specific determination of the wage standard for double-wage damages, please refer to "58. How is the wage standard for double-wage damages determined?"

For example, Ms. Li entered a job on March 1, 2024, and the employer has not signed an employment contract with her. If we do not consider the limitation of arbitration, she can demand double-wage damages for the period from April 1, 2023 to February 28, 2024 (a total of 11 months). This is the actionable period without considering the one-year limitation of arbitration.

The next step is to apply the statutory one-year limitation of arbitration time limit prescribed by the Labor Dispute Mediation and Arbitration Law. This depends on the time when Ms. Li files her labor arbitration application and whether the labor arbitration commission in the jurisdiction over Ms. Li adopts a divisible or indivisible arbitration limitation accounting. For detail on divisible or indivisible arbitration limitation accounting, please refer to "53. Is it too late for me to claim the double-wage damages?"

If the arbitration commission adopts the indivisible accounting method (such as in Beijing, Tianjin, Shandong, etc.): if Ms. Li files an arbitration application for double-wage damages within the aforementioned 11 months of actionable period, for example, on December 1, 2024, the liable period is from April 1 to December 1, 2024. If Ms. Li files an arbitration application between March 1, 2025 and February 28, 2026, for example, on August 1, 2025, then she can obtain the damages for the aforementioned 11 months as a whole (i.e., the period from April 1, 2024 to February 28, 2025). But if Ms. Li files an arbitration application on or after March 1, 2026, her claim of double-wage damages shall be rejected due to exceeding the limitation of arbitration.

If the arbitration commission adopts the divisible accounting method (such as in Guangdong, Shanghai, Chongqing, etc.): if Ms. Li files the arbitration claim within the aforementioned 11 months (for example, on December 1, 2024), the liable period is from April 1 to December 1, 2024. If Ms. Li files an arbitration application between March 1, 2025 and February 28, 2026, for example, on August 1, 2025, then she can obtain the damages for the period from August 1, 2024 to February 28, 2025 (a total of seven months) as per the principle of accounting each day and month in the divisible accounting method. But if Ms. Li files an arbitration application on or after March 1, 2026, her claim of double-wage damages shall be rejected due to exceeding the one-year limitation of arbitration.

53. Is it too late for me to claim the double-wage damages?

Answer: To calculate the double-wage damages that an employer should pay, it is necessary to first determine the actionable period. This refers to the period during which the employer should have signed an employment contract with the employee according to the statutory requirement but failed to do so. This involves considering the period during which the employer is legally obligated to sign the contract, as well as any limitations based on legal provisions or judicial practices to establish the starting point (such as the date when a permanent contract should have been signed) and the cut-off point (such as one year after a new employee's entry into the company).

The determined actionable period in the second step needs to be subject to the limitation of labor arbitration to ultimately determine the liable period. The Labor Dispute Mediation and Arbitration Law stipulates that the time limit for filing employment arbitration is one year, which is the so-called limitation of labor dispute arbitration. That is to say, the period for which employees may claim double-wage damages should be within one year after the right's formation. The practices implementing this rule can be divided into two types in legal practice.

The first type of practice is divisible arbitration limitation accounting. This type of practice considers that any claim of double-wage damages is a separatable, non-integrated right. Every day in the actionable period (on which a written employment contract should have been signed as required by the law but was not) shall be examined by the one-year limitation of arbitration, and the double-wage damages shall be determined based on the number of days or a time period within the limitation. Specifically, divisible arbitration limitation accounting is a practice of determining the liable period by accounting the overlapping period between the 12-month period before the filing date of the arbitration claim and the actionable period. The courts that have applied this practice include the Guangzhou and Shenzhen Intermediate People's Courts in Guangdong Province, the Jiujiang Intermediate People's Court in Jiangxi Province, the Chengdu Intermediate People's Court in Sichuan Province, the Huaian Intermediate Court in Jiangsu Province, the Anshan Intermediate Court in Liaoning Province, the Hefei Intermediate Court in Anhui Province, Chongqing High Court, and Shanghai the First Intermediate Court.[48]

The second category of practice is indivisible arbitration limitation accounting. This is the practice most courts follow by considering double-wage damages as indivisible, integral rights. In this practice, within one year, the limitation of arbitration, from the last day of the actionable period, employees must submit their labor arbitration application for double-wage damages. Employees following this can then receive double-wage damages for their entire actionable period. If their arbitration application is filed after this one-year period, the overall right to be awarded double-wage damages is extinguished. This is the practice of the vast majority of courts, including Tianjin City High Court, Shandong

48 Xiong Jinhui Labor Dispute Civil Judgment of Second Instance of Shenzhen Intermediate People's Court of Guangdong Province (2017) Yue 03 Min Zhong No. 1329; Guo Yuqing, Guangzhou Xinyi Trading Co., Ltd. Labor Dispute Civil Judgment of Second Instance of Guangzhou Intermediate People's Court of Guangdong Province (2019) Yue 01 Min Zhong No. 20726; Jiujiang City and New Energy Technology Development Co., Ltd., Xu Faqing Labor Dispute Second Instance Civil Judgment Jiangxi Jiujiang Intermediate People's Court Civil Judgment (2018) Gan 04 Min Zhong No. 2077; Labor Dispute Appeal between Sichuan Xinyun Labor Service Co., Ltd. and Liu Haijun Civil Judgment of Chengdu Intermediate People's Court of Sichuan Province (2014) C.M.Z.Z. No. 1402, No. 1403; Li Shuzhong and Huaian Ningxin Property Service Co., Ltd. Civil Judgment of Second Instance of Labor Dispute Civil Judgment of Intermediate People's Court of Huaian City, Jiangsu Province (2019) Su 08 Min Zhong No. 1476; Tiedong District Wangski Pet Products Beauty Shop, Gao Yipeng Labor Dispute Civil Judgment of Second Instance Civil Judgment of Anshan Intermediate People's Court of Liaoning Province (2023) Liao 03 Min Zhong No. 908; Anhui Chuangjinghui Precision Manufacturing Co., Ltd., Li Lei Labor Dispute Second Instance Civil Judgment Anhui Hefei Intermediate People's Court Civil Judgment (2020) Wan 01 Min Zhong No. 4380; Civil Judgment on the Retrial of Labor Dispute between Wen Xuan and China Metallurgical Construction Group Co., Ltd., Chongqing High People's Court Civil Judgment (2019) Yu Min Zai No. 94; WK v. Shanghai HY Concrete Co., Ltd. Labor Dispute Appeal Case, Shanghai the First Intermediate People's Court Civil Judgment (2011) Hu Yi Zhong Min San (Min) Zhong Zi No. 1775.

Provincial High Court, Qinghai Provincial High Court, Henan Provincial High Court and Tibet Autonomous Region High Court, Guangdong Province Foshan City Intermediate Court, Beijing City the Second Intermediate Court, Shizuishan City Intermediate Court of Ningxia Hui Autonomous Region, Chengde City Intermediate Court of Hebei Province, Shaoguan City Intermediate Court of Guangdong Province, Chongqing City the First Intermediate Court, and Gansu Provincial High Court.[49]

Let's take Mr. Zhang, an employee in Shenzhen, as an example to illustrate how to conduct the arbitration limitation accounting for double-wage damages. Mr. Zhang joined the company on January 1, 2023, and the company has not signed an employment contract with Mr. Zhang since. We can divide the consideration period into three segments. The first segment is from February 1, 2023 to December 31, 2023. This is the period during which the company is potentially actionable for not signing a labor contract with Mr. Zhang. The second segment is from January 1, 2024 to December 31, 2024, which is one year after the actionable period. The third segment is from January 1, 2025 onwards.

In the first and third segments, the liable periods determined by the divisible arbitration limitation accounting method and the indivisible arbitration limitation accounting method are the same. For example, if Mr. Zhang submits a labor arbitration application requesting double-wage damages on August 1, 2023, the liable period under both methods is from February 1, 2023 to August 1, 2023. If Mr. Zhang submits the arbitration application during the third segment, it will be rejected under both methods due to exceeding the one-year arbitration limitation.

The difference between the two methods lies in the consequences when Mr. Zhang submits the arbitration application during the second segment. Let's assume that on May 1, 2024, Mr. Zhang submits the claim to the labor arbitration committee for the company to compensate him double-wage damages for not signing an employment contract.

49 Tianjin Daan Electric Vehicle Co., Ltd., Civil Ruling on Labor Dispute Retrial Review and Trial Supervision of Jiaman Tianjin High Court Civil Ruling (2020) Jin Min Shen No. 1211. Ou Lianghong v. Zhaoyuan Zhengbang Machinery Co., Ltd. The civil judgment of Shandong Provincial People's High Court (2016) Lu Min Zai No. 400. Labor Dispute Case of Shen Xiaohong v. Qinghai University Civil Judgment of Qinghai High Court (2015) Qing Min Ti Zi No. 29. Luoyang Kaikai Food Development Co., Ltd. and Li Hongjun's application for retrial of labor disputes, Henan Provincial People's High Court Civil Ruling (2021) Yumin Shen 9853. "The employer's liability to pay double-wage damages to workers for not signing an employment contract should be regarded as a debt of regular payment with integrity and relevance, and the limitation period of arbitration shall be calculated from the final date of expiration of the performance period, that is, from the date of one year after the date a written employment contract should have been signed." Beijing Banmo International Engineering Design Co., Ltd. Tibet Branch v. Lin Labor Dispute Civil Trial Supervision Civil Ruling Tibet Autonomous Region High Court Civil Ruling (2021) Zang Min Shen No. 114. Labor Dispute between Cao Gangyan, Shanghai Wuzhu Garment Co., Ltd. and Wuzhu Garment (Foshan) Co., Ltd. Civil Judgment of Foshan Intermediate People's Court of Guangdong Province (2019) No. 06 Minzhong 13391. Civil Judgment of Second Instance of Labor Dispute between Beijing Huayuxing Property Management Co., Ltd. and Zhang Jianguo Civil Judgment of the Second Intermediate People's Court of Beijing (2021) Jing 02 Min Zhong No.11230. Shizuishan Huiyi Metallurgical Industry and Trade Co., Ltd. and Chen Zhanqing Labor Dispute Second Instance Civil Judgment Ningxia Hui Autonomous Region Shizuishan Intermediate People's Court Civil Judgment (2018) Ning 02 Min Zhong No. 822. Zhang Junru et al. v. Ji Jiantao Labor Dispute Case Civil Judgment of Chengde Intermediate People's Court of Hebei Province (2017) Ji 08 Min Zhong No. 3567. Civil Judgment of Second Instance of Labor Dispute between Li Wei and Chongqing Dongchuang Hotel Equipment Co., Ltd. Civil Judgment of the First Intermediate People's Court of Chongqing (2019) Yu 01 Min Zhong No. 5982. Civil Judgment of the Second Instance of the Labor Dispute Case between Tang Hui and Zhenjiang District Jinda Oumeida Firm Civil Judgment of Shaoguan Intermediate People's Court of Guangdong Province (2020) Yue 02 Min Zhong No. 1924. Zhang Hongle v. Gansu Lanzhou Intermediate People's Court, the Gansu High People's Court (2019) Gan Min Shen No. 2045.

Under the divisible arbitration limitation accounting method, based on its principle of "overlapping the period backdating one year from the arbitration application date and the actionable period," the liable period is from May 2, 2023 to December 31, 2023, totaling eight months. However, under the indivisible arbitration limitation accounting method, based on the principle of "indivisible, integral rights," the liable period is the entire actionable period, from February 1, 2023 to December 31, 2023, totaling 11 months. Clearly, the indivisible arbitration limitation accounting method is more favorable to employees claiming double-wage damages.

The amount of the double-wage damages is the paid wages in the corresponding liable period determined by the aforementioned method. Please refer to "58. How is the wage standard for double-wage damages determined?"

54. How are double-wage damages calculated for not signing a permanent employment contract?

Answer: Article 82 of the Employment Contract Law also stipulates that employers should compensate double-wage damages to employees who should have signed indefinite-term contracts but did not. This is a type of double-wage damages with fewer legislative considerations than the one for new employees not signing an employment contract.

When calculating this type of double-wage damages against employers, we mainly consider whether different types of not signing permanent employment contracts involve a legal obligation to sign the contract, and the actionable period and liable period, accounted from the former when applying the limitation of arbitration, and the wage standard for the liable period.

According to "55. Under what circumstances must employers sign permanent employment contracts with employees?", currently, there are three scenarios where employers should sign permanent contracts with their employees.

The first scenario is where employees have worked continuously for ten years and request to sign permanent contracts with the employer. Currently, most courts nationwide generally follow the rules for signing employment contracts with new employees, with the actionable period starting 1 month after the employee requests to sign (e.g., the starting point) and ending 1 year after the request (e.g., the cut-off point), for a maximum period of 11 months.[50] However, after the implementation of Article 4 of the 2023 Consultation Draft on the Interpretation of the Supreme People's Court on the Application of Law in the Trial of Labor Dispute Cases (II), this period will be changed to a maximum of 12 months.

The second scenario is where employees have signed two consecutive fixed-term employment contracts and meet the conditions for signing permanent contracts. In most cases, the actionable period starts the day after the second fixed-term contract expires and ends 1 year later, for a maximum period of 12 months.[51] However, some cases suggest that

50 Xuchang Wanli Transportation Group Co., Ltd. v. Ma Haixia Labor Dispute, the Henan High People's Court (2015) Yu Fa Min Ti Zi No. 00102. Chen Yilong v. Beijing Huanan Building Co., Ltd., the Beijing High People's Court (2014) Gao Min Shen Zi No. 01185. The court determined that if an employee has worked continuously for over ten years and has requested to sign a permanent contract, the employer's "failure to sign a written permanent employment contract falls under the category of not signing a written employment contract. Therefore, the period for paying double-wage damages shall not exceed eleven months." Xu Xiaoming v. Guangzhou Wohua Fire Engineering Co., Ltd., the Guangdong High People's Court (2020) Yue Min Shen 4037.

51 Yu Jianhua v. Shandong Yingtian Law Firm, the Shandong High People's Court (2018) Lu Min Shen 3237. Wen Xuan v. China Metallurgical Construction Group Co., Ltd., the Chongqing High People's Court

the actionable period starts 1 month after the expiration of the second fixed-term contract and ends 1 year later, for a maximum period of 11 months.[52] After the implementation of Article 4 of the 2023 Consultation Draft on the Interpretation of the Supreme People's Court on the Application of Law in the Trial of Labor Dispute Cases (II), this period will be unified to a maximum of 12 months.

Both parties signing a third fixed-term contract after having signed two consecutive fixed-term contracts is a confusing issue. In such cases, most courts consider this as the employee waiving the right to permanent contract by signing the third fixed-term contract; unless there is fraud, coercion, taking advantage of vulnerability, or other statutory circumstances, the employer shall not be liable for double-wage damages for not signing a permanent contract with the employee. This is also the rule under Article 16 of the 2023 Consultation Draft on the Interpretation of the Supreme People's Court on the Application of Law in the Trial of Labor Dispute Cases (II). This is also one of the exemptions from double-wage damages. For the consequences of signing a third fixed-term contract, please refer to "56. Should a permanent employment contract be signed after two consecutive fixed-term employment contracts?"

The third scenario when an employer should sign a permanent employment contract is where a new employee has taken up the role for one year but has not signed an employment contract. Article 14 of the Employment Contract Law stipulates that in this circumstance, it is deemed that both parties have signed a permanent contract upon the expiration of the one-year period. Although Article 7 of the Regulations on the Implementation of the Employment Contract Law stipulates that the employer should immediately sign a permanent contract with the employee, ostensibly rendering that the employer should have signed the contract but did not, judicial practice shows that even if the employer fails to do so afterward, they are not liable for double-wage damages for the subsequent period.

After determining the actionable period for the aforementioned scenarios, calculating double-wage damages still requires using limitation of arbitration to finally determine the liable period (see "53. Is it too late for me to claim the double-wage damages?") and then conduct the calculation based on the relevant wages standard (see "58. How is the wage standard for double-wage damages determined?").

We notice that there are individual, exceptional court decisions denying employers' obligations of signing a permanent employment contract and consequent double-wage. They stated that the provision in the 2020 Supreme Court's Judicial Interoperation, "deeming

(2019) Yu Min Zai No. 94. In this case, the employee signed two consecutive fixed-term contracts. The court confirmed that the actionable period for double-wage damages started from the day after the expiration of the second fixed-term contract and stated that there was no similar cut-off point for the accountability of double-wage damages as in the case of new employees, having been employed for one year without a signed employment contract in place.

52 Zhang Hongle v. Gansu Lanzhou Intermediate People's Court, the Gansu High People's Court (2019) Gan Min Shen No. 2045. In this case, after signing two consecutive fixed-term contracts, the parties did not sign a new contract. The court held that the actionable period for double-wage damages for not signing a permanent contract should be based on the rules for new employees, starting from the day when the contract should have been signed to 1 year later, totaling 11 months. Ma Hong v. Dingyan Town People's Government, Rugao City, the Jiangsu High People'sCourt, (2018) Su Min Shen No. 2945. In this case, the employee had already signed two consecutive fixed-term employment contracts. The court held that: "if the employer violates laws or regulations by failing to sign a permanent employment contract with the employee, the starting point for paying double-wage damages to the employee shall be the next date after one month following the expiration of the contract, up to the date before a new permanent employment contract is signed, for a maximum period of 11 months."

both parties to have signed permanent employment contract," shall apply to the situation where employers should have signed the contract but did not, and that consequently, the employers are not liable to double-wage damages.[53] This practice is tantamount to excluding any right of claiming double-wage damages for any case of not signing permanent employment contracts and is currently not universal practice in judicial practice. The implementation of Article 4 of the 2023 Consultation Draft on the Interpretation of the Supreme People's Court on the Application of Law in the Trial of Labor Dispute Cases (II) shall end this judicial practice.

55. Under what circumstances must employers sign permanent employment contracts with employees?

Answer: A permanent employment contract does not have a termination deadline, providing the highest employment security for employees. Employers are prohibited from terminating or dissolving employment relationships without legal reasons. According to the Employment Contract Law, an employer must sign a permanent employment contract with an employee under the following circumstances.

The first circumstance is where the employee has worked continuously for ten years for the employer and the employee has requested a permanent employment, including the situations where the parties are in a current fixed-term employment contract, or their contract is just expiring but both parties are willing to extend the employment. The main issue here is how to identify "continuous work." There are two possibilities. The first situation is that the employment relationship was suspended for a period of time (for example, the employee did not work and the employer did not pay wages) during which the two parties maintained the employment relationship. This is typically not considered "continuous work."[54] However, some courts, such as Shanghai High Court, consider that long-term

53 Li Jinling v. Kuitun Xinzhong Automobile Trading Co., Ltd., the Ili Kazakh Autonomous Prefecture Branch of the Xinjiang Uygur Autonomous Region High People's Court (2018) Xin 40 Min Zhong No. 868. The court interpreted Article 16 of the 2000 Supreme People's Court Judicial Interpretation, "deeming the parties to have continuously signed a permanent employment contract" (i.e., Article 34 of the 2020 Supreme Court's Judicial Interpretation), stating that the employer was not liable for double-wage damages for not signing a permanent employment contact with the employee. Kong Xiangguo v. Yili Yibei Coal Co., Ltd., the Ili Kazakh Autonomous Prefecture Branch of the Xinjiang Uygur Autonomous Region High People's (2017) Xin 40 Min Zhong No. 1539. Liu Aimin v. Qihe Zhongyuan Automobile Trading Co., Ltd., the Dezhou Intermediate People's Court in Shandong Province (2022) Lu 14 Min Zhong No. 266.

54 Jing Ruling and Huarun Tianneng Xuzhou Coal and Electricity Co., Ltd. Daliu Coal Mine Labor Dispute Appeal Case Civil Judgment of Xuzhou Intermediate People's Court of Jiangsu Province (2011) Xu Min Zhong Zi No. 1555. "Since July 2001. Jing Ruling did not provide services to Daliu Coal Mine, Daliu Coal Mine did not pay remuneration to Jing Ruling, and the employment relationship between the two parties was suspended. As the premise for Jing Ruling and Daliu Coal Mine to sign a permanent employment contract is that Jing Ruling has worked continuously for ten years in Daliu Coal Mine, although the employment relationship between the two parties has lasted for more than ten years, it does not constitute the situation of working continuously for ten years." The labor Dispute Appeal Case between Zhu Junkang and Hongda Salt Industry Co., Ltd. of Hebukesaier Mongolian Autonomous County, Tacheng Intermediate Court of Ili Kazakh Autonomous Prefecture, Xinjiang Uygur Autonomous Region, Civil Judgment (2014) Ta Min Yi Zhong Zi No. 922. "In this case, the employee went home on waiting-for-work in April 2001. After the restructuring, the employer did not terminate the employment relationship in an explicit way, and the appellant did not sign an employment contract with a new employer, nor did he provide labor. Therefore, the court found that the employment relationship between the two parties was suspended and did not recognize that they had worked continuously for ten years."

unpaid leave may result in continuous work.[55] The second situation is that the worker has gone through a formal termination procedure after working for a period of time, and then rejoins the employer. This situation constitutes an interruption of employment relationships between the two parties and does not meet the threshold of "continuous work" required by law. Once the aforementioned suspension and interruption of the employment relationship have occurred, the duration of continuous work for the employer should be recalculated.

The second circumstance is where two consecutive fixed-term contracts have been signed and completed, both parties continue their employment relationship, and a permanent employment contract is supposed to be signed according to the new rule stipulated in the 2008 Employment Contract Law. Subsequently, there have been numerous complex situations in judicial practice that are not explicitly addressed in the law, including how to define "consecutive two contracts," the consequences of both parties signing a third fixed-term contract, the consequences when both parties do not renew the contract after the expiration of the second fixed-term contract but continue the employment relationship, and whether the employer has the right to terminate the second fixed-term contract on the ground of contract expiration. Please refer to "56. Should a permanent employment contract be signed after two consecutive fixed-term employment contracts?"

The third circumstance is where an employer fails to sign a written employment contract with the employee when the employee has taken up the job for one year. Although Article 7 of the Regulations on the Implementation of the Employment Contract Law stipulates that employees in this situation must immediately sign permanent employment contracts with the employer, Article 14 of the Employment Contract Law, "deeming the employer and the employee have signed a permanent employment contract," and its corresponding judicial practice do not impose liability of double-wage damages on the employers not complying with the requirement of subsequent signing of the contract. This can be considered a circumstance where the law requests signing of permanent contracts but where violations lead to no legal consequences.

56. Should a permanent employment contract be signed after two consecutive fixed-term employment contracts?

Answer: The Employment Contract Law set a new rule stipulating that if two consecutive fixed-term contracts have been signed and fulfilled, and both parties wish to continue the employment, and the employee requests a permanent contract, the employer is obligated to sign a permanent employment contract with the employee.[56] This rule, however, has led to conflicting judicial decisions in practice.

There are usually four problems.

The first problem is how to identify "two consecutive times." "Two consecutive times" means that there is no interruption between two fixed-term employment contracts. But a special case is where there is a short interruption between the two fixed-term employment contracts, during which the employer pays social insurance contribution but does not pay wages, and the employee does not work for the employer. In this case, the two fixed

55 Administrative Ruling Document of the Administrative Adjudication Supervision over Administrative Cases of the Shanghai Social Insurance Administration Center—Shanghai High People's Court Administrative Ruling Document (2016) HuXingShen 196.

56 Item 3, Paragraph 2, Article 14 of the Employment Contract Law.

employment contracts might be regarded as consecutive,[57] and in some places, such as Shanxi Province, if the interruption between two fixed employment contracts is less than six months, it is regarded as two consecutive fixed-term contracts.[58]

If both parties change the contract duration after signing the first fixed-term employment contract, this situation cannot be regarded as two consecutive employment contracts, but should be regarded as a condition change of the first employment contract.[59] In addition, another situation is that the employer and the employee first sign a probation contract and then sign a fixed-term contract after the expiration of the probation contract. Because the legal consequence of signing a sole probation agreement is a fixed-term employment contract without a probation period,[60] after the expiration of the subsequent fixed-term contract, the employer and the employee are deemed to have signed two consecutive fixed-term employment contracts.

The second problem is the consequence of both parties signing a third fixed-term employment contract after the expiration of the second fixed-term contract. At present, most courts nationwide, including those in Guangdong Province, Jilin Province, Guizhou Province, Sichuan Province, Zhejiang Province, JiangXi Province, Changsha City of Hunan Province, Hezhou City of Guangxi Zhuang Autonomous Region, and Weihai City of Shandong Province, hold that the signing of a third fixed-term contract is the consent of the employee to give up the right to a permanent employment contract, and that the voluntarily signed third fixed-term employment contract is effective and binding.[61] For example,

57 Qingyang Company of Gansu Tobacco Company and Li Xianghong confirmed the Civil Judgment of Second Instance of Employment Relationships Dispute, Qingyang Intermediate People's Court of Gansu Province Civil Judgment (2012) Qing Zhong Min Zhong Zi No. 604. In this case, the two parties did not sign an employment contract for four months from July to November 2008, the employer did not pay wages and the employee did not leave the employer to find another job, and the employer continued to pay social insurance premiums for Li Xianghong. The court held that the above behavior was acquiescence to the existence of an employment relationship between the two parties rather than interruption, so the two employment contracts were continuous, and they are two consecutive employment contracts.

58 Article 11 of the Regulations of Shaanxi Province on Employment Contracts stipulates that if an employer and a worker sign a fixed-term employment contract again within six months from the date of termination or termination of the previous fixed-term employment contract, they shall be deemed to be two consecutive fixed-term employment contracts.

59 Zeng Wanxing and Chongqing Guangda Machinery Factory Co., Ltd. Labor Dispute Civil Judgment of First Instance Chongqing Jiangjin District People's Court Civil Judgment (2016) Yu 0116 Min Chu No. 5484. In the case, the two parties signed an employment contract in December 2013 for a period up to November 2016, which had not yet expired. The two parties then signed another contract in February 2014 for a period up to December 2014. The court held that the contract shall be regarded as the change of the original contract conditions by both parties and does not constitute signing two consecutive fixed-term employment contracts.

60 Article 19 of the Employment Contract Law.

61 Li Weidong v. Jiangxi Lantie Security Service Co., Ltd. Employment Dispute Retrial Civil Ruling Jiangxi High People's Court Civil Ruling (2020) Gan Min Shen No. 910. Fuquan Fenglin World Hotel Co., Ltd., Xue Xiaoying Labor Dispute Civil Judgment of Second Instance Civil Judgment of the Intermediate People's Court of Qiannan Buyi and Miao Autonomous Prefecture, Guizhou Province (2021) Qian 27 Min Zhong 3593. "Xue Xiaoying signed two consecutive fixed-term employment contracts. instead of requiring Fenglin Company to sign a permanent employment contract, she has signed a one-year fixed-term employment contract again. This should be regarded as a disposition of its own rights." Cen Yong, Civil Ruling on Labor Dispute Retrial Review and Trial Supervision of Beijing Yinhe Wanjia Electronic Technology Co., Ltd. Civil Ruling of Chengdu Intermediate People's Court of Sichuan Province (2020) Chuan 01 Min Shen No. 164, Shi Mei, Guangdong Nanyou Foreign Service Co., Ltd. Civil Judgment of Second Instance of Labor Dispute of Guangzhou Intermediate People's Court of Guangdong Province (2018) Guangdong 01 Minzhong No. 23176. Xu Cheng v. Zhenhai Refining and Chemical Company of China Petroleum & Chemical Corporation and other labor disputes Civil Ruling of Zhejiang High Court (2015) Zhe Min Shen Zi No. 1078. Baimei, Zhoushan Archipelago New Area Haina Service Co., Ltd. Labor Dispute Civil Judgment of Second Instance Zhoushan

in the case of Li Weidong v. Jiangxi Lantie Security Service Co., Ltd., the Jiangxi High Court held that "there is no evidence to prove that Lantie Company engaged in fraud, coercion, or vulnerability-advantage-taking of Li Weidong when renewing the fixed-term employment labor contract. Li Weidong's request for the third employment contract to be a permanent contract after the expiration of the contract performance violates the principle of good faith."

Only a very few court decisions, while citing Article 34 of the 2020 Supreme Court's Judicial Interpretation, consider that in this circumstance, it is deemed that the parties have already signed a permanent contract and that the employer is no longer liable for signing the contract and double-wage damages.[62]

The third problem is the nature of the employment relationship between the two parties who have not renewed the contract after the expiration of the second fixed-term contract but continue the employment. The Intermediate People's Court of Chenzhou City in Hunan Province, Guilin City in Guangxi Autonomous Region, and Shenyang City in Liaoning Province have decisions holding that after the expiration of the second fixed-term contract, the contract should be signed within one month as with a newly hired employee, the two parties are in a de facto employment relationship, and that when the contract has not been signed for one year, the two parties are deemed to have established a permanent contract relationship.[63] However, the Second Intermediate People's Court of Beijing and intermediate courts of Wuhu City of Anhui Province, Xi'an City of Shaanxi Province, and Beihai City of Guangxi Autonomous Region have decisions stating that

---

Intermediate People's Court of Zhejiang Province Civil Judgment (2022) Zhe 09 Min Zhong No. 370. Hunan Tanheng Expressway Development Co., Ltd., Liu Fang Labor Dispute Second Instance Civil Judgment Hunan Changsha Intermediate People's Court Civil Judgment (2020) Xiang 01 Min Zhong No. 4763. Zhong Guoxing and Jinji Pharmaceutical Co., Ltd. Civil Judgment of the Second Instance of Labor Dispute Civil Judgment of Hezhou Intermediate People's Court of Guangxi Zhuang Autonomous Region (2019) Gui 11 Min Zhong No. 1027. Wang Guozhong and Weihai Hemingway Group Co., Ltd. Civil Judgment of Second Instance of Labor Dispute Civil Judgment of Weihai Intermediate People's Court of Shandong Province (2018) Lu 10 Min Zhong No. 422. Article 13 of Jilin Provincial People's High Court's Answers to Questions on the Application of Law in the Trial of Labor Dispute Cases (II) stipulates: "If two fixed-term employment contracts have been signed, shall the employer have the right to terminate the employment contract after the expiration of the second fixed-term employment contract? If the employer claims not to sign a permanent employment contract with the employee on the grounds of the expiration of the (second) employment contract, it shall not be supported. Unless the worker agrees to terminate or sign a fixed-term employment contract."

62 Article 34 of the Interpretation of the Supreme People's Court on the Application of Law in the Trial of Labor Dispute Cases (I) (Judicial Interpretation [2020] No. 26): "After the expiration of the employment contract, if the employee still works in the former employer and the former employer does not raise any objection, it shall be deemed that both parties agree to continue to perform the employment contract under the original conditions. If one party proposes to terminate the employment relationship, the people's court shall support it. According to Article 14 of the Employment Contract Law, if an employer should have signed a permanent employment contract with a worker but fails to do so, the people's court may deem that there is a permanent employment contract relationship between the two parties, and determine the rights and obligations of the two parties based on the original employment contract."

63 Wang Yonghong and Hunan Huaxin Rare Precious Science and Technology Co., Ltd. Civil Judgment of the Second Instance of Labor Dispute Civil Judgment of the Intermediate People's Court of Chenzhou City, Hunan Province (2019) Xiang 10 Min Zhong No. 2540. The court held that there was a permanent contract relationship between the two parties from one year after the expiration of the second contract, but did not specify the nature of the contract between the two parties within one year after the expiration. Han Yonglin, Civil Judgment of Second Instance of Labor Dispute of Funeral and Funeral Administration of Xing'an County Civil Judgment of Guilin Intermediate People's Court of Guangxi Zhuang Autonomous Region (2020) Gui 03 Min Zhong No. 1903. Shenyang University Education and Training School, Cheng Lin Labor Dispute Civil Judgment of Second Instance Civil Judgment of Shenyang Intermediate People's Court of Liaoning Province (2022) Liao 01 Min Zhong No. 1886 1.

if the two parties continue their employment relationship on the second day after the expiration of the second fixed-term contract, the relationship will automatically become permanent employment.[64]

The fourth issue is whether the employer has the right to terminate the second fixed-term contract. Article 14 of the Employment Contract Law concerning the conclusion of two consecutive fixed-term contracts is silent about the right of the employer to terminate the contract. As for the right of termination of the employer before the expiration of the second fixed-term contract, there are two approaches in court decisions in practice.

The first practice is in the view that once the employee, before the expiration of the second fixed-term contract, notifies the employer of the intention to have a permanent contact after the expiration, the employer must sign a permanent contract with the employee upon the expiration, if there are no situations provided in Article 39 and items 1 and 2 of Article 40 of the Employment Contract Law.

That is, employers have no right of termination upon expiration of the second fixed-term contract unless the employee is at serious fault or health-incompetent or ability-incompetent. This is the view of most courts, including Guangdong Provincial High Court, the Sichuan Provincial High Court, the Jilin Provincial High Court, the Chongqing Municipal High Court, the Jiangsu Provincial High Court, Beijing the Second and Third Intermediate Courts, the Shenzhen, Guangzhou, and Qingyuan Intermediate Courts of Guangdong Province, the Qingdao Intermediate Court of Shandong Province, Tianjin the First Intermediate Court, and the Changchun Intermediate Court of Jilin Province.[65]

---

64 Wuhu Anhua Glass Co., Ltd. and Jin Xiaomei Labor Dispute Civil Judgment of Second Instance Wuhu Intermediate People's Court of Anhui Province Civil Judgment (2017) Wan 02 Min Zhong No. 1041. Zhou Lei, Shaanxi Qingyang Environmental Science and Technology Co., Ltd. Civil Judgment of Second Instance of Labor Dispute Civil Judgment of Xi'an Intermediate People's Court of Shaanxi Province (2022) Shaanxi 01 Minzhong No. 11010. Beihai Haohai Real Estate Development Co., Ltd. and Liu Guangxuan Labor Dispute Civil Judgment of Second Instance Civil Judgment of Beihai Intermediate People's Court of Guangxi Zhuang Autonomous Region (2018) Gui 05 Min Zhong No. 871. Civil Judgment of First Instance of Labor Dispute between CIC Credit Guarantee Co., Ltd. and Yi Zhonghua Civil Judgment of Beijing the Second Intermediate People's Court (2018) Jing 02 Min Chu No. 282.

65 Beijing Tianzheng Zhongguang Real Estate Co., Ltd. and Li Zhongguang Labor Dispute Second Trial Civil Judgment (2023) Beijing the Second Intermediate People's Court Civil Judgment (Jing 02 Min Zhong No. 2299). Tianjin Bailitai Ceramics Co., Ltd. and Wu Shuli's Civil Judgment on Labor Disputes in the Second Instance of Tianjin the First Intermediate People's Court (2021) Jin 01 Min Zhong No. 4510. "The appellant and the respondent have entered into fixed-term employment contracts twice in a row, and the employee resignation approval form provided by the appellant states that the reason for resignation is 'disagree because I have not reached the retirement age'. Moreover, the appellant has not provided evidence to prove that the appellant is in the circumstances specified in Article 39 and Article 40 (1) and (2) of the Employment Contract Law of the People's Republic of China. Therefore, the appellant should have entered into a permanent employment contract with the respondent." Guo Qiang, Changchun Economic Development Group Property Service Co., Ltd. Economic Compensation Dispute Civil Second Trial Civil Judgment Letter of Jilin Province Changchun Intermediate People's Court Civil Judgment Letter (2022) Ji 01 Min Zhong 1920. Li Yankun, Qingdao Public Transport Group Shibei Bus Co., Ltd. Labor Dispute Civil Second Trial Civil Judgment Letter of Qingdao Intermediate People's Court in Shandong Province (2022) Lu 02 Min Zhong 16126. Jiang Wanmei and Qingyuan Huiye Property Management Service Co., Ltd. Employment Contract Dispute Civil Second Trial Civil Judgment Letter Guangdong Qingyuan Intermediate People's Court Civil Judgment Letter (2021) Yue 18 Min Zhong No. 1809. The court believes that if the employee fails to renew the contract before the expiration of the second contract, the two parties' contract will expire and terminate. He Baolan, Shangrao New Thinking Human Resources Co., Ltd. Labor Dispute Second Trial Civil Judgment, Jiangxi Shangrao Intermediate People's Court Civil Judgment (2020) Gan 11 Min Zhong No. 14. Sichuan Jiabao Media Co., Ltd. and Yang Wei's Civil Ruling on Labor Dispute Retrial Review and Trial Supervision Sichuan Provincial High People's Court Civil Ruling (2019) Chuanminshen No. 6019. The Civil Ruling of Chongqing High Court in the case of employment contract dispute between Ning Xianxian and Wute Electronics (Chongqing) Co.,

For example, in the Li Zhongguang Case in 2023, Bejing the Second Intermediate Court held that, "This court is in the view that in this case, Li Zhongguang and Zhongguang Real Estate Co., Ltd. had entered into two consecutive fixed-term employment contracts. Before the expiration of the second employment contract, Li Zhongguang had submitted a written request to Zhongguang Real Estate Co., Ltd. for signing a permanent employment contract. Both parties must sign a permanent employment contract in accordance with the law."

The second approach is that a few courts, including Shanghai High Court, Henan High Court, and Dalian Intermediate Court of Liaoning Province, hold that the employer has a veto power before the expiration of the second fixed-term contract, and that the renewal of the permanent contract by both parties must be based on the premise that both parties reach an agreement on the continuation of the employment relationship.[66] The 2020 Supreme Court's Judicial Interpretation also seems to imply that the employer has the right to unilaterally terminate the second fixed-term contract after its expiration.[67]

Ltd. (2015) Yugao Famin Shen Zi No. 00383. Xing Zhihua and Suzhou Port University Sipei Technology Vocational College Employment Contract Dispute Application Case Jiangsu Provincial High People's Court Civil Judgment (2014) Su Shen Er Min Shen Zi No. 0632. Article 13 of the Reply to the Application of Law in the Trial of Labor Dispute Cases by the High Court of Jilin Province (II): "Does the employer have the right to terminate the fixed-term employment contract after two consecutive fixed-term employment contracts expires? If the employer claims not to enter into a permanent employment contract with the employee based on the termination of the employment contract after the second fixed term employment contract expires, it will not be supported unless the employee consents to terminate or sign a fixed term employment contract." Guangzhou Greenland Real Estate Development Co., Ltd. Labor Dispute Civil Second Trial Civil Judgment (2022) Yue 01 Min Zhong 24675, Guangzhou Intermediate People's Court, Guangdong Province. Beijing Shaanxi Building Co., Ltd. Chang'an Hotel and Wang Fuping Labor Dispute Second Trial Civil Judgment (2021) Beijing the Third Intermediate People's Court Civil Judgment (Jing 03 Min Zhong No. 170). In this case, the employee did not actively request renewal before the expiration of the contract and claimed in the lawsuit that he had expressed willingness to renew the contract in communication with the employer. The employer failed to refute this, so it was determined that the termination of the contract after the expiration of the contract was illegal. Guotai Daming Precision Machinery (Shenzhen) Co., Ltd. and Ouqianhua Labor Dispute Second Trial Civil Judgment Letter of Shenzhen Intermediate People's Court in Guangdong Province (2020) Yue 03 Min Zhong 17549. "This clause should be understood as: when the second fixed-term employment contract expires, the employer has no right to terminate the employment contract. Unless the employee decides not to renew the employment contract or proposes to enter into a fixed-term employment contract, the employer and the employee should enter into a permanent employment contract." Li Tongxiang v. Guangzhou Shibang Human Resources Co., Ltd. Employment Dispute Retrial Civil Judgment Guangdong High People's Court Civil Judgment (2018) Yue Min Zai No. 275.

66 Geng Xiaojun and Henan Branch of Huajin Securities Co., Ltd. applied for retrial of labor disputes. Civil Ruling of Henan High Court (2022) Yu Min Shen No. 2561. "According to the above-mentioned statutory provisions, the situation in which a permanent employment contract must be signed refers to the situation in which the employer has signed two consecutive fixed-term employment contracts with the employee, is renewing the employee's employment contract for the third time, and the employee proposes to sign a permanent employment contract. Therefore, the precondition for the application of this clause is that both parties reach a mutual agreement on the third renewal of the employment contract. In this case, before the expiration of the employment contract between the two parties, Huajin Securities Co., Ltd. made it clear that it would not renew the employment contract with Geng Xiaojun after the expiration, and issued a Notice of Termination of Employment contract to Geng Xiaojun on October 8, 2021. It also does not conform to the situation that 'the employer and the worker may sign a permanent employment contract through negotiation'." Civil Ruling on Trial and Supervision of Employment Contract Dispute between Zhao Liying and Aramark Service Industry (China) Co., Ltd. Shanghai Branch Civil Ruling of Shanghai High Court (2019) Hu Min Shen No. 1423. Gao Xuelong v. Mavro Parts (Dalian) Co., Ltd. Civil Judgment of Dalian Intermediate People's Court of Liaoning Province (2015) D.M.W.Z.Z. No. 5.

67 Article 34 of the Interpretation of the Supreme People's Court on the Application of Law in the Trial of Labor Dispute Cases (I) (Judicial Interpretation [2020] No. 26) states that after the expiration of the employment contract, if the employee still works at the former employer and the former employer does not express any

57. How are double-wage damages calculated for not signing a new contract after the expiration of a fixed-term employment contract?

Answer: The issue of double-wage damages when both parties continue to perform the employment relationship after the expiration of their fixed-term contract without signing a new contract involves two questions: whether the employer is obligated to sign a new contract, and how to calculate the liable period for double-wage damages if such obligation exists.

There is a divergence among courts regarding whether the employer has an obligation to sign a new contract after the expiration of the fixed-term contract, mainly due to different interpretations of "the Interpretation on Several Issues Concerning the Application of Law in the Trial of Labor Dispute Cases by the Supreme People's Court in 2020." Article 34 of the Supreme People's Court's judicial interpretation states that "after the expiration of an employment contract, if the employee continues to work for the employer without objection from the employer, it shall be deemed that both parties agree to continue to perform the employment contract under the original conditions." However, it is unclear whether this provision implies the existence of a new employment contract with the same terms and conditions as the original contract and no further need to sign a new contract, as the Supreme Court did not provide further clarification and explanation.

Court decisions from the High Courts of Henan Province, Guizhou Province, Jiangxi Province, Tianjin Municipality, Anhui Province, and Hubei Province, and Guangdong Province Shenzhen City Intermediate People's Court, have cited the judicial interpretation of the Supreme Court and held that this situation constitutes the signing of a new labor contract, thereby rejecting requests for double-wage damages.[68] However, there are also contradictory rulings from courts such as the High Courts of Guangxi Zhuang Autonomous Region, Xinjiang Uygur Autonomous Region, and Chongqing Municipality.[69]

---

objection, it shall be deemed that both parties agree to continue to perform the employment contract under the original conditions. If one party proposes to terminate the employment relationship, the people's court shall support it.

68 Shenzhen Zhongzhou Investment Holding Co., Ltd. v. Huang Yujin Labor Contract Dispute Case Guangdong Shenzhen Intermediate People's Court Civil Judgment (2016) Yue 03 Min Zhong No. 11048; Zhang Changhui v. Zhaoqing Jinfu Toy Co., Ltd., Guangdong High People's Court Civil Ruling (2014) Yue Gao Fa Min Shen Zi No. 2155; Hu Biqin v. Kaili Friendly Gynecological Hospital, Guizhou High People's Court (2020) Qian Min Shen No. 3662; Wang Yongjie v. Banumaodu Hot Pot Co., Ltd., Henan High People's Court Civil Ruling (2021) Yu Min Shen No. 2737. Qiu Xiaoming v. Jiangxi Huameiao Tungsten Industry Co., Ltd., Jiangxi High People's Court Civil Ruling (2016) Gan Min Shen No. 628; Song Wenbin v. PetroChina Beijing Natural Gas Pipeline Co., Ltd., Tianjin High People's Court Civil Ruling (2017) Jin Min Shen No. 369; Qu Dan v. Tongfang Energy (Friendship) Heat Co., Ltd., Heilongjiang High People's Court Civil Ruling (2017) Hei Min Shen 1822. Liang Liping, et al. v. Zhenlai County Local Taxation Bureau, Jilin High People's Court Civil Ruling (2017) Ji Min Shen No. 1531; Cui Shenglai v. Anhui Hongguang Enterprise Investment Group Co., Ltd., Anhui High People's Court Civil Judgment (2019) Wan Min Zai No. 149.

69 Shenzhen Chuanchuan Technology Development Co., Ltd. v. Hu Xuezhang, Guangdong Shenzhen Intermediate People's Court Civil Judgment (2017) Yue 03 Min Zhong No. 15288; Chen Yuhe v. Zhanjiang Mingjing Property Service Co., Ltd., Guangdong High People's Court Civil Ruling (2015) Yue Gao Fa Min Shen Zi No. 1661; Liu Mingshan v. Harbin Shanmu Labor Dispatch Co., Ltd., Heilongjiang High People's Court Civil Judgment (2020) Hei Min Zai No. 291; Chongqing Kaidi Automobile Sales Service Co., Ltd. v. Tan Zhen, Chongqing High People's Court Civil Ruling (2020) Yu Min Shen No. 2740; Xu Junhong v. Wuhan Kaibisi Electric Power Equipment Co., Ltd., Hubei High People's Court Civil Judgment (2020) E Min Zai No. 156; Wu Jihong v. Guangxi Vinylon Group Co., Ltd., Guangxi Zhuang Autonomous Region High People's Court Civil Ruling (2014) Gui Min Shen Zi No. 790; Tang Pei v. Xinjiang Zhaotai Environmental Protection Co., Ltd., Xinjiang Uygur Autonomous Region High People's Court Civil Ruling (2016) Xin Min Shen No. 617; Zhao

Additionally, some courts, like the High Courts of Guangdong Province, Heilongjiang Province, Jilin Province, and Guangdong Province Shenzhen City Intermediate People's Court, have issued contradictory rulings. Most Chinese courts appear to consider that an employer is not liable for double-wage damages for not extending a fixed-term employment contract with the employee.

The next issue is how to determine the liable period for double-wage damages if the employer is obligated to sign a new contract after the expiration of the fixed-term contract. The liable period should first be determined based on the obligation to sign an employment contract as prescribed by law to identify the actionable period, in which the starting point and cut-off point (if any) of the actionable period should be determined. Currently, courts around the country have two approaches to determine the starting point. One is to set the starting point as the next date after one month of the expiration of the fixed-term contract, similar to the one-month grace period for new employees. Courts in Shandong Province and Fujian Province adhere to this view.[70]

Another approach is to find that the day after the expiration of a fixed-term contract is the starting point. For example, in the case of Gong Jinping in 2022, Judge Sun Chengsong of Beijing the Third Intermediate People's Court stated, "The employer should have anticipated the legal consequences of the expiration of the original employment contract and the continuation of employment, so there is no need to provide a one-month grace period. The day after the expiration of the original employment contract is the day when the employer should have signed a new employment contract and bear the legal consequences for not doing so."[71]

It is worth noting that Article 4 of the 2023 Consultation Draft on the Interpretation of the Supreme People's Court on the Application of Law in the Trial of Labor Dispute Cases (II) clarifies this issue. It stipulates: If an employer should have signed a fixed-term contract with an employee but did not, the period for calculating double-wage damages starts from the day following one month after the date the employer should have signed the employment contract. This means that if both parties wish to continue the employment relationship after the expiration of the fixed-term employment contract, the employer should sign the contract within one month after the contract expires. Otherwise, the employer shall be liable for double-wage damages. This means the starting point for calculating the double-wage damages shall be regulated as the next date of the one-month expiration date of the fixed-term employment contract.

The next issue after determining the actionable period is the cut-off point. Currently, the court decisions we have seen all found the cut-off point as the one-year date of the

---

Huaiyi v. Jilin Henglian Precision Casting Technology Co., Ltd., Jilin High People's Court Civil Ruling (2022) Ji Min Shen No. 215.

70 Tian Dingli v. Power Department of China National Heavy Duty Truck Group Jinan Power Co., Ltd., Shandong High People's Court Civil Ruling (2018) Lu Min Shen No. 4835. In this case, the court agreed with the original judgment's finding that the renewal of the fixed-term contract shoud align with the one-month grace-period rule of contract signing for new employees. Wuyishan Xingcun Linzhi Kindergarten v. Jiang Xuanying, Fujian High People's Court Civil Ruling (2019) Min Min Shen No. 539.

71 Wang Zhongxin v. Beijing Fengtai Hospital, Beijing High People's Court Civil Judgment (2021) Jing Min Zai No. 87. the court's final judgment confirms the determination of the original judgment, namely, that the starting point for double-wage damages for not signing a contract after the expiration of a fixed-term contract (not meeting the conditions for a permanent contract) is the day after the expiration. Beijing Wushengchang Automobile Sales Service Co., Ltd. v. Gong Jinping, Beijing, the Third Intermediate People's Court Civil Judgment (2022) Jing 03 Min Zhong No. 6983.

expiration of the fixed-term contract, referring to the one-year cut-off rule for newly-hired employees signing employment contracts (Article 14 of the Employment Contract Law).

According to the foregoing rules in judicial practice for starting point and cut-off point, the actionable period for not signing an employment contract following the expiration of a fixed-term contract is a maximum of either 11 months (if the starting point is the next day after 1 month of the expiration) or 12 months (if the starting point is the next day after the expiration).

Once the actionable period is determined, it is necessary to account the liable period based on the one-year limitation of arbitration. Please refer to "53. Is it too late for me to claim the double-wage damages?" for details. Then, we determine double-wage damages based on the employee's wages during the liable period. Please refer to "58. How is the wage standard for double-wage damages determined?"

The aforementioned analyses refer to situations where fixed-term contracts are not signed, excluding where two consecutive fixed-term contracts expire (which may lead to the obligation of signing a permanent employment contract). For the issue of double-wage damages for the latter, please refer to "54. How are double-wage damages calculated for not signing a permanent employment contract?" and "56. Should a permanent employment contract be signed after two consecutive fixed-term employment contracts?"

58. How is the wage standard for double-wage damages determined?

Answer: Double-wage damages for not signing an employment contract (commonly known as double-wage damages) refers to, because of the employer's violation of statutory provisions by not signing a written employment contract with the employee, the consequent punitive damages that the employer is liable to the employee, calculated as an additional amount equal to the employee's wages corresponding to the period during which the employer should have signed the contract but did not, subject to statutory and practical time restrictions such as accountability cut-off and one-year limitation of arbitration.

Therefore, to calculate the amount of double-wage damages, it is necessary to determine the liable period and the wage standard for the liable period.

In practice, the main issues for the wage standard are whether the wage standard is based on the received wages or the due wages, whether it includes overtime pay, whether it includes income not paid on a monthly basis (such as year-end bonus), and how to determine the wage standard when the wage agreement is unclear.

First, most courts across the country use the due wages rather than the received wages as the basis for determining the wage standard for double-wage damages. The law does not specify whether the wage standard for determining double-wage damages should be based on the received wages or the due wages. The received wages are the amount after deducting the employee's social security contributions and personal income tax from the due wages, so the due wages are higher than the received wages. Currently, courts across the country generally consider social security contributions and personal income tax themselves as part of the income, so they use the due wages amount to determine the wage standard for double-wage damages.

Second, there are two completely different approaches among courts nationwide regarding whether overtime pay should be included in the wage standard for double-wage damages. Courts in Shanghai City, Beijing City, Tianjin City, Zhejiang Province, Anhui Province, Jiangxi Province, Liaoning Province, Gansu Province, Xinjiang Autonomous

Region, Fujian Province, Heilongjiang Province, and other places stipulate that overtime pay should not be included in the wage standard for double-wage damages.[72]

The Supreme People's Court's Civil Division, published in the "Frontiers of Civil Trial" 2014 article "Disputes over Proxy-signed Employment Contracts and Their Handlings," advocates that the wage standard for double-wage damages should be the employee's normal working time wage.[73] However, for wages entirely composed of commissions,

---

72 Shanghai Fande Beauty Center First Branch v. Liu Xiner, Shanghai the Second Intermediate People's Court Civil Judgment (2020) Hu 02 Min Zhong No. 307. The court held, "According to the regulations for determining the calculation base for double-wage damages, if both parties to the employment relationship have agreed on the monthly wage, the calculation base for double-wage damages should be determined based on the normal working time monthly wage agreed upon by both parties; if both parties have not agreed or the agreement on the monthly wage is unclear, the normal working time monthly wage should be determined according to Article 18 of the Employment Contract Law, and the determined wage amount should be used as the calculation base for double-wage damages; if the wage amount for normal working time cannot be determined even according to Article 18 of the Employment Contract Law, the monthly income actually received by the employee after deducting overtime pay, non-routine bonuses, welfare, and risk-related items should be used to determine the normal working time monthly wage." the Beijing High People's Court's "Answers to Legal Issues in the Adjudication of Labor Dispute Cases" stipulates in Article 21: When calculating the wage standard for double-wage damages, the base wage, position wage, job wage, seniority wage, rank wage, and other monthly paid wage components, which are due wages for employees' normal work, with the characteristics of continuity, stability, and relatively fixed amounts, should be used as the calculation base for double-wage damages for not signing employment contracts. Generally, non-fixed payments such as commission wages and bonuses are not used as the calculation base for double-wage damages for not signing employment contracts; The "Implementation Rules for Several Issues Concerning the Implementation of the Economic Redundancy in Tianjin in 2018" stipulates in Article 4 that the wage standard for double-wage damages should be calculated based on the wages that the employee should receive for normal working hours, excluding the following two items: (1) labor remuneration with a payment period exceeding one month, such as quarterly bonuses, semi-annual bonuses, year-end bonuses, year-end double pay, and business commissions settled on a quarterly, semi-annual, or annual basis; (2) labor remuneration with an undetermined payment period, such as one-time bonuses, allowances paid under special circumstances, and subsidies; The Zhejiang Labor Arbitration Committee's "Guiding Opinions on Handling Several Issues in Labor Dispute Cases (Trial)" (Zhe Arbitration [2009] No. 2) states in Article 38: Overtime pay and the double-wage damages according to Article 82 of the Employment Contract Law should be based on the standard wages corresponding to the employee's position. Zhu Jiulong v. Anhui Sanxiang Technical Consulting Co., Ltd., Anhui Hefei Intermediate People's Court Civil Judgment (2021) Wan 01 Min Zhong No. 4719; Article 11 of the "Answers to Several Issues Concerning the Handling of Labor Dispute Cases (Trial)" by the Jiangxi Provincial Higher People's Court and the Department of Human Resources and Social Security in 2020. Lanzhou Chen Zuolin Chenji Catering Service Co., Ltd., v. Ba Tingting, Gansu Province Lanzhou Intermediate People's Court Civil Judgment (2022) Gan 01 Min Zhong Zi No. 4646. The court held: "The determination of the base for double-wage damages should be based on the monthly wage for normal working hours after deducting overtime pay, unconventional bonuses, welfare, and risk-related items." Dalian Nianqiang Food Co., Ltd. v. Gu Jibin, Liaoning Dalian Intermediate People's Court Civil Judgment (2022) Liao 02 Min Zhong No. 8855. The court held: "Except for the paid annual leave wage of RMB 300 included in the February 2021 wages, other commission wages, subsidies, and return goods rewards are remuneration that Gu Jibin has obtained for normal work and should be used as the basis for calculating the double-wage damages." Wu Meiru v. Shenyang Luer Business Information Consulting Co., Ltd., Liaoning Shenyang Intermediate People's Court Civil Judgment (2022) Liao 01 Min Zhong No. 10318. Liu Changping v. Urumqi Dadequan Trading Co., Ltd., Xinjiang Uygur Autonomous Region High People's Court Civil Ruling (2015) Xin Min Shen Zi No. 232. The court held: "The base for calculating double-wage damages for not signing employment contract should be determined based on the normal working time monthly wage obtained by the employee after deducting overtime pay, bonuses, commissions, and other items." Hu Jianping v. Xiamen Xiaohutong Catering Management Co., Ltd. and Huang Xiaobing, Fujian Provincial High Court (2015) Min Min Shen Zi No. 2091. Zhao Yongpan v. Harbin Hesheng Labor Dispatch Co., Ltd., Heilongjiang Provincial High Court Civil Ruling (2019) Hei Min Shen No. 3514. The court held: "It is not inappropriate for the second-instance court to deduct the transportation subsidy of RMB 100, overtime subsidy of RMB 2,400, and social security subsidy of RMB 1,000, which belong to welfare income and overtime pay in nature, and to consider the total of 6,500 RMB of basic wage and performance wage as the calculation base for double-wage damages."

73 Supreme People's Court Civil First Division: "Disputes over Proxy-Signed Employment Contracts and Their Handling," published in *Frontiers of Civil Adjudication*, Volume 1, People's Court Press, 2014 edition,

there are precedents that no longer distinguish between normal working time wages and overtime pay, and the wage standard for double-wage damages is determined based on the actual due wages (i.e., the commissions).

Courts in Guangdong, Jilin, Chongqing, and Jiangsu Provinces hold the view that according to the Regulations on the Composition of Total Wages by the National Bureau of Statistics, overtime pay should be included in the wage standard for double-wage damages.[74]

Third, it seems that most courts hold that basic wages, position allowances, subsidies, etc. paid on a monthly basis should be included in the wage standard for double-wage damages, while non-fixed payments such as quarterly bonuses, year-end bonuses, commissions, etc. should not be included.[75] However, if quarterly bonuses or year-end bonuses are paid on a fixed basis, there are court decisions where they are included in the wage base for double-wage damages after being averaged monthly.

Finally, if both parties dispute on different wage standards, and the standard cannot be determined, it should be determined first through negotiation as stipulated in Article 18 of the Employment Contract Law, followed by the comparable position standards in collective contracts, and then by the principle of equal pay for equal work. Of course, if the employee's monthly wage is below the local minimum wage standard, the wage amount for double-wage damages should be topped up to the minimum wage standard.

2.4 Probation Period and Validity of Employment

59. How long a probation period can an employer provide for a newly recruited employee?

Answer: The length of the probation period the employer may agree with a newly recruited employee depends on the type of the employee.

For full-time employees, if the term of the employment contract is three months or more but less than one year, the probation period shall not exceed one month; if the term of the

pages 291–294. "If both parties in the employment relationship have an agreement on the monthly wage, the calculation base for double-wage damages should be determined based on the monthly wage for normal working hours as agreed upon by both parties."

74 Guangdong Ruisheng Machinery Manufacturing Co., Ltd., v. Su Shengren, Guangdong Foshan Intermediate People's Court Civil Judgment (2022) Yue 06 Min Zhong Zi No. 14814; Guangdong Wanyang Zhongchuang City Real Estate Co., Ltd., v. Guo Zhiming, Guangdong Provincial High People's Court Civil Ruling (2019) Yue Min Shen No. 12560; Jilin Province He Hotel Management Co., Ltd., v. Lu, Jilin Provincial High Court Civil Ruling (2023) Ji Min Shen No. 4130; Chongqing Xingangcheng (Hong Kong) Shopping Plaza Co., Ltd. v. Xu Fangfang, Chongqing the First Intermediate Court Civil (2020) Yu 01 Min Zhong Zi No. 6413. Article 2 of the "Guiding Opinions on the Trial of Labor and Personnel Dispute Cases (II)" by the Jiangsu Provincial High Court stipulates, "For employers who fail to sign a written employment contract with employees, the double-wage damages payable each month shall be determined based on the employee's monthly due wages, including hourly or piecework wages, overtime pay, bonuses, allowances, and subsidies. If the employee's monthly wage includes quarterly bonuses, semi-annual bonuses, or year-end bonuses, the actual bonus amount for that month shall be determined after apportionment."

75 Liu Tao v. Jiangxi Broadcasting Television Network Transmission Co., Ltd., Jiangxi Provincial High Court (2020) Gan Min Shen No. 1018; Beijing Zhongheng Judicial Appraisal Institute et al. Labor Dispute Second Instance Civil Judgment, Beijing the Third Intermediate People's Court (2023) Jing 03 Min Zhong Zi No. 342; 2020 Jiangxi Provincial High Court, Human Resources and Social Security Department, Article 11 of "Answers to Several Issues Regarding the Handling of Labor Dispute Cases"; Article 6 of "Implementation Rules on the Implementation of the Economic Redundancy in Tianjin"; Article 38 of Zhejiang Labor Arbitration Committee "Guiding Opinions on the Handling of Labor Dispute Cases (Trial)" (Zhe Zhong [2009] No. 2).

employment contract is one year or more but less than three years, the probation period shall not exceed two months; for a fixed-term employment contract of three years or more or a permanent employment contract, the probation period shall not be more than six months. A probation period shall not be stipulated in a fixed-term employment contract with a period less than three months or an assignment contract.[76]

If an employer has agreed on a probation period for a full-time employee under a three-party labor dispatch, the probation period shall also meet the aforementioned standards. If the host employer considers that the employee does not meet the hiring requirements, it may terminate the dispatch employment relationship and return the employee to the labor dispatch company (while the employment relationship between the worker and the dispatch employer remains).[77] For the labor dispatch of casual employees, of course, the host employer shall not provide a probation period.

The employer may apply and determine the length of the probation period according to the term of the employment contracts for employees on irregular and general work hours, referencing the probation rules applicable to ordinary full-time employees.[78] However, employers may not establish a probation period for casual workers.[79]

60. I am a newly recruited employee of the company. What rights and obligations do I have during the probation period?

Answer: During the probation period, the employer assesses your work abilities, and you evaluate whether the employer aligns with your career development goals. Despite uncertainties, this period is integral to the duration of your employment relationship, and you remain protected by the employment laws covering aspects such as minimum wage, employer contribution of social insurance, rest and vacation rights, and other worker entitlements.

If an employee was previously employed by the employer and is now rejoining, should the employer apply Article 19 of the Employment Contract Law, which states that "a same

76 Article 19 of the Employment Contract Law.

77 Wang Ping, Fujian Strait Human Resources Co., Ltd. Ningde Branch Labor Dispute Retrial Review and Trial Supervision Civil Ruling Fujian Provincial People's High Court Civil Ruling (2018) Min Min Shen No. 1573. The court held that "Ningde Strait Company is the dispatch employer in this case, forming an employment relationship with Wang Ping; Ningde Unicom is the host employer. According to the provisions of Article 39 of the Employment Contract Law, the host employer may terminate the employment contract if the worker has one of the following circumstances: (1) During the probation period, it is proved that the worker does not meet the hiring requirements; (2) It seriously violates the company rules and regulations. The employee may be returned to the labor dispatch employer, and the labor dispatch employer may terminate the employment contract with the employee in accordance with the relevant provisions."

78 Guan Yong and Huijia (Xiamen) Property Management Co., Ltd. Labor Dispute Civil Judgment of Second Instance Civil Judgment of Xiamen Intermediate People's Court of Fujian Province (2021) Min 02 Min Zhong No. 783. "The agreement of the employment contract between the two parties (employees are working on irregular hours) on the term of the contract is more than three years. The probation period of six months does not violate the provisions of Article 19 of the Employment Contract Law concerning the probation period." Labor Dispute Appeal Case between Zheng Chunsheng and Beijing Minhai Biotechnology Co., Ltd. Civil Judgment of Beijing the Second Intermediate People's Court (2014) Er Zhong Min Zhong Zi No. 02957. "This Court considers that if an employment relationship has been established but a written employment contract has not been signed at the same time, a written employment contract shall be signed within one month from the date of employment. A probation period may be stipulated in an employment contract. For an employment contract with a fixed term of more than three years or a permanent contract, the probation period shall not exceed six months … as Zheng Chunsheng's work role is on the general work hours."

79 Article 70 of the Employment Contract Law.

employer can only agree on one probation period with the same employee," and must not provide a second probation period for the employee? Currently, courts in different regions hold differing opinions. One opinion, for example, held by the Guangdong High Court and the Beijing Second Intermediate People's Court, states that an employer cannot set a second probation period based on the literal meaning of the law.[80] However, the Shanghai First Intermediate People's Court and the Shenzhen Longgang District Court hold opposite views.[81]

During the probation period, the wage paid by the employer to the employee shall not be less than 80% of the regular wage stipulated in the employment contract and shall not be less than the minimum wage standard.[82] For example, if your employment contract stipulates that your wage is RMB 5,000, your probation wage shall not be less than RMB 4,000; otherwise, the employer is obligated to make up the difference.

If the employer is not satisfied with the probationary employee and wants to dismiss the employee, it must also meet the legal requirement that the employee "does not meet the hiring requirements"[83] rather than what many people think, that employers can dismiss probationary employees at will. In addition, if a host employer is not satisfied with a probationary dispatched new employee under labor dispatch, the employee can be returned to the labor dispatch employer.

The length of the probation period shall not exceed the length prescribed by law. Please refer to "59. How long a probation period can an employer provide for a newly recruited employee?" If the agreement on probation period violates the legal provisions, for example, the length of time exceeds the scope permitted by law or the probation period agreement is illegal, the probation period shall be considered as the regular contract period. The employer's termination of the employee's contract during this so-called "probation period" is likely to constitute an illegal dismissal.

Sometimes, the two parties may have agreed on a probation period when the employee joined the company, but later extended the probation period. If the employee does not agree, the extension is invalid. If the employee approves the extension, the period beyond the statutory allowable limit is considered part of the regular contract period. Regarding the extended probation within the statutory allowable period, courts around the country hold two perspectives: one deeming it legal and the other considering it illegal, each carrying corresponding legal consequences. For details, please refer to "61. What legal consequences will an employer face for extending a newly hired employee's probation period?"

80 Wang Zonggui v. Zhongshan Boyi Electric Co., Ltd., Retrial and Supervision of Labor Contract Dispute Civil Ruling, Guangdong High People's Court, Civil Ruling (2018) Yue Min Shen No. 12712. Sichuan Yingcai Property Management Co., Ltd. v. Xu Yumei, Application to Revoke Arbitration Award, Special Procedure Civil Ruling, Nanchong Intermediate People's Court of Sichuan Province, Civil Ruling (2020) Chuan 13 Min Te No. 29. Huangjia Precious Metals Management Co., Ltd. Beijing Branch v. Zhang Xuefang, Labor Dispute Appeal Case, Beijing Second Intermediate People's Court, Civil Judgment (2017) Jing 02 Min Zhong No. 5076.

81 Tang Zhiquan v. Shenzhen Gaode Color Printing and Packaging Co., Ltd., Labor Contract Dispute, First Instance Civil Judgment, People's Court of Longgang District, Shenzhen City, Guangdong Province, Civil Judgment (2019) Yue 0307 Min Chu No. 18895. Zhu Rui, "Li Chen vs. Shuguang Company Labor Contract Dispute Case—Is It Illegal for the 'Former Employer' to Agree on a Probation Period Again After Returning to Work Two Months After Resignation?" Yan Qinshun v. Yunnan Xinduchang Real Estate Development Co., Ltd., Labor Dispute Case, Xishan District People's Court of Kunming City, Civil Judgment (2016) Yun 0112 Min Chu No. 7535.

82 Article 20 of the Employment Contract Law.

83 Article 39 of the Employment Contract Law.

During the probation period, in addition to adhering to professional ethics, employees are obligated to provide three days' notice to the employer if they decide to resign, for example, due to dissatisfaction with the working environment.[84] Otherwise, you may bear the liability of compensating the employer for the loss caused by your immediate resignation. Please refer to "124. Should an employee compensate the employer for the losses caused by their fault?"

61. What legal consequences will an employer face for extending a newly hired employee's probation period?

Answer: First, we need to analyze whether extending a newly hired employee's probation period is legal. According to the Employment Contract Law, an employee can undergo only one probation period with a single employer. Judicial decisions show that the legality of extending an employee's probation period depends on whether the employee agrees the extension, the finding of the nature of the extension, and whether it causes the probation period to exceed the statutory limit.

If the employer unilaterally extends the probation period without the consent of the employee, the extension is illegal.[85] If the employer stipulates or both parties agree to extend the probation period beyond the statutory probation period, the excess period is illegal, even if the employee has agreed to it. Any illegal extension of the probation period shall at least be recognized as the regular employment contract period.

What is rather controversial now is the situation where both parties agree to extend a probation period, and the extension does not exceed the statutory probation period. Regarding whether this extension constitutes a change of probation period or a second probation period in violation of the Employment Contract Law, Chinese courts have differing views.

Some courts, including the Shanghai High Court, Guangdong Province Shenzhen City Intermediate Court, the Xianyang Intermediate Court of Shaanxi Province, and the Hangzhou and Jinhua Intermediate Courts of Zhejiang Province, held that the extension of a probation period agreed by both parties is legal and effective as long as the whole probation period does not exceed the statutory time limit.[86] However, other courts, including

84 Article 37 of the Employment Contract Law

85 Wang Yueping, Guangdong Wanyin Installation Engineering Co., Ltd. Civil Judgment of Second Instance of Labor Dispute Guangzhou Intermediate People's Court of Guangdong Province Civil Judgment (2020) Yue 01 Min Zhong 21125, No. 21126, "The unilateral extension of the probation period when the probation period expires violates the law."

86 Civil Ruling on Trial and Supervision of Other Labor Disputes between Zhang Jianqiao and Shanghai Huanyue Garment Co., Ltd. Civil Ruling of Shanghai High Court (2018) Hu Min Shen No. 2786. "The probation period originally agreed by Zhang Jianqiao and Huanyue Company is 3 months. Although it has been extended since then, the reason for the extension is that Zhang Jianqiao's work performance was not good and further investigation is needed. The extended probation period does not exceed the statutory period, and the wages of Zhang Jianqiao has not been reduced during the probation period. All have been consented by Zhang Jianqiao himself." Labor Dispute Appeal between Hua Xiaolong and Zhongyan Xinshangmeng Electronic Commerce Co., Ltd. Civil Judgment of Hangzhou Intermediate People's Court of Zhejiang Province (2015) Zhe Hang Min Zhong Zi No. 3127. Liu Dan and Shenzhen Market and Quality Supervision and Administration Commission Labor Dispute Appeal Case Civil Judgment of Shenzhen Intermediate People's Court of Guangdong Province (2017) Yue 03 Min Zhong No. 3849. Civil Judgment of the Labor Dispute Case between Fu Shaofeng and China Gezhouba Group No. 3 Engineering Co., Ltd. Civil Judgment of the Intermediate People's Court of Xianyang City, Shaanxi Province (2019) Shan 04 Min Zhong No. 784. The two parties re-signed a permanent

Beijing High Court and the First Intermediate Court, Xiamen Intermediate Court of Fujian Province, and Guangdong Province Guangzhou City Intermediate Court, have decisions ruling that the extension of the probation period is equivalent to a second probation period in disguise, so that the agreement to extend the probation period is invalid.[87]

The second issue is the legal consequences for extending the probation period if it is illegal. The consequence is that according to Article 83 of the Employment Contract Law, the employer should pay probation period damages at the monthly wages of the last month's probation period during the extended period that has been fulfilled.[88] For example, Ms. Li signed a permanent contract with the employer, which stipulated that the probation period was six months, the wage during the probation period was RMB 4,000, and the wage during the regular employment period was RMB 5,000, but the employer later stipulated that the probation period should be extended for three months, so the employer should pay Ms. Li RMB 15,000 (3 * 5,000) as the probation period damages for violating the provisions of the probation period ("probation damages").

62. Is it legal for an employer to require a current employee to undergo a second probation period?

Answer: The probation period is a period during which an employer conducts capability and suitability tests on a newly hired employee at the beginning stage of the employment contract. If the employee does not meet the hiring requirements, the employer can terminate the employment relationship with the employee without compensation. Employers may establish a second probation period for employees in two situations.

The first situation is change of the employee's position. If the employee's position is changed within the same employer, even it is a promotion, according to the provisions of

---

employment contract and changed the probation period from two months to six months, which was found to be legal by the court. Civil Judgment of the Second Instance of the Labor Dispute between Hua Xiaoming and Pujiang Changzhu Huazhen Real Estate Co., Ltd. Civil Judgment of the Intermediate People's Court of Jinhua City, Zhejiang Province (2020) Zhe 07 Min Zhong No. 4315. "The appellant agrees to extend the probation period voluntarily, because the total probation period after the extension is still within the legal period (not more than six months). Therefore, the first instance decision is not improper in finding that it did not constitute employer providing for multiple probation periods for the same employee, and that the probation period agreement between the two parties was legal and effective."

87 Fazhijin Information Technology Co., Ltd. v. Wu Qinghua Labor Dispute Civil Ruling of Beijing High Court (2017) Jing Min Shen No. 1290. Labor Dispute between Tan Chusi and Xiamen Zhongjin Machinery Co., Ltd. and Xiamen Honghai Machinery Co., Ltd. Civil Judgment of Xiamen Intermediate People's Court of Fujian Province (2015) XMZZ No. 2434. Civil Judgment of Second Instance on the Labor Dispute between Taiji Aisi (China) Investment Co., Ltd. and Yu Jiao Civil Judgment of Intermediate People's Court of Guangzhou City, Guangdong Province (2017) Yue 01 Min Zhong No. 22937. In the case, both parties agreed to extend the three-month probation period of the three-year fixed-term contract to six months, and the court held that such extension was illegal. Civil Judgment of the Second Instance of Labor Dispute between Lingtu Education Consulting (Beijing) Co., Ltd. and Wang Xiuhua Civil Judgment of the First Intermediate People's Court of Beijing (2020) Jing 01 Min Zhong No. 5195. "Regardless of whether Lingtu Education Consulting (Beijing) Co., Ltd. and Wang Xiuhua have reached an agreement on the extension of the probation period, the act of re-agreeing on the probation period has violated the mandatory provisions of law."

88 Article 83 of the Employment Contract Law of the People's Republic of China stipulates that if an employer violates the provisions of this Law on providing a probation period for their employees, the labor administrative authority shall order it to make corrections; if the probation period agreed upon in violation of the law has been fulfilled, the employer shall pay damages to the worker for the period that has been fulfilled beyond the statutory probation period based on the monthly wage of the worker at the end of the probation period.

the Employment Contract Law, the employer must not request the employee to undergo a new probation period.[89]

But if the position change is an internal transfer between subordinate enterprises within a group company, there are different treatments in judicial practice at present. Some cases confirm that this internal transfer does not constitute a change of employer, so the transfer-in employer shall not set a probation period for the employee.[90] However, some court decisions hold that different employers under a group company are independent legal persons, and it is not against the law to provide a probation period again.[91]

These precedents demonstrate a trend in determining whether an employer can set a new probation period for its employee (or whether the job transfer constitutes a change of employer); the courts tend to examine the roles played by the employer and the employee during the transfer process based on the purpose of probation period laws (i.e., providing employers with a reasonable trial period to assess new employees). If the transfer is entirely driven by the parent company (such as a group company) or the receiving company, with no involvement or influence from the employee, then the receiving company should not set a probation period again; if the employee actively participates in or even initiates the transfer process, then the receiving company has grounds to set a probation period to assess the employee. The employee's length of service should also be considered as a factor in determining whether it is reasonable to set a probation period again.

The second scenario involves a change in the legal entity of the employer. These changes include changes in equity ownership, such as through acquisition or merger, renaming of the employer, or merger or division of the employer. In the case of renaming of the employer, it is unquestionable that the employer cannot require existing employees to undergo a new probation period. In the event of a change in equity ownership, the employer cannot set a new probation period for existing employees. This is because the Employment Contract Law clearly stipulates that only one probation period can be agreed upon between the same employer and the same employee, and a change in the controlling shareholder of the employer does not legally transform the employer into a different entity. This differs from the rules in common law countries such as New Zealand, where new controlling shareholders have the right to require existing employees to undergo a new probation period because the employer under the New Zealand law is changed.

Employers involved in mergers or divisions should also not require existing employees to undergo a new probation period. Article 34 of the Employment Contract Law states: "In the event of merger or division of the employer, the original employment contract shall

89 Article 19 of the Employment Contract Law stipulates that the same employer and the same worker can only agree on one probation period.

90 In the case of the labor dispute between Ma Dayong and Changchun Shengji Real Estate Development Co., Ltd., Changchun Kuancheng District People's Court Civil Judgment (2013) KMCZ No. 1613, "The Court holds that during the performance of the employment contract between the plaintiff and Hengda Changji (Shenyang) Real Estate Co., Ltd., transferring the plaintiff to the defendant, the employer, is an internal position transfer. The defendant signing an employment contract with the plaintiff again with another probation period violates the relevant provisions of the Employment Contract Law."

91 Wang Hong and Jiangxi Haorun Investment Co., Ltd. Civil Judgment of the First Instance of Labor Dispute Jiangxi Nanchang Economic and Technological Development Zone People's Court Civil Judgment (2020) Gan 0192 Min Chu No. 1275. "The same employer and worker can only agree on one probation period, the plaintiff has worked in Hongkelong Group, Huaying Company, and the defendant Haorun Company successively. Although the three companies are related, they are different independent and legitimate business entities."

remain valid, and the employer who inherits its rights and obligations shall continue to perform the employment contract." Therefore, the employer after the merger or division cannot change its obligations under the original employment contract (i.e., there can only be one probation period for the same employee) to set a new probation period that may lead to the employee being dismissed without compensation.

A rather obscure question is whether it is legal for an employer to set a probation period for an employee's position transfer when the employee has not undergone one when initially hired. This does not appear to violate the principle of "one probation period for one employee in one employer." However, we believe this is not legal because it would empower the employer to arbitrarily dismiss an employee who has already established a stable employment relationship, which contradicts the principle of the employment laws protecting the rights of workers.

As legislations and judicial decisions are unclear, a more reasonable approach should be based on the purpose of the probation law (that is, the employer has a reasonable probation period for new employees). We can assess the role played by employees in the transfer process: if the transfer is entirely led by the parent company (such as the group company) or the transfer-in employer, and the employee does not participate in or influence the process, the transfer-in company should not impose a probation period for the employee. If the employee actively participates in the transfer process or even applies for the job, the transfer-in company should have a reason to set a probation period to examine the employee. The length of service of the employee should also be a factor taken into account in the reestablishment of a probation period.

In addition, when an employer is acquired (or a major equity change occurs), the new controlling party may not set a new probation period for the existing employees, because the Employment Contract Law clearly stipulates that the same employer and the same employee can only set one probation period, and the change of the controlling party of the employer will not lead to the employer becoming a different employer in law. This is quite different from the rule in a common law country, for example, New Zealand, where a new controlling shareholder may set new probation for current employees.

The above rules are applicable not only to employees on permanent and fixed-term contracts but also to those on labor dispatch and irregular and general work hours.

63. An employer notified its employee of termination only after the probation period. Is it legal?

Answer: Whether this kind of termination of employment is legal depends on the grounds on which the employee terminates the employee. There are two kinds of circumstances.

The first situation is that the employer terminates the employment relationship with an employee on the ground that the employee in the probation period does not meet the hiring requirements. In this case, the employment laws do not stipulate that the employer's notice of termination of the probation period must be made at or before the expiration of the probation period. Therefore, as long as the employer notifies the employee within a reasonable time after the expiration of the probation period, it can still effectively terminate the employment relationship on the ground of not meeting hiring requirements.[92]

---

92 Zhao Lei, Jiangxi Guanhao Commercial Operation Management Co., Ltd. Civil Judgment of the Second Instance of Labor Dispute Civil Case, Civil Judgment of the Intermediate People's Court of Fuzhou City,

The second situation is that the employer terminates the employment relationship for serious violation of company rules and regulations or other reasons.[93] In this case, it means that the employer has acquiesced that the employee does not have a situation of not meeting the standard of hiring requirements, and that the employee has become a regular employee. Therefore, whether the dismissal is legal or not depends on whether the company has established the substantive grounds for the dismissal and whether the employer has followed a legal procedure in the dismissal.

Of course, the employer can terminate the employee's employment relationship immediately any time before the probation period expires on the ground of not meeting the hiring requirements. The Employment Contract Law only stipulates that employees should give three-day notice for resignation during the probation period, but does not request prior notice for employers to terminate employees. The judgments of courts across the county generally hold that employers have the right to terminate their employees immediately during the probation period on the ground of not meeting hiring requirements.[94]

64. Is the employment contract I signed invalid?

Answer: Article 26 of the Employment Contract Law stipulates the circumstances for which an employment contract is invalid. If either party to the employment contract commits fraud, coercion, or taking advantage of vulnerability, so that the other party signs the employment contract against its true intention, the employment contract shall be invalid.[95] Any party can legally dissolve the invalid employment contract.

The most common dispute arises when employees provide false certificates of academic and/or professional qualifications during the recruitment process. If the employee's behavior causes the employer to recruit the employee against its true intention, it shall constitute fraud in principle, and the employer shall have the right to terminate the contract accordingly. Having examined numerous current cases nationwide, we summarize

---

Jiangxi Province (2022) Gan 10 Min Zhong No. 708. After the expiration of the probation, the employer notified the employee that he was not hired, and the employer claimed in the lawsuit that the reason for the termination was not meeting the hiring requirements in the probation period. The court finally found that the termination of the probation period was legal.

93 Other reasons stipulated in Article 39 of the Employment Contract Law include corruption to damage the interests of the company, multiple employment relationships, employee crime, invalidity of the contract, etc.

94 Labor dispute between Shanghai Lianghong Printing Co., Ltd. and Tang, Shanghai the Second Intermediate People's Court (2014) Hu Er Zhong Min San (Min) Zhong Zi No. 89. "The Employment Contract Law stipulates that if the employee is proved not to be up to hiring requirements during the probation period, the employer may terminate the employment contract immediately without any liability for damages or compensations." Civil Judgment of Second Instance on Labor Dispute between Zhong Wencheng and Sunac (Beijing) Cultural Tourism Planning & Research Institute Co., Ltd. Civil Judgment of Beijing the Third Intermediate People's Court (2020) Jing 03 Min Zhong No. 12016. (The right of immediate termination of the employer within the probation period was upheld in the first instance, and the second-instance decision upheld the first instance.) Civil Judgment of the Second Instance of the Labor Dispute Case between Li Ziqing and Rudy Van Gelderen Civil Judgment of Dongguan Intermediate People's Court of Guangdong Province (2020) Yue 19 Min Zhong No. 6795. "The employee can terminate the contract by notifying the employer three days in advance during the probation period (the regular contract period requires one month notice in advance). If the employer proves that the worker does not meet the hiring requirements, the employment contract can be immediately terminated (regular contract period requires serious violation of company rules and regulations, etc.)."

95 This statutory provision also stipulates that if the employer exempts itself from legal responsibility, excludes the rights of the employee, or violates the mandatory provisions of laws and administrative regulations, it is also invalid. These two types of invalidity usually refer to partial invalidity of employment contract, which is different from the overall invalidity of the employment contract discussed in this Q&A article.

the following factors that may affect the court's determination of whether an employer can terminate the contract due to the employee's fraud.

The first factor is the materiality of false qualifications provided by the employee. Employees who have provided only non-substantive false information do not necessarily commit fraud that leads to invalidation of the employment contract. For example, in the case of Xu Hongqi before Beijing High Court in 2022, the court held that the employee only concealed a period of work experience, and the employer did not prove that this led to the hiring of the employee against its real intention, so that the employer's claim that the employment contract was invalid because of academic qualification or professional fraud was not made out.[96]

In the 2018 case of Sui Yongjie, as another example, the court found that the employee had committed fraud by providing a false special-equipment-operation certificate during the contract negotiation process. Although the employee later obtained a genuine operation certificate, the court determined that the fraud had reached a level sufficient to cause the employer to violate its true intention. Therefore, the court found that the employer was entitled to legally terminate the employee.[97]

The second factor is the length of time that the employee has served the employer after a recruitment fraud. There are conflicting practices in courts around the country. Cases from the Intermediate People's Court of Suzhou City, Jiangsu Province, and the Intermediate People's Court of Hangzhou City, Zhejiang Province hold that there should be a reasonable time limit for fraud investigations of false academic and professional qualifications, and that the employer should not terminate the employee's employment contract for fraud after a long period of performance of the employment contract.[98] However, cases from the Guangdong Provincial High Court, Shenzhen Intermediate Court, and Guangzhou

96 Beijing Shanjie Investment Management Co., Ltd. and Xu Hongqi Labor Dispute Retrial and Trial Supervision Civil Ruling Letter Beijing High Court Civil Ruling Letter (2022) Jingminshen No. 1161.

97 Ba Jingyan, Zhang Douyuan: "The Impact of Failure to Fulfill the Obligation of Truthful Explanation on the Effectiveness of Employment contracts at the Time of Employment," published in *People's Justice · Cases*, Issue 8, 2018, p. 39. "Regarding the appeal case of labor dispute between Civil Aviation Air Traffic Control Technology and Equipment Development Co., Ltd. and Sui Yongjie, the court holds that the invalidity of the employment contract is determined to be due to fraudulent behavior committed by the employee when signing the employment contract. Even though Sui Yongjie obtained a genuine special-equipment-operation certificate after the false certificate was discovered, he cannot deny the fact that he signed the employment contract through fraudulent means. An invalid employment contract has no legal effect since its conclusion, so Sui Yongjie's claim that the employment contract between both parties is valid lacks factual and legal basis, and the court does not accept it. The scope of the employee's obligation of explanation should be judged based on both formal and substantive standards. In terms of form, the employer should clearly and fully inform the employee of the information and supporting materials that need to be provided; Substantively, the content required by the employer to be explained by the employee shall not violate the provisions of laws and administrative regulations, and shall have a direct and inevitable connection with the employee's role. The failure of a worker to truthfully explain does not necessarily constitute fraud. Only where the information that is not truthfully explained is directly related to the employment and where failure to truthfully explain causes the employer to make an expression of intention to enter into the employment contract, a fraud can be established."

98 Civil Judgment of the Intermediate People's Court of Suzhou City, Jiangsu Province (2017) Su 05 Min Zhong 6577 on the labor Dispute Appeal Case between Xingguang Fine Chemical (Zhangjiagang) Co., Ltd. and Shi Xiaofeng. The Civil Judgment of the Intermediate People's Court of Suzhou City, Jiangsu Province (2016) Su 05 Min Zhong No. 7008 regarding the labor Dispute Appeal Case between Shi Xiaofeng and Xingguang Fine Chemical (Zhangjiagang) Co., Ltd. Hangzhou Wenqin Shanxiao Investment Management Co., Ltd. and Li Dairan labor Dispute Appeal Case. Zhejiang Hangzhou Intermediate People's Court Civil Judgment (2015) Zhehang Minzhong Zi No. 1614.

Intermediate Court assert that employers are still entitled to terminate the employment contract based on recruitment fraud even after the employee's long-time service.[99]

The third factor is relevant provisions of the employer's company rules and regulations. If the company rules and regulations clearly stipulate that any false information of academic or professional qualifications provided by an employee is dishonest and thus constitutes a serious violation of company rules and regulations, it would be more legitimate for the employer to terminate the employee in question on this ground. For example, in the case of Jiekun before Guangzhou Intermediate People's Court of Guangdong Province in 2020, the employee had worked for 16 years with false academic qualifications. The company rules and regulations clearly stipulated that providing false academic qualifications was a serious violation of the company rules and regulations, and the court ruled that it was legal to establish fraud and to terminate the employee's employment relationship.[100] Of course, it must be noted that the company rules and regulations must be documents binding on employees through legal procedures. Please refer to "121. Is it legally permissible for my employer to discipline me?"

Another common phenomenon is establishing an employment relationship with an employer in the name of another. Courts usually find that this situation constitutes fraud and leads to the invalidity of the employment contract. The legal consequence of this invalidity is that the employer has the right to legally terminate the employment contract. However, the impostor has had a de facto relationship with the employer and has the right to receive wages, overtime wages, other employment remunerations, work injury entitlements, and other entitlements that all employees should receive.[101] The employee can also request the employer to pay double-wage damages in the absence of a written employment contract.[102] But if the employer has signed an employment contract with the impostor in

99 In the case of labor dispute review and trial supervision between Zhu Daorong and Guangdong Electronic Vocational and Technical School, Guangdong Provincial People's High Court Civil Ruling (2015) No. 1031. The employee has signed three employment contracts for more than five years with false academic titles. The court found the three employment contracts invalid and that the Notice of Termination of Employment relationship shall not be revoked. Shenzhen Kailu Innovation Technology Co., Ltd., Li Weilan Labor Dispute Second Instance Civil Judgment, Shenzhen Intermediate People's Court of Guangdong Province Civil Judgment (2019) Guangdong 03 Minzhong 20539. In the case, the employee provided false academic qualifications. Four years after the commencement, the employer terminated the employment on the ground of fraud. The court of first instance found academic fraud but considered that pursuit should be within reasonable length of time. The judgment of the second instance set it aside ruling that termination based on fraud was legal.

100 Civil Judgment of Second Instance of Labor Dispute between Qu Jiekun and Guangzhou Seagull Housing Industry Co., Ltd. Civil Judgment of Guangzhou Intermediate People's Court of Guangdong Province (2020) Yue 01 Min Zhong No. 9312.

101 Civil Ruling on Labor Dispute Retrial between the retrial applicant Wu Suoxia and the respondents Hebei Haichuan Human Resources Service Co., Ltd., Yanshan County Haichuan Human Resources Co., Ltd. Tianjin Development Zone Branch and Jiaxing Precision Injection Molding (Tianjin) Co. Ltd. Civil Ruling of Tianjin High Court (2015) JGMSZ No. 0701. Shandong Chaowei Ciyao Power Supply Co., Ltd. and Huang Yunzhong Labor Dispute Second Instance Civil Judgment Shandong Tai'an Intermediate People's Court Civil Judgment (2018) Lu 09 Min Zhong No. 1912. The impostor died in a traffic accident after entering the role, and the court found that the impostor had an actual employment relationship with the employer. Civil Judgment of the Second Instance of Labor Dispute between Jiangsu Xinling Construction Labor Engineering Co., Ltd. and Hu Caili Civil Judgment of the third Intermediate People's Court of Beijing (2018) Jing 03 Min Zhong No. 8761. The court held that the impostor employee was entitled to work injury entitlements.

102 Civil Judgment of Second Instance of Labor Dispute between Beijing Tiezhen Security Technology Service Co., Ltd. and Cheng Guilian, etc. Civil Judgment of Beijing the Second Intermediate People's Court (2020) Jing 02 Min Zhong No. 4509.

another's name, it shall be deemed that the employment contract has been signed, and there is no liability of double-wage damages.

Accordingly, when an employee is terminated by the employer on the ground of an invalid employment contract, the employee should check the reasons for the invalidity specified on the termination notice, and determine which type of the invalidity it is and whether the employer has a factual basis for it, in order to assess whether the termination is lawful or not.

65. Is it legal for my employer to sign an assignment contract with me?

Answer: An assignment contract is a type of employment contract newly stipulated in the Employment Contract Law (not in the Labor Law), which is applicable to the completion of a specific work task for a period of time. The purpose is to facilitate the employer to flexibly employ personnel for specific work projects.

The law does not stipulate how to legally sign an assignment employment contract. In judicial practice, a common dispute is that an employment contract under the name of assignment employment contract is actually a fixed-term or other type of employment contract. There are great differences in legal consequences; for example, if an employer signs two consecutive fixed-term employment contracts with an employee, it must sign a permanent employment contract with the employee for the third time. For example, in the case of Xia Hanming in 2020, the Nanjing Intermediate Court of Jiangsu Province held that since employees had cross-signed two fixed-term contracts and two assignment contracts, there was no fact that they had signed two consecutive fixed-term contracts, so the employee's claim for a permanent contract was not established.[103]

From the detailed analyses of the court cases that define the nature of an assignment contract, we can see that whether the work assignment contract signed by both parties is essentially another type of employment contract depends on the following factors: whether the contract term is clear, whether the work assignment is temporary, and whether there is a history of repeated contract signing in the past.

For example, in the case of Rao Renbi before Yibin Intermediate Court of Sichuan Province in 2016, it was held that the employee, a security guard, signed several contracts with the employer, a school, to complete certain tasks with clear starting and ending dates, and the nature of the guard's work was mechanical and repetitive, which did not have the characteristics of the final completion of established objectives, so the assignment contracts were actually fixed-term contracts.[104] Another example is that in the case of Zhang Erping in 2021, the Intermediate People's Court of Haixi Mongolian-Tibetan Autonomous Prefecture of Qinghai Province held that the employee had been engaged in drilling work arranged by the employer for 12 years, the nature of his work was a long-term business of the employer, and that therefore, the nature of assignment contracts was not made out.[105]

---

103 Civil Judgment of the Second Instance of the Labor Dispute between Xia Hanming, the Eighth Construction Branch of China Jiangsu International Economic and Technical Cooperation Group Co., Ltd., China Jiangsu International Economic and Technical Cooperation Group Co., Ltd., and the Foreign Engineering Branch of China Jiangsu International Economy and Technology Cooperation Group Ltd. Civil Judgment of Nanjing Intermediate People's Court of Jiangsu Province (2020) Su 01 Min Zhong No. 5.

104 Rao Renbi and Changning County Huatan Town Junior Middle School Labor Dispute Appeal Case, Sichuan Yibin Intermediate People's Court Civil Judgment (2016) Chuan 15 Min Zhong No. 2157.

105 Zhang Erping, Civil Judgment of the Second Instance of Labor Dispute and Personnel Dispute of Golmud Geological Engineering Survey Institute of Geology and Mineral Resources, Civil Judgment of the

However, court decisions also recognize that stable annual seasonal work can constitute a legitimate assignment contract.[106] There are even court decisions finding that the assignment contract after long-term work or multiple fixed-term contracts may be transformed into a permanent employment contract.[107] These reflect the undeveloped state of this area of law in China.

In order to safeguard the rights and interests of employees, the Employment Contract Law stipulates that assignment employment contracts must not include a probation period. If both parties terminate the employment relationship after the completion of the work task, the employer shall also pay economic compensation to the employees according to their service years after 2008.[108]

66. Is my labor dispatch contract invalid?

Answer: A labor dispatch contract means that a human resources company (dispatch employer) signs an employment contract with an employee, and the employee is dispatched to work for a third-party company (the host employer). In principle, you should be an employee of the human resources company. However, in practice, labor dispatches are often to be considered invalid because they violate the law.

The determination of the invalidity of labor dispatch is an uncertain issue from law to judicial practice in China. Invalid labor dispatch includes three circumstances: false labor dispatch (including illegal labor outsourcing; see "21. My company has signed a labor outsourcing agreement with a human resources company. Is this legal?"), dispatch employer lacking qualifications, and labor dispatch violating the "three characteristics" of labor dispatch.

The first situation is that false labor dispatch leads to invalidity.[109] The employment laws do not provide a systematic definition of what is false labor dispatch. Generally speaking, a host employer pretends to sign a dispatch contract with dispatched employees

---

Intermediate People's Court of Haixi Mongolian-Tibetan Autonomous Prefecture of Qinghai Province (2021) Qing 28 Min Zhong No. 583.

106 Labor Dispute between Chen Xiaoqing and Ruian Dahu Shoes Co., Ltd. Civil Judgment of Intermediate People's Court of Wenzhou City, Zhejiang Province (2015) Zhe Wen Min Zhong Zi No. 1572.

107 Lichuan Forest Public Security Bureau and Zhang Huiling's Civil Judgment of the Second Instance of Labor Disputes, Civil Judgment of the Intermediate People's Court of Enshi Tujia and Miao Autonomous Prefecture, Hubei Province (2018) No. 1420. In the case, the public security organ, the employer, signed a contract with the employees to complete a certain task for the purpose of "engaging in auxiliary work." The court held that the task was not clear, so the employer could not terminate the employee's contract, which essentially evolved into a permanent employment contract. Liao Xiaoyu v. Shenzhen Futian District Hospital of Traditional Chinese Medicine Labor Dispute Guangdong Provincial People's High Court Civil Ruling (2015) Yue Gao Fa Min Shen Zi No. 489. A nurse signed several fixed-term contracts within nine years of joining the hospital. The last year of the contract was an assignment contract. The court determined that the last contract should be deemed as a permanent contract.

108 Article 22 of the Regulations on the Implementation of the Employment Contract Law stipulates that if an employment contract with a term of completion of a certain task is terminated due to the completion of the task, the employer shall pay economic compensation to the worker in accordance with the provisions of Article 47 of the Employment Contract Law. The transitional clause of Article 97 of the Employment Contract Law. Yin Hequn appealed the labor dispute of Beijing Simplot Food Processing Co., Ltd. Civil Judgment of the Second Intermediate People's Court of Beijing (2016) Jing 02 Min Zhong No. 6194. "The court held that the employer had been signing assignment contracts with employees and had paid economic compensation after 2008, so there was no case of arrears of economic compensation for employees."

109 Liang Yongzhen, Shunfeng Automobile Sales Service Co., Ltd. of Duanzhou District, Zhaoqing City, and other civil judgments on retrial of labor disputes, Guangdong Provincial High Court (2022) Yue Min Zai No. 30. "To sum up, the above-mentioned acts of Shunfeng Company and Zhuobo Company do not conform to

and a dispatch employer, but in reality, the dispatch employer does not undertake any employment management of the employees. This kind of labor dispatch violates the honest principle of Chinese civil law by concealing the purpose of a direct employment relationship in the form of a lawful labor dispatch, making it invalid. Only Article 67 of the Employment Contract Law stipulates a type of false labor dispatch, namely, the practice of host employers setting up a dispatch company to dispatch employees to itself, which is referred to "reverse dispatch" in judicial practice.

The second situation is that the human resources company does not have the qualification of labor dispatch. Whether this situation leads to the invalidity of labor dispatch is a point of conflict in judicial practice. For example, in the 2017 case of Zhongche Group Xi'an Vehicle Factory, Shaanxi Provincial High Court ruled that the labor dispatch was invalid due to the dispatch employer lacking the qualification,[110] while some other cases determined that the labor dispatch qualification requirement falls under the realm of administrative management and thus will not lead to the invalidity of labor dispatch.[111]

The third situation is that labor dispatch violates the "three characteristics" of temporary, alternative, and auxiliary work under the Employment Contract Law. The temporary characteristic means that labor dispatch work shall not exceed six months. Whether this situation leads to the invalidity of labor dispatch has two opposite judicial practices. One is that the violation of the three characteristics of labor dispatch will not lead to the invalidity of labor dispatch;[112] the other is the opposite.[113]

---

the relevant provisions of the Employment Contract Law of the People's Republic of China on labor dispatch. Shunfeng Company's act of evading the main responsibility by means of false labor dispatch should be invalid."

110 Zhongche Group Xi'an Vehicle Factory v. Xi'an Vehicle Factory Industry and Trade Corporation Rubber and Plastic Products Company and other companies, Shaanxi Provincial People's High Court (2017) Shan Min Shen No. 278. "After examination, the Court holds that … because the rubber and plastic products company does not have the qualification to operate the labor dispatch business, the Labor Employment Agreement signed between the company and the applicant, Zhongche Group Xi'an Vehicle Factory, lacks the content of the labor dispatch agreement stipulated by law. Therefore, the original trial finding that the labor dispatch behavior of the rubber and plastic products company was invalid is correct."

111 Wu Zhixiong v. Ezhou Gedian Weimin Labor Service Station employment dispute second instance civil judgment Hubei Province Ezhou Intermediate People's Court Civil Judgment (2020) E 07 Min Zhong No. 363. "The mandatory provisions of Article 57 of the Law on dispatch are administrative provisions, not validity-related provisions, and the failure to obtain the qualification of labor dispatch does not mean that the dispatch is invalid." Wang Yamei and Zichang Oil Production Plant of Yanchang Oilfield Co., Ltd., Civil Judgment of the Second Instance of Labor Dispute, Shaanxi Yan'an Intermediate Court (2019) Shan06 MinZhong No. 152. "Regarding the appellant's claim that Zichang Dingli Human Resources Co., Ltd. does not have the qualifications to engage in labor dispatch, its registered capital does not conform to the law, and it has not obtained operational permit in labor dispatch, after examination, we considered that the above-mentioned provisions are administrative norms and do not constitute the situation of 'violating the mandatory provisions of laws and administrative regulations' in Article 52 of the Contract Law."

112 Labor Dispute Appeal Case between Li Kexing and State Grid Shanxi Electric Power Company, Shanxi Provincial People's High Court (2017) Jin 04 Min Zhong No. 2704. Article 4 of the 2014 Summary of the Meeting on Several Issues Concerning the Application of Law to Labor Dispatch jointly issued by the Shanghai Human Resources and Social Security Bureau and the Shanghai High Court. It states that violation of the three characteristics of labor dispatch does not lead to invalidity of labor dispatch.

113 Article 30, paragraph 1, of the Regulations on the Protection of Workers' Rights and Interests in Chongqing in 2011 stipulates that the use of dispatched workers in non-temporary, auxiliary and alternative roles shall be regarded as the direct establishment of employment relationships between the host employers and the dispatched workers. Article 30 of the Regulations on the Protection of Workers' Rights and Interests in Liaoning Province in 2013 and Article 31 of the Regulations on the Protection of Workers' Rights and Interests in Shantou Special Economic Zone in 2015. Civil Judgment of Second Instance of Labor Dispute between Shi Jingwang and Xuzhou Mining Group Co., Ltd. and Jiahe Coal Mine of Xuzhou Mining Group Co., Ltd., Intermediate People's Court of Xuzhou City, Jiangsu Province (2017) Su 03 Min Zhong No. 6802.

The legal consequence of an invalid labor dispatch is that the employee(s) and the host employer has formed a direct employment relationship, and the employee can directly claim the rights under the employment laws against the host employer. At the same time, in the above three situations, the labor dispatch employer will inevitably be at fault for the invalidity of the labor dispatch, so the employees can also require the labor dispatch employer to bear a joint and several liability according to Article 92 of the Employment Contract Law.

An interesting question arises: After the invalidation of labor dispatch, how is the contract period of the de facto employment relationship between the host employer and the employee determined? The law does not provide specific regulations, and judicial precedents are also rare in this regard.[114]

67. What is the current judicial rule for invalid labor dispatch in China?

Answer: As shown in "66. Is my labor dispatch contract invalid?", there are framework defects in the law of invalidity of labor dispatch in China. We have observed that for invalid labor dispatches in relation to three situations (false labor dispatch, labor dispatch companies lacking qualifications, and labor dispatch violating the "three characteristics"), relevant judicial decisions all proceeded legal analyses and assessments revolving around employment relationships, the nature of dependence or subordination of workers to employers. Therefore, the underlying rules of invalid labor dispatch in current judicial judgments in China involve examining two main factors.

Combined with the analyses of the current judicial decisions and according to the essential characteristics of the subordination or dependence of employment relationships, a more feasible principle to assess the validity of labor dispatch can be as follows:

Judging whether the labor dispatch is invalid depends mainly on two factors. The first part is the substantive characteristics of the relationship between the host employer and the employees, which includes, first, whether the nature of the job position is auxiliary. For example, the work of an accountant dispatched to an accounting firm is obviously not auxiliary, and there is a higher likelihood of a direct employment relationship. Second is whether the job position is temporary or not. If the position of the dispatched employee is permanent, the employee is more likely to be judged as a direct employee of the host employer. Finally, it includes the degree of integration of the employee into the host employer, and whether the company unifies the management of the dispatched employee with other ordinary employees in daily management. This part is key and core in determining the validity of labor dispatch.

The second part is the agreements provided in the labor dispatch contract signed by the human resources company, the host employer, and the employees, the contents of which stipulate who is the employer of the employees, and whether the host employer treats the employees as employees or as external service personnel. If the labor dispatch contract clearly stipulates that the human resources company is the employer and the host employer is only the third-party controller, it should be more inclined to the absence of direct employment relationships. The way the host employer treats the employees and the

114 It appears that there are precedents suggesting that after the invalidation of labor dispatch, the contract period between the dispatched employee and the host employer should be determined with reference to the fixed term of the labor dispatch contract.

employees' perception of the relationship are also important considerations. If evidence shows that both the host employer and the employees believe that there are employment relationships between the two parties, and the employer treats the employees as general employees, direct employment relationships are more likely to exist.

This judgment of invalidity of labor dispatch is similar to the distinction between contractors and employees, the core of which is to judge whether the relevant workers are employees of the employer that actually uses their labor, according to the essence of the employment relationship and the understanding of both parties (or three parties). But, the difference between the two is that labor dispatch must include employment relationships, either between the employees and the dispatch employer, or between the employees and the host employer, while for the latter relationship, the worker may be an independent contractor, not subordinate to the company that receives services.

CHAPTER 3

Employee Entitlements

Introduction

The core issue of the employment laws is to determine what statutory rights employees are entitled to after establishing an employment relationship with the employer. This chapter provides detailed explanations of various types of entitlements relating to rest or leave, and the benefits for employees' illnesses and injuries.

The questions and answers in this chapter explain in detail the following rights of employees: public holidays, the calculation of overtime wages for public holidays, standard work hours and special work hour systems, the issue of employees' time-off in lieu to offset overtime hours, the entitlements of paid annual leave and the unused annual leave pay, the entitlements of employees' medical care leave for illness or non-work-related injury, the entitlements of medical care leave for special types of employees, the entitlements of medical care leave for employees with cancers and special diseases, application for sick leave and company rules and regulations during sick leave, the work injury entitlements and the identification of special types of work-related injuries, the treatment of overlapping tort compensation and work injury entitlements, the extension of the paid work injury leave, work-related disabled employees' entitlements, the identification and catalogue of occupational diseases, the liabilities for occupational diseases found after employment termination, the liabilities of multiple employers for occupational diseases of the same employee, bereavement leave, maternity and paternity leave benefits, special protection rules for female workers, equal pay for equal work for both genders, high-temperature allowance, and the right to work-breaks.

This chapter also explains certain complex issues, including situations where conflicts arise when an employee has completed the treatment period of medical care leave, or paid work injury leave expires, but no conclusion has been reached in the labor capacity appraisal, and the employee has not yet fully recovered, or where an employee claims for mental damages, or commercial insurance and work injury liability co-exist, and the specific compensation items for work injuries or occupational diseases. We provide practical suggestions accordingly.

3.1 Employee Leaves and Special Entitlements

68. As an employee, what are my basic leave rights?

Answer: According to Chinese employment laws, a full-time employee usually has the following basic rights: paid public holidays, overtime pay or leave for working on public

DOI: 10.4324/9781003583301-3

holidays, overtime pay or time-off in lieu for working overtime on weekdays and weekend days, paid annual leave, paid bereavement leave, paid breaks, unpaid lunch breaks, maternity and paternity leave, equal pay rights for equal work, minimum wage protection, etc. Please see Table 3.1 for all types of employee entitlements.

The rights of various types of employees with different types of entitlements are covered in the following question and answer passages.

69. What are the public holidays for employees?

Answer: Current public holidays in China include New Year's Day (January 1), Spring Festival (the first, second, and third days of the first lunar month), Qing-Ming Day (the day for tomb sweeping in the lunar calendar), Labor Day (May 1), Dragon Boat Festival (on the day of the Dragon Boat Festival in the lunar calendar), Mid-Autumn Festival (on the day of the Mid-Autumn Festival in the lunar calendar), and National Day (October 1, 2, and 3).

Holidays and anniversaries for some citizens include Women's Day for female employees (half a day on March 8), Youth Day for employees between the ages of 14 and 28 (half a day on May 4), and customary holidays for ethnic minorities.

Workers in the standard work hour system, including employees on permanent, fixed-term, and work assignment contracts, and labor dispatch, do not have to work on public holidays, and the employer is obligated to pay the ordinary wages of employees. If a public holiday falls on a day used by an employee as annual leave, weekend day, paid sick leave, or bereavement leave, the public holiday shall be taken additionally or be encashed in the form of unused annual leave.

If a full-time employee works overtime on public holidays, the employer shall pay 300% of the ordinary wage for the number of hours of overtime work, and in principle, the overtime wage shall not be replaced by time-off in lieu.[1] However, if eligible employees work on public holidays such as Women's Day and Youth Day, the employers do not need to pay overtime wages.[2]

Should employees on non-standard work hours be paid three times overtime wages for working overtime on public holidays? At present, judicial decisions are not very clear on this point. If the employment contract of a casual employee stipulates that the employee is required to work on public holidays, the employee shall abide by the agreement, but the employee shall be entitled to three times ordinary pay for the public holidays' work.[3]

---

1 Article 44 of the Labor Law.

2 Letter of the General Office of the Ministry of Labor and Social Security on Wage Issues Related to Holidays for Some Citizens (LaoSheTing Letter [2000] No.18): "In accordance with the provisions of the State Council's Measures for Holidays on National New Year's Festivals and Memorial Days (Decree No. 270 of the State Council) on holidays for some citizens such as Women's Day and Youth Day, during the holidays for these citizens who participate in celebrations organized by society or employers, their employers shall pay wages as if they normally work. No overtime wages shall be paid. If the festival falls on Saturday or Sunday and the employer arranges employees to work overtime, it shall pay overtime wages on weekend days according to law."

3 Civil Judgment of the Second Instance of the Labor Dispute Case between Haiyun and Fuyang Branch of China United Network Communications Co., Ltd., Civil Judgment of Fuyang Intermediate People's Court of Anhui Province (2016) No. 3420. "Casual workers are entitled to the right to rest on public holidays according to the employment contract and the provisions of national laws and regulations." Li Meiyi v. Haikou Xinhua Zhengda Airport Service Co., Ltd. Shenzhen Branch, etc. Employment Dispute Civil Second Instance Civil Judgment Guangdong Shenzhen Intermediate People's Court Civil Judgment (2021) Yue 03 Min Zhong No. 6207.

Table 3.1 Types of employees' entitlements

	Permanent	*Fixed term*	*Labor dispatch*	*Casual*	*assignment contract*	*Irregular and general work hours*
Public holiday	11 days per year and partial civil leave	11 days per year and partial civil leave	11 days per year and partial civil leave	Employee must work if the contract provides for, but normally overtime wages should be paid.	11 days per year and partial civil leave	11 days per year and partial civil leave
Overtime pays	Yes	Yes	Yes	No settled law in judicial practice.	Yes	For the general work hours, there are overtime wages on public holidays, and others depend on whether work hours exceed the standard work hours. Overtime pay rules for irregular work hours vary regionally.
Time-off in lieu	Yes	Yes	Yes	No	Yes	Yes, they are systems of alternative leave arrangement for busy and idle periods.
Paid annual leave	5 to 15 days, depending on accumulative service years of employees who have worked for more than one year for the current employer.	5 to 15 days, depending on accumulative service years of employees who have worked for more than one year for the current employer.	5 to 15 days, depending on accumulative service years of employees who have worked for more than one year for the current employer.	No	5 to 15 days, depending on accumulative service years of employees who have worked for more than one year for the current employer.	At present, the court has different views: yes or no.

(*Continued*)

Table 3.1 (Continued)

	Permanent	*Fixed term*	*Labor dispatch*	*Casual*	*assignment contract*	*Irregular and general work hours*
Paid sick leave	3 to 24 months in certain period, depending on accumulative service years and service years for the employer	3 to 24 months in certain period, depending on accumulative service years and service years for the employer	3 to 24 months in certain period, depending on accumulative service years and service years for the employer	No	3 to 24 months in certain period, depending on accumulative service years and service years for the employer	3 to 24 months in certain period, depending on accumulative service years and service years for the employer
Paid bereavement leave	Yes	Yes	Yes	No settled law in judicial practice	Yes	Yes
Work injury entitlements	Yes	Yes	Yes	Yes	Yes	Yes
Paternity leave	More than 15 days	More than 15 days	More than 15 days	No	More than 15 days	More than 15 days
Three-protected-period entitlement	Yes	Yes	Yes	No	Yes	Yes
Special protection for women workers	Yes	Yes	Yes	Yes	Yes	Yes
Minimum wage protection	Yes	Yes	Yes	Yes	Yes	Yes
Break	Yes	Yes	Yes	Yes	Yes	Yes
Physical Protection of Dismissal Procedure	Yes	Yes	Yes	No	Yes	Yes

"Three protected periods" refers to female employees' pregnancy, maternity, and lactation periods.

70. I am an HR manager. How do I calculate overtime pay for employees?

Answer: Introduced below is the overtime wage computation of standard hour system, including permanent employment contracts, fixed-term contracts, labor dispatch, and assignment contract.

There are three kinds of overtime wages for employees, namely, overtime wages on weekdays, weekend days, and public holidays. These three types of overtime pay depend on the overtime hours of three types done by the employee, whether the employee has taken time-off in lieu, and the different statutory overtime pay rates.

For the number of hours for calculating the employee's overtime pay, you should first consider whether there is time-off in lieu. Please refer to "72. Can employees' time-off in lieu be used to offset overtime hours?"

Having offset overtime hours by time-off in lieu, the employer needs to calculate net overtime hours of each type of overtime. The hourly rate for weekday overtime hours is 150% of the employee's ordinary hourly wage; overtime hours on weekend days, 200%; overtime hours in public holidays, 300%.

For example, an employee with a normal monthly wage of RMB 5,000 had, in this month, 30 hours of overtime on weekdays, 8 hours of overtime on weekends, and 16 hours of overtime on public holidays. The company should endeavor to arrange for the employee to take time-off in lieu for the 8 hours on weekends, so that only 30 hours of overtime on weekends and 16 hours of overtime on public holidays need to be paid for. However, if the time-off in lieu is not arranged, the overtime wages of the employee is RMB 3,132 (5,000/(21.75 * 8) * (30 * 150% + 8 * 200% + 16 * 300%)). Note that 21.75 represents the annual average number of working days per month in China, and thus, 174 hours (21.75*8) is the annual average number of working hours per month in China.

The 150%, 200%, and 300% in the above calculation formula are the standard rates of overtime wages stipulated in the Employment Contract Law. At present, the practice of most courts across the country, such as Guangdong Provincial High Court,[4] is to calculate according to this. However, some courts hold that the foregoing multiplier should deduct 100% for the wages already paid. That is, the calculation rate of overtime pay on public holidays is 200% (300% − 100%). Sichuan Chengdu Intermediate Court, Shandong Zibo Zhangdian District Court, and Shandong Jinan Changqing District Court held in their judgments that 100% should be deducted from the rate of overtime wages for public holidays because ordinary wages were already paid for the public holidays, so the rate should be calculated as 200%. The Changqing District Court of Jinan,[5] Shandong Province, even

4 Wu Jinjun v. Shenzhen Xindongsheng Property Management Co., Ltd. Guangzhou Branch Labor Dispute Civil Ruling of Guangdong Provincial People's High Court (2016) Yue Min Shen No. 589.

5 Civil Judgment (2020) Chuan 01 Min Zhong No. 9503 of the Intermediate People's Court of Chengdu City, Sichuan Province, issued by Zhao Jinying and Chenghua District Xiangan Building Materials Business Department on the second instance of labor disputes. "Because public holidays are paid holidays, the employer should pay additional two times wages when paying overtime wages." Lu Zhen, Zibo Fire Carving Catering Management Co., Ltd. Civil Judgment of First Instance for Labor Remuneration Dispute, Civil Judgment of People's Court of Zhangdian District, Zibo City, Shandong Province (2022) Lu 0303 Min Chu 8371, Shandong Leshengyuan Ecological Agriculture Co., Ltd., and the Civil Judgment of the First Instance of Congratulations on Labor Dispute Civil Judgment of the People's Court of Changqing District, Jinan City, Shandong Province (2021) Lu 0113 Min Chu No. 624. "Both parties have no objection on 4-day overtime on public holidays, and the Court confirms that during the probation period from July to September 2019, according to the work record of every Saturday, Overtime on weekend days is 13 days in total. To sum up, after deducting the one-time wage that has been paid normally, Leshengyuan Company shall pay Zhuhe overtime wages of RMB 18,193.3

held that weekend overtime wages should be paid at only 100% of the ordinary wage, as 100% of the ordinary wage should be deducted.

It should be noted that the calculation base of the overtime wage, the ordinary hourly wage, should not be lower than the minimum wage standard. If the base is lower than the minimum wage standard, the minimum wage standard should apply if there is no other way to determine a higher ordinary hourly wage.

For the calculation of overtime pay under special work hour systems, please refer to "71. How do I calculate overtime pay under special work hour systems?"

71. How do I calculate overtime pay under special work hour systems?

Answer: Special work hour systems include part-time, irregular, and general work hours. They have different rules for calculating overtime pay.

The practices of courts vary from place to place on whether the overtime pay to casual employees is applicable or not. One approach, as held by the courts of Guangdong Province, including Shenzhen City, is that casual employees' overtime pay is applicable for public holidays only but not for overtime on weekdays and weekends.[6] The other approach, as adopted in Beijing, Jinan City in Shandong Province, and Nanning City in Guangxi, is not to recognize casual employees' right to any overtime pay at all.[7] Another way is to stipulate the minimum wage standard for casual public holidays by local laws and regulations. For example, Beijing stipulates that the minimum hourly wage standard for casual workers on public holidays during 2023–2024 is RMB 62, and there is no need to implement the overtime wage rules for public holidays.[8]

Article 13 of the Provisional Regulations on Wage Payment stipulates that if the work hours of employees under the general work hour system exceed the standard work hours in an accounting cycle, the exceeding hours shall be paid overtime wages, which shall include three kinds of overtime wages, namely, weekdays, weekend days, and public holidays. In addition, the 1995 Ministry of Labor's Opinions on the implementation of the Labor Law, as well as local decisions, hold that employees should be paid three times overtime wages for working on public holidays, regardless of whether their total work

in total (i.e., RMB 423.1 × (22 days + 13 days) × 100% + RMB 423.1 × 4 days × 200%), in which the overtime on weekend days is calculated at the rate of 100%."

6 The labor dispute appeal case between Hong Anyun and Guangdong Southern Newspaper Media Group Co., Ltd., Guangzhou Intermediate People's Court of Guangdong Province issued the Civil Judgment (2011) S.Z.F.M.Y.Z.Z. No. 2049 and No. 2050. The court supported the casual worker's overtime wage on public holidays, but rejected the request for overtime wage on weekdays and weekend days.

7 Lin Zhenmei and Guangxi Nanguo Logistics Co., Ltd. Employment contract Dispute Appeal Case Nanning Intermediate People's Court of Guangxi Zhuang Autonomous Region Civil Judgment (2017) Gui 01 Min Zhong No. 3930. Civil Judgment of the Second Instance of the Labor Dispute between Wang Dingshu and the Infrastructure Maintenance Center of the Civil Aviation Administration of China Civil Judgment of the Second Intermediate People's Court of Beijing (2018) Jing 02 Min Zhong 9593 (in this case, the court even considered that casual work did not constitute an employment relationship and rejected all requests for overtime wages). Civil Judgment on the Labor Dispute between Wei Guangxin and Donghao Automobile Company Civil Judgment of Jinan Intermediate People's Court of Shandong Province (2020) Lu 01 Min Zhong No. 5963.

8 Beijing stipulates that from September 1, 2023, the hourly minimum wage for casual employees is RMB 26.4 per hour, and the hourly minimum wage for casual employees on public holidays is RMB 62 per hour. Article 18 of the 2007 Regulations on Payment of Wages in Beijing stipulates that casual workers are not subject to the rule of triple overtime pay when working on public holidays.

hours during the accounting period exceed the standard work hours.[9] At present, courts around the country are basically consistent in implementing this provision.

The overtime wage rule for employees on irregular work hours is also the abovementioned Article 13, which stipulates that "workers under the system of irregular work hours are not subject to the above provisions." This rule is puzzling. At present, courts around the country have three types of understanding. One approach, as held by the Shenzhen City Intermediate Court, Shanxi Provincial High Court, and Shanghai High Court, is that employees on irregular work hours have no right to claim overtime wages for weekdays and weekend days, but have the right to overtime wages for public holidays.[10] The second view, held by the High Court of Guangxi Zhuang Autonomous Region, is that employees on irregular work hours are entitled to overtime wages for public holidays, and whether overtime wages can be obtained for weekdays and weekend days depends on whether the total work hours exceed the standard work hours in the accounting cycle.[11] The third is the mainstream view, as held by the Guangdong Provincial High Court, Beijing City High Court, Shandong Provincial High Court, Guizhou Provincial High Court, Sichuan Provincial High Court, Jiangsu Provincial High Court, Chongqing City High Court, and Tianjin the First Intermediate Court, rejecting any overtime wage rights of employees on irregular work hours, and that the aforementioned rule completely excludes the overtime wage rights of employees on irregular work hours for their work on weekdays, weekend days, and public holidays.[12]

---

9 The former Ministry of Labor, "The Opinions on Several Issues Concerning the Implementation of the Labor Law of the People's Republic of China" (Laobufa [1995] 309), article 62, "For worker on irregular and general work hours, their work days in weekend are considered as normal weekdays; When workday happens to be public holiday, their pays should apply item 3 of article 44 of the Labor Law." Ma Dawei v. Lingzhi Fashion (Tianjin) Co., Ltd. and other labor disputes Beijing High Court Civil Ruling (2016) Jing Min Shen No. 2381. The court seems to imply that employees on general work hours should be paid overtime wages for public holidays. Qingzhou Ginza Mall Co., Ltd., Li Xiaofeng Labor Dispute Civil Judgment of Second Instance Civil Judgment of Weifang Intermediate People's Court of Shandong Province (2023) Lu 07 Min Zhong No. 1666. Li Jiezhu v. Guangzhou Nanlian Air Catering Co., Ltd. (Guangzhou Intermediate People's Court of Guangdong Province, Civil Judgment [2011] S.Z.F.M.Y.Z.Z. No. 749). "For the staff who implement the workhour system of general work hours, the work hours in weekends (other than public holiday) shall be considered as normal work hours. However, the hours worked that are exceeding the standard work hours shall be considered as overtime hours."

10 Li Meiyi, Haikou Xinhua Zhengda Airport Service Co., Ltd. Shenzhen Branch, etc. Employment Dispute Civil Second Instance Civil Judgment Guangdong Shenzhen Intermediate People's Court Civil Judgment (2021) Yue 03 Min Zhong No. 6207. Li Jin and Beijing Dawang Food Co., Ltd. Taiyuan Branch Labor Dispute Retrial Shanxi Provincial People's High Court Civil Ruling (2022) Jin Min Shen No. 328. "Employees on irregular work hours are not entitled to overtime wages except for public holidays work." Chen Kaiqi and Deyou Real Estate Brokerage Co., Ltd. Shenzhen Branch Employment Contract Dispute Trial Supervision Civil Ruling Shanghai High Court Civil Ruling (2021) Hu Min Shen No. 1128. The court only supports overtime wages on public holidays, but not on weekdays and weekend days.

11 Xie Yulong, Guangxi Guanyang Rural Commercial Bank Co., Ltd. and other civil applications for retrial review of labor disputes Civil Ruling of the High Court of Guangxi Zhuang Autonomous Region (2022) Guimin Shen No. 5355. The Guangxi High Court held that the hours the employee on irregular hours worked on weekdays and weekend days did not exceed the standard hours. Therefore, it does not support overtime wages on weekdays and weekend days, but supports the request for overtime wages on public holidays.

12 *People's Court Daily*, October 22, 2015, 6th edition: Case Selection, (2015) YZMZZ No. 0686, Tianjin the First Intermediate People's Court rules the case of Meng Tong v. Tianjin Suning Yunshang labor dispute. "According to Article 13 of the Provisional Regulations on Wage Payment, workers on the system of irregular work hours are not entitled to overtime wages. That is to say, for overtime hours employees work on weekdays, weekend days, and public holidays, the employers are not obligated to pay overtime wages." Civil Ruling on Labor Dispute Retrial Review and Trial Supervision between Liu Zhenshu and Beijing Brothers Moving Service Co., Ltd. Civil Ruling of Beijing High Court (2021) Jing Min Shen No. 5189. "His role is

72. Can employees' time-off in lieu be used to offset overtime hours?

Answer: So-called time-off in lieu offsetting overtime hours is when an employee takes alternative leave after overtime work, and consequently, the employer does not have to pay overtime wages for those hours. Obviously, it is one of the preconditions for accurately calculating the overtime wages of employees to distinguish different types of overtime and find out whether the time-off in lieu can offset the number of overtime hours. Whether an employee's time-off in lieu can be used to offset overtime hours depends on what kind of overtime hours the employee's time-off in lieu is used to offset.

First of all, employees' time-off in lieu may be offsetting a number of overtime hours on weekend days (that is, at weekends). Moreover, the employment laws require employers to prioritize time-off in lieu for overtime work on employees' weekend days, and only if this is impossible may the employer choose to pay overtime wages. Second, overtime hours on public holidays are not allowed to be offset by time-off in lieu; that is to say, employees must be paid overtime wages for overtime hours on public holidays regardless of whether they have time-off in lieu or not.[13]

Finally, as to whether overtime hours in weekdays can be settled by time-off in lieu, the prevailing practice of courts around the country appears to recognize the effectiveness of the leave in lieu.[14] However, some courts around the county, such as the Shenzhen Intermediate People's Court, hold the opposite opinion. For example, in the case of Zeng Yingyu before the Shenzhen Intermediate People's Court in 2020, the court emphasized that the law does not allow time-off in lieu for overtime hours on weekdays and public

on irregular work hours, thus his claims for overtime wages on weekend days and public holidays lack legal basis." Civil Ruling on Retrial Review and Trial Supervision of Labor Disputes between Su Jijin and Shandong Yantai Dongda Labor Affairs Service Center Civil Ruling of Shandong High Court (2020) Lu Min Shen No. 11446. Civil Ruling on Labor Dispute Appeal and Application for Retrial between Hu Zongyin and Chongqing Chuangang Logistics Group Co., Ltd. Civil Ruling of Chongqing High Court (2020) Yu Min Shen No. 3096. Li Hao, Jiangsu Jingdong Information Technology Co., Ltd. Labor Dispute Retrial Review and Trial Supervision Civil Ruling Guangdong Provincial People's High Court Civil Ruling (2019) Yue Min Shen No. 11195. The court held that the irregular work hour system does not apply overtime wages for public holidays. Mao Shiju, Hezhang County Power Supply Bureau Labor Dispute Retrial Review and Trial Supervision Civil Ruling Guizhou Provincial People's High Court Civil Ruling (2018) Qian Min Shen No. 1122. Chen Guojun and Chengdu Quancheng Debang Logistics Co., Ltd. Civil Ruling on Labor Dispute Retrial Review and Trial Supervision Civil Ruling of Sichuan Provincial People's High Court (2020) CMS No. 2768. Labor Dispute between Jiang Qianhe and Jiangsu Nanjing Long-distance Bus Passenger Transport Group Co., Ltd. Civil Ruling of Jiangsu Provincial People's High Court (2017) Sumin Shen No. 3991.

13 The case of labor dispute between China Southern Fund Management Co., Ltd. and XIEXUEJUN, Shenzhen Intermediate People's Court of Guangdong Province issued the Civil Judgment (2015) S.Z.F.L.Z.Z. No. 5199. In this case, the employee's days of time-off in lieu exceeded the number of days of overtime work on weekend days, but the court still refused to use the surplus days of time-off in lieu to offset the days of public holidays overtime.

14 Zhejiang Sunflower Solar Energy Technology Co., Ltd., Zhang Feng Labor Dispute Second Instance Civil Judgment Zhejiang Shaoxing Intermediate People's Court Civil Judgment (2019) Zhe 06 Min Zhong No. 2281. In the case, the court recognized the company's rules that overtime on weekdays shall not be paid overtime wages but can be taken time-off in lieu." Zhang Weiwei and Halliburton (China) Energy Services Co., Ltd., Civil Judgment of the Second Intermediate People's Court of Tianjin (2018) No. 3872. "The Court of First Instance holds that overtime on public holidays is different from overtime on weekdays and weekend days, and that it contains certain humanistic and ethical needs. Therefore, overtime on public holidays is not allowed to take time-off in lieu."

holidays, so overtime wages must be calculated according to the actual number of overtime hours on weekdays and public holidays without deduction of time-off in lieu, if any.[15]

In principle, employers have the right to arrange the time-off in lieu for employees, but they shall reasonably notify the employee in advance[16] and shall not cause unreasonable inconvenience to the life and work of the employees.

73. How does the law prescribe employees' entitlement of paid annual leave?

Answer: Paid annual leave refers to the paid leave that employees who meet certain conditions are entitled to for their health, well-being, and work–life balance. Whether employees are entitled to annual leave treatment from their employer should first depend on the type of their employment contract; casual workers are not entitled to paid annual leave.[17]

The number of days of paid annual leave for full-time employees on permanent, fixed-term, work assignment, and labor dispatch contracts, as well as full-time employees on irregular and general work hours, shall be determined based on their individual consecutive work days for their employers and accumulative service years, according to the Regulations on Paid Annual Leave for Employees.

Employees with less than one year of continuous service are not yet entitled to paid annual leave. Employees who have recently worked continuously for more than one year shall be entitled to various levels of paid annual leave according to their accumulative service years, as follows: (1) 5 days of annual leave for employees whose accumulative service years are more than 1 year but less than 10 years; (2) 10 days of annual leave for employees whose accumulative service years are more than 10 years but less than 20 years; (3) 15 days of annual leave for employees whose accumulative service years are more than 20 years.[18]

Exceptions to the aforementioned rules are: employees who enjoy winter and summer vacations (such as school teachers), employees who have had more than 20 days of paid personal leave, employees with an accumulative service of more than 1 year and less than 10 years who have taken sick leave for more than 2 months, employees with an accumulative service of more than 10 years and less than 20 years who have taken sick leave for more than 3 months, and employees who have accumulative service of more than 20 years

15 Shenzhen Kedun Technology Co., Ltd. and Zeng Yingyu's Civil Judgment of Second Instance of Labor Dispute Civil Judgment of Shenzhen Intermediate People's Court of Guangdong Province (2020) Yue 03 Min Zhong 27737. "According to the provisions of Article 44 of the Labor Law of the People's Republic of China, overtime on weekend days can be taken time-off in lieu. This law does not stipulate that overtime work on weekdays and on public holidays can be taken time-off in lieu. Since Kedun Company confirmed Zeng Yingyu's weekdays' overtime hours, this court confirms that the court of first instance ruling that Kedun Company should pay Zeng Yingyu the weekday's overtime wages of RMB 2,172.41 has factual and legal basis."

16 He Chengsheng and Oupai Home Furnishing Group Co., Ltd. Civil Judgment of the First Instance of Labor Dispute Civil Judgment of the People's Court of Baiyun District, Guangzhou City, Guangdong Province (2023) Yue 0111 Min Chu No. 686. "Although Oupai Company has the right to arrange overtime and time-off in lieu, it shall express its intention and notify He Chengsheng of such arrangement."

17 Li Jingru and Inner Mongolia Entry-Exit Inspection and Quarantine Bureau of the People's Republic of China, Inner Mongolia Entry-Exit Inspection and Quarantine Bureau Organ Service Center Labor Dispute Retrial Review and Trial Supervision Civil Ruling Inner Mongolia Autonomous Region High Court Civil Ruling (2019) No. 3801. "According to Article 2 of the Implementation Measures for Regulations on Paid Annual Leave for Employees and Article 2 of the Reply of the General Office of the Ministry of Human Resources and Social Security on Relevant Issues Concerning the Implementation Measures for the Regulations on Paid Annual Leave for Employees (No. 149, 2009), the hours of casual employees are different from those of full-time employees and they are not entitled to paid annual leave."

18 Article 3 of the Regulations on Paid Annual Leave for Employees in 2008.

and who have had over 4 months' sick leave. In these exceptional cases, an employee is not entitled to paid annual leave for the year.[19]

It is worth noting that although the precondition of "one year of continuous work" for annual leave stipulated by law theoretically includes the period of time before the current employment,[20] in practice, the policy generally implemented by enterprises is basically one year of continuous work for the current employer, because it is not easy for an employee to realize the "seamless continuity" of employment relationships between two employers in practice.[21] For example, if an employee joins their current employer after a two months' break following termination by their previous employer, the service years of the employee in the previous employer cannot be continuously included into their service years for the current employer. In addition, the condition of "one year of continuous work" also means that an employee who resigns within one year has no right to claim any unused annual leave pay.[22]

Another practical problem with paid annual leave is the treatment of overlapping other holidays. First of all, public holidays and weekend days are not absorbed by paid annual leave.[23] For example, if an employee takes ten days of paid annual leave that spans two weekend days, the employee will be counted as having used eight days of paid annual leave instead of ten days. Similarly, paid annual leave should not be absorbed by other leave periods, including sick leave, bereavement leave, and maternity leave.

Employers have the right to arrange annual leave for employees according to the needs of production and operation, but it shall reasonably consider the opinions and requirements of employees.[24]

At present, there are different decisions in courts around the country on whether full-time employees on irregular work hours and general work hours have the right to paid annual leave. One way is to consider that employees under the work hour system of

19 Article 4 of the Regulations on Paid Annual Leave for Employees in 2008.

20 The Reply of the General Office of the Ministry of Human Resources and Social Security on the Implementation Measures for Paid Annual Leave for Employees (No. 149, 2009) stipulates that "12 months of continuous work" includes both the circumstances of 12 months of continuous work for the same employer and 12 months of continuous work for different employers.

21 Civil Judgment of the First Instance of the Labor Dispute between He Mouying and Guangzhou Hengsheng International Travel Service Co., Ltd. Civil Judgment of the People's Court of Haizhu District, Guangzhou City, Guangdong Province (2020) Yue 0105 Min Chu No. 20193. "This Court holds that as long as a worker has worked continuously for more than one year, they meet the requirement for annual leave. For example, workers must work continuously for one year for the same employer or work seamlessly for more than one year for different employers before they are entailed to annual leave."

22 Civil Judgment of the Second Instance of Labor Dispute between Yang Limin and Guodu Security Branch of Beijing Security Service Corporation Civil Judgment of the Second Intermediate People's Court of Beijing (2022) Jing 02 Min Zhong No. 7564. "Concerning unused annual leave pay, because Yang Limin has worked in Guodu Branch for less than one year … the Court does not support this claim." However, there are also cases on the contrary: Ningbo Jinlai Machinery Manufacturing Co., Ltd., Civil Judgment of the Second Instance of Hu Qiangquan Labor Dispute Civil Judgment of Ningbo Intermediate People's Court of Zhejiang Province (2020) Zhe 02 Min Zhong No. 470. "Because Hu Qiangquan's work in Jinlai Company is less than one year, the average monthly wage should be calculated based on the actual working months … therefore, Jinlai Company should pay Hu Qiangquan annual leave pay."

23 Article 3 of the Regulations on Paid Annual Leave for Employees in 2008.

24 Article 9 of the Implementation Measures for the Regulations on Paid Annual Leave for Employees in 2008 stipulates that employers shall make overall arrangements for annual leave according to the specific conditions of production and work and taking into account the wishes of employees themselves. If the employer is unable to arrange annual leave for employees or arrange annual leave across one year due to business needs, it shall obtain the consent of the employees themselves.

irregular and general work hours have the same right to paid annual leave as other types of full-time employees;[25] the other way is to consider that irregular and general work hours, as special forms of employment, do not apply to the entitlement of paid annual leave.[26]

74. How should employers manage employees' paid annual leave?

Answer: According to Article 5 of the Regulations on Paid Annual Leave for Employees and the one-year limitation of labor arbitration, annual leave can be arranged to be taken in the year after the year the employee become entitled to the leave, or can be encashed into unused annual leave pay.[27]

Employers should manage employees' paid annual leave in accordance with the aforesaid rule. Let's consider a case to illustrate the managing and calculating method. It is assumed that Mr. Zhang joined the company on May 1, 2021, and his average monthly wage has been RMB 5,500, including RMB 500 overtime wages.

Before May 1, 2022, Mr. Zhang's service length was less than one year, so he was not entitled to paid annual leave.

Between May 1, 2022 and May 1, 2023, Mr. Zhang was entitled to five days of paid annual leave from the first year (May 2021 to May 2022).[28] Before May 1, 2023, Mr. Zhang can apply to the company to take the leave, and the HR manager of the company may also arrange for Mr. Zhang to take the leave based on the recommendation from the supervisor of Mr. Zhang's department.

Between May 1, 2023, and May 1, 2024, Mr. Zhang became entitled to another five days of paid annual leave from the second year (May 2022 to May 2023). For the remaining unused days of the first year's five-day annual leave, Mr. Zhang can apply to take them, or the employer may arrange the same, and the employer can also pay for them in the form of unused annual leave. For the second year's five-day annual leave, Mr. Zhang can apply to take it, or the employer may arrange the same, from May 1, 2023, to May 1, 2024; if it's not realistic to arrange for this five-day annual leave to be taken, the employer can reschedule it within one year from May 1, 2024, or pay the corresponding unused annual leave pay.

The calculating method for the first year's unused annual leave pay is (Mr. Zhang's monthly wage/21.75) * 5 * 200%.

---

25 Xiao Haiyan and other civil judgments of the second instance of labor disputes Civil Judgment of the Third Intermediate People's Court of Beijing (2022) Jing 03 Min Zhong No. 312; even workers with irregular hours also have the right to take annual leave. Whether workers are entitled to paid annual leave is not related to the applicable system. Hubei Zhengda Co., Ltd. and Huang Dongfang Labor Dispute Civil Judgment of Second Instance Civil Judgment of Suizhou Intermediate People's Court of Hubei Province (2022) E 13 Min Zhong No. 329. According to Article 45 of the Labor Law of the People's Republic of China and Article 3 of the Implementation Measures for the Regulations on Paid Annual Leave for Employees, employees who have worked continuously for more than 12 months are entitled to paid annual leave, which does not exclude the right to paid annual leave for workers who work irregularly according to the system.

26 According to the provisions of Article 11 of Zhejiang Provincial Labor and Social Security Department's Opinions on Implementing the System of Paid Annual leave for Employees (No. 36, 2009), the rule of three-time wages for unused annual leave does not apply to employees who have been approved to implement the system of irregular work hours. The civil ruling of retrial review and trial supervision of labor disputes between Wang Guoqing and Beijing Zhenzhong Taxi Co., Ltd., the civil ruling of Beijing High Court (2021) Jinminshen No. 4771: "and Wang Guoqing was on the irregular workhour system. It is not improper (for the lower courts) not to support Wang Guoqing's claim for payment of wages, overtime pay, and unused annual leave pay against Zhenzhong Company."

27 Article 5 of the Regulations on Paid Annual Leave for Employees in 2008.

28 Article 3 of the Regulations on Paid Annual Leave for Employees in 2008.

For example, if Mr. Zhang's five-day annual leave in the first year ultimately is not used, the unused annual leave wage for the first year should be RMB 2,299 (5,000/21.75*5*200%). Here, RMB 5,000 represents Mr. Zhang's average monthly salary for the previous 12 months, excluding overtime pay (RMB 5,500 – RMB 500). Additionally, the calculating multiplier of 200% for the unused annual leave wage is derived from deducting the already paid regular wage of 100% from the 300% specified in Article 5 of the Regulations on Paid Annual Leave for Employees.[29] Currently, judicial practices across different regions also adhere to the 200% calculation.

In the equation, Mr. Zhang's monthly wage is equal to the average monthly wage from Mr. Zhang's previous 12 months without overtime pay, that is, RMB 5,000 (5,500 – 500). In addition, the unused annual leave pay ratio, according to the Regulations, appears to be 300%; but 100% of the ordinary wage already paid should be deducted, so the ultimate ratio of the pay calculation should be 200%. At present, judicial practices in various regions show the ratio being 200%.

75. How should employers manage employees' accrued annual leave over the years?

Answer: In "74. How should employers manage employees' paid annual leave?", we explained the calculation of the unused annual leave pay for the previous year. But one headache is that employees sometimes accumulate unused annual leave from several past years. Due to the one-year limitation of labor dispute arbitration under the Labor Dispute Mediation and Arbitration, employees cannot take or encash any annual leave days that have exceeded the limitation unless the employer agrees otherwise. Therefore, how to handle accumulated annual leave days from the past few years, while applying the rule of limitation of arbitration, is an issue that both HR managers and employees need to understand.

Let's take Mr. Zhang, who joined the company on May 1, 2021, as an example. Assume that Mr. Zhang did not use his annual leave in the first year (2021–2022), the second year (2022–2023), or the third year (2023–2024) and did not ask the employer to pay for the unused annual leave. Mr. Zhang resigned on September 1, 2024, in the fourth year. Mr. Zhang's monthly wage, which is RMB 5,000, has not changed in the past four years. How shall Mr. Zhang's unused annual leave be settled?

At the time of Mr. Zhang's resignation, the most important issues are whether the unused annual leave days from each year have exceeded the limitation of arbitration, and how to calculate Mr. Zhang's annual leave days for the last year, in which he did not work for a full year.

According to the provisions of the Labor Dispute Arbitration and Mediation Law, the limitation of employment arbitration is one year. According to Article 9 of the Implementation Measures for the Regulations on Paid Annual Leave for Employees, the annual leave not taken in a current year is allowed to be taken in the next year. Hence, the

29 According to Article 11 of the Implementation Measures for Regulations on Paid Annual Leave for Employees in 2008, the daily wage income for calculating the unused annual leave pay shall be calculated by dividing the employee's monthly wage by the number of days of monthly wage calculation (21.75 days). The term "monthly wage" as mentioned in the preceding paragraph refers to the average monthly wage of an employee excluding overtime wages from the 12 months before the employer should pay the unused annual leave pay. If the service for the employer is less than 12 months, the average monthly wage shall be calculated according to the actual month.

limitation of arbitration for an employee's application for unused annual leave pay should be within two years from the date the employee becomes entitled to the annual leave days; the employee should should use the days or request unused annual leave pay within the period.

The five days of Mr. Zhang's annual leave from the first year (2021–2022) can be used between May 1, 2022, and May 1, 2023. If they are not used, starting from May 1 2023, Mr. Zhang must claim the unused annual leave pay before May 1, 2024; otherwise, it will exceed the one-year limitation of arbitration. Since Mr. Zhang did not raise the claim to the employer before May 1, 2024, the five days of annual leave from the first year have exceeded the limitation of arbitration; even if he applied to the Employment Arbitration Committee, he would not be upheld. Of course, the law does not prohibit the employer from paying Mr. Zhang the unused annual leave pay from the first year beyond the limitation of arbitration.

According to the same review method, Mr. Zhang's total ten days of unused annual leave in the second and third years (up to May 1, 2024) do not exceed the limitation of arbitration, and the employer shall settle and pay Mr. Zhang at the time of resignation. The calculation method is: 5000/21.75 * 10 * 200% = RMB 4,598.

Now, we turn to the second issue. Mr. Zhang only worked part of the fourth year (from May 1, 2024 to September 1, 2024, 123 days in total). The number of days of annual leave not taken from this period shall be calculated as: 123/365 * 5 = 1.68 days. The part less than one day shall be ignored, so Mr. Zhang's unused annual leave in the fourth year is one day. The employer shall settle and pay Mr. Zhang RMB 460 (5,000/21.75 * 1 * 200%) for unused annual leave.

Of course, if Mr. Zhang has used part of the days, the employer should settle Mr. Zhang's unused annual leave pay based on the remaining days.

It should be noted that the current method of calculating unused annual leave pay in practice is very complex. Article 5 of the 2023 consultation draft on the Interpretation of the Supreme People's Court on the Application of Law in the Trial of Labor Dispute Cases (II) simplifies this rule, equating the limitation of arbitration for unused annual leave pay with the one for wage remuneration. This means that if the Supreme Court's Judicial Interpretation II comes into effect, employees can request double-wage damages for unused annual leave days within one year from the termination date of the employment relationship, regardless of which year during the employment contract period the unused annual leave days come from. This will change the past practice, where the limitation of arbitration might expire during the employment contract period.

In addition, if Mr. Zhang's employer has agreed on annual leave days that exceed the statutory number (for example, Mr. Zhang is entitled to eight days of annual leave instead of the statutory five days after working for one year), whether the extra days that have not been taken should be encashed is not stipulated by law at present. Judicial practice is that encashment agreement by both parties for extra days shall be binding.[30] If there is no related agreement or stipulation between the two parties in the employment contract or

30 Civil Judgment of First Instance of Labor Dispute between Yu Chunyan and Beijing Foreign Enterprise Deco Human Resources Service Shanghai Co., Ltd. Civil Judgment of Beijing Fengtai District People's Court (2021) Jing 0106 Min Chu No. 1789.

company rules and regulations, the prevailing practice in various regions (such as Beijing, Guangzhou, etc.) is that employees are not entitled to encashment for the extra days.[31]

76. I am an employee. What bereavement entitlements do I have?

Answer: Whether you have the right to bereavement leave depends first, on what type of employee you are. If you are a casual employee, you are probably not entitled to bereavement leave. If you are an employee of irregular or general work hours, dispatched employee, or assignment contract employee, you should have the same bereavement rights as full-time employees do, as long as you have an employment relationship with your employer. Length of service or other conditions do not prevent you from having the entitlement to bereavement leave.

At present, the local regulations on bereavement leave formulated in all parts of the country are based on the 1980 rules of the State Administration of Labor and the Ministry of Finance on Bereavement Leave, which generally stipulate that if an employee's immediate family member dies, they shall be given three days of paid bereavement leave, and if a long journey is needed for the funeral, they shall be given additional travel leave.[32] The aforementioned immediate family members are limited to the employee's own parents, current spouse, children, and of course, adoptive parents and adopted children. Parents-in-law are not immediate family members.[33]

The number of days of bereavement leave for employees in some regions exceeds the aforementioned three-day standard. For example, some places in Guangdong (including Shenzhen) implement five-day bereavement leave. Sichuan Province also stipulates additional travel leave in addtion to five-day bereavement leave.[34]

Bereavement leave is based on the death of an immediate family member, similar to sick leave based on illness, and cannot be accumulated and carried forward to next year. This differs from the rule for annual leave, which permits accumulation, rollover to the next year, and encashment of unused annual leave.

---

31 Hennes & Mauritz (Shanghai) Trading Co., Ltd., v. Lei Wu, etc. Employment Dispute Civil Second Instance Civil Judgment Guangdong Guangzhou Intermediate People's Court Civil Judgment (2022) Yue 01 Min Zhong No. 9211. "In addition, Lei Wu and Haines Guangzhou Branch did not agree that additional welfare annual leave beyond the statutory annual leave should be compensated when it was not taken, so Haines Guangzhou Branch is not obligated to pay the unused additional annual leave pay." Civil Judgment of Second Instance of Labor Dispute between Zhang Jihong and Huamei Fortune (Beijing) Technology Co., Ltd. Civil Judgment of the Second Intermediate People's Court of Beijing (2021) Jing 02 Min Zhong No. 4343.

32 The State Administration of Labor and the Ministry of Finance in 1980, the Notice on the Issue of Marriage and Bereavement Leave and Travel for Employees of State-owned Enterprises, and the Guangdong Provincial Department of Labor, the Interim Provisions on Holiday Benefits and Death Pension Benefits for Employees of Enterprises in Guangdong Province (Yue Lao Xin [1997] No. 115).

33 Civil Judgment of Second Instance of Labor Dispute between Zhou Qiming and Beijing Kaixie Hotel Co., Ltd. Civil Judgment of Beijing the Second Intermediate People's Court (2022) Jing 02 Min Zhong No. 11969.

34 Li Qiugui, Qingyuan Fangyuan New Materials Co., Ltd. Employment Contract Dispute Civil Judgment of Second Instance Civil Judgment of Guangdong Province Qingyuan City Intermediate People's Court (2021) Yue 18 Min Zhong No. 1774, Guangdong Provincial Labor Department Interim Provisions on Holiday Treatment and Death Pension Treatment for Employees of Enterprises in Guangdong Province (Yue Lao Xin [1997] No. 115), Sichuan Provincial Labor Department the Reply to the Provisions on Marriage and Bereavement Leave for Enterprise Employees (Chuan Lao Xian [1993] No. 95) (five days of bereavement leave, plus travel leave), Wang Shuqiang v. Shenzhen Weihua Cargo Transportation Co., Ltd. and other motor vehicle traffic accident liability disputes, Civil Judgment of Shenzhen Intermediate People's Court of Guangdong Province (2014) Shen Zhong Fa Min Zhong Zi No. 1055.

77. My wife is about to give birth. What are my paternity leave rights?

Answer: If you are an employee of an employer, you are entitled to paid paternity leave from your employer when your wife gives birth. The number of days of paternity leave varies from place to place: for example, 15 days in Guangdong and Shandong Provinces, and 20 days in Hunan and Sichuan Provinces.

The law does not clearly stipulate whether employees who do not take their entitled paternity leave should be compensated for the unused paternity leave as with unused annual leave pay. This is a legal issue that varies in different courts in different places. The Guangzhou Intermediate Court has a case in 2021 ordering employers to pay employees' unused paternity leave pay,[35] but Guangdong Provincial High Court, Beijing, Shanghai, and other courts have cases that do not support unused paternity leave pay.[36] Some judgments from courts in Beijing, Shenzhen City of Guangdong Province, and Changsha City of Hunan Province hold that the employer preventing use of paternity leave is a prerequisite for the obligation of unused paternity leave pay; that is, if an employee does not request paternity leave, the employer is not liable to pay unused paternity leave pay.[37]

This divergence is so stark that even within the same place or court, opposite judgments may occur. For example, in the case of Dai Yinping in 2021, the Shenzhen Intermediate Court held that the employer did not prevent the use of the paternity leave, so there was

---

35 Zeng Xianyu, Guangdong Haosheng Chaofeng Garments Co., Ltd. Labor Dispute Civil Judgment of Second Instance Civil Judgment of Guangzhou Intermediate People's Court of Guangdong Province (2021) Yue 01 Min Zhong No. 18784 (The court held that the pay for the employee who did not take paternity leave was calculated according to the normal wages based on the actual number of days of paternity leave not taken.)

36 Zhong Youhong and Shenlan Technology (Shanghai) Co., Ltd. Employment Contract Dispute Civil Case of Second Instance Civil Judgment Shanghai the First Intermediate People's Court Civil Judgment (2021) Hu 01 Min Zhong No. 10197. Yang Shouan, Civil Ruling on Labor Dispute Retrial Review and Trial Supervision of Dongjiang Mould (Shenzhen) Co., Ltd. Civil Ruling of Guangdong Provincial People's High Court (2020) No. 5442. "The law does not explicitly stipulate that in the case that workers have not taken or partially taken paternity leave, employers are obligated to unused paternity leave pay." Ma Huijie and Beijing Daxing District Maternal and Child Health and Family Planning Service Center Labor Dispute Second Instance Civil Judgment Beijing the Second Intermediate People's Court Civil Judgment (2021) Jing 02 Min Zhong No. 7662 (the court held that the employer had paid the monthly wage in full and did not need to pay the unused paternity leave pay separately). Civil Judgment of the Second Instance of Personnel Dispute between Han Shimin and Shenzhen Huacai Optoelectronics Co., Ltd. Civil Judgment of the Intermediate People's Court of Shenzhen City, Guangdong Province (2020) Yue 03 Min Zhong No. 4413 (the law does not stipulate that unused paternity leave must be compensated). Civil Judgment of First Instance on Employment contract Dispute between Wu Fei and Suzhou Aoteming Pharmaceutical Technology Co., Ltd. Civil Judgment of the People's Court of Suzhou Industrial Park, Jiangsu Province (2021) Su 0591 Minchu 14924.

37 Zhang Xin and Hunan Lanqiao Human Resources Group Co., Ltd. Civil Judgment of the Second Instance of Labor Dispute Civil Judgment of Changsha Intermediate People's Court of Hunan Province (2021) Hunan 01 Minzhong No. 12018. "Zhang Xin did not submit evidence to prove that the number of days he did not take paternity leave was caused by Lanqiao Company. Therefore, there is no factual and legal basis for Zhang Xin's request for Lanqiao Company to pay wages for the number of days of untaken paternity leave, and the Court does not support the claim." Labor Dispute between Dai Yinping and Shenzhen Chuangxiang Architectural Decoration Engineering Co., Ltd. Civil Judgment of Shenzhen Intermediate People's Court of Guangdong Province (2021) Yue 03 Minzhong No. 18348. In this case, the employee did not apply for the paternity leave, the company only paid normal wages, and the court found that the employee could not get unused paternity leave pay because he failed to prove that not taking it was due to the employer. Therefore, the employer does not need to pay additional wages for paternity leave. Civil Ruling of Jilin Provincial People's High Court (2021) Ji Min Shen No. 1541 (the court held that the untaken paternity leave was not because of the company's refusal, so the "overtime wage" of paternity leave was not upheld). Civil Judgment of the Second Instance of Labor Dispute between Chongji Technology (Beijing) Co., Ltd. and Chen Yang Civil Judgment of the Third Intermediate People's Court of Beijing (2022) Jing 03 Min Zhong No. 1548 (the employee did not prove that his request for paternity leave was refused, so the unused paternity leave pay was not upheld).

no need to pay unused paternity leave pay; but in the case of Han Shimin in 2020, the same court held that the law did not stipulate that the employer must pay unused paternity leave. In another example, in the case of Ma Huijie in 2021, the Second Intermediate People's Court of Beijing held that since the employer paid the normal wages, it did not need to pay additional unused paternity leave pay; but in the case of Chen Yang in 2022, the Third Intermediate People's Court of Beijing implied that only when the application for paternity leave was rejected by the employer was the employer obligated to pay unused paternity leave pay.

If applicable, the method by which courts calculate unused paternity leave pay is generally based on the employee's normal daily wage rate. However, there are exceptional cases where the calculation is based on overtime wage at two times the normal rate.[38] Additionally, the right to claim unused paternity leave pay must be exercised within one year from the employee's wife's laboring date; otherwise, the limitation of arbitration shall be exceeded.

Employees on labor dispatch, assignment contract, or irregular or general work hours, except casual employees, should also be entitled to paid paternity leave.[39]

Note that paternity leave only applies to employees whose female wives give birth, as China does not recognize same-sex marriages. Furthermore, paid paternity leave only applies to lawful marriage and childbirth; for example, giving birth without marriage registration does not enable eligibility for paid paternity leave. Of course, employers are free to provide paid paternity leave to related employees beyond statutory provisions.

78. How do labor regulations stipulate the high-temperature allowance?

Answer: The high-temperature allowance is an additional allowance that employers under the employment laws should pay to employees working in designated high-temperature environments during the high-temperature season.

According to Article 17 of the Management Rules for Heatstroke Prevention and Cooling Measures in various parts of the country,[40] the payment of high-temperature allowances should meet the following conditions: first, the outdoor working environment for workers is 35°C or above, or the indoor working environment is 33°C or above; second, most provinces and cities ,including Beijing, Shanghai, Guangdong, etc., have stipulated restrictive conditions in specific high-temperature months. That is, employers are only obligated to pay high-temperature allowances if the aforementioned working environment temperatures are met during specific high-temperature months. However, certain provinces and cities, such as Tianjin, Chongqing, etc., do not have such restrictions, and

38 Dong Shiwei, Shandong Taishan Shengliyuan Glass Co., Ltd. and other civil judgments of the second instance of labor disputes Civil Judgment of the Intermediate People's Court of Tai'an City, Shandong Province (2022) Lu 09 Min Zhong No. 4164 (the court calculated it according to twice the normal wage for the number of days not taken, as the normal wages had already been paid).

39 Civil Judgment of First Instance of Labor Dispute between Jiao Xiaopeng and Beijing Branch of Breakthrough Lubricating Oil Co., Ltd. Civil Judgment of Beijing Daxing District People's Court (2019) Jing 0115 Min Chu No. 1870 (the employee is on the irregular work hour system and is entitled to take paternity leave).

40 Notice on the Management Rules for Heatstroke Prevention and Cooling Measures (the State Administration of Work Safety, the Ministry of Health, the Ministry of Human Resources and Social Security, and the All-China Federation of Trade Unions, An Jian Zong An Jian [2012] No. 89).

the payment of high-temperature allowances is based solely on temperature and not on specific months. Please refer to Table 3.2.

According to the aforementioned conditions, if the employer installs air conditioning equipment, employees working indoors generally do not have the right to receive high-temperature allowance, even if the local weather forecast predicts temperatures exceeding the specified 33°C standard. Employees engaged in outdoor night shifts during the high-temperature season are also unlikely to be able to claim high-temperature allowances.[41]

In cases where employees claim high-temperature allowances, they typically only need to provide local meteorological reports proving that the temperature has reached or exceeded 33°C (indoors) or 35°C (outdoors). If the employer argues against the obligation to pay high-temperature allowances, they must bear the onus to prove that the actual workplace temperature for the employee is lower than that temperature. For example, they may demonstrate that the workplace has air conditioning, resulting in indoor temperatures below 33°C, or that the outdoor temperature at the actual workplace or during the employee's work hours is below 35°C.[42]

The issue of the limitation of arbitration for employees seeking compensation for unpaid high-temperature allowances refers to how long employees have to make compensation claims after the months in which they were entitled to receive high-temperature allowances have passed (otherwise, they lose the opportunity for compensation). Currently, courts across the country, including the Guangdong Provincial High Court, Fujian Provincial High Court, Jiangsu Provincial High Court, etc., consider high-temperature allowances as special benefits, not part of labor remuneration. Therefore, they are strictly subject to the one-year limitation of arbitration.[43]

Judicial decisions apply a monthly and daily review against the limitation of arbitration for high-temperature allowances. For example, say Ms. Li filed a labor arbitration claim on August 20, 2024, asserting that her employer failed to pay her high-temperature allowances for June, July, and August 2023. If the employer pays her monthly wages on the 15th of next month , the labor arbitration committee would likely uphold Ms. Li's claim for the

41 Li Renlong, Dongguan Zhonghong Adhesive Products Co., Ltd. Labor Dispute Retrial Review and Trial Supervision Civil Ruling, Guangdong High People's Court Civil Ruling (2020) Yue Min Shen No. 2305. In this case, the court held: "Li Renlong confirmed his job position as a night shift security guard, working from 8:00 PM to 8:00 AM. He is not a high-temperature operation personnel and does not meet the conditions for receiving high-temperature allowances."

42 Case of Labor Dispute Application between Lai Fuling and Zhongshan Caixing Property Management Co., Ltd. Guangdong High People's Court Civil Ruling (2014) Yue Gao Fa Min Shen Zi No. 508. The court held that the worker must first prove that the labor provided meets the above conditions … Article 11 of the Management Measures for the Payment of High-Temperature Allowances jointly issued by the Guangdong Provincial Department of Human Resources and Social Security and other departments stipulates that employers must record the high-temperature works and the issuance of high-temperature allowances, and bears the burden of proof for such records. Case of Labor Dispute between Zhou Yusheng and Shenzhen Baodi Hardware Plastic Products Co., Ltd. Shenzhen Intermediate People's Court Civil Judgment (2016) Yue 03 Min Zhong Zi No. 3465. The court pointed out: "Baodi Company failed to provide evidence that the workplace temperature for Zhou Yusheng during August and September 2014 and June 2015 was below 33°C or that effective measures were taken to reduce the workplace temperature to below 33°C, and should bear the adverse consequences of failing to provide evidence."

43 Li Rongxing, Labor Dispute Retrial Review and Trial Supervision Civil Ruling, Fujian High People's Court Civil Ruling (2020) Min Shen No. 4539. Shang Yongjun, Labor Dispute Retrial Review and Trial Supervision Civil Ruling, Guangdong High People's Court Civil Ruling (2020) Yue Min Shen No. 9138. Le Guoyou v. Jiangsu Vocational College of Economics and Trade, Labor Dispute Case, Jiangsu High People's Court Civil Ruling (2017) Su Min Shen No. 1600.

Table 3.2 Nationwide high-temperature allowance rules

Regions	*Payment amount (RMB per month)*	*Payment period*
Beijing City	180 (outdoor) 120 (indoor)	June to August
Zhejiang Province	300 (outdoor) 200 (indoor)	June to September
Shanxi (山西) Province	240	June to August
Shanghai City	300	June to September
Tianjin City	12% of municipal average daily wages of previous year	June to September
Jiangsu Province	300	June to September
Liaojing Province	200	July to September
Fujian Province	260 (or 12 per day)	May to September
Inner Mongolia Autonomous Region	180	Days when temperature condition of working is met
Guangdong Province	300	June to October
Hunan Province	300	July to September
Guangxi Autonomous Region	250–300	June to October
Jiangxi Province	300 (outdoor) 200 (indoor)	Juneto September
Shandong Province	300 (outdoor) 180 (indoor)	June to September
Gansu Province	12 per day (outdoor or high-temperature work) 8 per day (other work)	June to September
Hubei Province	12 per day	June to September
Henan Province	10 per day	June to September
Shanxi (陕西) Province	25 per day	June to September
Hainan Province	10 per day	April to October
Yunnan Province	10 per day	Days when temperature condition of working is met
Jilin Province	200	June to August
Sichuan Province	10–18 per day in various regions	Days when temperature condition of working is met
Xinjiang Autonomous Region	10–20 per day	June to August
Ningxia Autonomous Region	12 per day (outdoor or high-temperature work) 8 per day (other work)	June to September
Chongqing City	No less than 5, 10, 15 per day (according to different temperature levels)	Days when temperature condition of working is met
Guizhou Province	8 per day or 168 per month	June to September

high-temperature allowance for August 2023, because her high-temperature allowance for August 2023 should have been paid on September 15, 2023, and she must file a labor arbitration claim for it before September 15, 2024, which she did. On the same principle, the arbitration claims for the high-temperature allowances for June and July 2023 have exceeded the one-year limitation of arbitration, because Ms. Li should have filed the claim for the June 2023 high-temperature allowance by July 15, 2024, and for the July 2023 high-temperature allowance by August 15, 2024.

It is important to note that employers are not allowed to substitute heatstroke prevention and cooling drinks for high-temperature allowances (Article 11 of the Management Rules). Additionally, the high-temperature allowance should not be included in the minimum wage standard (i.e., employees' wages after deducting high-temperature allowances should not fall below the minimum wage standard).

79. I am an employee. What is my work-break entitlement?

Answer: At present, the employment laws and relevant regulations do not provide for paid work-breaks, although work-breaks are statutory rights of employees. Judicial practices around the country generally treat work-breaks as unpaid.

The explanatory definition of Article 3 of the Labor Law, as indicated in the "Interpretation of the Labor Law of the People's Republic of China," which is compiled and published by the Legislative Affairs Commission of the Standing Committee of the National People's Congress in China, is as follows: "The rest time stipulated in the Labor Law includes work-breaks, rest time between two work days, weekend days, public holidays and annual leave, family visit leave, marriage and bereavement leave, personal leave, maternity leave, Sick leave, etc."

The book's interpretation of Article 38 of the Labor Law reads:

[T]he current type and content of rest times in our country are as follows: first, the rest time within a workday. It is referred to the time of work-break and meal-break during work hours in each work day, which is also called break-time. Work-break and meal-break vary depending on workers' job and work nature, typically taking 1 to 2 hours but no less than half an hour. Break time normally starts after 4 hours of consecutive work and is not considered paid work time. For those jobs that cannot apply fixed break time due to an unbroken production process, employees involved should still be arranged for a meal break … In other words, the definition does not consider work-break as work time and therefore not as paid break.

This problem is obscure in judicial practice. Limited decisions show that Chinese courts have held that work-breaks do not qualify as work hours. An interesting case is the 2016 Dou Hongbo case before the Suzhou Intermediate People's Court in Jiangsu Province, in which the judge implied that in his judgment, the nature of a work-break, that is, the time for employees to meet their physiological needs (going to the toilet), should be a paid interval or break.[44]

44 Dou Hongbo and Sanyo Electronic Parts (Suzhou) Co., Ltd., Labor Dispute Appeal, Civil Judgment of Intermediate People's Court of Suzhou City, Jiangsu Province (2016) Su 05 Min Zhong No. 9724. "Therefore, the Court holds that Sanyo Company has given employees the necessary time to solve their physiological needs and recover their physical strength outside the break time. Employees are free to use their rest time, engaging in activities unrelated to work and production, which should not be regarded as work hours." Wang Yanping and Shenzhen Shangpinxuan Culture Communication Co., Ltd. Labor Dispute Appeal Case Civil Judgment

For the right of female employees to take breaks under special protection, please see "89. What are the special protections for female employees under the employment laws?"

3.2 Sick Leave and Female Employee Rights

80. I am sick; how should I apply for leave from the employer?

Answer: An employee who falls ill and cannot go to work should endeavor to apply for sick leave, because this causes a certain degree of inconvenience and disruption to the employer's business operation, although absence due to sickness is understandable. Leave due to illness shall be handled in accordance with the company rules and regulations, employment contract agreements, and professional ethics.

Generally speaking, you should inform the employer of your illness by telephone, text message, or email as soon as possible, notifying the time when you can't go to work, requesting the number of days of sick leave, and providing hospital certificates such as sick leave forms. If the employee cannot notify the employer immediately due to illness, notification should be conducted as soon as possible when the condition is alleviated.

If an employee has the ability to notify the employer but delays or even does not notify the employer, they may have violated the company rules and regulations and may even lose the right to sick pay. For example, in the case of Yuan Hongye before the Second Intermediate People's Court of Beijing, the employee did not ask for leave from the employer after he was injured; the court held that the employee's notification to the employer was after the company terminated the employment relationship, so the claim for sick leave wage was not upheld.[45]

Of course, the employer should not be too harsh when the employee is really sick and should treat the employee's delayed leave leniently, respect the opinions of medical institutions, approve the employee's sick leave in time, and provide the employee with sick leave entitlements.

China's sick leave application practice reflects a strict cultural work discipline both in Asia and in China itself; even a half-day sick leave application is a necessary procedure. This is distinct from the lenient or soft work culture in Western countries such as New Zealand, in which only a notice of "feeling unwell" is required for a couple of days' sick leave.

of Shenzhen Intermediate People's Court of Guangdong Province (2014) Shenzhong Falao Zhong Zi No. 2432. "In addition, the attendance time on the attendance sheet is only recorded two items of sign-in and sign-out. Real work hours therefore are not reflected as the break time is not deducted." The Civil Ruling of Jiangsu High Court (2011) S.S.E.M.S.Z. No. 436 on the labor dispute case between Weng Yunzhong and Company A. "The applicant for retrial, Weng Yunzhong, claimed that the break time was overtime, which had no legal basis, and his application for retrial is not established."

45 Yuan Hongye and Diahs (Beijing) Multimedia Co., Ltd., in the case of labor dispute appeal, Beijing the Second Intermediate People's Court Civil Judgment (2015) No. 06925. "Because Yuan Hongye did not ask for leave in time and provide corresponding proof for the situation that he needed to take sick leave again because of his fall, and the time when he mailed the diagnosis certificate and the special certificate for sick leave to Dijes Company was also after Dijes Company made the decision to terminate the employment contract, therefore, it is not improper for the court of the first instance to reject Yuan Hongye claim of the sick leave pay from April 1, 2014 to April 11, 2014 and the wages from April 29, 2014 to May 14, 2014."

81. I am an employee. How many days of paid sick leave am I entitled to?

Answer: According to the 1994 Regulations on Medical Care Leave for Enterprise Employees with Illness or Non-Work-Related Injuries issued by the former Ministry of Labor, paid sick leave refers to the right of employees to receive paid time off when they are personally ill (excluding occupational diseases caused by work) or injured (excluding work-related injuries). The number of days allowed for paid sick leave is referred to as medical care leave.

Whether you are eligible for paid sick leave depends on the type of employee you belong to.

For full-time employees on standard hours, all employees are entitled to paid sick leave. However, the number of days of paid leave varies depending on the individual employee's total length of past employment services (accumulative service years) and consecutive length of employment with the current employer (service years for current employer).[46] The maximum total length of the first medical care leave when you fall ill for the first time in your current employment is determined by your total length of service (including service for other employers) and your consecutive length of service in the current employer. Please refer to Table 3.3 for more details prescribed by the former Ministry of Labor. Please note that the number of sick leave days to which an employee is entitled is calculated on a variable duration basis, not a calendar year.

It should be noted that each province and city may have specific local regulations regarding length of medical care leave. This table applies only to certain provinces and cities, such as Guangdong Province, including Shenzhen City, but other provinces and cities may have different rules regarding the number of days for medical care leave.

82. How should our company pay our employees during their sick leave?

Answer: Apart from the entitled number of days of medical care leave, the second issue is how employees' pay is treated during this period. In Shenzhen City, according to the Shenzhen City's Regulations on Wage Payment, the pay for employees during the medical care leave is set at 60% of their own wages.

Similarly, just as there are differences in the number of sick leave days among different regions, there are also slight variations in pay entitlements during medical care leave in different provinces and cities. For example, in Shandong Province, it is stipulated that within 180 days of illness, the pay entitlement is 70% of the employee's own wage. If the duration exceeds 180 days, it is 60% of the employee's own wage. In Zhejiang Province, the sick leave wage is determined based on whether the illness exceeds six months, ranging from 40% to 80% of the employee's own wage based on the total length of services.[47]

46 The accumulative service years refers to the actual service years referred to in the Regulations on Medical Care Leave for Enterprise Employees with Illness or Non-work-related Injuries, and it refers to the total accumulative length of service of the employee, including the periods with the current employer and other employers. Article 3 of the Reply of the General Office of the Ministry of Labor to the Request for Instructions on How to Understand "Continuous Service Years for the Same Employer" and "Service Years for Current Employer" (Lao Ban Fa [1996] 191). "When calculating medical care leave and economic compensation, 'Service Years for Current Employer' and 'Continuous Service years for the Same Employer' are the same concept. The medical care leave previously taken by an employee according to law shall not be deducted from them."

47 Shandong Provincial Department of Labor on forwarding Labor Ministry "Regulations on Medical Care Leave for Enterprise Employees with Illness or Non-work-related Injuries" (LuLaoFa [1995] 67). "Enterprise

Table 3.3 Medical care leave

Accumulative service years	*Service years for current employer*	*Medical care leave (months)*	*Computation duration (months)*
Less than 10 years	Less than 5 years	3	6
Less than 10 years	More than 5 years (inclusive) and less than 10 years	6	12
More than 10 years	Less than 5 years	6	12
More than 10 years (inclusive)	More than 5 years (inclusive) and less than 10 years	9	15
More than 10 years (inclusive)	More than 10 years (inclusive) and less than 15 years	12	18
More than 10 years (inclusive)	More than 15 years (inclusive) and less than 20 years	18	24
More than 10 years (inclusive)	More than 20 years	24	30

In Shanghai, it ranges from 40% to 100% of the employee's wage; in Chongqing from 60% to 95%; in Guangzhou from 45% to 70%. It should be noted that the employee's own wage should be based on the regular hours and does not include overtime pay.[48] The sick leave pay for employees in any region must not be lower than 80% of the local minimum wage standard.[49]

employees who are sick or non-work-related injured, during medical care leave, if the accumulative total of medical care leave does not exceed 180 days, the sick leave pay shall be at 70% of their wages; If the accumulative period exceeds 180 days, 60% of their wages." Zhejiang Province: Notice on Forwarding Regulations on Medical Care Leave for Enterprise Employees with Illness or Non-work-related Injuries of the Ministry of Labor (ZLXH [1995] No. 231). Notice of Shanghai Municipal Labor and Social Security Bureau on the Calculation of Sick Leave Wages, Notice of Shanghai Municipal Labor Bureau on Strengthening the Management of Sick Leave for Enterprise Employees and Guaranteeing the Life of Employees during Sick Leave (Hu Lao Bao Fa [95] No. 83). According to whether the sick leave exceeds half a year and the length of service, the employee's wages during the medical care leave are 40% to 100% of their wages. The Interim Provisions on the Treatment of Sick Leave for Employees of Enterprises in Chongqing (effective date: July 1, 2000). The wages during the medical care leave are 60% to 95% of the employee's wages, depending on whether the sick leave exceeds half a year and the length of continuous service. The Measures for the Implementation of the Management of the Medical Care Leave for Illness or Non-work-related Injury of Guangzhou Employees (Sui Lao Fu Zi [1998] No. 5). Depending on whether an employee takes sick leave for more than half a year within one-year period and their consecutive service years, the wages during the medical care leave are 45% to 70% of their wages.

48 Zhejiang Labor Department in Forwarding Ministry of Labor's "Regulations on Medical Care Leave for Enterprise Employees with Illness or Non-work-related Injuries" provides: "Employees who suffer illness or non-work-related injuries and whose accumulative sick leave is 6 months or less shall be paid medical care leave pay based on their continuous lengths of service. The standard is: if the continuous length of service is less than ten years, the pay is the employee's wages (excluding overtime wages, bonuses, allowances, and price living allowances)." Civil Judgment of the Second Instance of the Labor Dispute between Xu Aimei and the Power Department of Jinan Power Co., Ltd. of Sinotruk Group Civil Judgment of Jinan Intermediate People's Court of Shandong Province (2019) Lu 01 Min Zhong No. 7616. To Shenzhen Branch of Zhuofeigao Circuit Board (Qujiang) Co., Ltd. v. Wang Qiang Labor Dispute Case Civil Judgment of Qujiang District People's Court of Shaoguan City (2014) S.QF.M.Y.C.Z. No. 509.

49 Article 59 of the Opinions on Several Issues Concerning the Implementation of the Labor Law of the People's Republic of China, 1995. During the period when an employee is ill or non-work-related injured, the enterprise shall pay their sick leave wage or disease relief fee according to the relevant provisions during the

To explain how the number of sick leave days and the corresponding wages are calculated for an employee within a computation duration, let's consider a case study: Ms. Li, an employee in Shenzhen on a permanent employment contract, earns a monthly wage of RMB 5,000. Her total length of service is less than five years, and her length of service for the current employer is less than three years. Starting from March 11, 2023, she took sick leave.

According to the Medical Care Leave table set forth in "81. I am an employee. How many days of paid sick leave am I entitled to?", Ms. Li is entitled to a maximum of three months of sick leave within a six-month computation duration. In other words, within the 6-month period from March 11 to September 10, Ms. Li is entitled to a maximum accumulated 90 days or 3 months of sick leave. As long as her total sick leave days do not exceed 90 days, she can take sick leave in a single instance or multiple instances, and her wage during the medical care leave will be RMB 3,000 (5,000 * 60%).

If Ms. Li's wage is not RMB 5,000 but RMB 2,000, her sick leave wage would be RMB 1,200 if calculated at 60% (2,000 * 60%). According to the rule that the sick leave wage must not be lower than 80% of the local minimum wage standard, and since the minimum wage in Shenzhen is RMB 2,360 in 2023, the employee's sick leave wage should be RMB 1,888 (2,360 * 80%) instead of RMB 1,200.

It is important to note that after completion of a first sick leave computation duration, employees are still entitled to a new sick leave based on their current length of service. Using the above example, if Ms. Li falls ill again on a later date after September 10, 2023, such as October 12, her total length of service would still fall under the first tier, entitling her the same accumulated 90 days and a monthly wage of RMB 3,000 during any sick leave days in the period from October 12 to April 11 of the following year (6 months of computation duration).

83. Are casual employees and employees on irregular and general work hours entitled to paid sick leave?

Answer: Whether casual employees are entitled to sick leave, as full-time employees are, is not explicitly stated in the laws and regulations. Employers are only required to contribute to work injury insurance and bear the responsibility for work-related compensations for casual employees, without the obligation to contribute to other types of social insurance programs, including medical insurance. Currently, there are two different views in judicial practices regarding whether casual employees have the right to receive sick leave wage during medical care leave. Some courts, such as Chongqing, Jinan and Guangzhou courts, held that this right should not be denied to casual employees,[50] while some courts, such as Changsha and Shenyang courts, made contrary decisions.[51]

---

prescribed medical care leave. The sick leave wage or disease relief fee may be paid at a rate lower than the local minimum wage standard, but not at a rate lower than 80% of the minimum wage standard.

50 Civil Judgment of First Instance of Labor Dispute between Nanning Yijing Information Service Co., Ltd. and Yang Zhengqiu Civil Judgment of Huaiyin District People's Court of Jinan City (2020) Lu 0104 Min Chu No. 1725, Yang Min v. Chongqing Yujiang Taxi Co., Ltd. Labor Dispute Case Civil Judgment of People's Court of Banan District of Chongqing (2016) Yu 0113 14143 in the Early Republic of China, Labor Dispute Appeal Case between Guangzhou Midi Garments Co., Ltd. and Xiao Liudi, etc. Civil Judgment of Guangzhou Intermediate People's Court of Guangdong Province (2014) S.Z.F.M.Y.Z.Z. No. 7353.

51 Zhang Ning v. Liaoning Cui Xi Newcore Trading Co., Ltd. Employment Dispute Second-Instance Civil Judgment, Shenyang Intermediate People's Court of Liaoning Province, Civil Judgment (2019) Liao 01 Min

Where local regulations or court decisions support the entitlement of casual employees to medical care leave, these employees' pay during medical care leave should certainly refer to the pay to full-time employees as described above, but the issue of the number of days of leave is rarely discussed in detail in judicial decisions, and it may be necessary to refer to the number of days worked by the employee in proportion to the number of days worked by full-time employees.

The work systems of general work hours and irregular work hours are quasi-full-time work hour systems. Therefore, the entitlements of employees under these two systems for the medical care leave should refer to the aforementioned standards for full-time employees. Please see "81. I am an employee. How many days of paid sick leave am I entitled to?" and "75. How should our company pay our employees during their sick leave?"

84. How long can an employee with cancer take medical care leave?

Answer: Regarding the matter of medical care leave for employees with cancers or other special diseases, the former Ministry of Labor's 1994 "Notice on Implementing the Regulations on Medical Care Leave for Enterprise Employees with Illness or Non-work-related Injuries" has provided ambiguously for a 24-month medical care leave.[52]

This document and provisions have led to a huge divergence in the implementation of the 1994 Regulations on Medical Care Leave for Enterprise Employees with Illness or Non-work-related Injuries in China's judicial system on whether the accumulative service years should be taken into account to decide the 24-month medical care leave.

Henan Province, Chongqing City, Guangdong Province (including Shenzhen City), Xuancheng City of Anhui Province, Wuhan City of Hubei Province, Shanghai City, and other places still strictly follow the medical care leave form and do not recognize employees' automatic 24-month medical care leave when they suffer from cancer or a special disease, but must consider the accumulative service years of employees: for example, the case of Li Siwei of Jiangmen before Guangdong Provincial High Court in 2018, the case of Jiang Meizhou before Shenzhen Intermediate Court in 2018, and the case of Zhongding Seiko Technology Company before Xuancheng Intermediate Court of Anhui Province in 2022.[53]

Zhong No. 14332. Li v. Hunan Limousine Co., Ltd, Changsha Intermediate People's Court Civil Judgment (2011) Chang Zhong Min 04 Zhong Zi No. 0338.

52 Original Ministry of Labor in Notice on the Implementation of "Regulations on Medical Care Leave for Enterprise Employees with Illness or Non-work-related Injuries" (Laobufa [1995] 236) (hereafter referred to as "the notice of medical care leave") made further explanatory provision that "for those employees suffering from special diseases (such as cancer, mental disease, and paralysis) and who cannot recover within 24 months, their medical care leave may be extended upon approval by their employer and labor administrative authority."

53 In 2015, the Shanghai Municipal Government issued the Regulations on the Standard of Medical Care Leave for Workers Suffering from Illness or Non-work-related Injuries during the Implementation of Employment Contracts (Hu Fu Fa [2015] No. 40), which stipulates that "the medical care leave shall be set according to the service years of the workers in the employers. If a worker is identified by the Labor Capacity Appraisal Committee as completely incapacitated but does not meet the conditions for retirement or resignation, the medical care leave shall be extended. The extended medical care leave shall be specifically agreed upon by the employer and the worker, but the total period of the extended medical care leave and the medical care leave stipulated in the preceding article shall not be less than 24 months." The Notice on the Opinions on Several Issues Concerning the Implementation of the Interim Provisions on the Treatment of Sick Leave for Employees of Enterprises in Chongqing (Yu Lao Ban Fa [2000] 233) stipulates that "for some employees suffering from special diseases (such as cancer, mental illness, paralysis, etc.), if they can not recover within the medical care leave they have taken, appropriate extension of medical care leave shall be approved by the enterprise and the administrative departments of labor and social security in the districts and counties (cities) where they are located. In principle, the extended medical care leave shall not exceed the original medical

However, courts in Beijing, Shanghai, Anhui Province (Huaibei City, Chuzhou City, Huainan City, and Tongling City), Jiangsu Province (Provincial People's High Court, Nanjing City, Xuzhou City, and Wuxi City), Changsha City of Hunan Province, Xinjiang (Provincial People's High Court and Urumqi City), and other places hold a completely opposite view, ruling that as long as employees suffer from a cancer or special disease, they can get 24 months of medical care leave regardless of their total length of service.[54]

Another question is what the scope of special diseases is for the latter approach (that is, regardless of the total length of service, employees with cancer or special diseases shall get 24 months). The special diseases referred to in the 1994 notice of the former Ministry of Labor simply stipulated three situations: cancer, mental illness, or paralysis. Are there other similar diseases that can also be regarded as special diseases? According to decisions from courts around the country, there are other diseases, including secondary pneumonia, paraplegia, and even hemiplegia, that fall under the scope of special diseases.[55] Employees with these diseases shall be given a 24-month medical care leave.

care leave." Li Siwei, Civil Ruling of Employment Contract Dispute Retrial Review and Trial Supervision of Jiangmen New Hengda Economic and Trade Co., Ltd. Civil Ruling of Guangdong Provincial People's High Court (2018) Yue Min Shen No. 1994, Jiang Meizhou, Civil Judgment of Second Instance of Labor Dispute of Shenzhen Shenkeda Intelligent Equipment Co., Ltd. Civil Judgment of Shenzhen Intermediate People's Court of Guangdong Province (2018) Yue 03 Min Zhong 20373, Wang v. Anhui Zhongding Precision Technology Co., Ltd. Guangde Branch Labor Dispute Civil Judgment of Second Instance Anhui Xuancheng Intermediate People's Court Civil Judgment (2022) Wan 18 Min Zhong No. 1419, Anhui Yaxia Industrial Co., Ltd., Yu Wenting and other civil judgments of the second instance of labor disputes, Anhui Xuancheng Intermediate People's Court Civil Judgment (2022) Wan 18 Min Zhong No. 2800. "When read with the context of the notice, the 'appropriate extension of medical care leave' stipulated in Article 2 is a flexible provision for the maximum medical care leave of 24 months in Article 3 of the Regulations on Medical Care Leave for Enterprise Employees with Illness or Non-work-related Injuries; Moreover, 'appropriate extension of medical care leave' needs to meet the conditions of 'approval by enterprises and competent labor administrative authorities', which does not mean that 'workers suffering from special diseases (such as cancer, mental diseases, paralysis, etc.)' are entitled to a 24-month medical care leave regardless of their service years and conditions."

54 Beijing Century Yongxin Automobile Repair Co., Ltd. and other, civil judgments of the second instance of labor disputes Civil Judgment of the First Intermediate People's Court of Beijing (2021) Jing 01 Min Zhong No. 8724. In this case, the employee suffered from a cancer, the employer dismissed the employee after nearly two years, and the employee sued for punitive damages. The court held that the medical care leave for cancer was 24 months. Huang Huiying v. Shenzhen Huaziyi Industrial Development Co., Ltd. Shanghai Branch, Employment Contract Dispute Appeal Case Shanghai the First Intermediate People's Court Civil Judgment (2017) Hu 01 Min Zhong No. 9536. Anhui Jingxin Electronics Co., Ltd., v. Ma, Civil Judgment of the Intermediate People's Court of Huaibei City, Anhui Province (2022) No. 127. The court held that: "regardless of the actual service years, as long as the disease can not be cured within the prescribed medical care leave, the medical care leave can be extended, and the extended medical care leave does not exceed 24 months. It does not need to be approved by the enterprise or the competent labor administrative authority." Huainan Bole Human Resources Management Co., Ltd., v. Rongjun, Labor Dispute Second Instance Civil Judgment Anhui Huainan Intermediate People's Court Civil Judgment (2020) Wan 04 Min Zhong No. 1400. Nanjing Liuhe Branch of Xuzhou Enhua Unified Pharmaceutical Chain Sales Co., Ltd. v. Liu Xiaohong, Nanjing Intermediate People's Court of Jiangsu Province (2020) Su 01 Min Zhong No. 6592. People's Government of Wusong Town, Yian District, Tongling City v. Peng Qian, Tongling Intermediate People's Court of Anhui Province (2020) Wan 07 Min Zhong No. 236. Wei v. Chutian Science and Technology Co., Ltd., Civil Judgement of Changsha Intermediate People's Court of Hunan Province (2019) Xiang 01 Min Zhong No. 11739. Jiangsu Tongmao Industrial Co., Ltd. v. Zhou Labor Dispute Second Instance Civil Judgment Jiangsu Xuzhou Intermediate People's Court Civil Judgment (2019) Su 03 Min Zhong No. 7827. Yan Yu v. Jiangsu Taikun Information Service Co., Ltd., Civil Judgment of Intermediate People's Court of Wuxi City, Jiangsu Province (2019) Su 02 Min Zhong No. 3798. He & Li, Civil Judgment (2017) Xin 01 Min Zai No. 75 of Intermediate People's Court of Urumqi, Xinjiang Uygur Autonomous Region. Li Shubao v. Huai'an Rongsheng Yuantong Express Co., Ltd. Civil Judgment (2017) Su Min Zai No. 315 of High Court of Jiangsu Province.

55 Guizhou Jinxing Gold Mining Co., Ltd. v. Zhang Xilong, Civil Judgment of the Second Instance of Employment Contract Dispute of the Intermediate People's Court of Buyi and Miao Autonomous Prefecture in

Therefore, how long the medical care leave should be granted to an employee suffering from a cancer depends on the province or city where the company is located or where the employment is performed. If the company or the employment performance is in the province or city where the first approach is taken, the employee can obtain a total number of days of medical care leave according to the table of medical care leave, taking into account the employee's accumulative service years and service years for the current employer. If the company or the employment performance is in the provinces or cities applying the second practice, the employee should be given 24 months of medical care leave directly if the employee's disease is within the scope of special diseases or cancers. Of course, if the employer has strong financial ability, it can also give the employee treatment beyond the legal standard to help the unfortunate employee.

85. What should I do if an employee of my company has not recovered after the expiration of the medical care leave?

Answer: The law stipulates that the purpose of the medical care leave for illness or non-work-related injuries is on the one hand, to ensure employees' entitlements to medical care leave during the period of treatment for the sickness or injuries and on the other hand, to set an upper limit of liability for the employer, so that the employer can conditionally and legally terminate the employment relationship after the expiration of the medical care leave.

If an employee has not recovered after the expiration of the medical care leave, the following situations may occur.

The first situation is that the employee does not have a medical certificate to continue treatment, including circumstances where the employee has recovered or the employee just personally feels that he has not recovered. In this case, in principle, the employee should return to work. The employee should abide by company rules and regulations and should not unreasonably refuse to work. Of course, the employer can also consider the possibility that the employee may not recover physically and adjust the position of the employee based on their ability when necessary. If the employee's employment contract has expired at this time, the company can terminate the employment relationship.

The second situation is that the employee has a medical certificate requiring continuous treatment, but no application for labor capacity appraisal has been submitted. The most common situation is that although the employee has a medical certificate that requires recuperation or treatment, it does not show that the employee is disabled. At this time, from the legal point of view, the employer can be regarded as having exhausted its obligations through the employee's medical care leave, and can terminate the contract according to Article 40 of the Employment Contract Law. That is, the company must first arrange a position transfer for the employee, and if the employee is still not competent for the job, the company can terminate the employment relationship and pay economic

---

Southwest Guizhou Province (2020) Qian 23 Min Zhong Zi No. 1957. The court held that: "not only limited to cancer, mental disease, and paralysis, but also includes other special diseases that are difficult to recover within 24 months. Zhang Xilong's secondary pneumonia could not be cured within 24 months and should also be included in the scope." Ding Wei v. Chuzhou Public Resources Trading Center, Labor Dispute Second Instance Civil Judgment Chuzhou Intermediate People's Court of Anhui Province Civil Judgment (2021) Wan 11 Min Zhong No. 733 (lower limb paraplegia). Huang v. Anhui Kezheng New Materials Co., Ltd., Civil Judgment of Second Instance of Labor Dispute of Civil Judgment of Xuancheng Intermediate People's Court of Anhui Province (2020) Wan 18 Min Zhong No. 1302 (Hemiplegia Caused by Cerebral Hemorrhage).

compensation. Please refer to "164. How do I calculate economic compensation?" If the employee's employment contract has expired at this time, the company can also terminate the employment relationship on the grounds of contract expiration.

When the employer implements the aforementioned procedure of position transfer and termination, the employee may not be able to go to work because he has not recovered. At this time, the employer shall not terminate the employee's employment relationship for serious violation of company rules and regulations in principle; otherwise, it may constitute illegal dismissal.[56] The correct practice for the employer is to terminate the job on the ground that the employee has not recovered sufficiently to return to work after the position transfer, being heath-incompetent for the job, and the employer pays the employee economic compensation. Of course, if the employee still unreasonably refuses to communicate with the employer after the employer reaches out, and also refuses to negotiate the return and position transfer, the employer can also dismiss the employee for serious violation of company rules and regulations.

It should be noted that if the employee has obviously lost part or all of their labor capacity, the employer should apply for, or remind the employee to apply for and cooperate with, the labor capacity appraisal (even if the fixed-term employment contract has expired), instead of directly terminating the employee's employment contract on the ground of the aforementioned medical care leave expiration.[57] Of course, if the employee refuses to cooperate with the appraisal after the employer has applied for the labor capacity appraisal and does not return to work, this may also constitute a serious violation of company rules and regulations, and the employee may be legally terminated.[58]

---

56 Appeal of labor dispute between Yichang Yiren Human Resource Service Co., Ltd. and Deng Qingsong Civil Judgment of Intermediate People's Court of Yichang City, Hubei Province (2015) E Yichang Zhong Min San Zhong Zi No. 00058.

57 Civil Judgment of the Second Instance of the Labor Dispute between Guang'an Security Group Co., Ltd. and Liu Jianguo Civil Judgment of the Intermediate People's Court of Guang'an City, Sichuan Province (2020) Chuan 16 Min Zhong No. 1371. In this case, the court held that after the expiration of the medical care leave for acute stroke, the employee was dismissed directly according to his health incompetence at the expiration of the medical care leave without assessing the necessity for labor capacity appraisal, and that was an illegal dismissal. Sheyang Yongan Machinery Co., Ltd. and Zhou Juntao Labor Dispute Appeal Case Jiangsu Yancheng Intermediate People's Court Civil Judgment (2018) Su 09 Min Zhong No. 192. In this case, after the expiration of the medical care leave of an employee suffering from schizophrenia, the employer dismissed the employee on the grounds of health incompetence after the expiration of the medical care leave without applying for labor capacity appraisal. The court held that this constituted illegal dismissal. However, there are also cases to the contrary. Gangyongde and Liaoning Shiling Property Co., Ltd. Huanggu Branch Labor Dispute Second Instance Judgment, Liaoning Shenyang Intermediate People's Court Civil Judgment (2022) Liao 01 Minzhong No. 11945. In the case, the employee's labor capacity due to cerebral hemorrhage was identified as total incapacity. Before the conclusion of the appraisal, the employer terminated the employment contract by paying economic compensation and payment in lieu of notice on the ground of health incompetence at the end of the medical care leave. The court held that workers who have lost their labor capacity should withdraw from their roles, indicating that the law allows employers to terminate their employment contracts according to law. Moreover, the employee had initiated employment arbitration to claim punitive damages for the termination of the employment contract before the conclusion of the labor capacity appraisal, indicating that he recognized the fact that the employment contract had been terminated and he did not advocate the restoration of the employment relationship. Therefore, the conclusion of the labor capacity appraisal cannot prevent the company from exercising the right to terminate the contract according to law before that. We believe that the real reason is not that the employer has the right to terminate before the appraisal conclusion, but that the employee has recognized the fact of termination by claiming punitive damages for illegal termination, rendering the employee's abandonment of the entitlements after the labor capacity appraisal.

58 Civil Judgment of the Second Instance of the Labor Dispute between Wang Xiuhong and Beijing Muleidi Fashion Co., Ltd. Civil Judgment of the Third Intermediate People's Court of Beijing (2022) Jing 03

The third situation is that the employee has obtained a labor capacity appraisal. If the appraisal result confirms that there is no disability, the employer may require the employee to return to their position, or the employer may consider the possibility that the employee has not physically recovered and then transfer them to an appropriate job according to Article 40 of the Employment Contract Law. If the employee still refuses or is not competent for the job, the employer may terminate the contract. If the employee's employment contract has expired at this time, the company can also terminate the employment relationship on the ground of contract expiration. If the employee is identified as disabled, they shall proceed with illness-retirement or a position transfer according to the disability level of the employee. Please refer to "86. The labor capacity appraisal has a conclusion after my medical care leave expires. What should I do?"

The fourth situation is that the employee has applied for labor capacity appraisal, or has applied for extension of medical treatment due to a medical entity's requirement for further treatment or special diseases (such as cancer, mental illness, or paralysis), and is currently waiting for the appraisal conclusion or approval of extension of medical treatment.[59] In this case, even if the employee's fixed-term contract has expired, the employer shall not terminate the employment relationship and shall continue to pay the employee's wage according to the standard of medical care leave. Please see "75. How should our company pay our employees during their sick leave?"

We have observed that the treatment of employment relationships after the expiration of employees' medical care leave for illness and non-work-related injury lacks legal rules, causing uncertainties in practice. This situation is very similar to the treatment of employment relationships after the expiration of work-related injury leave for work-related injuries and occupational diseases.

86. The labor capacity appraisal has a conclusion after my medical care leave expires. What should I do?

Answer: The standard for labor capacity appraisal for employees who suffer illnesses or non-work-related injuries is the same as that applying to the appraisal for employees who suffer work-related injuries or occupational diseases. The conclusions of these appraisals reflect the state of employees' labor capacities or disability levels.

According to the 1994 Regulations on Medical Care Leave for Enterprise Employees with Illness or Non-work-related Injuries, employers shall handle employment relationships between the two parties in accordance with the results of the employees' labor capacity appraisal disability level.

The first situation is that the result found no disability. Employees have no right to request the entitlements of disability from the employer. Both parties may continue to perform the employment contract or terminate the contract. If the employer terminates the

Min Zhong No. 8532. "After the expiration of the medical care leave, Wang Xiuhong refused to go to work and refused to cooperate with the labor capacity appraisal, so the termination of the employment relationship with Wang XiuHong is legal."

59 Article 76 of the Opinions on Several Issues Concerning the Implementation of the Labor Law of the People's Republic of China by the Ministry of Labor. "For some employees who suffer from special diseases (such as cancer, mental illness, paralysis, etc.) and who cannot recover within 24 months, the medical care leave may be extended appropriately with the approval of the enterprise and the local labor administrative authority."

employment relationship because the employee is health-incompetent for the work after the expiration of the medical care leave, it shall pay economic compensation.

The second circumstance is that the labor capacity appraisal conclusion shows a disability class of 1 to 4. The employer can terminate the medical care leave, arrange for the employee to stand down from the job, and then terminate the employment. The employee shall proceed with a medical retirement due to illness or non-work-related injury and begin to receive retirement benefits. Employers do not need to pay economic compensation for the termination of such employment contracts.[60]

The third circumstance is that the labor capacity appraisal conclusion shows a disability class of 5 to 10. The employer can terminate the employment contract, pay economic compensation (1 year of service equals a month's wage, plus 30-day prior notice or payment for notice in lieu) and medical treatment allowance (not less than 6 months of wages). Please refer to "153. Under what circumstances should our company pay medical treatment allowance to our employees?" and "164. How do I calculate economic compensation?"

Of course, if employees or employers are not satisfied with the conclusion of the labor capacity appraisal, they have the right to apply to the provincial labor capacity appraisal committee for re-appraisal within 15 days after receiving the conclusion of the appraisal.[61]

If the employer violates the above obligations to terminate the employment contract of an injured or sick employee, it shall be liable for punitive damages. Please refer to "165. How do I calculate punitive damages for illegal termination of the employment relationship?" If an employer illegally terminated the employment contract of an employee whose labor capacity is assessed to be within Class 5 to 10, for example, it did not comply with the aforementioned position transfer procedure, it shall also bear the liability of punitive damages and medical treatment allowance.

87. I suffer from a chronic illness and am currently in a lawsuit with my employer. Must I go to work?

Answer: An employee must abide by the employer's company rules and regulations during the employment relationship. If you are sick and unable to go to work, you should communicate with your employer in a timely manner and provide a medical leave certificate from the medical institution so that you may take leave and get sick leave treatments.

Violation of such rules, even if you are really sick and unable to go to work, is a violation of the company rules and regulations, or even if the company rules and regulations do not so stipulate, is also a violation of professional ethics. The employer has the right to impose disciplinary action on you or even dismiss you in accordance with the company rules and regulations or the employment laws.

For example, in the case of Peng Weiming before Jiangsu Provincial High Court in 2021, the employee suffered from hemiplegia caused by sudden cerebral infarction during

60 Civil Judgment of the Second Instance of the Labor Dispute between Zhao and Zhao Zhigang Civil Judgment of the Intermediate People's Court of Hefei City, Anhui Province (2019) Wan 01 Min Zhong No. 1319. The court held that the employee was completely incapable of working with disability level between Class 1 and 4, and there was no need to pay economic compensation for the medical retirement.

61 Article 16 of the Measures for the Administration of Labor Capacity Appraisal of Injured Workers in 2014.

his security work, did not return to work for a long time during the course of an employment dispute case, and did not follow the sick leave procedure. Duhui Property Company terminated the employment relationship for serious violation of company rules and regulations. The court held that the termination was valid.[62] The case shows that employees should abide by company rules and regulations such as leave of absence even if they are ill due to work reasons.

Of course, in practice, if the employer makes unreasonable use of company rules and regulations and takes too harsh disciplinary measures against sick employees, it is also illegal. The employer should reasonably consider the employee's illness and the possibility and ability of communication between the employee and the employer, give the employee a fair grace period, and take the initiative to contact and take care of the sick employee. The employee, even if they are injured at work or suffer from an occupational disease, should keep communicating with the employer and provide medical treatment or medical assessment information to the employer in time.

It should be noted that employees are not necessarily entitled to sick leave treatment even if they have a sick leave certificate from the hospital. Please refer to "85. What should I do if an employee of my company has not recovered after the expiration of the medical care leave?"

88. I'm a pregnant employee. What are my rights?

Answer: Most types of female employees, including those on irregular or general work hours and the full-time standard hours system, are entitled to the same protections for female workers, including special protection for female workers, prenatal examination, maternity leave, and expenses related to childbirth.

Article 6 of Special Provisions on Labor Protection for Female Employees provides that pregnant female workers' antenatal examination time is deemed to be work hours. Therefore, employers should agree to a female employee's request for reasonable leave for prenatal examination, including routine prenatal examinations arranged by medical institutions and additional prenatal examinations because the employee feels unwell, and pay the employee normal wages during the prenatal examinations.

According to the Special Provisions on Labor Protection for Female Employees, a female employee is entitled to 98 days of paid maternity leave, including 15 days of prenatal leave; in the case of dystocia, the maternity leave is increased by 15 days (but 30 days are added in Guangdong Province, including Shenzhen City); in the case of multiple births, the maternity leave is increased by 15 days for each additional baby. For example, if a female employee in Shenzhen has dystocia and has triplets, the employee is entitled to 158 days of paid maternity leave (98 + 30 + 2 * 15). The definition of dystocia is generally based on hospital discharge records. At present, some court decisions have considered

62 Peng Weiming and Nanjing Duhui Property Management Co., Ltd. Labor Dispute Appeal, Application for Civil Ruling Jiangsu Provincial People's High Court Civil Ruling (2021) No. 1061. The employee suffered from hemiplegia caused by sudden cerebral infarction during security work, did not return to work for a long time during the labor dispute period, and did not follow a sick leave procedure. After that, Duhui Property Company terminated the employment relationship for serious violation of company rules and regulations. The court held that the termination was legal and effective.

cesarean section and the use of fetal aspiration as dystocia,[63] and lateral incision is not necessarily recognized as dystocia.[64]

According to the aforementioned provisions, a female employee who miscarries after less than 4 months of pregnancy is entitled to 15 days of paid maternity leave; a female employee who miscarries after more than 4 months of pregnancy is entitled to 42 days of paid maternity leave.

The maternity leave pay rate for a female employee is an individual wage that is equal to the average wages from the 12 months before her maternity leave. For an employee under maternity insurance, the Maternity Insurance Fund shall pay maternity allowance at the average monthly wage of all employees of the employer in the previous year. The shortfall between the maternity allowance and the individual wage shall be compensated to the employee by the employer;[65] the excess the employee receives shall be paid to the employer. However, if the employer is in a state of shutdown, the maternity leave pay of the employee shall be calculated according to the standard shutdown wage.[66] The cost of prenatal examination and medical expenses for childbirth shall be borne by the Social Insurance Bureau, but if the employer has not purchased maternity insurance for its employees, these expenses shall be borne by the employer.[67]

Article 9 of the Special Provisions on Labor Protection for Female Employees stipulates that employers shall not arrange overtime work or night shifts for female workers who are breastfeeding infants under one year of age. Employers should arrange one hour of lactation time for breastfeeding female employees during each day's work hours, and female employees who give birth to multiple children shall be granted an additional one-hour lactation time for each additional child. Lactation time is considered paid work hours.

In principle, a female pregnant part-time employee should be given the same special protection for female employees, including paid prenatal examination, one hour of breastfeeding, rest between work shifts, etc. However, since her employer is not obligated to contribute to maternity insurance for the employee (only to work injury insurance), the employer does not need to provide maternity leave benefits for the employee.

63 Hunan Runzhi Jinfu Information Technology Co., Ltd., Xiao Jing Labor Dispute Civil Judgment of Second Instance Civil Judgment of Changsha Intermediate People's Court of Hunan Province (2021) Xiang 01 Min Zhong No. 10659. Civil Judgment of Second Instance of Labor Dispute between Shenzhen Sanlida Electrical Appliance Technology Co., Ltd. and Zhao Genhui Civil Judgment of Shenzhen Intermediate People's Court of Guangdong Province (2019) Guangdong 03 Minzhong No. 28210. Civil Judgment of First Instance of Labor Dispute between Changle Aijie Stomatological Hospital and Guo Fengjuan Civil Judgment of People's Court of Changle County, Shandong Province (2020) Lu 0725 Min Chu No. 1904.

64 Civil Judgment of Second Instance of Labor Dispute Case between Chen Xinzhu and Liaoning Tianhao Drinks Co., Ltd. Civil Judgment of Shenyang Intermediate People's Court of Liaoning Province (2019) Liao 01 Min Zhong No. 2373.

65 Civil Ruling on Labor Dispute Retrial Review and Trial Supervision of Yangliu and Huatai Innovation Asset Management (Tianjin) Co., Ltd. Civil Ruling of Beijing High Court (2021) Jing Min Shen No. 5071.

66 Civil Judgment on Labor Dispute Retrial of Wu and Xiamen Cele Industrial Co., Ltd. Civil Judgment of Fujian Provincial People's High Court (2019) Min Min Zai No. 312.

67 The second paragraph of Article 8 of the Special Provisions on Labor Protection for Female Employees stipulates: "the medical expenses for childbirth or abortion of female workers shall be paid from the maternity insurance fund for those who have already participated in maternity insurance in accordance with the items and standards stipulated in the maternity insurance, and shall be paid by the employer for those who have not participated in maternity insurance."

89. What are the special protections for female employees under the employment laws?

Answer: According to the Special Provisions on Labor Protection for Female Employees, employers must not cut the pay of, terminate the employment contract of, or dismiss female employees because they are pregnant, have given birth, or are feeding infants.

For employees who have been pregnant for over seven months, the employer must not arrange overtime work or night shifts and shall provide appropriate work-breaks for them. Employers shall also refrain from scheduling overtime and night shifts for lactating employees. All other categories of female employees should receive the same protection.

In particular, an employer must not terminate the employment relationship with a full-time female employee in the three protected periods (pregnancy, maternity, and lactation) in accordance with the provisions of Articles 40 and 41 of the Employment Contract Law (including the grounds of health incompetence and ability incompetence, major change in objective situation, and economic redundancy). Any fixed-term employment contract with a female employee in the three protected periods shall not be dissolved on the ground of contract expiration unless and until her three protected periods expire.

The same employment security protection shall apply to female employees on irregular and general work hours, labor dispatch, and assignment contract. Female part-time employees, however, are not necessarily under the protection, as both parties may terminate the employment relationship at any time in accordance with the Employment Contract Law.

90. Female employees earn less than male employees. Does the employer violate the principle of equal pay for equal work?

Answer: Employees engaged in the same or similar work should receive the same or close remuneration. This is called equal pay for equal work in China's employment law. The Employment Contract Law has two rules on equal pay for equal work: the first is that an employee's remuneration should be determined first, by the provisions in the employment contract, second, by collective contract in absence of the provisions, and third, by the principle of equal pay for equal work in the absence of the former two (Articles 11 and 18).

The second is that employees on labor dispatch receive equal pay for work equal to that which normal employees do (Article 63). Additionally, Articles 41 and 42 of the 2022 Law on the Protection of Women's Rights and Interests also stipulate that gender discrimination against women in labor and social security is prohibited.

Judging from relevant judicial decisions, the cases that found no violation of equal pay for equal work and rejected claims for wage discrepancies account for an absolute majority. Only in a few cases, such as the case of Liu Li before Heilongjiang Provincial High Court in 2018 and the case of Yang Quanyou before Shihezi City Court in Xinjiang in 2016, did the courts find that the employers violated the principle of equal pay for equal work.[68]

68 Liu Li, Harbin Radio and Television Station Labor Dispute Retrial Review and Trial Supervision Civil Ruling Heilongjiang Provincial People's High Court Civil Ruling (2018) Hei Min Shen No. 3392. This is a rare case; the court remitted the case for retrial on the ground that the comparative position employee's wages items were different from those of the plaintiff workers and that the principle of equal pay for equal work was violated. Labor Dispute between Yang Quanyou and Shihezi Zhongyuan Labor Dispatch Co., Ltd. Civil Judgment (2016) Bing 9001 Min Chu No. 6016 of the People's Court of Shihezi City, Xinjiang Uygur Autonomous

There are many reasons for courts not finding violation of equal pay for equal work in legal practice. The first situation is that some courts found that employees failed to prove the nature of their roles to be the same as that of the comparative roles, or that even if a role was similar, the qualifications and experience of the two were different. While the employee had agreed upon the wages in their employment contract, there was no violation of the principle of equal pay for equal work.

In the second situation, some courts held that equal pay for equal work does not mean exactly the same pay, and that a reasonable difference should not be regarded as a violation of equal pay for equal work, if the nature of the role and the seniority of the employee and the comparator employee are taken into account,[69] or directly ruled that agreement in the employment contract prevails over the principle of equal pay for equal work under the Article 11 of the Employment Contract Law.

The third situation is the common phenomenon where employees inside and outside establishments, such as state-owned companies or other business organizations, normally receive unequal pay in reality. Many court cases have explicitly stated that employment contracts within the establishment are incomparable to those of outsiders.[70] This sad reality in the current employment relationship system probably stems from the convention in the past hierarchical employment management system.

3.3 Employers Handling Work Injuries

91. What circumstances should be identified as work injuries?

Answer: Work injury determination is an administrative procedure conducted by social insurance agencies to examine the causes of employee injuries or occupational diseases and their relevance to their work. If it is determined to be a work injury (including occupational disease), the employee shall be entitled to work injury treatments; otherwise, the employee can only claim medical treatments for illness or non-work-related injury.

Work injury determination is a complex issue in practice, and it includes the following situations.

Region. The court held that the employer implemented different annual wages for permanent workers and contract workers, which violated the principle of equal pay for equal work, and the court supported the request for wage difference.

69 Du Zhiwei and Guangzhou Public Security Bureau Liwan District Branch Organ Service Center Labor Dispute Retrial Case, Guangdong Provincial People's High Court Civil Ruling (2017) No. 852. Harbin Pharmaceutical Group Pharmaceutical General Factory v. Lv Xinyou Labor Dispute Case, Heilongjiang Provincial People's High Court Civil Ruling (2015) No. 208, Heilongjiang Province. Labor Dispute Case of Tao Baoping v. Jiangsu Hongyun Property Management Co., Ltd. Civil Judgment of Gangzha District People's Court of Nantong City, Jiangsu Province (2017) Su 0611 Min Chu No. 1108.

70 Civil Ruling on Labor Dispute Retrial Review and Trial Supervision of Xiong Yan and Gongan County Experimental Kindergarten Civil Ruling of the High Court of Hubei Province (2015) E Min Shen Zi No. 00971. Civil Ruling on Labor Dispute Retrial Review of Yang Chunhai and Siping Local Taxation Bureau Civil Ruling of the High Court of Jilin Province (2016) Ji Min Shen Zi No. 92. Wang Ling v. Xiangxi Tujia and Miao Autonomous Prefecture Central Sub-branch of the People's Bank of China and other labor disputes, Hunan Provincial People's High Court Civil Ruling (2016) Xiang Min Shen No. 1344. The court held that the dispatched employees could not be compared with the employees regulated by the bank management law within the establishment. Civil Ruling of Qinghai High Court (2022) Qing Min Shen No. 541. "But the relationship between the respondent and the applicant is an employment relationship, not a civil servant relationship. The wage distribution system of government institutions is different from that of enterprises."

The first situation is the most typical work-related injuries, including accidental injuries and occupational diseases that occur in workplaces during work time for work reasons.

The second is accidental injuries related to travel for work, including on the way to and from work on normal routes, or on out-of-office work, or on business trips. Under the Regulations on Work Injury Insurance and the relevant interpretation of the Supreme Court, a traffic accident on the way to or from work is deemed to be a work-related injury if it occurs at a reasonable time and on a reasonable route, and the main responsibility is not attributable to the employee.[71] For example, an accident occurring to an employee taking a shower in a hotel during a business trip should not be classified as a work-related injury. Although some court decisions strictly limit the situation of work-related injuries on the way to and from work to traffic accidents only,[72] some courts, such as the Guangdong Provincial High Court, have extended it in practice to other, non-traffic accidents of which the main responsibility is not attributable to the employee.[73]

The third is accidents related to workplace reasons, including accidents occurring in rest rooms, dormitories, canteens, and other places, or accidents during preparing or finishing work, violent accidental injuries relevant to work duties, or deaths within 48 hours after work from a sudden illness that occurred during work.[74] The characteristics of identifying such cases as work-related injuries are that the more the employer controls and manages the site, the closer the incident time is to the work, and the more the reasons are related to the work and unrelated to personal matters, the more likely they are to be identified as work-related injuries. For example, if an employee is injured due to a quarrel for work reasons, as long as the employee did not intend it or was not mostly at fault, this

71 The Regulations on Work Injury Insurance stipulate that if an employee is injured by a traffic accident that is not their main responsibility on their way to and from work, it shall be recognized as a work-related injury. "On the way to and from work" here includes not only commuting between work and residence, employer dormitory, or residence of spouse, parents, and child within a reasonable time, but also traveling for activities needed for daily work and life within a reasonable time, such as picking up and delivering children to and from work. The Provisions of the Supreme People's Court on Several Issues Concerning the Trial of Administrative Cases of Work Injury Insurances make it clear that the reasonable route between the place of work and the place of residence of spouses, parents, and children within a reasonable time belongs to "on the way to and from work."

72 Sun & Chu v. Huoshan County Human Resources and Social Security Bureau Labor and Social Security Administration (Labor, Social Security) First Instance Administrative Judgment Anhui Huoshan County People's Court Administrative Judgment (2017) Anhui 1525 Line 33. (In this case, the court found that the accident in which an employee was hit by falling rocks on his way to work was not a work-related injury.)

73 Yu Shunying et al. v. Zhuhai Human Resources and Social Security Bureau and other labor and social security reconsideration disputes retrial case, Guangdong Provincial People's High Court Administrative Ruling (2017) No. 237. "Zhuhai Municipal People's Social Bureau investigated the scene of the incident, and combined with existing evidence materials, believed that Yu Shunying accidentally fell down while riding a bicycle. There is no evidence to prove that other parties are responsible for the accident. It is caused by Shunying's own reasons and does not bear the element of 'the employee does not assume main responsibility' (of work-related injury on the way from and to work)."

74 Civil Judgment of the First Instance of Labor Dispute between Ningxia Branch of Shenzhen Guangtian Group Co., Ltd., Shenzhen Guangtian Group Co., Ltd. and Wang Jinchen Civil Judgment of the People's Court of Jinfeng District, Yinchuan City, Ningxia Hui Autonomous Region (2019) Ning 0106 Min Chu No. 956. (In this case, the employee accidentally fell into the fire well on his way back to the dormitory after work, and this was identified as a work-related injury.)

can generally be identified as a work-related injury.[75] However, injuries caused by violent crimes committed by others do not necessarily constitute work-related injuries.[76]

The fourth type is the special cases of work-related injuries, encompassing injuries suffered for rescue and disaster relief, as well as the recurrence of old work-related injury. Some courts have extended the scope of identifying work-related injuries from rescue and disaster relief to other acts of safeguarding public interests, such as brave acts for justice on the way to work.[77] Recurrence of old work-related injuries, including the ordinary recurrence of old work-related injuries and the recurrence of old injuries of demobilized soldiers, should give rise to the work injury entitlements.[78]

It should be noted that the employer's work-related injury liability is a kind of no-fault liability. In general, even if the employee is injured due to the fault of an illegal operation of their own, it will not affect the identification of work injury. However, according to Article 16 of the Regulations on Work Injury Insurance, if an employee commits a crime or violates the Public Security Administration law, or the employee becomes a casualty due to drunkenness, suicide, or other serious acts, it cannot be recognized as a work-related injury.

92. What is an employee's occupational disease?

Answer: Occupational diseases are specific diseases that employees suffer from due to their work in employment. According to the 2018 Occupational Disease Prevention and Control Law, whether an employee's illness is an occupational disease depends on two conditions being met at the same time: one is that the illness is caused by "occupational activities," and the other is that the illness falls within the scope of the "Classification and Catalogue of Occupational Diseases."

The diagnosis and identification of occupational diseases are carried out by specialized medical institutions, and the Occupational Disease Diagnosis Certificate issued by them is the main basis for determining whether employees suffer from occupational diseases. When diagnosing and identifying occupational diseases, the medical institution shall investigate the patient's occupational history, the history of exposure to occupational hazards, and the situation of occupational hazards in the workplace. To determine the causal link in the first condition, "illness due to occupational activities," the institution applies

---

75 Labor dispute between Zhongshan Dongcheng Furniture Co., Ltd. and Wang Xiangcai, the second civil judgment of the Intermediate People's Court of Zhongshan City, Guangdong Province (2021) No. 1864. "Wang Xiangcai had a certain fault in his own injury, even if he violated the company rules and regulations, as long as he was not intentionally injured himself, violent injuries suffered during work hours and in the workplace due to the action of their duties have been recognized as work-related injuries, and the employee should be treated with work injury insurance entitlements according to law."

76 Zhang Xiaofeng & Zhang Labor Dispute Retrial Review and Trial Supervision Civil Ruling Guangdong Provincial People's High Court Civil Ruling (2017) Guangdong Minshen No. 10110. "But Zhuo Ziping was injured by violent crimes committed by outsiders, not by performing his duties." (In this case, it is impossible to see from the judgment under what specific circumstances the victim case occurred, and it is impossible to judge whether it was due to the performance of work duties.)

77 Hengyang Yiluge Liquor Co., Ltd. v. Gong Guoyun, Lei Chunyun, Ye Zhengzheng, Gong Labor Dispute Second Instance Civil Judgment Hunan Hengyang Intermediate People's Court Civil Judgment (2016) Xiang 04 Min Zhong No. 24. Gong was on his way home from work at about 2 a.m. on October 13, 2012. His was identified as a work-related death by Hengyang Human Resources and Social Security Bureau because of his brave act for justice.

78 Articles 15 (3) and 36 of the 2003 Regulations on Work Injury Insurance (note: Articles 15 [3] and 38 of the 2010 Regulations on Work Injury Insurance).

the principle of "the diagnosis should confirm an occupational disease in the absence of evidence to negate the inevitable connection between occupational hazards and clinical manifestations in patient."[79] For the second condition of occupational disease identification, please refer to "93. What types of diseases are occupational diseases?"

That is to say, if an employee suffers from a disease of the type specified in the Classification and Catalogue of Occupational Diseases that is caused by other reasons, he is not deemed to have contracted an occupational disease. For example, if an employee suffers from chemical poisoning because he does his own decoration and spray painting at home in his spare time, but the employee is only an office clerk and is not exposed to chemical hazards at work, the employee can only claim medical care leave for illness or non-work-related injury rather than paid work injury leave for occupational disease. Of course, if the employee also has a slight exposure to chemical hazards in the work environment of the employer, it is necessary to determine whether the employer should bear the liability according to the certificate of diagnosis and identification by the medical institution following the aforementioned causal-link judgement principle.

Employees who are diagnosed and identified to have contracted occupational diseases shall be entitled to work injury entitlements, including the paid work injury leave, disability treatment, etc. When an employee who has engaged in the work affected by occupational hazards intends to end their role, the employer shall not terminate the employment relationship with the employee if it has not arranged an off-role occupational health examination for the employee.[80] It is illegal for the employer to terminate the employee's employment relationship in violation of this regulation, and it shall bear the liability of punitive damages or reinstatement of the employment relationship.[81] If an employee who has engaged in occupational hazard work has not undergone off-role occupational health examination, or an employee with a suspected occupational disease is in the period of diagnosis and observation, or an employee has lost part or all of their labor capacity due to an occupational disease, the employer must not dismiss the employee on the grounds of health or ability incompetence, major change in objective situation, or economic redundancy.[82]

93. What types of diseases are occupational diseases?

Answer: According to the provisions of the Classification and Catalogue of Occupational Diseases in 2013, occupational diseases include occupational pneumoconiosis and other respiratory diseases, occupational skin diseases, occupational ophthalmopathy, occupational ear, nose, throat, and oral diseases, occupational chemical poisoning, occupational diseases caused by physical factors, occupational radiation disease, occupational

---

79 Article 46 of the Occupational Disease Prevention and Control Law of 2018.

80 Article 35 of the Occupational Disease Prevention and Control Law of 2018 states that "workers who have not undergone off-role occupational health examination shall not be terminated or dissolved their employment contracts." Article 22 of of the Consultation Draft on the Interpretation of the Supreme People's Court on the Application of Law in the Trial of Labor Dispute Cases (II).

81 Hebi Huitong Construction Engineering Co., Ltd., Yao Jicheng and other civil applications for retrial of labor disputes to review the civil ruling of Henan Provincial People's High Court (2022) Yumin Shen No. 1631. In the case, the court held that the employer had terminated the employment relationship by stopping paying wages and arranging work for the employee who was engaged in occupational hazards. The employer did not arrange the off-role occupational health examination, and the court found the termination illegal and that the employer must pay punitive damages.

82 Article 42 of the Employment Contract Law.

infectious disease, occupational tumor, and other occupational diseases. The most common occupational diseases include pneumoconiosis, noise-induced deafness, leukemia caused by chemical pollution, contact dermatitis, and various chemical poisonings.

The recognition of occupational disease must satisfy the condition that the type of disease in question falls within the scope of the aforementioned occupational diseases. Therefore, if an employee suffers from a disease that does not fall within this scope, it is not an occupational disease even if it is due to their occupational activity or work. For example, if an employee is infected by a coworker's COVID-19 in the workplace, it is not an occupational disease. However, if a medical staff member or a police officer is unfortunately infected with AIDS due to work contact, it is an occupational disease. This is the second condition for the identification of occupational diseases.

To determine whether an employee has contracted an occupational disease, and whether the first condition for the identification of occupational diseases, "illness due to occupational activities," is met, please refer to "92. What is an employee's occupational disease?"

94. How do I handle work injury recurrence?

Answer: Work injury recurrence refers to the situation in which an employee has had a work-related injury or occupational disease and has recovered or stabilized after a period of treatment and recuperation, but later, the same injury or disease recurs again. Work injury recurrence also includes the recurrence of old injuries of demobilized soldiers.[83]

Employers shall provide the same treatments to the employees with work injury recurrence as to those with ordinary work-related injuries and occupational diseases. Please refer to "99. What are the entitlements for employees with work-related injuries or occupational diseases?" That is to say, although the employer has an upper limit of liability for each case of work-related injury and occupational disease (that is, usually no more than 12 months of paid work injury leave), there is no limit on the number of work injury recurrences.[84]

Work injury recurrence is legally equivalent to restarting the treatment of work-related injuries of an employee. Therefore, the statutory procedure in confirming whether the injury or illness of employees is considered to be work injury recurrence and the corresponding length of the paid work injury leave should still be handled by local labor capacity appraisal committees. Of course, if either party is not satisfied with the conclusion of

83 In the Regulation on Work Injury Insurance of 2003, there is another wording referring to the recurrence of old injuries, which is specifically used to refer to the recurrence of old injuries after military personnel are transferred to civilian work. At present, the two terms are used interchangeably in judicial decisions.

84 Wang & Liu, Civil Judgment on Labor Dispute, Shenzhen Intermediate People's Court of Guangdong Province (2015) Shen Zhong Fa Lao Zai Zi No. 7. "According to this, if the work-related injury recurs, the injured worker can still receive the benefits of the paid work injury leave in accordance with the provisions of Article 33 of the Regulations on Work Injury Insurance, in addition to the previous paid work injury leave. Therefore, according to the above provisions, Wang Jin may be entitled to 24 months of paid work injury leave for his work injury recurrence." In the summary of the judgment of the Supreme People's Court in the case of Deng Jinlong v. Shenzhen Social Insurance Fund Administration in the 11th Bulletin of 2019, it was stated that the maximum paid work injury leave stipulated in Article 33, paragraph 2, of the Regulations on Work Injury Insurance of the State Council and Article 16, paragraph 1, of the Regulations on Work Injury Insurance of Guangdong Province shall not exceed 24 months. This should mean that the maximum paid work injury leave that the injured workers are entitled to for medical treatment, 24 months, is the entitlement for each injury rather than an accumulative maximum period for all injuries.

the appraisal committee, they may apply to the provincial labor capacity appraisal committee for re-appraisal within 15 days.

There are two special circumstances of work injury recurrence: one is the work injury recurrence of retirees, and the other is work injury recurrence of an employee that occurs with a new employer.

As for how to deal with the treatment of retirees who suffer from work injury recurrence, the prevailing practice of domestic courts is that retirees have terminated their employment relationships with their former employers and receive monthly pensions, so the former employers do not need to bear the wages during the period of paid work injury leave, medical expenses for the work injuries (which are borne by the social insurance fund), hospitalization meal allowances, or nursing fees.[85] However, some courts around the country, such as Shandong Provincial High Court and Yueyang Intermediate Court of Hunan Province, ruled in cases that medical expenses were to be borne by the former employer according to the provisions of the Ministry of Labor in 1964.[86] In addition, if the employer fails to purchase work injury insurance for employees before their retirement, resulting in employees being unable to receive the entitlements of work injury recurrence, the former employer should still bear the medical expenses, nursing fees, and hospitalization meal allowance.

Another special case of work injury recurrence is when an employee had a work injury while working for an employer, but has the work injury recurrence while working for a new employer. The legal rules and judicial practice are unclear. Currently, there appear to be no published judicial decisions on this issue, but some courts hold that the entitlements for an employee with work injuries (which include work injury recurrence) should be based on the existence of the employment relationship and the fact that the employee has not received a one-off work injury allowance. Therefore, it appears that the new employer should bear the relevant liability for the employee suffering from the work injury recurrence due to the old work injury from the former employer.[87] However, according to the

85 Xin Deqing and Jilin Province (Fanjiatun) Sugar Refinery Labor Dispute Application Case Supreme People's Court Civil Ruling (2012) Min Shen Zi No. 1091. The court held that for the one-off treatment fee and the continuing treatment fee for the work injury recurrence, it was not improper for the original trial to reject Xin Deqing's lawsuit based on the fact that Xin Deqing had undergone the retirement formalities, had signed the Agreement on Termination of Work-related Injury Relationship of Work-related Injury Personnel (including Temporary Workers) with the Sugar Refinery and that Xin Deqing had not raised any objection to the ruling No. 80 within the objection period. Wang Yuchun, Liaoning Automation Instrument Complete Factory (First Name) and other civil applications for retrial of labor disputes Civil Ruling of Liaoning Provincial People's High Court (2021) Liao Min Shen No. 1494. The court held that the treatment of work injury recurrence after retirement did not belong to the above-mentioned paid work injury leave and therefore, it is correct that the original trial did not support the claim of nursing fees during hospitalization.

86 1964 Reply of the Ministry of Internal Affairs and the Ministry of Labor on the Treatment Expenses for Wound Recurrence of Retired Workers Injured at Work ([64] Nei Cheng Zi No. 4 [64] Zhong Lao Xin Zi No. 25). Chen Yuzhong, Civil Judgment of Labor Dispute Retrial of China Weapons and Equipment Group Co., Ltd. Civil Judgment of Yueyang Intermediate People's Court of Hunan Province (2019) Xiang 06 Min Zai No. 1. Yanjian Group No. 15 Construction and Installation Co., Ltd. and Sun Jingyan Labor Dispute Civil Application for Retrial Review Civil Ruling Shandong High Court Civil Ruling (2022) Lu Min Shen No. 1888. The court held that the employer should bear the nursing fee for the work injury recurrence of the retired employee.

87 Yang Zhengquan, Sichuan Xingwen County Yuping Cement Co., Ltd. Civil Ruling on Labor Dispute Retrial Review and Trial Supervision, Sichuan High Court Civil Ruling (2018) Chuan Min Shen No. 2591. The court held that: "Workers who receive benefits of work-related injuries due to the work injury recurrence should be based on the premise that the injured worker and the former employer still retain employment relationship and the worker has not received one-off work injury medical allowance."

regulations of the former Ministry of Labor, if an employee is diagnosed with a recurrence of an occupational disease for which the former employer is responsible, the former employer should still bear the liability for the work injury.[88] This problem and conflict need to be solved through future legislative amendments.

95. What should the employer do if an employee has not recovered after the expiration of the paid work injury leave?

Answer: The general principle of the employment laws is to provide protection for employees to cure their injuries as far as possible, and to set the paid work injury leave as the upper limit of the employer's obligation for injured employees.

If an employee has not recovered after the expiration of the paid work injury leave (including extension[s] of the paid work injury leave) for the occurrence of work-related injury or occupational disease, there will be many uncertain and complex situations in the relationship with the employer. From a practical point of view, the following situations may occur after the expiration of the paid work injury leave, based on factors such as the employee's own physical feelings, the treatment opinions of medical institutions, the application for extension of the paid work injury leave, and the conclusion of the labor capacity appraisal.

The first situation is that the employee feels that they are not cured and are not able to work, but there is no hospital medical certificate in support or labor capacity appraisal to determine the result of disability. In this case, there is no basis for entitlements of work injury or even general illness, and the employee should return to work. If the employee is unable to perform their original work upon returning, the employer should assign other work; if the employee is still incompetent, the employer may terminate the employment relationship and pay economic compensation.[89] The employee's refusal to return to work may constitute a violation of the company rules and regulations.

The second situation is that the employee has already obtained the conclusion of the labor capacity appraisal. If the conclusion has determined that the employee has a disability of a certain class, the employer is obligated to deal with the situation based on disability caused by the work-related injury or occupational disease, including arranging an appropriate job for the employee, or retaining the employment relationship but withdrawing the employee from the role, or terminating the employment relationship, and the employer and the Work Injury Insurance Fund shall pay the compensations stipulated by

---

88 Articles 8 and 9 of the Opinions of the Ministry of Human Resources and Social Security on Several Issues Concerning the Implementation of the Regulations on Work Injury Insurance (Renshebufa [2013] No. 34) stipulate that those who have been exposed to occupational hazards, who were not found to suffer from occupational diseases at that time, and who have been diagnosed or identified as having occupational diseases after leaving their roles, may still be identified as being work-injured after termination and should be paid work injury entitlements by the Work Injury Fund and the employer, in accordance with the rules of Regulations on Work Injury Insurance. Employers who have not purchased work injury insurance for the employee shall pay the entitlements to the employee in accordance with the rules of the Regulations on Work Injury Insurance.

89 The law does not specify how to handle a situation where an employee, after the expiration of a paid work injury leave, has no disability rating but is unable to perform their original work. Judicial precedents indicate that the employer should refer to Article 40, Item 1 of the Employment Contract Law, which deals with employees being unable to perform their work after medical care leave, for example, Cao Yi v. Changzhou Dongfang Special Steel Co., Ltd., the civil second-instance judgment of the labor dispute of Changzhou Intermediate People's Court of Jiangsu Province (2022) Su 04 Min Zhong No. 1008.

the law. Please refer to "98. What should we do upon the completion of the labor capacity appraisal for an employee with a work-related injury or an occupational disease?"

The third situation is that the employee has a medical certificate to continue treatment and has applied for an extension of paid work injury leave. While waiting for the approval of the application, the employment relationship between the two parties still exists. If the extension is approved, the employee may continue to be entitled to the paid work injury leave during the approved period; if the application is not approved, the employee may continue to use non-work-related illness or injury medical care leave based on the medical certificate. For specific handling, please refer to "97. How does our company handle matters related to the application for extension of the paid work injury leave?"

The fourth situation is that the employee has a medical certificate to continue the treatment and has not applied for an extension of paid work injury leave but has applied for a labor capacity appraisal. Judging from judicial decisions in various places, the prevailing view is that the employers must not terminate the employees, and the employees can at least receive the medical care leave entitlements for ordinary illness or non-work-related injury. Please refer to "96. An employee's paid work injury leave has expired, but the application for labor capacity appraisal is being processed. How should the employer pay the employee?"

Employees should communicate with the employer in good faith and provide the employer with information about their treatments and medical certificates. If an employee refuses to communicate with the company or return to work, in extreme cases, the company may have the right to terminate the employee's employment relationship for absenteeism.[90] On the other hand, the employer cannot arbitrarily terminate the employment relationship just because the employee has not returned to work after the paid work injury leave expires. Employers should be considerate of employees' injuries and illnesses, communicate with the employees in good faith and patiently, and remind employees to apply for labor capacity appraisal. If employers do not consider these factors and directly terminate the employment relationships with employees, it is likely to constitute illegal dismissal.[91]

The fifth situation is that after the expiration of the paid work injury leave, the employee does not return to work, does not apply for an extension of the paid work injury leave, and does not apply for a labor capacity appraisal. In this case, even if there is a medical certificate for continued treatment, the employer should be regarded as having exhausted the responsibility for work injuries and can terminate the employment relationship or regard the employee as actively terminating the employment relationship.[92]

---

90 Civil Ruling of Hubei Provincial People's High Court (2021) E Min Shen No. 1005. In this case, the employee did not recover after the expiration of the paid work injury leave, but he neither applied for extension nor returned to work. The court found that the employer had legally terminated the employee on the ground of serious violation of company rules and regulations.

91 Li Fangping, Zhejiang Wansheng Talent Information Service Co., Ltd. Ningbo Branch Labor Dispute Second Instance Civil Judgment Zhejiang Ningbo Intermediate People's Court Civil Judgment (2021) Zhe 02 Min Zhong No. 2892. In this case, the employee's extended paid work injury leaves expired, but the doctor's advice requested continued recuperation, and the employee still had not applied for labor capacity appraisal. The court found that the employer's direct termination of the employee was illegal.

92 Labor dispute between Rizhao Xincheng Construction Co., Ltd. and Li Hongquan, Civil Judgment of Rizhao Intermediate People's Court of Shandong Province (2016) Lu 11 Min Zhong 495. "After the expiration of paid work injury leave, Li Hongquan did not return to work in Xincheng Company, neither asked for leave from Xincheng Company nor applied for an extension of the paid work injury leave. He terminated the

We are of the view that the prime reason for the five situations mentioned above being so complicated is that the legal rules are not clear. Article 33 of the Regulations on Work Injury Insurance, "An injured worker, who still needs medical treatment after the expiration of the paid work injury leave, shall continue to be entitled to medical treatments for work injury," does not foresee the possible complex situations and stipulates detailed, feasible rights and obligations of both employers and employees. In addition, the inadequate functional design of medical institutions in the management of employees' work injuries (such as employers applying for extension of paid work injury leave and labor capacity appraisal on behalf of employees) and the inefficiency of labor capacity appraisal institutions (such as some appraisals taking a protracted time) also increase the uncertainty and the likelihood of disputes between employers and employees.

96. **An employee's paid work injury leave has expired, but the application for labor capacity appraisal is being processed. How should the employer pay the employee?**

Answer: The duration between the expiry of paid work injury leave and the processing of a labor capacity appraisal application is a special period of time, during which both the employer and the employee need to wait for the labor capacity appraisal result in order to decide whether the employee should be entitled to compensations from the Work Injury Insurance Fund and whether the employment should continue. Therefore, the employer should not terminate the employment relationship during this period.

At present, there are the following judicial practices for the wage standards for employees with work-related injuries and occupational diseases during the period. The first approach is that the wage applies to the standard for medical care leave, which is held by the prevailing judicial decisions, including cases from Beijing, Tianjin, Chongqing, Shandong, Jiangxi, Shenzhen, Huanggang City of Hubei Province, Jincheng City of Shanxi Province, and Nanping City of Fujian Province;[93] the second approach is to apply

---

employment relationship with Xincheng Company by his actual actions." Qin Zhengfa and Wenzhou Tongye Construction Engineering Co., Ltd. Civil Judgment of Intermediate People's Court of Hefei City, Anhui Province (2015) No. 02588.

93 Zhou Ling and UFI Network Technology Co., Ltd. Civil Judgment of the Second Instance of Labor Dispute Beijing the First Intermediate People's Court Civil Judgment (2023) Beijing 01 Min Zhong No. 1928. In this case, the employee was identified as having a work-related injury, but neither party applied for a labor capacity appraisal before the employer terminated the employment contract. The court found that the employer did not inform the employee of the consequences of not applying for a labor capacity appraisal, so the relationship between the two parties continued before the conclusion of the later labor capacity appraisal, and that the employer should pay the wages at the standard of sick leave pay during the period of waiting for the conclusion. Article 9 of the Notice on the Measures for the Administration of the Paid Work Injury Leave for Injured Workers in Chongqing stipulates that "when the paid work injury leave expires or the paid work injury leave terminates, the labor capacity appraisal shall be carried out. During the period of labor capacity appraisal, the employer shall pay the living allowance monthly for those who cannot return to work, and the standard shall not be lower than the sick leave wage during the medical care leave due to illness." Article 9 of the Measures for the Administration of the Paid Work Injury Leave for Injured Workers in Shandong Province. Article 11 of the Interim Measures for the Administration of the Paid work Injury Leave for Injured Workers in Jiangxi Province. In the case of the labor dispute appeal between Huang Shanming and Nanping Train Depot of Nanchang Railway Administration, the Intermediate People's Court of Nanping City, Fujian Province, Civil Judgment (2015) Nan Min Zhong Zi No. 529. "The injured workers who still need treatment after the expiration of the paid work injury leave are only entitled to 'medical treatment entitlements for work-related injuries'; Huang Shanming's understanding of 'medical treatment entitlements for work-related injuries' being equivalent to original wages and welfare benefits is exaggeratory, wrong interpretation. Therefore, Huang Shanming's appeal has no legal basis and shall be rejected." In 2023, the Tianjin High Court issued the sixth of eight typical cases of labor disputes: Wang v. a hotel labor dispute. The court ruled that Wang had been

the minimum wage standard in some cases in Shaanxi Province and Zhangzhou City of Fujian Province;[94] the third approach is the wage standard for paid work injury leave, taken by decisions from the Second Intermediate Court of Tianjin, Huaian Intermediate Court of Jiangsu Province, and Xiamen Intermediate Court of Fujian Province;[95] the fourth approach is Shanghai cases, which hold that the wages for work-injured workers who are illegally employed are determined according to the average monthly wages of the workers in the previous year in the overall planning region (which is likely to be the Shanghai Region);[96] the fifth approach is cases from Huaian Economic Development Zone Court of Jiangsu Province, Benxi Intermediate Court of Liaoning Province, and Ezhou Intermediate Court of Hubei Province pointing out that if an employee does not go to work before the result of the labor capacity appraisal, the employer does not need to pay the employee's wage during that period.[97]

---

identified as having a work-related injury and should receive the benefits of work-related injury in accordance with the relevant provisions. Wang did not return to work on the grounds of illness after the expiration of the paid work injury leave, which was handled by the hotel as medical care leave. After the expiration of the medical care leave, Wang still refused to be on duty on the grounds of illness ...." Ni v. Hubei Honglu Steel Structure Co., Ltd., Civil Judgment of Second Instance of Labor Dispute, Huanggang Intermediate People's Court of Hubei Province (2022) E 11 Min Zhong No. 1472. Civil Judgment of Second Instance of Labor Dispute between Feng Hulin and Jincheng Yameijie Environmental Sanitation Clearance and Transportation Co., Ltd. Civil Judgment of Shanxi Jincheng Intermediate People's Court (2020) Jin 05 Min Zhong No. 877. Civil Judgment of First Instance of Labor Dispute between Wu Chengpeng and Beijing CBRE Property Management Services Co., Ltd. Shenzhen Branch and Beijing CBRE Property Management Services Co., Ltd. Civil Judgment of People's Court of Futian District, Shenzhen City, Guangdong Province (2018) Yue 0304 Min Chu No. 871.

94 Ren Xiangjian and Shaanxi Hengyuan Investment Group Zhaojialiang Coal Mine Co., Ltd. Civil Ruling on Labor Dispute Appeal and Application for Retrial Civil Ruling of Shaanxi High Court (2020) Shan Min Shen No. 1395. Civil Judgment of the First Instance of Labor Dispute between Shen Guoqing and Xintai Construction Group Co., Ltd. Civil Judgment of the People's Court of Xiangcheng District, Zhangzhou City, Fujian Province (2020) Min 0602 Min Chu No. 3392. "The defendant must pay the plaintiff the minimum wage from the expiration of the paid work injury leave to the plaintiff's disability appraisal result (i.e. July 13, 2018 to December 20, 2019)."

95 Tianjin Xingjian Weiye Metal Products Co., Ltd., Liu Jianwei Labor Dispute Civil Judgment of Second Instance Civil Judgment of Tianjin the Second Intermediate People's Court (2021) Jin 02 Min Zhong No. 7855. The court held that the employer should pay the employee his earned wages, i.e., the wages for the paid work injury leave, during the labor capacity appraisal. Civil Judgment of the Second Instance of the Labor Dispute between Jiangsu Lvye Construction Development Co., Ltd. and Liu Guoqing Civil Judgment of the Intermediate People's Court of Huai'an City, Jiangsu Province (2020) Su 08 Min Zhong No. 166. The court held that: "with regard to the wages during the period from paid work injury leave to labor capacity appraisal, if the employer is unable to arrange work from the expiration of the paid work injury leave to the end of the labor capacity appraisal, the original wages and welfare benefits shall be paid." Qiuyedi (Xiamen) Outdoor Equipment Technology Co., Ltd. and Li Caihui Labor Dispute Second Instance Civil Judgment Fujian Xiamen Intermediate People's Court Civil Judgment (2020) Min 02 Min Zhong No. 4701. The employee in this case was identified as having a work-related injury four months after the injury, and the conclusion of the labor capacity appraisal about nine months later was that there was no disability level and the paid work injury leave was three months. The employee was hospitalized or went to outpatient clinics many times before the conclusion of the labor capacity appraisal and basically did not go to work. The court ruled that after the expiration of the paid work injury leave, the wage treatment before the labor capacity appraisal was equal to that of paid work injury leave.

96 The plaintiff Yang Guanwang sued the defendant Shanghai Angyou Kitchen Equipment Co., Ltd. for other labor disputes. Shanghai Fengxian District People's Court Civil Judgment (2015) Feng Min San (Min) Chu Zi No. 3470. "This case should be applied to the relevant provisions of the One-off Compensation Measures for Casualties of Illegal Host Employers. According to the provisions of Articles 4 and 5 of the Measures, the defendant shall pay the plaintiff's living expenses and one-off compensation during the period of treatment before the labor capacity appraisal, and the standard shall be determined according to the local employees' average monthly wage of the previous year in the overall planning region."

97 He Guohua, Jiangsu Jiantai Construction Labor Service Co., Ltd. Civil Judgment of the First Instance of Labor Dispute Civil Judgment of the People's Court of Huaian Economic and Technological Development

Although employers cannot terminate employment relationships with employees before the completion of the labor capacity appraisal and after the expiration of the paid work injury leave or the medical care leave,[98] if an employee does not have a medical certificate for resting or further treatment during this period, the employee should certainly return to work. If the employee refuses to go to work without justifiable reasons, the employer is entitled to refuse to pay wages or even dismiss the employee for violation of the company rules and regulations.

Obviously, there are concerning inconsistencies in the judicial decisions about the treatment after the expiration of the paid work injury leave and before the completion of labor capacity appraisals. We believe that the fundamental reason lies in the defects of legal rules and the system of labor capacity appraisal. The system of the application and approval process of labor capacity appraisal calls for reforms to increase the certainty and predictability of application initiation, approval time, and results, and on this basis, shorten the length of this uncertain period and clarify the treatment rules during this period.

97. How does our company handle matters related to the application for extension of the paid work injury leave?

Answer: If a work-injured employee has not yet recovered and needs treatment after the expiration of the paid work injury leave, they need to apply for an extension of the paid work injury leave. The application for such an extension shall be submitted by the employee (or the employer) to the relevant labor capacity appraisal committee,[99] or by the employee to the employer, according to the treatment opinions of the medical institution.[100]

Zone, Jiangsu Province (2021) Su 0891 Min Chu No. 3334. The court held that the employee was found to have no disability and did not support the wages and benefits from the expiration of the period of paid work injury leave to the conclusion of the labor capacity appraisal. In the labor dispute appeal case between Benxi Fuhong Real Estate Development and Construction Co., Ltd. and Fang Weixin, the Intermediate People's Court of Benxi City, Liaoning Province, the Civil Judgment (2015) BMYZZ No. 00409. In the case, the employee's paid work injury leave was six months. The labor capacity appraisal, being Class 9 disability, was issued at six and a half months after the injury. The medical advice after the leave expired was one month's rest. The second-instance court changed the seven and a half months of paid work injury leave found by the first-instance court into six and a half months of paid work injury leave, finding the one-month rest requested by the medical advice as unpaid. Merchandise Club (Hubei) Electronic Commerce Co., Ltd. and Luolong Labor Dispute Civil Judgment of Second Instance Civil Judgment of Ezhou Intermediate People's Court of Hubei Province (2021) E 07 Min Zhong No. 642. "But this court rejects Luo Long's claim of sick leave pay after expiration of the paid work injury leave as it has no legal basis."

98 Local regulations and judicial decisions all support this principle, for example, Article 12 of the Measures for the Administration of the Paid Work Injury Leave of Injured Workers in Beijing in 2004 and Article 6 of Shanghai Municipal Human Resources and Social Security Bureau Opinions on Several Issues Concerning Work-Related Injury Insurance in the City (Hu Ren She Gui [2024] No. 6).

99 According to Article 8 of the Measures for the Administration of the Paid Work Injury Leave for Injured Workers in Tianjin, if the paid work injury leave for injured workers expires and they are unable to resume their work and still need treatment, the injured workers or the employers shall submit an application for extension of the paid work injury leave to the labor capacity appraisal committee in advance, and the labor capacity appraisal committee shall decide whether or not to extend the period of the paid work injury leave for injured workers. Before the decision, workers with work-related injuries can still receive the benefits of paid work injury leave. Shen Zhixin, Guangzhou Taisheng Human Resource Service Co., Ltd. Civil Judgment of the Second Instance of Labor Dispute Civil Judgment of Guangzhou Intermediate People's Court of Guangdong Province (2019) Yue 01 Min Zhong No. 15113.

100 Li Yanjun and Tianshui Xinhua Printing Factory Labor Dispute Appeal Case Tianshui Intermediate People's Court of Gansu Province Civil Judgment (2015) Tian Min San Zhong Zi No. 65. "According to the Regulations on Work Injury Insurance, injured workers who still need treatment after the expiration of the

The specific way of application depends on the local regulations of the province or city where the employee is located. The employee should be mindful to submit the application before the expiration of the paid work injury leave (for example, Shandong Province requires employees to submit their applications to the employer five days in advance so as to reserve time for the employer to submit the application to the local labor capacity appraisal committee), in order not to delay thc processing. If the employer agrees to extend the paid work-injury leave, the employee may continue to receive the relevant treatments. The labor capacity appraisal committee reviews whether to grant an extension of the paid work injury leave, usually based on professional opinions of medical institutions as to whether the employee's injury or illness requires further medical treatments.

In practice, it is often the case that an original paid work injury leave has expired but the application for extension of the paid work injury leave is under review, which is prone to cause disputes during this uncertain period. The employer is not allowed to terminate the employment contract during this period, because the extension application may be approved to extend the paid work injury leave, and the situation that the employee has not recovered may also mean that the employee will be identified as disabled, leading to further entitlements related to disability under the employment laws.

In current judicial practice, there are three ways to deal with the wage entitlement of employees when they are waiting for approval to extend the paid work injury leave. The first is that the wage of employees is paid at the standard rate for paid work injury leave, held by courts in Tianjin and Shanxi Province; the second is that the standard of wage is that for medical care leave, held by Chongqing City;[101] and the third is the local minimum wage, held by the case of Shaanxi Provincial High Court.[102] Of course, the extension of the employee's paid work injury leave is subject to the length of the maximum period of 12 or 24 months.[103]

From the basic principles of the employment laws regarding paid work injury leave, the period during which employees wait for the extension approval of the paid work injury leave is similar to the period during which they await the labor capacity appraisal (please refer to "96. An employee's paid work injury leave has expired, but the application for

---

paid work injury leave shall continue to receive medical benefits for work-related injuries. In the absence of a written notice to Li Yanjun, the employer stopped Li Yanjun's wage pay illegally, knowing that Li Yanjun was still in the medical care leave for work-related injuries, and treated him as absenteeism, which was obviously improper." Article 7 of the Administrative Measures of Shandong Province for the Period of Paid Work Injury Leave for Injured Workers: If the period of paid work injury leave for injured workers expires, the injury condition is not stable or has not recovered, and the injured workers cannot resume work and still need treatment, they shall submit a written application for extension of the period of paid work injury leave to the employer within five working days before the expiration of the period, and submit a leave certificate issued by the agreed medical institution.

101 Article 9 of the Measures for the Administration of the Paid Work Injury Leave for Injured Workers in Chongqing stipulates: When the paid work injury leave expires or the paid work injury leave terminates, the labor capacity appraisal shall be carried out. During the period of labor capacity appraisal, the wages during the paid work injury leave shall be suspended, and the employer shall pay a living allowance monthly for those who cannot work, and the standard shall not be lower than the sick leave wage during medical care leave due to illness.

102 Ren Xiangjian and Shaanxi Hengyuan Investment Group Zhaojialiang Coal Mine Co., Ltd. Civil Ruling on Labor Dispute Appeal and Application for Retrial Shaanxi High Court Civil Ruling (2020) Shan Min Shen No. 1395. The court held that although the employee did not work during the period of work-related injury determination and labor capacity appraisal, the employee should also be paid the minimum wage.

103 Labor Dispute Application Case between Jiang Zhiyong and Shenzhen Ming'an Security Service Company Civil Ruling of Guangdong Provincial People's High Court (2013) Yue Gao Fa Min Shen Zi No. 1494.

labor capacity appraisal is being processed. How should the employer pay the employee?"). Both periods exhibit similar characteristics of uncertain outcomes, and the wage treatment for employees during these two periods should be the same. Therefore, future legal revisions are needed to enhance the predictability of legal expectations.

98. What should we do upon the completion of the labor capacity appraisal for an employee with a work-related injury or an occupational disease?

Answer: The purpose of the labor capacity appraisal after an employee suffers a work-related injury or an occupational disease is to determine the disability class or labor capacity of the employee, in order to decide how to deal with the employment relationship and how the Work Injury Insurance Fund and the employer compensate and support the employee.

After the completion of the labor capacity appraisal, there are the following situations.

The first situation is that the employee does not have a disability of any class. In this case, the employee shall continue to take the paid work injury leave, or if the paid work injury leave has expired, he may take medical care leave for general illness if there is a medical certificate issued by a medical institution, or return to work.

The second situation is that the employee has a disability of Class 1 to 4. The two parties shall retain the employment relationship, the employee shall stand down from the role, and the Work Injury Insurance Fund shall pay the employee a monthly disability subsidy and a one-off disability allowance according to the disability level. The employer must not terminate the employee. However, if the employment is terminated based on the employee's request,[104] the Work Injury Insurance Fund shall pay a one-off work injury medical allowance;[105] consequently, afterwards, the employee can no longer be entitled to the treatments of work-related injury, including disability subsidy and assistive device costs.[106]

The third situation is that the employee has a disability of Class 5 to 6. The Work Injury Insurance Fund pays a one-off disability allowance to the employee. The two parties shall retain the employment relationship, and the employer must arrange an appropriate role for the employee; if this is not possible, the employer is responsible for paying the employee's monthly disability subsidy. The employer must not terminate the employee. The employee, however, may negotiate with the employer to terminate the contract, in which case the Work Injury Insurance Fund pays a one-off work injury medical allowance, and the employer pays a one-off employment subsidy for disability and economic compensation. However, the employee shall no longer be eligible for further work injury entitlements.

The fourth situation is that the employee has a disability of Class 7 to 10. The Work Injury Insurance Fund pays a one-off disability allowance. The two parties shall retain the employment relationship, and the employer shall arrange an appropriate role for the

104 The civil ruling on the review and judicial supervision of the labor dispute between the Dongning County Xingshun Coal Mine and Yang Changcai, the Civil Ruling (2019) Hei Min Shen 4065 by the Heilongjiang Higher People's Court. In this case, the court held that the provision of the "Regulations on Work Injury Insurance" regarding the retention of employment relationships for employees disabled at a level from Class 1 to 4 after a work injury only restricts the employer's right to termination but does not preclude the employee's right to request termination.

105 Article 38 of the Social Insurance Law of 2018.

106 In the case of Guo Jinguang v. Fujian Quanzhou Donghai Construction Co., Ltd., Fujian Provincial People's High Court Civil Ruling (2017) Min Min Shen No. 252.

employee. If the employer terminates or dissolves the employment relationship due to not being able to arrange an appropriate role, or for other reasons such as mutual negotiation, the Work Injury Insurance Fund shall pay a one-off work injury medical allowance, and the employer shall pay a one-off employment subsidy for disability and economic compensation. However, the employee shall no longer be eligible for further work injury entitlements.

The fifth situation is the death of the employee due to work injuries or occupational diseases. The Work Injury Insurance Fund shall pay the family members a funeral allowance, a one-off work death allowance, and a family support pension.

The above allowance and compensation items are the rights that disabled employees or family members of a deceased employee are entitled to according to the law. If an employer illegally terminates the employment relationship of an disabled employee in order to evade the obligations, rather than complying with the aforementioned rules, the disabled employee shall still have the right to request to reinstate the employment relationship, or claim and receive the compensation for these items in one lump sum as well as the punitive damages for illegal termination of employment.[107]

In any of the above cases, the disabled employee has the right to obtain nursing fees and assistive device costs paid by the Work Injury Insurance Fund according to the result of the labor capacity appraisal. The nursing fees shall be paid at 50%, 40%, or 30% of the local employees' average monthly wage of the previous year in the overall planning region at the three different levels, namely, the total inability for self-care, the major inability for self-care, and the partial inability for self-care, according to the result of the labor capacity appraisal. The injured employee can also be entitled to assistive device costs (including artificial limbs, orthoses, artificial eyes, dentures, and wheelchairs) according to confirmation from the labor capacity appraisal committee.

The standards for the various entitlements stipulated by each province and city may vary slightly. For example, for the monthly disability subsidy, some places determine it based on the individual's wage, while others calculate it based on the local average wage for employees. There are also different regulations in different places regarding the number of months' wage payments on which the one-time work injury medical allowance is based. Please refer to Table 3.4 for more details.

In addition, if an employer does not purchase work injury insurance, all the expenses that the Work Injury Insurance Fund should pay should be borne by the employer. In addition, part-time employees and those on irregular and general work hours are also entitled to the same work injury entitlements as other employees, such as full-time employees.[108]

---

107 Tianjin Benlaixian Network Technology Co., Ltd., Li Feng Labor Dispute Retrial Review and Trial Supervision Civil Ruling Tianjin High Court Civil Ruling (2021) Jinmin Shen No. 177. The court held that the Regulations on Work Injury Insurance stipulated that even when an injured worker voluntarily proposes to terminate the employment contract and the term of the employment contract expires, the employer is still obligated to pay a one-off employment subsidy for disability. Thus, when the employer terminates the employment contract illegally, the employee should be more entitled to the aforementioned entitlements under work injury insurance.

108 Civil Judgment of the Second Instance of Labor Dispute between Beijing SF Express Co., Ltd. and Sun Yunxing Civil Judgment of the Third Intermediate People's Court of Beijing (2022) Jing 03 Min Zhong No. 13598. In the case, the court held that casual employees should also be entitled to work injury benefits such as paid work injury leave according to their own wages. Sun Yi and Tianjin Lovol Heavy Industry Group Co., Ltd. Labor Dispute Appeal Case Tianjin the First Intermediate People's Court Civil Judgment (2013) YZMSZZ No. 644. This case is about the work injury entitlements of employees under the general work hour system.

Table 3.4 Shenzhen work injury entitlements

Disability	*Work injury medical expenses*	*Hospitalization meal allowance*	*Nursing fees during the paid work injury leave*	*Wage during paid work injury leave*	*Monthly disability subsidy and nursing fee for post disability identification*	*One-off disability allowance*	*One-off work injury medical allowance upon employment termination*	*One-off employment subsidy for disability upon employment termination*	*Assistive device cost*
No disability	Covered by WIIF	Employers pay 70% of daily allowance for business trip and, if treatment in another region is necessary, expenses of travel, meals, and accommodation	If inability of self-care exists during PWIL, employer arranges nursing or pays nursing fees at average wages of local workers in previous year	Employers provide original wages and benefits for a maximum of 24 months	Not applicable	Not applicable	Not applicable	Not applicable	Covered by WIIF
Class 1 to 4					The nursing fee is paid by WIIF at 50%, 40%, or 30% of local workers' average wage The disability subsidy is paid by WIIF at 90%, 85%, 80%, or 75% of individual wage	Covered by WIIF at 27, 25, 23, or 21 times individual wage	Covered by WIIF at 15, 14, 13, or 12 times individual wage	Not applicable	
Class 5 to 6					Disability subsidy: if job assignment is impossible, employers pay at 70% or 60% of individual wage. No nursing fees	Covered by WIIF at 18 or 16 times individual wage	Covered by WIIF at 10 or 8 times individual wage	Employers pay 50 or 40 months of individual wages	
Class 7 to 10					Not applicable	Covered by WIIF at 6, 4, 2, or 1 times individual wage	Covered by WIIF at 10 or 8 times individual wage	Employers pay 25, 15, 8, or 4 months of individual wages	

(*Continued*)

Table 3.4 (Continued)

Disability	*Work injury medical expenses*	*Hospitalization meal allowance*	*Nursing fees during the paid work injury leave*	*Wage during paid work injury leave*	*Monthly disability subsidy and nursing fee for post disability identification*	*One-off disability allowance*	*One-off work injury medical allowance upon employment termination*	*One-off employment subsidy for disability upon employment termination*	*Assistive device cost*
Work death	1) Funeral allowance: RMB 13,730 applicable between July 1, 2023 and June 30, 2024 (six times local average employees' salary from the previous year) 2) One-off work death allowance: RMB 985,660 (20 times national municipal residents' average disposable income in previous year, RMB 49,283 in 2022) 3) Family support pension shall be paid monthly at a certain portion, with the spouse, orphan, or parent who is widow or widower receiving 40%, and other family members receiving 30% of the individual wages of the deceased employee, for family members who have no labor capacity. For the scope of family members to be supported and the conditions for support, please refer to the Regulations on the Scope of Deceased Employees' Family Members for Pension Support.								

Notes: WIIF refers to Work Injury Insurance Fund, PWIL refers to paid work injury leave.

1. Employers who do not purchase work injury insurance or purchase the insurance at a level lower than the statutory standard shall bear all payments that should have been covered by WIIF, including the discrepancies required to reach the standard entitlements.
2. Individual wage refers to an employee's 12-month average wages on which the work injury insurance contribution was based before the work-related injury or occupational disease, subject to a cap of 300%, and a bottom of 60%, of the local average workers' wage in the overall planning region.
3. The food allowance for a business trip in Guangdong Province in 2015 is RMB 100 per day.
4. Employers are responsible for employees who are unable to care for themselves during paid work injury leave. If an employer fails to provide care or allows the employee to arrange the care, the employer shall pay nursing fees under the following circumstances. The nursing fee is determined based on actual invoices if a nurse was hired during hospitalization. If a relative with a stable income provided the care, the fee is based on the relative's income level (verified by a relevant income certificate, but normally not exceeding the local average employees' salary from the previous year). If a relative with no stable income provided the care, the nursing fee is based on the market price.

3.4 Employee Entitlements for Work Injuries

Under Chinese employment law, the concept of work injuries consists of work-related injury and occupational disease.

99. What are the entitlements for employees with work-related injuries or occupational diseases?

Answer: The entitlements for employees with work-related injury and occupational disease are collectively referred to as work injury entitlements under the employment laws. Employers should treat all types of employees who suffer from work-related injuries and occupational disease equally, including casual employees and employees on irregular and general work hours.[109]

The work injury entitlements include two parts. The first part is the entitlements related to the disability identified by the labor capacity appraisal, including compensations and employment relationship treatments. Please refer to "98. What should we do upon the completion of the labor capacity appraisal for an employee with a work-related injury or an occupational disease?" The second part is related to the entitlements of payments for employees' injuries or illnesses, including the following parts.

The first is the wages for the paid work injury leave. Paid work injury leave is a period of leave for treating employees' work-related injury or occupational disease while receiving the same pay as before the work-related injury. This paid period is also the upper limit of employers' liability for work-related injuries or occupational diseases stipulated by law. During the paid work injury leave, employers must not refuse to grant work injury entitlements to employees with work-related injuries and occupational diseases on the grounds of procedural requirements such as leave application in the company's system.[110]

The determination of the length of a paid work injury leave is an important factor affecting the treatment of the employee, and it is usually directly related to the severity of the injury or the illness and the method and progress of the treatment of the employee. The length of this period shall be determined by the labor capacity appraisal committee or the employer according to the medical certificate or in accordance with the provisions of the local classification catalogue of the paid work injury leave.[111] It is generally not exceeding 12 months and may be extended to 24 months under special circumstances.[112] The courts may decide the length of the paid work injury leave according to the injury,

109 Article 9 of the Provisions of the Ministry of Human Resources and Social Security on the Implementation of the Social Insurance Law of the People's Republic of China stipulates that "[i]f an employee (including casual employees) is employed in two or more employers at the same time, each employer shall pay a work injury insurance premium for the employee separately. If an employee suffers from work-related injury, the employer for which the employee worked and was injured shall bear the liability of work injury insurance according to law."

110 Xuzhou Mining Group Co., Ltd. Jiahe Coal Mine Kaolin Factory and Pan Xiutuan Labor Dispute Appeal Case Civil Judgment of Xuzhou Intermediate People's Court of Jiangsu Province (2014) Xu Min Zhong Zi No. 3817. "It is the legal right of the injured workers to receive the benefits of paid work injury leave. During the leave, no matter how the injured workers apply for leave from their employers, the nature of the paid work injury leave will not change."

111 For example, the Classified Catalogue of the Paid Work Injury Leave for Injured Workers in Henan Province.

112 Article 33 of the Regulations on Work Injury Insurance stipulates that the paid work injury leave shall generally not exceed 12 months, and that for serious injuries or special circumstances, the leave may be appropriately extended upon confirmation by labor capacity appraisal committees of prefecture-level cities.

local regulations, and other circumstances in judicial proceedings, if the labor capacity appraisal committee or the employer has not determined the same.[113]

The wages of an employee during the paid work injury leave shall remain unchanged as the original wages and welfare benefits. The wage rate shall be determined based on the employee's average wage from the 12 months prior to the work injury. At present, courts around the country have two approaches to determine the standard of the average wage. The first approach, held by some courts such as the Shenzhen Intermediate Court, is that the average wage does not include overtime wages.[114] The second approach, held by Jiangsu Provincial High Court and Guangzhou Intermediate Court, is that the average wage includes overtime wages.[115] If the employee has worked for less than 12 months before the work injury, it shall be determined according to the average monthly wage of

113 Civil Judgment of Second Instance of Labor Dispute between Zhang Xueliang and Tang Jiachang Civil Judgment of Intermediate People's Court of Jiangmen City, Guangdong Province (2018) Yue 07 Min Zhong No. 1782 (in this case, neither party applied to the Labor Capacity Appraisal Committee for confirmation of the paid work injury leave); Shenzhen Guangchengda Construction Labor Subcontracting Co., Ltd., Wang Shengwu Labor Dispute Second Instance Civil Judgment Liaoning Province Panjin Intermediate People's Court Civil Judgment (2020) Liao 11 Min Zhong No. 666. "Injured workers who still need treatment after the expiration of the paid work injury leave shall continue to receive medical treatment for work-related injuries. From the above law and combined with judicial practice, the paid work injury leave generally includes two stages: hospitalization period and discharge period determined by medical advice."

114 Du Haigang and Wuhan Geely Youhang Technology Co., Ltd. Civil Application for Retrial Review of Labor Disputes Civil Ruling No. 5794 of Hubei High Court (2021). "But since paid work injury leave pay does not include overtime pay, the overtime wage items should be deducted." Hebi Coal and Electricity Co., Ltd. No. 6 Coal Mine and Li Xidong Labor Dispute Appeal Case, Hebi Intermediate People's Court of Henan Province Civil Judgment (2015) He Min Zhong Zi No. 498, Liu Sunbiao v. Dongguan Changan Caijia Hotel Labor Dispute Case Civil Judgment of the Second People's Court of Dongguan City, Guangdong Province (2012) Dong Er Fa Min Yi Chu Zi No. 7272, Shenzhen Nanyou Fire Safety Engineering Co., Ltd. v. Li Haixia Labor Dispute Case Civil Judgment of the First People's Court of Dongguan City, Guangdong Province (2015) Dong Yi Fa Dong Min Yi Chu Zi No. 1878, Wang Lin v. Shenzhen Fufa Hardware Co., Ltd. Labor Dispute Case Shenzhen Bao'an District People's Court Civil Judgment (2011) Shen Bao Fa Min Lao Chu Zi No. 295, Shenzhen Hanwang Plastic Electronics Co., Ltd. Ling Xiao Labor Dispute Civil Judgment of Second Instance Civil Judgment of Intermediate People's Court of Shenzhen, Guangdong Province (2020) Yue 03 Min Zhong No. 9840.

115 Shenyang Coking Coal Co., Ltd. Xima Coal Mine, Wang Qiang Labor Dispute Civil Judgment of Second Instance Civil Judgment of Liaoyang Intermediate People's Court of Liaoning Province (2022) Liao 10 Min Zhong No. 1187. "Concerning the determination of the wage standard, the employee's wages mentioned in the Regulations on Work Injury Insurance refers to the average monthly contribution wage of the injured workers from the 12 months before they suffer from accidents or occupational diseases. Therefore, this court does not support Xima Coal Mine's claim that the overtime wage should be deducted from the wage recognition standard." Case of labor dispute retrial between Mingshuo Computer (Suzhou) Co., Ltd. and Cao Ailing Civil Ruling of Jiangsu Provincial People's High Court (2020) Su Min Shen No. 4338. "Regarding whether overtime wages should be included in the calculation base of wages for paid work injury leave, the purpose that system of paid work injury leave sets up is to ensure the standard of life of work-related injury workers during medical treatment is not affected by the injury; Article 33 of the Regulations on Work Injury Insurance also stipulates that [d]uring paid work injury leave, the original wages and welfare benefits remain unchanged. Cao Ailing was unable to work overtime due to the work-related injury; it is not improper that the courts of the fist and second instance comprehensively considered the actual situation of this case, from the perspective of fairness, calculated the average monthly wage based on the actual income of Cao Ailing from the 12 months before her injury, and used it as the base for calculating and paying the wage during the period of paid work injury leave." Civil Judgment of Guangzhou Intermediate People's Court of Guangdong Province (2020) No. 01 Minzhong 18083. "The court of first instance held that the 'original wage and welfare benefits' during the paid work injury leave only referred to the wages for normal work hours excluding overtime wages. This a wrong understanding of the law application, and this court corrects the judgment according to the law."

the actual work period or according to the employment contract. The original non-wage welfare benefits of employees, such as board and lodging, should remain unchanged.[116]

The second part is the treatment of medical expenses for work injuries. As long as the employer has paid work injury insurance for employees, the work injury fund managed by the government will bear the medical expenses involved in work-related injury or occupational disease. This is the basic mechanism of the work injury insurance system to protect and support employees who suffer from work-related injury and occupational disease incidents.

There are two issues in the practice of work injury medical expenses: the first is that some employers do not buy social insurance for their employees, including work injury insurance. In this case, the employer should bear the medical expenses that should have covered by the Work Injury Insurance Fund.[117] The second is the problem of who should bear the expenses of medical items beyond the coverage of the Work Injury Insurance Fund for the work injury. At present, the prevailing court decisions at the provincial high court level are that employers are not liable to bear the expenses; that is, the employees themselves who suffer from work-related injuries and occupational diseases shall cover the expenses.[118] However, there are also some opposite cases, such as the case of Xiao Haiyang before Xicheng District of Beijing in 2015, in which Judge Li Xi comprehensively analyzed that the liability for expenses beyond the scope of work injury insurance should be borne by the employer from the perspective of no-fault liability, tort law, and the principle of occupational disease liability for work injury.[119] The practice of employees bearing costs that are not reimbursed by the Work Injury Insurance Fund causes significant injustice, and this problem should be solved through legislative amendments.

The third is the hospitalization meal allowance. The employer shall be responsible for the payment of a hospitalization meal allowance to an employee with work-related injuries and occupational diseases. The amount to be paid is based on the days of hospitalization treatment of the employee and the local daily allowance standards. This local standard usually ranges from RMB 30 to 50 per day (for example, the standard of the hospitalization meal allowance in Guangzhou and Shenzhen is RMB 50 per day).

---

116 Deng Xiang, Guangzhou Yuehao Hotel Management Co., Ltd. Labor Dispute Retrial Civil Judgment Guangdong Provincial People's High Court Civil Judgment (2018) Yue Min Zai No. 28 and No. 29.

117 Article 60 of the Regulation on Work Injury Insurance of 2003.

118 Du Haigang and Wuhan Geely Youxing Technology Co., Ltd. Civil Application for Retrial Review of Labor Disputes Civil Ruling of Hubei High Court (2021) E Min Shen No. 5794. Xie Zhifu, Civil Ruling on Labor Dispute Retrial Review and Trial Supervision of Ganlin Town Central Primary School in Jiajiang County, Civil Ruling of Sichuan Provincial People's High Court (2020) Chuan Min Shen No. 1294. Lin Chengwen, Ningde Wanda Plaza Co., Ltd. Wanda Jiahua Hotel Labor Dispute Retrial Review and Trial Supervision Civil Ruling Fujian Provincial People's High Court Civil Ruling (2017) Min Min Shen No. 2852.

119 Qin Guangkui and Chongqing Zhongtianhai Construction Engineering (Group) Co., Ltd. Labor Dispute Retrial Civil Judgment No. 16 of Chongqing the Fourth Intermediate People's Court (2022). "Work-related injury liability is a statutory no-fault liability, so medical expenses beyond the catalogue of work-related injury medical insurance should still be borne by the employer in principle. Unless the employer can provide evidence to prove that there is obvious non-necessity and non-rationality between the use of drugs beyond the scope of the medical insurance catalogue for work-related injuries and the treatment of work-related injuries." Guyuan Garden Management Institute v. Guo Labor Dispute Civil Second Instance Civil Judgment of Guyuan Intermediate People's Court of Ningxia Hui Autonomous Region (2022) Ning 04 Min Zhong No. 1534. Wuhu Zhongshan Technology Co., Ltd. and Gaofeng Labor Dispute Appeal Case Civil Judgment of Wuhu Intermediate People's Court of Anhui Province (2019) Wan 02 Min Zhong No. 862. Xiao Haiyang and Beijing Xicheng District Children's Amateur Sports School Labor Dispute First Instance Civil Judgment Beijing Xicheng District People's Court Civil Judgment (2015) Xi Min Chu Zi No. 36640.

The fourth is the nursing fee during the paid work injury leave. Employers should be responsible for the care of employees who are unable to care for themselves during the paid work injury leave. In practice, employers usually pay nursing fees instead. There are two practical problems in the payment of nursing fees: the first is that, since the condition for the payment of nursing fees is that employees suffering from work-related injuries or occupational diseases cannot take care of themselves during the paid work injury leave, who is capable of judging an employee's inability for self-care is often a controversial issue. In some places, it is based on the opinions of medical institutions.[120] The second issue is that the standards for nursing fees vary in different regions. For example, in Henan Province, the standard is set at 40% of the average wage in the overall region for the previous year, while in Anhui Province, it is set at 80%. Tianjin Municipality specifies that employers can determine this standard on their own.[121] Additionally, certain courts reference the standards for nursing fees as the nursing fees for post disability identification.

The fifth is the nursing fees for post disability identification. If the employer has already purchased work injury insurance for the employee, the Work Injury Insurance Fund is responsible for monthly payment of the nursing fee after the disability level has been identified by the labor capacity appraisal. According to Article 32 of the 2003 "Regulations on Work Injury Insurance," the nursing fee is paid at three different levels: complete inability of self-care, major inability of self-care, and partial inability of self-care. The standards for these levels are 50%, 40%, or 30% of the local employees' average monthly wage in the overall planning region of the previous year, respectively.

A special situation is that if an employee resigns during the paid work injury leave, it is generally regarded as giving up the paid work injury leave entitlements after the termination, but if the employer dismisses the employee illegally, the employer should still bear all the employee's benefits in the period.

100. Can an employee who continues working after work injury request both paid wages and work injury leave pay?

Answer: The nature of paid work injury leave is that employers bear the obligation of wage pay during the period while the employees stop work for treatments of their work injuries (including work-related injuries and occupational diseases). It is a special situation in practice when an employee who is entitled to a paid work injury leave does not rest but go to work. Currently, there are two ways for courts around the county to deal with this situation.

---

120 With reference to Article 16 of the Opinions of the Department of Human Resources and Social Security of Henan Province on Several Issues Concerning Work Injury Insurances (YuRenSheGongShang [2012] No. 15), if an injured worker who is unable to take care of himself needs nursing during the paid work injury leave, the medical institution that receives him shall issue a certificate. The employer shall arrange a person to take care of him or pay the accompanying fee monthly according to the standard of 40% of the local employees' average monthly wage of the previous year in the overall planning region.

121 Tianjin Labor and Social Security Bureau on the Reply to the Inquiry on the Issues Related to the Standards for Payment of Wages, Benefits, and Nursing Fees for Work Injured Workers during the Paid Work Injury Leave, the JinLaoBan No. 11 of 2005. According to Article 29 of the Measures for the Implementation of the Regulations on Work Injury Insurance in Anhui Province, if an injured worker requires care during the paid work injury leave or during the treatment period of work injury recurrence, employers are responsible for providing care or paying a monthly nursing fee based on certificate from medical institutions. The standard of the nursing fees is set at 80% of the local employees' average monthly wage of the previous year in the overall planning region.

The first is that the employee cannot obtain the work injury leave pay together with the actual wages paid to the employee in the same period, and that the employer must only pay whichever is higher.[122] The courts for this practice include the Shandong Provincial High Court, the Shenzhen and Foshan Intermediate Courts of Guangdong Province, the Guangde Intermediate Court of Anhui Province, and the Xiamen Intermediate Court of Fujian Province.

The second approach is that the pay for the paid work injury leave is the legal entitlement of employees suffering from work injuries, and the law does not stipulate that the employees are not entitled to the actual wages for work during the paid work injury leave. In other words, the employees are entitled to both. The case of Taiyuan Chemical Industry Group Construction Co., Ltd. before Qingxu County Court of Shanxi Province in 2019 reflects this practice.[123]

It is a rather obscure question whether employees are entitled to both the wages for the paid work injury leave and wages for actual work. Disappointingly, the Xiamen Intermediate Court of Fujian Province made contradictory judgments on the same issue in the case of Li Xiya in 2020 and the case of Li Caihui in 2020. We believe that this needs to be clarified by future legal amendments.

101. An employee who suffered a car accident injury on his way home has been compensated by the at-fault party. Can he additionally get work injury entitlements?

Answer: In principle, if an employee suffers from a third party's tort damage, and it is identified as a work-related injury, the employee has the right to claim against both the tortfeasor and the subjects of work-related injury obligations (including the social insurance institutions and the employer). Article 8 of the Provisions of the Supreme People's Court on Several Issues Concerning the Trial of Administrative Cases of Work Injury Insurance in 2014 stipulates that work injury and tort are two different compensational legal relationships, and employees can claim their rights through both avenues. However, in practice, employers and the Work Injury Insurance Fund may be able to deduct certain items when paying for the employees' entitlements.

If the injured employee has obtained income loss from the tortfeasor, can he request the employer to pay the wages for paid work injury leave? At present, courts around the country have two practices. One Supreme People's Court's communique case in 2021, the

122 Civil Judgment of First Instance on Labor Dispute between Weier Pump Manufacturing Co., Ltd. and Lei Tishun People's Court of Guangde City, Anhui Province (2020) Wan 1822 Min Chu No. 3597, Song Guangjun v. Qingdao Sizhou Electric Power Equipment Co., Ltd. (Original enterprise name: Alstom Sizhou Electric Power Equipment [Qingdao] Co., Ltd.) Labor Dispute Civil Ruling of Shandong Provincial People's High Court (2014) Lu Min Shen Zi No. 863, Tianhong Digital Commercial Co. Liu Bao et al. Labor Dispute Civil Judgment of Second Instance Civil Judgment of Shenzhen Intermediate People's Court of Guangdong Province (2021) Yue 03 Min Zhong No. 28976. Xiamen Kangbaifu Sports Goods Co., Ltd., Li Xiya Labor Dispute Second Instance Civil Judgment Fujian Xiamen Intermediate People's Court Civil Judgment (2020) Min 02 Min Zhong No. 2437. Civil Judgment of Second Instance of Foshan Jiayingshun Metal Co., Ltd. and District Boren Labor Dispute Civil Judgment of Foshan Intermediate People's Court of Guangdong Province (2019) Yue 06 Min Zhong No. 11820.

123 Qiuyedi (Xiamen) Outdoor Equipment Technology Co., Ltd. and Li Caihui's Civil Judgment of the Second Instance of Labor Dispute, Xiamen Intermediate People's Court of Fujian Province, Civil Judgment (2020) Min 02 Min Zhong 4701. The court held that "the wage earned is the remuneration for Li Caihui's work done, and it does not conflict with his legally entitled work injury pay." Taiyuan Chemical Industry Group Engineering Construction Co., Ltd. v. Zhao, Civil Judgment of the First Instance of Labor Dispute, the People's Court of Qingxu County, Shanxi Province (2019) Jin 0121 No. 2177.

Henan Provincial High Court, the Beijing High Court, the Hebei Provincial High Court, and the Hubei Provincial High Court hold that the wages for paid work injury leave are different in nature from the income loss, and the employees can have both.[124] However, there are contrary decisions or local regulations in Guangdong Provincial High Court, Beijing the Third Intermediate Court, Chenzhou Intermediate Court of Hunan Province, Jiangsu Provincial High Court, Tianjin the First Intermediate Court, Shanghai City, and Changchun City of Jilin Province.[125]

For the situations where tortfeasors have compensated for medical expenses, assistive device costs, nursing fees, funeral allowance, and so on, most courts around the country are of the view that employers or social insurance institutions do not have to pay those items any more. For example, Article 8, paragraph 3, of the Provisions of the Supreme People's Court on Several Issues Concerning the Trial of Administrative Cases of Work Injury Insurance in 2014 stipulates that social insurance institutions are not obligated to repeatedly pay the medical expenses if the tortfeasors have already done so. Guangdong Province allows the Work Injury Insurance Fund to deduct the medical expenses, assistive device costs, and funeral allowance paid by a tortfeasor for the work-related injury that the employee has suffered, and also allows the employer to deduct the income loss paid by the tortfeasor from the wages for the paid work injury leave.[126]

---

124 The case of the bulletin of the Supreme People's Court, the sixth issue of 2021, shows that the wages during the period of paid work injury leave and the compensation from a third party can both be obtained. Jiaozuo Longfeng Fur Enterprise Co., Ltd., Wang Yanfeng Labor Dispute Retrial Review and Trial Supervision Civil Ruling Henan High Court Civil Ruling (2020) Yu Min Shen No. 1606. Wang Zhesan and Beijing Xinnongyuan Real Estate Development Co., Ltd. Labor Dispute Retrial Civil Judgment Beijing High Court Civil Judgment (2018) Jing Min Zai No. 81. Wang Zhiwei, Shuai Shaodong Labor Dispute Retrial Review and Trial Supervision Civil Ruling Hebei Provincial People's High Court Civil Ruling (2018) Ji Min Shen No. 2867. Luotian Xinpusheng Pharmaceutical Co., Ltd., He Guoping Labor Dispute Retrial Review and Trial Supervision Civil Ruling Hubei Provincial People's High Court Civil Ruling (2018) E Min Shen No. 2773.

125 Chenzhou Beihu District Ean Automobile Sales Service Co., Ltd., Li Fuyun Labor Dispute Civil Judgment of Second Instance Civil Judgment of Hunan Chenzhou Intermediate People's Court (2022) Xiang 10 Min Zhong No. 2042. Beijing Jialian Port Restaurant and Meng Lingshan Labor Dispute Civil Judgment of Second Instance Civil Judgment of the Third Intermediate People's Court of Beijing (2021) Jing 03 Min Zhong No. 6578. Huizhou Xiaoxing Construction Engineering Co., Ltd., Zhang Haiyuan Labor Dispute Retrial Review and Trial Supervision Civil Ruling Guangdong Provincial People's High Court Civil Ruling (2020) Yue Min Shen No. 310. Baoding Tianwei Electric Wire Co., Ltd. and Yang Guifang's Application for Labor Dispute Civil Ruling of Jiangsu Provincial People's High Court (2014) Su Shen Er Min Shen Zi No. 01304. Tianjin Security Service Corporation Nankai Branch and Yan Fuming Labor Dispute Appeal Case Tianjin the First Intermediate People's Court Civil Judgment (2015) YZMSZZ No. 0779. Civil Judgment of First Instance on Other Labor Disputes between Tongwei Digital Technology (Shanghai) Co., Ltd. and Wang Yongqing Civil Judgment of Shanghai Changning District People's Court (2018) Hu 0105 16669 of the Early Republic of China. Article 45 of the Measures for the Implementation of Work Injury Insurance in Shanghai stipulates that "the wages and benefits for the paid work injury leave, one-time disability allowance, one-off disability allowance, one-off work death allowance and other work-related injury insurance benefits paid in advance by the employer or the work injury fund shall be correspondingly paid back by the injured worker or their close relatives after receiving compensation from a third party." Notice of the General Office of Changchun Municipal People's Government on the Implementation of the Regulations on Work Injury Insurance and Several Provisions on the Implementation of the Regulations on Work Injury Insurance in Jilin Province (Changfu Ban Fa [2003] 93) Article 4 "On the Treatment of Work Injury Insurance" Item 5 stipulates that "work-related injury accidents caused by civil liability of a third party shall be treated in accordance with the principle of 'work injury entitlements are not concurrently available'."

126 Article 6 of the Summary of the Symposium of the Guangdong Provincial Labor and Personnel Dispute Arbitration Commission of the Guangdong Provincial People's High Court on Several Issues Concerning the Trial of Labor and Personnel Dispute Cases (Guangdong High Law [2012] 284), "If an employee's work-related injury is caused by the infringement of a third party, who has assumed the liability for tort compensation, and the employee or their close relatives have also requested the employer for work-related compensations, the

If the tortfeasor has already paid the nursing fees, nutrition fees, and hospitalization meal allowance, some courts, such as the Guizhou Provincial High Court, allow the employer or social insurance institution not to repeat the payment,[127] but some courts have rendered opposite judgments.[128]

102. If I develop pneumoconiosis after leaving my job, should the employer bear the responsibility?

Answer: If you have not been exposed to pneumoconiosis-related occupational hazards after you left your employer, the employer may still need to assume the responsibility for pneumoconiosis that is discovered after the termination.

Articles 8 and 9 of the Opinions of the Ministry of Human Resources and Social Security on Several Issues Concerning the Implementation of the Regulations on Work Injury Insurance (Renshebufa 2013 No. 34) stipulate that those who have been exposed to occupational hazards, who were not found to suffer from occupational diseases at that time, and who have been diagnosed or identified as occupational diseases after leaving their roles, may still be identified as having a work injury and, according to Regulations on Work Injury Insurance, to receive payments from the Work Injury Insurance Fund and the employers. In the absence of work injury insurance for an employee, the employer shall bear the liabilities of items and standards under the Regulations on Work Injury Insurance.

Therefore, whether the employer you left is responsible for your occupational disease depends mainly on whether your previous role is the occupational hazard role related to pneumoconiosis, and whether the employer arranged for you to have the off-role occupational health examination.

A typical case is Li Farong, one of the ten typical cases of labor disputes in the Fifth Intermediate Court of Chongqing in 2014, in which the employee was found to have pneumoconiosis seven years after leaving a coal mine. Because the employer did not arrange for the employee to have an off-role occupational health examination, and the pneumoconiosis disease was related to the employee's underground work for the employer, the court ordered the employer to bear the liability for work injury.[129]

---

employer's liability for work injury insurance shall be deducted from medical expenses, assistive device costs, and funeral allowance." Huizhou Xiaoxing Construction Engineering Co., Ltd., Zhang Haiyuan Labor Dispute Retrial Review and Trial Supervision Civil Ruling, Guangdong Provincial People's High Court Civil Ruling (2020) No. 310. However, in the treatment of work injury insurance and compensation for personal injury, medical expenses, assistive device costs, nursing fees, and income loss (wages during the period of paid work injury leave) cannot be compensated repeatedly. Guiyang Huaxi Fashion Wedding Photography Department v. Ou Labor Dispute Retrial Review and Trial Supervision Civil Ruling, Guizhou Provincial People's High Court Civil Ruling (2018) No. 3267. "The final decision of the court of the second instance is not improper in that it deducted the actual expenses such as medical expenses, nursing fees, nutrition fees, transportation expenses, and funeral allowance paid by the traffic accident tortfeasor from the work injury insurance liabilities of the case, considering that the compensation arising from the actual cost is duplicate compensation."

127 Guiyang Huaxi Fashion Wedding Photography Department v. Ou Labor Dispute Retrial Review and Trial Supervision Civil Ruling Guizhou Provincial People's High Court Civil Ruling (2018) Qian Min Shen No. 3267.

128 Wang Fuqun, China Railway Zhengzhou Bureau Group Co., Ltd. Civil Ruling on Labor Dispute Civil Application for Retrial Review Henan High Court Civil Ruling (2021) Yu Min Shen No. 1290. The court held that the hospitalization meal allowance and nursing fee could be paid repeatedly.

129 Chongqing Fifth Intermediate People's Court Labor Dispute Ten Typical Cases (2014) II: Li Farong and Yonglong Coal Mine Labor Dispute Appeal Case—when miners leave their jobs without physical examination, the former employer, a coal mine, should be responsible. The court held that Yonglong Coal Mine did not

Even if you have undergone an off-role occupational health examination and were not diagnosed with pneumoconiosis when you left, and if pneumoconiosis is later discovered, the former employer may still be liable for work injury. In a case heard by the Chengde City Intermediate People's Court in Hebei Province in 2015, the employee underwent an off-role occupational health examination when leaving the former employer, and no abnormalities were found. However, during a pre-role occupational health examination four months later, pneumoconiosis was discovered. The court determined that because there was a de facto relationship between the employee and the former employer, the employee was still entitled to apply to the Social Insurance Bureau for work injury determination and to claim from the former employer and the Work Injury Insurance Fund for his work injury entitlements.[130]

If you have been exposed to occupational hazards related to pneumoconiosis with both your former employer and the current employer, the question of who should bear the responsibility for work injury found at the current employer is a complex legal issue. Please refer to "103. Which employer is liable for the occupational disease suffered by an employee who had been exposed to the occupational hazard in the workplaces of both former and current employers?"

103. Which employer is liable for the occupational disease suffered by an employee who had been exposed to the occupational hazard in the workplaces of both former and current employers?

Answer: When an employee is diagnosed with an occupational disease while working for their current employer, the question of liability arises for both the former and present employers. Liability and the extent thereof depend on the off-role and pre-role occupational health examinations of the employee, as well as the status of the occupational hazards at both the employers.

First of all, it is necessary to examine whether the former employer arranged an off-role occupational health examination for the employee when he left his role, and whether the current employer arranged a pre-role occupational health examination for the employee when he took up his role. This is the legal obligation of the employers in the management of occupational hazards.[131] If the former employer arranged the off-role occupational health examination, and the examination result was normal, the current employer shall bear the occupational disease treatment of the employee alone, and the former employer shall not bear the responsibility.

Second, however, if the off-role occupational health examination of the former employer has found that the employee suffers from the occupational disease, whether the current employer should bear the responsibility depends on the relationship between the type of

---

arrange a health check-up for Li Farong before he left the role in accordance with the law, so it could not prove that Li Farong's pneumoconiosis was contracted after he left the mine, and decided that Yonglong Coal Mine should bear the corresponding liability for compensation for work-related injuries.

130 Judgment of the Second Instance of the Civil Dispute between Chengde Tianbao Mining Group Iron Feng Mining Co., Ltd. and Wang Xiaoguang, Hebei Chengde Intermediate People's Court, Civil Judgment (2015) Cheng Min Zhong Zi No. 01672.

131 Article 35 of the Law of the People's Republic of China on the Prevention and Control of Occupational Diseases in 2018 stipulates that employers must arrange an off-role occupational health examination for employees engaged in occupational hazards, and arrange a pre-role occupational health examination for employees engaged in occupational hazards.

occupational disease found and the working environment of the two employers, the degree of exacerbation of the occupational disease with the current employer, and the compliance of the two employers in the management of occupational hazards. The court will weigh and determine comprehensively.

If it is impossible to find out which employer is responsible for the occupational disease of the employee because neither of the two employers arranged the pre-role and off-role occupational health examination for the employee, then the two employers are likely to be jointly and severally liable for the occupational disease treatment of the employee.[132]

104. Can commercial accident insurance for an employee offset the employer's work-related injury liabilities?

Answer: Some employers buy commercial accident insurance for their employees in addition to work injury insurance. It is a common question whether the employer can use the commercial insurance compensations to substitute or offset a partial or full amount of the work injury compensations it bears, or from the other perspective, whether the employees are entitled to both work-related injury compensations and commercial insurance compensations when they are injured at work.

It is a legal and mandatory obligation for employers to purchase work injury insurance for employees and provide them with work injury entitlements when they suffer from work-related injury. Therefore, in general, courts hold that compensation from commercial insurance belongs to another legal relationship than the work-related injury compensation relationship between the employers and the social insurance authority and the employees, or that it is an additional benefit besides work-related injury compensation.[133] The prevailing practice is that employees are entitled to both.

There are two exceptional circumstances where commercial insurances can offset the work-related injury compensations: the first is that the employee agrees the offset in the work-related injury settlement; the second is that both parties have an explicit agreement beforehand that the insurance claim proceeds from the commercial insurer belong to the employer.[134] These two situations essentially confirm that the employer possesses the

132 The appeal case of labor disputes between Sicong Coal Mine of Chaling County and Gaotang Mining Co., Ltd. of Youxian County, the Civil Judgment of Zhuzhou Intermediate People's Court of Hunan Province (2017) No. 213 of Hunan 02 Minzhong. "Because neither the appellant Sicong Coal Mine nor the appellant Gaotang Mining Co., Ltd. had Chen Dingshan occuptional-health examined, it is impossible to confirm the specific formation time of Chen Dingshan's pneumoconiosis and the degree of occupational disease during his work in the two employers. Therefore, it is not inappropriate for the court of first instance to rule that the two employers are jointly and severally liable for Chen Dingshan's third-level disability of pneumoconiosis."

133 Shanghai Zhenshu Furniture Co., Ltd. v. Zhu Jiafu Work Injury Insurance Treatment Dispute Shanghai Qingpu District People's Court Civil Judgment (2014) Qing Min Si (Min) Chu Zi No. 406. In 2017, the Guangdong Provincial People's High Court released the seventh of ten typical cases of labor disputes: the case of work injury insurance treatment disputes between Tong and Yuhai Dongguan Branch—commercial insurance and work injury insurance treatment can both be available. Xinjiang Jinshantui Construction Machinery Co., Ltd. and Li Zongjun Labor Dispute Retrial Review and Trial Supervision Civil Ruling of the High Court of Xinjiang Uygur Autonomous Region (2020) Xin Min Shen No. 912.

134 Beijing Jindingsheng Lifting Construction Machinery Equipment Co., Ltd. and Chen Guijun Labor Dispute Appeal Case Beijing the Second Intermediate People's Court Civil Judgment (2016) Jing 02 Min Zhong No. 2150. In the case, the employee agreed to offset the work-related injury compensation with commercial insurance, which was recognized by the court. Xiamen Feiyue Express Logistics Co., Ltd. and Zhong Xiaoqing Labor Dispute Second Instance Civil Judgment Fujian Xiamen Intermediate People's Court Civil Judgment (2019) Min 02 Min Zhong No. 773. "However, Feiyue Company did not provide evidence in this case to prove the source of funds for the payment of the commercial insurance premium and the agreement

ownership of the insurance claim proceeds, so that the insurer's compensating the work-injured employee is tantamount to the employer's discharging its statutory obligations to its work-injured employee.

For example, Ms. Li's employer purchased an accident-injury insurance for her, but did not purchase work injury insurance for her. After Mrs. Li had a work-related accident, the employer should pay RMB 50,000 for work-related injury compensation. Commercial insurance paid Ms. Li RMB 30,000 as insurance compensation. Under normal circumstances, Ms. Li has the right to receive RMB 50,000 from the employer and RMB 30,000 from commercial insurance compensation. However, if Ms. Li agrees that the commercial insurance compensation can offset work-related injury compensation, or the two parties have agreed in advance that the ownership of the commercial insurance compensation belongs to the employer or that commercial insurance can offset work-related injury compensation, the employer only needs to pay RMB 20,000 of the discrepancy.

105. Can employees claim for mental damages in employment disputes?

Answer: Mental damages are legal concepts used under Chinese civil tort law. In principle, mental damages are not applicable in labor dispute cases under the employment laws. For example, in the case of Yu Likun v. Fuxin Mining Bureau Badaochao Coal Mine Bankruptcy Liquidation Team in 2016, the Supreme People's Court pointed out that the provisions of the Interpretation of the Supreme People's Court on Several Issues concerning the Application of Law in the Trial of Labor Dispute Cases regarding the scope of labor dispute claims do not include mental damages, and that therefore, the lower courts striking out the employee's mental damages claim is in alignment with legal rules.[135] So do the Supreme Court's subsequent judicial interpretations on labor dispute issues.

However, there are still exceptions in judicial decisions from courts across the country that support claims for mental damages in labor dispute cases. Based on the decisions, these exceptions include five categories of situations. The first category involves cases where employers lose employees' personal files. For example, in the case of Deng Jincai v. Huadian City Supply and Marketing Cooperative Union in 2019, the final judgment of the Jilin Provincial High Court awarded the employee RMB 5,000 in compensation for mental distress due to the loss of the employee's file by the employer.[136]

The second category involves recruitment discrimination. For example, in a guiding case issued by the Supreme People's Court in 2022, the case of Yan Jialin v. Zhejiang Sheraton Resort Co., Ltd., a job applicant was not hired after submitting a resume, and the reason shown on her mobile app was that she was from Henan Province. The court ruled that the employer must pay RMB 10,000 in compensation for mental distress due

---

between the two parties on the ownership of the claim compensation." Civil Ruling on Retrial Review and Trial Supervision of Contract Disputes between Tan Wenlian and He Moudeng, etc. Civil Ruling of Sichuan High Court (2021) Chuan Min Shen No. 1125.

135 Yu Likun v. Fuxin Mining Bureau Badao Hao Coal Mine Bankruptcy Liquidation Team Labor Dispute Retrial Case, Supreme People's Court of the People's Republic of China, Civil Ruling (2016) Supreme Law Min Shen No. 3363.

136 Deng Jincai v. Huadian City Supply and Marketing Cooperative Union and China Pacific Property Insurance Co., Ltd. Huadian Branch Labor Dispute Retrial Review Civil Ruling, Jilin Provincial High People's Court, Civil Ruling (2019) Ji Min Shen No. 2890.

to regional discrimination.[137] However, it seems that recruitment discrimination cases do not fall under employment disputes, and workers should file civil lawsuits with courts.[138]

The third category involves cases where employers' working environment is extremely poor, resulting in serious mental consequences. According to the Employment Contract Law, employers are obliged to provide normal or contractually agreed working conditions. If the employer fails to manage the company properly and allows certain employees to discriminate against, harass, or bully other employees, resulting in severe mental suffering and mental illness to the victimized employees, the court may uphold their claims for mental damages. However, there are virtually no successful cases of this type shown in published judgments.

The fourth category involves cases where employees suffer serious consequences due to work-related injuries or occupational diseases. Although there are precedents from the Supreme People's Court and local courts that do not support claims for mental damages by employees injured at work or suffering from occupational diseases, some courts have made contrary judgments in cases with severe consequences. In these cases, there are more instances involving occupational diseases than work-related injuries, likely because employers often have a higher degree of fault when it comes to employees suffering from occupational diseases. Claims for mental damages by family members of employees who died due to work-related injuries or occupational diseases (i.e., work death) typically are not upheld. For more details, please refer to "106. Are employees suffering from occupational diseases or work-related injuries entitled to mental damages?"

The final exceptional circumstance is when the administrative actions of the Social Insurance Bureau cause mental harm to the worker, and the worker has the right to claim mental damages. For example, in the case of Men Aijing v. Henan Zhengzhou City Human Resources and Social Security Bureau Administrative Litigation in 2019, the Zhengzhou City Social Security Bureau committed illegal administrative acts while processing medical insurance registration procedures for workers. A worker sued for mental damages. The Supreme Court held that the State Compensation Law allows workers to claim mental damages from social security agencies. However, in this case, the worker failed to provide evidence of serious mental harm consequences, so the claim for mental damages was not upheld.[139]

Therefore, exceptions supporting claims for mental damages in labor dispute cases should meet the following two criteria.

First, there must be serious consequences. This is based on Article 8 of the Interpretation of the Supreme People's Court on Several Issues concerning the Determination of Civil

137 Notice from the Supreme People's Court on the Release of the 32nd Batch of Guiding Cases (Fa [2022] No. 167), Guiding Case No. 185, Yan Jialin v. Zhejiang Xilaideng Holiday Resort Co., Ltd. Equal Employment Rights Dispute Case.

138 Judgment of the Second Instance of the Civil Labor Dispute Case between Xie Zhongsheng and Huizhou Haopeng Technology Co., Ltd., Guangdong Province Huizhou Intermediate People's Court, Civil Judgment (2021) Yue 13 Min Zhong No. 849. The court held that, according to Article 62 of the Employment Promotion Law of the People's Republic of China: "In violation of the provisions of this Law, if employment discrimination is committed, the worker may bring a lawsuit to the People's Court." Therefore, claims for mental damages due to recruitment discrimination do not fall under labor disputes and should be directly filed as a civil lawsuit in court.

139 Men Aijing v. Henan Province Zhengzhou City Human Resources and Social Security Bureau Other Labor and Social Security Compensation Dispute Retrial Case, Administrative Ruling of the Supreme People's Court of the People's Republic of China (2019) Zui Gao Fa Xing Shen No. 11320.

Tort Liability for Mental Damage (Judicial Interpretation [2001] No. 7), which states that compensation for mental harm caused by tortious acts, but without serious consequences, is generally not supported. Under the employment laws, these serious consequences may include disabilities caused by work-related injuries or occupational diseases, suicides by the victim or family members, severe mental illnesses caused by employers' failure to provide a normal working environment, and exceptional discrimination during the recruitment process.

Judicial decisions also indicate that serious consequences are a necessary condition for claiming mental damages. For example, in the case of Huang Guanghua v. Heyuan City Ideal Comprehensive Market Operation and Management Co., Ltd., the Guangdong Provincial High Court held that the employer's illegal dismissal and non-compliance with social insurance payments did not result in serious consequences, and the employer had already borne corresponding liabilities, and that the claim for mental damages was not upheld.[140]

Second, there must be a causal relationship between the conduct of a party to the employment relationship and the aforementioned serious consequences. For example, in the case of Zhang Shanshan v. Zhonggong Gaokao Maintenance Technology Co., Ltd., the employee claimed that the employer's working environment caused her depression and claimed for mental damages. The Beijing High Court held that the employee failed to provide evidence of a causal relationship between the working environment and depression and that the claim for mental damages was not supported.[141]

106. Are employees suffering from occupational diseases or work-related injuries entitled to mental damages?

Answer: Mental damages is a legal concept used in Chinese civil law, specifically in the realm of tort law, and is rarely applied in the field of employment law. The issue of employees claiming mental damages for severe loss of labor capacity due to occupational diseases or work-related injury is currently handled differently by courts around the country. However, the prevailing court decisions appear to be in favor of such claims.

For mental damages claims based on occupational diseases, Guangdong Provincial High Court, Shenzhen Intermediate Court, Jiangxi Provincial High Court, and Jiangsu Provincial High Court all have decisions ruling that the law does not prohibit employees suffering from occupational diseases from demanding that at-fault employers bear the liability of mental damages and/or other civil legal compensation, in addition to the statutory entitlements for occupational diseases.[142] However, some courts do not uphold the mental

140 Huang Guanghua v. Heyuan City Ideal Comprehensive Market Operation and Management Co., Ltd. Labor Dispute Civil Application Retrial Review Civil Ruling, Civil Ruling of Guangdong Provincial High People's Court (2021) Guangdong Civil Application No. 6030.

141 Zhang Shanshan v. Zhonggong Gaoke Maintenance Technology Co., Ltd. Labor Dispute Retrial Case, Civil Ruling of Beijing High People's Court (2023) Beijing Civil Application No. 3159.

142 Article 58 of the Occupational Disease Prevention and Control Law of 2018 states that "in addition to receiving work injury insurance benefits according to law, occupational disease patients who still have the right to compensation in accordance with relevant civil laws shall have the right to claim compensation from the employer." Kunteng Precision Industry (Shenzhen) Co., Ltd. and Zhang Gaoming Labor Dispute Civil Judgment of Second Instance Civil Judgment of Shenzhen Intermediate People's Court of Guangdong Province (2019) Yue 03 Min Zhong No. 27444. In the case, the employee suffered from silicosis Phase II, his work capacity was identified as Class 4 disability, and the court ordered the employer to pay RMB 90,000 of mental damages. Jiangxi Jiujiang Southern Cement Co., Ltd. v. Qian Fangmei and other labor disputes,

damages claim due to occupational diseases, such as the case of Huang Anxu before the Shaanxi Provincial High Court in 2021.[143]

For mental damages based on work-related injuries, courts around the country have different handlings. Judging from the cases at the provincial high court level, the Guangdong Provincial High Court, the Zhejiang Provincial High Court, the Xinjiang Autonomous Region High Court, and the Shandong Provincial High Court hold that employees who suffer from work injuries can only request work injury entitlements according to the Regulations on Work Injury Insurance, and that mental damages are not supportable.[144] The Yunnan Provincial High Court, on the other hand, holds a completely opposite view and supports the claim of mental damages for employees involved in work injuries.[145]

Claims for mental damages from survivors of employees who died of work-related injuries or occupational diseases (commonly referred to as work death) usually are not upheld by labor arbitration committees or courts. For example, in the case of Du Guimei et al. v. China Railway First Group Co., Ltd., the Shaanxi Provincial High Court held that according to the provisions of the Interpretation of the Supreme People's Court on Several Issues Concerning the Application of Law in the Trial of Personal Injury Compensation Cases, claims related to work deaths only apply to the Regulations on Work Injury Insurance, that the Regulations on Work Injury Insurance, however, does not allow mental damages, and that therefore, compensation for work-related deaths should not include mental damages.[146]

Jiangxi Provincial People's High Court Civil Ruling No.309 (2017). The court held that there was a fault in the employer's failure to carry out occupational health examination during the employment period for employees engaged in occupational hazards. Therefore, the employer shall bear a discretionary 20% of the compensation liability for one-off work death allowance according to the standard of work-related death, and order the employer to pay a discretionary six months' sick leave wages. Wang v. Zhangjiagang Jinmao Investment Development Co., Ltd., Jiangsu Provincial People's High Court Civil Ruling (2014) Su Shen Er Min Shen Zi No. 01555. The court ordered the payment of RMB 35,000 for mental damages because of aplastic anemia and Class 4 disability caused by high paint concentration poisoning in the working environment of the employer. Chen Honghuan, Huizhou Chaoba Battery Co., Ltd. Labor Dispute Retrial Review and Trial Supervision Civil Ruling Guangdong Provincial People's High Court Civil Ruling (2018) Guangdong Minshen No. 11817. The employee suffered from occupational disease Class 5 disability, and the court ordered RMB 15,000 of mental damages and RMB 6,000 of nutrition fees.

143 Huang Anxu and Shaanxi Zhenbang Energy-saving Technology Co., Ltd. Labor Dispute Retrial Shaanxi Provincial People's High Court Civil Ruling (2021) Shan Min Shen No. 962. The employee died of occupational disease, and the court did not support the request for mental damages.

144 Article 3 of the Interpretation of the Supreme People's Court on Several Issues Concerning the Application of Law in the Trial of Personal Injury Compensation Cases in 2022 stipulates that "if an employee of an employer who should participate in the overall planning of work injury insurance according to law suffers personal injury due to work-related injury accidents, and if the employee or their close relatives sue the employer to the people's court for civil compensation, the court shall inform them to deal with the case in accordance with the provisions of the Regulations on Work Injury Insurance." Cheng Yeyun v. Yuhuan County Chumen Sanzhong Furniture Factory Labor Dispute Case Zhejiang Provincial People's High Court Civil Ruling (2015) Zhe Min Shen No. 570. In the case, the court rejected the request of the injured employee for mental damages. Labor Dispute Application between Wu Xiaoyun and Puning Chengfa Garment Manufacturing Co., Ltd. Civil Ruling of Guangdong Provincial People's High Court (2014) Yue Gao Fa Min Shen Zi No. 475. Xinyuan County Guqiang Construction and Installation Co., Ltd. and Yan Jiayun Labor Dispute Second Instance Civil Judgment Xinjiang Uygur Autonomous Region High Court Yili Kazakh Autonomous Prefecture Branch (2015) YZMZZ No. 86. Li Xingjun v. Rizhao Jinhe Boyuan Biochemical Co., Ltd. Labor Dispute Civil Ruling of Shandong High Court (2016) Lu Min Shen No. 1588.

145 Application for Labor Dispute between Yunnan Luliang Chemical Industry Co., Ltd. and Hu Likun Civil Ruling of Yunnan High Court (2014) YGMSZ No. 347.

146 Du Guimei et al. v. China Railway No. 1 Group Co., Ltd. Labor Dispute Appeal Case, Civil Ruling of Shaanxi High People's Court (2017) Shaanxi Civil Application No. 2534.

CHAPTER 4

Performance of Employment Contract

Introduction

The performance of the labor contract constitutes a relatively stable relationship between the employer and the employee. This chapter provides detailed explanations regarding social insurance, wage calculation (including equity incentives) and payment, disciplinary actions by the employer against employees, position transfers and salary adjustments, as well as the responsibilities of the employer for violating labor laws.

This chapter offers Q&A explanations for the following practical issues: the calculation of monthly wages, the protection of minimum wage, wages payment during business closure and epidemic lockdown, piecework wage and package wage system, whether night shift allowances conform to overtime wage rules, employees' rights on bonus or commission after termination, employees' right to spare time, validity of employer's company rules and regulations and disciplinary actions, fines imposed on employees, the legitimacy of suspension investigation, the compensation for the loss caused by an employee's fault, the person liable for compensation for the loss caused by the employee's duty act, position transfer of employees controlled by multiple employers, multiple employers' mixed employment, the legal issues of position transfer and wage reduction for employees, deputies related to equity incentive, and administrative and criminal liability for employers and their responsible persons in the case of violations of the employment laws.

This chapter also delves into some complicated employment law issues, including unjustified wage (or overtime wage) deductions and arrears, compensation liabilities for employees who cause damages to their employers, mixed employment, equity incentive, and collective work stoppage.

4.1 Wage Entitlements, Calculation, and Payment

107. How are employees' received wages calculated?

Answer: Although an employment contract may specify the wages that the employer should pay, the employer is entitled to lawfully deduct certain items that the employee is required to contribute or pay, such as for social insurance and personal income tax. The calculation of the wage the employee receives is equal to due wage plus overtime pay plus unused time-off in lieu pay or unused annual leave pay, and then deducting allowable deduction items, namely:

Net wage = Due wage + Overtime pay + Unused Annual Leave Pay − Allowable Deduction Items

DOI: 10.4324/9781003583301-4

First, employees' payable hourly wages for normal work hours must not fall below the local minimum hourly rate standard, and the calculation base for their overtime wages shall also not be lower than the standard. In other words, due to unpaid leave and social insurance deduction, an employee earning the minimum wage may actually receive a lower wage than the minimum wage standard.

The second is the calculation of overtime pay. Different rates and rules apply to the three different types of overtime, e.g., weekday, weekend, and public holiday overtime. For detailed calculations of these three types of overtime please refer to "70. I am an HR manager. How do I calculate overtime pay for employees?"

Third, allowable deduction items are certain legally permitted items that employers can deduct from employees' wages, including personal income tax, social insurance contributions (employees' contributions to pension, medical, and unemployment insurances), and other allowable deductions.

Sometimes, with mutual agreement or upon employees' request, employees may receive encashment pay for unused annual leave. Please refer to "74. How should employers manage employees' paid annual leave?" Additionally, employers may deduct incorrectly overpaid wages, court-mandated wage deductions, and expenses such as rent and utilities agreed upon by both parties if employers provide accommodation.

108. My wage is lower than the minimum wage. Is this legal?

Answer: The prerequisite for minimum wage issues and minimum wage protection is the existence of an employment relationship. If you are in a contractor relationship with the company that receives your work services, then the service fee issue needs to be reviewed according to the Contract Law. Even if you personally understand that the relationship between both parties constitute an employment relationship, your service fees are still not protected by minimum wage regulations.[1] To determine whether there is an employment relationship or a contractor relationship, please refer to "12. How do I distinguish between an employment relationship and a contractor relationship?"

If there is an employment relationship between you and the company, the company must pay you not less than the minimum hourly wage.

It should be noted that the minimum wage under the protection of the employment laws in China is hourly rate protection based on actual work hours rather than protection of the wage rate in the pay cycle. For example, Mr. Zhang, whose due wage is the local minimum wage, in a particular month worked less than standard hours (i.e., 174 hours per month). His payable wages for the month will be less than the local minimum wage. Even if he worked full standard hours in the month, his received wages will still be under

1 Judgment on Labor Dispute Civil Second Trial for Zhang and Yu Mengchi, Wuhan Intermediate People's Court of Hubei Province Civil Judgment (2022) E01 Min Zhong No. 20197. Judgment on Labor Dispute Civil Second Trial for Meng Qingmei and Tai'an the First Middle School of Shandong Province, Tai'an Intermediate People's Court of Shandong Province Civil Judgment (2022) Lu 09 Min Zhong No. 3116. In these cases, the court distinguished between the employment relationship and the contractor relationship based on the point at which the employee reached the retirement age to qualify for pension insurance. Before this point, the relationship was considered an employment relationship and was subject to minimum wage protection, while after this point, it was considered a contractor relationship and not subject to minimum wage protection. Judgment on Labor Dispute between Longshan Health Center of Dianbai District and Li Meili, Maoming Intermediate People's Court of Guangdong Province Civil Judgment (2015) Mao Zhong Fa Min Er Zhong Zi No. 254. "Contractor relationships are not subject to the requirements of the minimum wage standard."

the local minimum wage standard due to legitimate deductions such as social insurance contributions.

In addition, the minimum wage standard for casual employees is different from that for full-time employees. For example, the monthly minimum wage standard for full-time employees in Shenzhen in 2023 is RMB 2,360 per month (the hourly wage is RMB 13.6); the hourly minimum wage for casual employees is RMB 22.2.

109. How should employees be paid during an employer's business closure?

Answer: According to the Provisional Regulations on Wage Payment and local regulations in various provinces and cities, in the event of an employer's suspension of work or production due to reasons not attributable to the employees, the employer should pay wages based on the contracted wage standard (or the actual wage standard, whichever is higher) for the first wage payment period of the suspension. Starting from the second wage payment period of the suspension, the employer should pay employees who have provided normal labor no less than the local minimum wage standard, and those who have not provided normal labor should receive living expenses at the local standard.[2]

The living expense standard is generally 70%–80% of the local minimum wage standard. For example, in Guangdong Province (including Shenzhen), the living expense standard is 80% of the minimum wage, while in Beijing and Shandong Province, it is 70%. An exception is Shanghai, where the living expense standard is not lower than the minimum wage standard regardless of whether employees provide normal labor during the suspension period.[3]

In practice, three issues should be noted:

First, the employer must have legitimate reasons for suspending work or production. These reasons may include changes in government policies, the impact of natural disasters, or external market environment changes. Infectious disease outbreaks such as the COVID-19 pandemic may also constitute legitimate reasons for suspending work or production. However, if an employer maliciously exploits the suspension to reduce employee wages or even force employees to resign, employees may have the right to proceed a forced resignation due to the employer's failure to provide labor conditions as stipulated in Article 38 of the Employment Contract Law, and may claim economic compensation from the employer. For detailed information on forced resignation, please refer to "143. Are employers liable for economic compensation for employees' forced resignation?"

Second, an employer's suspension of work or production can be either complete or partial. The wage treatment for the employees affected by a partial suspension should comply with the Provisional Regulations on Wage Payment and relevant local regulations. Employees who are not affected by the suspension should be able to continue to work normally and receive regular wage treatment. However, employers should be mindful that partial suspension of work or production typically involves the shutdown of entire departments or production lines, and employers should not use partial suspension as an excuse to implement wage reductions or waiting-for-work for individual positions or personnel.

---

2 Article 12 of the Provisional Regulations on Wage Payment (Laobufa [1994] No. 489.

3 Article 12 of the Shanghai Municipal Enterprise Wage Payment Measures of 2016, Article 31 of the Shandong Province Enterprise Wage Payment Regulations of 2021, Article 27 of the Beijing Municipal Wage Payment Regulations of 2007, and Article 39 of the 2016 Guangdong Province Wage Payment Regulations.

Third, the Provisional Regulations on Wage Payment uses the vague term "wage payment period" to specify the employers' wage payment obligations for the first wage payment period after the suspension and beyond, and theoretically, employees may be on weekly or annual, in addition to monthly, wages. In practice, however, wage payment periods in China are typically monthly. Therefore, the wage treatment for employees affected by the suspension is based on the original wage standard for the first month, and then based on the minimum wage standard (for those providing normal labor) or the local living expense standard (for those not providing normal labor) for the second month. There is no scenario where the employer pays for the first week and the second week, or the first year and the second year, of the suspension.

110. Should employers pay wages to employees during an epidemic lockdown?

Answer: Lockdown due to a pandemic falls into the situations where the employer stops operation due to no fault of the employees, as stipulated in the Provisional Regulations on Wage Payment. For detailed rules, please refer to "109. How should employees be paid during an employer's business closure?"

According to the Provisional Regulations on Wage Payment and the regulations by the Ministry of Human Resources and Social Security on the COVID-19 epidemic, for the first month of lockdown, employers are obligated to pay employees according to the wage standard stipulated in employees' individual employment contracts (or actual wages, whichever is higher). For the second month, employers shall pay wages no less than the local minimum wage standard to the employees who have provided normal work, and pay the living expenses of the local standard to the employees who have not provided normal work.[4]

According to local regulations around the country, standards of living expenses are generally 70%–80% of the local minimum wage standard. For example, the standard of living expenses in Shenzhen City is 80% of the local minimum wage.[5]

Therefore, during a lockdown due to an epidemic, employers are obligated to pay wages to their employees at their individual wage level, the local minimum wage, or living expenses, depending on the length of the lockdown and whether employees provide normal work for the employer.

4 Article 12 of the Provisional Regulations on Wage Payment (LaoBuFa [1994] No. 489), Article 2 of the Notice of the Office of the Ministry of Human Resources and Social Security on Proper Handling Employment Relationships during the Prevention and Control of Pneumonia Infected by the New Coronavirus (RenSheTingMingDian No.5 [2020]) stipulates: "If an enterprise stops production within a wage payment cycle, it shall pay wages to its employees in accordance with the standards stipulated in the employment contract. In case of more than one wage payment cycle, if the employee provides normal work, the wage paid by the enterprise to the employee shall not be lower than the local minimum wage standard. If the staff and workers do not provide normal work, the enterprise shall pay living expenses, of which the standards shall be implemented in accordance with the provisions of the provinces, autonomous regions and municipalities directly under the Central Government."

5 The Notice of Liaoning Provincial Department of Human Resources and Social Security on Forwarding the Notice of the General Office of the Ministry of Human Resources and Social Security on Proper Handling Employment Relationships during the Prevention and Control of Pneumonia Infected by the New Coronavirus stipulates that the standard of living expenses is 70% of the minimum wage standard. Henan Provincial Department of Human Resource on forwarding RenSheTingMingDian No. 5 (2020), the Proper Handling Employment relationships during the Prevention and Control of Pneumonia Infected by the New Coronavirus (Yu She Ming Dian [2022] No. 2). The standard of living expenses shall not be less than 80% of the minimum wage. Article 28 of the 2022 Shenzhen Employees' Wage Payment Regulations.

111. Is it legal for employers to pay only the minimum wage during the central furlough period of irregular and general work hours?

Answer: Whether the employer is in breach of the employment laws depends on the level of the employee's normal wages. If the employee's normal wages far exceed the local minimum wage, it is probably illegal for the employer to do so.

The system of irregular or general work hours is essentially to adjust the standard work hour system to a certain extent due to industrial characteristics or seasonal changes. Employees work in the central work period and rest in the central furlough period, but their average weekly or monthly work hours in the accounting cycle are still the same as or close to the standard work hours. Therefore, during the period of central furlough, in principle, the employer should pay wages according to the employees' normal wages, and during the period of central work, the employer should pay the employees roughly the same level of wages.

In exceptional cases, employees on the general work hours may work for hours that exceed the standard work hours within the accounting cycle, indicating the presence of overtime during the cycle. Therefore, the wages for these employees during the central work period may be higher than the aforementioned balanced wage level, as they include overtime pay. Employees on irregular work hours may not be entitled to overtime pay, and thus, the aforementioned imbalance of pay may not occur. For overtime pay calculation for irregular and general work hour systems, please refer to "71. How do I calculate overtime pay under special work hour systems?"

That is to say, under both the systems of irregular work hours and normal work hours, the work hours of employees are not balanced, but the payment of wages is largely balanced.[6] Therefore, if an employer pays the employee's wages during the central furlough period at a rate much lower than the employee's normal wages, it is likely to be illegal.

112. How do I calculate the wages of employees under the piecework wage system?

Answer: Unlike the standard hours system, where wages are calculated based on work hours, the piecework wage system is a type of system where wages are calculated based on the number of completed work units, such as the number of products completed on an assembly line or the number of newspapers delivered to customers. It reflects the principle of more pay for more work done.

Similarly to the standard work hour system, the piecework wage system enables employees to receive overtime pay; that is to say, wages under the piecework system may include both normal-time and overtime wages. Two prerequisites must be met for overtime pay under the piecework wage system: first, the employee must have fulfilled their piecework quota, and second, the employee also must have completed work units outside of normal work hours.[7]

We use a case to illustrate how to calculate piecework wages. Under the piecework wage system, employee Mr. Zhang's employment contract stipulates that his monthly

6 Labor dispute appeal case between Shanghai Tuoxin Special Painting Co., Ltd. and Deng Qiuzhen, Fujian Fuzhou Intermediate People's Court Civil Judgment (2017) Min 01 Min Zhong 7077. The court found that the average monthly wage of the employee on irregular hours was RMB 4,000, and that it was illegal for the employer to unilaterally change the wage treatment of the employee by paying only the basic wage to the employee during the rotational furlough period.

7 Article 13 of the Provisional Regulations on Wage Payment.

piecework quota is 1,000 pieces, and the piecework unit price is RMB 2. In a particular month, Mr. Zhang completed 1,100 pieces during normal work hours, 200 pieces during weekday overtime hours, and 50 pieces on weekend days. How should Mr. Zhang's wages for that month be calculated?

The calculation result of Mr. Zhang's wages for that month is RMB 2,900, including RMB 2,200 (1,100 * 2) for normal work hour wage, RMB 600 (200 * 2 * 150%) for weekday overtime wage, and RMB 100 (50 * 2 * 200%) for weekend overtime wage. If Mr. Zhang only completed 800 pieces within normal work hours, then his normal work hours wage is RMB 2,000 (1,000 * 2). Accordingly, the number of pieces for overtime hours should be 200 pieces less (1,000 − 800), as the 200 pieces have been deducted from overtime production to top up the piecework quota (e.g., 1,000 pieces) for normal work hours production.

Therefore, the main factors affecting wages for piecework employees are the piecework quota and the piecework unit price. Article 37 of the Labor Law stipulates that employers must reasonably determine a piecework quota and piecework unit price. For how to determine whether a piecework quota and piecework unit price formulated by an employer are reasonable, please refer to "113. Are the piecework quota and piecework unit price set by the employer reasonable?"

In practice, common phenomena include employers not setting a piecework quota for their employees or setting unreasonable piecework quotas and piecework unit prices. In such cases, the common practice among courts nationwide is not to recognize the effectiveness of the piecework wage system. Instead, they apply the standard work hour system to determine whether the wages are insufficient for the work hours done, based on the local minimum hourly wage.[8]

113. Are the piecework quota and piecework unit price set by the employer reasonable?

Answer: As explained in "112. How do I calculate the wages of employees under the piecework wage system?", employees' wages under a piecework wage system are determined by piecework quota and piecework unit price, normally dictated by employers. The reasonableness of the two, therefore, is vital.

If piecework quota and piecework unit price are applied in computing an employee's wage, there are two main factors to consider in determining whether piecework quota and piecework unit price are reasonable from current judicial practice and regional regulations.

The first is the minimum wage bottom line factor, i.e., an employee's average hourly wages under a piecework system must not be lower than the local minimum wage standard, having taken into account the employee's working hours on workdays, weekend days, and public holidays. This is the minimum wage protection for piecework employees under

8 Gao Ying, Meihekou Branch of China United Network Communications Co., Ltd. and other civil applications for retrial of labor disputes Civil Ruling Jilin Provincial People's High Court Civil Ruling (2021) Ji Min Shen No. 3698. In this case, the court held that both parties could not prove the existence of piecework quota, so it could not be determined that both parties implemented the piecework wage system. Shenzhen Intermediate People's Court's Guidelines on the Trial of Labor Dispute Cases, Article 63. "If the two parties agreed to implement the piecework wage system, but the existing evidence cannot deduce the piecework quota for normal work hours, and if the calculated hourly wages of the employee is no less than the minimum wage standard, according to the worker's wages, work hours, and legal overtime ratios, it can be concluded that overtime wages have been included in the wages paid by the employer." Liu Fei and Nantong Yide Logistics Co., Ltd. Labor Dispute Appeal, Application for Civil Ruling Jiangsu Provincial People's High Court Civil Ruling (2018) Sumin Shen No. 1013. The court held that when the piecework quota could not be determined, the standard work hour system could be directly used to calculate whether the overtime wages were insufficient.

the employment laws. For example, Mr. Zhang's piecework quota is 1,000, and the piecework unit price is RMB 2. In a particular month, he completed 1,100 units in normal work hours (standard 174 hours per month in China), 200 units in 40 hours of weekday overtime, and 50 units in 10 hours of weekend day overtime; and his wage is RMB 2,900 under the piecework wage system (see "112. How do I calculate the wages of employees under the piecework wage system?"). Mr. Zhang's average hourly wage under the standard work hour system is RMB 11.4 (2,900 / [174 + 40 * 150% + 10 * 200%]). If the local minimum hourly wage is RMB 22, Mr. Zhang's wage obviously falls under the minimum wage standard. Therefore, the piecework quota and piecework unit price are not reasonable. Mr. Zhang's wages must be adjusted to RMB 5,588 (22 * [174 + 40 * 200% + 10 * 200%]) based on the minimum hourly wage.

The second factor is industrial practice. Reasonableness also requires a piecework quota conforming to the industry standard or a fair level in the industry in terms of the productivity of an individual employee. Courts may invalidate overly high piecework quotas. However, as to who (the employer or the employee) is responsible for proving the reasonableness or unreasonableness of the piecework quota, courts around the country adopt different practices at present. In the case of Shen Xulan in 2015, the Shenzhen Intermediate Court held that the employer should be responsible for proving the rationality of the piecework quota.[9] The reason is probably that Guangdong Province has a regulation in place requesting that at least 70% of staff should be able to complete the piecework quota within normal work hours.[10] However, there are also decisions ruling that employees are obligated to prove the unreasonableness of their piecework quotas.

A more reasonable approach may be to compare piecework wages under a piecework wage system with industry wage guidance prices. A typical case is Li Jian before Huzhou Intermediate Court of Zhejiang Province in 2015.[11] If the piecework quota and piecework unit price are found to be unreasonable, the court should determine a reasonable piecework unit price or piecework quota according to the industry wage guidance. However, due to the lack of guidance from legislation and judicial interpretation, this approach may go further than the courts are willing to intervene. In practice, if courts find that a set of piecework quota and piecework unit price is unreasonable, they normally resort to the minimum wage standard under the standard work hour system to calculate the employees' wages.

---

9 Xue Chengsong, Wenzhou Shenshi Stationery Co., Ltd. Civil Judgment of the Second Instance of Labor Dispute Civil Judgment of Wenzhou Intermediate People's Court of Zhejiang Province (2020) No. 5193. "The employer implements the piecework wage system for workers, and if the workers claim overtime wages, they shall mainly examine whether the piecework wage piecework quota is reasonable. However, Xue Chengsong did not prove that he and Shenshi Company had agreed on the piecework wage quota or that there was an industry standard that could be referred to." Labor dispute between Shen Xulan and Shenzhen Weimei Children's Products Co., Ltd., Shenzhen Intermediate People's Court of Guangdong Province issued a civil judgment (2015) Shen Zhong Fa Lao Zhong Zi No. 662. The court held that the employer had not submitted evidence to prove the rationality of the piecework quota, so it was examined whether the hourly wage of employees was lower than the minimum wage standard according to the conversion of the standard work hour system.

10 Article 21 of the Guangdong Province Wage Payment Regulations. "Where piecework wages are implemented, the employer shall scientifically and reasonably determine the piecework quota and piecework unit price and publish them. In principle, the piecework quota determined shall enable more than 70% of the workers in the same role of the employer to complete within the standard work hours."

11 In the labor dispute appeal case between Li Jian and Huzhou Tianyang Cable Co., Ltd., Zhejiang Huzhou Intermediate People's Court Civil Judgment (2015) Zhe Hu Min Zhong Zi No. 222. The court compared the median wage standard of the wage guidance price of the same industry with the wages of the employees and concluded that the piecework quota was reasonable.

114. How are wages calculated under the package wage system?

Answer: The package wage system refers to a wage system where employees' monthly wages, agreed upon by the employers and employees, include a certain number of overtime hours as part of the packaged pay. Instead of providing additional overtime pay after employees do overtime work within the agreed number of overtime hours, the employers pay a fixed agreed wage package. Therefore, the package wage is a "package" wage that includes both normal and overtime wages, and is normally applied to employees with a fixed overtime arrangement.

To compute the normal work hour wage included in a package wage in a particular month, it is necessary to reverse the calculation method of overtime wages. For example, Ms. Li's contract stipulates a monthly package wage of RMB 5,000, including 10 hours of overtime on weekdays and 4 hours of overtime at weekends. Let's assume that her normal hourly rate is H. The calculation equation is: $H * 21.75 * 8 + H * 10 * 150\% + H * 4 * 200\% = 5{,}000$. Her normal hourly wage is RMB 25.38, and thus, her normal work hour wage is RMB 4,416 in the month.

Having obtained Ms. Li's normal hourly rate, we can further calculate overtime wages if she worked more overtime hours than provided in the contract. For example, in another specific month, she worked 15 hours of weekday overtime and 8 hours of weekend overtime in addition to her normal work hours in this month, meaning that she had additional 5 hours of weekday overtime and 4 hours of weekend overtime outside her original package. Therefore, her wage payable this month is RMB 5,394 ($5{,}000 + [15 - 10] * 25.38 * 150\% + [8 - 4] * 25.38 * 200\%$).

115. An employer pays night allowance under the minimum wage to an employee on night duty. Is it legal?

Answer: Whether it is lawful for the employer to do so depends on whether the nature of the employee being on night duty falls under work or overtime work.

As for whether an employee being on night duty under a standard work hour system (such as permanent, fixed term, labor dispatch, or assignment contract) falls under overtime work, current practices in court cases predominantly consider factors such as work requirements for employees on night shift, their freedom of movement, whether they can rest and sleep, and other relevant factors to determine whether being on night duty qualifies as overtime work, thereby obliging the employer to pay overtime wages.[12]

---

12 Wu Guangyong, Shenzhen Yantian District People's Hospital Labor Dispute Civil Judgment of Second Instance Civil Judgment of Shenzhen Intermediate People's Court of Guangdong Province (2021) Yue 03 Min Zhong No. 25131. The court held that the labor intensity, free activities, and work tasks of the employee on duty in the hospital determined that the shift was not overtime. Zhongkai Agricultural Engineering College and Ma Jinbao Labor Dispute Civil Judgment of Second Instance Civil Judgment of Guangzhou Intermediate People's Court of Guangdong Province (2022) Yue 01 Min Zhong 11354. The court held that "directly restricting and affecting their right to leave their roles for rest and free activities led the work to be overtime." Yuan Xiaoping, Jiangxi Wannianqing Science and Technology Industrial Park Co., Ltd. Civil Judgment of the Second Instance of Labor Dispute Civil Judgment of the Intermediate People's Court of Nanchang City, Jiangxi Province (2020) Gan 01 Min Zhong No. 513. The court held that the time for employees to sleep on night shift and eat on day shift was not overtime. Article 8 of the Answers to Several Difficult Questions on the Trial of Labor Dispute Cases by the Civil First Division of Zhejiang Provincial People's High Court stipulates that "the nature of the work of security guards, communication room guards, warehouse keepers, and other personnel who live and eat 24 hours a day in their employer's place has its particularity. If because of working place needs and genuine employer's requirement, employees cannot sleep. They should be considered working; Where accommodations

A more reasonable test for assessment may be that during night duty, the greater responsibility the employees assume, the less freedom they have to leave the workplace, and the more frequently they must wake up to work, the more likely it is that their night duty will be considered overtime work, and consequently, the more likely that the trivial night allowance constitutes an underpaid overtime wage; however, if an employee basically sleeps in the rest room and rarely needs to get up to work, the employee is free to leave the workplace for a short time, and the responsibility of the duty is relatively low, it is probably not overtime work, it may, therefore, be reasonable for the employer to pay a small amount of night allowance. At present, the prevailing court decisions also hold that when an employee has a trivial night shift task and can take a rest, the employee's claims for overtime pay shall not be upheld once night allowance has been paid.[13]

If the employee's night duty is recognized as overtime, can the night allowance paid by the employer offset the overtime wages that the employer should pay? There are very few such court cases. Some courts held that night allowance could not offset overtime wages unless both parties agreed otherwise.[14] However, for the sake of fairness, we believe that employers requesting night allowance to offset payable overtime wages is reasonable.

For other special types of employees, if the employees are classified as employees on irregular hours, even if their night duty is considered to be work, they may only be eligible for overtime wages for night duties on public holidays, or in some regions, they may not be eligible for overtime pay at all. If they are employees on general work hours, even if their night duty is considered work, they still need to calculate whether their total hours within the accounting cycle exceed the standard work hours to be eligible for overtime wages. If they are part-time employees, and their night duty is considered work, they may still only be eligible for overtime wages for night duties on public holidays, or in some regions, they may not be eligible for overtime pay at all. Please refer to "71. How do I calculate overtime pay under special work hour systems?"

116. Are companies still obligated to pay commissions or bonuses promised to employees after the employees leave?

Answer: Performance-based commissions or bonuses are considered part of labor compensation, as defined by the 1990 Regulations on the Composition of Total Wages issued

---

or rest facilities are provided, work hours should deduct time for sleep and rest, excluding the hours not for normal work, and the employer must pay overtime for work hours exceeding the standard hours. In judicial practice, the following factors can be considered comprehensively: whether the employer has applied to the labor administrative authority for the examination and approval of the general workhour system and the irregular workhour system for the role (attention should be paid to valid granted period and the number of people granted); whether the employer has equipped the workers with necessary rest facilities in the workplace; the requirements for the specific work content and work intensity of the employee in the work system or company rules and regulations (to judge whether the employee's work in accordance with the system will lead to the fact that it is impossible to rest); the number of people on duty arranged by the employer (that is, to consider whether the employee has the possibility of taking turns to have a rest)."

13 In the labor dispute appeal case between He Maorong and Chongqing Golden Phoenix Talent Exchange Service Co., Ltd., Civil Judgment of the First Intermediate People's Court of Chongqing (2015) Yu Yi Zhong Fa Min Zhong Zi No. 02792, the court held that the employee's request for overtime pay was not supported because the night shift allowance had been paid and the employee could sleep on duty.

14 Qingdao Licang District Lekang Hospital, Zhang Jinyuan Labor Dispute Retrial Review and Trial Supervision Civil Ruling Shandong Provincial People's High Court Civil Ruling (2020) Lu Min Shen No. 772. The court held that the two parties did not explicitly agree that the night shift allowance was overtime pay, so the additional calculation of overtime pay was not improper.

by the National Bureau of Statistics. They are a fundamental obligation of employers under employment contracts. Therefore, whether an employee is still employed or has left, the employer is obligated to pay the commissions or bonuses agreed upon or promised by the employer.

For example, in the Supreme People's Court's Guiding Case No. 182 of 2022, the labor dispute case of Peng Yuxiang v. Nanjing Urban Construction Development (Group) Co., Ltd., the employer formulated a reward scheme stipulating that if an employee successfully introduced commodity housing projects, the company promised to pay the employee a certain percentage of the expected profit or revenue from the introduced projects as a reward. The employee introduced six commodity housing projects during their employment and applied for the rewards, but the company did not pay when the employee resigned. The employee then filed a labor arbitration claim demanding RMB 1.69 million. The final judgment of the Nanjing Intermediate People's Court of Jiangsu Province held that the reward promised by the company is part of the wages, and the employer has the obligation to pay the employee when the conditions for the reward are met. The court ultimately ruled that the employer should pay the employee a reward of nearly RMB 1.26 million.[15]

In practice, employers may argue that the company's reward scheme should be approved by the company's management before payment, and since the approval process has not been completed, the conditions for payment of the bonus have not been met, so there is no need to pay. However, the Nanjing Intermediate People's Court in Peng Yuxiang case held that employers should honor the reward commitment to employees, and the approval of the reward by the company's leadership should not constitute a substantive condition preventing the employer from fulfilling the payment of the reward.

If commissions and bonuses were formed many years ago but have not been paid by the company, can employees demand payment after resignation? This issue involves the limitation of arbitration for commissions and bonuses. Since commissions and bonuses are considered wages, if an employee files this type of labor arbitration claims within one year after resignation, the claim will not be struck out due to the expiration of the limitation. The labor arbitration committee should review whether there is a basis for the commission or bonus and then make a ruling on whether the employer should pay. Please refer to "27. Is there a time limitation for employees or employers to file an employment arbitration application?"

117. My employer significantly reduced my wages. Is it legal?

Answer: The wage standards agreed upon in the employment contract or being implemented by both parties are protected by employment law, and wage reduction may impose significant impact on employees' financial stability. In principle, employers may not reduce the agreed-upon wage standards specified in the employment contract or decrease wages after an actual wage increase(s) without the employees' consent. However, in practice, aside from instances where employees explicitly agree to a wage reduction, there are two potential legally permissible exceptions to wage reductions.

15 Supreme People's Court Guiding Case No. 182: Peng Yuxiang v. Nanjing Urban Construction Development (Group) Co., Ltd., Labor Compensation Dispute Case. Published in the *Supreme People's Court Gazette*, 2022, Issue No. 10 (Total No. 314), Pages 16–18.

The first scenario involves the employee accepting the effectiveness of a wage reduction during the performance of the employment contract. If, after an employee's wage was unilaterally reduced for a certain period, the employee does not raise objections, this may be deemed as the employee consenting to the wage reduction. According to the 2020 Supreme Court's Judicial Interpretation, if a change to an employment contract has been implemented in practice for more than one month, the courts shall not uphold either party's assertion that the change is invalid due to its not being in written form.[16] This provision is widely applied in various court cases concerning employee wage reductions. Courts generally consider that if an employee, after experiencing a wage reduction, continues to perform their duties for more than one month (presumably after receiving more than one month of wages) and does not raise objections, it is deemed that both parties have effectively modified the wage standards through practical performance.[17]

A typical situation is where an employment contract between two parties has provided for a higher wage standard, but from the beginning of the performance of the employment contract, the employee's wage is paid at a lower standard, and the employee has not raised any objection for more than one month. In this case, the courts usually apply the 2020 Supreme Court's Judicial Interpretation to find that both parties have changed the contract agreement by actual performance, and that this change is valid and binding.[18]

The second scenario is when the employer transfers the position of an employee, leading to a reasonable reduction of the employee's wages. If the employer's position transfer for the employee is lawful, the adjustment of the employee's wages, either decreasing or increasing, may be deemed lawful. Courts typically assess the legitimacy of such position transfer and wage reductions by considering the business needs of the employer and the impact on the employee. It is crucial to note that under this comprehensive evaluation of multiple factors, excessively reducing an employee's wage may adversely affect the

16 Article 43 of the Interpretation of the Supreme People's Court on the Application of Law in the Trial of Labor Dispute Cases (I) (Judicial Interpretation [2020] No. 26) stipulates that "if the employer and the worker have changed the employment contract by mutual agreement, although not in written form, but have actually fulfilled the orally changed employment contract for more than one month, and the content of the changed employment contract does not violate laws and regulations, the people's court shall not support either party's claim that the alteration of the employment contract is invalid on the grounds that it is not in written form."

17 Wang Junbiao and Shenzhen Jinyang Electronics Co., Ltd. Labor Dispute Second Instance Civil Judgment Guangdong Province Shenzhen Intermediate People's Court Civil Judgment (2016) Yue 03 Minzhong No. 13128. "Jinyang Company changed Wang Junbiao's monthly wage from RMB 36,000 to RMB 26,000 since February 2015, which constitutes a change of employment contract, and both sides have actually fulfilled it for eight months. Wang Junbiao had no evidence to prove that he had raised objections during this period, which is regarded as approval." Civil Judgment of Second Instance on Labor Dispute between Shen QiNan and Evergrande Real Estate Group Pearl River Delta Real Estate Development Co., Ltd. (2018) Yue 01 Min Zhong No. 12856. "Although the above change is not in writing, it has been actually performed for more than one month, and Shen Qinan knew the above change and did not raise any objection … it is considered as both parties … reached mutual agreement."

18 Zeng Jian and Beijing Boshida Refrigeration and Air Conditioning Technology Co., Ltd. and other civil judgments of the second instance of labor disputes, Beijing the First Intermediate Court, Civil Judgment (2016) Jing 01 Min Zhong No. 5953. In the case, the contract provided that the wage standard was the monthly wage standard of employees of Beijing Refrigeration Society, but it was actually paid according to the minimum wage from 2005 to 2014; the court found it valid. Civil Judgment of the First Instance of the Employment Contract Dispute between Worewen Construction and Installation Materials (Shanghai) Co., Ltd. and Yan Xinbin, Shanghai City Minhang District Court Civil Judgment (2017) Hu 0112 Min Chu No. 16443, "Since the plaintiff has never paid the above quarterly award to the defendant since the defendant took office, it can be concluded that the above agreement has been changed in the way of actual performance."

legality of the position transfer itself. For further details, please refer to "129. How should an employer legally transfer the position of an employee?"

The lawfulness of wage reduction has a significant impact on both parties in the employment relationship. If an employer unlawfully reduces an employee's wage, they should fulfill the obligation to retroactively pay the withheld wages due to the unjustified wage deduction. In some cases, it may even lead to employees' forced resignation, resulting in the liability for the employer to pay economic compensation. Please refer to "143. Are employers liable for economic compensation for employees' forced resignation?"

4.2 Employer Management and Disciplinary Actions

118. How do Chinese laws and judicial practices address workplace human rights issues?

Answer: Discrimination, bullying, and harassment in employment relationships or the workplace are increasingly concerning issues in employment laws across various countries. The rules in Chinese labor law are relatively underdeveloped in these areas, and there are few relevant precedents in the practice of employment law in China. Our evaluation of the human rights rules established by current Chinese laws and judicial practices is as follows.

The first is wage discrimination. The Employment Contract Law stipulates the principle of equal pay for equal work, but this principle is not truly followed in judicial practice. For example, there are significant differences in wages between employees inside and outside the system of state-owned enterprises. Please refer to "90. Female employees earn less than male employees. Does the employer violate the principle of equal pay for equal work?"

The second is gender region discrimination. Although Articles 41 and 42 of the 2022 Law on the Protection of Women's Rights and Interests stipulates that discrimination against women in labor and social security is prohibited, the retirement age for women (50 or above for worker employees or 55 or above for cadre employees) differs from that for men (60 or above).[19] Employers are not allowed to discriminate against employees based on gender or region during recruitment. For example, there is a judicial case where an employer was ordered to pay RMB 10,000 in compensation for discriminating against people from Henan Province during the recruitment process.

The third is job discrimination. In labor judicial practice, courts usually consider that position transfer of employees by employers based on discrimination or insult is illegal and invalid. This is a practical rule of the anti-discrimination principle in labor management. Additionally, even if the difference in retirement age between women and men only reflects the characteristics of Chinese social culture, the different retirement ages for female workers and female cadres as stipulated by law should be considered unfair job or occupational discrimination (see "146. How does the law stipulate the statutory retirement age?").

19 In September 2024, the Standing Committee of the National People's Congress of China announced the "Decision on Implementing the Gradual Delay of the Statutory Retirement Age," stipulating that starting from 2025, over the course of 15 years, the statutory retirement age for male employees will be gradually extended from the original 60 years to 63 years, and for female employees from the original 50 and 55 years to 55 and 58 years, respectively.

The fourth is harassment. Article 11 of 2012 Special Provisions on Labor Protection for Female Employees stipulates that employers should prevent and stop sexual harassment of female employees. However, in labor judicial practice, disputes about sexual harassment usually concern disputes about violations of company rules and regulations due to sexual harassment by employees against other employees,[20] rather than disputes in which employers are held liable for civil or employment compensation. In Chinese employment practice, it is usually foreign-funded enterprises or a few local enterprises in Chinese developed cities that stipulate in their company rules and regulations or employment contracts that sexual harassment constitutes a violation of labor obligations by employees.

Fifth, in general, in labor judicial practice, it is very rare for employers to be held liable for compensation because employees have been discriminated against, bullied, or harassed. Judicial cases resulting in compensation for employees primarily involve recruitment discrimination; in other cases, it is very rare for employees who have been discriminated against, bullied, or harassed to receive compensation from employers, as such compensation usually involves mental damages. The threshold for permitting mental damages under Chinese law is relatively high, usually requiring severe consequences (such as mental disorders, suicide, etc.). See "105. Can employees claim for mental damages in employment disputes?"

119. Can employers contact employees outside work hours?

Answer: In normal circumstances, employers should refrain from contacting their employees outside their normal work hours, as this can disrupt the employees' private time.

However, in exceptional circumstances, an employer may still be entitled to contact an employee outside normal work hours. These circumstances include emergencies, important situations requiring early notification or contact, employee absence or being out of contact, employee being on call or working from home, employee being on sick leave, and employee being suspended from work. The guiding principle is that employers should treat employees honestly and in good faith, respecting their personal time.

Likewise, employees should also treat employers honestly and in good faith. They should understand that employers may need to contact them due to business needs and should not overly emphasize privacy at the expense of the legitimate interests of employers.

120. What kinds of company rules and regulations are binding on employees?

Answer: Lawful company rules and regulations, labor discipline, and basic professional ethics are binding on employees' work behavior and performance.

First, company rules and regulations are binding. Company rules and regulations of employers are the institutional documents for the company's management of employees' behavior and performance in its production and operation. Article 4 of the Employment Contract Law stipulates that company rules and regulations must protect employees' employment rights and ensure that employees fulfill their obligations. What kinds of company rules and regulations can effectively bind employees?

20 Zheng v. Honeywell Automation Control (China) Co., Ltd., labor contract dispute case, Shanghai First Intermediate People's Court, (2021) Hu 01 Min Zhong No. 2032, Supreme People's Court Guiding Case No. 181 in the 32nd batch, *Supreme People's Court Gazette*, Issue 10, 2022 (Total Issue 314), pp. 13–16.

On the one hand, the content of labor discipline in company rules and regulations and employment contracts should be legal, and the content that violates the law is invalid. For example, the following provisions in a company's rules and regulations or employment contract are illegal and consequently invalid: the length of the employee's working hours exceeding the maximum time allowed by the Labor Law,[21] the provision of poorest-performance-out system,[22] restricting the employee's right to resign,[23] monthly deduction limits of the employee compensating the employer exceeding the national or local regulations, or that an employee must pay a deposit as a guarantee for the employment relations.[24] Of course, if the contents of company rules and regulations or employment contracts are invalid, only the illegal parts are invalid, not affecting the validity of other legal parts.

On the other hand, the company rules and regulations of the employer should be formulated through legal procedures so as to be binding on the employees. The Employment Contract Law requires employers to publicize or inform employees of the company rules and regulations they have formulated.[25] In practice, employees signing training forms related to the company rules and regulations,[26] signing the text of the company rules and regulations or their notices, the employer sending or informing employees of the company rules and regulations by mass email or in management software, evidence of study or discussion of the company rules and regulations at employee congress, and even provisions mentioning the company rules and regulations in employment contracts signed by employees,[27] may all constitute evidence that the employer has publicized or informed the company rules and regulations to the employees, thus fulfilling its obligation to formulate

21 In the case of Zhang and a courier company in the second batch of typical cases of labor disputes issued by the Supreme Court in 2021, the length of working hours of employees stipulated by the unit exceeded the working hours permitted by the Labor Law, and the court ruled that the rules and regulations of the unit were illegal and could not be used as a basis for punishing employees.

22 Zijin Property Insurance Co., Ltd. Nanjing Branch v. Zhang Chenli Employment Dispute Second Instance Civil Judgment Jiangsu Nanjing Intermediate People's Court Civil Judgment (2018) Su 01 Min Zhong No. 10443. The court held that the poorest-performance-out system stipulated in the employer's company rules and regulations was invalid due to violation of the law.

23 Liu Yongzhi, Guangdong Yu'an Industrial Co., Ltd. Civil Judgment of Second Instance of Labor Dispute Civil Judgment of Meizhou Intermediate People's Court of Guangdong Province (2022) Yue 14 Min Zhong No. 1966. "Article 32 of the above-mentioned Employment Contract restricts Liu Yongzhi's right to terminate the contract and excludes Liu Yongzhi's legitimate rights, rendering it invalid."

24 Civil Judgment of Second Instance of Labor Dispute between Pan-China Innovation (Beijing) Monitoring Instrument Co., Ltd. and Sun Wence Civil Judgment of Beijing the First Intermediate People's Court (2022) Jing 01 Min Zhong No. 10829. The court found that the provisions of the company rules and regulations on the collection of employee risk deposits violated the provisions of the Employment Contract Law that employers must not collect guarantees or property from workers, so they were not binding.

25 Article 4 of the Employment Contract Law: "The employer must publicize the company rules and regulations and decisions on major matters directly related to the vital interests of the workers, or inform the workers."

26 Li Minggeng, Shenzhen Hengfeng Property Management Co., Ltd. Labor Dispute Civil Application for Retrial Review Civil Ruling Guangdong Provincial Higher People's Court Civil Ruling (2021) Yue Min Shen No. 5784. "Although Li Minggeng claims that the company rules and regulations of Hengfeng Company have not gone through democratic and publicity procedures, Li Minggeng has signed the Training Sign-in Form, and thus Hengfeng Company has completed the publicity and training procedures."

27 Application for retrial of labor dispute between Zhang Machao and Henan Youqi Human Resources Management Co., Ltd. Civil Ruling of Henan Higher People's Court (2022) Yu Min Shen No. 3832. The court held that the employment contract between the two parties had stipulated that the employee should abide by the company rules and regulations. Zheng v. Honeywell Automation Control (China) Co., Ltd., labor contract dispute case, Shanghai First Intermediate People's Court, (2021) Hu 01 Min Zhong No. 2032, Supreme People's Court Guiding Case No. 181 in the 32nd batch, *Supreme People's Court Gazette*, Issue 10, 2022 (Total Issue 314), pp. 13–16.

company rules and regulations through legal procedures. As for the provisions of employment contracts on labor discipline, of course, employment contracts must be signed by employees so as to produce binding force.

Second, lawful labor discipline is binding on employees. Article 3 of the Labor Law provides that employees must abide by company labor discipline, and Article 4 of the Employment Contract Law and Article 19 of the Labor Law also stipulate that employment contracts or company rules and regulations should include clauses of labor discipline; thus, labor discipline is an institutional document similar to company rules and regulations. Therefore, the content of labor discipline must be lawful, as company rules and regulations are; unlawful labor discipline is not binding.

Meanwhile, as labor discipline is normally established through the conclusion of an employment contract, with the nature of an individual agreement between an employee and the employer, it is not required to undergo the public notice or notification that company rules and regulations are subject to.

Third, professional ethics is binding. From the perspective of judicial cases, even if an employee's violation of professional ethics does not violate the company rules and regulations or the provisions of the employment contract, the employer can also impose disciplinary actions on the employee according to professional ethics. Professional ethics can be divided into basic professional ethics and special professional ethics. The former usually includes the honesty and credibility of employees, the duty of loyalty to their employer, and treating colleagues in a friendly way; the latter is related to the role responsibilities of employees, and behavior constituting a serious violation of professional ethics in some specific positions may well not be a violation of professional ethics in other positions. For example, drivers or pilots must not drink alcohol at work, while sales representatives may do so normally at work. Whether an employee's behavior violates professional ethics needs to be judged under specific circumstances.

In judicial practice, some acts that violate professional ethics may directly constitute the grounds for legal dismissal. These behaviors include the behavior of being absent from work without approval for several consecutive days (the current judicial practice in various places is that being absent from work for three consecutive days is a serious violation of company rules and regulations),[28] serious misconduct in specific positions (such as the aforementioned driver's drinking at work), and acts that seriously violate the employee's duty of loyalty or other basic professional ethics (such as gross negligence and corruption and criminal acts as stipulated in Article 39 of the Employment Contract Law).[29]

---

28 Wang Xiangzhang v. Shanghai Sinopec Chemical Logistics Co., Ltd. Employment Contract Dispute Case Shanghai First Intermediate People's Court Civil Judgment (2018) Hu 01 Min Zhong No. 2148. The court held that long-term absenteeism of employees, even not violating the company rules and regulations, was a violation of basic professional ethics and serious violations of discipline, and the dismissal was legal.

29 Jiangxi Zhifang CNC Power Co., Ltd., Chen Liyin Labor Dispute Second Instance Civil Judgment Jiangxi Nanchang Intermediate People's Court Civil Judgment (2019) Gan 01 Min Zhong No. 796. The court held that Article 3 of the Labor Law stipulates the obligations of employees to abide by professional ethics, so even if there are no relevant provisions in the company rules and regulations, employees can also be legally dismissed if their behavior seriously violates professional ethics. The labor dispute appeal case between Wang Yuewen and Yida Property Management Co., Ltd. Dalian Branch, Liaoning Province Dalian Intermediate People's Court Civil Judgment (2017) Liao 02 Min Zhong No. 1611. The court held that even though there was no stipulation in the company rules and regulations, the employee's behavior of buying and drinking alcohol at work seriously violated the basic professional ethics, and the dismissal of the employee was legal. Civil Ruling on Labor Dispute Retrial Review and Trial Supervision of Gaoxianghua and Fujian New Huadu

121. Is it legally permissible for my employer to discipline me?

Answer: China's Employment Contract Law allows employers to take disciplinary actions against employees. Disciplinary action is a measure taken by employer to punish an employee's misconduct according to the company rules and regulations, the employee's employment contract, and professional ethics, so as to maintain the order of company's management, punish and warn the employee, and help the employee correct themselves. In practice, disciplinary actions usually include warnings, demerits, fines, dismissals, and other measures.

The employer shall examine the legality of the company's punishment rules and the legality of the punishment.

On the one hand, employers should impose disciplinary actions on employees in accordance with effective company rules and regulations, employment contract provisions, and professional ethics. Please refer to "120. What kinds of company rules and regulations are binding on employees?"

On the other hand, the employer's disciplinary actions against employees must be fair and reasonable.

The fairness and reasonableness of disciplinary actions first require employers to follow reasonable procedures in implementing the disciplinary actions. When an employer knows that an employee may have violated the company rules and regulations, the first step is to start the investigation reasonably; that is, starting the investigation for disciplinary action should be based on plausible evidence rather than hearsay. The second step is to inform the employee of the decision of the investigation and the reasons for the investigation, and to solicit the employee's opinions and explanations. Asking questions frankly is the basis of communicating in good faith and solving problems. The third step is that employees should be given an appropriate time to respond. There are also specific things that the employer should be aware of if the investigation of an incident requires suspension of the employee (please see "122. Is it legal for my company to suspend an employee for a performance investigation?"). The fourth step is to carefully consider the employee's explanation before disciplinary action is decided, and if necessary, multiple rounds of communication can be conducted to find out the relevant facts.

The fairness and reasonableness of disciplinary actions should also require the employer to follow the principles of objectivity, non-repetition of punishment, and timely punishment. Employers should impose disciplinary actions on employees objectively and should not subjectively exaggerate the improper nature of employees' behavior. For example, if an employee is unable to ask for leave in time because of illness, the employer should consider the specific situation of the employee objectively instead of simply and roughly identifying the employee as absent from work. The employer shall not repeatedly punish the employee in different ways for the same violation of discipline. For example, in the case of Beijing Shider Automobile Parts Co., Ltd. in 2023, the Beijing High Court held

---

Comprehensive Department Store Co., Ltd. Fujian Provincial People's High Court Civil Ruling (2020) Min Min Shen No. 2157. The court held that although the supermarket employee's action did not constitute theft under the company rules and regulations, the fraud of changing price tags constituted a violation of basic professional ethics, so the dismissal of the employee was legal. Zhang and Ai Dennison (China) Co., Ltd. Tianjin Binhai Branch other labor disputes, personnel disputes retrial Tianjin High Court Civil Ruling (2020) Jin Min Shen No. 1689. The court held that the employee's violation of the privacy of the superior seriously violated professional ethics, and the dismissal of the employee was legal.

that the employer had given a verbal warning to the employee for violation of company rules and regulations but dismissed the employee three months later, and that this was a repeated punishment and therefore, an illegal dismissal.[30] Employers should also punish employees reasonably promptly for violations of company rules and regulations. A disciplinary action that exceeds a reasonable time may result in a disciplinary action that the court finds to be unlawful.[31]

Finally, employers can consider the cumulative effects of an employee's misconduct. Sometimes, an employee's violation of company rules and regulations, employment contract, or professional ethics alone may not be enough to constitute a disciplinary action, but if the cumulative factors are taken into account, the employer may have the right to discipline them. For example, in the case of Li Huasen before the Guangdong Provincial Higher People's Court in 2018, the employee had already received a number of disciplinary actions but did not reach the level of a serious violation of discipline, and later, he violated professional ethics. The court found that the accumulation of these factors was enough to amount to serious violation of company rules and regulations and that the dismissal was legal.[32]

122. Is it legal for my company to suspend an employee for a performance investigation?

Answer: The employment laws and relevant laws and regulations do not have specific provisions on suspension investigation. Because a suspension may have an adverse effect on the employee's reputation and psychology, normally, the employer's initiation and conduct of suspension investigations on the employee must be fair and reasonable.

From the perspective of case law, the first decisions of a suspension investigation must be based on reasonable facts,[33] and the reason for the suspension investigation should be that the employee has seriously violated the company rules and regulations or that the employer's business operation would be negatively affected without a suspension investigation. Second, when the employer has a legitimate reason(s) to suspend the employee, it might be able to reduce the employee's wages (for example, only pay the local minimum wage).[34] However, the company rules and regulations allowing a pay cut or paying full wages to the employee during the suspension investigation will render the suspension

30 Civil Ruling on Labor Dispute Retrial Review and Trial Supervision between Beijing Shider Automobile Parts Co., Ltd. and Lin Yasen Civil Ruling of Beijing Higher People's Court (2023) Jing Min Shen No. 1024.

31 Yan Zhihong and State Grid Shanxi Electric Power Company Taiyuan Power Supply Company Labor Dispute Second Instance Civil Judgment Shanxi Taiyuan Intermediate People's Court Civil Judgment (2020) Jin 01 Min Zhong No. 2923. The court held that the employer did not punish the employees for their long-term absence from work in a timely manner and did not strictly abide by the company rules and regulations, so it was illegal termination of the employment contract.

32 Li Huasen v. Guangdong Fenni Technology Co., Ltd., Labor Contract Dispute Retrial Review and Trial Supervision Civil Ruling, Guangdong High People's Court Civil Ruling (2018) Yue Min Shen No. 7667.

33 Chengdu Feida Real Estate Co., Ltd. and Yang Xuefen Labor Dispute Appeal Case Chengdu Intermediate People's Court of Sichuan Province Civil Judgment (2015) C.M.Z.Z. No. 4910. The court held that the employer's unilateral decision to initiate a suspension investigation without evidence of employees violating company rules and regulations was unlawful.

34 Judgment of Second Instance of Labor Dispute between Qi Wei and Dalian Bangqi Island Hotel Group Co., Ltd. Civil Judgment of Dalian Intermediate People's Court of Liaoning Province (2022) Liao 02 Min Zhong No. 5925. Civil Ruling on Labor Dispute Retrial Review and Trial Supervision of Tao Mingda and Chengdu Organic Chemistry Co., Ltd. of Chinese Academy of Sciences Civil Ruling of Sichuan High Court (2021) Chuan Min Shen No. 1278.

investigation more legitimate.[35] Lastly, suspension investigations cannot be indefinite and should be completed within a reasonable period.[36] If the ground for a suspension investigation is untenable, the investigation may be considered illegal, and the employer must provide a conclusion stating that the employee is not guilty and pay the employee's full wages for the suspension investigation if there is a pay cut.[37]

An appropriate way to enhance the lawfulness of an employer's action of suspension investigation is to stipulate grounds, procedures, and measures of suspension investigation in its company rules and regulations.

Therefore, whether your company's action of suspension investigation is legitimate depends on comprehensive assessments on whether the reasons for the suspension investigation are sufficient, the extent of reducing the employee's wages during the suspension investigation, the timeframe in which the investigation is completed, and whether your company has listened to and considered explanations by the employee before and during the investigation. Establishing specific provisions for suspension investigations in your company rules and regulations is also a recommended practice, particularly if the grounds for the investigation are performance issues with low culpability.

123. Can an employer impose a fine on an employee and deduct their wages?

Answer: A fine imposed on an employee refers to a financial penalty involving the deduction of the employee's wages by the employer because the employee violated company rules and regulations or a provision(s) of the employment contract (without causing direct economic loss). Whether employers are entitled to impose a fine, or economic penalty, on their employees is a controversial issue in the judicial practice. At present, courts around the country have two completely different practices.

One practice is to consider that employers have the right to impose fines. These courts have held that the right to impose fines is part of employers' management autonomy, but that fines should usually be limited so as not to affect their employees' subsistence. Some courts, such as the Jiangsu Provincial High Court, the Jilin Provincial High Court, Tianjin High Court, courts in Jiaozuo City in Henan Province, Baiyin City in Gansu Province, Chengde City, Shanghai City and Shenzhen City of Guangdong Province, in Hebei Province, held that as long as company rules and regulations include provisions for fines, and the company rules and regulations are valid, imposing fines is legal if the 20% limit of wage deduction under the Regulations on Rewards and Punishments for Enterprises' Employees,[38] and the remnant wages after deduction of fines being no less

35 Civil Judgment of Second Instance on the Labor Dispute Case between Feruni Ceramiche Sdn Bhd and Xi Jiaojun, Zou Qifeng, Xie Shuren, etc., Civil Judgment of Intermediate People's Court of Foshan City, Guangdong Province (2020) Yue 06 Min Zhong No. 1024. The court seems to think that the full payment of the suspended employee's wage during the suspension investigation makes the suspension investigation measure more legitimate.

36 Shenzhen Haige Jingu Industrial Technology Co., Ltd. and Kaolin Labor Dispute Second Instance Civil Judgment of Shenzhen Intermediate People's Court of Guangdong Province (2019) Yue 03 Minzhong No. 20640.

37 Civil Judgment of Second Instance of Hu Bin's Labor Dispute Civil Judgment of the Second Beijing Intermediate People's Court (2022) Jing 02 Min Zhong No. 7501.

38 Article 17 of the repealed Regulations on Rewards and Punishments for Enterprises' Employees. Hebei Iron and Steel Group Mining Co., Ltd. Chengde Mining Branch, Zhao Zhenfeng Labor Dispute Second Instance Civil Judgment Hebei Chengde Intermediate People's Court Civil Judgment (2018) Ji 08 Min Zhong No. 2116. The court held that the key to the legality of the fine lies in the validity of the company rules and

than the local minimum wage standard,[39] are observed. In accordance with its local regulations, Shenzhen City stipulates that total fines imposed on an employee must not exceed 30% of their monthly wages.[40]

Another practice is that employers have no right to impose fines at all. Courts in some regions, including the High Court of Hubei Province, Shanxi(山西) High Court, Guangdong Provincial High Court, Beijing City, Ningbo City of Zhejiang Province, Chenzhou City of Hunan Province, Xinjiang, Chengdu of Sichuan Province, Shizuishan of Ningxia, Fuyang of Anhui Province, Changsha of Hunan Province, Chongqing Municipality, Ordos of Inner Mongolia, and other courts, have decisions ruling that since the foundation for the right to impose fines, the Regulations on Rewards and Punishments for Enterprises' Employees has been repealed, the imposition of fines by employers on employees is unlawful.[41]

---

regulations on the fine. Labor Dispute Appeal between Wang Guangen and Xuzhou Qiangsheng City Gas Co., Ltd. Civil Judgment of Xuzhou Intermediate People's Court of Jiangsu Province (2010) Xu Min Zhong Zi No. 2118. Nanjing Jiangnan Bus Passenger Transport Co., Ltd. and Zhang Ling Labor Dispute Appeal and Application Civil Ruling Jiangsu Provincial People's High Court Civil Ruling (2019) SuminShen No. 943. The court held that effective company rules and regulations were the basis for the fine. Guo Dongjun and Gansu Liuhua (Group) Co., Ltd. Civil Judgment of the Second Instance of Labor Dispute Civil Judgment of Baiyin Intermediate People's Court of Gansu Province (2015) Bai Zhong Min Yi Zhong Zi No. 347. Henan Jinkai Group Wuzhi Luyu Chemical Co., Ltd. and Zhang Hongxia Labor Dispute Appeal Case Civil Judgment of Jiaozuo Intermediate People's Court of Henan Province (2017) Yu 08 Min Zhong No. 1421. Deng Chao and Jilin Gongzhuling Rural Commercial Bank Co., Ltd. Labor Dispute Retrial Review Civil Ruling Jilin Provincial People's High Court Civil Ruling (2018) Ji Min Shen No. 1460. Yin Yinghua v. third branch of Tianjin Binhai New Area Public Transport Group Co., Ltd., Employment Dispute Retrial Review and Judicial Supervision Civil Ruling Tianjin High People's Court Civil Ruling (2021) Jin Min Shen No. 654. Guizhou Yibai Pharmaceutical Co., Ltd. v. Zhou Tie, Employment Contract Dispute Second Instance Civil Judgment Shanghai First Intermediate People's Court Civil Judgment (2022) Hu 01 Min Zhong No. 10340.

39 Article 16 of the Provisional Regulations on Wage Payment.

40 Article 16 of 2019 Regulations on the Promotion of Harmonious Employment Relations in Shenzhen Special Economic Zone.

41 Yu Caiwen v. Foshan Shunde Jinding Accounting Consulting Co., Ltd. et al. Employment Contract Dispute Case Guangdong High People's Court Civil Ruling (2017) Yue Min Shen No. 7481. Hubei Tianliqi New Materials Co., Ltd. v. Wei Chunyan Labor Dispute Civil Ruling of Hubei High Court (2016) E Min Shen No. 806. Civil Judgment of the Second Instance of the Labor Dispute Case between Li Jianchun and Chenzhou Kailong Hotel Co., Ltd. and Chenzhou Yuquan Hotel Co., Ltd. Civil Judgment of Hunan Chenzhou Intermediate People's Court (2018) Xiang 10 Min Zhong No. 939. Civil Judgment of the Second Instance of Labor Dispute between Liu Houping and Changqing Transportation Branch of China Petroleum Transportation Co., Ltd. Civil Judgment of the Intermediate People's Court of Ordos City, Inner Mongolia Autonomous Region (2018) No. 1818. Appeal Case of Labor Dispute between the Second Social Welfare Institute of Wanzhou District of Chongqing and Pan Zhongyu Civil Judgment of the Second Intermediate People's Court of Chongqing (2010) Yu Er Zhong Fa Min Zhong Zi No. 1208. Hunan Caixin Global International Travel Service and Tian Rong Labor Dispute Appeal Case Changsha Intermediate People's Court Civil Judgment (2012) Chang Zhong Min Si Zhong Zi No. 1734. Fuyang Guomao Hotel Investment Management Co., Ltd. and Liu Liying, etc. Civil Judgment of Fuyang Intermediate People's Court of Anhui Province (2013) Fu Min Yi Zhong Zi No. 00041. Labor Dispute Appeal Case between Wang Mingjiang and Pingluo Chiyu Mechanical Engineering Co., Ltd. Civil Judgment of Shizuishan Intermediate People's Court of Ningxia Hui Autonomous Region (2015) Shi Min Zhong Zi No. 724. China Railway 23rd Bureau Group No. 4 Engineering Co., Ltd. and Hu Qiaochu Labor Dispute Civil Judgment of Second Instance Chengdu Intermediate People's Court of Sichuan Province Civil Judgment (2020) Chuan 01 Min Zhong No. 7845. Civil Judgment of the Second Instance of Labor Dispute between Zhu Sen and Xinjiang Kunlun Iron and Steel Co., Ltd. Civil Judgment of the Intermediate People's Court of the Sixth Division of Xinjiang Production and Construction Corps (2020) Bing 06 Min Zhong No. 312. Yang v. Shanxi Shouyang Duanwang Mining Group Co., Ltd., Employment Dispute Retrial Review and Judicial Supervision Civil Ruling Shanxi High People's Court Civil Ruling (2019) Jin Min Shen No. 1387. Yu Caiwen v. Foshan Shunde Jinding Accounting Consulting Co., Ltd. et al. Employment Contract Dispute Guangdong High People's Court Civil Ruling (2017) Yue Min Shen No. 7481. Li Jian v. Ningbo Xinjie Concrete Products Co., Ltd. Employment Dispute Zhejiang Ningbo Intermediate People's Court (2011) Zhe Yong Min

Therefore, whether an employer has the right to impose fines on employees depends on the specific practices of the courts of different provinces and municipalities where the employer is located or where the employment is performed.

Employers' imposition of fines on employees and employers' claim for employees to compensate for losses caused by their faults are different. They are normally applied independently: the former usually applies when an employee's behavior violates management norms, affecting the company's management order and labor discipline; the latter usually applies when an employee's fault causes actual losses to the company, and the employee should partially compensate.

Regarding compensation for losses caused by an employee's fault to the employer, please refer to "124. Should an employee compensate the employer for the losses caused by their fault?"

124. Should an employee compensate the employer for the losses caused by their fault?

Answer: The overall principle of handling cases where in-service employees cause losses to the employer due to their faults under Chinese employment laws is to rigorously examine the cause of the loss and limit the amount of compensation borne by employees. According to Article 16 of the effective 1994 Provisional Regulations on Wage Payment, if an employee's fault causes economic losses to the employer, the employer may demand compensation for the economic losses according to the terms of the labor contract.

Based on this provision and relevant judicial precedents, the following four conditions must all be met for employees to be liable for employers' losses.

First, the employee must have engaged in behavior that violates the terms of the employment contract, valid company rules and regulations, or professional ethics. There are differing viewpoints in judicial decisions regarding which aforementioned norm(s) is a valid basis on which employees compensate for economic losses. In the 2019 case of Quanzhou Sheshi Weaving Co., Ltd. v. Zeng Fanhe, the court ruled that according to Article 16 of the Provisional Regulations on Wage Payment, claims for losses caused by employees' negligence cannot solely rely on company rules and regulations without employment contract provision(s).[42] However, in the 2020 case of Hunan Wugang Rural Commercial Bank Co., Ltd. v. Tang Guanghong, the Hunan Provincial High Court held that employee compensation for economic losses should be governed by provisions in employment contract or legally established company rules and regulations.[43]

Yi Zhong Zi No. 576. X Company v. Fu, Employment Dispute Second Instance Civil Judgment Beijing First Intermediate People's Court Civil Judgment (2024) Jing 01 Min Zhong No. 2344.

42 Quanzhou Sheshi Weaving Co., Ltd., Zeng Fanhe Labor Dispute Retrial Review and Trial Supervision Civil Ruling Fujian Provincial People's High Court Civil Ruling (2019) Min Min Shen No. 2290. The court held that an employer only relying on company rules and regulations without an employment contract agreement cannot claim compensation for losses caused by employees' dereliction of duty. Hunan Wugang Rural Commercial Bank Co., Ltd., Tang Guanghong Labor Dispute Retrial Review and Trial Supervision Civil Ruling Hunan Provincial People's High Court Civil Ruling (2020) Xiangmin Shen No. 315. "For the situation where workers should be liable for compensation for losses caused to the employer, it must be based on the agreement in the employment contract or the provisions in the legally formulated company rules and regulations of the enterprise."

43 Hunan Wugang Rural Commercial Bank Co., Ltd., Tang Guanghong Labor Dispute Retrial Review and Trial Supervision Civil Ruling Hunan Provincial People's High Court Civil Ruling (2020) Xiangmin Shen No. 315.

In the 2021 case of Beijing Zhongsheng Health Management Co., Ltd. v. Hu Yanlin, Beijing High Court Judge Duan Chunmei was not shackled to confining herself solely to the company rules and regulations or employment contract provisions as the basis. Instead, she pointed out that the employee failed to fulfill the duty of cautious work and adhere to professional ethics, resulting in the company being defrauded of funds, and therefore should bear partial liability for the loss.[44]

Regardless of provisions of the employment contract, legally binding company rules and regulations, or implied employee professional ethics, they all constitute obligations that employees should fulfill in the performance of their employment contracts. The employment laws should certainly establish legal responsibilities for employees who violate these obligations. Therefore, the provisions of employment contract and valid company rules and regulations, as well as professional ethics, should all serve as the basis for employee compensation for economic losses rather than being limited to only one aspect.

Second, employees should only be held accountable when the nature of their misconduct is particularly egregious (such as intentional or gross negligence). Employers are the primary beneficiaries of business profits and should naturally be the main bearers of business risks. If an employee's behavior is not particularly egregious and even falls within the normal course of work, such as the normal proportion of defects produced by assembly line workers, then the consequences should certainly be borne by the employer. The law should punish behaviors of higher degrees of misconduct by employees.

For instance, in the 2020 case between Hunan Wugang Rural Commercial Bank Co., Ltd. and Tang Guanghong, Judge Jiang Lin of the Hunan Provincial High Court pointed out: "In cases where workers cause losses to employers and should bear compensation liability, this should be based on … the worker having subjective intention or gross negligence in causing the loss." The Xinjiang High Court held a similar view in the 2023 case between Xinjiang Zunmao Hongfu Hotel Co., Ltd. and Wang Guohua.[45] In the 2020 case of Liao Gaobo in Guangdong Provincial High Court, the court determined that the employee's malicious theft of the company's source code resulted in losses to the company, and the employee should compensate the company with a sum of RMB 150,000.[46]

Third, there must be a causal relationship between the employee's misconduct and the economic loss. The determination of this causal relationship should involve an objective analysis of the contribution of the employee's wrongdoing to the loss. It should assess whether the wrongdoing is a decisive factor in the loss, rather than merely applying the test of "but for the employee's wrongdoing, the loss would not have occurred." Generally, the stronger the causal connection between the employer's loss and the employee's misconduct, the more likely it is that the employee should bear compensation liability, and the higher the proportion of compensation. Other factors to consider include the specific

44 Beijing Zhongsheng Health Management Co., Ltd. and others v. Hu Yanlin Labor Dispute Retrial Review and Trial Supervision Civil Ruling, Beijing High People's Court Civil Ruling (2021) Jing Min Shen 5876.

45 Xinjiang Zunmao Hongfu Hotel Co., Ltd., Wang Guohua Labor Dispute Civil Trial Supervision Civil Ruling, Xinjiang Uygur Autonomous Region Higher People's Court Civil Ruling (2023) Xin Min Shen 435. Hunan Wugang Rural Commercial Bank Co., Ltd., Tang Guanghong Labor Dispute Retrial Review and Trial Supervision Civil Ruling, Hunan Provincial High People's Court Civil Ruling (2020) Xiang Min Shen 315.

46 Liao Gaobo v. Zhuhai Ruijing Juyuan Technology Co., Ltd. Labor Dispute Retrial Review and Trial Supervision Civil Ruling, Guangdong Provincial High People's Court Civil Ruling (2020) Yue Min Shen 12508.

background of the employee's wrongdoing, whether there is a high degree of subjective malice, and serious violations of professional ethics.

Especially, consideration should be given to whether the employer itself is at fault in management for not taking necessary preventive or remedial measures, as employee misconduct leading to loss is often a result of poor company management.

Fourth, employers must have suffered actual and direct economic losses. The employer must provide evidence to prove that such losses do indeed exist rather than merely demonstrating interference or inconvenience caused to the company's operations by the employee's act. Judicial precedents show that in many cases where employers claimed compensation from employees, courts did not uphold their claims because the employers failed to submit evidence of actual losses. After all, employers must prove the facts they assert with evidence in judicial proceedings. Chinese contract law distinguishes between direct losses and indirect losses, the latter also known as foreseeable profit, which is the loss of profit that the non-breaching party could have obtained but did not due to the breach of contract. The losses that employers can claim should be direct losses rather than foreseeable profit.

Therefore, when considering the aforementioned four conditions in determining the employee's compensation liability, courts generally, based on the principle of protecting vulnerable employees, consider overall factors such as the degree of employee misconduct, the employee's income level, the completeness of the employer's management system and the degree of poor management, the severity of the consequences of the loss, the presence of fault factors in other parties, etc.[47] Ultimately, they reach a fair and reasonable conclusion on whether the employee should compensate and the amount of compensation.

Finally, when employers require employees to compensate the economic loss and deduct the employees' wages, monthly deduction amounts must not exceed 20% of the employees' wages, and the employees' wages after deduction must not fall short of local minimum wage standard.[48] Some places, such as Shenzhen, Guangdong Province, stipulate that the monthly deduction must not exceed 30% of the wages.

The aforementioned is a general situation in which an employee causes tangible losses to the employer due to their fault during the performance of the employment contract. As for employees' liabilities for unlawful resignation, please see "177. Is an employee liable for the employer's losses caused by inadequate notice of resignation?" For departed employees causing losses to their employers by infringing trade secrets of the employers and/or violating the obligations of non-competition, we will deal with the issues concerning trade secrets and non-competition in Chapter 6.

125. What are the legal consequences of an employee being transferred between two employers?

Answer: The arrangement by one employer for an employee to transfer to another employer, not due to the employee's own reasons, may lead to two main types of disputes:

47 Beijing Dongxing Hengyuan Import and Export Co., Ltd. v. Tang Min Labor Dispute Retrial Review and Trial Supervision Civil Ruling, Beijing Higher People's Court Civil Ruling (2020) Jing Min Shen 5751.

48 Article 16 of the Provisional Regulations on Wage Payment stipulates that "if a worker causes economic losses to the employer due to their own reasons, the employer may claim compensation for the economic losses in accordance with the agreement of the employment contract. Compensation for economic losses may be deducted from the wages of the worker. However, the monthly deduction shall not exceed 20% of the worker's monthly wage. If the remaining wage after deduction is lower than the local monthly minimum wage standard, it shall be paid according to the minimum wage standard."

first, when the employee's employment terminates in the latter employer, whether their service years at the former employer should be included for calculating economic compensation, meaning whether the employee's service years can be continuously calculated between the two employers; second, when the employee does not sign an employment contract with the latter employer, whether the calculation of double-wage damages is affected by the employment contract's signing status of the former employer.

Regarding the first issue, the Supreme Court's judicial interpretation in 2020 has a clear provision. Any position transfer or change arranged by the employer(s), not due to the employee's own reasons (including status changes of the employer, such as equity change, company mergers and divisions, transfers or mixed employment between affiliated companies, etc.), the employee's service years should be continuously calculated between the two employers. However, if the employee has already received economic compensation when leaving the previous employer, then only the service years of the latter employer should be calculated.[49]

For the second issue, the liability for double-wage damages is related to whether there is mixed employment among multiple companies. If these companies engage in mixed employment with an employee, meaning multiple companies simultaneously use the employee and sign employment contracts or purchase social insurance for the employee in rotation, the legal consequence of mixed employment is that these companies are considered as one employer. If the first company signs an employment contract with the employee, it is considered that other employers have signed an employment contract with the employee.[50] Similarly, if the first company does not sign an employment contract with the employee for one year, then other employers shall be deemed to have signed a permanent employment contract with the employee, based on Article 14 of the Employment Contract law, because they are considered as one employer. Please refer to "126. What are the legal consequences of multiple employers using a full-time employee at the same time?" for the identification of mixed employment and its legal consequences.

49 Article 46 of the Interpretation of the Supreme People's Court on the Application of Law in the Trial of Labor Dispute Cases (I) (Judicial Interpretation [2020] No. 26).

50 The Supreme People's Court issued the Annual Excellent Cases of the National Court System in 2019. Shenzhen Chain Golden Internet Finance Service Co., Ltd. and Xie Xiulian, the Guangdong Shenzhen Intermediate People's Court, Civil Judgment (2018) Yue 03 Min Zhong No. 13950. In this case, the employee requested Chain Golden Finance Company to compensate double-wage damages. However, during the period for the claim, the employee had an employment contract with Fullwood Company, a related company of Chain Golden Finance Company. There was a fact of mixed employment between the two companies regarding this employee. The court held that Chain Golden Finance Company did not have malicious mixed employment, so it did not support the claim for double-wage damages. The Civil Judgment of the Second Trial of Labor Dispute between Chen Mouli and Zhangpu County Certain Construction Investment Co., Ltd., the Fujian Zhangzhou Intermediate People's Court, Civil Judgment (2023) Min 06 Min Zhong No. 1380. The Civil Judgment of the Second Trial of Labor Dispute between Wang Shaojun and Xinhua Six and Feed Co., Ltd. Juxian Branch, the Shandong Rizhao Intermediate People's Court, Civil Judgment (2023) Lu 11 Min Zhong No. 64. The court considered that the transfer of employees to related companies should be regarded as the continuation of the employment between related companies and did not support the employees' request for double-wage damages. Article 16 of the "Labor Dispute Adjudication and Arbitration Coordination Working Conference Minutes" issued by the Dongguan Intermediate People's Court and the Dongguan Labor Dispute Arbitration Committee, as well as the documents from Hefei City, explicitly state that "if a worker has employment relationships with multiple employers who share mixed employment or have an affiliate relationship, and signs an employment contract with one of the employers, if the worker claims other employers to pay double-wage damages for not signing employment contract, the claim shall not be supported."

However, if there is no mixed employment among the companies, but a clear sequence of employment relationships, then the examination of double-wage damages should separately consider the responsibility for double-wage damages of each employer for the employee, rather than treating two or more employers as one.[51] For example, if employee Ms. Li is transferred from Company A to Company B and no longer works for Company A, and Ms. Li claims double-wage damages because she did not sign an employment contract with either Company A or Company B, then we should take into account the one-year limitation of arbitration and examine the liabilities of Company A and Company B respectively. For details, please refer to "52. How are double-wage damages calculated for a newly joined employee?"

126. What are the legal consequences of multiple employers using a full-time employee at the same time?

Answer: Compared with the common situation that a full-time employee only serves one employer, it is a special employment phenomenon for multiple employers to use one employee at the same time. This phenomenon may lead to the identification of mixed employment, and these employers are considered to constitute an employment relationship with the employee at the same time, and jointly assume the employer's obligations and liabilities under the Labor Law for the employee.

There is no clear definition of mixed employment in the employment laws; it is is a term produced in judicial precedents and the practice of the employment laws, referring to the rights and obligations relationship under the employment laws between multiple employers and the same full-time employee at the same time and known to all parties. These rights and obligations lead to multiple employment relationships. Mixed employment is obviously different from the multiple employment relationship of part-time employment, which is stipulated in Section 3 of Chapter 5 of the Employment Contract Law. Mixed employment is also different from a multiple employment relationship established by full-time employees illegally and privately.

As can be seen from judicial precedents, courts usually judge whether there is mixed employment based on the signing of multiple labor contracts, the factual employment relationship (such as work content, workplace, etc.), subject(s) of salary payment, subject(s) of social insurance contribution, and control of the ownership structure of the employers.

For example, in the labor dispute between Wang Jiangping and China Youth (Beijing) Investment Fund Management Co., Ltd. in 2019, the Beijing High Court held that there was a factual employment relationship between the employee and several companies, so the mixed employment was established.[52] In the 2020 case of a labor dispute between Beijing Jiayu Xiangmei Enduring Cosmetics Co., Ltd. and Yang Fan, the Beijing Higher People's Court confirmed the establishment of mixed employment based on the attendance records of the employee in several companies, the payment of wages to the employee by several companies and shareholders, and the coincidence of shareholders in several companies.[53]

---

51 Article 46 of the Interpretation of the Supreme People's Court on the Application of Law in the Trial of Labor Dispute Cases (I) (Judicial Interpretation [2020] No. 26).

52 Wang Jiangping et al. and Guozhongqing (Beijing) Investment Fund Management Co., Ltd. Civil Ruling of Beijing Higher People's Court (2019) Jing Min Shen No. 4597.

53 Beijing Jiayu Xiangmei Enduring Cosmetics Co., Ltd. and Yang Fan labor dispute retrial review and trial supervision civil ruling Beijing Higher People's Court Civil Ruling (2020) Jing Min Shen No. 3790.

In the 2022 case of a labor dispute between Wendeng Branch of Zhuoda Property Service Co., Ltd. and Jin Wanzhong, Shandong Provincial High Court held that before the expiration of the employment contract between the employee and the head office, the employee began to work for the branch, and the branch purchased social insurance and paid wages for him, and that mixed employment was therefore established.[54]

Mixed employment among multiple companies is often a feature of mixed operation among these companies. Mixed operation often refers to the common use of capital, personnel, equipment, premises, and other production factors by multiple affiliated companies for joint operation, and the common use of employees is of course a very common feature.

Therefore, in judicial practice, the courts sometimes cite the criteria for determining mixed operation between a company and its shareholders under the Company Law, that is, the criteria for determining merger of personality in Article 10 of the Summary of the National Courts' Civil and Commercial Trial Work Conference in 2019, to conduct a comprehensive analysis of merger of capital, financial management and records, personnel, business scope, equipment, residence, and equity control to determine whether mixed employment is established.

For example, in the case of the labor dispute between Pan Congxi and Yueyang Fuerkang Absorbent Cotton Co., Ltd. and Hunan Fuerkang Medical and Health Materials Co., Ltd. in 2022, Judge Hu Fujun of Yueyang Intermediate Court of Hunan Province cited the criteria for determining merger of corporate personality in the Summary of the National Courts' Civil and Commercial Trial Work Conference in 2019 in analyzing whether the two companies constituted mixed employment of the employee.[55] In the labor dispute between Xie Moujin and Guangzhou Baishun Synthetic Materials Co., Ltd. in 2023, the Guangzhou Intermediate Court of Guangdong Province, based on the fact that the two companies had similar names, the same office location, overlapping managers, and similar business scope, found that using mixed employment was highly probable.[56]

The establishment of mixed employment means that multiple companies should bear common employer obligations and liabilities to one employee, or be regarded as one employer. These companies should be jointly and severally liable for the employee's wages, overtime wages, unused annual leave pay, high-temperature allowances, work injury entitlements, entitlements of medical care leave, and the economic compensation or punitive damages after termination, unless there are express contractual agreements between the employee and the employers. If the employee has signed an employment contract with one company, it may mean that they have signed an employment contract with all other companies and may not be able to claim double-wage damages from other companies. It may also mean that the employee's service years in the calculation of the employee's entitlements to economic compensation or punitive damages may include their

---

54 Civil Ruling on Civil Application for Retrial Review of Labor Contract Dispute between Wendeng Branch of Zhuoda Property Service Co., Ltd. and Jin Wanzhong Shandong Higher People's Court Civil Ruling (2022) Lu Min Shen No. 7669.

55 Pan Yanxi v. Yueyang Fuerkang Absorbent Cotton Co., Ltd., Hunan Fuerkang Medical and Sanitary Materials Co., Ltd. and other civil judgments of the second instance of labor dispute civil judgment of Yueyang Intermediate People's Court of Hunan Province (2022) Xiang 06 Min Zhong No. 2981.

56 Xie Moujin, Guangzhou Baishun Synthetic Materials Co., Ltd. and other civil judgments of labor dispute civil second instance, Guangzhou Intermediate People's Court of Guangdong Province Civil Judgment (2023) Yue 01 Min Zhong No. 34642, 34643.

service years in more than one company.[57] This is stipulated by Article 9 of the 2023 Consultation Draft on the Interpretation of the Supreme People's Court on the Application of Law in the Trial of Labor Dispute Cases (II).

For example, in the labor dispute case between Zhou Huamai and Zhejiang Heduoduo Cultural Industry Development Co., Ltd. in 2023, Judge Yang Zongbo of Wenzhou Intermediate People's Court of Zhejiang Province pointed out that in the case of mixed employment, "in order to prevent multiple companies from evading their employment responsibilities and to effectively protect the employee's legal rights and interests, in the case where it is impossible to accurately identify the employer, it can be determined that the affiliated companies shall bear joint and several liability."[58] In addition, in the enforcement stage of labor dispute judgments, the courts can also add affiliated companies as the persons subject to enforcement based on the mixed operation and property merger between the companies, so as to pay off the employee's labor remuneration or compensations.

127. Who is liable for damages to a third party caused by an employee who is working for the employer?

Answer: The bearer of liability for damages caused by an employee during work depends on the nature of the employee's actions. Article 1191 of the Civil Code stipulates: "If an employee of an employer causes harm to another person while performing work tasks, the employer shall bear tort liability."

This legal provision clarifies that the premise for the employer to bear the liability for damages is that the employee's tortious act was "in the performance of work tasks." In other words, if the employee's action was in the performance of work tasks, the employer must assume responsibility. Otherwise, the action is considered a personal act of the employee, and the liability for damages to others should be borne by the employee instead of the employer.

There is no clear legal definition in the current effective laws for determining whether an employee's act constitutes "performance of work tasks." Generally, undisputed common sense is that an employee's act authorized or instructed by the employer is considered performance of work tasks. However, in judicial practice, there are often cases where the employee acts without the employer's instruction or authorization. Article 9 of the now-invalid 2003 the Interpretation of the Supreme People's Court on Several Issues Concerning the Application of Law in the Trial of Personal Injury Compensation Cases once provided that if an employee's act, though not authorized or instructed by the employer, has inherent connections with the employee's duties, it also constitutes "engaging in employment activities," which is virtually identical to "performance of work tasks."[59] However, the latest revision of this judicial interpretation and other laws have not inherited or listed this. We believe this is an oversight in legislative revision.

57 Article 46 of the 2020 Supreme Court's Judicial Interpretation stipulates that when multiple affiliated companies sign labor contracts with employees in turn, the length of service of employees shall be calculated continuously.

58 Zhou Huamai, Zhejiang Heduo Cultural Industry Development Co., Ltd. Civil Judgment of Second Instance of Labor Dispute Civil Judgment of Wenzhou Intermediate People's Court of Zhejiang Province (2023) Zhe 03 Min Zhong No. 6060.

59 Article 9 of the 2003 Interpretation of the Supreme People's Court on Several Issues Concerning the Application of Law in the Trial of Personal Injury Compensation Cases (Judicial Interpretation [2003] No. 20) stipulates that "if an employee causes damage to others in their employment activities, the employer shall be

In fact, courts nationwide still use "inherent connections" as the test for determining whether an employer should bear liability for an employee's tortious act. For example, in the 2024 case of Chabuchaer Xibe Autonomous County v. Wu, a staff member of a village committee caused a fire by the unauthorized burning of weeds, which damaged seedlings, and the Xinjiang High Court ruled that Wu's act was a job-related behavior with inherent connections to the village committee's management work;, thus, the village committee should bear the liability for Wu's act.[60]

As can be seen from judicial precedents, the determination of "inherent connections" should mainly examine the nature of the act, the employee's work responsibilities, and the purpose and consequences of the act. For example, if a driver causes harm to another person while delivering goods for the company under the influence of alcohol, this act is inherently connected to the work tasks, and the employer should bear the liability.[61] However, if the employee causes harm while driving under the influence after work, the employer should not be liable. Similarly, in the 2024 Xinjiang High Court case, Wu's action and consequences were closely related to his management work, so the village committee should bear the liability.

There are two situations regarding whether the employee should bear personal liability. The first situation, as mentioned earlier, is that if the employee's tortious act is not in the performance of the employer's work tasks, or is not inherently related to the employee's duties, the act is a personal act, and the liability for damages should be borne by the employee personally rather than by the employer.

The second situation is that the employee's tortious act is in the performance of the employer's work tasks. Article 1191 of the Civil Code does not explicitly state that in this situation, the employee does not bear joint liability. In judicial practice, whether the employee bears joint liability with the employer depends on whether the employee's act was intentional or grossly negligent.

On the one hand, even if the harmed party does not pursue personal liability of the employee, the employer may still seek compensation from the employee for violating company rules, the employment contract, or professional ethics.[62] However, such claims are strictly limited and are different from the employee directly bearing civil liability. Please refer to "124. Should an employee compensate the employer for the losses caused by their fault?"

On the other hand, if the employee's tortious act in the performance of work tasks is intentional or grossly negligent, the employee may bear joint liability with the employer.

---

liable for compensation; if the employee causes damage to others intentionally or in gross negligence, he shall be jointly and severally liable with the employer. If the employer is jointly and severally liable for compensation, it may recover the compensation from the employee. The term 'engaging in employment activities' as mentioned in the preceding paragraph refers to engaging in production and operation activities or other labor activities within the scope authorized or instructed by the employer. If an employee's behavior is beyond the scope of authorization, but its manifestation is the action of their duties or has inherent connection to the action of their duties, it shall be recognized as 'engaging in employment activities'."

60 Chabuchaer Xibe Autonomous County Villagers' Committee v. Wu Property Damage Compensation Dispute Second Instance Civil Judgment Xinjiang Uygur Autonomous Region High People's Court Ili Kazakh Autonomous Prefecture Branch (2024) Xin 40 Min Zhong No. 215.

61 Anyang Wanfeng Logistics Co., Ltd. v. Zhang Yi et al. Motor Vehicle Traffic Accident Liability Dispute Hubei Provincial People's High Court Civil Ruling (2017) E Min Shen No. 3351.

62 Article 1191 of the Civil Code stipulates that: "if a staff member of an employer causes damage to others due to actions of their work tasks, the employer shall bear tort liability."

China's basic legal principle on civil tort is to punish faults and compensate for losses. For example, in the 2019 Sichuan High Court case of Li Changjun, the court stated that the law does not prohibit the victim from seeking compensation from the tortfeasor personally, based on the Supreme Court's interpretation on personal injury compensation cases.[63]

Similarly, in the 2017 case of Loudi Huize Economic and Trade Co., Ltd., Huize Company supplied building materials to Zaozhuang Company, and an employee of Huize Company conspired with others to resell the building materials, causing losses to Zaozhuang Company; the Supreme Court ruled that the employee's act was in the performance of work tasks and caused losses to Zaozhuang Company, and thus, the employee should bear joint liability with Huize Company.[64]

In summary, if the employee's tortious act is not in the performance of work tasks, the employee should bear personal liability. If the employee's tortious act is in the performance of work tasks, the employer must bear liability. In this case, the employee may bear personal liability in two situations: either the employer imposes an economic penalty on the employee based on their company's rules and regulations and the employee's faults after compensating the harmed party, or the harmed party seeks joint liability from the employee (with the employer) for the intentional or grossly negligent act.

128. Under what circumstances can an employer transfer the positions of its employees?

Answer: Under Chinese employment legislations and practice, an employer is entitled to transfer the position of an employee by mutual agreement and under six other lawful circumstances.

Position transfer by mutual agreement may be the easiest and the most convenient way. According to the provisions of Article 35 of the Employment Contract Law, an employer can legally and effectively transfer the position of an employee after negotiation and obtaining the employee's consent. Moreover, employers often stipulate in employment contracts or company rules and regulations that they have the right to transfer their employees to other specific roles or relevant roles, or do so based on the needs of business operation or management or under specific circumstances.

The other six lawful circumstances for position transfer are stipulated in the provisions of Article 40 and Article 41 of the Employment Contract Law and the principles of the employment law, Employers may transfer the position of their employee under the following six exceptional circumstances.

The first situation is position transfer based on the employee's physical or mental incompetence to work in their position after the expiration of medical care leave (or the expiration of the paid work injury leave). We call it health incompetence. This is a lawful position transfer according to Article 40 (1). The health state in connection with the work capacity of the employee determines the availability of this type of position transfer.

63 Li Changjun and Sichuan Aonong Biotechnology Co., Ltd. Civil Ruling on Labor Dispute Retrial Review and Trial Supervision Sichuan Provincial People's High Court Civil Ruling (2019) Chuan Min Shen No. 5196. In this case, the employee drove a scrapped vehicle to perform the work tasks of the employer and caused damage to another vehicle, and the victim sued the employee and the employer as co-defendants. The employer finally assumed the liability for compensation.

64 Loudi Huize Economic and Trade Co., Ltd. v. Zaozhuang Daoqiao Engineering Co., Ltd. Construction Project Contract and Property Damage Compensation Dispute Retrial Case Supreme People's Court of the People's Republic of China Civil Ruling (2017) Zuigao Fa Min Shen No. 218.

Whether a pay cut is lawful in a position transfer is an interconnected issue with the lawfulness of position transfer itself, and it is often a matter with a degree of uncertainty.[65] For example, a reasonable position transfer due to an employee's health state may be rendered illegal due to an overly large pay cut.

The second situation is the position transfer of ability-incompetent employees. Article 40 (2) allows employers to arrange training or position transfer for ability-incompetent employees. This is incompetence due to employees' individual ability instead of their health state. We call it ability incompetence. Therefore, an employer intending this transfer must first prove that its employee is not competent for their job. Cases show that the most common situation is that employers failed in proving ability incompetence, resulting in illegal position transfer.[66] Employers proving ability incompetence often need to refer to employees' job descriptions or company rules and regulations and to base the proof on performance review of the employee.

The third situation is the position transfer due to major change in objective situation. According to Article 40(3), in the case of major change in the objective situation on which an employment contract was based at the time of its conclusion, the employer must first negotiate with the employee for a change of employment conditions, including a position transfer, before it proceeds to terminate the employment contract. This is the rule under the employment laws allowing employers to transfer the positions of employees in the case of changes in circumstance rendering the performance of the roles unnecessary or unreasonable, so as to improve the operational efficiency of the employers' businesses. As for how to identify a major change in objective situation, please refer to "157. My employer terminates my employment contract on the ground of major change in objective situation. Is it legal?"

The fourth situation is the position transfer due to major change in objective during economic redundancies. Article 41 (4) stipulates that when a "major change in objective situation" based on which the employment contract was concluded leads to business hardships, the employer, subject to statutory requirements, may lay off employees. Although the article does not mention the right of position transfer, we consider that the employer is certainly entitled to transfer the position of the employee to relieve the difficulties the employer faces before the ultimate redundancy. As for the circumstances and extent of major change in objective situation during economic redundancy, please refer to "155. How can employers experiencing business hardship legally reduce their workforce to survive?"

65 Civil Ruling on Labor Dispute Retrial Review and Trial Supervision between Liu Qi and Beijing Metro Operation Co., Ltd. the Second Branch, Civil Ruling of Beijing High Court (2019) Jing Min Shen No. 1674. The court held that "the employee could not return back to work upon expiration of medical care leave, and the employer conducting position transfer for him to a role with lower labor intensity is not a malicious demotion and wage cut." The labor dispute appeal case between Zeng Hong and Shenzhen Long-distance Bus Passenger Transport Co., Ltd., the Intermediate People's Court of Shenzhen City, Guangdong Province, Civil Judgment (2017) Yue 03 Min Zhong No. 1039. In the case, the employee was unable to work as a driver after the expiration of the medical care leave, and the employer transferred him to a position with the same wage. The court held that the transfer did not reduce his benefits and was not insulting, and that the transfer was legal.

66 Guangzhou Yingda Imaging Equipment Co., Ltd. v. Mai Weiyu Labor Dispute Guangdong Provincial People's High Court Civil Ruling (2016) Yue Min Shen No. 1990. The court found that the employer did not prove that the employee was not competent for the work or that the transfer did not substantially degrade the work conditions, so the position transfer was illegal.

The fifth scenario is the employer's position transfer as agreed upon by employment contract or provided by company rules and regulations. Employers often stipulate in the employment contract or company rules and regulations that they have the right to reassign employees to specific positions, or that the employer may do so due to operational needs or other circumstances defined by the employer. The more explicit and reasonable the agreement on position transfers, the more legitimate and justifiable the position transfer is considered to be. This type of position transfer is contract provided or regulation stipulated in advance, unlike position transfer based on mutual agreement.

The sixth situation is lawful position transfer without mutual agreement or statutory circumstances. Employers in this situation must follow substantive and procedural requirements to legally transfer the positions of their employees. Please refer to "129. How should an employer legally transfer the position of an employee?"

129. How should an employer legally transfer the position of an employee?

Answer: Position transfer is a situation of employment variation where an employee retains their employment but changes their position to another role. Position transfer without mutual agreement or a statutory circumstance is a complex legal issue and involves a delicate balance between employees' employment security, career development, and employers' management autonomy and business interests. The lawfulness of a position transfer requires substantive and procedural lawfulness during the process.

According to the existing court decisions throughout the country, the substantive legality of an employer transferring employees' position depends on the comprehensive consideration of the following factors: available agreement(s) on position transfer (for example, a scope of positions),[67] the rationality and necessity of the employer's production and operation needs, whether the position transfer is insulting and punitive,[68] negative impacts of the impugned position transfer on the employees, including wages, commuting costs, etc., whether the employee's personal situation is taken into account,[69] and whether

67 Chi Yanwei, Hebei Huadian Shijiazhuang Yuhua Thermal Power Co., Ltd. Civil Judgment of the Second Instance of Labor Dispute, Shijiazhuang Intermediate People's Court of Hebei Province Civil Judgment (2018) Ji 01 Minzhong No. 13665. The two parties' employment contract stipulated that the company had the right to transfer the position of the employee. The court held that the employment contract did not specify the position of the employee and that there was little difference in the working environment and treatment of the position to which the employee was to be transferred, so the transfer was reasonable. The labor dispute case of Zhang Jianzhong v. Nantong Yide Logistics Co., Ltd., Jiangsu Provincial People's High Court Civil Ruling (2017) Sumin Shen No. 4822. The employment contract stipulated "driver," and the court held that the employer's reassigning the employee to different driving positions did not constitute position transfer.

68 Civil Ruling on Labor Dispute Retrial Review and Trial Supervision of Qin Zhong and Dongyang Rubber and Plastics (Guangzhou) Co., Ltd. (2018) Yue Min Shen No. 6677, Civil Ruling of Guangdong Provincial People's High Court. "The employer transferred the position of the employee due to the organizational restructuring, did not reduce the wages, nor was it insulting and punitive, so the transfer was legal."

69 Wang Zhongwei, Guangzhou FAW Bus Co., Ltd. Civil Judgment of the Second Instance of Labor Dispute Civil Judgment of Guangzhou Intermediate People's Court of Guangdong Province (2021) Yue 01 Min Zhong No. 2228. In the case, the employer transferred the employee from a bus driver to a minibus driver due to the business practice of routing position transfer, and the court held that the employer had considered the employee's personal situation, and the treatment did not change, so the transfer was legal. Civil Judgment of the Second Instance of the Labor Dispute between Beijing Pinggu Grain and Oil Industry and Trade Co., Ltd. and Cui Dongyan Civil Judgment of the Third Intermediate People's Court of Beijing (2022) Jing 03 Min Zhong No. 11629. "No party to the employment contract has the right to unilaterally change the conditions of the employment contract, although the employer may, according to the needs of production and operation, exercise the right of appropriate unilateral position transfer of workers, but the transfer should be reasonable, that is, the transfer should take into account the needs of production and operation or the individual ability of workers, the

the employee has actually accepted and both parties have actually fulfilled the contract of the changed position (including actual work and wages payment).[70] The general principle is to compare the employee's employment security and career development and the employer's management autonomy and business interests to determine the lawfulness of a position transfer.

On the other hand, the employer should abide by procedural lawfulness in dealing with position transfers of employees. Employers should adopt a fair, reasonable, and good-faith attitude to deal with position transfer, especially for employees who are not competent for their work for special reasons, such as disability after medical care leave or expiration of paid work injury leave, to maintain good faith. Employers should inform employees of the proposed position transfer and the reasons for the transfer, and consider the employees' view, rather than treat them simply, roughly, and arbitrarily, or even dismiss them.[71] Accordingly, employees should also maintain a good-faith attitude of communication rather than relying on health reasons for capricious absenteeism.[72]

The lawfulness of the position transfer of employees has an important impact on the employer. If the transfer is legal, the employee's refusal to come to work may constitute absenteeism and may lead to lawful dismissal; if the transfer is illegal, the employee may refuse to enroll in the new position, and the employer will not be able to execute normal management on the employee, resulting in the consequences of management disability. The employee may even be able to assert forced resignation and claim economic compensation.

It is worth noting that Article 20 of the 2023 Consultation Draft on the Interpretation of the Supreme People's Court on the Application of Law in the Trial of Labor Dispute Cases (II) stipulates that a position transfer is illegal if any of the following circumstances exist: it does not comply with the employment contract or the employer's company rules and regulations, it is not due to the employer's objective production and business needs and there are adverse changes to the employee's wages and other working conditions without necessary assistance or compensation measures, the employee is objectively unable to perform the transferred position, or there are discriminatory or insulting circumstances. This Judicial Interpretation (II) also stipulates that if the employer illegally transfers the position, the employee has the right to claim that the employer does not provide contractual

---

wage level after the transfer being equal to that of the previous position, the transfer being not insulting and punitive, and the transfer not increasing the labor cost of workers."

70 Luo Haibo, Changsha Yicai Human Resources Consulting Co., Ltd. Civil Judgment of the Second Instance of Labor Dispute Civil Judgment of Changsha Intermediate People's Court of Hunan Province (2017) Xiang 01 Min Zhong No. 8280. The employee's wage was reduced after medical care leave expired and he worked for nearly a year, and thus, the court did not support the claim that the employer's wage reduction violated the law.

71 Hunan Bus Public Transport Co., Ltd., Zhou Lixin Labor Dispute Retrial Review and Trial Supervision Civil Ruling Hunan Provincial People's High Court Civil Ruling (2019) Xiang Min Shen No. 707. The employee was not competent for the work after the expiration of the medical care leave, and the employer terminated the employee on the ground of the employee's serious violation of company rules and regulations because the employee did not go to work during the negotiation process. The court held that the employer should communicate in good faith with humanistic care, and that the forced dismissal was illegal.

72 Tong Jie, Liaoning Anji United Automobile Logistics Co., Ltd. Labor Dispute Retrial Review and Trial Supervision Civil Ruling Liaoning Provincial People's High Court Civil Ruling (2019) Liao Min Shen No. 5984. After the expiration of the employee's medical care leave, the employer issued seven work notices, but the employee ignored them and continued to be absent from work, and the court found that the employee's dismissal was legal.

working conditions, request the termination of the employment contract, and demand economic compensation.

There are several specific circumstances under which employers may legally transfer the positions of their employees based on negotiation or statutory situations. Please refer to "128. Under what circumstances can an employer transfer the positions of its employees?"

4.3 Strike, Equity Incentive, and Employer Misconduct

130. Are employees entitled to collective strike?

Answer: Under Chinese employment laws, there is no legal concept of "strike." In judicial practice, "collective work stoppage" instead of "strike" is in use. Generally speaking, the Chinese employment law system, based on concerns for maintaining social stability and the emphasis on developing the national economy under the reform and opening-up policy, does not recognize the right of employees to engage in collective work stoppages.

Although the "Employment Contract Law" and the "Labor Law" stipulate the right of employees in collective negotiation of employment contracts, they do not specify the right of employees to engage in collective work stoppages or set up the statutory conditions for collective work stoppages. While these laws specify that individual employees have the rights to stop work due to illness, work-related injuries, or leave, they also do not specify the right of employees to stop work individually due to disputes.

As can be seen from judicial decisions, the basic attitude of the courts toward collective work stoppages by employees is not to recognize the legality of such actions. Published cases involving collective work stoppages at the provincial high court level generally show that courts tend to support employers in terminating the employment relationships of striking employees. When examining the legality of an employer's termination of collective work stoppage employees, courts typically consider the maliciousness of the collective work stoppage behavior, the legitimacy of the demands made by the striking employees, the reasonableness of the employer's response to the employees' demands, the duration of the work stoppage, and the effectiveness of the rules and regulations to determine whether the employer's disciplinary actions against the employees, including termination of the employment relationship, are legal.

If a collective work stoppage behavior involves actions such as seriously disrupting production or besieging the company, courts usually deem the company's dismissal measures as lawful. The reason for this judicial practice is likely the punitive attitude of the courts toward employees who disrupt production and harm major interests of the employer.

For example, in the 2020 case of Huaying Optoelectronics Co., Ltd. before Fujian Provincial High Court, employees engaged in actions such as besieging warehouses to prevent shipments and sitting quietly after punching in for attendance; in the 2015 case of Nokia Communication Co., Ltd. Dongguan Branch before Guangdong Provincial High Court, employees engaged in actions such as blocking traffic in and out of the employer's premises and sitting quietly while holding banners; and in the 2013 case of Wuxi Mashan Yonghong Heat Exchanger Co., Ltd. before Jiangsu Provincial High Court, employees engaged in actions such as trying to obstruct the startup of company production equipment and then shutting down the equipment. The courts all deemed the dismissal of these employees by the companies as lawful.

The demands of employees engaging in collective work stoppages and the reasonableness of the employer's response are also factors to consider. Although courts tend to examine the legality of an employer's termination of employees engaged in collective work stoppages leniently (compared with the legality of ordinary individual dismissal), there are also decisions where courts held that employers should reasonably respond to employees' legitimate demands, and failure to do so would constitute illegal dismissal. For example, in a 2011 case between SJ Company and SCL before the Shanghai the First Intermediate People's Court, the court found that the employees' concerns about workplace pollution and the request for increased income due to domestic inflation were understandable, and that the employer did not engage in reasonable consultations, and thus, that the company's dismissal of the employees was deemed illegal.

The duration of the collective work stoppage and the effectiveness of the company's rules and regulations are also factors to consider, as the legality of an employer's dismissal of an employee must ultimately consider the behavior of the dismissed employee and the corresponding institutional basis. For more details, please refer to "154. What requirements should an employer meet to legally terminate an employee?" However, in judicial practice, the threshold of legality in the review by courts for employees dismissed due to collective work stoppages seems to be lower than in the cases of normal dismissals of individual employees.

Please refer to "131. Are there any reference judgments on the legality of dismissing employees who participated in collective strikes?" for the aforementioned cases.

131. Are there any reference judgments on the legality of dismissing employees who participated in collective strikes?

Answer: We searched and compiled the following cases from six provincial high courts and one intermediate court for readers' reference.

Labor Dispute Case between Zheng Mingquan and Huaying Optoelectronics Co., Ltd. before Fujian High Court in 2020. In the case, over 600 employees stopped working collectively due to the company's relocation, merger, and concerns about changes of the employer in their employment contracts. Zheng Mingquan participated in the collective strike for over two weeks, staying at the company daily after clocking in and participating in blocking the warehouse to prevent shipments. The court reviewed and found that the company's rules and regulations were established through a democratic procedure and thus, were legally valid. The termination of the employee by the company for serious violations of these rules and regulations was deemed lawful.[73]

Labor Contract Dispute Case between Wang Yuehong and Wuxi Mashan Yonghong Heat Exchanger Co., Ltd. before the Jiangsu High Court in 2013. In the case, all employees of a workshop of the company went on strike due to wage disputes. On the second day of the strike, Wang Yuehong participated in obstructing the company's production equipment startup and shutting down the equipment. The company terminated Wang Yuehong's employment contract based on the company rules and regulations, which stipulated that strike constitutes one of the grounds for employment termination. The court considered

73 Zheng Mingquan v. Huaying Optoelectronics Co., Ltd. Labor Dispute Retrial Review and Trial Supervision Civil Ruling Fujian Provincial Higher People's Court Civil Ruling (2020) Min Shen No. 3502.

that since the company had informed the employees of the rules and regulations, the termination of the employee based on these binding rules was lawful.[74]

Labor Contract Dispute Case between Wang Fengfeng and Hubei Tengfei Talent Co., Ltd. before Hubei High Court in 2019. In the case, Wang Fengfeng participated in a one-day collective strike due to wage disputes. According to the company's rules and regulations, a strike resulting in a half-hour work stoppage constituted grounds for contract termination, based on which the company terminated the employee's contract. The court considered the rules and regulations to be legally valid, thus ruling the termination of the employee's contract as lawful.[75]

Labor Contract Dispute Case between Yang Jianqin and Dongguan Jianchang Industrial Co., Ltd. before Guangdong High Court in 2018. In the case, the company notified employees of a planned change from hourly wages to piecework wages. In response, employees collectively stopped working and refused to provide labor after clocking in.

Later on, the company compromised and agreed to maintain the hourly wage unchanged, but the employees still continued the collective strike for a total of ten days. Yang Jianqin participated in the entire collective strike and was dismissed by the company. Although the court did not specify whether the company's rules and regulations were valid, it deemed the employee's actions as serious violations of basic labor rules and regulations, thus ruling the termination of the employment relationship with the employee by the company as lawful.[76]

Labor Contract Dispute Case between Qin Zhenye and Nokia Telecommunications Dongguan Branch before Guangdong High Court in 2015. In the case, employees of the company went on strike for two days due to dissatisfaction with modifications to the employee handbook, engaging in activities such as blocking traffic in and out of the company and staging sit-ins with protest banners. The company terminated Qin Zhenye based on the original employee handbook. The court considered the employee handbook to be legally valid, thus ruling the termination of the employee's contract by the company as lawful.[77]

Li Rongshu, Xu Hailiang, and Geoxi Shoes (Shenzhen) Co., Ltd. before Guangdong High Court in 2016. In the case, employees of the company went on strike for over five days due to wage and benefits issues and service years issues after the enterprise merger. The employee fully participated in this. The court considered that although the company had not informed employees of the merger in advance, it made positive commitments to employees afterward and did not refuse negotiation with employee representatives. Therefore, the company's termination of the employee for serious disciplinary violations based on valid rules and regulations was deemed lawful.[78]

---

74 Wang Yuehong v. Wuxi Mashan Yonghong Heat Exchanger Co., Ltd. Labor Contract Dispute Application Case Jiangsu Provincial Higher People's Court Civil Ruling (2013) Su Shen Er Min Shen Zi No. 762.

75 Wang Fengfeng v. Hubei Tengfei Talent Co., Ltd. Labor Contract Dispute Retrial Review and Trial Supervision Civil Ruling Hubei Provincial Higher People's Court Civil Ruling (2019) E Min Shen No. 3757.

76 Yang Jianqin v. Dongguan Jianchang Industrial Co., Ltd. Labor Contract Dispute Retrial Review and Trial Supervision Civil Ruling Guangdong Provincial Higher People's Court Civil Ruling (2018) Yue Min Shen No. 12621.

77 Qin Zhenye v. Nokia Telecommunications Ltd. Dongguan Branch, Nokia Telecommunications Ltd. Labor Contract Dispute Retrial Review and Trial Supervision Civil Ruling Guangdong Provincial Higher People's Court Civil Ruling (2015) Yue Gao Fa Min Shen Zi No. 1466.

78 Li Rongshu, Xu Hailiang, and others v. Geoxi Shoes (Shenzhen) Co., Ltd. Administrative Review and Trial Supervision Case on Labor and Social Security Administration Guangdong Provincial Higher People's

Labor Contract Dispute Case between SJ Company and SCL before the Shanghai First Intermediate People's Court in 2011. In the case, over 20 employees of the company went on strike for over 5 days due to concerns about toxic air in the workplace and demands for increasing wages and benefits. The employee participated in the strike for three days. The company terminated the employee based on the provision in the employee handbook stating that three days of absence without leave could result in contract termination. The court deemed the company's termination of the employee unlawful since the company failed to reasonably negotiate with the employee regarding concerns about workplace pollution and reasonable requests for increasing income given the exacerbation of domestic inflation.[79]

132. What is the equity incentive agreement between employer and employee?

Answer: An equity incentive agreement refers to a conditional agreement signed by a limited company (including a joint stock limited company) and/or its affiliate and an employee on granting, holding, and transferring the company's equity; its purpose is to reward the employee's past contribution and as a long-term incentive for the employee to work hard in the future so as to achieve the company's development goals and achieve a win-win situation with the employee. Equity incentives include equity and equity options (that is, equity granted or exercised under certain conditions, also known as restricted equity or shares).

The foregoing definition we have made is derived from relevant regulations. The Notice on Improving Income Tax Policies on Equity Incentives and Technology Shares in 2016 stipulates that restricted shares granted to an employee by a non-listed company refer to a certain amount of equity of the company granted to incentive objects by the company in accordance with pre-determined conditions; the incentive object can only dispose of the equity if its service years or performance objectives meet the conditions stipulated in the equity incentive plan.[80] The Measures for the Administration of Equity Incentives of Listed Companies in 2018 stipulates: "The term 'equity incentive' as mentioned in the Measures refers to the long-term incentive given by a listed company to its directors, senior managers and other employees with the company's shares as the subject matter."[81]

There are three types of employment law disputes involved in equity incentive agreements.

The first type of dispute is whether issues related to employees' rights and interests arising from equity incentives fall under labor disputes. The regulations of the State Administration of Taxation, judicial decisions, and the consultation draft on the Supreme Court's proposed judicial interpretation on labor dispute (II) all hold that the disputes over the rights and interests generated by equity incentives belong to labor disputes. This is the situation when the signing party of the equity incentive agreement is the employer. Please refer to "133. Is the dispute between an employer and an employee arising from the equity incentive agreement a labor dispute?"

Court Civil Ruling (2016) Yue Min Shen No. 512–546.

79 SJ Company v. SCL Labor Contract Dispute Appeal Case Shanghai First Intermediate People's Court Civil Judgment (2011) Hu Yi Zhong Min San (Min) Zhong Zi No. 1714.

80 Article 1 (1) and (3) of the Notice of the Ministry of Finance and the State Administration of Taxation on Improving the Income Tax Policies on Equity Incentives and Technology Shares (Fiscal and Tax [2016] 101).

81 Article 2 of the Measures for the Administration of Equity Incentives of Listed Companies (Order No. 148 of the China Securities Regulatory Commission).

The second type of dispute is over how to deal with the situation where the granting subject of the equity incentive is not the employer but a third party associated with the employer. According to the relevant labor dispute judicial principle, the arbitration committee or the court will treat both the employer and its affiliated companies as joint defendants when handling matters related to the rights and obligations under equity incentive agreements. However, if the affiliated company that granted the equity is located overseas, the labor arbitration commission or court will generally strike out such a case. Please refer to "134. The employer is not the signing subject of the equity incentive. Who is liable under the equity incentive agreement in the labor dispute?"

The third type of dispute is whether employees can obtain the substantive entity rights and interests according to the equity incentive agreement. The content of equity incentive agreements between two parties and the relevant implementation system are the key to employees' equity incentive rights and interests. Employers or the third-party affiliated companies must strictly abide by relevant provisions of equity incentive agreements, and carefully handle termination of the employees' employment relationship and employees' performance appraisals. Employees should also strictly abide by the equity incentive agreement to obtain the corresponding rights and interests. See "135. An employee agreeing to an equity incentive agreement did not receive the equity benefits. Is it legal?"

Equity incentive is a new form of labor remuneration in China. It is a legal issue across the fields of Securities Law, Company Law, and the employment laws. Its relevant judicial precedents and legal rules are in the initial stage of development and need further improvement and observation.

133. Is the dispute between an employer and an employee arising from the equity incentive agreement a labor dispute?

Answer: Whether a dispute between an employer and an employee arising from their equity incentive agreement is a labor dispute or an equity contract dispute is related to the procedural issue regarding whether the employer or employee should file a labor arbitration application to the labor arbitration committee or file a civil action of equity contract to the court.

According to our observation on judicial decisions, in principle, disputes arising from equity incentive agreements involving an employee's rights and interests arising from grant, holding, or transfer of equity are labor disputes if the incentive does not lead to the employee becoming a shareholder holding a substantial portion of shares. However, it is not a labor dispute for an employee to claim to exercise the power of a shareholder under the company law (such as voting power) based on the equity they hold.

First of all, China's tax regulations regard equity incentive income as employees' remuneration. For example, the Notice of the State Administration of Taxation on the Levy of Individual Income Tax on Individual Stock Option Income and the Notice of the State Administration of Taxation on the Levy of Individual Income Tax on Equity Incentives both regard employee's stock option or equity incentive related income as "wage, salary income" to calculate and levy individual income tax.

Second, judicial precedents show that courts usually hold that equity incentive is a conditional salary with economic benefits paid by employers to employees. For example, in the case of Boyan Science and Technology (Shenzhen) Co., Ltd. and Wen Jian Labor dispute in 2017, Judge Luo Yingqing of Shenzhen Intermediate Court of Guangdong

Province pointed out that "although the equity incentive is not paid in the form of legal currency as emphasized by the Labor Law when it is granted, its equity incentive price is significantly lower than the stock market price. When an employee exercises the right, it will inevitably bring the benefit of price difference to the employee, which can be realized in the form of legal currency. Based on the above analysis, the restricted stock granted to Wen Jian in this case should be part of the remuneration, and the dispute caused by the repurchase and cancellation of Wen Jian's restricted stock has the typical characteristics of employment relationship in which employees accept employer management, constraints and incentives. It is obviously different from the ordinary civil contract disputes between equal civil subjects."[82]

Finally, Article 1 of the Consultation Draft on the Interpretation of the Supreme People's Court on the Application of Law in the Trial of Labor Dispute Cases (II) in 2023 also preliminarily stipulates that where an employer pays an employee labor remunerations based on an equity incentive agreement under an employment relationship, the dispute arising from the employee's request for the employer to pay the subject matter of equity incentive or compensate for the loss of equity incentive is a labor dispute, except for disputes arising from the exercise of the power related to the equity.

134. The employer is not the signing subject of the equity incentive. Who is liable under the equity incentive agreement in the labor dispute?

Answer: The disputants in a labor dispute case involving equity incentive are normally the parties to the equity incentive agreement, i.e., the employer and the employee; however, a party to an equity incentive agreement can also be a third party, for instance, an affiliated company of the employer, rather than the employer itself. A typical situation is that an employee of a company signs an equity incentive agreement with the parent company in relation to the equity of the parent company.

This raises a question. Who, the employer or the third-party affiliated company, shall be liable under the equity incentive agreement in a labor dispute case? Or, to put it another way, can the labor arbitration committee assume jurisdiction over the equity incentive issues?

Specifically, the employer may argue that the equity incentive agreement is not signed by our company, and the equity involved in the agreement is not our company's equity, so it is unreasonable to require our company to assume the obligations; at the same time, the third-party affiliated company may also argue that the labor dispute case is employee suing employer, and thus, it has nothing to do with our company as a non-employer.

At present, there are few published judicial precedents. The handling principle in the courts' relevant precedents is largely as follows: if the third-party affiliated company is a domestic company, it can be put as a co-defendant to bear the joint and several liabilities for the loss of the employee's equity incentive, or as a co-defendant to bear the liability for the disposal of equity in the equity incentive; however, if the third party is an overseas company, the employee's claim against the affiliated company is likely to be struck out.

The potential reason for this treatment principle may be that the equity incentive of the third-party affiliated company to the employee is apparently based on the performance of

82 Boyan Technology (Shenzhen) Co., Ltd. and Wen Jian labor dispute appeal case Shenzhen Intermediate People's Court of Guangdong Province Civil Judgment (2017) Yue 03 Min Zhong No. 1326.

the employment relationship between the employee and the employer. The affiliated company therefore becomes the performing party of the employer's obligations to pay labor remuneration to the employee, and the court ordering the affiliated company to assume the obligations under the equity incentive agreement in the labor dispute case is the implementation of the employment laws regarding the employee's labor remuneration.

For example, in the case of Boyan Technology (Shenzhen) Co., Ltd. and Wen Jian labor dispute in 2017, the employee and the employer's holding parent company signed an equity incentive agreement, and then the holding parent company cancelled the employee's equity according to the agreement. The employee sued the employer and the parent company for joint and several damages for the cancellation of their shares. The Shenzhen Intermediate Court ruled that the holding parent company is "the issuing subject of the incentive plan, the actual granting subject, and the decision-making subject of lifting the restriction or repurchase and cancellation of the restricted stock granted to Wen Jian involved in the case, and it shall be jointly and severally liable for the compensation for the loss of repurchase and cancellation of Wen Jian's restricted stock according to law."[83]

For another example, in the case of the labor dispute between Dou Hengli and Jingdong Technology Holding Co., Ltd. in 2021, Judge Huo Zhiyong of Beijing Daxing District Court found: "Dou Hengli did not provide labor to Jingdong Financial Group, and the reason for which the group granted Dou Henli restricted stock is based on the existence of an employment relationship between JingDong Technology and Dou Hengli, and the grant object, grant conditions, and right-exercise conditions of the stock option in the case are based on several factors in the employment relationship. That is to say, the dispute related to stock repurchase in this case arises from the employment relationship. Based on foregoing reasoning and the affiliate relationship between the two defendants, this court considers that it is not inappropriate for Dou Hengli to take Jingdong Technology Company and Jingdong Financial Group as the defendants in this case."[84]

However, if the third-party affiliate is an offshore company, the situation differs. There are obstacles in the enforcement of a judgment for a Chinese court to request foreign companies to fulfill labor remuneration obligations, and the issues of foreign companies' equity should also be regulated by foreign company law according to the principle of exclusive jurisdiction, so Chinese courts are inclined not to hear disputes involving foreign companies' equity.

For example, in the case of the labor dispute between Zhang Chen and Beijing Dasheng Zhixing Technology Co., Ltd. in 2020, the employee signed a share option agreement with a New York–listed Cayman Islands company indirectly controlled by the employer, which stipulated the judicial jurisdiction of the Hong Kong court. Later, the employer dismissed the employee, and the result of the lawsuit was that the employment relationship terminated due to contract expiration. The employee then filed a labor arbitration claiming the employer to cash in the stock options. The Beijing High Court and the two lower courts

83 Boyan Technology (Shenzhen) Co., Ltd. and Wen Jian labor dispute appeal case Shenzhen Intermediate People's Court of Guangdong Province Civil Judgment (2017) Yue 03 Min Zhong No. 1326.

84 Dou Hengli and Jingdong Science and Technology Holding Co., Ltd. and other labor dispute civil judgment of first instance Beijing Daxing District People's Court Civil Judgment (2021) Jing 0115 MinChu No. 12024.

struck out the employee's claim on the grounds of the Chinese court lacking jurisdiction and the wrong subject to cash in the stock options.[85]

In the labor dispute between Liang Ping and Tianjin Bona Aijieer Technology Co., Ltd. in 2021, the Hong Kong controlling shareholder of the employer signed a stock arrangement agreement with the employee, stipulating that when the employee met certain conditions, the controlling shareholder would recommend for another overseas listed company, Danaher Corporation, to grant the employee shares of the listed company or pay the stock price. Another affiliate company paid the employee more than RMB 910,000 in payments marked as "stock option." The employer terminated the employment relationship with the employee on the grounds of major change in objective situation, and the employee filed a labor arbitration application to request the employer to pay labor remunerations based on the stock arrangement agreement. The Beijing High Court and the two lower courts struck out the claim on the grounds that the equity involved was real equity rather than virtual equity, resulting in the matter not being a labor dispute, and that the employer was not the subject of granting equity or rewards.[86]

Therefore, at present, in determining whether a third-party affiliated company should bear responsibility in a labor dispute case between an employee and an employer, the courts primarily weigh the balance between protecting the employee's labor remuneration–associated equity incentive and the convenience of judicial procedures for third-party affiliated companies to fulfill their obligations related to equity incentive, and make a trade-off decision.

135. An employee agreeing to an equity incentive agreement did not receive the equity benefits. Is it legal?

Answer: Equity incentive essentially is the labor remuneration paid by an employer or its affiliated company based on the employee's performance of the employment contract (please refer to "133. Is the dispute between an employer and an employee arising from the equity incentive agreement a labor dispute?"). Therefore, the equity incentive agreement is a part of the salary provisions in the employment contract in a broad sense. The employer or its affiliated company and the employee shall abide and be bound by the agreement. Whether the employee can obtain the equity benefits under the equity incentive depends on the specific provisions in the equity incentive agreement.

For example, in the case of a labor dispute between Yang Guiru and Beijing Upper Nebula Investment Center (Limited Partnership) in 2022, the Beijing High Court held that employees' rights and interests' issues based on the equity incentive agreement, including equity unlocking conditions, dividend income, equity transfer price difference, etc., should be determined by examining the conditions stipulated in the equity incentive agreement.[87]

85 Zhang Chen and Beijing Dasheng Zhixing Technology Co., Ltd. Civil Ruling on Retrial Review and Trial Supervision Civil Ruling of Beijing Higher People's Court (2020) Jing Min Shen No. 1858.

86 Liang Ping and Tianjin Bona Aijieer Technology Co., Ltd. Civil Ruling on Retrial Review and Trial Supervision Civil Ruling of Beijing Higher People's Court (2021) Jing Min Shen No. 7200.

87 Yang Guiru and Beijing Shangshang Xingyun Investment Center (Limited Partnership), etc. Civil Ruling on Retrial Review and Trial Supervision Civil Ruling of Beijing Higher People's Court (2022) Jing Min Shen No. 5733.

One of the most common disputes over equity incentive rights and interests is the dispute over the loss of equity incentive rights and interests due to the employee's departure, because equity incentive agreements usually have provisions related to this situation.

For example, in the case of the labor dispute between Red Fox Information Technology (Shenzhen) Co., Ltd. and Wang Qinsheng in 2020, the Guangdong Provincial High Court held that the equity incentive agreement involved clearly stipulated that if an employee resigned due to their own reasons, the employer had the right to recover the unpaid employee's internal equity and cash incentives free of charge, and that since the employee's resignation was not found to be forced resignation, the employee lost the agreed equity incentive bonus due to resignation.[88]

However, an employer's illegal termination of an employee may cause the employee not to lose the equity incentive rights and interests, because the basic principle of civil law in China is that if one party to the contract maliciously prevents the fulfillment of a contract condition, the condition shall be deemed to have been fulfilled.[89] For example, in the second of the ten typical cases of labor and personnel disputes, an appeal case of the labor contract dispute between Wu and an electronic company, published by the Intermediate People's Court of Suzhou City, Jiangsu Province in 2022, the hearing court pointed out: "The employer‘s illegal termination of the employment contract led to the cancellation of employee's stock options or restricted stocks. Since the employer failed to provide evidence to prove that the employee does not meet other incentive conditions, the employee's claim against the employer for the loss of stock options or restricted stock during the corresponding assessment period must be upheld."

However, if there is no causal relationship between the employer's illegal termination and the employee's inability to obtain the equity incentive benefits, the employee may still be unable to obtain the benefits. For example, in the case of the labor dispute between Tian Yong and Beijing Alibaba Cloud Computing Technology Co., Ltd. in 2021, the Third Intermediate Court of Beijing held that although the employer conducted illegal termination before the expiration of the employee's fixed-term employment contract, the consequence of the employee's reinstatement was still a termination after the expiration of the contract, that the employee was still unable to obtain the restricted shares that could be granted under the equity incentive agreement, so that there was no causal relationship between the employer's illegal termination and the employee's loss of restricted shares, and that the employer did not need to compensate for the loss of incentive equity income.[90]

Cancellation of employees' equity incentive rights and interests based on employees' performance appraisal results is another possible dispute. Employers or the third-party affiliated companies must strictly abide by the provisions stipulated in the equity incentive agreement, and be fair and reasonable in substance and procedure when canceling the employee's equity incentive rights and interests, otherwise they may also bear adverse consequences. For example, in the case of Boyan Technology (Shenzhen) Co., Ltd. and

88 Red Fox Information Technology (Shenzhen) Co., Ltd. and Wang Qinsheng Labor Contract Dispute Retrial Review and Trial Supervision Civil Ruling Guangdong Provincial Higher People's Court Civil Ruling (2020) Yue Min Shen No. 2332.

89 Article 159 of the Civil Code stipulates that for a conditional civil act, if a party improperly prevents the condition from being fulfilled for their own benefit, the condition shall be deemed to have been fulfilled.

90 Tian Yong and Beijing Alibaba Cloud Computing Technology Co., Ltd., etc. Civil Judgment of the Second Instance of Labor Dispute Civil Judgment of the Third Intermediate People's Court of Beijing (2021) Jing 03 Min Zhong No. 14356.

Wen Jian labor dispute in 2017, a third-party affiliated company conducted a performance assessment on the employee and cancelled his granted restricted stocks based on the results of the assessment, and the employee claimed that their cancellation was unreasonable and demanded compensation. The Shenzhen Intermediate Court held that the court's examination of the cancellation of shares by the affiliated company is not to interfere with the company's autonomy in employment management in assessing their staff, but to examine the legitimacy of the affiliated company's implementation of the company's rules and regulations, which is entirely within the scope of the court's judicial function under the employment laws.[91]

Therefore, when dealing with the rights and interests of employees' equity incentives, employers or third-party affiliated companies should strictly abide by the relevant provisions of the equity incentive agreement and carefully handle the termination of the employment relationship and employee performance assessment. Employees should also strictly abide by the equity incentive agreement to obtain the corresponding rights and interests.

136. What are unjustified wage deduction and unjustified wage arrear by employer?

Answer: The concepts of unjustified wage deduction and unjustified wage arrear were put forward in the Labor Law. Article 50 of the law stipulates that wages shall be paid monthly to employees in the form of currency, and employees' wages must not be deducted or delayed without reason.

Unjustified wage deduction means that the employer deducts or fails to pay the full amount of due wages to the employee without justified reasons, and clearly refuses to pay; unjustified wage arrear means that the employer fails to pay all or part of the employee's wages at the statutory or agreed time for wage payment without justified reasons, forming wage arrear, and does not explicitly refuse to pay the amount. A similar definition was made in the Guidelines for the Trial of Labor Dispute Cases of Jiangsu Provincial Higher People's Court in 2010.[92] One of the legal ramifications of unjustified wage deduction or unjustified wage arrear is that the employee may be forced to resign and claim against the employer for economic compensation.

Based on the analyses of judicial decisions, we believe that unjustified wage deduction and unjustified wage arrear by an employer that causes forced resignation should meet two conditions. The first is that the employer has subjective malice for the deduction or arrear of the wage.[93] Judicial precedents and legal rules show that an employer is not subjectively malicious and has a justified reason for the following situations: legal fines

91 Boyan Technology (Shenzhen) Co., Ltd. and Wen Jian labor dispute appeal case Shenzhen Intermediate People's Court of Guangdong Province Civil Judgment (2017) Yue 03 Min Zhong No. 1326.

92 According to Article 2 of Section 3 of Chapter 2 of the Guidelines for the Trial of Labor Dispute Cases of Jiangsu Provincial Higher People's Court in 2010, unjustified wage deduction means that an employer deducts the wage due to the employee without justified reasons (less payment, explicit refusal to pay the remaining part of the wage). The two sides dispute over the amount of the paid wages. Unjustified arrear of labor remuneration refers to the employer's failure to pay the employee's wage beyond the stipulated or agreed payment time without justified reasons. The employer and the employee have no dispute over the specific amount of the labor remuneration that the employee should have received, and the employer has not refused to pay the employee the wage, but the dispute is over the time of payment.

93 Sichuan Baiteng Technology Co., Ltd., v. Lv Dianquan labor dispute retrial civil judgment Sichuan Provincial Higher People's Court Civil Judgment (2020) ChuanMinZai No. 217. The court held that the failure of Baiteng Technology Company to pay the cash wages from August to October 2017 due to Lv Dianquan's

or economic penalties on employees, wage deductions in accordance with company rules and regulations,[94] legal wage deductions based on mutual agreement (such as charges for accommodation, meals, etc.[95]), the wage reduction caused by the reduction of the working hours,[96] and the corresponding wage reduction after the legal position transfer. An employer does not have a justified reason but bears no subjective malice in the following cases: the company delays or deducts the payment of wages due to operational difficulties or an epidemic,[97] or the employer has a non-malicious misunderstanding of the amount of wages,[98] or the employer can provide reasonable explanations for the wage pay incompliance.[99]

The second condition is that the amount of unjustified wage arrear or deduction is relatively significant in the total amount of the wages. This is an implicit condition inferred by common sense. The reason why the employment law punishes employers for unjustified wage arrear or deduction is that the wage is the basic guarantee for employees' livelihood, and the act of deduction or arrear infringes employees' fundamental rights and interests; a small amount of deduction or arrear, which accounts for a small proportion of the total amount of the employee's wage, obviously has a slight impact on the rights and interests of the employee, so it is not appropriate to punish the employer by serious means such as termination of the employment relationship and economic compensation. Instead, the two sides should be encouraged to resolve such minor contradictions through negotiation.

---

failure to submit the invoice could not be attributed to Baiteng Technology Company, and Baiteng Technology Company did not have the subjective malice of unjustified wage arrear. Nor was it a unjustified wage deduction.

94 Civil Ruling on Labor Dispute Retrial Review and Trial Supervision of Xie Jiahan and Guangzhou Nanlian Air Catering Co., Ltd. Civil Ruling of Guangdong Provincial People's High Court (2019) Yue Min Shen No. 9323. The court held that the employer's deducting the reward part of the wages according to the company rules and regulations did not constitute an unjustified wage deduction.

95 Wang Jianguo v. Shenzhen Longgang District Security Service Co., Ltd., Shenzhen Hongweiyuan Investment Co., Ltd., etc. Civil Ruling on Retrial Review and Trial Supervision of Labor Remuneration Dispute Civil Ruling of Guangdong Provincial Higher People's Court (2015) Yue Gao Fa Min Shen Zi No. 1879.

96 Yu Mingqiang v. Guangdong Jinnuo Property Management Service Co., Ltd. Civil Application for Retrial Review of Labor Contract Dispute Civil Ruling of Guangdong Higher People's Court (2021) Yue Min Shen No. 4568. Ye Jinping, Hubei Xinyangfeng Fertilizer Co., Ltd. Civil Ruling on Retrial Review and Trial Supervision of Labor Contract Disputes Civil Ruling of Hubei Higher People's Court (2019) E Min Shen No. 3327.

97 Xu Bo v. Jilin Zixin Pharmaceutical Co., Ltd. Civil judgment of labor dispute civil retrial Civil judgment of Jilin Provincial Higher People's Court (2023) Ji Min Zai No. 18. In this case, the court held that the employer's wage arrear to the employee was due to operational difficulties, and that it had subsequently paid the wage in a timely manner, so this did not constitute an unjustified wage arrear.

98 Civil Ruling on Trial and Supervision of Labor Contract Dispute between Chen Xiliang and Shanghai Hanqing Hi-tech Co., Ltd. Civil Ruling of Shanghai Higher People's Court (2019) Hu Min Shen No. 2282. The court held that regarding whether there was an unjustified wage deduction, there was a dispute between the two parties on whether to adopt the piecework system for wage calculation. Based on the evidence of both parties and the contents of previous labor contracts, the original effective judgment's rejection of Chen Xiliang's claim on the unjustified wage deduction by Hanqing Company was recognized by this court. Fu Fengzhu, Jiangsu Hongbo Glass Products Co., Ltd. and Taixing Aibo Glass Products Co., Ltd. in the civil judgment of the second instance of labor disputes, the civil judgment of the Intermediate People's Court of Taizhou City, Jiangsu Province (2019) Su 12 Min Zhong 741. The court held that "the employer's failure to pay labor remuneration in time and in full was caused by calculation standard dispute for genuine, objective reasons shall not constitute the legitimate ground for employee's termination."

99 The labor dispute case between Li Shaohua and the respondent Xinxiang Ruifeng Chemical Industry Co., Ltd., Henan High Court Civil Ruling (2009) Yu Fa Min Shen Zi No. 3080. The court held that if the employer has a reasonable explanation for the wage arrears, it does not constitute unjustified wage arrear, and the resignation of employee does not constitute forced resignation. Labor Dispute Case of Zheng Shikai v. Yada Technology Group Co., Ltd. Civil Ruling of Zhejiang High Court (2014) ZMSZ No. 1132.

For example, in the case of Wang Xiaofei and Kunshan Xinxin Talent Service Co., Ltd. and Dingmei (Kunshan) New Material Technology Co., Ltd. in 2018, Judge Zhu Li of the Intermediate Court of Suzhou City, Jiangsu Province, said: "Because the wage arrear involved is small, and there is no evidence to prove that it is a malicious act of withholding. Therefore, it does not constitute a legitimate reason for the appellant to request the termination of the contract and claim economic compensation."[100]

Unjustified wage deduction and unjustified wage arrear have two legal consequences. The first is that the employee can proceed forced resignation and claim for economic compensation; please see "143. Are employers liable for economic compensation for employees' forced resignation?" Second, according to Article 85 of the Employment Contract Law, if the employer, after being ordered by the labor administrative authority to correct, still fails to pay the wages owed, it shall be liable for supplementary punitive damages ranging from 50% to 100% of the wage amount owed. Please refer to "171. Under what circumstances should employers be liable for supplementary damages?"

Whether the aforementioned unjustified deduction or arrear of wages also applies to overtime wages is a delicate issue, which involves a problem brought about by Article 45 of the 2020 Supreme Court's Judicial Interpretation, providing that refusing to pay overtime wages constitutes a lawful ground for an employee's forced resignation. At present, most court precedents hold that the aforementioned wages include overtime wage, but some courts hold the opposite view. Please refer to "138. What is employer's refusal to pay overtime wage?"

137. What is the difference in limitation of arbitration between unjustified wage deduction and unjustified wage arrear?

Answer: According to the introduction of "136. What are unjustified wage deduction and unjustified wage arrear by employer?", unjustified wage deduction means that the employer explicitly indicates that it will not pay or will pay less than the employee wage that should be paid, while unjustified wage arrear refers to the situation where the employer is willing to pay the wage that should be paid, but cannot pay on time.

The difference between the two lies in whether the employer has a clear intention not to pay or to underpay the wage that the employee should be paid. For example, Ms. Li's wage is RMB 5,000 per month, but the employer only pays RMB 4,500 to Ms. Li in a certain month without justification. Unless the employer tells Ms. Li that the difference of RMB 500 will be paid to her later, the employer's action constitutes a unjustified wage deduction, not an unjustified wage arrear.

The distinction between unjustified wage deduction and unjustified wage arrear may lead to differences in limitation of arbitration. Article 27 of the Labor Dispute Mediation and Arbitration Law stipulates two kinds of limitations of arbitration. One is the general limitation of arbitration, requesting that an employee or employer must file a claim within one year from the date when the party knows or should have known of the infringement of the rights, including economic compensation, double-wage damages, etc. The second is a special limitation of arbitration that applies only to labor remuneration arrears; the

100 Wang Xiaofei v. Kunshan Xinxin Talent Service Co., Ltd. and Dingmei (Kunshan) New Material Technology Co., Ltd. Civil Judgment of Second Instance of Labor Dispute Civil Judgment of Intermediate People's Court of Suzhou City, Jiangsu Province (2018) Su 05 Min Zhong No. 8821.

employee's claim for the arrears of labor remuneration must be made within one year from the date of termination of the employment relationship between the two parties, and the period of compensation for the arrears of labor remuneration may exceed one year. For details, please refer to "27. Is there a time limitation for employees or employers to file an employment arbitration application?"

The problem is whether the employer's unjustified wage deduction falls under the "labor remuneration arrear" stipulated in the special limitation of arbitration. There are two approaches in courts nationwide.

The first view holds that both unjustified wage deduction and unjustified wage arrear are applicable to special limitation of arbitration; it is supported by cases from Beijing High Court, Xinjiang High Court, Shandong High Court, Shenzhen Intermediate Court, and Shanghai the First Intermediate Court.[101] For example, in the case of Wuqiang and Beijing Dongtao Co., Ltd., the employee sued the employer for unpaid overtime wage. The Beijing Higher People's Court held that when the employer paid the overtime wage every month, the employee should have known the insufficient amount of the overtime wage (that is, the unjustified wage deduction). Therefore, the special limitation of arbitration of Article 27 of the Labor Dispute Mediation and Arbitration Law shall be applied: the employee should have raised the claim within one year after the employment termination. Especially in the case of Zibo Boshan Xinglong Shopping Mall Co., Ltd. and Chen Lisheng in 2018, Judge Fan Cuizhen of Shandong Provincial High Court pointed out that: "the legislation of the limitation rule in Article 27 of the Labor Dispute Mediation and Arbitration Law was intended to protect the legitimate rights and interests of employees to claim labor remuneration, that labor remuneration arrear should be interpreted in a broad sense and should include items such as overtime wage."

The second view advocates that only unjustified wage arrear is applicable to special limitation of arbitration and that the unjustified wage deduction should be strictly applied to the general limitation of arbitration for one year, which is shown in cases from Jiangsu Provincial High Court, Fujian Provincial High Court, and Hubei Provincial High Court. For example, in the case of the labor dispute between Wu Zhigang and Xuzhou Water Conservancy Construction Co., Ltd. in 2019, the employee, during the waiting-for-work period of the employment relationship, filed a labor arbitration to claim the payment of the living expenses unjustifiably deducted for ten years (that is, wages). The Jiangsu Provincial High Court held that the unjustified wage deduction was different from the unjustified wage arrear and should be applied to the one-year general limitation, so it rejected the employee's claim. In the case of the labor dispute between Chen Ge and Pingtan Yuying Middle School in 2016, Fujian Provincial High Court held that unjustified wage deduction and arrear on labor remuneration are not the same concept. The employee's claim for

101 Civil Ruling of Beijing Higher People's Court (2021) Jing Min Shen No. 557 Civil Ruling of Labor Dispute application for retrial between Wu Qiang and Beijing Dongtao Co., Ltd. Liu Xiaojin, Xinjiang Bohai Cement Co., Ltd. Civil Ruling of the Second Instance of Labor Dispute Civil Ruling of the Higher People's Court of Xinjiang Uygur Autonomous Region (2023) Xin Min Shen No. 114. Zibo Boshan Xinglong Shopping Mall Co., Ltd., Chen Lisheng Labor Contract Dispute Retrial Review and Trial Supervision Civil Ruling Shandong Provincial Higher People's Court Civil Ruling (2018) Lu Minshen No. 6376. Konka Group Co., Ltd. v. Wu Xiuni Employment Dispute Second Instance Judgment Guangdong Shenzhen Intermediate People's Court Civil Judgment (2019) Yue 03 Min Zhong Zi No. 33454. Xu v. Huari Scientific Instruments (Shanghai) Co., Ltd. Employment Contract Dispute Appeal Case Shanghai Second Intermediate People's Court Civil Judgment (2010) Hu Er Zhong Min 3 (Min) Zhong Zi No. 257.

unjustified deduction of the year-end bonus shall be exercised within one year from the date of the acknowledgment.[102]

138. What is employer's refusal to pay overtime wage?

Answer: Paragraph 4 of Article 45 of the 2020 Supreme Court's Judicial Interpretation stipulates that if an employer refuses to pay the employee overtime wage and causes the employee to resign, it constitutes lawful ground for a forced resignation of the employee. The employer should pay economic compensation (see "143. Are employers liable for economic compensation for employees' forced resignation?")

Paragraph 4 of Article 45 (employer's refusal to pay the employee overtime wage), paralleled as unjustified wage deduction and unjustified wage arrear, are all legitimate reasons for an employee's forced resignation. As can be seen from the court decisions, refusal to pay an employee overtime wage refers to the situation where the employer commits unjustified wage deduction or unjustified wage arrear, and then the employee raises a request of payment to the employer, but the employer illegally refuses the request to pay the overtime wages.[103]

The article of the Judicial Interpretation seems to imply that among the legal grounds for an employee's forced resignation, overtime wage is different from wage: unjustified wage deduction or arrear are legitimate grounds for an employee's forced resignation; however, the employee's resignation based on overtime wages can only constitute forced resignation after the employer refuses to pay the overtime wage. If an employee's resignation cannot be found to be forced resignation, it shall be deemed as voluntary, rendering no economic compensation for the employee.

As a result of this nuanced difference, some courts have ruled that employees who file forced resignation on the grounds of arrears or deduction of overtime wages cannot obtain economic compensation.[104] However, the jurisprudence of mainstream courts still holds that the unjustified deduction or arrear of overtime wages can constitute a legitimate reason for forced resignation without the precondition of the employer's refusal.[105] For example, in the case of the labor contract dispute between Shenzhen Jieyuan Property Management Co., Ltd. and Wang Lin in 2018, the Guangdong Provincial High Court pointed out: as mentioned above, Jieyuan Company did not pay overtime wages to

---

102 Wu Zhigang and Xuzhou Water Conservancy Engineering Construction Co., Ltd. Civil Ruling of Jiangsu Provincial Higher People's Court (2019) Sumin Shen No. 7997. Ye Jinping, Hubei Xinyangfeng Fertilizer Co., Ltd. Civil Ruling on Retrial Review and Trial Supervision of Labor Contract Disputes Civil Ruling of Hubei Higher People's Court (2019) E Min Shen No. 3327. Chen Ge v. Pingtan Yuying Middle School labor dispute retrial Fujian Provincial Higher People's Court Civil Judgment (2016) Min Min Zai No. 71.

103 Civil Judgment of Second Instance of Labor Contract Dispute between He Xianglong and Chengdu Youyun Internet Technology Co., Ltd. Civil Judgment of Chengdu Intermediate People's Court of Sichuan Province (2020) Chuan 01 Min Zhong No. 3471. Shenzhen Zhonghai Commercial Service Co., Ltd., Huang Binggui labor dispute civil judgment of second instance civil judgment of Shenzhen Intermediate People's Court of Guangdong Province (2021) Yue 03 Min Zhong No. 237.

104 Hong Xuechun and Zhejiang Tongtianxing Group Co., Ltd., labor dispute case, civil judgment of Zhejiang Quzhou Intermediate People's Court (2015) ZQMZZ No. 329. Sun Xuefeng and Weifang New Era School Recover the Civil Judgment of the Second Instance of the Labor Remuneration Dispute Civil Judgment of Weifang Intermediate People's Court of Shandong Province (2021) Lu 07 Min Zhong No. 8138.

105 Du Ying and Beijing Huaqianshu Information Technology Co., Ltd. Dongcheng Branch labor dispute civil judgment of first instance Beijing Dongcheng District People's Court civil judgment (2020) Jing 0101 Min Chu No. 4844. Shi Jianqiang, Tianjin Shengshi Kaiyuan Automobile Sales Co., Ltd. Civil Judgment of Second Instance of Tianjin Third Intermediate People's Court (2022) Jin 03 Min Zhong No. 116.

Wang Lin in full. The reason for which Wang Lin raised forced resignation due to Jieyuan Company's unjustified overtime wage deduction is established.[106]

Therefore, an employer's explicit refusal to pay overtime wage certainly constitutes a legitimate ground for an employee's forced resignation and the employer's consequent liability of economic compensation; if the employer commits an unjustified overtime wage deduction or arrear, most of the courts consider that it constitutes a legitimate reason for the employee's forced resignation, and a few courts have the opposite stance.

139. What administrative penalties may be imposed on employers who violate employment law?

Answer: Under China's employment law system, labor inspection agencies under the labor administrative authorities at or above the county-level or district-level governments are responsible for supervising and inspecting the compliance of employers with the Labor Law and the Employment Contract Law. They have the authority to enter the premises of employers to review documents and conduct on-site inspections. The public security organs (the police) have the power to impose penalties on employers who infringe upon the personal rights (such as restriction upon personal liberty of workers) of employees, and various levels of trade union organizations also have the right to supervise employers.[107]

Employers are subject to corresponding administrative penalties for the following illegal acts.

First, if an employer violates Article 41 of the Labor Law regarding overtime hours (i.e., employees' monthly overtime hours shall not exceed 36 hours),[108] the labor inspection agency may issue a warning, order rectification, and impose fines (according to Article 25 of the Regulations on Labor Security Supervision, the fine amount can be calculated based on RMB 100 to 500 multiplied by the number of employees who worked overtime exceeding the limit).[109]

Second, if an employer delays or refuses to pay employees' wages or economic compensation, the labor inspection department may order payment (Article 91 of the Labor Law).

Third, if an employer's labor safety facilities and labor environment conditions are not up to standard, or if they fail to provide employees with the necessary labor protection articles or labor protection facilities, the labor inspection agency may order rectification and impose fines.[110] If the employer seriously violates this provision (such as seriously endangering the safety or health of employees), they may be ordered to suspend production and rectify (Article 92 of the Labor Law).

Fourth, employers must not use child labor (under the age of 16); otherwise, the market supervision and administration department may impose a fine on the employer, and in

106 Shenzhen Jieyuan Property Management Co., Ltd., Wang Lin Labor Contract Dispute Retrial Review and Trial Supervision Civil Ruling Guangdong Provincial Higher People's Court Civil Ruling (2018) Guangdong Minshen No. 13414.

107 Articles 85, 86, and 88 of the Labor Law.

108 Although this provision set the rule that daily overtime must not exceed 3 hours, the monthly 36-hour limit is the most frequently applied in labor inspections.

109 However, in employment law practice in China, employees' monthly overtime exceeding 36 hours is universal, and the labor inspection agencies do not implement the law strictly.

110 Regulations on Labor Security Supervision do not provide detailed implementation rules for the fine.

the case of serious violation, the department may revoke the employer's business license (Article 94 of the Labor Law).[111]

Fifth, if an employer employs juvenile workers (aged 16 to 18) to engage in underground or mining work, hazardous or poisonous operations, or Level 4 intensity operations, or fails to arrange for them to undergo medical examinations as required,[112] or violates the special protection provisions for female employees, the labor inspection agency may order rectification and impose fines (according to Article 23 of the Regulations on Labor Security Supervision, the employer may be fined RMB 1,000 to 5,000 per juvenile worker or female employee infringed upon [Article 23 of the Regulations on Labor Security Supervision]).

The circumstances that violate the special protection for female workers include: (1) arranging for female workers to engage in underground mining, labor with the intensity of the fourth level of physical labor as specified by the state, or other prohibited labor activities; (2) arranging for female workers to work at heights, in low temperatures, cold water, or labor with the intensity of the third level of physical labor as specified by the state during menstruation; (3) arranging for female workers to engage in labor with the intensity of the third level of physical labor as specified by the state during pregnancy or labor activities prohibited during pregnancy; (4) arranging night shifts for female workers who are more than seven months pregnant or extending their working hours; (5) granting maternity leave of less than 90 days to female workers after childbirth; (6) arranging for female workers to engage in labor with the intensity of the third level of physical labor as specified by the state or other labor activities prohibited during lactation before their infants are one year old, and extending their working hours or arranging night shifts for them.

Sixth, if an employer forces employees to work through violence, threats, or illegal restrictions on personal liberty, or insults, corporal punishment, beatings, illegal searches, and detention of workers, the public security organs may impose detention for up to 15 days, fines (RMB 200 to 1,000), or warnings on the responsible persons (Article 96 of the Labor Law and Article 40 of the Public Security Administration Punishment Law).

Seventh, if an employer illegally terminates a labor contract or deliberately delays the signing of a labor contract, the labor inspection agency may order rectification (Article 98 of the Labor Law).

Eighth, if an employer fails to contribute to social insurance premiums without reason, the labor administrative authorities shall order it to make payment within a specified period; if it fails to do so, it may be charged with a late fee (Article 100 of the Labor Law). If an employer conceals the total wage amount or number of employees when declaring the payable amount of social insurance contributions to the social insurance agency, the labor security administrative department shall order correction and impose a fine of more than one time but less than three times the concealed wage amount (Article 27 of the Regulations on Labor Security Supervision).

Ninth, if an employer obstructs or resists labor inspection, refuses to correct after being ordered to do so, refuses to declare or conceals facts, destroys evidence, or refuses

111 Regulations on Labor Security Supervision do not provide detailed implementation rules for the fine.

112 Article 6 of the "Special Protection Provisions for Juvenile Workers" stipulates that employers should conduct regular health examinations for juvenile workers according to the following requirements: (1) before arranging work positions; (2) after 1 year of employment; (3) after reaching the age of 18, and the time since the last medical examination has exceeded 6 months.

to implement labor administrative decisions, it may be fined between RMB 2,000 and 20,000 (Article 30 of the "Regulations on Labor Security Supervision").

140. Can employers or their representatives be held criminally liable for violating employment law?

Answer: The Criminal Law stipulates certain circumstances in which employers or relevant responsible persons who violate the employment laws or other employment-related laws shall bear criminal responsibility.

The first is the crime of major labor safety accidents (Article 135 of the "Criminal Law"). This refers to cases where the safety production facilities or conditions do not meet national regulations, resulting in one to two deaths, or three to nine serious injuries, or economic losses of RMB 1 million or more but less than RMB 5 million. The directly responsible managerial personnel and other directly responsible personnel shall be sentenced to imprisonment of less than three years or criminal detention; if the accident causes death of three or more people or economic losses exceeding RMB 5 million, they shall be sentenced to imprisonment of three to seven years.

The second is the crime of major responsibility accidents (Article 134 of the "Criminal Law"). This refers to cases where violations of safety management regulations in production or operations result in one to two deaths, or three to nine serious injuries, or economic losses of RMB 1 million or more but less than RMB 5 million. The directly responsible managerial personnel and other directly responsible personnel shall be sentenced to imprisonment of less than three years or criminal detention; if the accident causes death of three or more people or economic losses exceeding RMB 5 million, they shall be sentenced to imprisonment of three to seven years.

The third is the crime of compelling others to engage in hazardous operations in violation of regulations (Article 134 of the "Criminal Law"). This refers to cases where responsible persons force others to engage in hazardous operations against regulations, or knowingly fail to eliminate significant accident risks but still organize operations, resulting in one to two deaths, or three to nine serious injuries, or economic losses of RMB 1 million or more but less than RMB 5 million. The responsible person shall be sentenced to imprisonment of less than five years or criminal detention; if the accident causes the death of three or more people or economic losses exceeding RMB 5 million, they shall be sentenced to imprisonment of more than five years.

The fourth is the crime of forced labor. The directly responsible person who uses violence, threats, or restriction of personal liberty to compel others to work shall be sentenced to imprisonment of less than three years or criminal detention, and fined. If the aforementioned actions result in casualties, occupational diseases, forcing women to engage in labor with the intensity of the fourth level or prohibited labor, forcing women in the three protected periods to engage in labor with the intensity of the third level or prohibited labor, or forcing minors aged 16 to 18 to engage in labor with the intensity of the fourth level or other hazardous labor, the directly responsible person shall be sentenced to imprisonment of three to ten years, and fined.[113] Those who knowingly recruit or transport

113 Article 31 of the Notice of the Supreme People's Procuratorate and the Ministry of Public Security on Issuing the Provisions of the Supreme People's Procuratorate and the Ministry of Public Security on the Standards for Filing and Prosecutions of Criminal Cases Under the Jurisdiction of Public Security Organs (1) GongTongZi (2008) No. 36.

employees or assist in the forced labor of employees as mentioned above shall be punished according to the provisions of the preceding paragraph. If an employer commits the first two crimes, it shall be fined.[114]

The fifth is the crime of employing child labor to engage in hazardous, intensive labor. The directly responsible person who violates labor management regulations by employing minors under the age of 16 to engage in excessive physical labor, or work at heights, underground, or in hazardous environments such as explosive, flammable, radioactive, or toxic environments, or uses deception to employ minors in hazardous labor, or causes injury or serious health hazards to minors under the age of 16, or employs three or more such minors,[115] shall be sentenced to imprisonment of less than three years or criminal detention, and fined. In cases of particularly serious circumstances, imprisonment of three to seven years and a fine shall be imposed.[116]

The sixth is the crime of refusing to pay labor remuneration.[117] This refers to the directly responsible person evading payment of labor remuneration through methods such as transferring property or absconding, or having the ability to pay but refusing to pay labor remuneration and still refusing to pay the same after being ordered by relevant government authorities to pay. If the aforementioned unpaid labor remuneration is one employee being owed three months' wages with the amount reaching RMB 5,000 to 20,000 or ten people being owed wages with the amount of wage arrears reaching RMB 30,000 to 100,000,[118] the punishments are imprisonment of less than three years or criminal detention and fines, or fines alone; if the number of employees and amounts owed exceeds the aforementioned standards, or if it causes serious consequences such as collective demonstrative petitioning and disrupting social order,[119] imprisonment of three to seven years and fines shall be imposed. If an employer commits the crimes, it shall be fined. If the aforementioned acts have not caused serious consequences, and the labor remuneration is paid to the workers before a prosecution is initiated and corresponding compensation liability is assumed according to law, the punishment may be mitigated or exempted.

In addition, directly responsible persons of employers may also be held criminally responsible for illegal detention under Article 238 of the Criminal Law, intentional body harm under Article 234, or other crimes related to safety management regulations,

---

114 Article 244 of the Criminal Law.

115 Article 32 of the Notice of the Supreme People's Procuratorate and the Ministry of Public Security on Issuing the Provisions of the Supreme People's Procuratorate and the Ministry of Public Security on the Standards for Filing and Prosecutions of Criminal Cases Under the Jurisdiction of Public Security Organs (1) GongTongZi (2008) No. 36.

116 Article 244A of the Criminal Law.

117 Article 276A of the Criminal Law.

118 Article 7 of Supplementary Provisions for the Notice of the Supreme People's Procuratorate and the Ministry of Public Security on Issuing the Provisions of the Supreme People's Procuratorate and the Ministry of Public Security on the Standards for Filing and Prosecutions of Criminal Cases Under the Jurisdiction of Public Security Organs (1) GongTongZi (2017) No. 12.

119 One of the five typical cases issued by the Supreme People's Procuratorate on punishment according to the law of the crime of refusing to pay labor remuneration: the case of Chai before the Intermediate People's Court of Jinzhou City, Liaoning Province, in 2023. The procuratorate considered that the case involved a large number of victims, with an exceptionally large amount of wages owed. Not only did the perpetrator abscond and conceal the whereabouts of the funds involved, but they also refused to pay the owed wages and intentionally misled the group of victimized migrant workers to collectively petition, severely disrupting local social order. This situation falls under the circumstances specified in Article 276A of the Criminal Law of the People's Republic of China, involving "serious consequences," warranting the application of an escalated statutory penalty.

including the crime of major engineering safety accidents under Article 137, the crime of major safety accidents in educational facilities under Article 138, the crime of fire safety responsibility accidents under Article 139, and the crime of failure to report or falsely report safety accidents under Article 139A, of the Criminal Law. Directly responsible persons of employers shall also bear corresponding criminal responsibility if they use violence or threats to obstruct the supervision and inspection work of labor administrative authorities, which may constitute the crime of obstructing official duties under Article 277 of the Criminal Law.

The sentencing and scope of responsible persons for the aforementioned criminal responsibilities are based on the "Interpretation of the Supreme People's Court and the Supreme People's Procuratorate on Several Issues Concerning the Application of Law in Handling Criminal Cases Endangering Production Safety" issued in 2015, and the various provisions on the jurisdiction of public security organs in handling criminal cases and supplementary regulations issued by the Supreme People's Procuratorate and the Ministry of Public Security from 2008 to the present.

CHAPTER 5

Employment Termination

Introduction

Employment termination means the end of the employment relationship. Employment relationships may be dissolved or terminated in a number of ways, which may involve grounds of termination or dissolution and the calculation of related compensation or damages.

The questions and answers in this chapter mainly explain the following practical issues: the process of lawful resignation, the identification of forced resignation, the issue of whether economic compensation is available due to employer relocation, the treatment of disputed reasons for termination, compensations for illegal resignation of employees, training service agreements, determination of employees' statutory retirement age, termination of employees who have reached retirement age, treatment of employees who have reached retirement age during medical care leave, treatment of employees who are incompetent for the work after the expiration of medical care leave, employment termination due to ability incompetence, automatic extension of the fixed-term employment contract due to medical care leave, medical treatment allowance for disability due to illness or non-work-related injury, notification of the trade union to terminate the employment contract by the employer, termination in the case of an employee's serious violation of company rules and regulations, termination due to an employee's poor performance, employment termination due to the employer's closure, termination in the case of economic redundancy and major change in objective situation and the differences between them, termination protection for special types of employees and female employees during the three protected periods, management of employees who have committed crime, termination due to gross negligence and corruption, treatment of an employee's multiple employment relationships, calculation and heedful issues for economic compensation and punitive damages, payment in lieu of notice, wage losses due to employment termination, reinstatement after illegal termination, validity of the compensation agreement between both parties, entitlements of survivors of employees deceased due to illnesses or non-work-related injuries, conditions and amount of unemployment insurance benefits, and personal liability of shareholders of employers for labor dispute debts.

This chapter provides in-depth analyses of the substantive and procedural aspects of employers terminating employees, including the procedure of notifying the trade union, handling of a fixed-term employment contract that expires during the period of medical care leave, reinstation after illegal dismissal, and the departed employee compensating

DOI: 10.4324/9781003583301-5

the employer's losses. It also offers detailed explanations of the calculation of relevant compensation and remedies through case examples.

5.1 Resignation, Retirement, and Party Demise

141. What are the processes for termination of employment relationships?

Answer: Termination or dissolution of employment relationship may occur in the following seven ways.

The first is termination of employment contract by mutual agreement (Article 36 of the Employment Contract Law). Normally, in termination by mutual agreement, both parties sign a clear settlement agreement. In practice, there may be situations where the reason for termination is disputed, where the employee claims dismissal by the employer, while the employer insists that the employee resigned. This normally is considered as termination by mutual agreement in judicial practice. Please refer to "145. My boss fired me, but now he claims I resigned. What can I do?"

The second is employee resignation (Article 37 of the Employment Contract Law). Please see "142. I don't want to work for my employer any more. How should I resign?"

The third is forced resignation (see Article 38 of the Employment Contract Law), including situations where the employer makes it unbearable for the employee to continue work, for example, the employer illegally deducting the employee's wage, and immediate termination due to the employee having been subjected to forced labor or risk of physical harm. For details of forced resignation, please refer to "143. Are employers liable for economic compensation for employees' forced resignation?" and "144. I had to resign due to the relocation of my employer. Am I entitled to economic compensation?"

The fourth is termination of the employment relationship on the following grounds (Article 39 of the Employment Contract Law): employees' serious violation of company rules and regulations (see "154. What requirements should an employer meet to legally terminate an employee?"), employees having committed crimes (see "161. My employee is sentenced to imprisonment for committing a crime. Can we terminate his employment?"), employees' gross negligence and corruption (see "162. My employer fired me for gross negligence and corruption. Is it legal?"), the employee having multiple employment relationships (see "163. One of my employees is also working for another company. Can we fire him?"), invalid employment contracts (see "64. Is the employment contract I signed invalid?", and employees being considered not up to the hiring requirements during the probation period (see "63. An employer notified its employee of termination only after the probation period. Is it legal?").

The fifth is termination due to employees' health incompetence for work after medical care leave (see "85. What should I do if an employee of my company has not recovered after the expiration of the medical care leave?"), the employee being ability incompetent (see "158. Can we terminate an employee's employment due to his poor performance?"), and major change in objective situation (see "157. My employer terminates my employment contract on the ground of major change in objective situation. Is it legal?") (Article 40 of Employment Contract Law).

The sixth is termination due to economic redundancy (Article 41 of the Employment Contract Law). Please refer to "155. How can employers experiencing business hardship legally reduce their workforce to survive?"

The seventh is termination due to employment contract expiration, the work assignment contract ending, the employee reaching retirement age (see "148. Can an employer terminate an employee who has reached retirement age?"), death of the employee, the employer's bankruptcy, the license being revoked or canceled, or the operation period expiring (see "151. What should employees do if their employer goes bankrupt, is deregistered, or is ordered to close?", Article 44 of the Employment Contract Law).

142. I don't want to work for my employer any more. How should I resign?

Answer: The Employment Contract Law stipulates that employees have the right to decide to resign, but they should comply with the requirement of advance notice stipulated by law. The employee must give three days' advance notice during the probation period and one month's advance notice during the regular contract period.[1]

The law does not stipulate the form of resignation, although employees can resign orally, but in order to make the evidence clear, it is better for employees to resign in writing, such as by writing an email or submitting a resignation letter.

After the employee's resignation letter is received by the employer, it will take legal effect unless the employee has no or limited civil capacity.[2] Because the employee's right to unilaterally terminate the employment contract is a type of formation right in Chinese civil law, the right holder's unilateral expression of intention (without the consent of the party receiving the notice) produces legal effect.[3] That is to say, the employment relationship between the two parties is effectively terminated at the time set on the resignation letter (for example, 30 days later).[4] In practice, many employers stipulate a company management procedure of approval, but in law this procedure does not produce effect; whether the employer's management approves or not, the employment relationship between the two parties is to be terminated based on the resignation.

The employee's resignation takes effect once it is delivered to the employer. Even if the employee goes back on their word after resignation, it does not necessarily have the effect of withdrawing their resignation. If the employer disagrees with the employee's withdrawal or make no indication, the employee's resignation has taken effect.[5] Of course, if the employer agrees to withdraw, it is a consensus between the two parties that the

---

1 Article 37 of the Employment Contract Law.

2 Audit Center of Anshan Iron and Steel Group Co., Ltd., Feng Jianqiu Labor Dispute Civil Judgment of Second Instance Civil Judgment (2021) Liao 03 Min Zhong No. 553 of Intermediate People's Court of Anshan City, Liaoning Province. The court held that the employee's resignation was invalid as he was in a bipolar affective disorder manic episode without civil capacity.

3 Liu Zizhen v. Hubei Vocational College of Finance and Taxation Labor Dispute Civil Ruling of Hubei High Court (2016) E Min Shen No. 2514.

4 Civil Ruling on Labor Dispute Retrial Review and Trial Supervision of Zhao Wenxuan and Guangzhou Tongyu International Hotel Co., Ltd. Civil Ruling of Guangdong Provincial People's High Court (2020) Yue Min Shen No. 271.

5 Civil Judgment of the Second Instance of the Labor Dispute between Qin Qingfeng and Xuzhou Meritor Axle Co., Ltd. Civil Judgment of Xuzhou Intermediate People's Court of Jiangsu Province (2020) Su 03 Min Zhong No. 2027. The court held that the employee's resignation letter had legal effect after it was delivered to the employer, and his withdrawal of resignation did not affect the resignation, so the employee's claim for economic compensation was not established.

employer will continue to employ the employee, and the two parties will continue to perform the current employment relationship.[6]

If the employee violates the obligation to give advance notice and resigns immediately or leaves without notice, it may cause disruption or difficulty to the employer's business operation. This is a violation of the employee's obligation of good faith, and the employer has the right to claim compensation for any economic losses caused by the employee. In practice, the employer should provide evidence to prove the existence of the economic losses, the compensation rule for losses in the employment contract or effective company rules and regulations, and the causal relationship between the employee's illegal resignation without advance notice and the occurrence of the economic losses. Please refer to "124. Should an employee compensate the employer for the losses caused by their fault?"

143. Are employers liable for economic compensation for employees' forced resignation?

Answer: Both the Employment Contract Law and the 2020 Supreme Court's Judicial Interpretation stipulate that if an employee is forced to resign for a specific statutory reason, the employer is liable to economic compensation. Therefore, the key issue is under what circumstances the employee is forced to resign. Legally established forced resignations include the following situations.

The first situation is unjustified wage deduction and unjustified wage arrear, which also include overtime wages deduction or arrear. Unjustified wage deduction means the circumstance in which an employer deducts or fails to pay the full amount of an employee's wages that should have been paid without justified reasons, with clear intention of refusing to pay. Unjustified wage arrear means the circumstance in which an employer fails to make its employee's full or partial wage payment at the statutory or agreed-upon wage payment time without justified reasons, while not explicitly refusing to pay the amount. If an employer delays or fails to pay wages in full with justified reasons or without subjective malice, it does not constitute unjustified wage deduction or arrears. This includes legal fines imposed on employees by the employer, reduced wages due to decreased working hours, wage reductions resulting from legal position transfers, lawful or agreed-upon deductions for expenses, wage calculation errors, disputes arising from differing understandings of wages by the employer, or wage payment incompliance caused by business difficulties. According to the 2020 Supreme Court's Judicial Interpretation, employers' paying wages below the local minimum wage standard is also a legitimate reason for forced resignation, as it can also be regarded as a broad type of employer's unjustified wage deduction. Please see "136. What are unjustified wage deduction and unjustified wage arrear by employer?"

If an employer makes an unjustified wage deduction or unjustified wage arrear, and an employee resigns explicitly for this reason, the employer is liable for economic compensation to the employee.

6 Zhang XX, Qingdao Yuantai Taihe Industrial Co., Ltd. Civil Judgment of the Second Instance of Labor Dispute Civil Judgment of Qingdao Intermediate People's Court of Shandong Province (2021) Lu 02 Min Zhong No. 4196. "Zhang XX has withdrawn his resignation application submitted on August 19, 2019 with clear intention and actual behavior. And the intention and actual behavior of the withdrawal have been approved by Yuantai Taihe Company."

The second situation is where social insurance has not been purchased legally. Due to the objective reality of insufficient social insurance contributions in China, it appears that courts all over the country use non-contribution, rather than insufficient contribution, to social insurance as the legitimate reason for employees' forced resignation.[7] Moreover, court decisions and local regulations in Guangdong Province, Shenzhen City, and Maanshan City in Anhui Province show that employees are obligated to request their employers to purchase social insurance in advance, and only if the employers still fail to do so are they entitled to forced resignation.[8]

China's social insurance system also includes the housing provident fund, but in judicial practice, employers' failure to pay the housing provident fund generally does not constitute a legitimate ground for forced resignation.[9]

The third situation involves labor protection, labor conditions, illegal company rules and regulations, and invalid employment contracts. If an employer fails to provide labor protection or working conditions to the employee as agreed, the employee shall be responsible for proving that the working conditions fell below the agreed or statutory standards in order to establish a legitimate forced resignation.[10] As for the situation where

7 Chen Ru and Taizhou Hengyuan New Building Material Machinery Co., Ltd. Labor Dispute Appeal and Application Civil Ruling Jiangsu Provincial People's High Court Civil Ruling (2019) Sumin Shen No. 4318. The court held that as long as the social insurance is paid, even if the amount is insufficient, it does not constitute a reason for forced resignation. Cao Hongjun and Liaoning Jindiyang Ceramics Co., Ltd. Labor Dispute Judgment of Second Instance Civil Judgment of Shenyang Intermediate People's Court of Liaoning Province (2023) Liao 01 Min Zhong No. 5861. The court held that the employer was in arrears of wages due to economic hardship and had agreed to top up the insufficient social insurance, so it did not constitute forced resignation. Li Chuangao and Enshi Longfeng Investment and Development Co., Ltd. Labor Dispute Retrial Review and Trial Supervision Civil Ruling Hubei Provincial People's High Court Civil Ruling (2018) E Min Shen No. 1571. The court held that failure to pay social insurance in full does not constitute a reason under Article 38 of the Employment Contract Law.

8 The second paragraph of Article 15 of the Regulations on the Promotion of Harmonious Employment Relationships in Shenzhen Special Economic Zone stipulates that if an employer fails to pay social insurance premiums for a worker in accordance with the law, the worker shall require the employer to pay them; if the employer fails to pay them within one month, the worker may terminate the employment contract and require the employer to pay economic compensation. Civil Ruling on Labor Dispute Retrial Review and Trial Supervision of Jiayida Electric Industry (Shenzhen) Co., Ltd. and Jiang Xiaoju Civil Ruling of Guangdong Provincial People's High Court (2020) Yue Min Shen No. 10635. The court held that both parties agreed that the social insurance premium should be paid to the employee instead of to the social insurance authority, but the employee requested the employer to purchase the social insurance on multiple occasions, while the employer failed to do so, and that the employee was forced to resign. Labor Dispute between Yuan Zuoqin and Maanshan Huada Metallurgical Machinery Co., Ltd. Civil Judgment of Maanshan Intermediate People's Court of Anhui Province (2016) Wan 05 Min Zhong No. 730. The court held that in the case that both parties agreed not to pay social insurance, the employee should first ask the employer to buy social insurance, and if the employer refused, it would constitute a legitimate reason for forced resignation.

9 Civil Judgment of the Second Instance of Labor Dispute between Zhu Xiaodong and Suzhou Huisi Human Resources Co., Ltd. and Jinlong United Automobile Industry (Suzhou) Co., Ltd. Civil Judgment of the Intermediate People's Court of Suzhou City, Jiangsu Province (2019) Su 05 Min Zhong No. 4047. The court held that the failure of the employer to pay the housing provident fund was not a legitimate cause of forced resignation. Judgment of Second Instance of Labor Dispute between Miao Liang and Xuzhou Tianyu Gas Power Generation Co., Ltd. Civil Judgment of Intermediate People's Court of Xuzhou City, Jiangsu Province (2021) Su 03 Min Zhong No. 2546.

10 Civil Judgment of the Second Instance of the Labor Dispute between Liu Kun and Beijing Minrui Human Resources Management Co., Ltd. Civil Judgment of the Third Intermediate People's Court of Beijing (2014) No. 3 Zhong Min Zhong Zi No. 05578. The employee resigned on the ground that allergy caused by the decoration odor of the employer's office constituted the failure to provide appropriate working conditions, and the court held that the employee failed to prove that the decoration odor had caused the allergic reaction. Therefore, the claim was rejected. Cai Xueping v. Dalian Hongyou Auto Parts Co., Ltd. Labor Dispute Retrial

the employer's company rules and regulations are detrimental to the rights and interests of employees, the court cases appear to consider that, while examining the tenability of a claimed forced resignation due to unlawful company rules and regulations, the court should review whether the unlawful company rules and regulations have direct, actual impact on the employee, and the employee is responsible for proving the causal relationship between the rules and the impact.[11] In the case of an invalid employment contract, the employee is obligated to prove that the employer has entered into an employment contract against the employee's true intention by means of fraud.[12] The above situations are rarely successful paths for employees in judicial practice.

The fourth situation is that employer restricts the personal liberty of an employee or endangers their personal safety by means of violence or violation of regulations. In this case, the employee can terminate the employment contract immediately without notifying the employer in advance. In practice, this kind of employer's violation certainly exists, but it is rare in judicial decisions, probably because of employees' insufficient ability to prove the existence of these violations.

It should be noted that a legitimate forced resignation normally requires that the employee has clearly indicated the specific reason for the forced resignation at the time of resignation. Most court decisions hold that if the resignation does not specify the reason for the claimed forced resignation or claims that the resignation is due to personal reasons, but later, the employee claims for economic compensation, courts usually do not find forced resignation or uphold economic compensation.[13] However, a few courts, including the Shaanxi Provincial High Court and the Inner Mongolia Autonomous Region High Court, have rejected the prerequisite, holding that as long as there is legitimate reason(s) forcing employees to resign, employees are not obligated to specify the reason(s) for resignation.[14]

Case Dalian Intermediate People's Court of Liaoning Province Civil Judgment (2015) D.S.M.Z.Z.Z. No. 13. The court held that the employee did not prove that the substation's labor protection fell below the legal requirements and that it did not find forced resignation.

11 Wen Ninghua, Dongguan Hengxing Electronic Hardware Co., Ltd. Labor Dispute Civil Judgment of Second Instance Civil Judgment of Dongguan Intermediate People's Court of Guangdong Province (2021) Yue 19 Minzhong No. 10904. The employee resigned because he was dissatisfied with the position transfer and later claimed that the company rules and regulations violated the law, leading to his forced resignation. The court found that the real reason for the resignation of the employee was that he was dissatisfied with the position transfer, not the company rules and regulations.

12 Article 26 of the Employment Contract Law, in which the act of the employer excluding the rights of workers and exempting itself from responsibility can be classified as the illegal part of the company rules and regulations.

13 Li Hui, Shenzhen Chuanyi Interactive Technology Co., Ltd. Labor Dispute Retrial Review and Trial Supervision Civil Ruling Guangdong Provincial People's High Court Civil Ruling (2017) Yue Minshen No. 10038. The court held that the employee's claim of forced resignation was based on the employer not signing an employment contract with him, failure of purchase of social insurance and provident fund, and arrears of wages; however, he did not provide evidence to prove that he had indicated the reasons in his resignation. Therefore, the request for economic compensation is not supported. Civil Ruling on Labor Dispute Retrial Review and Trial Supervision of Zhang Hongzhu and Jining Zhongxin Taxi Co., Ltd. Civil Ruling of Shandong Provincial People's High Court (2018) Lu Min Shen No. 5285. The court held that the employee resigned for personal reasons and later claimed forced resignation on the grounds of unjustified wage deduction and social insurance issues, and that the claim of forced resignation was not established. Civil Ruling on Labor Dispute Retrial Review and Trial Supervision of Wang Chengwei and Sichuan Electric Appliance Group Co., Ltd. Civil Ruling of Sichuan High Court (2019) Chuan Min Shen No. 2277. The employee's resignation report stated that "he had to leave the company for some reason," and the court found that he was not forced to resign.

14 Xi'an Jindun Escort Co., Ltd. and Liu Pengfei Labor Dispute Appeal and Application for Retrial Civil Ruling Shaanxi Provincial People's High Court Civil Ruling (2021) Shan Min Shen No. 153. The court held that the employer did not pay social insurance to employees, and that even if the employee did not explicitly

144. I had to resign due to the relocation of my employer. Am I entitled to economic compensation?

Answer: The Employment Contract Law stipulates that the employer is obligated to provide the employee with the agreed-upon work conditions. They include the agreed-upon work location because changing work location affects the employee's commuting time and costs. Hence, if such relocation constitutes a failure to provide the employee with the agreed-upon work conditions, the employee may be forced to resign in accordance with Article 38 of the Employment Contract Law, and therefore has the right to claim economic compensation against the employer.

Whether you meet the threshold of the aforementioned forced resignation, first of all, you need to see whether the work location(s) stipulated in your employment contract include the new location that your employer moved to. If so, you do not have right to claim economic compensation, because it is you who violated the provision of the employment contract by refusing to move to the new work location that has been agreed upon.

If your employment contract does not stipulate that work location as your place of work, the general principle is that the courts will examine the impact of the change of location on you and the remedial measures taken by the employer. If the company moved too far away and the company does not provide mitigatory measures, such as offering transportation expenses or a commuter bus, you who are forced to resign should receive economic compensation.[15] Otherwise, the courts may consider that the employer has tried its best to mitigate the adverse effects of the relocation on you, and that your resignation is merely a unilateral resignation for personal reasons, instead of a forced resignation that entails economic compensation.

Some regional courts have some specific judicial guidance or guidance decisions. For example, the 2015 judicial guidance of the Shenzhen Intermediate People's Court stipulates that relocation within the administrative region of Shenzhen does not justify an employee's forced resignation and consequent economic compensation.[16] Guangdong Provincial High Court also rendered a case ruling that relocation within the same municipal administrative region does not constitute a condition for an employee's forced resignation.[17] However, Guangdong Provincial High Court has a case ruling that even if relocation is within the same city, if the distance is too far, it also constitutes a change

---

put this forward at the time of resignation, it constituted a reason for forced resignation. Huolinguole Baisheng Commerce and Trade Co., Ltd. and Wang Xiaoai Labor Dispute Retrial Review and Trial Supervision Civil Ruling Inner Mongolia Autonomous Region High Court Civil Ruling (2020) No. 2166. The court held that although the employee did not explicitly indicate the employer's failure to pay social insurance as the reason for his resignation in his resignation letter, objectively, it was a fact that the employer did not pay social insurance ... it can be concluded that the employer has not paid social insurance according to law, and the employee has unilaterally terminated the employment contract according to law.

15 Anhui Shiqiang New Materials Co., Ltd., Zhang Lingzhi Labor Dispute Retrial Review and Trial Supervision Civil Ruling Anhui High Court Civil Ruling (2020) Wan Min Shen No. 3218. Because in the case the workplace was relocated too far, Anhui Shiqiang Materials Co., Ltd. did not provide sufficient evidence to prove that it fulfilled the corresponding assistance obligations, so the court ordered economic compensation. Retrial of labor dispute between Shenzhen Qianhai Tianxin Jiuzhou Commercial Factoring Co., Ltd. and Shi Kunjie Civil Ruling of Guangdong Provincial People's High Court (2021) Yue Min Shen No. 13716.

16 Article 80 of the 2015 Shenzhen Intermediate Court's Guidelines for Adjudicating Labor Dispute Cases.

17 Liu Miaohua, Huang Guangming, Zhang Guoqiu, Feng Weichao, Labor Dispute Review and Trial Supervision of Zhuhai Songli Electrical Appliances Co., Ltd. Civil Ruling of Guangdong Provincial People's High Court (2017) Yue Min Shen No. 6391–6394.

in working conditions, and employees who are forced to resign should receive economic compensation.[18]

145. My boss fired me, but now he claims I resigned. What can I do?

Answer: The relationship between an employer and an employee often worsens before or after they end the employment. It is not uncommon that both parties accept the termination, but disagree on the cause: the employee may maintain that they were dismissed by the employer, and the employer may insist that the employee resigned. Both parties may stick to their own arguments, making it difficult to judge the truth.

Obviously, the legal consequences of different processes of termination are completely different. Needless to say, if the court finds that the termination of employment relationships was made by the employer, and the ground of the termination is untenable, there will be serious consequences for the employer in the form of punitive damages. If the court finds that the employee resigned, the employer bears no liability of punitive damages or anything else. Therefore, it is a very important issue to determine how an employment relationship was terminated.

The current practices of the courts vary in different situations.

The first situation is termination with clear evidence, including clear terminating party, termination process, and relatively clear reasons. In this case, the court will generally judge on the basis of evidence such as resignation letters of employees, notices of termination issued by employers, and the merits of each case. This is a relatively simple situation.

The second situation is unequivocal termination by mutual agreement, that is, termination proposed by the employer and agreed by the employee. For example, an employer persuades an employee to resign, and the employee subsequently submits a resignation letter.[19] This situation is also relatively simple, requiring only the establishment of facts. It should be noted that an employee's voluntarily proposing to terminate and the employer subsequently agreeing to the proposal, in principle, constitutes a unilateral resignation of the employee rather than termination by mutual agreement.

The third situation is the most difficult situation: both parties dispute the cause of termination of the employment relationship. Typically, employers claim the employee's resignation or abandonment of their job, while employees assert that the employer dismissed them, and there is no evidence to prove either claim. In this case, the courts are likely to find, in compromise, a termination of the employment contract by constructive mutual agreement between the two parties.[20]

---

18 Guangzhou Jingyong Sports Goods Co., Ltd., He Guiping Labor Dispute Retrial Review and Trial Supervision Civil Ruling Guangdong Provincial People's High Court Civil Ruling (2018) Yue Minshen No. 10250.

19 Guilin Suning Yunshang Sales Co., Ltd. and Zeng Liang Labor Dispute Second Instance Civil Judgment Guilin City Intermediate People's Court of Guangxi Zhuang Autonomous Region Civil Judgment (2015) Gui Min Si Zhong Zi No. 627. The employer persuaded the employee to resign because of the employee's violation of company rules and regulations, and then, the employee resigned; the court held that this was a mutual agreement to terminate the contract.

20 Ma Zhengcong, China Merchants Property Management Co., Ltd. Dongguan Branch Labor Dispute Retrial Review and Trial Supervision Civil Ruling Guangdong Provincial People's High Court Civil Ruling (2018) Yue Min Shen No. 117. "As both parties hold different opinions on the reasons for the termination of employment relationships, and there is no evidence to prove … this case is regarded as the termination of employment relationship by mutual agreement." Huang Zhixian, Civil Ruling of Labor Dispute Retrial Review and Trial Supervision of Zhenmiao Hospital of Changfeng County, Civil Ruling of Anhui High Court

The fourth situation is that the two parties have been deadlocked and disputed repeatedly for a long time in the employment relationship, each sticking to their own argument, and finally ended the employment relationship. In this case, the courts are likely to find that the employment relationship is terminated by constructive mutual agreement between the two parties. A typical example is where employees have been in long-term waiting-for-work because of illness or work-related injuries and occupational diseases, and the two parties have repeatedly disputed.[21]

The fifth situation is that both parties are at fault in the termination of the employment relationship, and the courts, for the sake of fairness, determine that both parties have reached a constructive termination by mutual agreement. For example, in the case of Cai Wuqiang before Guangdong Provincial High Court in 2020, the employer did not dismiss the employee but demoted them due to the latter's serious violation of company rules and regulations. Four months later, the disagreement between the two parties became irreconcilable. The employer terminated the employee, resorting to the original violation of company rules and regulations. The court held that both parties were at fault in the case and that it was fair to find a constructive termination by mutual agreement.[22]

This frequent occurrence in China, where employers and employees hold conflicting views on the reasons for the termination of the employment relationship, reflects a relatively low level of credibility and trust in social life and the resulting reduced reliance on witness testimony by judicial authorities.

146. How does the law stipulate the statutory retirement age?

Answer: The statutory retirement age is the age at which employees may start to receive pension benefits and employers can terminate the employment relationship with the employee in accordance with the Employment Contract Law.

Before the end of 2024, the national statutory retirement age for enterprise employees was 60 years for male employers, 50 years for female worker employees, and 55 years for female cadre employees. The retirement age for those engaged in underground, high-temperature, high-altitude, particularly heavy physical labor, or other work harmful to their health is 55 years for men and 45 years for women. For employees who are completely

---

(2020) Wan Min Shen No. 732. Civil Ruling of the Supreme People's Court of the People's Republic of China (2016) S.F.M.J. No. 35 in the employment contract dispute case of Liu Hanbo v. Linak Transmission Systems (Shenzhen) Co., Ltd. "The employee who returned hometown for the Spring Festival without asking for leave was an unauthorised absence, and he was refused to return to the employer after one month. The court held that this situation constituted termination of employment by mutual agreement with the employer's proposal and the employee's consent."

21 Liaoning Dalong Gold Investment Co., Ltd. v. Gu Yingxue Labor Dispute Liaoning Provincial People's High Court Civil Ruling (2014) Liao Shen Yi Min Shen Zi No. 1293. Civil Ruling of Guangdong Provincial People's High Court on Labor Dispute Retrial Review and Trial Supervision of Zhuguang Street Community Health Service Center, Yuexiu District, Guangzhou (2017) No. 3273. Ronglin Plastics (Fujian) Co., Ltd. and Sun Yang Labor Dispute Civil Judgment of Second Instance Civil Judgment of Fuzhou Intermediate People's Court of Fujian Province (2019) Min 01 Min Zhong No. 5328. Although the employer claimed that the employee resigned but failed to prove this, the court found the termination of employment relationship being mutual agreement three months after the employee's resignation application.

22 Civil Ruling on Labor Dispute Retrial Review and Trial Supervision of Cai Wuqiang and China Resources Concrete (Zhanjiang) Co., Ltd. Civil Ruling of Guangdong Provincial People's High Court (2020) Yue Min Shen No. 8268. The employee forged a signature for false reimbursement, but the employer only demoted the employee; then, the disagreement between the two parties continued, and the employer ultimately terminated the employee for serious violation of company rules and regulations four months later. The court held that both parties were at fault and found constructive termination of employment by mutual agreement.

incapacitated due to illness or non-work-related issues, certified by the labor appraisal committee, the retirement age is 50 years for men and 45 years for women.[23]

Starting from 2025, the aforesaid retirement age shall be gradually extended. In September 2024, the Standing Committee of the National People's Congress of China announced the "Decision on Implementing the Gradual Delay of the Statutory Retirement Age," stipulating that starting from 2025, over the course of 15 years, the statutory retirement age for male employees will be gradually extended from the original 60 years to 63 years, and for female employees from the original 50 and 55 years to 55 and 58 years, respectively.

A common disputed issue with the aforementioned rule is the retirement age of female employees. As mentioned above, the retirement age for female employees distinguishes the status of cadres and workers. Female cadre employees retire at the age of 55 or above, and female worker employees retire at the age of 50 or above.

Female cadres are those in management and technical positions; others are female workers. At present, there appears to be no law stipulating what type of position falls within the scope of management positions, but court decisions usually take management personnel higher than department managers, including financial, technical, and marketing directors and other members of management, as employees in management positions. Technical positions do not appear to have a specific rule defining their scope. In judicial practice, the employee's current position, the employee's employment contract agreement, the government's personnel file records, and social insurance payment registration in this regard may affect the identification of a female employee when disputes occur. At present, there are three practices provided in regional laws and regulations and the judicial decisions.

The first approach is based on the position of a female employee when she reaches the retirement age. For example, Beijing decides whether a female employee is a worker or a cadre according to whether her position is a management or technical position at a female worker employee's retirement age (i.e., 50 or above).[24]

The second approach is to not only look at the female employee's position at retirement age, but also consider the length of time she has been in the management or technical position. For example, in Guangdong Province (including Shenzhen), if a female employee has worked in a management position for more than 1 year before reaching the retirement age, the retirement age should be 55 or above; otherwise, the employee should retire at the age of 50 or above as a worker. Fujian Province requires female employees to work in management positions for more than 5 years before the retirement age to be eligible to retire at the age of 55 or above as cadre.

---

23 The former Ministry of Labor and Social Security issued on March 9, 1999 the Notice on Stopping and Correcting the Relevant Issues Concerning the Early Retirement of Enterprise Employees in Violation of State Regulations (No. 8, 1999, issued by the Ministry of Labor and Social Security).

24 Beijing Xunfengguang Communication Technology Development Co., Ltd. and Liu Yongxia Labor Dispute Second Instance Civil Judgment Beijing the First intermediate People's Court Civil Judgment (2022) Beijing 01 Min Zhong No. 778. "At present, the Beijing Municipal People's Society Department does not determine the retirement age of female workers according to the status of cadres and workers. It is judged according to the difference between management positions and professional and technical positions and non-management positions, and based on the position and job responsibilities signed in the last employment contract before retirement."

The third approach is to determine female employees' identities as cadres or workers based on their social insurance registration status.[25]

Please refer to "147. What are the current national and local regulations and referable case law on retirement age?" This discriminatory rule artificially creates numerous unnecessary disputes: female employees may insist they are cadres, being entitled to retire at the age of 55 or above, while employers request the employees to retire at the age of 50 or above as workers. The conflicts in retirement age rules for different types of employees increase the uncertainty of the law and dispute costs, and reflect discriminations in gender, position, and identify. We call for future legislative amendments to simplify and unify the rules and eliminate the legislative gender, position, and identity discrimination.

147. What are the current national and local regulations and referable case law on retirement age?

Answer: For readers' reference, we have complied the following national regulations, judicial decisions, and local regulations of Guangdong Province, Liaoning Province, Fujian Province, Jiangsu Province, Sichuan Province, and Chongqing Municipality.

Article 75 of the Former Ministry of Labor's LaoBuFa (1995) No. 309 file stipulates that the retirement age and condition for employees who transitioned from a former worker position to a current cadre or technical position or from a former cadre or technical position to a current worker position, during the employer's transition into the employment contract system, shall be determined according to national regulations in relation to their current position.

Article 3 (1) (2) of the Measures of the Department of Human Resources and Social Security of Guangdong Province on the Qualification of Enterprise Employees Participating in Basic Pension Insurance (Yue Ren She Gui [2019] No. 1) stipulates that identifying female cadre or worker employees shall be in accordance with the Circular of the Ministry of Labor and Social Security on Stopping and Correcting the Problems Related to the Early Retirement of Enterprise Employees in Violation of State Regulations (YueLaoXin [1999] No. 114) and the Opinions on the Handling of the Problems Related to the Implementation of Document YueLaoXin [1999] No. 114) (YueLaoShe [2000] No. 200). The retirement age for those who work in workers' positions is 50 years, and for

25 Guangdong Foshan Intermediate People's Court (2021) Civil Judgment Yue 06 Min Zhong No. 6398. The judgment of the second instance of the labor dispute between Xu Yonghong and Guangfo Commercial and Trade City Development Co., Ltd. in Nanhai District of Foshan City. "This Court holds that whether an employee is a worker or a cadre, and whether her retirement age should be 50 or 55 years old, belongs to the scope of the authority of the social security administrative department. Since Xu Yonghong did not submit to the social security administrative department to identify her as a cadre, the court of first instance finding Xu Yonghong a female worker, based on the state of her social insurance, purchased by Guangfo Trade City Development Company for Xu Yonghong, of 'female worker', and her retirement age being 50, is not inappropriate, and this court maintains the decision." Chen Xiaohui v. Jiangxi Xinhua Distribution Group Co., Ltd., Jiangxi Provincial People's High Court Civil Ruling (2017) No. 645. "Chen Xiaohui was a worker when she entered the Xinhua Bookstore in Quannan County, and the status of the worker in her resume remained unchanged after that. Although she was appointed as the manager of the Xinhua Bookstore in Longnan County in 2002, it does not mean that she had the status of national cadres. The cadre status of the staff of the employer can not be determined only by the employer and the position, but should be determined by the governmental organization personnel department according to the relevant procedures. Chen Xiaohui's personnel files do not have the relevant materials identifying her as a cadre by the organization personnel department. Chen Xiaohui's claim that she has worked in a management position for many years and should be applied the standard of retirement age of 55 years old lacks legal basis."

those who work in management and technical positions, it is 55 years. The current position shall be determined as per the position set on the employment contract, or the current position in which the employee has been working for more than one year.

Liyoubi (Dalian) Machinery Co., Ltd. and Xu Huashan Labor Dispute Retrial Liaoning Provincial People's High Court Civil Ruling (2018) Liao Min Shen No. 3198. "The current position is determined as the management position agreed-upon in the employment contract."

Article 1 (7) of the Notice of the Ministry of Labor and Social Security of Fujian Province on Regulating the Management of Examination and Approval of Retirement of Employees (Min Lao She [2001] No. 362) stipulates that the retirement age of female employees shall be determined according to their positions before retirement. Among them, female cadres who have worked continuously for 5 years in their positions before retirement shall retire at the age of 50; female workers who have worked in management positions for 5 consecutive years before retirement shall retire at the age of 55.

Article 13, Paragraph 1 of the "Implementation Measures for Basic Pension Insurance for Employees in Enterprises in Jiangsu Province" (Su Ren She Gui [2022] No. 1) stipulates that female workers retire at the age of 50, female cadres retire at the age of 55, or although they are female workers, they retire at the age of female cadres under the following circumstances: working in management or technical positions at the age of 50, or working in management or technical positions after the age of 45 and having accumulated more than 5 years in such positions. Additionally, sole traders, flexible employment female insured persons, female unemployed persons who retain the pension insurance relationship, and female insured persons with rural household registration also retire at the age of 55.

The Reply of Chongqing Municipal Human Resources and Social Security Bureau on the Retirement of Personnel Participating in the Basic Pension Insurance for Enterprise Employees (Yu Ren She Han [2015] No. 118) explicitly states: "All types of enterprises that have established a personnel system open for management position competition and promotion and demotion shall abolish enterprises' administrative stratum. Enterprises shall no longer apply the administrative level of state organs, and managers are no longer entitled to the administrative level treatment of cadres of state organs, breaking the traditional boundaries between 'cadres' and 'workers' and changing identity management into position management. The status of female workers and cadres is defined by enterprises as management positions and non-management positions."

Article 55 of the Detailed Rules for the Implementation of the Combination of Social Overall Planning and Personal Accounts of Basic Pension Insurance for Enterprise Employees in Chengdu (CLSF [2006] No. 134) stipulates: "The normal retirement age of enterprise employees shall be implemented in accordance with the current provisions of the state and the province, that is, male employees being 60 years old, and female employees working in management and technical positions being 55 years old, and female workers working on production, operation, and service positions being the age of 50."

The Opinions of Hunan Province on Several Policy Issues Concerning the Improvement of the Basic Pension Insurance System for Enterprise Employees (XLSZZ (2006) No. 13) further clarifies the retirement age of female employees and the specific criteria for distinguishing them: the retirement age of female employees employed as cadres granted by competent personnel administrative department is 55 years old; the retirement age of female workers who started work before and after the implementation of the Labor Law shall be determined based on their long-term positions; the retirement age for those who have worked for a long time in management positions shall be 55 years old; and the retirement age for those who have worked for a long time in production positions shall be 50 years old; those who hold certain administrative positions in the employer or are not directly engaged in the production activities of the employer or are not directly engaged in the front-line production, service, and service positions in the industry shall be determined as management positions. Employees who have worked on management positions for a long time and whose accumulative service is longer than that of production positions shall be considered to have worked on management positions for a long time, and their retirement age shall be 55; on the contrary, the retirement age is 50 years old for long-term work in production positions.

Notice on Improving the Retirement Age of Female Employees in Enterprises issued by Jiangxi Provincial Department of Human Resources and Social Security (GRSF [2019] No. 4). When a female employee in an enterprise reaches the age of 50, if she works in a management (technical) position, the retirement age shall be 55 years old; if she works in a worker position, the retirement age shall be 50 years old.

Li v. Shenzhen Nepstar Health Pharmacy Chain Co., Ltd. and other, Shenzhen Intermediate People's Court (2016) Yue 03 Min Zhong No22042. Ms. Li internally retired as a cadre and now serves as a quality management manager. The court ruled that she should be identified as a cadre based on her current position.

Guangzhou Wangji Catering Service Co., Ltd. v. Chen Xinyi labor dispute, Guangdong Huadu City (District) People's Court first-instance civil judgment (2022) Yue 0114 Min Chu No. 12031. The court stated that: "Chen Xinyi has worked in this position for more than one year. According to the above provisions, regardless her status in participating social insurance, her identity should be determined by her current position. Chen Xinyi's position was a management role before her termination; thus, her statutory retirement age should be 55 years old."

148. Can an employer terminate an employee who has reached retirement age?

Answer: This is a rather complicated legal issue in law and practice. Article 44 of the Employment Contract Law stipulates that if a worker begins to receive basic pension insurance benefits in accordance with the law, the employment contract shall be terminated. However, Article 21 of the Regulations on the Implementation of the Employment Contract Law stipulates that when a worker reaches statutory retirement age, the employment contract shall be terminated. The former provision encompasses two conditions: reaching retirement age and receiving pension, while the latter only indicates the retirement ages.

This divergence is also reflected at the law enforcement level. The Supreme Court holds that termination of the employment relationship must meet the two conditions of age and basic pension insurance benefits simultaneously, while the Ministry of Human Resources is of the view that termination of employment relationships between the two parties only requires the age condition.[26] It merits mention that the conclusion may be different if the

26 Reply of the Civil First Division of the Supreme People's Court on the Criteria for Determining the Termination of Employment Relationships between Workers (including Migrant Workers) Who Have Reached

employee reaches retirement age but is still within the period of medical treatment (see "149. Can an employer terminate an employee who has reached retirement age during their medical treatment?")

If the employee reaches statutory retirement age and begins to receive basic pension insurance, applications of the two statutory provisions will not make difference, as the situation satisfies both aforesaid statutory provisions.

However, in the practice of China's employment law, it is not unusual that employers and employees have not purchased pension insurance, or, if they have, the pension insurance contribution duration is less than 15 years, the statutory requirement for a pension. In both cases, employees have reached retirement age but cannot receive pension benefits. For them, the two aforementioned provisions will bring about distinct legal consequences. That is to say, under the former provision, which requires two conditions, reaching retirement age and receiving pension benefits, employers may not be able to terminate them while they are under the latter provision, which requires reaching retirement age only. This obviously makes a huge difference.

At present, the legal consequences of reaching retirement age without receiving a pension are reflected in four types of court practices around the country.

The first is automatic termination of the employment relationship. This practice holds that as long as employees reach retirement age, whether or not employees receive basic pension insurance benefits, the employment relationship between the two parties will automatically terminate. The provinces and cities or courts for this practice include Beijing High Court, Shanghai High Court, Jilin Provincial High Court, Chongqing High Court, Zhejiang Provincial High Court, Guangdong Provincial High Court, and Chengdu City of Sichuan province.[27]

---

or Exceeded the Statutory Retirement Age and Employers ([2015] Min Yi Ta Zi No. 6): for the termination of employment contract relations between workers (including migrant workers) who have reached or exceeded the statutory retirement age and employers, the standard should be whether the worker receives the pension insurance treatment or receives the pension. The Reply of the Ministry of Human Resources and Social Security to Recommendation No. 6979 of the Second Session of the 13th National People's Congress, Ren She Jian Zi [2019] No. 37: "the main consideration of Article 21 of the Regulations on the Implementation of the Employment Contract Law is that when workers reach the statutory retirement age, they no longer meet the subject qualification stipulated by the employment laws and regulations, thus the employment contract dissolves … the employment contract of an employee who has reached statutory retirement age shall dissolve. If a worker over the statutory retirement age is willing to continue working, the relationship between the employer and the worker may be handled as a contractor relationship, and the rights and obligations of both parties shall be adjusted according to the civil legal relationship."

27 Civil Ruling on Retrial Review of Labor Dispute Case between Mao Yunchang and Lalin Irrigation District Management Center of Fuyu City Civil Ruling of Jilin Provincial People's High Court (2020) Ji Min Shen No. 2196. Civil Ruling on Labor Dispute Appeal and Application for Retrial between Zhang Fuxiu and Chongqing Wanglong Industrial (Group) Co., Ltd. Civil Ruling of Chongqing High Court (2020) Yu Min Shen No. 873. Geng Huaxian v. Jinhua SEG Dyeing and Finishing Co., Ltd. Labor Dispute Civil Ruling of Zhejiang Provincial People's High Court (2017) Zhe Min Shen No. 669. Civil Ruling on Labor Dispute Retrial Review and Trial Supervision of Tang Yuanzhong and Guangzhou Holly Garment Co., Ltd. Civil Ruling of Guangdong Provincial People's High Court (2020) Yue Min Shen No. 1061. The court held that the employment relationship was terminated if the worker had reached the statutory retirement age or had received the basic pension insurance benefits. Civil Ruling on Labor Dispute Retrial Review and Trial Supervision between Tian Xinjian and Beijing Sunshine Jinyu Pension Service Co., Ltd., Beijing High Court (2023) Jing Min Shen No. 94. "The employment contract is terminated when the worker reaches the statutory retirement age. According to the above provisions and the original court investigation, Tian Xinjian reached the age of 60, the statutory retirement age, on November 11, 2018. The court of second instance confirmed that Tian Xinjian and Sunshine Jinyu Company had employment relationships from February 10, 2017 to November 11, 2018, and that it was correct for both parties to have a contractor relationship thereafter. Tian Xinjian's claim that he did not receive

The second approach is that the employment relationship automatically continues. This approach considers that according to the opinion of the Civil First Division of the Supreme People's Court, the employment relationship between an employer and an employee who has reached retirement age but has not received basic pension insurance benefits will not automatically terminate but continue. The representative case is the case of Li Xiuyu before Fujian Province Nanping City Intermediate Court in 2018, which is one of the exemplary cases issued by the Supreme Court in 2019. In addition, Henan Province Zhengzhou City Intermediate Court, Jiangxi Provincial High Court, Shandong Provincial High Court, and Inner Mongolia Autonomous Region High Court also implement this practice.[28]

The third approach is that the employment relationship will terminate or continue conditionally. Under this practice, courts examine the causes of employees' failure to receive pension insurance benefits. If the employer is at fault, the employment relationship between the two parties will continue. Otherwise, the employment relationship between the two parties will be terminated and converted into a contractor relationship. This

pension insurance benefits, believing that there was still a special employment relationship between the two parties, lacks legal basis, and it was not improper that the court of first instance rejected it." In the sixth of the ten typical cases of labor disputes in Chengdu Court in 2015, the case of labor disputes between Wang and a company, the post-retirement-age work injury entitlements for workers who have been working until the statutory retirement age do not include a one-off employment subsidy for disability. Civil Ruling on Trial and Supervision of Other Labor Disputes between Wang Jianning and Shanghai Jahwa United Co., Ltd. Civil Ruling of Shanghai High Court (2019) Hu Min Shen No. 1311 (the employment relationship will be terminated naturally after the employee reaches the statutory retirement age). Article 16 of the Opinions of the Guangdong Provincial Labor and Personnel Dispute Arbitration Commission of the Guangdong Provincial People's High Court on the Connection between Labor and Personnel Dispute Arbitration and Litigation stipulates that if a worker reaches the statutory retirement age or has already received the basic pension insurance benefits, the employment relationship shall be terminated naturally.

28 The Supreme People's Court issued an excellent case of the national court system in 2019, the Center for Disease Control and Prevention of Nanping City v. Li Xiuyu's labor dispute appeal case, the Intermediate People's Court of Nanping City, Fujian Province (2018) Min 07 Min Zhong 562: "but for those who have reached the statutory retirement age and have not received pension insurance benefits or pensions in accordance with the law, the formation of employment relationships is not prohibited. Laws and regulations do not prohibit the use of employees over the statutory retirement age. Li Xiuyu reached the statutory retirement age during the employment tenure (November 2010), but did not receive pension insurance benefits or receive pension according to law, so it should be recognized that there is an employment relationship between Li Xiuyu and Nanping CDC." Labor dispute Sun Changsheng v. Zhengzhou Xinxicheng Property Service Co., Ltd, Henan Zhengzhou Intermediate People's Court (2014) Zheng Min Yi Zhong Zi No. 219. "In the case, Sun Changsheng was over 60 years old when he worked in Zhengzhou Xinxicheng Property Service Co., Ltd., but he was a peasant who did not receive the pension insurance benefits for employees and did not receive pension. The new-style rural pension insurance received monthly has the nature of social welfare, which is different from the employee pension insurance. This case does not meet the conditions for handling contractor relationships stipulated in Article 7 of the 2010 Interpretation of the Supreme People's Court on Several Issues Concerning the Application of Law in the Trial of Labor Dispute Cases (III), and the formation of de facto relationships between the two parties should not be handled as contractor relationships." In 2019, the High Court of Jiangxi Province and the Department of Human Resources and Social Security of Jiangxi Province jointly released the fifth of ten typical cases of labor and personnel disputes: the case of labor disputes between Huang and a company in Shun'an (when an employee reaches retirement age, the employment relationship is not automatically terminated). Zhong Quanxiu, Civil Ruling of Labor Dispute Retrial of Xingguo County Urban Environmental Sanitation Management Institute, Civil Ruling of Jiangxi Provincial People's High Court (2019) Gan Min Zai No. 144. Tai'an Xiaotianting Hotel Management Co., Ltd. and Yang Wenxin Labor Dispute Civil Application for Retrial Review Civil Ruling Shandong High Court Civil Ruling (2021) Lu Min Shen No. 6928. Inner Mongolia Morning News Agency and Ding Xueyun Labor Dispute Retrial Review and Trial Supervision Civil Ruling Inner Mongolia Autonomous Region High Court Civil Ruling (2020) No. 2849.

approach is adopted by Tianjin High Court, Liaoning Provincial High Court, Xinjiang Uygur Autonomous Region High Court, and Hunan Provincial High Court.[29]

The fourth approach is that when employees reach retirement age, employment relationships will not automatically terminate, but the employer has the option to terminate; the employment relationship shall terminate if the employer informs the employee of the same. Otherwise, the relationship continues. This practice is adopted in the Hubei Provincial High Court, the Gansu Provincial High Court, the Henan Provincial High Court, and the Shanxi Provincial High Court.[30]

In summary, when an employee reaches statutory retirement age and receives the basic pension insurance benefits, the employer may notify the employee of the termination of the employment relationship. No economic compensation is required. However, if the employee is not receiving the basic pension insurance benefits at their retirement age, the nature of the relationship between the two parties and how the employer can deal with it will depend on the province or city where the employer is located. Different regions implement different practices regarding whether the two parties can terminate or continue the employment relationship. Please note that the aforementioned basic pension insurance is limited to the pension insurance for employees, excluding urban resident social pension insurance and new-style rural pension insurance.

From the above analyses, it is obvious that the determination of the nature of employment relationships between the two parties when an employee reaches statutory retirement

29 The second paragraph of Article 10 of the Guidelines for the Trial of Labor Dispute Cases in Tianjin Court stipulates that if a worker who has reached the statutory retirement age has not yet received the basic pension insurance benefits or has not yet received the pension due to the employer's reasons, the actual employment relationship between the worker and the former employer shall be handled in accordance with the employment relationship. Zhou Huachun and Tianjin Chengtong Decoration Engineering Co., Ltd. Other labor disputes and personnel disputes retrial Tianjin High Court Civil Ruling (2020) Jin Min Shen No. 703. Wang Huailin, Liaoning Yuanshenglong Machinery Co., Ltd. Civil Ruling on Labor Dispute Civil Application for Retrial Review, Liaoning Provincial People's High Court Civil Ruling (2021) Liao Min Shen No. 6807. Urumqi Meixinyuan Property Service Co., Ltd. and Ma Donghua Labor Dispute Civil Judgment of Civil Retrial, Xinjiang High Court (2022) Xinmin Zai No. 229. "In this case, Ma Donghua did not receive the basic pension insurance benefits, so the provisions of Article 44 (2) of the Employment Contract Law of the People's Republic of China could not be directly applied. Article 21 of the Regulations on the Implementation of the Employment Contract Law of the People's Republic of China, which stipulates that 'when a worker reaches the statutory retirement age, the employment contract shall be terminated,' should be applied in this case. Of course, from the original intention of this article, if the employer is directly granted the right to terminate the employment contract because the worker reaches the statutory retirement age, it will also cause damage to the legitimate rights and interests of workers to a certain extent. Therefore, the examination of the application of Article 21 of the Regulations on the Implementation of the Employment Contract Law of the People's Republic of China should also specifically examine whether the reasons the workers can not receive basic pension insurance benefits are related to employers." The High Court of Hunan Province issued the fourth "100 Excellent Judgment Documents" and "100 Excellent Court Trials," the Civil Judgment of Changsha Intermediate People's Court of Hunan Province (2021) Xiang 01 Min Zhong 452 in the labor dispute appeal case between Hunan Louyuan Hotel Co., Ltd. and Zhang Mou; Li Guangli v. Gaizhou Environmental Health Service Center Labor Dispute Civil Application for Retrial Review Civil Ruling, Liaoning Provincial People's High Court (2021) Liao Min Shen No. 8056.

30 Xiangyang Hongri Wanli Dregs Transportation Co., Ltd., Bu Haibo Labor Dispute Retrial Review and Trial Supervision Civil Ruling Hubei Provincial People's High Court Civil Ruling (2020) E Min Shen No. 2293. Zhang Caihe, Weiyuan County Maikang Security Co., Ltd. Civil Ruling of Second Instance of Labor Dispute Civil Ruling of Gansu Provincial People's High Court (2022) Gan Min Shen No. 740. Application for retrial of labor dispute between Xinzheng Tiansu Building Materials Co., Ltd. and Gu Jinqin, etc. Civil Ruling of Henan High Court (2022) Yu Min Shen No. 3817. Wheat Research Institute of Shanxi Agricultural University, Zhang Genlin Labor Dispute Civil Trial Supervision Civil Ruling Shanxi High Court Civil Ruling (2022) Jin Min Shen No. 1014.

age is a contradictory and complex problem in judicial practice. It carries serious consequences for both employees and employers in terms of the legality of termination of employment at retirement age and potential corresponding punitive damages and other liabilities.

Fundamentally, the predicament of reaching retirement age without receiving pension benefits stems from incomplete coverage of the social insurance system and the flawed legal system in China. Therefore, in the near future, the Supreme Court or legislative bodies should simplify and unify rules based on the principle of balancing the interests of employees, employers, and the state. In the long run, achieving universal coverage of social insurance and unified standards for urban and rural areas should be established in labor governance.

149. Can an employer terminate an employee who has reached retirement age during their medical treatment?

Answer: Employees who reach retirement age during the treatment period for illness or injury fall into two categories: those on paid work injury leave and those on medical care leave for illness or non-work-related injury. Currently, the law does not stipulate the obligations of employers in these two situations, and there are few relevant court decisions. However, based on the conclusion of "148. Can an employer terminate an employee who has reached retirement age?", the basic judicial principle appears to be that the rights and obligations of the employer depend on whether the employer has the right to terminate the employment relationship on the ground of employee having reached retirement age, whether the employment or contractor relationship is actually terminated, and the basic principle of protecting the interests of the employee (especially those on paid work injury leave).

If an employee on paid work injury leave not only reaches the statutory retirement age but also receives basic pension insurance benefits, although the court may decide that the employment is dissolved, it may order that the employer is still obligated to pay the employee for the paid work injury leave, but is possibly entitled to a deduction of the amount of the pension insurance benefits the employee receives.[31]

If an employee on paid work injury leave has reached the statutory retirement age but has not received basic pension benefits, the court may determine this as a continuation of a special employment relationship, entitling the employee to benefits for work injury. The employer cannot terminate the employment relationship and must bear the obligation of paying wages for the paid work injury leave. For example, in the 2014 case of Hangzhou Landun Property Service Co., Ltd., although the employee had reached retirement age, they had not received pension benefits. Judge Zhang Weiguo of Zhejiang Provincial High Court stated: "When Li Suhua reached retirement age, she was still in the paid work injury

31 Guangzhou Elite Sporting Goods Co., Ltd. v. Li Shuhua Employment Dispute Civil Second Trial Civil Judgment, Guangzhou Intermediate People's Court of Guangdong Province Civil Judgment (2022) Yue 01 Min Zhong No. 20443. X Company v. Wang, Work-Related Injury Insurance Benefit Dispute Civil Second Trial Civil Judgment, Shizuishan Intermediate People's Court of Ningxia Hui Autonomous Region Civil Judgment (2024) Ning 02 Min Zhong No. 16. In the aforementioned two cases, the employees had reached retirement age and were receiving pension insurance. The court in both cases ordered the employers to pay wages for the paid work injury leave. However, in the latter case, the court did not permit the employer to deduct the pension insurance amount from the wages paid.

leave; therefore, the employment relationship between both parties should have continued and she was entitled to the benefits of paid work injury leave."[32]

For an employee in the second category, who is on medical care leave for illness or non-work-related injury and reaches retirement age while receiving pension insurance benefits, at present, the practice in most provincial and municipal courts in China is that when employees reach retirement age, the employment contract is terminated, and the employer no longer assumes the responsibility of the employee's unexpired medical care leave, including the payment of wages during the medical care leave. These courts include Shenzhen Intermediate Court of Guangdong Province, Jiangsu Provincial High Court, Shanghai the Second Intermediate Court, Zhuzhou Intermediate Court of Hunan Province, Liaocheng City of Shandong Province, Qingdao Intermediate Court, Fifth Intermediate Court of Chongqing City, intermediate courts of Xianyang City of Shaanxi Province, and Hanzhong Intermediate Court.[33] However, we noticed that Hunan Province Changsha City Intermediate Court had a different practice.[34]

For employees who are on medical care leave for illness or non-work-related injury and have reached retirement age but have not received pension insurance benefits, the situation is more complex. This involves factors such as how different regional courts determine whether the employment relationship between the parties should have dissolved on the ground of retirement age, whether the employment or contractor relationship has actually ended, and the reason why the employee has not received pension benefits. Please refer to "148. Can an employer terminate an employee who has reached retirement age?" Anyway, it appears that courts offer much weaker protection for employees on medical care leave compared with those on paid work injury leave.

---

32 Hangzhou Landun Property Service Co., Ltd. v. Li Suhua Employment Dispute Case, Zhejiang Provincial High Court Civil Ruling (2014) Zhe Min Shen Zi No. 894. X Steel Company v. Zhang Work-Related Injury Insurance Benefit Dispute Second Civil Trial, Lianyungang Intermediate People's Court of Jiangsu Province Civil Judgment (2024) Su 07 Min Zhong No. 3216.

33 Jiang Chunhong v. Changzhou Yida Garment Co., Ltd., Labor Dispute Appeal and Application for Civil Ruling Jiangsu Provincial People's High Court Civil Ruling (2019) Su Minshen No. 2670. Zhu Yinxiu v. Guangzhou Wang Laoji Da Health Enterprise Development Co., Ltd., Civil Judgment of the Second Instance of Labor Dispute, Civil Judgment of Hunan Zhuzhou Intermediate People's Court (2021) Xiang 02 Min Zhong No. 612. Hu Fenglan v. Shandong Shengshilong Garments Co., Ltd., Labor Dispute Civil Judgment of Second Instance Civil Judgment of Liaocheng Intermediate People's Court of Shandong Province (2021) Lu 15 Min Zhong No. 2676. Guo Qiuying v. Qingdao Tianmo Yatai Auto Parts Co., Ltd., Civil Judgment of Second Instance of Labor Dispute Civil Judgment of Qingdao Intermediate People's Court of Shandong Province (2021) Lu 02 Min Zhong No. 7553. Northwest Branch of China Construction Eighth Engineering Bureau Co., Ltd., v. Xi'an Weiyang Security Service Co., Ltd. and others, civil judgments of second instance of labor disputes, Civil Judgment of Xianyang Intermediate People's Court of Shaanxi Province (2021) Shan 04 Min Zhong No. 2393. Mou Yilin v. Jiuqi Yisu Hotel of Hantai District of Hanzhong City, Civil Judgment of Second Instance of Labor Dispute, Intermediate People's Court of Hanzhong City, Shaanxi Province (2023) Shan 07 Min Zhong No. 253. Huang Xiaofei v. Shanghai Hongkou District Quyang Community Service Management Center, Labor Dispute Second Instance Civil Judgment Shanghai the Second Intermediate People's Court Civil Judgment (2018) Hu 02 Min Zhong No. 7743. Wang Xuemei v. Shenzhen Xinjitai Spray Pump Co., Ltd., Civil Judgment of Second Instance of Labor Dispute, Shenzhen Intermediate People's Court of Guangdong Province, Civil Judgment (2018) Yue 03 Min Zhong No. 11486. Chongqing Yuchun Technology Co., Ltd. v. Chen Jianfen, Civil Judgment of the Second Instance of Labor Dispute, the Fifth Intermediate People's Court of Chongqing (2019) Yu 05 Min Zhong No. 598.

34 Changsha Branch of Kunshan Runhua Commercial Co., Ltd. and Leftist Red Labor Dispute Civil Judgment of Second Instance Civil Judgment of Changsha Intermediate People's Court of Hunan Province (2021) Xiang 01 Minzhong No. 16254. The employees continued working for more than four years after reaching retirement age. The court held that the employee had the right to receive medical care leave entitlement and the employer could not terminate the employment.

In a word, whether the employer can dissolve the employment contract when the employee reaches the retirement age during medical treatment is a complicated issue; it requires further research on judicial decisions and legislative amendments striking a balance between the rights and interests of employees, employers, and the state.

150. What should employers do if their employee dies from illness or non-work-related injury?

Answer: An employee's death due to illness or non-work-related injury will first lead to the termination of both parties' employment contracts. According to Article 46 of the Employment Contract Law, the employer is not required to pay economic compensation for such termination of employment contract. Instead, the survivors of the employee who died of illness or non-work-related injury may receive compensations, such as funeral allowance and condolence allowance.

The "Interim Measures for Survivor Benefits of Enterprise Employees' Basic Pension Insurance" issued by the Ministry of Human Resources and Social Security and the Ministry of Finance in 2021 and effective from September 1, 2021, provides rules on benefits for survivors of employees who die of illnesses or non-work-related injuries, based on Article 17 of the Social Insurance Law of 2018. This interim measure has changed the rules (including relevant allowance amounts) for the payment of funeral and condolence allowances under past local regulations formulated according to the Regulations on Scope of Family Members Supported by Workers Who Died of Work Injuries issued in 2003.

Under this new rule, there are several practical issues.

The first issue is whether funeral and condolence allowances should be governed by past local regulations or the Interim Measures. Undoubtedly, the rules for funeral and condolence allowances under past local regulations should apply to cases of death due to illnesses or non-work-related injuries before September 1, 2021. In light of judicial decisions for deaths due to illnesses or non-work-related injuries after this date, the Interim Measures should generally apply, but[35] there are instances where if the employers did not purchase pension insurance for their employees, past local regulations may still apply.[36] Currently, due to the limited number of relevant judicial decisions published, the specific application of the law remains to be observed.

The second question is whether the employer should bear the funeral and condolence allowances. If the Interim Measures applies, funeral and condolence allowances are covered by the social insurance fund as long as the employee participated in basic pension insurance. If past local regulations apply, it depends on whether specific local regulation stipulates that these expenses should be covered by the social insurance fund; if not, the employer should bear the cost. However, if the employee did not participate in pension insurance, regardless of whether the Interim Measures applies, the employer should bear these costs. For example, in the case of Zhang Sanheng in 2022, the Hunan Yongzhou Intermediate People's Court ruled that since the tea restaurant hired an employee without purchasing pension insurance for him, the lower court's decision ordering the company

35 Tang and others v. Yu and others Labor Dispute Civil Second Instance Civil Judgment Guangzhou Intermediate People's Court of Guangdong Province Civil Judgment (2023) Yue 01 Min Zhong Zi No. 15386.

36 Xinhui District Huicheng Qiongai Beauty Center v. Cai Jinqiu and others Labor Dispute Civil First Instance Civil Judgment Xinhui District People's Court of Jiangmen City, Guangdong Province Civil Judgment (2022) Yue 0705 Min Chu No. 4930.

to bear funeral and condolence allowances based on the Interim Measures was deemed appropriate.[37] Moreover, if the contribution base for the employee's pension insurance is lower than the actual salary of the employee, the employee may also have the right to demand that the employer pay the shortfall in funeral and condolence allowances due to the insufficient contribution.

The third question is who is eligible to receive funeral and condolence allowances. This actually also relates to whether these allowances should be paid out, because if there were no eligible survivors to receive them, the social insurance fund or the employer would not have an obligation to pay. The Interim Measures does not specify the scope of survivors, but based on limited judicial precedents, the scope of survivors should be determined according to the provisions of the 2003 "Regulations on Scope of Family Members Supported by Workers Who Died of Work Injuries." For example, in the case of Shandong Dingliang Fire Technology Co., Ltd. in 2022, the Shandong Provincial High People's Court held that the scope of survivors stipulated in Article 17 of the Social Insurance Law should be determined according to the 2003 "Regulations on Scope of Family Members Supported by Workers Who Died of Work Injuries," which are those provided in the third condition in the next paragraph.[38]

Therefore, according to the "Regulations on Scope of Family Members Supported by Workers Who Died of Work Injuries," the scope of survivors must meet the following three conditions simultaneously: first, the survivors only include the deceased employee's spouse, children, parents, grandparents, grandparents-in-law, grandchildren, grandchildren-in-law, and siblings; second, the survivors must have relied on the deceased employee as their main source of livelihood before the employee's death; third, the survivors must fall under one of the following situations: 1) spouse or parent had been of complete incapacity; 2) spouse or parent is male over 60 years old or female over 55 years old; 3) children under 18 years old; 4) both parents of the deceased employee have died, their paternal grandfather and maternal grandfather are 60 years old or older, and their paternal grandmother and maternal grandmother are 55 years old or older; (5) the children of the deceased employee have died or are completely incapacitated, and their grandchildren and maternal grandchildren are under 18 years old; 6) siblings who are under 18 years old and whose parents have died or are of complete incapacity and so on.

However, considering that the funeral and condolence allowances under this Interim Measures are one-time assessments and payments, unlike the previous periodic payments for supporting survivors, whether the condolence allowance will be reviewed for the scope of survivors in future judicial practice remains to be further observed.

The fourth issue concerns the standards for funeral and condolence allowances. According to the Interim Measures, the standard for funeral allowance is calculated as twice the average monthly disposable income per capita of urban residents in the province (including autonomous regions and municipalities directly under the Central Government) in the previous year at the time of the insured person's death. The standard for condolence allowance to survivors is as follows: for employees who are still working, if the length of

37 Luo 3 v. Zhang Sanhang and others Labor Dispute Civil Second Instance Civil Judgment Intermediate People's Court of Yongzhou City, Hunan Province Civil Judgment (2022) Xiang 11 Min Zhong Zi No. 3955.

38 Shandong Dingliang Fire Technology Co., Ltd., Gao Minghua, Labor Dispute Civil Application for Retrial Civil Review Civil Decision Shandong Provincial High People's Court Civil Decision (2022) Lu Min Shen No. 6295.

service is less than 5 years, they will receive an allowance equivalent to 3 months of the average monthly disposable income per capita of urban residents in the previous year; if the length of service is between 5 and 10 years, they will receive an allowance for 6 months; if the length of service is between 10 and 15 years (inclusive), they will receive an allowance for 9 months; if the length of service exceeds 15 years, for each additional year of service, the allowance will be increased by 1 month. For those with a length of service of more than 30 years, the maximum number of months for the allowance is 24, calculated based on 30-year service. For retirees, the maximum number of months for the allowance is determined based on the length of service during their employment (calculated in the same way as for employees who are still working), and for each year of receiving basic pension, the number of months for the allowance is reduced by one, with a minimum nine-month allowance. If the funeral and condolence allowances are governed by current local regulations, they will be determined according to the local regulations.

This interim measure changes the previous practice of providing regular life allowances for supporting survivors. Previously, the life allowance (i.e., condolence allowance) for supporting relatives was paid periodically, and the amount depended on the number of eligible survivors. For example, the life allowance for minor children should be paid monthly until they reach the age of 18, and the amount of allowance would vary depending on whether there were one or more minor children. Under the Interim Measures, the condolence allowance for survivors is determined and assessed as a one-off and paid as a one-off.

Finally, Article 2 of the Interim Measures stipulates that the funeral and condolence allowances apply not only to death of employees but also to death of retirees. Retirees who are not covered by the pension will not have the costs covered by the social insurance fund. However, whether survivors of such retirees have the right to demand that the last employer the retirees worked for bears these costs needs further observation of judicial practices in different regions, as those retirees' inability to receive pension insurance benefits may be due to the failure of multiple employers to contribute social insurance for them.

151. What should employees do if their employer goes bankrupt, is deregistered, or is ordered to close?

Answer: When an employer goes bankrupt, undergoes company deregistration, or is ordered to close, the employment relationship between the employer and its employees is terminated as the employer, the operating entity, ceases to exist. According to Article 46 of the Employment Contract Law, the employer should pay economic compensation to all employees who are still in service.

Article 113 of the 2006 Enterprise Bankruptcy Law stipulates that the bankruptcy estate should prioritize payment of labor remuneration or compensation, including wages, medical benefits, disability allowances, condolence allowances, outstanding basic pension insurance and basic medical insurance contributions owed to employees' insurance accounts, as well as compensation required by laws and regulations. When a company is deregistered or closed, its remaining assets should also be used to pay these labor remunerations or compensations.

In practice, it is common for employers facing bankruptcy, deregistration, or closure to have insufficient assets to pay the labor remunerations or compensations owed. In such cases, employees may consider whether they can hold the employer's shareholders, controllers, or responsible persons personally liable. See "175. Is the boss of a limited liability company personally liable for outstanding wages?" and "174. Can employees hold their employer's boss personally liable for their labor remunerations or compensations?"

5.2 Employer-Initiated Employment Termination

152. How should employers handle the procedure of notifying the trade union when terminating employees?

Answer: Article 43 of the Employment Contract Law stipulates that employers must notify the trade union if they intend to unilaterally terminate an employee's employment contract. The terminations include terminations under Article 39 of the Employment Contract Law, for serious violation of company rules and regulations, invalid contract, multiple employment relationships, termination in the probation period, gross negligence and corruption, and employee's crime; terminations under Article 40, for ability incompetence, health incompetence, and major change in objective situation; and terminations under Article 41, economic redundancy. Employers' failure to comply with this procedural requirement of notifying the trade union may result in illegal termination of the employment contract.

The first issue is how to implement the procedure for notifying the union. According to the aforementioned Article 43 of the Law, a compliant procedure of notifying the trade union is that the employer shall notify the trade union of the details of the termination of the employment relationship, including the ground(s) for the termination (such as ability incompetence, provided in Article 40 of the Employment Contract Law, or serious violation of company rules and regulations, in Article 39), factual basis, and relevant evidence, and the employer must reply to the objection of the trade union in writing. Although the wording of the statutory provision does not indicate that the first notice must be in written form, the current judicial decisions around the country do not recognize the oral form of the first notice to the trade union. For example, in the case of Wan Guoqiong in 2022, the Beijing the First Intermediate Court found that the employer had notified the chairman of the trade union orally and submitted audio recording evidence, but the court still held that the employer had not fulfilled the procedure requirement of notifying the trade union.[39]

In practice, if an employer fails to notify the trade union in the process of terminating an employee, it may be able to take remedial measures. Article 47 of the judicial interpretation of the Supreme People's Court on labor disputes in 2020 provides a corrective procedure for employers who terminated an employee without notifying the trade union under Article 39 and Article 40 of the Employment Contract Law. For example, an employer terminated an employee's employment contract on the ground of serious violation of company rules and regulations and did not notify the trade union. The employment arbitration committee found that the employer did not fulfill the procedural requirement, finding illegal dismissal and ordering punitive damages, even though the employee substantively and seriously violated the company rules and regulations. However, if the employer notifies

39 Beijing Zhongnong Dadi Science and Technology Development Co., Ltd. Jinma Hotel v. Wan Guoqiong, Labor Dispute Civil Judgment of Second Instance Beijing the First intermediate People's Court Civil Judgment (2022) Jing 01 Min Zhong No. 5649.

the trade union before appeal to the court, the court shall consider that the employer has corrected the procedural defect and shall quash the arbitration order, ruling the dismissal as lawful.[40]

The second issue is how employers that have no trade unions in place can implement the procedure. Currently, courts around the country adopt two different practices. The first practice is that these employers are exempted from the procedural obligation, and the other is that these employers must notify their local trade union organization.

Courts in most parts of the country adopt the first practice, that employers without a trade union are not subject to this procedural requirement and that they do not have to notify any trade union for unilateral terminations. At present, the courts of Guangdong Province, including Shenzhen, Guangzhou, Beijing, Shanghai, Chongqing, Hunan, and Jilin, hold this attitude. Referable court cases are the 2021 case of Panlong Eco-agricultural Demonstration Park of Xiangtan before Chu Yongfeng of Hunan Provincial High Court, the 2020 case of Jingbangda Logistics Company before Chongqing High Court, the 2019 case of Hu Jingyan before Shanghai High Court, and the 2014 case of Zhejiang Hengdian Baiya Clothing before Jinhua Intermediate Court.[41]

Jiangsu and Zhejiang Provinces adopt the second approach. The Regulations on Employment Contracts of Jiangsu Province stipulate that an employer who has not yet established a trade union shall notify the trade union where the employer is located of the termination.[42] Therefore, Jiangsu Province implements the practice of notifying local trade unions (for example, the case of Zhao Xiaomian before Nanjing Intermediate Court of Jiangsu Province in 2016). In 2016, the Ningbo Intermediate Court of Zhejiang also ordered the employer to notify the local trade union in the case of CITIC Logistics Flying Company; however, in the 2019 case of Ruan Xiaofei, the Hangzhou Intermediate People's Court in Zhejiang adopted the approach that if a trade union has not been established, there is no need to notify the local trade union.[43]

---

40 However, the Supreme Court's Interpretation does not mention whether the correction measure is applicable for the termination under Article 41 of the Employment Contract Law, the economic redundancy.

41 Chu Yongfeng v. Xiangtan Panlong Ecological Agriculture Demonstration Park Co., Ltd. Employment Dispute Retrial Review and Judicial Supervision Civil Ruling Hunan Provincial High Court Civil Ruling (2021) XiangMinShen No. 1318. Lv Sirong v. Chongqing Jingbangda Logistics Co., Ltd. Employment Dispute Appeal and Retrial Application Civil Ruling Chongqing High Court Civil Ruling (2020) YuMinShen No. 2420. Hu Jingyun v. Shanghai Yiju Precision Tools Co., Ltd. Employment Contract Dispute Judicial Supervision Civil Ruling Shanghai High Court Civil Ruling (2019) HuMinShen No. 1062. Inscom IT (Shenzhen) Co., Ltd., Qu Sumei Labor Dispute Civil Judgment of Second Instance Civil Judgment of Guangzhou Intermediate People's Court of Guangdong Province (2021) Yue 01 Min Zhong No. 27685. Wang Guofeng and Shenzhen West Bus Co., Ltd. and Other Companies Labor Dispute Appeal Case Civil Judgment of Shenzhen Intermediate People's Court of Guangdong Province (2016) Yue 03 Min Zhong No. 7136. Civil Judgment of Second Instance of Labor Dispute between Chen Chen and Beijing Founder Apabi Technology Co., Ltd. Civil Judgment of Beijing the First Intermediate People's Court (2022) Jing 01 Min Zhong No. 4823. Li Gen v. Changchun Menshi Trading Co., Ltd. Employment Dispute Retrial Review Civil Ruling Jilin Provincial High Court Civil Ruling (2021) JiMinShen No. 777.

42 The second paragraph of Article 31 of the Regulations of Jiangsu Province on Employment Contracts stipulates that if an employer unilaterally terminates an employment contract, it shall notify the trade union of the reasons in advance; if the employer has not yet established a trade union, it shall notify the trade union of the place where the employer is located.

43 CITIC Logistics Feichi Co., Ltd. Daxie Branch v. Zhao Ziqian Employment Dispute Appeal Case Zhejiang Ningbo Intermediate People's Court Civil Judgment (2016) Zhe02MinZhong No. 1258. Ruan Xiaofei v. Xiangfu Town Ruanjiaqiao Village Economic Cooperative, Hangzhou Employment Dispute Second Instance Civil Judgment Zhejiang Hangzhou Intermediate People's Court Civil Judgment (2019) Zhe01MinZhong No. 6001.

An exceptional case reflects the uncertainty of employment law practice. In the case of Jianhua Building Materials Company before Huizhou Intermediate Court of Guangdong Province in 2019, the court held that the employer, with 500 people, had violated the provision of the Trade Union Law that a trade union must be established in an employer with over 25 employees, which was illegal in itself. Even if the employer notified the local general trade unions, the illegal procedure cannot be remedied.[44]

The bizarre regulation and practice of notifying local trade unions, which are unlikely to have any connections with the employee, and the remedial correction of notifying a trade union before the court proceedings, reflects the undeveloped state of trade unions' functionality in China.

153. Under what circumstances should our company pay medical treatment allowance to our employees?

Answer: Medical treatment allowance is an additional subsidy for employees who leave their roles due to illness or non-work-related injury, and the amount is not less than six months' wages. The two preconditions for employers to pay the medical treatment allowance to an employee are that the employer terminates the employee on the ground of the employee being health incompetent after expiration of the medical care leave (provided that the employee is still health incompetent after a position transfer), and that the employee's labor capacity is identified as Class 5 to 10.

The basis of the specified amount of medical treatment allowance and these two premise conditions are under 1997 "Notice on Interpretation of Certain Issues of the Document [1996] No. 354 of the Ministry of Labor" and Article 35 of 1995 "The Opinions on Several Issues Concerning the Implementation of the Labor Law of the People's Republic of China" by the Ministry of Labor.[45] For employees with severe or terminal illness, some courts around the country still follow the practice of increasing the medical treatment allowance by 50% or 100% (for example, Guilin Intermediate Court of Guangxi Autonomous Region and Jiangsu Province),[46] and some courts increase the medical treatment allowance by discretion.

44 Civil Judgment in the Second Instance of the Labor Dispute Case between Jianhua Building Materials (Huizhou) Co., Ltd. and Liu Wen Cheng—Guangdong Huizhou Intermediate People's Court Civil Judgment (2019) Yue 13 Min Zhong 6566.

45 Article 22 of the Notice on Several Issues Regarding the Implementation of the Labor Contract System by the Ministry of Labor (Laobufa [1996] No. 354) and the Notice from the General Office of the Ministry of Labor on the Interpretation of Issues Related to the Document Laobufa No. [1996] 354 (Laobanfa [1997] No. 18). "When an employee falls ill or is non-work-related injured, and the employment contract is terminated upon expiration, if the employee is assessed by the Labor Appraisal Committee as disability class 5–10, the employer should provide medical allowance not less than six months' wages. Additionally, for those suffering from serious illnesses and terminal diseases, an additional medical allowance should be provided." Article 35 of "the Opinions on Several Issues Concerning the Implementation of the Labor Law of the People's Republic of China" issued in 1995. "If, after the expiration of the medical care leave, the employee is unable to resume their original job or engage in alternative work arranged by the employer, the Labor Appraisal Committee shall assess the employee's labor capacity referencing the standard for assessing disabilities caused by work-related injuries or occupational diseases … for those assessed disability class 5 to 10, the employer has the right to terminate the employment contract and is required to provide the stipulated economic compensation and medical treatment allowance."

46 Deng Chaoyu, Guilin Hospital of Traditional Chinese Medicine Labor Dispute Civil Judgment of Second Instance Civil Judgment of Guilin Intermediate People's Court of Guangxi Zhuang Autonomous Region (2021) Gui 03 Min Zhong No. 2437. Article 34 of the Regulations on Employment Contracts of Jiangsu Province still follows the practice of increasing the medical treatment allowance for those suffering from severe and incurable diseases by 50% and 100%, respectively.

Judicial decisions show that if an employer illegally terminates the employment contract of an employee whose labor capacity has been identified as Class 5 to 10, for example, by not complying with the statutory negotiation procedure for position transfer, it shall bear the liabilities of both the medical treatment allowance and the punitive damages.[47]

For the monthly wage base when computing the medical treatment allowance, at present, courts around the country have two types of practice. One practice applies the average normal-work-hours wage (excluding overtime wages) from the prior 12 months, for example, in Beijing and Guangzhou;[48] the other adopts the average monthly wages including overtime wages from the prior 12 months, which is the same as the base for calculating economic compensation, by courts in Shanghai, Chongqing, Nanjing, Jiangsu, and Guangdong, including Guangzhou and Dongguan courts.[49]

154. What requirements should an employer meet to legally terminate an employee?

Answer: There are differences in the determination criteria for the legality of terminating an employment relationship based on different grounds, so we first list different types of termination by an employer and then discuss and analyze them in normal and special scenarios later.

The types of employment relationship termination initiated by an employer can be categorized into the following scenarios: 1) mutual agreement termination;[50] 2) termination on the ground of the employee's not meeting hiring requirements during the probationary period; 3) termination on the ground of expiration of a fixed-term employment contract; 4) termination on the ground of employee's incompetence (including health or ability incompetence); 5) termination on the ground of employee's serious violation of company

47 The Guangdong Provincial People's High Court issued the second of eight typical cases of judicial protection for the disabled: a labor dispute between Yang and a technology company—to safeguard the employment rights and interests of disabled workers, the people's court ruled in accordance with the law that it was illegal for employers to terminate employment relationships during the medical care leave of disabled workers. In addition to paying punitive damages to disabled workers, the employer was also ordered to pay sick leave wages during the remaining medical care leave and medical treatment allowance, so as to effectively safeguard the rights and interests of disabled workers in medical insurance and ensure the equal participation of disabled persons in social life.

48 Civil Ruling on Labor Dispute Retrial Review and Trial Supervision between Han Wenjiang and Beijing Hezhong Huatai Taxi Co., Ltd. Civil Ruling of Beijing High Court (2021) Jing Min Shen No. 7816. Zhang Hua v. Guangzhou Zhuojiang Electronic Technology Co., Ltd. Employment Contract Dispute Retrial Case Guangdong Provincial Higher People's Court Civil Ruling (2020) Yue Min Shen No. 9541. Xu Meiqin, Feng Jiancheng, and Guangzhou Xianglong Real Estate Development Co., Ltd. Civil Judgment of Guangzhou Intermediate People's Court of Guangdong Province (2012) S.Z.F.M.Y.Z.Z. No. 4037.

49 Labor Dispute between Peng Yongkun and Guangzhou Yuexiu Real Estate Engineering Management Co., Ltd. Guangzhou Intermediate People's Court of Guangdong Province Civil Judgment (2017) Yue 01 Min Zhong No. 6284. Jin v. Shanghai A Co., Ltd., Civil Judgment of Shanghai Xuhui District People's Court (2010) Xu Min Yi (Min) Chu Zi No. 3404. Civil Judgment of the First Instance of Labor Dispute between Yang Haibo and Chongqing Midea General Refrigeration Equipment Co., Ltd. Civil Judgment of the People's Court of Nan'an District of Chongqing (2018) Yu 0108 Min Chu No. 9344. Civil Judgment on the Labor Dispute between Nanjing Handian Real Estate Development Co., Ltd. and Chen Rui Civil Judgment of Nanjing Intermediate People's Court of Jiangsu Province (2016) Su 01 Min Zhong No. 841. Civil Judgment of Second Instance of Labor Dispute between Chen Chen and Beijing Founder Apabi Technology Co., Ltd. Civil Judgment of Beijing the First Intermediate People's Court (2022) Jing 01 Min Zhong No. 4823. Chen Zhenhua v. Shenzhen Luohu District Public Security Bureau Employment Dispute Case Guangdong Provincial Higher People's Court Civil Ruling (2015) Yue Gao Fa Min Shen Zi No. 483.

50 If the employee initiates the termination of the employment relationship, it is usually considered a resignation. Therefore, mutual agreement to terminate the employment relationship typically refers to a termination proposed by the employer with the employee agreeing to it.

rules and regulations; 6) termination on the ground of employee being criminally liable; 7) termination on the ground of employee's gross negligence or corruption; 8) termination on the ground of major change in objective condition; 9) economic redundancy; 10) termination on the ground of the employee making the employment contract invalid.

Normal scenarios where employers initiate the termination of employees are Scenarios 2 and 4 to 9. Lawful terminations in these scenarios normally involve two main aspects. The first is that the termination must be in accordance with substantive legal requirements, such as legitimate grounds, factual basis, statutory or regulatory rules, or legally binding company institutional rules (see "120. What kinds of company rules and regulations are binding on employees?"); the second is that the termination must meet procedural legal requirements. This may involve the employer fulfilling certain statutory or regulatory procedural obligations or reasonable procedural obligations, such as notifying the trade union or the labor administrative authority (see "121. Is it legally permissible for my employer to discipline me?" and "152. How should employers handle the procedure of notifying the trade union when terminating employees?").

We take Scenario 5, the employer terminating the employment contract on the ground of serious violation of company rules and regulations, as an example to explain. Two conditions must be met for lawful termination.

The first is that the employee must have seriously violated the employer's legally binding institutional rules (including company rules and regulations, provisions of contractual agreements, and basic professional ethics). The employer must prove that the employee has committed the misconduct, that the company has established legally binding institutional rules, and that the employee's misconduct reached the threshold for dismissal as stipulated by these rules. The second is that the termination procedure must comply with statutory procedural requirements. The employer must prove that they have fulfilled the obligation of notifying the trade union when terminating the employee (unless the company has not established a trade union and the local court does not require an alternative notification of the local trade union). Additionally, the employer should adhere to the fair and reasonable procedures outlined in the company rules and regulations or the employment contract when handling the termination. We recommended that the employer reasonably consider and implement procedures such as advance notice, objective investigation of the incident, and careful consideration of the employee's explanation to strengthen the legality of the termination of the employment relationship.

In Scenario 2, terminating an employee during the probationary period on the ground of the employee not meeting hiring requirements, the employer can immediately terminate the relationship if it can prove the employee does not meet the requirements; therefore, it is crucial for the employer to clearly define the hiring requirements in the employment contract and outline the methods for assessing whether the employee meets the standard. The employer must notify the trade union, as Article 43 of the Employment Contract Law stipulates that employers must do so when unilaterally terminating an employment relationship, and this requirement is often overlooked in practice, resulting in few judicial decisions being available in this regard.[51]

51 Chen Renkuan v. Dongguan Jinyao Garment Co., Ltd. Labor Contract Dispute, Guangdong High People's Court, Civil Ruling (2014) Yue Gao Fa Min Shen Zi No. 1962.

In Scenario 4, terminating an employee on the ground of health incompetence or ability incompetence, the employer must arrange a position transfer for the employee; if the employee is still incompetent, the employer should notify the trade union and notify the employee of the termination with 30 days' notice (or a payment in lieu of notice) (see "85. What should I do if an employee of my company has not recovered after the expiration of the medical care leave?" and "158. Can we terminate an employee's employment due to his poor performance?").

In Scenario 6 (terminating employees who are criminally liable), Scenario 7 (terminating employees on the ground of gross negligence or corruption), and Scenario 10 (terminating employees on the ground of the employee making the employment contract invalid), employers must notify the trade union before they terminate the employment. In Scenario 8, terminating an employee on the ground of major change in objective condition, the employer must first negotiate with the employee for position transfer. If this fails, the employer then may notify the trade union and terminate the employee with a 30-day notice (or a payment in lieu of notice). In Scenario 9, economic redundancy, the employer must notify the trade union or the employee congress and then the labor administrative authority before it terminates the employees.

Special scenarios of employer-initiated termination of an employee's employment relationship include Scenarios 1 and 3. In Scenario 1, mutual agreement termination, both parties typically sign an agreement of employment termination, arranging matters such as economic compensation. In Scenario 3, terminating a fixed-term employment contract on the ground of expiration, the employer only needs to notify the employee of the intention not to renew the contract. Judicial precedents show that employers are not required to notify trade unions for termination on the ground of expiration of fixed-term employment contracts or mutual agreement terminations.[52]

A lawful dismissal of employees does not attract liability of any compensation; otherwise, the employer must pay punitive damages or reinstate the employee upon the employee's labor dispute claim.[53] Please refer to "165. How do I calculate punitive damages for illegal termination of the employment relationship?"

155. How can employers experiencing business hardship legally reduce their workforce to survive?

Answer: Your company wanting to reduce the number of employees because of economic hardship may constitute an economic redundancy. Economic redundancy refers to the

52 Gan Qi v. Jiangsu Kelu Automobile Transportation Co., Ltd. Labor Contract Dispute Appeal and Application Civil Ruling, Jiangsu High People's Court, Civil Ruling (2018) Su Min Shen No. 4568 (the court explicitly stated in this case that the Employment Contract Law does not require the employer to notify the trade union when terminating the employment relationship on the ground of the expiration of the employment contract). Tang Chuanyu v. Guangzhou Tonglida Property Management Co., Ltd., Guangzhou Red Sea Human Resources Group Co., Ltd., and Guangzhou Red Sea Human Resources Group Co., Ltd. Zengcheng Branch, Labor Dispute Case, Guangdong High People's Court, Civil Ruling (2015) Yue Gao Fa Min Shen Zi Nos. 408, 409 (the court explicitly stated in this case that the employer is not required to notify the trade union when terminating the employment relationship by mutual agreement).

53 Article 48 of the Employment Contract Law of the People's Republic of China stipulates that if an employer dissolves or terminates an employment contract in violation of the provisions of this Law, and the worker requests to continue to perform the employment contract, the employer shall continue to perform the employment contract; if the worker does not request to continue performing the employment contract, or if the employment contract can no longer be performed, the employer shall pay punitive damages in accordance with Article 87 of this Law.

situation provided in Article 41 of the Employment Contract Law, where an employer can legally lay off employees when facing severe business hardship.

According to this regulation, economic redundancy bears two characteristics: first, it applies to collective layoffs of more than 20 people or more than 10% of the total number of employees; second, applicable circumstances include bankrupt reorganization, serious operational hardships, and business transfer (including major technological innovation, operational adjustment, and other major change in objective situation, which all cause or have the nature of operational hardship), that make it impossible to perform the employment contract.

According to the aforementioned characteristics, the law not only requires a legal number of redundant employees for a legal economic redundancy, but also requires economic redundancy to meet substantive and procedural requirements.

The substantive conditions of economic redundancy include one of three situations.

The first situation is that the employer is reorganized according to the bankruptcy law in China. If the company is unable to repay its debts that are due, is insolvent, or clearly lacks the capacity, or it is impossible to repay the debts, the company or its creditors may apply to the court for reorganization. If the court grants reorganization, the company will meet the substantive condition for economic redundancy. This kind of reorganization must be decided by the court; the reorganization decided by the company itself does not fulfill the requirement under the first situation.

The second situation is that the company encounters serious operational hardships. As for how to identify "serious operational hardship," in the past, some regions have stipulated rules such as two years or three years of financial losses, a certain shutdown rate, and the proportion of employees that have been in waiting-for-work.[54] However, as these rules may be too stringent on employers, in practice, the courts usually examine whether the employers have suffered losses based on evidence such as financial reports or company board or trade union documents in the past two or three years. For example, in the case of Huanghua and Lejin Electronics Company before Beijing High Court in 2020, the company provided four years of financial audit reports and documents from the board of directors and the trade union. The court considered them sufficient to prove the existence of serious operational

54 On September 5, 1994, Article 27 of the Ministry of Labor's Explanation on Several Articles of the Labor Law of the People's Republic of China stipulates: "The definition of serious operational hardships shall be interpreted in accordance with the provisions of local governments." The Tianjin Municipal Labor and Social Security Bureau, the Interim Provisions on the Economic Redundancy by Enterprises in Tianjin (Jin Lao Ban [2001] No. 241), stipulates that the following conditions shall be met at the same time if serious operational hardships really require the redundancy: (1) the actual losses in production and operation have lasted for more than three consecutive years (the year of financial final accounts), the amount of losses has increased year by year, and there is no obvious improvement in the production and operation conditions; (2) the operating rate is less than 60% for two consecutive years, and more than 50% of the employees are laid off and waiting for work; (3) the wages of the employees on duty for more than six consecutive months cannot be paid according to the minimum wage standard stipulated by this Municipality. The former Beijing Municipal Department of Labor's Regulations on Beijing City Enterprises' economic redundancy (Jing Lao Jiu Fa [1995] No. 56, abolished), stipulates that serious operational hardships are "three consecutive years of operating losses and the amount of losses increasing year by year, insolvency, 80% of the workers being suspended from work, and they being unable to pay the living expenses of workers according to the minimum living standard for six consecutive months." Zhejiang Province Former Labor Department, Zhe Lao Li (1995) No. 2, Notice on Forwarding the Regulation on Enterprise Economy Redundancy Personnel, "The reference standard for employers being economic redundancy due to serious operational hardship is: due to market reasons, having insufficient production orders in two consecutive years, causing half shut-down with no hope of turnaround."

hardships. The case of Yashili (Ma'anshan) Sales Company before Guangzhou Intermediate Court of Guangdong Province in 2019 also reflects a similar determining principle.[55]

The third situation is that business transfer requires redundancy. This business transfer includes productional transfer, major technological innovation, operational adjustment, and other major changes in objective economic conditions on which the employment contract is based at the time of its conclusion, which make it impossible to continue the employment contract. For this type of redundancy, some courts consider that employers must first negotiate with the employees to alter their contracts. If this fails, the employer may then implement the procedure of notifying the trade union or the employee congress, considering their responses, and reporting to the labor administrative authority before implementing the economic redundancy.[56]

Economic redundancy must also follow legal procedures. Employers must report to the labor administrative authority after notifying their trade union or employee congress and considering their response. An economic redundancy in violation of these procedures will be considered an unlawful dismissal. Among them, the procedure of informing the trade union or employee congress and listening to their opinions must be strictly observed; violating this will result in illegal dismissals. However, whether failure to report to the labor administrative authority, after notification of the trade union or employee congress, constitutes a procedural illegality is controversial in judicial practice. The 2014 Wang Haiying case before the Second Intermediate People's Court of Beijing held that failure to report to the labor administrative authority was only a minor flaw in the procedure and did not affect the legitimacy of the redundancy.[57]

Employers must notify trade unions or employee congresses one month in advance of economic redundancy, or pay one month's wage in lieu of notice, and pay economic compensation. Employers violating the rules on numbers of employees to be laid off, or substantive or procedural requirements, shall lead to illegal termination and the liability of punitive damages. For the calculation method of payment in lieu of notice, economic compensation, and punitive damages, please refer to "168. How do I calculate the payment in lieu of notice?", "164. How do I calculate economic compensation?", and "165. How do I calculate punitive damages for illegal termination of the employment relationship?"

It should be noted that certain types of employees are legally protected from dismissal when employers implement economic redundancy (see "160. What types of employees are entitled to special non-termination protection in employers' layoffs?"); additionally, if an employer believes that the business cannot continue, it is entitled to unilaterally decide

55 Huang Hua v. LG Electronics (China) Co., Ltd. Employment Dispute Retrial Review and Judicial Supervision Civil Ruling Beijing High Court Civil Ruling (2020) Jing Min Shen No. 2694. Xie v. Yashili Dairy (Ma'anshan) Sales Co., Ltd., et al. Employment Dispute Case Guangdong Guangzhou Intermediate People's Court Civil Judgment (2018) Yue 01 Min Zhong No. 6115. Liu Yan, Heilongjiang Longshi Star Media Co., Ltd. Civil Judgment of the Second Instance of Labor Dispute Civil Judgment of Harbin Intermediate People's Court of Heilongjiang Province (2018) Hei 01 Min Zhong No. 8311. Zheng Ying, Fuzhou Huarong Property Management Co., Ltd. Civil Judgment of Second Instance of Labor Dispute Civil Judgment of Fuzhou Intermediate People's Court of Fujian Province (2020) Min 01 Min Zhong No. 4099 (loss for two years).

56 Guangdong Baodian Minghui Trademark Co., Ltd. v. Huang Chunfa, Labor Dispute Appeal Case Dongguan Intermediate People's Court of Guangdong Province Civil Judgment (2014) Dong Zhong Fa Min Wu Zhong Zi No. 864.

57 Wang Haiying v. Dongjiang Mixiang Garden (Beijing) Catering Co., Ltd., Civil Judgment of Second Instance on Labor Dispute, the Second Beijing Intermediate People's Court (2014) Er Zhong Min Zhong Zi No. 08363.

to close the company without being influenced by staff's opinions,[58] but it must provide economic compensation to the employees in accordance with the law.

156. Can our company implement economic redundancy due to productional transfer, major technological innovation, or operational adjustment?

Answer: Economic redundancy is a term used by the courts in judicial practice to refer to the reduction of employees by employers under Article 41 of the Employment Contract Law.[59] From the textual meaning of this legal provision, employers certainly have the right to implement economic redundancy due to productional transfer, major technological innovation, or operational adjustments.

For example, in the 2015 case of Zhu Hong v. Guizhou Zunyi Jian'an Concrete Co., Ltd., the Guizhou Provincial High Court held that since the auxiliary position of the employer (outsourcing business) no longer existed, the employer's reduction of employees due to operational adjustment under Article 41 of the Employment Contract Law constituted a legitimate reason for economic redundancy.[60] In the 2018 case of Li Sicai v. Kaiping Guanghe Fermented Bean Curd Co., Ltd., the Jiangmen Intermediate People's Court of Guangdong Province held that the employer's purchase of automated machinery and equipment to replace manual operations constituted a major technological innovation, and the redundancy could be made based on Article 41 of the Employment Contract Law.[61]

What may be confusing is that productional transfer, major technological innovations, and operational adjustments themselves may also constitute major change in objective situation under Item 3 of Article 40 of the Employment Contract Law. In such cases, can Article 40 be applied when a redundancy is implemented due to productional transfer, major technological innovations, or operational adjustments? The procedural requirements for applying different articles are different; for economic redundancy under Article 41, notification to the labor administrative authority is required, while termination due to major change in objective situation under Article 40 does not require such notification.

We believe that the key to determining which article should be applied by the employer in such situations depends on the number of employees whose employment relations are to be terminated simultaneously. If this number exceeds 20, or if it is less than 20 but exceeds 10% of the total number of employees, then the employer must apply Article 41 to reduce employees, and cannot apply Article 40.

157. My employer terminates my employment contract on the ground of major change in objective situation. Is it legal?

Answer: Major change in objective situation, as stipulated in Article 40 of the Employment Contract Law, refers to the circumstance where the objective situation on which the

---

58 Article 44 of the Employment Contract Law.

59 Li Xiang v. Beijing Jinjiang Fuyuan Hotel Co., Ltd. Labor Dispute Retrial Review and Trial Supervision Civil Ruling, Beijing High People's Court Civil Ruling (2023) Jing Min Shen 3132. Xu Xianghong v. Shanghai Pudong Dongfeng Liberation Special Vehicle Co., Ltd. Labor Contract Dispute Trial Supervision Civil Ruling, Shanghai High People's Court Civil Ruling (2019) Hu Min Shen 446.

60 Zhu Hong v. Guizhou Zunyi Jian'an Concrete Co., Ltd. Labor Dispute Dispute Case, Guizhou Provincial High People's Court Civil Ruling (2015) Qian Gao Min Shen Zi No. 840.

61 Li Sicai v. Kaiping Guanghe Fermented Bean Curd Co., Ltd. Labor Dispute Second Instance Civil Judgment, Guangdong Province Jiangmen Intermediate People's Court Civil Judgment (2018) Yue 07 Min Zhong 147.

employment contract(s) is based has changed significantly, rendering it impossible to implement the employment contract(s), and subsequently, the employer and the employee have failed to reach an agreement on altering the content of the employment contract(s) through negotiation. In such a case, the employer may legally terminate the contract, conditional on paying economic compensation.

What kinds of situation constitute a major change in objective situation is not stipulated by law and is quite complex in practice. The former Ministry of Labor's interpretation of major change in objective situation refers to the occurrence of force majeure or other circumstances that make it impossible to implement the employment contract(s), including company relocation, merger, or transfer of company assets, but excluding economic redundancy.[62] From the perspective of judicial decisions, it appears that courts in various parts of China generally consider that major change in objective situation is limited to major changes in the external environment that cannot be changed and controlled by the companies, instead of general business disruptions or institutional adjustments to improve operations.[63] This is the view of the case of Qiu Lihong before Jilin Provincial High Court in 2017, which was issued by the Supreme Court as the first "100 Excellent Judgment Documents."

In practice, courts generally recognize the major change in objective situation caused by external reasons (especially government-led restructuring). For example, according to the Chen Fading case before the Taizhou Intermediate Court of Zhejiang Province in 2019, some employees lost their positions because their departments' management system was changed at the request of the government; therefore, this constitutes a major change in objective situation.[64] In the case of Zhang Wei v. Fushun Natural Resources Bureau before Liaoning Fushun Intermediate Court in 2019, the court held that the government-led reform of official vehicles leading to the layoff of drivers was a major change in objective situation.[65] The courts do not recognize those changes of general nature, especially the non-major changes in ordinary business situation decided by the company independently,

62 Article 26 of the Explanation on Several Articles of the Labor Law of the People's Republic of China issued by the former Ministry of Labor stipulates that the "objective situation" in this article refers to the occurrence of force majeure or other circumstances that make it impossible to perform all or part of the terms of the employment contract, such as enterprise relocation, merger, transfer of enterprise assets, etc. It also excludes the objective situation listed in Article 27 of this Law (referring to economic redundancy). Beijing Weibaifang Science and Trade Co., Ltd. and Jinmingguang Labor Dispute Second Instance Civil Judgment Beijing the First Intermediate People's Court Civil Judgment (2022) Jing 01 Minzhong No. 10196. "The deterioration of business conditions, the inability to continue operating, and the transfer of stores are within the scope of the company's business adjustment and the operational risks it should bear. It is not major change in objective situation that cannot be foreseen at the time of the conclusion of the contracts, such as the suspension of production and change of production due to force majeure or policy changes after the conclusion of the employment contract as stipulated in the aforementioned law."

63 The Supreme People's Court issued the first "100 Excellent Judgment Documents," Jilin Provincial High Court (2017) Jimin No. 296, Qiu Lihong v. Shentian Pharmaceutical (China) Co., Ltd. for retrial of labor disputes. "Therefore, the interpretation of 'major change in objective situation' should be limited to the major changes that occur in the external environment of the enterprise, that the enterprise cannot change or control. They are the facts that the enterprise has to face and accept, instead of the situation of ordinary poor business operation or the management mode changes for the enterprise pursuing higher profits."

64 Civil Judgment of Second Instance of Labor Dispute between Chen Legal and Yuhuan Market Development Service Center, Intermediate People's Court of Taizhou City, Zhejiang Province, (2019) Zhe 10 Min Zhong No. 664.

65 Fushun City Natural Resources Bureau v. Zhang Wei employment dispute second-instance civil judgment Liaoning Province Fushun City Intermediate People's Court Civil Judgment (2019) Liao 04 Min Zhong No. 627.

as major change in objective situation. For example, in the case of Li v. a foreign-invested company, one of the Ten Exemplary Labor Dispute cases in Beijing in 2016, the court decided that the internal adjustment of the enterprise was not a major change in objective situation.[66] The case of Yingsikang Information Technology (Shenzhen) Co., Ltd. before Guangzhou Intermediate Court of Guangdong Province in 2021 also points out that major changes in a company's equity do not necessarily constitute major change in objective situation.[67]

From many judicial decisions, what is vaguer and more controversial is whether the court should recognize a major change in objective situation when a company implements a strategic management adjustment. In the case of Feng v. Bei A Electronics Company before the Hangzhou Intermediate Court of Zhejiang Province in 2016, the court held that the fact that some employees had been dismissed from their departments had proved the existence of major change in objective situation, and in the case of Zhao Benfa before Guangdong Provincial High Court in 2018, the courts of the first and second instances in Guangzhou both held that the abolition of departments by the employer due to business strategy adjustment had been partially implemented, proving a major change in objective situation.[68] However, in the case of Zhou v. Online Information Company before Beijing the Third Intermediate People's Court in 2020, the court confirmed that the selling or out-outsourcing of departments or businesses as a whole did not necessarily constitute a major change in objective situation.[69] In the case of Xiamen ABB Switch Company before Fujian

66 The Beijing Municipal Bureau of Human Resources and Social Security released one of the top ten typical cases of labor disputes in 2016: the employment contract dispute between Li and a foreign-funded company—the internal adjustment of the enterprise is not a "major change in objective situation." "As an operator, when an employer signs an employment contract with an employee, it should foresee the possible fluctuations in the market and the possible changes in production and operation strategies. If it is really necessary to transfer the employee's position due to the needs of production and operation, the employment contract shall be changed or terminated in writing by mutual agreement. If no agreement can be reached, the employer can arrange the employee to work in similar or close positions, and can not arbitrarily reduce the wage standards of the employee, let alone simply terminate the employment contract."

67 Yinsikang Information Technology (Shenzhen) Co., Ltd., v. Qu Sumei Labor Dispute Civil Second Instance Civil Judgment Book Guangdong Province Guangzhou Intermediate People's Court Civil Judgment (2021) Yue 01 Min Zhong No. 27685.

68 Labor Dispute between Feng and Bei x Electronics (Hangzhou) Co., Ltd, Zhejiang Hangzhou Intermediate Court (2016) Zhe 01 Min Zhong No. 1515. Zhao Benfa, Guangzhou Nanyang Electrical Appliances Co., Ltd. Labor Dispute Retrial Civil Judgment Book Guangdong Provincial High People's Court Civil Judgment (2018) Yue Min Zai No. 194.

69 The Guangdong Provincial People's High Court issued the seventh of nine typical cases of labor disputes: Huang sued a real estate company for labor disputes—the termination of employment contracts on the grounds of changes in the company's equity is illegal. Beijing the Third Intermediate People's Court (2020) Beijing 03 Civil Judgment No. 3801, Zhou v. Online Information Company Labor Dispute—the criteria for determining major change in objective situation at the time of the conclusion of the employment contract. "The unpredictable major changes in the conclusion of the employment contract usually refer to force majeure caused by natural disasters, major changes in the employer's relocation, transfer of assets or suspension of production, change of production, transfer (or change) of system, due to changes in laws, regulations and policies, or major changes in the business scope of the employer with the nature of franchising. According to the statements and evidence of both sides in the trial, the online information company chose to outsource Zhou's department to a third party in order to reduce costs, improve efficiency, and improve audit efficiency in an all-round way. This situation does not belong to the objective situation on which the conclusion of the employment contract is based."

Xiamen Intermediate People's Court in 2018, the court held that the strategic adjustment of the company was not a major change in objective situation.[70]

This vagueness in practice is exacerbated further because of the confusion between the major change in objective situation under Article 40 and the major change in objective situation under Article 41 of the Employment Contract Law.[71] The law uses the same term in two different statutory provisions related to employment termination without distinguishing the applicable scopes. This is a regrettable legislative flaw, resulting in courts in practice suffering contradictions and confusions. Please see "159. What are the differences between terminations due to economic redundancy and the major change in objective situation?"

Therefore, if you are terminated by the employer on the ground of major change in objective situation under Article 40, you need to see how the employer explained the specific "objective situation" in the termination notice. If the employer encounters a major change in the external environment, it may be legal. On the contrary, if it is only a general business adjustment, it is unlikely to constitute a lawful termination. If the company was implementing an overall strategic adjustment, the legality of the termination may depend on whether the company encountered operational difficulties and has other reasonable grounds for termination.

If an employer intends to terminate the employment contract due to a major change in objective situation, it must first negotiate with the employee to change the content of the employment contract. If this fails, it must notify the employee one month in advance, or pay one month's wage in lieu of notice, and pay economic compensation. If major change in objective situation is not established, the employer is likely to have made an illegal dismissal and is liable for punitive damages. For the calculation method of payment in lieu of notice, economic compensation and punitive damages, please refer to "168. How do I calculate the payment in lieu of notice?", "164. How do I calculate economic compensation?", and "165. How do I calculate punitive damages for illegal termination of the employment relationship?"

158. Can we terminate an employee's employment due to his poor performance?

Answer: The Employment Contract Law stipulates two lawful circumstances under which an employer can terminate the labor relationship with an employee due to incompetence in work. One is when an employee is incompetent in their work due to injury or illness, which predominately arises from complex issues such as medical certification and labor capacity appraisal; please see "85. What should I do if an employee of my company has not recovered after the expiration of the medical care leave?" and "95. What should the employer do if an employee has not recovered after the expiration of the paid work injury leave?"

---

70 Xiamen ABB Switchgear Co., Ltd., v. Zhang Ping Labor Dispute Second Instance Civil Judgment Book Fujian Province Xiamen Intermediate People's Court Civil Judgment (2018) Min 02 Min Zhong No. 3177.

71 The Employment Contract Law, Article 40 (3), "where the objective situation based on which the employment was entered into has significantly changed, rendering the implement of the contact impossible, and both parties fail in reaching agreement in altering the contract after negotiation." Article 41 (4), "other circumstances where the objective situation based on which the employment contact was entered into has significantly changed, rendering performance of the contract impossible."

If your employee's performance is unsatisfactory, it likely falls under the other circumstance outlined in Article 40 of the Employment Contract Law, which allows termination of the employment relationship due to the employee's incompetence to perform their duties. To legally terminate the employment of an incompetent employee, the employer must meet four statutory conditions: first, the employee is incompetent in their work; second, the employer has provided training or transferred the employee to another position; third, the employee remains incompetent after the training or the position transfer; fourth, the employer has given a 30-day notice or paid payment in lieu of notice.

For the first and third conditions, the employer is obligated to provide evidence of the employee's incompetence. This evidence typically includes job descriptions or requirements stipulated in the employment contract and performance evaluations during the performance of the employment contract. Courts often find terminations unlawful when employers rely solely on their subjective judgments without providing sufficient evidence of incompetence.[72] In practice, some companies implement a policy of poorest-performance-out, in the belief that the fact of an employee's performance appraisal results being at the bottom automatically proves their incompetence. However, this is a mistaken belief. Employers must provide specific criteria or standards outlined in agreements or company rules and regulations to demonstrate an employee's incompetence.[73]

For the second condition, the employer should, based on objective evidence proving the employee's incompetence, either provide training for the employee or transfer them to a different position. The purpose of training provided by the employer should be to enhance the employee's job skills so that they can perform their duties competently. The training wages for the employee can be determined according to the agreements in the employment contract or the lawful company rules and regulations regarding training wages for employees who are deemed incompetent for their positions. However, these wages should not be lower than the local minimum wage standard. If the employer chooses to transfer the position of the employee, the legality of the transfer may involve complex legal considerations such as wage standards and procedural requirements, and therefore requires careful handling. For more details, please refer to "129. How should an employer legally transfer the position of an employee?"

For the fourth condition, the employer should choose either to provide a 30-day advance notice or to pay compensation in lieu of notice to legally terminate the employment relationship. An interesting question arises regarding the legal consequences of not complying with the statutory requirement of providing a 30-day advance notice for termination. Does it result in an illegal termination of the employment relationship? Judicial precedents indicate that the usual consequence is that the employer is automatically deemed liable for paying payment in lieu of notice, rather than being deemed to have illegally terminated the employment relationship due to procedural violations. For example, in the 2019 case of Huang YuJie and Foshan Shunde Jinhui Shun Electric Heating Materials Co., Ltd., where the employee was incompetent to perform his job duties upon the expiry of the medical

72 Yang Xinliang v. Ping An Technology (Shenzhen) Co., Ltd., Guangdong Provincial Higher People's Court Civil Ruling (2019) Yue Min Shen No. 11051. The court found that the employer failed to provide evidence proving that the employee was incompetent to perform their job duties. Therefore, the termination of the employment relationship by the employer was found illegal.

73 Gao Xiaogang, Yao Dongcai: "Review of the Effectiveness of the Poorest-Performance-Out Policy of Employers," published in *People's Judiciary • Case Studies*, Issue 11, 2020, Page 4.

care leave, the court found that the employer had failed to issue the 30-day notice for termination and therefore chose to make payment in lieu of notice, and ordered the employer to provide such payment.[74]

Employers following these principles when terminating incompetent employees should be prepared to provide economic compensation and possibly payment in lieu of notice. For further details, please refer to "164. How do I calculate economic compensation?" and "168. How do I calculate the payment in lieu of notice?" Violations of the aforementioned first three conditions may lead to illegal termination with the serious consequence of punitive damages. For more information, please see "165. How do I calculate punitive damages for illegal termination of the employment relationship?"

159. What are the differences between terminations due to economic redundancy and the major change in objective situation?

Answer: The major change in objective situation we usually refer to is the one under Article 40 (3) of the Employment Contract Law, by which employers may terminate their employees in the case of major change in objective situation and subsequent failure of negotiation, rather than the confusing major change in objective situation under Article 41 (4) of the law for economic redundancy.[75]

In order to distinguish the scope of application of these two statutory provisions, judicial practice tends to limit the Article 40–related major change in objective situation to the situation where employers are unable to retain employees due to major changes from the external environment, and define the Article 41–related major change in objective situation under economic redundancy as where employers are forced to lay off employees in batches due to serious operational hardships. Please refer to "157. My employer terminates my employment contract on the ground of major change in objective situation. Is it legal?" and "155. How can employers experiencing business hardship legally reduce their workforce to survive?"

Obviously, the aforementioned two circumstances may well coincide, although possibly being different, as an employer's internal business hardships may well be caused by changes in the external environment. The coincidence and distinction of these two legal provisions have caused wide ambiguity and confusion.

On the one hand, this will lead to employers feeling at a loss, as both legal provisions might be applicable. For example, if the number of employees to be laid off reaches the standard of economic redundancy (10% of staff or more than 20 employees), or if an employer having only 2 employees dismisses 1 employee (50% in layoff, reaching the percentage standard of the economic redundancy), the employer would be confused about whether the termination should be proceeded on the ground of Article 41–related major change in objective situation under economic redundancy or Article 40–related major changes in objective situation. The legal procedure requirements of the two in the

74 Huang Yujie v. Foshan Shunde Jinhui Shun Electric Heating Materials Co., Ltd., Guangdong Provincial Higher People's Court Civil Ruling (2019) Yue Min Shen Nos. 1989 and 1990.

75 The Employment Contract Law, Article 40 (3), "where the objective situation based on which the employment was entered into has significantly changed, rendering the implementation of the contract impossible, and both parties fail in reaching agreement in altering the contract after negotiation." Article 41 (4), "other circumstances where the objective situation based on which the employment contact was entered into has significantly changed, rendering performance of the contract impossible."

termination of employment relationships are distinct, the former requiring the employer to notify the trade union or employee congress and report to the labor administrative authority, while the latter requires the employer to negotiate with the employees for contract alterations. A mistaken choice of avenue may result in serious consequences such as punitive damages.

For example, in the case of Cheng Lizhuo before Liaoning Provincial High Court in 2014, due to equity restructuring, the employer terminated employees from multiple departments on the ground of Article 40–related major change in objective situation and placed them in other companies. The number of employees terminated obviously meets the characteristics of economic redundancy. Liaoning Provincial Procuratorate appealed, claiming that this was an economic redundancy under Article 41. Liaoning High Court, however, finally rejected the appeal and found that the transfer of equity making all employees in the departments redundant constituted an Article 40–related major change in objective situation. In another case, Zhang v. a cement company before Guangdong Province Huizhou Intermediate Court in 2016, the employer executed an economic redundancy due to serious operational hardship, while the number of employees laid off fell short of the statutory requirement on economic redundancy. The dismissal was therefore found illegal.[76]

Another prosecutorial appealed case, involving the confusion between the two types of major change in objective situation, had an opposite outcome. In the case of Xin Deshan before Shandong High Court in 2019, the employer laid off a batch of employees due to a government-led policy restructuring. The employer did not specify the legal basis of the layoff on the notices of dismissal to the employees involved, while pointing out later that the employees were ability incompetent even after training, and that the layoff was implemented based on the poorest-performance-out under the requirements of the policy restructuring. The decision of the second-instance court tended to hold that even if the number of terminated employees and other factors met the characteristics of economic redundancy, the layoff was still implemented under Article 40–related major change in objective situation. However, after the Shandong Provincial Procuratorate appealed, the Shandong Provincial High Court ultimately set aside the decision, upheld the procuratorate's stance that the layoff should be found to be economic redundancy, and found the layoff illegal due to mistaken choice of termination procedure.[77]

On the other hand, this ambiguity can also lead to situations where neither of the two legal provisions is applicable to a circumstance, leaving employers with no laws to rely on. For instance, an employer, facing a general business hardship, has to reduce the number of employees for an operational strategy adjustment to prevent potential serious challenges in the future. This is manifestly normal and reasonable managerial measure by any company in a market economy. However, under the Employment Contract Law, the employer may not be able to terminate the employments under the provisions of Article 41 for economic redundancy, as current judicial decisions seem to be limited to situations

---

76 Cheng Lizhuo v. Chaoyang Yilong Industrial Development Co., Ltd. Labor Dispute Case Liaoning Provincial High Court Civil Judgment (2014) Liao Shen Yi Min Kang Zi No. 42. Huizhou Intermediate People's Court announced the second typical case of labor disputes in 2016: the employment contract dispute between Zhang and a cement company—economic redundancy.

77 Civil Judgment on Civil Retrial of Labor Dispute between Xin Deshan and Weifang Xingsheng Highway Engineering Co., Ltd. Shandong Provincial People's High Court (2022) Lumin Zai No. 209.

where the employer has incurred losses for two or three consecutive years, and there are strict requirements regarding the number of employees to be laid off in economic redundancy. Please refer to "155. How can employers experiencing business hardship legally reduce their workforce to survive?" Additionally, a termination by the employer applying Article 40–related major change in objective situation may also not necessarily be legal, as the terminations resulting from such strategic adjustments may not necessarily meet the requirements of this legal provision. Please refer to "157. My employer terminates my employment contract on the ground of major change in objective situation. Is it legal?" Whether strategic adjustments by companies are permissible for legal layoffs under Article 40 or 41 of the Employment Contract Law is currently a highly contentious issue in judicial decisions, making it impossible to achieve consistent rulings. This brings serious uncertainty to businesses in China implementing their business strategies to mitigate market risks.

The divergent understandings and practices in these cases illustrate the defects of the law, which rigidly stipulates a number of grounds for employment terminations, providing no feasible implementation rules or interpretation for legal principles of lawful termination. We are of the view that this principle should be to balance the employers' rights in business survival and development and employees' labor rights and interests, and the employer's termination must conform to the fundamental principle of balanced fairness and reasonableness of the law under specific circumstances.

Future legislative amendments should consider merging these two legal provisions, allowing judges to take into account the legitimate, reasonable needs of business operations (including technological upgrading, strategic adjustment, operational efficiency, etc.[78]), the personal circumstances of employees (such as length of service, historical contribution, etc.), public order and good morals, and other factors, so that a judge may determine whether an enterprise is justified in terminating the employment contract(s) of a specific employee(s) in order to promote harmonious employment relations and social and economic development. Stipulating rigid provisions with a planned economic management mindset will either excessively restrict the development rights of companies or seriously damage the fair rights and interests of employees who are in particular difficulties. Employment law is the law of human nature, and judges should have discretion based on human nature, fairness, and justice.

160. What types of employees are entitled to special non-termination protection in employers' layoffs?

Answer: The employment laws in China tend to protect the security of employment contracts of specially vulnerable employees.

Article 42 of the Employment Contract Law stipulates that the following types of employees must not be terminated when the employer intends to terminate employment(s) due to health incompetence, ability incompetence, major change in objective situation of employer, or economic redundancy (that is, termination of employment contracts in accordance with Articles 40 and 41): 1) female employees in their three protected periods (pregnancy, maternity, and lactation); 2) employees with more than 15 years of service

78 Whether enterprises are allowed to lay off employees for the purpose of improving operational efficiency is an issue involving the principles of labor legislation. The current employment laws do not seem to allow it.

and less than 5 years toward retirement age; 3) employees with occupational diseases or work-related injuries who have lost all or part of their labor capacity; 4) employees who are on medical care leave due to illnesses or non-work-related injuries or on paid work injury leave due to work injury;[79] 5) employees who have been exposed to occupational hazards and have not undergone off-role occupational health examination; 6) employees suspected of occupational diseases who are under diagnosis or medical observation.

If an employee is terminated in violation of the aforementioned provisions, the employer's action shall be deemed to be an illegal termination of the employment relationship, and the employee shall be entitled to reinstatement to their position (or punitive damages without reinstatement), the loss of wages, and other compensations.

161. My employee is sentenced to imprisonment for committing a crime. Can we terminate his employment?

Answer: The Employment Contract Law and the Labor Law both stipulate that an employer can terminate the employment contract of an employee who is held criminally liable according to law. The aforementioned phrase, "held criminally liable according to law," includes the following situations: being sentenced to fixed-term imprisonment (including on suspension) by the courts, under criminal detention, being discharged of a conviction by a court, and being discharged of a prosecution by a procuratorate.[80] Employers do not need to pay economic compensation to terminate employees' employment for these reasons. This is similar to the situation of terminating employees who seriously violate company rules and regulations.

During the period when an employee's personal liberty is restricted by the police or the procuratorate due to a suspected crime, their employer may suspend the performance of the employment contract without paying wages, and may suspend the contribution of social insurance at the same time. If the investigation reveals that the employee is innocent, the employee may file a state compensation lawsuit for wages or other losses.[81]

It should be noted that if the employee is held criminally liable but the employer does not terminate the employee's employment contract, the employment relationship between the two parties still exists, and the employer should still contribute to their social insurance

---

79 The provisions of Article 33 of 2010 Regulations on Work-related Injury Insurance on the rights of employees during paid work injury leave implies that an employer may not terminate the employment relationship with an employee who has suffered a work injury during the period.

80 Article 29 of the Opinions on Several Issues Concerning the Implementation of the Labor Law of the People's Republic of China (Laobufa [1995] No. 309). "If the employee is held criminally liable according to law, the employer may terminate the employment contract in accordance with Article 25 of the Labor Law. Being held criminally liable according to law refers to: being exempted from prosecution by the people's procuratorate, being sentenced to criminal punishment by the people's court, or being exempted from criminal punishment according to Article 32 of the Criminal Law. If a worker is sentenced by a people's court to criminal detention or a suspended sentence of fixed-term imprisonment of not more than three years, the employer may terminate the employment contract."

81 Article 28 of the Opinions on Several Issues Concerning the Implementation of the Labor Law of the People's Republic of China (Laobufa [1995] No. 309). "If a worker is under confinement review, detention, or arrest by the relevant authorities for suspected crime, the employer may temporarily suspend the performance of the employment contract with the worker during the period when the worker's personal liberty is restricted. During the period of temporary suspension of the performance of the employment contract, the employer shall not assume the corresponding obligations stipulated in the employment contract. If a worker proves to have been wrongly restricted in their personal liberty, he may claim compensation from the relevant departments in accordance with the State Compensation Law for the loss of the worker during the period of temporary suspension of the performance of the employment contract."

while the employee is in detention or serving their sentence.[82] In addition, even if employees are held criminally liable, the employer has the obligation to properly keep the personnel files of the employees.[83] Finally, if the employee's criminal conviction or related criminal liability is finally revoked and the employee is found innocent, the employer shall reinstate the employment relationship,[84] unless the employment relationship cannot be reinstated or both parties have accepted the fact that the employment relationship has been actually terminated.[85]

162. My employer fired me for gross negligence and corruption. Is it legal?

Answer: You should first look carefully at the factual reasons and the legal or institutional basis for the employer's dismissal.

If the employer dismisses you on the grounds of "gross negligence and corruption causing major losses to employer" under Article 39 of the Employment Contract Law, it is necessary to see whether you have shown gross negligence or corruption in terms of your job description and have caused heavy losses to the employer. If that is the case, the termination by the employer is legal.

If the termination is based on your serious violation of the company rules and regulations on gross negligence or corruption, the first thing to see is whether the company rules and regulations are valid (see "121. Is it legally permissible for my employer to discipline me?"). Then, you need to check how the rule defines gross negligence or corruption to consider whether you have shown gross negligence or corruption in terms of your job description, and finally, examine whether the employer has notified the trade union before dismissing you (see "152. How should employers handle the procedure of notifying the

---

82 Hegang Gongchuang Re-employment Service Co., Ltd., Chen Xiaolei Labor Dispute Civil Judgment of Second Instance Heilongjiang Hegang Intermediate People's Court Civil Judgment (2022) Hei 04 Min Zhong No. 261. "The Court holds that, according to Article 39 of the Employment Contract Law, if the employee is held criminally liable according to law, the employer may terminate the employment contract. However, it cannot be considered that the employment contract is terminated naturally after the employee is convicted. The employer must serve the notice of termination of the employment contract to the employee and fulfill the obligation of notification in time. Otherwise, the employee still maintains employment relationship with the employer, and the employer should contribute to social insurance and provident fund for the employee."

83 Guo Engui and Dalian Dyeing and Chemical Group Co., Ltd. Civil Judgment (2020) Liao 02 Min Zhong No. 5245 of the Intermediate People's Court of Dalian City, Liaoning Province. The court held "Article 7 of the 2016 Personnel Files Law of the People's Republic of China stipulates: 'Personnel files departments and their workers are responsible for keeping the personnel files and supervising and guiding the work-related personnel files of their organisations.' Article 18 of the Provisions on Management of Employee's Personnel Files (LaoLiZi [1992] No. 33) stipulates: 'When an enterprise's employee is transferred, resigns, terminates their employment contract, or is dismissed, the employer to which the employee belongs shall transfer their personnel files to their new employer or the labor (organization and personnel) department of the street office where their registered permanent residence is located within one month. If an employee is punished by labor education or labor transformation and their former employer is going to employ them in the future, their file shall be kept by their former employer. The employer has the obligation to properly keep the employee's files. Even if the employee is dismissed, the employer should transfer the files out within the prescribed time limit.' Therefore, the court of the first instance rejected the the defendant's claim that it has no obligation to keep the plaintiff's personnel file because the plaintiff was held criminally liable and was dismissed."

84 Civil Ruling of the Supreme People's Court (2012) Min Zai Shen Zi No. 104, Huojia County Power Supply Co., Ltd. v. Lou Yuanwei Labor Dispute Retrial.

85 The labor disputes between Zhai Liujun and Pingdingshan Tian'an Coal Industry Co., Ltd., Henan Provincial People's High Court Civil Ruling (2013) Yu Fa Li Er Min Shen Zi No. 01984. In the case, the employee's criminal judgment was revoked, but the court took into account that the employee had received a one-off work injury medical allowance. Therefore, it is concluded that both parties have accepted the fact that the employment relationship has been terminated subjectively and objectively.

trade union when terminating employees?"). The termination should be lawful if the foregoing conditions are met.

In judicial practice, there are very few cases of lawful dismissal of employees on the grounds of "gross negligence and corruption causing major losses to employer," and the relevant cases are those in which employers claimed that employees had committed gross negligence or corruption causing major losses to the employer, but failed to provide evidence to prove it, rendering that the employees' impugned acts were not established.

This legal provision is basically in a state of sleep. On the one hand, employers generally stipulate gross negligence and corruption as serious violations of labor discipline in company rules and regulations so as to avoid the high threshold of "causing heavy losses." On the other hand, "corruption" itself is a serious act of dishonesty and a serious violation of professional ethics. According to the current decisions of courts nationwide, a serious violation of professional ethics is likely to be enough to constitute a legitimate reason for dismissal (even without the provisions of company rules and regulations). This also leads to the hollowing out of the statutory provision.

163. One of my employees is also working for another company. Can we fire him?

Answer: Article 39 of the Employment Contract Law stipulates that "if an employee establishes an employment relationship(s) with other employer(s) simultaneously, having a serious impact on the completion of their work tasks for the current employer, or refuses to make corrections after being put forward by the current employer," the employer may terminate the employment relationship with the employee without paying economic compensation.

In judicial practice, the most common application of this clause is that employees start or participate in the establishment of companies competing with their current employers during their tenure. The courts usually no longer entangle itself with whether they meet the legal requirements of "having a serious impact on the completion of their work tasks" but find that this is a serious violation of employees' professional ethics or agreed-upon obligations of non-competition or confidentiality, and rule that therefore, such terminations comply with the aforementioned statutory provision.[86]

It should be noted that this legal provision only applies to full-time employees. If an employee of your company is a casual employee, according to the provisions of the Employment Contract Law, a casual employee can establish casual employment relationships with more than one employer, and the employee does not violate the law. Of course, according to Article 71 of the Employment Contract Law, your company can also notify casual employees of termination at any time without paying economic compensation.

---

86 Civil Judgment of First Instance of labor dispute between Jiang Momo and Fujian Jiedian Information Technology Co., Ltd, the People's Court of Cangshan District, Fuzhou City, Fujian Province (2016) Min0104MinChu No. 3110. "According to the principle of 'revealing the heavy by the light', since an employer is entitled to terminate an employer who establishes employment relationships with other employers at the same time, which has a serious impact on the completion of the current work tasks, an employer should be more justifiable to terminate an employer who has set up a new company, which is even more serious act." The labor dispute appeal case of Xia Zhihui and Huashu Exploration Business Consulting (Hangzhou) Co., Ltd., the Civil Judgment of the Intermediate People's Court of Hangzhou City, Zhejiang Province (2017) Zhe 01 Min Zhong No. 667. In the case, the employee invested in the establishment of a competitive company with others during their tenure in the employer, and did not correct it after the employer raised the issue. The court held that this violated the principle of good faith and the duty of loyalty, as well as the provisions of the law on dual employment relationships, and that the termination was legal.

Employees on long-term unpaid leave waiting for their work, employees on irregular or general work hours during rotational furlough, or even full-time employees during their spare time establishing employment relationships with other employers, in principle, as long as it does not affect their current employer's work tasks, comply with legal provisions. The Supreme Court's judicial interpretation in 2020 evidently adopts this stance.[87]

5.3 Calculation of Termination Compensations

164. How do I calculate economic compensation?

Answer: According to the Employment Contract Law, economic compensation is applicable for employers to pay the employee in the following circumstances: employees are forced to resign, employment contracts expire and are dissolved, or the employer terminates employment on the grounds of health incompetence, ability incompetence, major change in objective situation, or economic redundancy.

The basic calculation rule of economic compensation is as follows: if an employee has worked continuously for several years for their employer, the employer shall pay the same number of months of wages as the economic compensation to the employee (the part of the service years less than 1 year is calculated as half a year if it is less than 6 months, and as 1 year if it exceeds 6 months); and the monthly wages for the economic compensation shall be the employee's average wages from the 12 months immediately before the termination.

We use a case to illustrate how economic compensation is calculated. Mr. Zhang has worked for his employer for 9 years and 2 months before his termination due to ability incompetence, and his average wage from the 12 months before the termination is RMB 9,000. Then, the economic compensation he should receive for his termination is RMB 85,500 (9.5 months * 9,000 RMB/month). According to Article 40 of the Employment Contract Law, the employer shall notify Mr. Zhang of the termination 30 days (1 month) in advance and pay the economic compensation at the time of the termination. The employer may pay RMB 9,000, one month's wages, as payment in lieu for the one-month notice, plus the aforementioned economic compensation. This is called N + 1 compensation in China.

The calculation of economic compensation is not necessarily always as straightforward as in Mr. Zhang's case. There are some specific issues in the accurate determination of the number of months and the monthly wage base, such as how to handle decimal months instead of an integer number of months, or whether the monthly wage base includes the year-end bonus, or the monthly wage base that exceeds three times local employees' average wages of the previous year shall be subject to a cap, and so on. Please refer to "166. What are the considerations for calculating economic compensation and punitive damages?"

87 Article 32 of the Interpretation of the Supreme People's Court on the Application of Law in the Trial of Labor Dispute Cases (I) (Judicial Interpretation [2020] No. 26): "Employees who are on long-term unpaid leave, internal retirees who have not reached the statutory retirement age, stood-down and waiting-for-work individuals, as well as employees of enterprises on temporary leave due to operational suspension, who file lawsuits due to employment disputes with a new employer, shall be handled by the People's Court in accordance with labor relations."

165. How do I calculate punitive damages for illegal termination of the employment relationship?

Answer: In the case that an employer illegally terminates an employee and the employee does not elect to claim for reinstatement, the employer is liable to pay punitive damages.

The calculation method for punitive damages is twice the amount of the economic compensation computed according to "164. How do I calculate economic compensation?" (the so-called 2N punitive damages). For example, if the length of service of Ms. Li's employee is nine years and two months, and the wage is RMB 5,000, the punitive damages is RMB 95,000 (5,000 * 9.5 * 2).

The calculation of punitive damages, just like that of economic compensation, also involves the same cap rule. That is to say, if the employee's monthly wage exceeds three times the local average employees' monthly salary from the previous year, the monthly wage standard for calculating punitive damages is three times the local employees' average monthly wages of the previous year, and the maximum number of months for calculating punitive damages is 12 months. This is the so-called double cap for punitive damages. For example, if Ms. Li has worked for 15 years for the employer, and the average wage from the 12 months immediately before the illegal termination is RMB 40,000, while the average monthly wage of local employees from the previous year is RMB 5,000, she is entitled to received punitive damages of RMB 360,000 (5,000 * 3 * 12 * 2) instead of RMB 1,200,000 (40,000 * 15 * 2).[88]

The double-capping rule setting was meant to restrict the overly high compensational burden on employers. However, it could have unintended consequences for some lawmakers. For example, two employees of an employer, Mr. Zhang and Ms. Li, both had 30 years of service and were both dismissed illegally by the employer. Mr. Zhang's average monthly wage from the 12 months before his departure, RMB 14,999, was narrowly less than three times the local employees' average monthly monthly wage of the previous year, RMB 15,000, while Ms. Li's was RMB 15,000. Mr. Zhang's punitive damages shall be RMB 899,940 (14,999 * 30 * 2). However, Mrs. Li's punitive damages will be RMB 360,000 (15,000 * 2 * 12). These two employees are in virtually the same situation (the difference of the two employees' monthly average wages is only RMB 1), but the amount of punitive damages is several-fold different, rendering the result obviously unfair. This is more evidence of China's employment laws legislation being busy creating rules while lacking prediction of practice.

Beginning in 2019, the cap for economic compensation and punitive damages in Beijing has been changed to three times the average monthly wage of employees in enterprise entities in Beijing (the cap standard in 2023 is 178476/12 * 3 = RMB 44,619), rather than three times the local employees' average monthly wage of the previous year.[89] Other regions, including Shanghai, Shenzhen, Guangzhou, Tianjin, Chongqing, Chengdu, and

88 Civil Judgment of Second Instance of Labor Dispute between Zhenyi Electronics (Shenzhen) Co., Ltd. and Yao Chaozhi Civil Judgment of Shenzhen Intermediate People's Court of Guangdong Province (2020) Yue 03 Min Zhong No. 12083. Civil Ruling on Labor Dispute Civil Application for Retrial by Yao Chaozhi and Zhenyi Electronics (Shenzhen) Co., Ltd. Civil Ruling of Guangdong Provincial People's High Court (2021) Yue Min Shen No. 4525.

89 Notice of Beijing Human Resources and Social Security Bureau on Calculating the Economic Compensation Cap Base According to the Average Wage of Employees in Legal Entities in 2019.

most other provinces and cities still apply the rule of three times the local employees' average monthly wage of the previous year.

The calculation of punitive damages is not necessarily always simple and straightforward. There are some specific issues in accurate determination of the number of months and the monthly wage base, such as how to handle decimal months instead of a integer number of months, or whether the monthly wage base includes the year-end bonus, or the monthly wage base that exceeds three times local employees' average wages of the previous year shall be subject to a cap, and so on. Please refer to "166. What are the considerations for calculating economic compensation and punitive damages?"

166. What are the considerations for calculating economic compensation and punitive damages?

Answer: Several issues need attention in calculating economic compensation and compensation.

First, the number of months calculated corresponding to service years is handled based on the rule of "rounding up on four and rounding up on five," instead of the common mathematical rule of "rounding down on four and rounding up on five." For example, Mr. Zhang worked for nine years and two months. As the two months is less than half a year, it will be rounded up to half a year. Mr. Zhang's length of service is regarded as nine and a half years, so he should get nine and a half months' wage. If Mr. Zhang worked for nine years and six or seven months, Mr. Zhang's length of service should be rounded up to ten years.

Second, unless otherwise agreed upon, the length of service for calculating economic compensation for an employee should only count the recent continuous length of service for the employer. For example, although the total service years Mr. Zhang has worked for the employer are 15 years, his recent continuous service years are only 9 years and 2 months, as he resigned and rejoined the company. Mr. Zhang can only get 9.5 months' wages as economic compensation instead of 15 months' wages (unless the employer recognizes otherwise).

In a case where an employee undergoes a position transfer that is not controlled by the employee, for example, being transferred by their former employer to an affiliated or even non-affiliated company, the length of service of the employee should be calculated continuously rather than only the service years in the new employer being accounted.[90] The employee's length of service shall not be affected by renaming, changes of shareholders, or division or merger of the employer. Please see "125. What are the legal consequences of an employee being transferred between two employers?" Additional, long-term unpaid leave does not dissolve the employment relationship; the employee's length of service for the employer therefore continues to accrue during the long-term unpaid leave. However, the nominal wages during the leave, being used for average monthly wages from the previous 12 months for computing economic compensation, shall be set at local minimum wages.[91]

90 Article 46 of the Interpretation of the Supreme People's Court on the Application of Law in the Trial of Labor Dispute Cases (I) (Judicial Interpretation [2020] No. 26).

91 The former Ministry of Labor and Personnel and the State Economic Commission issued the Notice on the Issue of Long-term Unpaid Leave for Employees of Enterprises. Original Ministry of Labor, Notice on Several Issues on Implementing Labor Contract System. In Article 7, "during the long-term unpaid leave, an

Third, the average monthly wages from the 12 months should be based on due wages (including monetary income such as bonuses, allowances, and overtime wages, excluding the value of tangible items provided by the employer) instead of received wages.[92] Non-monthly incomes such as year-end bonus and quarterly bonus should be included in the base,[93] and they should be proportionally allocated into bonus-related duration as the part of the income thereof, before the computation of the 12-month average monthly wages.[94] In addition, economic penalties legally deducted from employees' wages can be excluded from the incomes for computing the average monthly wage base.[95] Finally, this month's average wage base should not be lower than the local minimum wage standard; if employees work overtime, all wage income divided by work hours should not be lower than the local minimum hourly wage. Please note that if the employee's paid months are less than 12 months before the termination, the calculation of average monthly wages shall be based on actual paid months.

Fourth, if the employee's average monthly wage from the previous 12 months is equal to or over three times the local employees' average wages of the previous year, the average monthly wages for computing economic compensation or punitive damages shall be three times the local employees' average monthly wage of the previous year (rather than the employee's own average wage); and besides, the number of months for calculation shall not exceed 12 months even if the employee's service years are over 12 years. This is the so-called double cap for economic compensation and punitive damages calculation. That is to say, if Ms. Li's average monthly wage is RMB 40,000 and her service years are 15 years, and the local employees' average monthly wage of the previous year is RMB 5,000, Ms. Li's monthly wage base for calculating economic compensation shall be 15,000 (5000 * 3) instead of RMB 40,000, and her compensational service years shall be 12 years instead of 15 years. Therefore, Ms. Li's economic compensation is RMB 180,000 (15000 * 12) instead of RMB 600,000 (40,000 * 15).

---

employee remains the employment relationship with the employer, and the employee's service years continue counting; but the wage payment and welfare are different from that of the employment relationship." Reply of the Department of Labor and Social Security of Guangdong Province on the Calculation and Payment Base of Economic Compensation for the Termination of Employment Contract between the Enterprise and the Former Employee on Long-term Unpaid Leave (Yue Lao She Han [2000] No. 155). "In principle, the calculation and payment base of economic compensation or living allowance for the former employees on long-term paid leave can be calculated and paid according to the minimum wage standard of the year published by the local government which the enterprise is under."

92 Article 27 of the Regulations on the Implementation of the Employment Contract Law of the People's Republic of China stipulates: "The monthly wage of economic compensation stipulated in Article 47 of the Employment Contract Law shall be calculated according to the due wages of workers, including hourly wages or piecework wages, as well as monetary income such as bonuses, allowances, and subsidies."

93 Most courts apportion the year-end bonus to the income from the first 12 months. However, Liaoning Shenyang Intermediate People's Court appears to have a decision that the year-end bonus should not be included in the average monthly wage (Wang Zhihua, Foshan Abis Health Care Industry Co., Ltd. and Guangdong Jingxing Health Care Industry Co., Ltd. Civil Judgment of Liaoning Shenyang Intermediate People's Court (2022) Liao 01 Min Zhong 13376), while another case of Shenyang Intermediate People's Court held that year-end bonus should be counted into average monthly wage: Shenyang Yuanda Intelligent Industry Group Co., Ltd., Fu Mingyu Labor Dispute Civil Judgment of Second Instance Civil Judgment of Shenyang Intermediate People's Court of Liaoning Province (2023) Liao 01 Min Zhong No. 2133.

94 Shenzhen Yishihuolala Technology Co., Ltd. Beijing Branch, Shenzhen Yishihuolala Technology Co., Ltd. and other civil judgments of the second instance of labor disputes Civil Judgment of Linyi Intermediate People's Court of Shandong Province (2023) Lu 13 Min Zhong No. 1173.

95 Huang Jian v. Shenzhen Xichong Workers' Holiday Village Labor Dispute Case Civil Ruling of Guangdong Provincial People's High Court (2014) YGFMSZ No. 2161.

The fifth issue is the differential treatment of the length of service before and after January 1, 2008, the date when the Employment Contract Law came into effect and started to be implemented. If an employee joined an employer before this date, different policies for calculating economic compensation should be implemented for the two periods of service before and after January 1, 2008. Please refer to "167. How should I distinguish the calculation of economic compensation and punitive damages for service years before and after 2008?"

167. How should I distinguish the calculation of economic compensation and punitive damages for service years before and after 2008?

Answer: The implementation of the Employment Contract Law on January 1, 2008 changed the calculation rules of economic compensation. This piece of legislation specifically provides for a transitional, segmented treatment rule: the length of service of employees before 2008 is treated in accordance with the law before the implementation of the Law, and the length of service after 2008 is treated in accordance with the new rules under the Law.[96]

Specifically, under the following circumstances, the service years for calculating economic compensation shall only count for the period after January 1, 2008: 1) fixed-term contracts expire and are dissolved; 2) employees are forced to resign due to employers' non-compliance in social insurance; 3) employees are forced to resign due to the illegality of company rules and regulations; 4) employment contracts are invalid, resulting in employees being forced to resign. Employers are not liable to pay economic compensation for the foregoing four situations under the law before 2008; however, they are under the 2008 Employment Contract Law. For example, before 2008, an employer did not have to pay economic compensation for refusing to renew an expired fixed-term employment contract, while being liable if it did so after 2008.

We use a case to explain the aforementioned segmented treatment rule. Mr. Zhang joined a company in 2000. His monthly wage was RMB 8,000 when he was forced to resign in 2020 due to the company's non-compliance in social contribution. Before the implementation of the Employment Contract Law in 2008, the employee's resignation due to employer's non-compliance in social insurance was not statutorily compensable. Therefore, in accordance with the segmented treatment rule, Mr. Zhang's calculable length of service for economic compensation is only 12 years from 2008 to 2020, instead of 20 years from 2000 to 2020, rendering the compensable number of months 12 months instead of 20 months. Therefore, his entitled economic compensation should be RMB 96,000 (12 * 8,000).

As for whether the foregoing three types of resignations, due to non-compliance in social insurance, invalidity of employment contract, and illegality of company rules and regulations, are statutorily compensable forced resignations, please refer to "143. Are employers liable for economic compensation for employees' forced resignation?"

---

96 Article 97 of the Employment Contract Law: "Where an employment contract in existence on the implementation date of this Law is dissolved or terminated after the implementation of this Law, and economic compensation shall be made in accordance with Article 46 hereof, the number of years for economic compensation shall be calculated from the implementation date of this Law. Prior to the implementation of this law, in accordance with the relevant provisions at that time, the employer shall make economic compensation to the worker in accordance with the relevant provisions at that time."

It should be noted that although employers are liable for economic compensation for the foregoing four situations while distinguishing the service years before and after 1 January 2008 (e.g., the segmented treatment rule), the calculation of punitive damages due to illegal termination remains unaffected by the segmented treatment rule.[97] That is to say, in the same case as before, if Mr. Zhang is illegally dismissed in 2020, the punitive damages for illegal dismissal should be RMB 320,000 (20 * 2 * 8,000) instead of RMB 256,000 (8 * 8,000 + 12 * 2 * 8,000), following the segmented treatment rule to calculate the economic compensation for the years before 2008 and the punitive damages (which is double the economic compensation) for the period after 2008.[98]

168. How do I calculate the payment in lieu of notice?

Answer: According to Article 40 of the Employment Contract Law, an employer must give one month's notice in advance to terminate their employee on the grounds of the employee's health incompetence or ability incompetence and major change in objective situation. The employer must pay one month's wages in lieu of notice if it fails to give the one month's notice in advance or chooses immediate termination without continuing the one-month notice period.

The Labor Law and the Employment Contract Law do not stipulate the calculation method for the one-month wage in lieu of notice. At present, courts around the country take several approaches.

The first, held by Guangdong Provincial High Court, Shenzhen Intermediate Court, and Guangzhou Intermediate Court, is that the payment in lieu of notice is the same monthly wage standard for calculating economic compensation,. Specifically, the payment in lieu of notice is based on the employee's average monthly wages from the 12 months immediately before the termination. However, if this average monthly wage exceeds three times the local employees' average monthly wage of the previous year, the payment in lieu of notice is set at three times the local employees' average monthly wage of the previous year.[99] Please see "164. How do I calculate economic compensation?"

The second approach, typically taken by Xiangtan Intermediate Court and Hunan Province, refers to the employee's average wages from the 12 months immediately before the termination without the capping restriction.[100] The third approach is under the Regulations on the Implementation of the Employment Contract Law, which determine

97 Article 25 of the Regulations on the Implementation of the Employment Contract Law of the People's Republic of China, "If an employer dissolves or terminates an employment contract in violation of the provisions of the Employment Contract Law, it shall not pay economic compensation if it has paid punitive damages in accordance with the provisions of Article 87 of the Employment Contract Law. The calculation period of compensation shall be calculated from the date of employment."

98 Before 2008, employers were only liable for economic compensation in the case of illegal termination.

99 Labor Dispute between Li Gaoqin and Philips Jinkewei (Shenzhen) Industrial Co., Ltd. Civil Judgment of Shenzhen Intermediate People's Court of Guangdong Province (2015) S.Z.F.L.Z.Z. No. 648. Zhang Zhixiang and Ruiyunda Trading (Shanghai) Co., Ltd. Civil Judgment of the Second Instance of Labor Dispute Civil Judgment of Guangzhou Intermediate People's Court of Guangdong Province (2020) Yue 01 Min Zhong No. 25000 and No. 25001. Lv Yue and Huizhou Chuangcheng Development Co., Ltd. Civil Judgment of Second Instance of Labor Dispute Civil Judgment of Guangdong Provincial People's High Court (2019) Yue Min Zhong No. 1592.

100 Hunan Yipu Electric System Co., Ltd., Shuxiong, Sound Group Co., Ltd. Civil Judgment of Second Instance of Labor Dispute Hunan Xiangtan Intermediate People's Court Civil Judgment (2019) Xiang 03 Min Zhong No. 2178. Guo Jingshen et al. and Cao Xing et al. Labor Dispute Civil Judgment of Second Instance Beijing the First intermediate People's Court Civil Judgment (2021) Jing 01 Min Zhong No. 7032.

it as per the employee's wages of the previous month before the termination, including overtime wages. This amount is not subject to the cap and the average wage from the previous 12 months.[101]

Article 41 of the Employment Contract Law stipulates that an employer must notify the trade union or employee congress one month in advance when implementing economic redundancy, but it does not stipulate whether the employer is liable for payment in lieu of notice if it fails to notify. At present, the prevailing court decisions appears to refer to the practice of Article 40 of the Employment Contract Law. That is, if the employer does not give 30 days' notice in advance, it is liable for 1 month's wage in lieu of notice.[102] However, a few courts, such as Liaoning Province Shenyang Intermediate Court, held that the employer is not liable for payment in lieu of notice in economic redundancy.[103]

169. Are employers liable for wage losses after illegally terminating employees?

Answer: Article 48 of the Employment Contract Law stipulates that if an employer unlawfully terminates an employment contract, the employee can request reinstatement or claim punitive damages for the illegal termination of the employment contract, and the employee should choose only one from the two options. If the employee chooses to claim punitive damages for the illegal termination of the employment contract, thereby acknowledging the termination of the employment relationship, the employee has no right to claim compensation for wage losses after the termination of the employment relationship, regardless of whether they quickly find new employment.

The semantic exegesis of the statutory provision should be that the intent of the punitive damages is not only to punish the employer for illegal termination but also to compensate the employee for wage losses after the termination. Judicial practice follows this principle. For example, in the case of Zhu Changyin v. Wuxi Xianxing Silkworm Silk Mill in 2014, where the employee claimed punitive damages and wage losses after being unlawfully terminated by the employer, the Jiangsu High Court upheld the lower court's decision upholding the punitive damages but dismissing the claim for wage losses.[104]

Disputes over wage losses resulting from illegal dismissal by employers mainly arise in cases where employees request reinstatement of employment. In practice, after an employer serves a notice of termination of employment, employees typically cease work and then file an employment dispute arbitration application seeking reinstatement; and then, the employer stops wage payment. This includes two scenarios: the first scenario is where the labor arbitration commission or the court ultimately orders the reinstatement of

101 Article 20 of the Regulations on the Implementation of the Employment Contract Law of the People's Republic of China: "If an employer chooses to pay an additional month's wage to terminate the employment contract with an employee according to article 40 of the Employment Contract Law, the additional wage shall be determined according to the wage standard of the previous month of the employee."

102 Cen Dongming and Guangxin Maritime Heavy Industry Co., Ltd. Civil Judgment of Second Instance of Labor Dispute Civil Judgment (2021) Yue 20 Min Zhong No. 3226 of Intermediate People's Court of Zhongshan City, Guangdong Province, Guangxin. "The company has notified Cen Dongming to terminate the employment relationship one month in advance, so there is no legal basis for payment in lieu of notice claimed by Cen Dong Ming, and the court of first instance rejecting the claim is rightful."

103 Cai Heping, Shenyang Shidoke Electric Power Equipment Co., Ltd. Civil Judgment of Second Instance of Labor Dispute Civil Judgment of Shenyang Intermediate People's Court of Liaoning Province (2021) Liao 01 Min Zhong No. 11092.

104 Zhu Changyin v. Wuxi Xianxing Silkworm Silk Mill Labor Dispute Application Jiangsu High People's Court Civil Ruling (2014) Su Shen San Min Shen Zi No. 070.

the employment relationship; the second scenario is where the labor arbitration commission or the court determines that reinstatement of the position is objectively impossible.

In the first scenario, the courts usually rule that the employer should compensate the employee for the wage losses before reinstatement. However, the amount of wage loss compensation is determined based on various factors such as whether the employee provided service, the employee's wages or the local minimum wage standards, whether the employee had other sources of income, and whether the employee was at fault for the wage loss. For example, in a labor dispute case between Sui and a freight company in Beijing in 2023, the Beijing High Court found that the company illegally terminated the employment relationship and should reinstate the employee, and then determined by discretion the wage loss before reinstatement at 60% of the agreed salary.[105] In another case in 2021 involving Shi Yinghua and Jinzun Real Estate Development company in Beijing, the employee's labor arbitration application for reinstatement was upheld; However, the court did not uphold the claim of wage loss based on the fact that the employee had income from other employment after the termination and that there was no actual wage loss.[106]

It is worth noting that Article 25 of the 2023 Consultation Draft on the Interpretation of the Supreme People's Court on the Application of Law in the Trial of Labor Dispute Cases (II) stipulates that if an employer illegally dismisses an employee and the dismissal is illegal while reinstatement is realistic, the employer should compensate the employee's wage losses based on the normal wage standard (which excludes overtime wages), and that the labor arbitration committee or court should determine the proportion of compensation based on the faults of both parties, such as whether the employee delayed filing a labor arbitration, whether the employee has other employment relationships, and other factors.

For the second scenario, most court decisions tend to establish that the employment relationship cannot be restored and is thus terminated; therefore, the employer is not obligated to compensate the employee for wage losses incurred after the termination of the employment relationship. Examples of such judgments include the labor dispute case between Fu Haitao and Wuhan Jinma Kaixuan Real Estate Co., Ltd. in the Hubei High People's Court in 2023, the labor dispute case between Liu Xiaoying and Guangdong Nanyou Foreign Service Co., Ltd. in the Guangdong High People's Court in 2020, and the labor dispute case between Liu Xinyao and Mars Wrigley Confectionery (China) Co., Ltd. in the Beijing High People's Court in 2019.[107]

105 Sui v. a Certain Freight Transport Company Labor Dispute Retrial Review and Trial Supervision Civil Judgment Beijing High People's Court Civil Judgment (2023) Jing Civil Application No. 5972.

106 Shi Yinghua v. Beijing Jinzun Real Estate Development Co., Ltd. Labor Dispute Retrial Review and Trial Supervision Civil Judgment, Beijing High People's Court Civil Judgment (2021) Jing Civil Application No. 862.

107 Fu Haitao v. Wuhan Jinma Kaixuan Real Estate Co., Ltd., Hubei High People's Court (2023) EMinZai No. 66. In this case, the employer unlawfully terminated the employment relationship, and the employee requested reinstatement. However, the court determined that it was objectively impossible to reinstate the employee, so it did not support the claim for wage losses. Liu Xiaoying v. Guangdong Nanyou Foreign Service Co., Ltd., Guangdong High People's Court (2020) Yueshen Nos. 4720 and 4721. The court found that the employer illegally dismissed the employee, but the employment relationship could not be restored, and the employer had already paid punitive damages above the statutory standard. Therefore, the claim for wage losses was not supported. Liu Xinyao v. Mars Wrigley Confectionery (China) Co., Ltd., Beijing High People's Court (2019) Jingminshen No. 2106. In this case, the employer unlawfully terminated the employment relationship, but the employee only sued for compensation for wage losses and reinstatement of the employment relationship. The court ruled that the employment relationship could not be reinstated and therefore was terminated and then dismissed both claims.

In a few cases where the court orders the employer to compensate for wage losses, the finding of amount also takes into account factors such as whether the employer illegally dismissed the employee, whether the employee provided labor, the employee's wage level or the local minimum wage standard, whether the employee had other sources of income, and whether the employee was at fault for the wage loss. For example, in the 2021 labor dispute case between Ding Le and Chengdu Xinqin Garden Trade Co., Ltd., where the employer illegally dismissed the employee and it was objectively impossible to restore the employment relationship after a lengthy legal process, the Sichuan High People's Court ruled that the employer should compensate the employee for wage losses during the dispute period based on the minimum wage standard, considering that the employee did not provide labor and also bore some fault for the wage loss.[108]

170. Can I get unemployment insurance benefit after I lose my job?

Answer: An employee who has lost their job must meet all the three conditions to be eligible for unemployment insurance: minimum one year of contribution of unemployment insurance before becoming unemployed, the termination being non-voluntary, and having registered for unemployment and actively seeking employment without success.[109]

The aforementioned non-voluntary termination refers to the terminations of employment contracts caused by: forced resignation of employees, proposition by employers, mutual agreement, expiration of employment contracts, or employer's dissolution, including bankruptcy or revocation of license, etc.[110] Employees' resignations or employees' having already received pension insurance benefits do not constitute non-voluntary termination.

Employees who meet the aforementioned conditions receive unemployment insurance benefits in a lump sum payment rather than monthly after their unemployment. The calculation of unemployment insurance benefits involves multiplying the number of months, determined by the employee's years of contribution, by the local standard of unemployment insurance benefits. If the employee is unemployed again, the entitled number of months shall be recalculated based on the new contribution years. The accumulative number of months of unemployment insurance benefit each employee may receive shall not exceed 24 months.[111]

---

108 Ding Le v. Chengdu Xinqinyuan Commercial Trading Co., Ltd., Sichuan High People's Court (2021) ChuangMinZai No. 120.

109 Article 45 of the Social Insurance Law of the People's Republic of China in 2018 states that "an unemployed person who meets the following conditions shall receive unemployment insurance benefits from the unemployment insurance fund: (1) The employer and the unemployed person have paid unemployment insurance premiums for one year before the unemployment; (2) The employment is terminated by the unemployed person voluntarily; (3) The unemployed person has registered for unemployment and has job seeking requirements."

110 Article 16 of the Regulations on Unemployment Insurance of Guangdong Province in 2022.

111 Article 46 of the Social Insurance Law of the People's Republic of China in 2018. "If the employer and the unemployed person have paid contributions for more than one year but less than five years before unemployment, the maximum period for receiving unemployment insurance benefits shall be 12 months; if the employer and the unemployed person have paid contributions for more than five years but less than ten years, the maximum period for receiving unemployment insurance benefits shall be 18 months; If the accumulative payment is more than 10 years, the maximum period for receiving unemployment insurance benefits shall be 24 months. In case of re-unemployment after re-employment, the time of payment shall be recalculated, and the period of receiving unemployment insurance benefits shall be combined with the period of receiving unemployment insurance benefits that should have been received but not yet received in the previous unemployment,

For example, Mr. Zhang of Guangdong Province was unemployed after four years of working and contributing unemployment insurance, then re-employed after six months, and unemployed again after two years of working. Guangdong Province stipulates that if the contribution is less than four years, the unemployment insurance benefits shall be determined by the years of contribution, one year contribution enabling one month of unemployment insurance benefit,[112] and the local unemployment insurance benefit standard is RMB 1,000. How much unemployment insurance benefit can Mr. Zhang get?

When Mr. Zhang is unemployed for the first time, the contribution years are four years, so Mr. Zhang can receive unemployment insurance benefit of RMB 4,000 (4 * 1000). When Mr. Zhang is unemployed for the second time, the contribution duration is two years (because he has received unemployment insurance benefits for the first time, the payment period is reset to zero and re-accrued), so Mr. Zhang can still receive unemployment insurance benefit of RMB 2,000 (2 * 1000). It should be noted that since Mr. Zhang has received unemployment insurance benefit for a total of 6 months, the total amount of unemployment insurance benefit that Mr. Zhang may receive in the future cannot exceed 18 (24 − 6) months of unemployment insurance benefits.

If an employer has not purchased unemployment insurance for an employee, the employee has the right to claim the loss of the aforementioned unemployment insurance benefits from the employer. For example, in the previous case, if the employer did not purchase unemployment insurance for Mr. Zhang, then Mr. Zhang can claim the unemployment insurance benefits of RMB 4,000 from the first employer when he first becomes unemployed. For the second time he becomes unemployed, Mr. Zhang can claim RMB 2,000 of unemployment insurance benefits from the second employer who did not purchase unemployment insurance for him. However, compensation standards may vary across different regions due to local regulations. For instance, Chongqing Municipality requires employers to compensate 120% of the unemployment insurance benefits, while Guangxi Zhuang Autonomous Region stipulates double the amount of unemployment insurance compensation.[113]

This is a relatively obscure employee's employment right. Employees whose employer did not buy unemployment insurance, and whose employment was terminated on a non-voluntary basis, are entitled to claim from the employer for unemployment insurance benefit as well as economic compensation or punitive damages. If an employer who has purchased unemployment insurance for an employee fails to provide the employee with a certificate of termination of employment relationship in time, resulting in the employee's inability to apply for unemployment insurance benefits, they may also be liable for compensation for unemployment insurance benefits.[114]

---

and the maximum period shall not exceed 24 months." Article 47, "The standard of unemployment insurance benefits shall be determined by the people's governments of provinces, autonomous regions, or municipalities directly under the Central Government, and shall not be lower than the minimum living standard of urban residents."

112 Article 17 of the Regulations of Guangdong Province on Unemployment Insurance in 2022.

113 According to Article 13 of the "Implementation Measures for Chongqing Municipality's Unemployment Insurance Regulations." Articles 24 and 36 of the "Measures for Unemployment Insurance in the Guangxi Zhuang Autonomous Region."

114 Anhui High Court Releases Typical Case of Judicial Protection of Workers' Labor Rights in Anhui Province (2013–2016) No.10: Labor Dispute Case of Tao v. a Pharmaceutical Company in Huainan—If the employer terminates the employment contract illegally, it shall compensate the workers for economic compensation, unemployment insurance, etc.

171. Under what circumstances should employers be liable for supplementary damages?

Answer: Supplementary damages are different from punitive damages due to illegal termination of the employment relationship. The term refers to the liability employers must assume as stipulated in Article 85 of the Employment Contract Law: if an employer is involved in unjustified arrears or deductions of wages and overtime wages, payment of wages lower than the local minimum wage, or failure of payment of economic compensation, and subsequently fails to rectify the issues(s) after the labor administrative authority orders a correction, the employer is liable to pay supplementary damages ranging from 50% to 100% of the amount owed.[115] The term "supplementary damages" probably originates from judicial decisions.[116]

That is to say, if an employee is forced to resign under the employment laws, they not only have the right to request the employer to pay economic compensation, but also may ask the employer to pay additional damages when certain conditions are met. According to the provisions of that article of the Employment Contract Law, the aforementioned conditions are: first, the employee must first complain to the labor administrative authority about the unjustified wage arrears, wages lower than the local minimum wage, and failure of payment of economic compensation, etc.; second, the employer fails to respond to the labor administrative authority's correction order, the necessary pre-processing.

At present, the vast majority of court cases stipulate that the pre-processing of the labor administrative authority is the prerequisite for supplementary damages, including the cases from Guangzhou City of Guangdong Province, Jilin Province, Shandong Province, and Ningbo and Jiaxing Courts in Zhejiang Province.[117] However, this is a very obscure claim item. In the practical cases we have seen, virtually none of the employees took administrative complaint measures but directly initiated employment arbitration for these supplementary damages; therefore, their claims for the supplementary damages were not supported.

The case of Wu Hanmin before Hubei Provincial High Court in 2017 is a rare opposite case. The court held that the lower court's view that the supplementary damages are subject to the administrative pre-processing was a mistake in applying the law, and directly changed the judgment to the employee being entitled to the supplementary damages.[118]

---

115 It should be noted that these damages are totally different from the punitive damages for illegal termination under Article 87 of the Employment Contract Law.

116 For example, in the retrial case of the labor dispute between Sun Qixiang and Jilin Medas Light Alloy Co., Ltd., Civil Judgment No. (2020) ZuiGaoFaMinZai No. 50 issued by the Supreme People's Court of the People's Republic of China. In this case, the court referred to the damages under Article 85 of the Employment Contract Law as supplementary damages.

117 Civil Judgment of the Second Instance of Labor Dispute between Qu Jianzhong and Heli Forklift Co., Ltd. Civil Judgment of the Intermediate People's Court of Jiaxing City, Zhejiang Province (2019) Zhe 04 Min Zhong No. 487. Li Sicong, Ningbo Beilun Zixuan Entertainment Management Co., Ltd. and other civil judgments of the second instance of labor disputes, Zhejiang Ningbo Intermediate People's Court Civil Judgment (2021) Zhe 02 Min Zhong 4911. Liao Liping, Guangzhou Ruisheng Yanxi Trading Co., Ltd. and other civil judgments of the second instance of labor disputes, Guangzhou Intermediate People's Court of Guangdong Province, Civil Judgment (2021) Yue 01 Minzhong No. 26149. Guo Jian and COFCO Biochemical Energy (Gongzhuling) Co., Ltd. Labor Dispute Review Case Jilin Provincial People's High Court Civil Ruling (2016) Ji Min Shen No. 922. Civil Ruling on Labor Dispute Civil Application for Retrial Review by Pei Xiangqin and Weihai Keyuan International Freight Forwarding Co., Ltd. Civil Ruling of Shandong High Court (2022) Lu Min Shen No. 10218.

118 Civil Judgment on Labor Dispute Retrial of Wu Hanmin and Wuhan Baoan Group Co., Ltd. Civil Judgment of Hubei High Court (2017) E Min Zai No. 398.

5.4 Other Issues for Employment Termination

172. My medical care leave does not expire, but my fixed-term employment contract does. Can my employer terminate the employment contract?

Answer: Your employer now cannot terminate the employment contract on the ground of contract expiration. Article 42 of the Employment Contract Law stipulates that employers must not terminate the employment contract if an employee is ill or suffer from non-work injury and is on their prescribed medical care leave.

Unlike when an employee reaches the retirement age, when the employment contract of a fixed-term employee expires before the medical care leave does, the employee still has the right to continue to apply for and take the medical care leave according to a medical certificate from a medical institution, and the employer must extend the employment contract until the medical care leave expires (even if the employee has not recovered). Only then can the employment relationship be terminated on the ground of expiration of the employment contract. Please see "81. I am an employee. How many days of paid sick leave am I entitled to?" and "85. What should I do if an employee of my company has not recovered after the expiration of the medical care leave?"

If an employee suffers from a refractory disease that may affect their ability to work, the employer, before making a decision on the employment relationship, should obtain a labor capacity appraisal decision from the labor appraisal committee referencing the appraisal standards of disability degree for work-related injury or occupational disease.

For employees who are identified as Class 1 to 4 of disability, the employer shall stand them down from their positions, terminate their employment relationships, and proceed with medical retirement due to illness or non-work-related injuries. The employees shall receive the corresponding retirement entitlements; for employees who are identified as Class 5 to 10 of disability, the employer may terminate the employment contract and pay economic compensation (1 month's wage for 1 year's length of service, plus 30 days' notice in advance or a payment in lieu of notice) and medical subsidies (see "153. Under what circumstances should our company pay medical treatment allowance to our employees?"). For the calculation method for the economic compensation by the employer, please see "164. How do I calculate economic compensation?"

173. My employer illegally fired me. Can I request reinstatement?

Answer: Under Article 48 of the Employment Contract Law, if an employer unlawfully terminates an employee's employment relationship, the employee may request to be reinstated, e.g., continue performing the employment contract. Reinstatement is often very important for employees who are unlawfully terminated, as it may relate to their basic subsistence.

However, there are exceptions to the employer's obligation to reinstate. Although the aforementioned legal provision does not specify the application scope for the exception, based on current judicial decisions nationwide, the basic requirement for this exception is that the objective situation renders reinstatement impossible. These situations include the employer's organizational adjustments involving the position, the parties having completely lost basic trust and confidence, and the employee's position having had a substitute.

For example, in the 2017 case of Zhang Zhimin v. Eimer (Beijing) Holding Group Co., Ltd., the Third Beijing Intermediate People's Court held that the employee's position had been assigned to another person, that the original employment contract could no longer be performed, and that reinstatement was not upheld.[119] In the 2023 case of Yang Xuejing v. Swiss Reinsurance Company, the Beijing High People's Court held that the parties had clearly lost the basic trust to implement the employment contract due to the employee's complaint of the superior supervisor eavesdropping and secretly recording, that the parties had been involved in disputes for five years, and that it was impossible to continue to implement the contract.[120]

Employees can only elect either reinstatement or punitive damages as the claim. If an employee chooses to continue to implement the employment contract and be reinstated in the position, they cannot claim for punitive damages for illegal termination of the employment contract. The court may order the employer to pay punitive damages if the employee claims for reinstatement, which is subsequently found impossible. For the calculation method of punitive damages, please refer to "165. How do I calculate punitive damages for illegal termination of the employment relationship?"

174. Can employees hold their employer's boss personally liable for their labor remunerations or compensations?

Answer: Whether the boss of the company should compensate, with their personal assets as unlimited liability, employees' wages, economic compensation, and other employment entitlements (hereafter refer to employment debts or employment claim) first depends on the types of different employers. Compared with the insolvency distribution, the boss's personal liability for compensation is often a more effective way for employees to recover their employment claims.

The owner of a partnership enterprise shall generally bear personal liability for the employment debts to its employees. The partners of a general partnership and the general partners of a limited partnership shall bear unlimited joint and several liability for the debts of the enterprise, including employment debts. That is to say, employees can ask all or any of these partners to compensate their employment claims with their personal assets, without considering the distribution of liabilities among partners. Moreover, even if a partner withdraws from the partnership, if the employment debt occurs during their tenure as a partner, the partner is still liable for compensation. The only exception is limited partners in a limited partnership.[121]

The bosses of sole traders should also bear personal responsibility. According to Article 56 of "the Civil Code," debts incurred during the operation of the sole trader's business

119 Zhang Zhimin v. E-MERCK (Beijing) Holdings Group Co., Ltd. Labor Dispute Appeal Case Beijing the Third Intermediate People's Court Civil Judgment (2017) Jing 03 Min Zhong No. 4680.

120 Yang Xuejing v. Swiss Reinsurance Company Limited Beijing Branch, Labor Dispute Retrial Case Beijing High People's Court Civil Ruling (2023) Jing Min Shen 1496.

121 Article 2 of the Partnership Enterprise Law, "The term 'partnership enterprise' as mentioned in this Law refers to a general partnership enterprise or a limited partnership enterprise established within the territory of China by a natural person, legal person or other organization in accordance with this Law. A general partnership consists of general partners, who bear unlimited joint and several liability for the debts of the partnership. Where there are special provisions on the form of liability of general partners in this Law, such provisions shall prevail. A limited partnership consists of a general partner and a limited partner. The general partner is jointly and severally liable for the debts of the partnership, and the limited partner is liable for the debts of the partnership to the extent of their subscribed capital contribution." Article 53 stipulates: "a withdrawn partner shall bear unlimited joint and several liability for the debts of the partnership arising from causes prior to the withdrawal."

shall be borne by personal assets if the business is operated under their personal name, or by all family assets if it is operated under the family's name or in an undistinguishable way.

The owner of a sole proprietorship enterprise also needs to take personal responsibility for employment debts. Article 2 of the Sole Proprietorship Enterprise Law stipulates that "a sole proprietorship enterprise referred to in this Law means a business entity established within the territory of China in accordance with this Law, invested by a natural person, whose assets are personally owned by the investor, and whose investor bears unlimited liability for the debts of the entity with their personal assets."

For the most common limited liability company situation, owners or shareholders of limited liability companies do not bear personal liability for employment debts. However, there are exceptions. Please see "175. Is the boss of a limited liability company personally liable for outstanding wages?"

175. Is the boss of a limited liability company personally liable for outstanding wages?

Answer: In most circumstances, the shareholders or boss of a limited liability company do not need to bear personal liability for wages or other employment debts owed. This is because under the legal framework of a limited company, the company is only liable for the debts within the limits of the company's assets, isolating the owner from the liability.

Whether the boss or shareholder of a company should use their personal assets to repay the wages owed to their employees is the issue of "piercing the corporate veil" (or denial of legal personality) under the company law to pursue their personal liability to pay off debts. According to the Company Law, the judicial interpretation of the Supreme Court and judicial decisions, in the following exceptional cases, the shareholders or owners of a company shall bear the obligation to repay the debts of the company.

The first situation is the commingling of company assets and the personal assets of the boss and shareholder. Paragraph 3 of Article 23 of the Company Law stipulates that "if a shareholder of a one-person limited liability company cannot prove that the company's assets are independent of the shareholder's own assets, they shall bear joint and several liability for the company's debts." For example, in the case of Cao Jianqiao in 2021, the Intermediate People's Court of Zibo City, Shandong Province found that the shareholder failed to prove the independence of the company's assets and personal assets, and that there was a personal act of paying wages to employees, and thus, it ordered the shareholder to compensate for the wages owed to employees.[122]

The commingling of shareholders' property in an ordinary limited liability company is more complicated. The denial of the legal personality of a limited company is mainly based on Article 23 of the 2023 Company Law and the 2019 Summary of the National Courts' Civil and Commercial Trial Work Conference.[123] The Summary stipulates that the commingling

122 Cao Jianqiao, Wang Wenyu, and Other Labor Providers' Liability Dispute Civil Judgment of Second Instance Civil Judgment of Zibo Intermediate People's Court of Shandong Province (2021) Lu 03 Min Zhong No. 1668.

123 The 2019 Summary of the National Courts' Civil and Commercial Trial Work Conference points out that "Section 4 Denial of Corporate Personality. The independence of corporate personality and the limited liability of shareholders are the basic principles of the Company Law. In judicial practice, we should accurately grasp the spirit of Article 20, paragraph 3, of the Company Law (Note: this is paragraph 1 of Article 23 of the 2023 Company Law): First, only when shareholders abuse the independent status of corporate legal person and the limited liability of shareholders and act seriously damages the interests of the creditors of the company can it be applied. Damaging the interests of creditors mainly refers to the abuse of rights by shareholders to make

of shareholders' and company's assets should have the following characteristics: the first characteristic is that shareholders abuse the legal system of a limited liability company (mainly, shareholders encroach on the interests of the company);[124] the second characteristic is that this behavior causes the loss of creditors' interests. If it can be determined that the shareholders' and the company's assets are commingled, the shareholders should bear personal liability for the company's debts.

The second situation is that shareholders make false capital contributions or insufficient capital contributions, or withdraw capital contributions or help other shareholders to make false capital contributions when the company is established. As limited companies are publicly registered business entities, the law requires shareholders to make real capital contributions; otherwise, it is a dishonest act related to asset credibility to the general public and specific traders. When the company is unable to discharge its debts, creditors certainly have the right to require the shareholders to bear the liability within the scope of their false or insufficient capital contributions.

In practice, the biggest challenge for creditors (including employees) pursuing shareholders is evidence collection. Because shareholders' investment records and other information are controlled by the company, ordinary people and even lawyers may not be able to access them, and the courts are not necessarily willing to take the initiative to investigate and collect evidence in the process of hearing the case in China.

The third situation is that shareholders violate the law and harm the interests of creditors in the course of the company's operation, such as failing to liquidate in time after the

---

the company's property insufficient to pay off the creditor's rights to the company. Secondly, only the shareholders who abuse the independent status of legal person and the limited liability of shareholders bear joint and several liability for the company's debts, while other shareholders should not bear this liability. Thirdly, the denial of corporate personality is not a comprehensive, thorough, and permanent denial of the company's legal personality, but a breakthrough in the general rule that shareholders are not liable for the company's debts only in specific cases according to specific legal facts and legal relations, as exceptional decisions ordering them jointly and severally liable. 10. Personality commingling. To determine whether there is commingling between corporate personality and shareholder personality, the most fundamental criterion is whether the company has independent will and independent property, and the most important manifestation is whether the company's property and shareholder's property are commingled and cannot be distinguished. The following factors should be taken into consideration when determining whether it constitutes a personality commingling: (1) the shareholder uses the company's fund or property without compensation, and no financial records are made; (2) the shareholder uses the company's funds to repay the shareholder's debts, or uses the company's funds for affiliated companies without compensation, and no financial records are made; (3) there is no distinction between the account books of the company and the account books of the shareholder, which makes it impossible to distinguish the company's property from the shareholder's property; (4) there is no distinction between the shareholder's own income and the company's profits, which makes the interests of both parties unclear; (5) the company's property is recorded under the name of the shareholder and is occupied and used by the shareholder; (6) other circumstances of personality commingling. In the case of personality commingling, the following commingling often occurs at the same time: commingling of company business and shareholder business; commingling of company employees and shareholder employees, especially financial personnel; commingling of company residence and shareholder residence. When the people's court hears a case, the key is to examine whether it constitutes a personality commingling, but not to require the commingling of other aspects at the same time, which is often only the reinforcement of the personality commingling."

124 Article 10 of the Summary of the 2019 National Courts' Civil and Commercial Trial Work Conference points out that the most fundamental criterion for denying the personality of a legal person is whether the company has independent will and property, and the most important manifestation is whether the property of the company is commingled with that of shareholders and cannot be distinguished. We are of the view that this kind of non-independence and commingling actually includes two situations: the shareholders encroach on the company's property, or the company uses the shareholders' property. In judicial practice in China, the court denying legal personality and investigating the shareholder's responsibility covers only the first situation.

company's closure, abusing shareholders' power to transfer assets, and violating the law in the process of deregistration of the company (such as providing false information in deregistration procedures).

Paragraph 1 of Article 23 of the 2023 Company Law stipulates that shareholders of a company shall abide by laws, administrative regulations, and the articles of association, shall exercise their rights in accordance with the law, and shall not abuse the independent status of the company (a legal person) and the limited liability of shareholders to damage the interests of creditors of the company. Where any of the shareholders of a company evades the payment of its debts by abusing the independent status of legal person or the limited liabilities of the shareholders, thus seriously damaging the interests of any creditor, they shall bear joint and several liabilities for the debts of the company.

Article 19 of the Provisions of the Supreme People's Court on Several Issues Concerning the Application of the Company Law of the People's Republic of China (2) stipulates that "where shareholders of limited liability companies, directors and controlling shareholders of joint stock limited companies, and actual controllers of companies maliciously dispose of company assets after the dissolution of a company, causing losses to creditors, or cheat the company registration authority to revoke its registration with a false liquidation report without liquidation according to law, and the creditors claim for the corresponding liability for compensation for the debts of the company against them, the people's court shall uphold it according to law."

The fourth situation is that the shareholder undertakes a guarantee or a promise to pay off the company's debts. In this case, the shareholder should of course fulfill their liability for compensation according to their guarantee obligation and the promise to pay off the debts.

176. Under what circumstances may a departed employee need to compensate the former employer?

Answer: An employee may still liable for compensation for unlawfully terminating the employment relationship or violation of the agreed contractual obligations after the termination. There are five possible situations.

The first situation is that the employee did not resign according to the law, resulting in loss to the employer. This situation encompasses the employee's resignation with a less than three-day advance notice during the probation period and a less than one-month advance notice during the regular contract period. The critical question in determining the employee's liability for compensation in these cases is whether the employer has suffered actual direct losses and whether there is a causal relationship between the employee's illegal resignation and the alleged losses. Please see "177. Is an employee liable for the employer's losses caused by inadequate notice of resignation?"

The second situation is that the employee fails to fulfill the terms of the training service agreement signed by both parties, resulting in their liability for the contractual damages. The primary factors in determining employees' compensation obligations encompass the scope of training, determination of training fees and contractual damages, and the reasonableness of the service period agreement. Please refer to "179. Are employees who resign in breach of their training service agreements liable for contractual damages?"

The third situation is that the employee infringes on the employer's trade secret. If the employee has ever made contact with the trade secret, they are subject to an absolute protection obligation to refrain from illegally acquiring, disclosing, and using the secret. Any breach of the obligation shall result in the employee's liability for damages. Please refer to "181. How do employers protect their trade secrets?"

The fourth situation is that the employee violates the non-competition agreement signed with the employer. Non-competition is a measure permitted by law to restrict departed employees from engaging in competitive industries in order to proactively protect employers' trade secrets. Employees who violate the obligation of non-competition may be liable to pay contractual damages to the employer. Please see "197. What is non-competition and liability for breach of non-competition?"

The fifth situation is that employees' on-the-job misconduct causes losses to the employer that are found or occur after their employment has been terminated. This is a situation that is rare but is indeed documented in court decisions. Please see "178. Are employees who caused losses to their employers during their tenure liable for the same after their employments end?"

The liability of departing or departed employees to compensate their former employer's losses is a one-time, civil-like responsibility, distinct from the liability of current employees to compensate their employers' losses, which is subject to limitations on wage deductions. For detailed rules on the compensation of current employees for losses caused to the employer, please refer to "124. Should an employee compensate the employer for the losses caused by their fault?"

177. Is an employee liable for the employer's losses caused by inadequate notice of resignation?

Answer: Article 37 of the Employment Contract Law requires employees to provide a 30-day notice period for resignation during the regular contract period and a 3-day notice period during the probation period. If an employee resigns without adhering to the aforementioned legal requirements, and even departs without conducting any necessary handover procedures, it could potentially disrupt the employer's business operations or result in economic losses. As a result, the employee may be held liable for compensating the employer for any losses incurred.

According to Article 90 of the Employment Contract Law and Article 4 of the "Compensation Measures for Violations of the Labor Contract Provisions in the Labor Law" issued by the Ministry of Labor in 1995, the scope of compensation that employees should bear for resigning in violation of statutory rules includes the expenses incurred by the employer in recruiting and hiring them, as well as the direct economic losses caused to production and operation.[125] However, in practice, the most common losses related to employees' unlawful resignation are the direct economic losses to the employer.

---

125 Article 90 of the Employment Contract Law stipulates, "If an employee breaches this Law to terminate the employment contract, or breaches the confidentiality obligation or non-competition agreement stipulated in the labor contract, resulting in losses to the employer, the employee shall bear liability for compensation." According to Article 4 of the Notice of the Ministry of Labor on the Issuance of the "Compensation Measures for Violations of the Labor Contract Provisions in the Labor Law" (Laobufa [1995] No. 223), employees who violate the regulations or the provisions of their employment contract to terminate the employment contract, and cause losses to the employer, shall compensate the employer for the following losses: (1) the expenses incurred by the employer in recruiting and hiring them; (2) the training expenses paid by the employer, handled according to the agreement between the two parties if there is any; (3) the direct economic losses caused to

From judicial precedents, whether an employee needs to compensate the employer for losses due to their resignation and the amount of compensation depend on three conditions: whether the employee's resignation violates the provisions of the labor contract, company regulations, or statutory provisions; whether the employer has suffered actual losses; and whether there is a causal relationship between the employer's loss and the employee's resignation.

For the first condition, whether an employee's resignation violates the contractual agreement, company rules and regulations or statutory provisions can initially be judged based on whether they provided proper advance notice. If the employee did not comply with the legal requirement to provide 3 days' notice during the probation period or 30 days' notice during the regular contract period, or if the employee did not adhere to a longer notice period specified in the employment contract or company rules and regulations, then the employee's resignation would likely be considered a violation of the obligation to give advance notice. However, the employer also needs to examine the reason the employee provided for resigning. If the employee resigned because the employer violated Article 38 of the Employment Contract Law (for example, by unjustified deduction of the employee's wages), and this reason is substantiated, then the employee's resignation would be considered lawful. In such a case, the employer would not have a legal basis to demand compensation for losses from the employee.

The second condition is that the employer has actually suffered a direct loss. The employer should gather evidence to prove that the loss does exist, not merely the inconvenience and unhappiness caused by the employee's departure. Judicial decisions show that in numerous instances, employers' claims against employees for compensation for losses were not upheld by the courts simply because they failed to provide evidence of actual losses. Finally, the employer must prove the facts it alleges with evidence. If the courts determine that the employee's illegal resignation has indeed caused losses, they may determine the amount of losses in a discretionary way when the actual losses are difficult to determine.[126] The Chinese Contract Law distinguishes between direct losses and indirect losses, with the latter also referred to as loss of foreseeable profits, which are benefits that the non-breaching party could have obtained but did not due to the breach of contract by the breach party. The Compensation Measures for Violation of Labor Contract Provisions under the Labor Law stipulate that an employee's compensation obligation to the employer for illegal termination of the employment contract is limited to direct economic losses, which implies that such losses do not include loss of foreseeable profits.

The third condition is a causal relationship between the loss and the employee's illegal resignation.[127] Even if the court determines that the employer has suffered actual direct

---

production, operation, and work; (4) other expenses that should be compensated as stipulated in the employment contract.

126 Beijing Wanquanyuan Taxi Co., Ltd. and Wang Lixin Labor Dispute Civil Judgment of First Instance Beijing Pinggu District People's Court Civil Judgment (2021) Jing 0117 Min Chu No. 3750.

127 Guangdong Yingdu Law Firm v. Chen Ruimiao Labor Dispute Guangdong High Court Civil Ruling (2017) Yue Min Shen No. 5049. The employee (a lawyer) did not give a 30-day prior notice of the resignation. The court held that there was no direct connection between the employee's resignation and the client's cancellation of the service relationship, because the service contract did not stipulate that the service must only be provided by the employee. Civil Judgment of Second Instance of Labor Dispute between Liu Jinde and Shenzhen Dingfengda Precision Mould Injection Co., Ltd. Civil Judgment of Shenzhen Intermediate People's Court of Guangdong Province (2016) Yue 03 Min Zhong No. 4325. The court found that the employer failed to prove the losses or the causal link between the claimed losses and the employee's resignation without prior notice.

losses, whether the employee should bear the responsibility for compensation and the proportion of such responsibility still depends on the causal relationship. The judgment of the causal relationship should be based on an objective analysis of whether the contribution of the employee's illegal resignation to the loss is operating, rather than a possible consequence but for the employee's illegal resignation. Other factors that need to be considered include the specific background of the employee's resignation behavior and whether it has the characteristics of high subjective malice and constitutes a serious violation of professional ethics. Particularly, consideration should be given to see if the employer is at fault by failing to take preventive measures in its management. Normally, the higher the causation between the employee's unlawful resignation and the employer's loss, the more likely the employee is to be liable for the loss, and to bear a higher proportion in compensating the losses.

If we compare the conditions for employees to compensate their employers for losses due to breaching agreements or statutory provisions when resigning with the conditions for employees to compensate for losses caused to their employers while still being employed (please refer to "124. Should an employee compensate the employer for the losses caused by their fault?"), they are similar in the analysis of causality. Both involve a determination based on the elements of fault, loss, and causality, resembling a kind of liability akin to tort law. Additionally, determining and distributing losses in both cases requires considering the employer's management responsibility for the occurrence of the loss. However, the difference lies in the former being the responsibility of employees under the employment relationship, while the latter involves non-employee compensation obligations under the employment laws or employment contracts. For instance, in the former scenario, the employer can demand a one-time compensation based on general civil liability principles, but in the latter scenario, due to employment laws' tendency to strictly protect employees' interests, the compensation can only be deducted from the employee's wages on a monthly basis, subject to certain proportional limits.

178. Are employees who caused losses to their employers during their tenure liable for the same after their employments end?

Answer: The question of whether an employee should compensate their employer, after the employment terminates, for losses caused during their employment period seems to be a blank point in statutory provisions.

While Article 90 of the Employment Contract Law only stipulates that employees who illegally terminate their employment contracts (i.e., resign without prior notice), or violate confidentiality or non-competition obligations resulting in losses, should bear compensation responsibilities after employment termination, the 1994 Provisional Regulations on Wage Payment by the former Ministry of Labor only stipulate the compensation obligations of employees causing losses to employers while still being employed;[128] there are no laws or regulations governing whether and how employees should, after their employment terminates, compensate for losses caused during their employment period.

128 Article 16 of the 1994 Provisional Regulations on Wage Payment by the former Ministry of Labor: If the employee causes economic losses to the employer due to their own reasons, the employer may demand compensation for the economic losses according to the provisions of the labor contract.

As can be seen from judicial practice, the majority of court judgments indicate the following.

First, as long as employees' misconduct meets the criteria of intention or gross negligence, employers suffer losses, and there is a causal relationship between the misconducts and the losses, the employees still bear partial responsibility (due to the contribution of the employer's inherent management responsibilities). These liability criteria are similar to those for situations where employees resign without prior notice, causing losses to employers; please refer to "177. Is an employee liable for the employer's losses caused by inadequate notice of resignation?"

Second, these judgments typically cite Article 4 of the 1995 Compensation Measures for Violations of the Labor Contract Provisions in the Labor Law, which states that "employees who violate provisions or contractual agreements to terminate employment contracts, causing losses to employers, shall compensate employers." We believe this provision, from a semantic interpretation, should only apply to situations where employees resign without prior notice, as specified by law. However, this might be the most relevant or closest legal basis that courts can refer to in the absence of specific regulations, illustrating the courts' dilemma in the absence of relevant laws and regulations.

Furthermore, whether claiming the losses caused by employees' work-related faults during their employment period and the subsequent liability after termination for such losses fall under employment disputes or civil disputes remains contentious. While most cases are accepted, and therefore by implication classified, as employment disputes by labor arbitration committees and courts, there are a few instances (such as the 2013 case of Lang Wenjie v. Panjin Taihe Door and Window Manufacturing Co., Ltd. involving property damage compensation disputes) where courts have treated them as civil disputes. Such cases obviously fall outside the scope of the Employment Contract Law and the Supreme Court's 2020 Judicial Interpretation on Labor Disputes, suggesting the need to revise the scope of employment disputes in the judicial interpretation to include any disputes arising from labor relations.

Here are summaries of some court judgments that we have compiled for readers' reference.

In the case of Wang Juyin v. Nanning Haiqi Real Estate Development Co., Ltd. labor dispute in 2019, two accountants failed to report taxable items during their employment, resulting in a penalty of over RMB 50,000 imposed by the tax authority after their resignation. The Guangxi High Court ultimately ruled that the two former employees should bear 40% and 10% of the compensation for the losses, respectively.[129]

In the case of Lang Wenjie v. Panjin Taihe Doors and Windows Manufacturing Co., Ltd. property damage compensation dispute in 2013, an employee, as an engineering technician, made mistakes in measuring and designing window sizes, resulting in the company incurring a loss of over RMB 30,000 on a contracted project. The company deducted RMB 3,000 from the employee's wages for two months as compensation, and later, the employment contract was terminated by mutual agreement. After the employee resigned, the company sued the employee for compensation for the losses on the ground

129 Wang Juyin v. Nanning Haiqi Real Estate Development Co., Ltd. Labor Contract Dispute Reconsideration Review and Trial Supervision Civil Ruling, Guangxi Zhuang Autonomous Region Higher People's Court Civil Ruling (2019) Gui Min Shen 869.

of economic damages. The Panjin City Intermediate People's Court in Liaoning Province held that the employee's fault had caused the company's loss and ruled that the employee should bear 20% of the losses.[130]

In the case of Longchuan Hengxin Dental Hospital v. Cui Xiulan labor dispute in 2020, an employee, while employed as a dentist at the hospital, violated a no-moonlighting clause in the employment contract by opening a private clinic. The hospital subsequently terminated the employee's contract and filed an employment arbitration claim for compensation for losses. The labor arbitration committee struck out the claim. The Intermediate People's Court of Heyuan City, Guangdong Province, ruled that the employee, for violating the contract by engaging in unauthorized moonlighting, should compensate the hospital for its loss with a sum of RMB 100,000, equivalent to 30% of the standard income in the healthcare industry.[131]

In the case of Chen Honglu v. Qingdao Zhongda Yanjing Automobile Sales Co., Ltd., in 2022, the employee, a salesperson at an automobile sales company, engaged in serious violations of professional ethics during his employment, including forging customer signatures and allowing car delivery without receiving payment. These actions resulted in significant losses to the company. Although the labor arbitration application initiated by the company was not accepted (likely because the employee had already resigned and there was no employment relationship), the Qingdao City Intermediate People's Court in Shandong Province ruled that the employee should bear partial responsibility for the losses.[132]

In the case of Chuzhou Dingxing Refrigeration Equipment Engineering Co., Ltd. v. Lu Weili in 2018, an employee embezzled part of the group accident insurance premiums paid by the company, resulting in the employer having to pay extra compensation due to the shortfall in insurance compensation for an employee's personal injury accident. After the company terminated the employee's contract, it sued the employee for compensation for losses. The Intermediate People's Court of Chuzhou City, Anhui Province ruled that the employee should bear partial responsibility for the losses.[133]

In the case of Guizhou Haisan Decoration Engineering Co., Ltd. v. Song Zhaoyu in 2014, the employee, who served as a site manager for the decoration company, resigned after two years of employment. The company filed a labor arbitration claim for compensation for economic losses caused by the employee's intentional or gross negligence in managing the construction site during his employment. The court held that according to Article 90 of the Employment Contract Law, the employee's obligation to compensate is limited to losses arising from illegal termination of the employment contract or violation of confidentiality or non-competition obligations, and that the employee was not obligated

130 Lang Wenjie v. Panjin Taihe Door and Window Manufacturing Co., Ltd. Property Damage Compensation Dispute Appeal Case, Liaoning Panjin Intermediate People's Court Civil Judgment (2013) Pan Zhong Min Second Instance Case No. 00350.

131 Longchuan Hengxin Stomatological Hospital v. Cui Xiulan Labor Dispute Civil Second Instance Civil Judgment, Guangdong Heyuan Intermediate People's Court Civil Judgment (2020) Yue 16 Min Zhong No. 935.

132 Chen Honglu v. Qingdao Zhongda Yanjing Automobile Sales Co., Ltd. Labor Dispute Civil Second Instance Civil Judgment, Shandong Qingdao Intermediate People's Court Civil Judgment (2022) Lu 02 Min Zhong No. 4807.

133 Chuzhou Dingxing Refrigeration Equipment Engineering Co., Ltd. v. Lu Weili Labor Dispute Second Instance Civil Judgment, Anhui Chuzhou Intermediate People's Court Civil Judgment (2018) Wan 11 Min Zhong No. 3017.

to compensate for losses caused during employment, and therefore, the company's compensation claim was dismissed.[134]

179. Are employees who resign in breach of their training service agreements liable for contractual damages?

Answer: The penalty for training service agreement violation is the legally permissible liability for employers to recover their dedicated expenses in training employees and to penalize employees for breaches of mutual agreements on training service.

In principle, the penalty for an employee's violation of a training service agreement shall be calculated based on actually incurred training expenses in proportion to fulfilled and unfulfilled service duration. For example, in the case of He Mengyuan before Beijing Xicheng District Court in 2017, the pilot resigned before the service period set in the training agreement expired, and the court ordered the employee to pay RMB 1.31 million as the penalty.[135]

Whether employees have actually received training must be judged comprehensively according to the employment contract agreement and the nature of employees' participation in activities.[136] In principle, the training under training service agreements refers to trainings conducted through a third party training organization and paid by the employer to the third party, or trainings that are not conducted through a third party organization but that require special, expensive equipment, or training process, and for which the employers bear significant costs (such as pilot training). The general induction training or activities for employees within an employer's workplace are mainly ordinary internal trainings for production and operation, and should not be recognized as training in this regard.

Employers are responsible for providing evidence for the amount of training fees incurred, such as evidence of payment and receipt of training-related fees. When the amount of fees is hard to ascertain, the court may also decide on the basis of discretion or industry standards. For example, in the case of Xu Haiming before the Third Intermediate Court of Beijing in 2017 and the case of He Mengyuan before the Xicheng District Court of Beijing in 2017, the courts found the amount of training fee according to the actual costs and industry practices.[137] In addition, the Employment Contract Law explicitly stipulates that the scope of training fees only includes direct expenses related to training, such as

134 Guizhou Haisan Decoration Engineering Co., Ltd. v. Song Zhaoyu Labor Dispute Appeal Case, Guizhou Guiyang Intermediate People's Court Civil Judgment (2014) Zhuminsizhongzi No. 264.

135 He Mengyuan and China Post Aviation Co., Ltd. Civil Judgment of the First Instance of Labor Dispute, Beijing Xicheng District People's Court Civil Judgment (2017) Jing 0102 Minchu No. 5100. The pilot resigned in advance after signing the training agreement. The court ordered the employees to pay the training fee of RMB 1.31 million in proportion to the implementation of services according to the documents of the Civil Aviation Administration, rejecting the claim on contractual damages. The court of the second instance of the case upheld the original judgment.

136 Shenzhen Yataixing Industrial Co., Ltd. and BYD Automobile Industry Co., Ltd. Luo Zhikai Labor Dispute Second Instance Civil Judgment Shenzhen Intermediate People's Court of Guangdong Province Civil Judgment (2018) Yue 03 Min Zhong No. 4428. The court found that the employer's arrangement for employees to attend exhibitions abroad could not constitute training.

137 Xu Haiming and Aokai Airlines Co., Ltd. Labor Dispute Civil Judgment of Beijing the Third Intermediate People's Court (2017) No. 8973. "Regarding the determination of the amount of training fees, Aokai Airlines has submitted relevant evidence. It is not improper for the court of first instance to make a decision on the training fee payable by Xu Haiming based on the specific factors of the case, such as Xu Haiming's length of service, age and industry practice, taking into account the particularity of the aviation industry."

training course fees, travel expenses, etc. Therefore, both parties' mutual agreements on a discretionary training fee amount, or the wages of employees during the training period constituting the training fees, in the employment contract or training service agreement, shall be invalid.[138] Such expenses can be special benefits, such as accommodation spending paid for by employers for employees.[139]

The reasonableness of the length of the service period stipulated in the training agreement is also a problem that often arises in practice. The courts have different approaches. For example, Henan Pingdingshan Court held that the 15-year service period was not unreasonable in the case of Lan Zhuizhui in 2017, while Jiangsu Yancheng Intermediate Court held that it was obviously unreasonable for the employer to train employees for only two days but require them to serve for three years in the case of Zhou Min in 2022, ordering that the service period agreement was invalid.[140] Therefore, for the reasonableness of a training service period stipulated in the training service agreement, we should comprehensively examine the specific circumstances of the case, including the amount of training investment or expenses, the substitutability of training skills, and the length of the required service period.

The amount of contractual damages stipulated in a training service agreement must not exceed the training expenses and must be calculated according to the proportion of served period in the agreed-upon service period.[141] That is to say, even if the contractual damages exceed the actual training fees, the courts are still likely to calculate the compensation according to the proportion of served period and the amount of the actual training fees. For example, Mr. Zhang has agreed on a four-year training service period, and the employer has spent RMB 100,000 on the training for Mr. Zhang. If Mr. Zhang resigns at the end of the first year, the contractual damages should be RMB 75,000 ([4 − 1]/4 * 100,000). Even if the training agreement between the two parties stipulates a contractual damage of RMB 200,000, the court is likely to find the contractual damages as RMB 75,000.

However, if the parties stipulate both compensation for training fees and contractual damages in the training service agreement, there are two distinct court practices on

---

138 Guangdong High-tech Senior Technical School, Lin Yanghao Labor Dispute Civil Judgment of Second Instance Civil Judgment of Guangzhou Intermediate People's Court of Guangdong Province (2021) Yue 01 Min Zhong No. 22833. "According to Article 16 of the Regulations on the Implementation of the Employment Contract Law of the People's Republic of China, 'the training expenses provided in the paragraph 2 of Article 22 of the Employment Contract Law include the training expenses with invoices and paid by the employer for the professional and technical training of the workers, the travel expenses during the training period and other direct expenses incurred by the training for the workers.' The above provisions have clearly defined the scope of the training expenses. Although the Teacher Training Contract stipulates that wages and performance allowance during the training period will be included in the scope of training expenses, the provisions are inconsistent with the above statutory provisions. Therefore, the court of the first instance did not uphold the the high-tech school's claim that Lin Yanghao's wages during the training period should be included in the training expenses to calculate the contractual damages."

139 Article 26 of the 2023 Consultation Draft on the Interpretation of the Supreme People's Court on the Application of Law in the Trial of Labor Dispute Cases (II).

140 Dongtai Hongxue Art Training Co., Ltd. and Zhou Min Labor Dispute Civil Judgment of Second Instance Civil Judgment of Yancheng Intermediate People's Court of Jiangsu Province (2022) Su 09 Min Zhong No. 2265.

141 Article 22 of the Employment Contract Law of the People's Republic of China: "Where an employer provides special training fees for a worker and carries out professional and technical training for him, it may conclude an agreement with the worker to stipulate a service period. If a worker violates the agreement on the service period, he shall pay contractual damages to the employer in accordance with the agreement. The amount of contractual damages shall not exceed the training expenses provided by the employer."

whether both items can be upheld or just one. In the case of He Mengyuan in 2017, the Xicheng District Court of Beijing held that the employer could only selectively claim one of them, but the Pingdingshan Intermediate Court of Henan Province upheld both the employer's claims in the case of Lan Zhuizhui in 2017.[142]

Of course, the precondition for employees' being liable to compensate the employers for the penalty is that the employees breach the contract by resigning in advance. If the employer cannot prove the employee's resignation, and neither can the employee prove the employer's dismissal, the court may find that both parties terminated the employment contract by mutual agreement (please refer to "145. My boss fired me, but now he claims I resigned. What can I do?"). In addition, if the employee has a legitimate reason to terminate the contract, such as being forced to resign because of the employer's unjustified wage deduction, the employee is not liable for the contractual damages for breaching the training service agreement.[143] If the employer takes the initiative to terminate the employment contract, of course, the employee does not also have to bear the responsibility unless the employer legally terminates the employee due to the employee's serious violation of company rules and regulations.[144]

180. Is it legal for an employee to seek labor arbitration after reaching a compensation agreement with our company and already receiving payment?

Answer: Whether your employee can renege on the compensation agreement that has been signed and implemented depends on how the agreement is reached, whether the agreement is manifestly unfair, and whether the claim exceeds the limitation of arbitration.

The way the compensation agreement between the two parties is reached is very important. If the agreement is reached under the auspices of a court, a labor arbitration commission, or a state organ, the compensation agreement is legally binding or quasi-binding, and the employee may not go back on it. For example, in the case of Guangzhou Qiangye Company before Guangdong Provincial High Court in 2014, the court held that the mediation agreement reached by the two parties through the Labor Arbitration Commission could not be changed.[145]

---

142 The labor disputes Lantao v. Tianrui Group Co., Ltd., Henan Pingdingshan Intermediate People's Court Civil Judgment Yumin 04 Minzhong No. (2017) 927. The agreement stipulates that the service period is 15 years and the breach of contract shall lead to contractual damages. The court ruled that there was no basis for the employer to request such a long service period, and ordered that the employee compensate the employer training fee in proportion and a discretionary contractual damage of RMB 5,000.

143 The first paragraph of Article 26 of the Regulations on the Implementation of the Employment Contract Law of the People's Republic of China stipulates that if an employer and a worker have agreed on a service period, and the worker terminates the employment contract in accordance with the provisions of Article 38 of the Employment Contract Law, it is not a violation of the agreement on the service period, and the employer shall not require the worker to pay contractual damages.

144 Civil Second Instance Judgment on the Labor Dispute Case between Gao Wang and Jiangmen Dejun Petrochemical Transport Co., Ltd., Guangdong Province, Jiangmen Intermediate People's Court, Civil Judgment (2019) Yue 07 Min Zhong 3118. In the case, the training agreement stipulates that the company should reimburse training expenses, and the employee is required to serve for at least one year. The court determined that due to the employee's severe violation of company rules and regulations leading to the termination within 1 year of the commencement of the employment, the company is not obligated to reimburse the training expenses to the employee.

145 Retrial of work injury insurance treatment dispute between Peng and Guangzhou Qiangye Company Guangdong Provincial People's High Court, (2014) Yue Gao Fa Li Min Ti Zi No.6. Article 42 of the Law of the People's Republic of China on Mediation and Arbitration of Labor Disputes stipulates: Before making an award, the arbitration tribunal shall first mediate. If an agreement is reached through conciliation, the

If the two parties reach an agreement through negotiation, it is still necessary to examine whether the negotiation procedure and content of the agreement are fair and reasonable. The 2020 Supreme Court's Judicial Interpretation stipulates that an agreement reached between the employer and the employee on the payment of wages or economic compensation shall be recognized as valid if it does not violate mandatory provisions of law and there is no fraud, coercion, or taking advantage of vulnerability.[146] At present, the judicial decisions of courts all over the country also show that as long as the compensation agreement between the two parties is not significantly lower than the statutory standard, and there is no fraud when signing the agreement, the court generally recognizes the validity of the agreement.[147]

An employee intending to void a settlement agreement that they signed and that conflicts with the employment laws must file a claim with the labor arbitration committee or the court to cancel or alter the agreement within the statutory time limitation—within one year of the agreement's signing.

arbitration tribunal shall prepare a conciliation statement. The conciliation statement shall set forth the arbitration claims and the results of the agreement between the parties. The conciliation statement shall be signed by the arbitrators, sealed by the labor dispute arbitration commission, and served on both parties. The conciliation statement shall become legally effective after it is signed and accepted by both parties.

146 Article 35 of the Interpretation of the Supreme People's Court on the Application of Law in the Trial of Labor Dispute Cases (I) (Judicial Interpretation [2020] No. 26). "Where the agreement reached between a worker and an employer on the termination or dissolution of an employment contract, the payment of wages, overtime pay, economic compensation or punitive damages, etc., does not violate the law and if there is no fraud, coercion, or vulnerability-advantage-taking, it shall be recognized as valid. If there is a major misunderstanding or obvious unfairness in the agreement mentioned in the preceding paragraph, and the parties request cancellation, the people's court shall support it."

147 Shaanxi Zhuoyue Construction Labor Co., Ltd. v. Du Jinsong Labor Dispute Civil Ruling of Shaanxi Provincial People's High Court (2015) S.M.S.S.Z. No. 00251. The court held that work-related injury compensation must be in accordance with statutory standards. Guangzhou Yingshang Garments Co., Ltd., Peng Wentao Labor Dispute Civil Application for Retrial Review Civil Ruling Guangdong Provincial People's High Court Civil Ruling (2021) Yue Min Shen No. 8626. Zhengzhou Coal Group (Ruzhou) Fusheng Mining Co., Ltd. and Jiao Maoli's Application for Labor Dispute Civil Ruling of Henan Provincial People's High Court (2014) Yu Fa Li Er Min Shen Zi No. 00215. Henan Hengda Mechanical and Electrical Equipment Co., Ltd., Meng Qingkun Labor Dispute Retrial Civil Judgment Henan High Court Civil Judgment (2018) Yu Min Zai No. 1555.

CHAPTER 6

Trade Secrets and Non-competition

Introduction

Trade secret protection is a legal issue that spans labor law, tort liability law, and intellectual property law. Non-competition is also a significant area of recent judicial controversy with evolving Supreme Court rules and precedents, making both topics challenging in Chinese employment law. For employers, trade secrets and non-competition may involve major core business interests.

This chapter answers questions about the identification of trade secrets, the burden of proof for non-publicity of a trade secret, acts of infringement and their classification, judicial inconsistencies in the pursuit of employees' "customer poaching," situations of immunity of infringement of a trade secret, the types of right holders and infringers in trade secret cases, civil, administrative, and criminal liabilities for trade secret infringement, an overview of non-competition definitions and liabilities for breach of contract, the scope of individuals subject to non-competition obligations, non-competition during employment, handling of situations where non-competition allowance is not contractually stipulated, methods for terminating non-competition agreements, and dealing with excessive non-competition liquidated damages.

Laws related to trade secrets and non-competition are relatively underdeveloped areas in Chinese legal practice. This chapter, through the study of current judicial precedents and the evolution of laws and regulations, provides an in-depth analysis of "customer poaching," identification of commercial secret infringement, and immunities for such infringement, summarizing and deducing some judicial rules that, while not explicitly formulated, are practically applied in Chinese judicial practice.

In 2021, China promulgated and implemented the Personal Information Protection Act, which has received widespread international and domestic attention. Although this law has limited relevance to labor relations management, it significantly impacts businesses operating in China. Currently, judicial precedents involving the Personal Information Protection Act are rare, and its implementation and enforcement in China remain to be further observed.

6.1 Trade Secret Protection

181. How do employers protect their trade secrets?

Answer: Infringement of a company's trade secrets by an employee on or off the job not only violates the employee's professional ethics under the employment laws, but also

DOI: 10.4324/9781003583301-6

violates civil and even criminal laws. Trade secrets are certain information that needs protection. Two conditions must be met to determine that the employee's behavior constitutes infringement of trade secrets: one is that the information the employer owns belongs to a trade secret, and the second is that the employee has illegally infringed on the trade secret.

For any information owned by a company to be recognized as a trade secret, several requirements must be met, including the information being non-public information and of commercial value and the company having taken confidentiality measures. Please refer to "182. What are the legal criteria for information to qualify as a trade secret?" If the relevant information is not a trade secret, unless the information can be protected by other means, such as copyright and patent, your company cannot pursue the responsibility of the employee.

The employer also needs to prove that the employee has committed an infringement action of the trade secret, including stealing, disclosing, or using (including helping others to use) the trade secret. Please refer to "186. What are the types of infringement of trade secrets?" and "187. How do right holders of trade secrets prove infringement acts of trade secrets?" If the employer cannot prove that the employee has committed an act of infringing the company's trade secrets, the employee cannot be held accountable.

To pursue the employee's liability for compensation, the employer should also be able to confirm that the employee does not have a defense of immunity, including the impugned information being different from the employer's trade secrets, reverse engineering, no access to trade secrets, independent research and development, lawful acquisition, etc. Please refer to "191. What are the immunities for trade secret infringement in practice?"

According to the civil and criminal laws of China, the courts can order current or former employees who infringed on trade secrets to stop infringement, compensate for losses, and return and destroy trade secret information, and even order the employee to bear criminal responsibility. Competent governmental authorities may also impose administrative punishment on the infringer. Please see "193. What civil liabilities are trade secret infringers subject to?", "195. What criminal liabilities are trade secret infringers subject to?", and "194. What administrative liabilities are trade secret infringers subject to?"

The infringement type involving the illegal use of someone else's trade secret to produce products may require a comparison between the right holder's trade secret and the information used by the defendant. Alternatively, it may involve comparing the products produced by the right holder based on the trade secret with those produced by the defendant using the information in question. These two types of comparison have subtle implications for assessing infringement. The former (comparing information from both parties) produces the most direct evidence for assessing infringement, while the latter (comparing products from both parties) may not be sufficient to find infringement, even if the results show identity or substantial identity between the products of the right holder and that of the defendant, because, from a technical perspective, the defendant may use different information than the right holder's trade secret and produce products that are either identical or substantially identical to those of the right holder.[1] For example, different brewing processes may result in beers with the same flavor.

1 Gao Jing, On the Identification and Proof of Trade Secrets: Comments on the Case of Infringement of Trade Secrets by Shantou Southeast Company, Technology and Law, Page 47 of the 4th issue in 2010. The court held that the plaintiff should prove that the manufacturing method of the product was unique when proving infringement of the trade secret, a production method, by proving that the final products were identical. In

The aforementioned infringement of trade secrets is the most common form of infringement concerning technical information. In contrast, there is another special type of trade secret infringement related to business information, typically involving infringement of customer information, such as customer poaching behavior. Please refer to "189. Can an employer pursue a departed employee for customer poaching?"

182. What are the legal criteria for information to qualify as a trade secret?

Answer: Trade secrets are essentially intellectual property information generated by the right holder's investment of money, manpower, material resources, knowledge, experience, and time, including licensees' payment for use. Therefore, the law protects the right holder's interests in trade secrets. Ordinary information is not protected by law.

Article 9 of the 2019 Anti-Unfair Competition Law provides that "[t]rade secrets refer to technical information and business information that are not known to the public, can bring economic benefits to the right holder, are of instrumental nature, and have been taken confidentiality measures by the right holder." Therefore, the trade secret has three characteristics: the information is not known to the public, that is, it is not public; the information has commercial value; and the right holder has taken confidentiality measures. Without any of the above characteristics, information does not constitute a trade secret.

First, trade secrets must be information that is not known to the public, and public information does not belong to trade secrets. The term "not known to the public" refers to information of common sense or practice known to the public or personnel in the relevant industry, or information that cannot be obtained from public channels such as publications, networks, exhibition reports, etc., or information that cannot be obtained from observing the structure, dimensions, and materials of publicly marketed products. However, innovative information developed or processed from publicly available information may still constitute a trade secret if it bears the three characteristics of trade secrets.[2]

The second necessary condition of a trade secret is that the right holder has taken confidentiality measures for the information. Information not under confidentiality measures shall not constitute a trade secret.[3] When determining whether the right holder has taken confidentiality measures, the courts will consider the appropriateness of confidentiality

the absence of a confidentiality agreement between the plaintiff and the defendant, and because the defendant cooperated with the technical appraiser for on-site inspection and the appraisal could not confirm that the two methods were the same, the court ordered that the plaintiff should not be allowed to require the defendant to provide the manufacturing method, and therefore, the plaintiff lost the lawsuit.

2 Article 4 of the Provisions of the Supreme People's Court on Several Issues Concerning the Application of Law in the Trial of Civil Cases of Infringement of Trade Secrets (Judicial Interpretation [2020] No. 7). "Under any of the following circumstances, the people's court may determine that the relevant information is known to the public: (1) The information belongs to general knowledge or industry practice in its field; (2) The information only involves the size, structure, material, simple combination of components and other contents of the product, which can be directly obtained by the relevant personnel in the field by observing the listed products; (3) The information has been publicly disclosed in public publications or other media; (4) The information has been made public through public reports, exhibitions, and other means; (5) the relevant personnel in the field can obtain the information from other public channels. If the new information formed by sorting out, improving, and processing the information known to the public conforms to the rules of Article 3 of these Provisions, it shall be determined that the new information is not known to the public."

3 Liu Yulian and Huizhou Tianhong Shopping Mall Co., Ltd., Labor Dispute Appeal Case, Civil Judgment of Huizhou Intermediate People's Court of Guangdong Province (2017) Yue13MinZhong No. 2555. Civil Judgment of the Second Instance of the Labor Dispute Case between Lin Yu and Pan Jiao Dance Training School in Haizhou District Civil Judgment of Fuxin Intermediate People's Court of Liaoning Province (2019) Liao 09 Min Zhong No. 215.

measures according to the nature of trade secrets and their carriers, the commercial value of trade secrets, the degree of identifiability of confidentiality measures, the degree of correspondence between confidentiality measures and trade secrets, and the right holder's willingness to keep confidentiality.[4] For cases involving the reverse engineering defense, it is also necessary to see whether the products sold by the right holder in the market have measures against reverse engineering, and the company's internal confidentiality management measures alone may not be sufficient to pass the threshold of confidentiality measures having been taken. Please refer to "191. What are the immunities for trade secret infringement in practice?"

The third necessary condition for a trade secret is that the information has commercial value. This condition is the least controversial in practice. The right holder's use of the information for profit, the investment of funds and human resources in the information, the confidentiality measures taken, and the illegal acquisition of the information by employees or tortfeasors themselves can directly or indirectly prove the commercial value of the information.

In practice, common types of trade secrets include technical information and business information. Patents, trademarks, and copyrighted items do not qualify as trade secrets because they do not meet the condition of secrecy, "not known to the public." For instance, patents must disclose all technical details publicly. Another challenge in practice is whether customer information in business operations constitutes trade secrets. Please see "189. Can an employer pursue a departed employee for customer poaching?" and "190. What rule do Chinese courts tend to use in determining whether customer poaching constitutes infringement?" for details.

In the process of disputes, especially in the process of judicial proceedings, the most important factor affecting whether the three conditions of trade secrets are established may be the burden of proof involving complex legal issues. Why? Please refer to "183. How do right holders establish the legal existence of their trade secrets?"

4 The Provisions of the Supreme People's Court on Several Issues Concerning the Application of Law in the Trial of Civil Cases of Infringement of Trade Secrets (Judicial Interpretation [2020] No. 7), "Article 5, the reasonable confidentiality measures taken before the alleged infringement occur in order to prevent the disclosure of trade secrets shall be recognized by the people's court as the corresponding confidentiality measures referred to in Paragraph 4 of Article 9 of the Anti-Unfair Competition Law. The people's court shall determine whether the right holder has taken corresponding confidentiality measures according to the nature of the trade secret and its carrier, the commercial value of the trade secret, the identifiable degree of confidentiality measures, the corresponding degree of confidentiality measures and trade secrets, and the right holder's willingness to keep confidential. Article 6, the people's court shall determine that the right holder has taken corresponding confidentiality measures under any of the following circumstances, which are sufficient to prevent the disclosure of trade secrets under normal circumstances: (1) signing a confidentiality agreement or stipulating the obligation of confidentiality in the contract; (2) requiring employees, former employees, suppliers, customers, and visitors, who have access to or obtain trade secrets to keep them confidential by means of articles of association, training, company rules and regulations, written notification, etc.; (3) imposing differential management measures over, or restricting visitors' access to, production and operation facilities such as factory buildings and workshops involving secrets; (4) distinguishing and managing trade secrets and their carriers by means of marking, classifying, isolating, encrypting, sealing up, and restricting the scope of persons who can contact or obtain them; (5) taking measures to prohibit or restrict the use, access, storage, and reproduction of computer equipment, electronic equipment, network equipment, storage equipment, and software, that can access or obtain trade secrets; (6) requiring employees who leave their jobs to register, return, remove, or destroy the trade secrets and their carriers that they have access to or obtained, and to continue to undertake the obligation of confidentiality; (7) taking other reasonable confidentiality measures."

183. How do right holders establish the legal existence of their trade secrets?

Answer: According to "182. What arc the legal criteria for information to qualify as a trade secret?", if the right holder of a trade secret wants to stop the infringement or pursue the tortfeasor, they must prove the legal existence of the trade secrets they own. The legal existence of a trade secret has three conditions: the relevant information is non-public information, the information has commercial value, and the right holder has taken confidentiality measures for the information.

The key issue to prove the existence of trade secrets is the burden of proof, that is, whether a plaintiff should be responsible for proving the existence of trade secrets or the defendant should prove that trade secrets do not exist. Burden of proof is a complex but key issue in legal disputes, because according to the rules of evidence in Chinese law, the party who bears the burden of proof in a lawsuit heard by the court is likely to bear the consequences of losing the lawsuit if the evidence is insufficient to prove the facts they claim.

The identification of the first condition for the establishment of trade secrets is a very complex issue in law and practice. We conclude that for acquisition and disclosure trade secret torts (please refer to "186. What are the types of infringement of trade secrets?"), the court shall assign the burden of proof to the defendant to prove that the information is public information if the right holder has already demonstrated the confidentiality measures taken and the commercial value of the information. For use-based infringement, the court should first make a preliminary judgment on whether the information involved is more likely to be public or non-public information based on the preliminary existing evidence and the proposition and deposition made by both parties. If the prima facie conclusion is that the information is more likely to be public, the court should assign the burden of proof to the plaintiff to prove that the information is not public; otherwise, the defendant should be required to prove that it is public. The legal analysis process of this conclusion involves complex analyses of evolution of legislation and court decisions, and interested readers can refer to "184. How do right holders prove the non-publicity of trade secrets?" The average reader may only want to look at this conclusion.

As for the second condition (the commercial value of the related information) and the third condition (the right holder has taken confidentiality measures for the information) for the establishment of trade secrets, current judicial practice has a relatively definite understanding that the right holder of the related information (usually the plaintiff) should bear the burden of proof.

The evidence by which the right holder proves that their trade secret has commercial value may include the research and development process, investment of human resources and material resources, licensing others to use it, collecting technology licensing fees, and providing products or services containing the trade secret for profit. The confidentiality measures taken by the right holder can also prove the value of trade secrets.

The evidence for the right holder to prove that confidentiality measures have been taken includes signing a confidentiality agreement (which is the most common confidentiality measure), requiring relevant personnel to keep confidentiality through company rules and regulations, taking confidentiality management measures for trade secret–related sites, and managing trade secrets and their carriers by means of marking, classifying, isolating, encrypting, sealing, and restricting, as well as evidence such as confidentiality management measures for other third party equipment that may be exposed to trade secrets and carriers, and confidentiality management for departing employees. A person in a special position in a company, such as a director, assumes a statutory duty of confidentiality under the company law, so the fact that an employee holds the position may itself fulfill the condition of confidentiality measures.[5] In addition, the evidence of confidentiality measures also includes the measures taken by the right holder against reverse engineering.

184. How do right holders prove the non-publicity of trade secrets?

Answer: According to "183. How do right holders establish the legal existence of their trade secrets?", non-publicity of trade secrets is the prerequisite for existence of trade secrets and accountability for infringement. This short article provides an in-depth analysis and summary of China's current laws regarding trade secrets and judicial trial cases. It outlines a set of rules for determining who is responsible for proving, and how to prove, the confidentiality of trade secret information. Readers can skip the detailed legal analysis section and proceed directly to the conclusion.

This set of trial rules is not explicitly defined in current laws, nor is it uniformly summarized in judicial cases. However, it represents the potential rules that various local courts tend to apply in practice. This provides practical reference value for readers interested in understanding how trade secret disputes are handled.

The key issue to prove the existence of trade secrets is the burden of proof. When it comes to proving the non-publicity of trade secrets, the burden of proof becomes the issue of whether it is for the plaintiff to prove that the related information is not publicly available or for the defendant to prove the opposite. The consequence of the burden of proof in a court case is that the party who bears the burden of proof is likely to bear the consequences of losing the case if the evidence is insufficient to prove the facts it claims. The burden of proof is related to the success or failure of litigation.

At present, China's law and judicial practice do not give a clear answer to who should bear the burden of proof for the non-publicity of trade secrets.

The case of Nanjing Jinpeng Petrochemical Research Institute in 2015 shows that courts at all levels have not reached a stable consensus on the burden of proof for non-publicity of trade secret information. In the case, the plaintiff provided the defendant with a fuel additive technology, and the defendant paid nearly RMB 1 million for the use of the technology during the three-year contract period; the defendant then produced technically similar products for sale without authorization after the contract ended. The plaintiff sued the defendant for infringement of a technical trade secret. The first-instance court, Nanjing Liuhe District Court, found that the plaintiff had the burden of proof to prove that the technology was not public, and the plaintiff failed to apply for non-publicity appraisal, leading to the plaintiff having insufficient evidence and the consequent loss of the case.

5 Civil Ruling of the Supreme People's Court of the People's Republic of China (2020) Supreme Fa Min Shen No. 401, Civil Ruling of the Supreme People's Court of the People's Republic of China on Retrial Review and Trial Supervision of Disputes over Infringement of Trade secrets by Qingdao Melville Machinery and Equipment Import and Export Co., Ltd. and Xu Jingqing. "The seventh item of Article 149 of the Company Law of the People's Republic of China (Note: this is item 5 of Article 181 of the 2023 Company Law) stipulates: 'The directors and senior managers of a company shall not disclose the company's secrets without authorization.' Liu Yu, as a senior manager of the company, has the statutory obligation of confidentiality."

On the appeal of the case, the Nanjing Intermediate Court held that in view of the high cost of the technology license fee and the confidentiality clause provided in the contract, it was for the defendant to bear the burden of proof to prove that the technology was public, and it finally ruled that the trade secret was established and overturned the first-instance judgment.[6]

This case is a microcosm of the divergence in the understanding of the burden of proof of trade secrets in China's judicial decisions. In 2007, the Supreme Court's judicial interpretation of the Unfair Competition Law stipulates that the plaintiff shall be responsible for providing evidence to prove that trade secrets meet the legal conditions (including the non-publicity of trade secrets).[7] This rule has resulted in the plaintiff's heavy burden of proof to prove the non-publicity of trade secrets, and judicial decisions have been very divergent. The courts have not only held that the plaintiff assumes the obligation to prove non-publicity of the relevant information,[8] but also held that the defendant has the obligation to prove that the information is in the public domain.[9]

The amendment to the Anti-Unfair Competition Law in April 2019 tried to clarify the burden of proof for determining the non-publicity of trade secrets: "In the civil trial procedure of infringement of trade secrets, the right holder of trade secret shall first provide preliminary evidence to prove that they have taken confidentiality measures for the claimed trade secret and reasonably show that the trade secret has been infringed; then the suspected tortfeasor is obligated to prove that the trade secrets claimed by the right holder are not the trade secrets stipulated in this Law."[10] According to the revised law, the Supreme Court pointed out in the case of Jinan Sike Testing Technology Co., Ltd. in 2020 that "the right holder of trade secrets should first provide preliminary evidence to prove that they have taken corresponding confidentiality measures for the trade secrets they

---

6 Nanjing Jinpeng Petrochemical Research Institute v. Nanjing Rongsen Chemical Co., Ltd. for Infringement of Trade Secrets Nanjing Liuhe District People's Court Civil Judgment (2014) Liu Zhi Min Chu Zi No. 22. The Nanjing Intermediate People's Court in the judgment of the second instance quashed the first-instance judgment (Nanjing Intermediate People's Court of Jiangsu Province Civil Judgment (2015) NZMZZ No. 140) and confirmed that the technology should be presumed to be a trade secret after technology transfer and confidentiality agreement, and the defendant bears the burden of proof to prove its openness. This case shows that the allocation of the burden of proof for the disclosure of trade secrets is a complex issue.

7 Article 14 of the repealed Interpretation of the Supreme People's Court on Several Issues Concerning the Application of Law in the Trial of Civil Cases of Unfair Competition (Judicial Interpretation (2007) No. 2) stipulates: "in a suit, a party claiming that the other has infringed its trade secret shall bear the burden of proof for the fact that its trade secrets meet the legal conditions, that the information of the other party is identical or substantially identical as its trade secrets, and that the other party acted in an illegal manner. Among them, the evidence that the trade secret meets the legal conditions includes the carrier, specific content, commercial value of the trade secret and the specific confidentiality measures taken for the trade secret."

8 Civil Judgment of First Instance of Dispute over Infringement of Technical Secrets between Dongguan Qingsong Optics Co., Ltd. and Wei Zongtao Civil Judgment of Guangzhou Intellectual Property Court (2018) Yue 73 Min Chu No. 3114. The court held that the plaintiff failed to prove the difference between the product in circulation on the market and the drawing of the lens barrel mold that the plaintiff claimed to protect, so the trade secret did not exist. Civil Judgment of First Instance of Unfair Competition Dispute of Beijing Jisu Applied Technology Co., Ltd., Beijing Ganyun Applied Technology Co., Ltd., Jia Pengfei, etc. Handan Intermediate People's Court of Hebei Province Civil Judgment (2020) Ji 04 Min Chu No. 55.

9 Qingdao Shengfengda Industry and Trade Co., Ltd. v. Han Zhongxin and others for infringement of trade secrets, Qingdao Intermediate People's Court of Shandong Province issued a civil judgment (2006) Qing Min San Chu Zi No. 30. "This court held that it was a negative fact that certain information was not known to the public. As the plaintiff claimed that the technology of velvet belt machine was the first in China, it indicated that he believed that the technology was not known to the public. The burden of proof that the technical information has been known to the public should be borne by the defendant accused of infringing trade secrets."

10 Article 32 of the 2019 Anti-Unfair Competition Law.

claim to protect, and that the accused tortfeasor has perpetrated 'infringement'. Based on this, the right holder of trade secret does not need to provide evidence to prove that the trade secret they claim to protect is 'not known to the public', but that the accused tortfeasor must provide evidence to prove that the trade secret does not meet the requirement of 'not known to the public' rendering it is not the trade secret stipulated in the Anti-Unfair Competition Law."[11]

Although this burden of proof rule tries to strike a balance between the burden of proof on both sides and to reduce the burden of proof of the plaintiff, it still has manifest defects. From the perspective of judicial practice, there are generally three types of trade secret infringements (please refer to "186. What are the types of infringement of trade secrets?"): acquisition (where an employee wrongfully acquires a trade secret), disclosure (where an employee wrongfully discloses a trade secret to another person), and use (where an employee illegally uses, or helps other to use, a trade secret, for example, producing products).

The aforementioned new rule on burden of proof is appropriate for acquisition and disclosure torts. The right holder needs to preliminarily prove the confidentiality measures taken for the information, the commercial value of the information, and the tortious acts of the employee's unlawful acquisition or disclosure. Based on the existing evidence, the employee is of course obligated to prove that the information is not of the nature of non-publicity of trade secrets; otherwise, they should bear the tort liability. This is not very controversial.

However, when this rule is applied to use-based infringement, there is a serious defect, that the burden of proof on the right holder is unreasonably increased. The most common trade secret infringement is use-based infringement, where the right holder does not see the defendant's unlawful behavior of acquiring or disclosing, but only finds the infringement clues at the point of use, such as discovering products produced with the same technology as the right holder's trade secret. In this case, if the right holder has to "reasonably show that the trade secret has been infringed," there may be no other way than providing a technical appraisal report to compare the right holder's trade secret information with the technical information contained in the defendant's product to determine whether they are identical or substantially identical.

This means that the actual effect of this rule violates the original intention of reducing the burden of proof of the right holder, because the cost and technical complexity of the technical appraisal are far higher than those of the right holder proving the non-publicity of their trade secrets. Moreover, such a proof process actually requires the right holder to prove the existence of the infringement fact in advance, conflicting with the traditional practice of "proving rights first before proving infringement" in intellectual property infringement cases.

In fact, there are many cases, from the Supreme Court after the revision of the Anti-Unfair Competition Law in 2019, that do not follow the burden of proof when allocating the burden of proof between the two parties for the non-publicity of trade secrets. For example, in the case of Beijing Lizheng Software Co., Ltd. in 2020, the Supreme Court directly examined the nature of the information software database involved in the case and preliminarily

11 Jinan Sike Testing Technology Co., Ltd. v. Jinan Languang Electromechanical Technology Co., Ltd. Civil Judgment of the Supreme People's Court of the People's Republic of China (2020) SFZMZ No. 538.

identified its non-public nature, and then pointed out that although the defendant objected to the non-public nature of the information, he failed to provide evidence to refute it, and finally determined the establishment of trade secrets, taking account into confidentiality measures and commercial value.[12] This reminds us that the courts should first examine existing evidence to preliminarily judge the nature of the information, and then shift the onus to the unfavorable party to provide evidence to refute it.

Let's go back to the case of Nanjing Jinpeng Petrochemical Research Institute in 2015. The glaring facts in this case are that the defendant paid nearly RMB 1 million for using the technology and that the contract stipulated the defendant's obligation of confidentiality. This obviously constitutes a prima facie proof of the technology being non-public information, because no rational company would pay a high fee to use a publicly available technology. Therefore, the burden of proof should of course be assigned to the defendant: unless the defendant can prove that the technology is a publicly available technology, the non-publicity of the information is certainly established. In fact, the reasoning of the court of second instance echoed this in setting aside the first-instance judgment.

These cases show that the principle of balance of probability in civil evidence rules should be extended to shifting the burden of proof of both parties rather than limited to the judge's one-off allocation of burden of proof. If the version of fact claimed by one party prevails according to the existing evidence and propositions and depositions, the other party shall be responsible for proving that this version of fact is less likely than the fact claimed by itself. When a new fact prevails, one party should be given further opportunities to provide counter-evidence. In reality, facts of cases, particularly the sciences and technologies involved, are very complex, and it is difficult for judges to apply their legal knowledge to complex facts at one time. The courts should allow both sides to have multiple opportunities for proof, with the deepening of technology and factual disclosure, so as to find out the facts as closely as possible to the truth.

Therefore, we summarize the principle and rule in allocating the underlying burden of proof that courts across the country tend to use in practice as follows.

For use-based infringement cases, the courts first make a preliminary judgment on whether the relevant information is more likely to be public or non-public based on the preliminary existing evidence and the propositions and depositions of both parties. The factors to be considered in this alternative judgment include the content or technical features of the trade secret, the difficulty for both parties to prove the publicity (or non-publicity), the research and development investment of the right holder, the confidentiality measures taken by the right holder, whether the information is originally created by the right holder or is derived or transformed from information of a third party, evidence of the defendant's own research and development, the agreement or understanding of both parties on the nature of relevant information, etc. If the prima facie conclusion is that the information is more likely to be public, the courts allocate the burden of proof to the

12 Beijing Lizheng Software Co., Ltd. and Beijing Dacheng Huazhi Software Technology Co., Ltd. Civil Judgment of the Second Instance of Trade Secret Infringement Dispute Civil Judgment of the Supreme People's Court of the People's Republic of China (2020) Supreme Law Zhimin Zhong No. 1638. "The technical content of the trade secret involved in the case includes 66 database tables and 31 stored procedures/functions contained in the four databases LZMISCommon, LZMISPM, LZMISWF and LZ MISFrame of the 'Lizheng MIS System Database' software, which belong to the software background code files that are not easy for ordinary technicians to know and obtain. It is not known to the public, and the finding has factual and legal basis and can be confirmed."

plaintiff to prove that the information is not public; otherwise, the defendant should be required to prove that it is public.

If the case is an acquisition or disclosure infringement, the courts first consider the evidence of the acquisition or disclosure infringement, the confidentiality measures taken by the plaintiff, and the evidence of the commercial value of the information, provided by the plaintiff. If these evidences show that the defendant's unlawfulness (that is, unlawful acquisition and disclosure of the right holder's information) is established, then the courts assign the burden of proof to the defendant to prove that the information is publicly available. This path of burden of proof is consistent with the provisions of Article 32 of the Anti-Unfair Competition Law.

Right holders and infringement defendants can gather evidence based on this answer regarding the burden of proof for either pursuing infringement liability or defending against allegations of infringement.

185. What are the common types of trade secret information in practice?

Answer: In practice, information that may be a trade secret includes technical information such as structure, raw materials, components, formulas, materials, samples, patterns, propagation materials of new plant varieties, processes, methods or steps, algorithms, data, computer programs, and related documents, and business information such as management, sales, finance, planning, samples, bidding materials, customer information (including customer name, address, contact information and trading habits, intentions, and content), and data.[13]

Of course, patents, copyrights, and trademarks owned by right holders cannot be protected as trade secrets due to their public nature. Unpatented technologies (typically the formula of Coca-Cola drink) and unregistered layout designs of integrated circuits can, of course, be protected as trade secrets, and computer software source codes can also be protected as trade secrets even if they are published through software registration.[14]

As a special kind of trade secret, the scope of protection of computer software source code is a noteworthy issue. In practice, the common situation is that the computer source code requested for protection is a combination of independent innovation part code, open-source code, and third party authorized code. In the case of Anmei Weike (Beijing) Internet Technology Co., Ltd. before the Supreme Court in 2020, the court seems to consider that only part of the code of independent innovation of the right holder should be protected.[15] However, we believe that the source code of the three parts mentioned above

13 Article 1 of the Provisions of the Supreme People's Court on Several Issues Concerning the Application of Law in the Trial of Civil Cases of Infringement of Trade Secrets (Judicial Interpretation [2020] No. 7).

14 Shenzhen Huaer Blooming Network Technology Co., Ltd., Zhejiang Panxing Digital Intelligence Technology Co., Ltd. and other appeals for disputes over infringement of technical secrets, the Supreme People's Court of the People's Republic of China Civil Judgment (2021) No. 2298. The Supreme People's Court held that although some source codes were published in computer software registration, not all codes were published. Therefore, it can be identified as a trade secret. Beijing Yuanding Times Technology Co., Ltd., Qu Zhanbin, etc. Civil Judgment of the Second Instance of the Civil Dispute over Infringement of Technical Secrets Civil Judgment of the Supreme People's Court of the People's Republic of China (2021) SFZMZ No. 2389.

15 Anmei Weike (Beijing) Internet Technology Co., Ltd. and Lingbo Technology (Beijing) Co., Ltd., Zheng Guanghui, Wu Jianming, Shi Hongliang, and Xu Feng. Infringement of Computer Software Copyright and Infringement of Trade Secrets Civil Judgment of the Supreme People's Court of the People's Republic of China (2020) No. 1099. In the case, a former employee established a competitive software company. The right holder

normally is not a simple code superposition but an organic innovation and reconstruction. After a right holder has paid the third party authorization fee, they should be entitled to the trade secret of their software as a whole, as long as the whole code is non-public in terms of code expression and function.

The courts may comprehensively judge whether the relevant information is a trade secret according to an appraisal report, a novelty search report, evidence of the right holder's investment and development of the relevant information, and the legitimacy of the tortfeasor's means of obtaining the information.[16] The courts usually directly find business information such as financial information or a company's planned bidding information to be trade secrets.

186. What are the types of infringement of trade secrets?

Answer: Proving that the defendant has infringed upon trade secrets is another necessary condition for the right holder to pursue their legal liability. Different types of trade secret infringements have different evidentiary characteristics.

The Anti-Unfair Competition Law of 2019 stipulates that the infringement of trade secrets includes acquiring trade secrets by unlawful means (theft, bribery, fraud, coercion, etc.), disclosing trade secrets, or using or allowing others to use trade secrets in violation of laws or agreements, and a third party acquiring, disclosing, using, or allowing others to use a trade secret knowing of another's unlawful infringement of the trade secret.[17] Therefore, we can categorize infringements of trade secrets into three types: acquisition infringement, disclosure infringement, and use (including allowing others to use) infringement.

Acquisition and disclosure infringements only involve the initial stage of any use infringements. Tortfeasors illegally obtain the trade secret of the right holder or unlawfully disclose it to a third party, while the tortfeasors or the third party have not yet used the trade secret. The right holder needs to provide evidence of the tortfeasor's acquisition or disclosure of trade secrets.[18]

---

requested to identify trade secret infringement and software copyright infringement. The software source code of the right holder includes three parts: open-source code, third party licensed code, and self-developed code. The right holder did not specify the scope of the protected code, so the court determined that it could not support the existence of trade secrets, and the claim was rejected. There is a problem here. If the right holder uses the combination of open-source code and third party licensed code to make innovative software, it seems that it should still be protected, and cannot be understood as a simple stack of codes as this judgment considered.

16 Civil Ruling of the Supreme People's Court of the People's Republic of China (2015) No. 2035 on the application for retrial of disputes over infringement of trade secrets between Xinfa Pharmaceutical Co., Ltd. and Yifan Xinfu Pharmaceutical Co., Ltd. The court determined that the information was trade secrets according to the investment made by the right holder and the means of secret acquisition by the tortfeasor. It did not depend entirely on the trade secret appraisal report.

17 The first paragraph of Article 9 of the 2019 Anti-Unfair Competition Law stipulates: "An operator shall not commit any of the following acts of infringing upon trade secrets: (1) obtaining the trade secrets of the right holder by theft, bribery, fraud, coercion, or other unjustified means; (2) disclosing, using or allowing others to use the trade secrets of the right holder obtained by the means mentioned in the preceding item; (3) disclosing, using or allowing others to use the trade secrets in violation of the agreement or the requirements of the right holder to keep the trade secrets." The second paragraph of this article stipulates: "If a third party knows or should have known that an employee or former employee of the right holder of a trade secret or of other companies or individuals has committed the illegal acts listed in the preceding paragraph, but still obtains, discloses, uses or allows others to use the trade secret, it shall be deemed an infringement of the trade secret."

18 Beijing Anbiqi Biotechnology Co., Ltd. and Tang Yuanyuan Labor Dispute Retrial Review and Trial Supervision Civil Ruling Beijing High Court Civil Ruling (2022) Jing Min Shen No. 7501. The court held that

For example, in the case of Li Yuanli before Shenzhen Intermediate Court in 2015, the employee transferred financial data and confidential technical materials of the listed companies to his personal mailbox, and established a company for the same business as the employer, before his resignation. The court found that the plaintiff had proved that the employee had stolen trade secrets and that the employee must compensate RMB 30,000.[19]

These two types of cases rarely involve the comparison between the right holder's trade secrets and the information the tortfeasor acquired or disclosed, and the focus of proof is on the tortfeasor's behavior of acquisition or disclosure and the evidence of their illegal possession of the trade secrets.

The third type is use infringement. That is to say, the tortfeasor has illegally used the right holder's trade secret. It may be that the tortfeasor acquired or disclosed the trade secrets, or obtained the trade secret from another tortfeasor who illegally acquired or disclosed the trade secret. Use infringement is the most common type of infringement, which is characterized by the fact that the tortfeasor's unlawful acts of acquisition or disclosure are difficult to detect, and that the right holder can only trace the infringement from the production process or results of the tortfeasor's use of trade secrets.

The right holder pursuing use infringement usually needs to prove that the tortfeasor's production equipment, process, and final products or service process are relevant to the use of the trade secret. The proving process is usually to compare the trade secret with the aforementioned production equipment, service type, and the final product or service result to see whether the confidential points of the right holder's trade secret are identical or substantially identical to the technical features of the information accused of infringement,[20] comparing the differences in content features, uses, purposes, and effects while considering the influence of public information, third party owned information, and creative or non-creative changes.[21] For the technical secrets of the source code of

the employer had the obligation to prove that employees had access to trade secrets and that employees had used and disclosed trade secrets.

19 Shenzhen Huatai Testing Technology Co., Ltd. and Kong Lei, Li Yuanli, Shenzhen Yingbo Testing Technology Co., Ltd. Civil Judgment of the Second Instance of Infringement of Trade Secrets Civil Judgment of Shenzhen Intermediate People's Court of Guangdong Province (2015) No. 1222. The employee transferred the financial data and confidential technical materials of his employer, a listed company, to his personal mailbox and then set up a company with the same business as the company. The court found that the plaintiff had proved the trade secret and the theft of the trade secret by the employee, and that the employee should compensate RMB 30,000.

20 The civil judgment (2013) Hu Gao Min San (Zhi) Zhong Zi No. 93 of Shanghai High Court in the case of the dispute over the infringement of trade secrets between ST International Group and Xu Jie. The court held that in order to determine whether the trade secret of the right holder is infringed, it is first necessary to determine whether the technical information actually used by the alleged tortfeasor is identical or substantially identical to the trade secret of the right holder.

21 Article 13 of the Provisions of the Supreme People's Court on Several Issues Concerning the Application of Law in the Trial of Civil Cases of Infringement of Trade Secrets (Judicial Interpretation [2020] No. 7). "Where there is no substantial difference between the alleged infringing information and the trade secret, the people's court may determine that the alleged infringing information and the trade secret are substantially identical as referred to in Paragraph 2 of Article 32 of the Anti-Unfair Competition Law. The people's court may consider the following factors when determining whether the alleged infringing information is substantially identical as the trade secret as mentioned in the preceding paragraph: (1) the degree of similarities and differences between the alleged infringing information and the trade secret; (2) whether the relevant persons in the field are likely to think of the difference between the accused infringing information and the trade secret at the time of the alleged infringement; (3) whether there are substantial differences in the use, mode of use, purpose, and effect between the alleged infringing information and the trade secret; (4) the information related to the trade secret in the public domain; (5) other factors that need to be considered."

computer software, the court can even use the specific technology of comparing software to compare the computer software of the plaintiff and the defendant.[22]

It should be noted that the defendant's use of the right holder's trade secrets does not necessarily mean that the comparison results of the two are identical or substantially identical. If the defendant uses the trade secret of the right holder with partial innovation and transformation, the result of comparison may not be substantially identical. In this case, the defendant still constitutes an infringement of trade secrets.[23] That is to say, the key to comparison is to see whether the suspected infringing products (or production process) contain the confidentiality points of trade secrets, not necessarily all their technical features.

187. How do right holders of trade secrets prove infringement acts of trade secrets?

Answer: If a trade secret right holder wants to pursue the liability of a tortfeasor, they must prove the existence of the trade secret and the infringement act committed by the tortfeasor. Therefore, whether the right holder can prove the existence of the infringement act is a necessary condition for infringement damages.

According to "186. What are the types of infringement of trade secrets?", infringement of trade secrets includes three types of acts: acquisition, disclosure, and use.

In the case of acquisition and disclosure of a trade secret, the right holder usually only knows that the defendant has engaged in illegal acquisition or disclosure of trade secrets, but does not have evidence that the defendant has used the trade secrets, or use infringement has not yet occurred. According to the principles of Chinese civil law, in general, the right holder of intellectual property (including trade secrets) should be responsible for proving the existence of the defendant's infringement act. According to this principle, the burden of proof of infringement in the cases of acquisition and disclosure of trade secrets should certainly be borne by the right holder.

The right holder can provide the following evidence in the acquisition and disclosure infringement cases: email (for example, the defendant sends the company's trade secrets to their private mailbox through email), storage devices for storing trade secrets, technical drawings, the possibility or history of the tortfeasor's access to trade secrets, etc.

The burden of proof of use infringement is a very complex legal issue. Average readers may just want to see the following conclusion: for whether the infringement act exists or not, the courts should first examine the existing evidence, including the characteristics of the technology information, the history of employees' contact with the information involved, the unlawful nature of employees' series of acts on the information involved, their technical ability, and the evidence of research and development of both parties. If it is preliminarily judged that the probability of infringement is higher than that of non-infringement, the defendant shall bear the burden of proof to prove non-infringement

22 The High Court of Guangdong Province Released the Fourth of Six Typical Cases of Protecting Trade Secrets: Weidi Company v. Li Mouliang and Bell Company Infringement of Technical Secrets—Solving the "Difficulty of Infringement Comparison" in the Protection of Software Source Code Technical Secrets.

23 Jiaxing Zhonghua Chemical Co., Ltd., Shanghai Xinchen New Technology Co., Ltd. and Wanglong Group Co., Ltd., Ningbo Wanglong Science and Technology Company Limited, Xifu Shiwanglong Spices (Ningbo) Company Limited, Fu Xianggen, the Civil Judgment of the Supreme People's Court of the People's Republic of China (2020) ZGFZMZ No. 1667. "Use of a trade secret after modification or improvement of it, or adjustment, optimization, or improvement of relevant production and operation according to trade secrets, shall generally be found as use of the trade secret."

(typically to apply for a technical appraisal and prepay the appraisal fees); if the defendant cannot prove non-infringement, the infringement is established; and vice versa. Readers interested in reading a detailed legal analysis can see "188. How do right holders of trade secrets prove the acts of use infringement of trade secrets?"

188. How do right holders of trade secrets prove the acts of use infringement of trade secrets?

Answer: The use infringement of trade secrets is the most typical form of trade secret infringement, where the infringer unlawfully utilizes the trade secrets of the right holder, for instance, producing an industrial product using the trade secrets of the right holder. This type of infringement differs from acquisition infringement and disclosure infringement of trade secrets. See "186. What are the types of infringement of trade secrets?"

This article is a probing analysis of the current statutory provisions and judicial cases regarding use infringement of trade secrets, primarily focusing on technical trade secrets. It summarizes a rule of burden of proof allocation that Chinese courts tend to apply to prove the existence of acts of use infringement of trade secrets, assisting readers in determining the likely outcome of an act constituting trade secret infringement and understanding how the right holder should pursue the infringement liability and how the defendant should defend themselves against allegations of infringement. Readers can skip the detailed legal analysis and directly read the conclusion.

The burden of proof rule summarized in the conclusion is not explicitly stipulated in current laws, nor is it uniformly summarized in judicial cases. However, it represents a potential rule that courts across the country tend to apply in practice. This provides practical reference value for readers interested in understanding the handling of trade secret disputes, as the rule of burden of proof plays a crucial role for both right holders and alleged infringers in litigation. In simple terms, if the party bearing the burden of proof fails to provide sufficient evidence to support their claim, they are at risk of losing the case.

This answer article analyzes the deficiencies of the existing laws and cases on use infringement of trade secrets (mainly technical secrets) and deduces a reasonable rule for the allocation of the burden of proof for the infringement of trade secrets, so as to help both parties to predict a likely outcome on whether an act constitutes an infringement of trade secrets in China, the right holder to learn how to pursue infringement liability, and the defendant to establish non-infringement. Readers can skip the analysis section and go straight to the answer at the end.

The allocation of the burden of proof in trade secret infringement cases is a very complex legal issue. On the one hand, without the cooperation of the defendant in surrendering the alleged infringement information for comparison, the right holder cannot prove that the defendant's information infringes the trade secrets involved. On the other hand, if the right holder requests the defendant to provide their own information for comparison without good reasons, the defendant may suffer an unfair full disclosure of their own information that is self-developed and lawful.

The Anti-Unfair Competition Law, as amended in 2019, provides a two-step rule for the allocation of the burden of proof to prove the infringement of trade secrets: the first step is for the plaintiff to preliminarily prove that the defendant has access to the trade secret and that the information used by the defendant is substantially identical to the trade secret, or to prove that the trade secret has been disclosed or used or is at such risk; the second step is to shift the burden of proof to the defendant to prove that they have not infringed trade secrets.[24]

However, courts at all levels, including the Supreme People's Court, have not strictly followed this rule. In the case of Qu Zhanbin before the Supreme People's Court in 2021, the employee resigned after four years working as technical director and vice president of the plaintiff, a software company. Six days before his resignation, the employee set up a new software company (the defendant), with himself as the legal representative. The defendant then provided similar software project services to the plaintiff's customer, Luoyang Bank. If, according to the aforementioned rules, it appears that the plaintiff has proved the high risk of the former employee's disclosure or use of the trade secret (having contacted the trade secret, set up a new company, and provided services directly to the right holder's client), the burden of proof should be shifted to the defendant. However, the Supreme Court held that the plaintiff failed to prove that its software technical secrets were identical or substantially identical to the defendant's software, and ruled that the plaintiff lost the lawsuit.[25]

What is the problem with the aforementioned two-step burden of proof allocation rule? Perhaps in the eyes of the Supreme Court judge in the case of Qu Zhanbin in 2021, this rule lacks operability. There are two avenues for the plaintiff to fulfill the initial burden of proof: to prove that the defendant has access to trade secrets and that the information used by the defendant is substantially identical to the trade secret, or to prove that the trade secret is disclosed or used or at risk of this. The first avenue requires proving that the information of the plaintiff and the defendant is substantially identical, meaning that it is necessary to answer whether the defendant has the obligation to hand over their own information for the plaintiff to compare; and the technical comparison is likely to involve complex and expensive technical appraisal, which obviously is not a "preliminary proof." The second avenue is that the trade secret is at risk of being disclosed or used. What is the threshold for the degree of such risk? Must every employee who has had access to trade secrets of a right holder and who establishes a company surrender all their production and operation information to their former employer to prove that they have not infringed the trade secrets of the employer?

These analyses show that the two-step burden of proof allocation rule is a flawed one. For technical information in a use infringement case, the principle of balance of probability in civil evidence rules should be extended to shifting the burden of proof of both parties, rather than limited to the judge's one-off allocation of burden of proof. If the version of fact claimed by one party prevails according to the existing evidence and propositions and depositions, the other party shall be responsible for proving that this version of fact is less likely than the fact claimed by itself. When new evidence or facts arise,

24 Paragraph 2 of Article 32 of the 2019 Anti-Unfair Competition Law: "if the right holder of a trade secret provides preliminary evidence reasonably showing that the trade secret has been infringed, and provides one of the following evidences, the suspected tortfeasor shall prove that he has not infringed the trade secret: (1) There is evidence showing that the suspected tortfeasor has access to or opportunities to obtain the trade secret, and the information he uses is substantially identical as the trade secret; (2) There is evidence showing that the trade secret has been disclosed or used by the suspected tortfeasor or that there is a risk of disclosure or use; (3) There is other evidence showing that the trade secret has been infringed by the suspected tortfeasor."

25 Beijing Yuanding Times Technology Co., Ltd., Qu Zhanbin, etc. Civil Judgment of the Second Instance of the Civil Dispute over Infringement of Technical Secrets Civil Judgment of the Supreme People's Court of the People's Republic of China (2021) SFZMZ No. 2389.

both parties should be given further opportunities to provide evidence. In reality, facts of cases, particularly those with sciences and technologies involved, are very complex, and it is difficult for judges to apply their legal knowledge to complex facts at one time. The courts should allow both sides to have multiple opportunities for proof with the deepening of technology and factual disclosure, so as to find out the facts as closely as possible to the truth.

Take the case of Qu Zhanbin of the Supreme Court in 2021 as an example. The focus of the dispute between the two parties is whether the defendant and the employee have used the plaintiff's trade secret software to serve Luoyang Bank. The relevant factors are as follows: the employee was the vice president before his resignation, established a new software company (the defendant) with himself as the legal representative six days before his resignation, provided similar software system construction services to Luoyang Bank, the plaintiff's customer, immediately after the establishment of the defendant, and served Luoyang Bank while the employee worked in the plaintiff's company. The aforementioned factors, combined with the fact that the employee could also have infringed another trade secret of the former employer, customer information, are a strong tendentious signal of the employee's infringement of the employer's trade secret. That is, from the perspective of the judge, the probability of the existence of infringement is much higher than the opposite. Then, the burden of proof should be assigned to the defendant and the employee to prove his innocence. Unless the employee and the defendant company provide evidence of software development, or can prove that the software for service project for Luoyang Bank is completely different from the plaintiff's software, the infringement should be established. We are of the view that the Supreme Court's assignment of burden of proof to the plaintiff in the case is improper.

Therefore, we summarize the reasonable burden of proof allocation rule for proving act of use infringement, which courts across the country tend to apply in practice, as follows.

Courts first make a preliminary judgment on the probability of infringement or non-infringement based on the existing evidence and the proposition and depositions of both parties. The factors to be considered in this judgment include the timing and behavioral characteristics of the employee's exposure to trade secrets and suspicious infringement acts, the unlawful means of acquisition or disclosure trade secrets by the employee, the defendant's R & D details and investment, the defendant's past work experience and the ability of independent R & D, the method and characteristics of the employee's suspicious infringement acts after termination, the technical characteristics of trade secrets involved, whether the information is originally created by the right holder or comes from or is transformed from a third party, the agreement or recognition of the nature of the relevant information between the two parties, etc.

If the preliminary conclusion is that the employee or the defendant is more likely than not to have committed an infringement, the courts assign the burden of proof to the defendant to prove that it did not infringe. This is the key to who has the obligation to apply for and pay for the technical appraisal of comparison of trade secrets and information involved in the case. If the defendant refuses to apply for the comparative appraisal and fails to provide other exemption evidence, such as the evidence of independent research and development, the evidence of the possibility of its non-exposure to trade secrets, the non-use of trade secrets, the fact that the technology used is not substantially identical to the trade secrets of the right holder, or legal reverse engineering,[26] then the defendant should bear the consequences of the inability of proof, and the courts determine that the defendant has committed use infringement.

189. Can an employer pursue a departed employee for customer poaching?

Answer: The so-called departed employee poaching customers normally refers the departed employee taking advantage of the personal relationship established with the employer's customer or customer information in their possession to attract and persuade the customer to become a customer of their new employer or their own business.

If the employer and the employee have signed a non-competition agreement, the employer can certainly hold the employee responsible for poaching the customer according to the non-competition penalty. However, under trade secret law and practice, it is very difficult and highly uncertain for the employer to pursue the employee's liability for this type of activity.

Article 1 of the Provisions of the Supreme People's Court on Several Issues Concerning the Application of Law in the Trial of Civil Cases of Infringement of Trade Secrets in 2020 stipulates that the customer's name, address, contact information, trade habits, intentions, content, and other information contained in customer information are in-depth business information in trade secrets and shall be protected. However, Article 2 of this regulation appears to be based on the principle of free market competition, requiring that the scope of infringement of trade secrets shall be limited and that an employee's post-employment transaction with the former employer's customer without unlawful acts, especially the customer voluntarily trading with the employee or their current employer, should not be considered as trade secret infringement.[27] In practice, in most cases, employers' customers are willing to trade with departed employees or their new employers, and these transactions are usually based on in-depth business information; therefore, it is a problem that the Supreme Court's regulation cannot solve the dilemma of whether the situation of the departed employee trading with the former employer's customers should apply Article 1 to protect trade secrets, or apply Article 2 to deny trade secret infringement.

At present, there are also contradictory judgments and opinions in judicial decisions.

Some judgments are based on the aforementioned Article 1 to examine whether there is in-depth customer information in the case, including the customer's trading needs, habits, and information content as trade secrets. Employees using this in-depth information

---

26 Hubei Nayu New Energy Technology Co., Ltd., You Pengyu and other civil judgments of the second instance of disputes over infringement of technical secrets, Civil Judgment of the Supreme People's Court of the People's Republic of China (2022) ZGFZMZ No. 275. An employee had access to the computer containing technical secrets and had contacts with the employer's customers after entering the position. Four months later, he left his job and set up a company to produce coking inhibitors of the same kind, but the employee had no education or experience in producing the product. The court finally found that the plaintiff had completed the preliminary proof, and the defendant had not proved that he had not infringed, so the defendant was ordered to bear the responsibility.

27 Article 2 of the Provisions of the Supreme People's Court on Several Issues Concerning the Application of Law in the Trial of Civil Cases of Infringement of Trade Secrets (Judicial Interpretation [2020] No. 7). "The people's court shall not support a party's claim that a specific customer is a trade secret only on the ground of maintaining a long-term stable trading relationship with the specific customer. If a client conducts a transaction with the new employer of the former employee based on their trust in the employee, and after the employee terminates the role, it can be proved that the client voluntarily chooses to conduct a transaction with the employee or the new employer of the employee, the people's court shall determine that the employee has not obtained the trade secrets of the right holder by unjustified means."

and contacting customers constitutes infringement of trade secrets. In the case of Anmei Weike (Beijing) Internet Technology Co., Ltd. in 2020, the Supreme Court held that publicly available information such as the name list and addresses of customers does not constitute trade secrets; in the case of Qingdao Melville Machinery and Equipment Import and Export Co., Ltd. in 2020, an employer's senior manager did four transactions with a department of the Sudanese government in two or three years on behalf of the company. Later, the manager set up a company to trade with the customer through his wife, and the transaction items were largely the same as the company's original transaction. The Supreme Court ruled that it constituted an infringement of trade secrets.[28]

However, there are similar cases with the opposite result. In the case of Shijiazhuang Shimai Valve Manufacturing Co., Ltd. before the Supreme Court in 2020, a shareholder of the company and some others founded a new company engaged in the same business, trading with the company's customers. The Supreme Court held that the customers had not formed a long-term relationship with the company (only two transactions in one year), and there was no evidence showing that it involved specific trading needs, models, and other secret information, so it did not constitute trade secrets, nor did it constitute infringement.[29] Similarly, in the case of Kanhe before the Supreme Court in 2021, three employees set up a new company two years after joining an international logistics company and

28 Anmei Weike (Beijing) Internet Technology Co., Ltd. and Lingbo Technology (Beijing) Co., Ltd., Zheng Guanghui, Wu Jianming, Shi Hongliang and Xu Feng Infringement of Computer Software Copyright and Infringement of Trade Secrets Civil Judgment of the Supreme People's Court of the People's Republic of China (2020) No. 1099. The court held that "[a]ccording to the customer list submitted by Anmei Weike Company, the list is only a list of hotels, which can not show the special customer information different from the relevant public information, such as customer address, contact information, trading habits, intentions and contents, and the hotel name can be obtained through public channels, so it cannot constitute the trade secret of Anmei Weike Company." Qingdao Melville Machinery and Equipment Import and Export Co., Ltd., Xu Jingqing Civil Ruling on Retrial Review and Trial Supervision of Infringement of Trade Secrets Disputes, Civil Ruling of the Supreme People's Court of the People's Republic of China (2020) ZGFMS No. 401. In the case, the company's senior manager had represented the company four times in two or three years, trading with a government department of Sudan, a major customer. Later, the manager set up a company through his wife to trade with the client, and the content of the transaction was basically the same as the original transaction of the company. The court held that this constituted an infringement of trade secrets. Shenyang Industrial Pump Manufacturing Co., Ltd., Du Shaolong and other civil judgments of the second instance of civil disputes over infringement of trade secrets, Liaoning Provincial People's High Court Civil Judgment (2021) Liao Min Zhong No. 879. The court held that "Shenyang Industrial Pump Co., Ltd. cannot claim that the specific customer belongs to a trade secret merely on the ground of maintaining a long-term trading relationship with the specific customer so as to restrict the right of the customer to choose their own trading partners and other business entities to participate in competition. Customer's product requirements, product models, and technical parameters are very easy to be obtained by the relevant personnel in the field, and they are not confidential." Xu Shuzhen and Lianyungang Qunsi Electronic Commerce Technology Co., Ltd. in the case of labor dispute appeal, Jiangsu Lianyungang Intermediate People's Court Civil Judgment (2016) Su 07 Min Zhong No. 3313. In the case, the two parties signed a confidentiality and non-competition agreement but did not agree to pay non-competition allowance. Employees left the company, engaged in competitive business, and contacted the employer's customer group. The court held that the customer group belonged to the core business of the employer and was a trade secret, and that even if the non-competition allowance was not paid, it would not affect the employee's liability for contractual damages, and ordered the employee to compensate six months of wages, RMB 36,000, and the lawyer's fee.

29 Shijiazhuang Shimai Valve Manufacturing Co., Ltd. and Hebei Chuangmin Technology Co., Ltd. Civil Judgment of the Second Instance of the Dispute over Infringement of Trade Secrets Civil Judgment of the Supreme People's Court of the People's Republic of China (2020) ZGFZMZ No. 1695. In the case, a shareholder of the company established a new company with others and traded with a customer who had had two transactions with the company a year ago. The court found that the customer had no long-term relationship, and there was no evidence to show that there were specific trading needs, models, and other secret information, so it did not constitute a trade secret, nor did it constitute infringement.

poached 25 customers of the company. The Supreme Court set aside the second-instance judgment that found infringement, ruling that the content of the evidence (a VAT invoice) submitted by the plaintiff was not a trade secret, and the plaintiff's claim was rejected.[30]

Therefore, under the current law and case practice in China, an employee who has signed a valid non-competition agreement should certainly bear the liability for breach of contract, but whether the employee's trading with an employer's customer after leaving the company without a non-competition agreement constitutes an infringement of trade secrets is uncertain in different courts around the country. China's trade secret law regarding customer poaching needs appropriate amendments because it is hard to distinguish infringement and non-infringement, and law application and legal consequence are uncertain in the current system. Please refer to "190. What rule do Chinese courts tend to use in determining whether customer poaching constitutes infringement?"

190. What rule do Chinese courts tend to use in determining whether customer poaching constitutes infringement?

Answer: This article presents an in-depth analysis of the current statutory rules and judicial decisions in China regarding the handling of employee poaching behavior, summarizing a judicial rule for determining whether poaching constitutes infringement. This rule is not explicitly defined in current Chinese law, nor is it uniformly categorized in judicial practices, but it tends to be practically applied by courts across different regions. Readers may skip the detailed legal analysis below and refer directly to our conclusion.

We have observed that although the current judicial decisions tend to reduce the issue to whether customer information constitutes a trade secret, the courts' decisions appear to revolve around three types of factors to reach the conclusion of whether there is an infringement.

The first factor is the consideration of the legitimacy of the defendant's behavior. This factor should probably be the most important consideration, because the examination of trade secret infringement cases itself is to examine the illegality of infringement. Article 2 of the 2020 Supreme Court's regulation concerning trade secrets also refers to "obtaining the trade secrets of the right holder by unlawful means."[31] For example, in the case of Hou Lanyu before the Zhejiang High Court in 2020, the employee of a patent office took advantage of her work to obtain in-depth information about customers. Although she signed a commitment not to take away customers when she left, she still poached several

30 Kan He et al. and Anhui Jinling International Freight Forwarding Co., Ltd. in the retrial of the dispute over infringement of trade secrets (2021) Supreme Fa Min Zai No. 310. In the case, after working for more than two years, 3 employees of the International Freight Forwarding Co., Ltd. established the same business enterprise and began to trade with 25 customers of the company. The first- and second-instance judgment found infringement, but the Supreme Court found that the VAT invoice evidence submitted by the plaintiff could not prove that the customer information belonged to trade secrets, and rejected the plaintiff's claims. The appeal case of unfair competition disputes between Guangxi Hengsheng Electronic Technology Co., Ltd. and Tan Weiwei, the Civil Judgment of the High Court of Guangxi Zhuang Autonomous Region (2021) Gui Min Zhong No. 1196.

31 Paragraph 2 of Article 2 of the Provisions of the Supreme People's Court on Several Issues Concerning the Application of Law in the Trial of Civil Cases of Infringement of Trade Secrets (Judicial Interpretation [2020] No. 7). "If a client conducts a transaction with the new employer of the former employee based on their trust in the employee, and after the employee terminates the role, it can be proved that the client voluntarily chooses to conduct a transaction with the employee or the new employer of the employee, the people's court shall determine that the employee has not obtained the trade secrets of the right holder by unjustified means."

important customers in violation of the commitment and confidentiality agreement. The Zhejiang Provincial High Court held that even if these customers voluntarily traded with the employee out of trust, the employee's behavior was still accountable.[32]

The second factor is the interest of the right holder. The Article 2 of the aforementioned Supreme Court's regulation refers to the customer relationship as "long-term stable transactions," implying that long-term customers are an important interest of the right holder. In the case of Luoyang Ruichang Environmental Engineering Co., Ltd. in 2020, the Supreme Court pointed out "analyzing the time, manpower, and material costs invested by the right holder in the development of customers, as well as the long-term and stable transactions between the two parties" to assist in judging whether the information constituted "information not known to the public."[33] This also implies that the right holder's input is related to their interests in the customer relationship. Therefore, the more long-term the customers are, the more that has been invested in the development of the customer, and the more customers that have been poached, the greater are the rights and interests of the right holder, and the more trade secrets need to be protected.

The third category of factors is the interests of third parties and the general public. The aforementioned Article 2 of the Supreme Court's regulation on voluntary transactions by customers out of trust in employees implies that the right of customers to free choice of suppliers should not be excessively restricted. For example, in the case of Beijing Lima Software Information Technology Co., Ltd. in 2004, the Beijing High People's Court held that "the demander of a product or service has the right to freely choose their trading partners" and that "the customer's right to freely choose the trading partner should be respected." The court of Yiwu City, Zhejiang Province also pointed out in the case of Ningbo Luzun International Trade Co., Ltd. in 2019 that "customers have the right to freely choose the plaintiff or other market entities in conducting their transactions."[34]

32 Hou Lanyu and Hangzhou Hangcheng Patent Office Co., Ltd. Civil Ruling of Zhejiang Provincial People's High Court (2020) Zhe Min Shen No. 1941. In the case, the staff of the Patent Office obtained in-depth information on customers and took away important long-term customers. The court held that this constituted a trade secret infringement, even if the customers voluntarily traded with the employee; because the employee had promised not to take customers away when she left, there was accountability.

33 Luoyang Ruichang Environmental Engineering Co., Ltd. and Luoyang Mingyuan Petrochemical Technology Co., Ltd. and other civil disputes over infringement of trade secrets and technical secrets Civil Judgment of Second Instance Civil Judgment of the Supreme People's Court of the People's Republic of China (2020) ZGFZMZ No. 726. Hangzhou Jingda Electronic Technology Co., Ltd. and Chen Aiping Infringement of Trade Secrets Dispute Appeal Case Zhejiang Provincial People's High Court Civil Judgment (2004) Zhe Min San Zhong Zi No. 156. The court held that although some customer information is publicly available, as the company has worked hard to accumulate and collate such information, it belongs to trade secrets. Finally, the court ruled that the employee's illegal acquisition was an infringement of trade secrets but did not constitute the use of trade secrets; the court awarded a discretionary compensation.

34 Beijing Lima Software Information Technology Co., Ltd. and Beijing Institute of Machinery Industry Automation, etc. (Civil Judgment of Beijing High Court [2004] GMZZ No. 800) on the Dispute over Infringement of Trade Secrets and Unfair Competition. The court held that "in market competition, in general, the demander of products or services has the right to freely choose the trading partner. In this case, six companies, including Zhuzhou Electric Locomotive Research Institute, Nanyang Explosion-proof Group Co., Ltd., Harbin Volkswagen Food Group Co., Ltd., Changde Tobacco Machinery Co., Ltd. and Qinhuangdao Tobacco Machinery Company Limited, Changchun Railway Passenger Car Company Limited, turned to the Automation because of personnel changes within Lima Software Company. Their right to freely choose their trading partners should be respected, and there is nothing wrong with the Automation trading with them." Ningbo Luzun International Trade Co., Ltd. and Shen Shanqing, Yiwu Borui Import and Export Co., Ltd. Civil Judgment of First Instance on Infringement of Trade Secrets, Zhejiang Yiwu People's Court Civil Judgment (2019) Zhe 0782 Minchu No. 4102. The court held that "from the perspective of maintaining free competition

Fundamentally, the rules of protecting trade secrets should be set at a reasonable balance between punishing employees' unlawful acts, protecting legitimate rights and interests of right holders, and properly taking into account public interests, including the interests of third parties (such as customers).

Therefore, we summarize the potential judicial rules that courts across different regions tend to practically apply regarding whether "poaching clients constitutes trade secret infringement" as follows: courts are inclined to consider the balance of interests among the right holder, the defendant, and third-party interests and public interests, rather than solely focusing on whether specific client/customer information constitutes a trade secret.

First, courts will examine the legitimacy or illegitimacy of employee behavior based on the three elements of a trade secret, including the non-publicity and depth of client information, protective measures, and commercial value. The employee's behavior to be examined includes whether customer information was stolen or acquired legitimately, the reasonableness of contacting and transacting with clients, whether the employee established a company before departure, the presence of explicit commitments against customer poaching, awareness of the significant harm to the company's operations through customer poaching, and involvement in unlawful activities such as fraud, coercion, and theft, etc.

Second, the courts shall consider the legitimacy and significance of the rights related to the right holders, including the company's long-term investment in customer development and relationships, the extent of the impact of customer poaching on the company, and even factors such as favorable employment terms for the employee in question. Lastly, the courts shall consider third party or public interests, encompassing whether the third party clients are aware of the employee's obligations regarding confidentiality or non-solicitation and the duration of their cooperation with the right holder. Other factors may include whether there is collusion between the employee and the third party and whether the prohibition of transactions between the customer and the employee's company is fair.

Considering these factors as a whole, the courts will ultimately come down to judge whether it is fair and reasonable for the employee to poach the company's customers without punishment; it is no longer necessary to narrowly confine the problem to whether the customer information constitutes a trade secret. Considering the above factors, if it is unfair and unreasonable not to punish the employee for customer poaching, the employee's behavior of customer poaching will constitute infringement. Otherwise, it does not constitute infringement.

This potential rule of precedent could effectively explain the contradictions and conflicts in judicial practice regarding cases involving customer poaching, as well as decisions in which courts acknowledge that customer information constitutes a trade secret but do not uphold prohibiting customers from engaging in transactions with departed employees (i.e., using such trade secrets).

191. What are the immunities for trade secret infringement in practice?

Answer: Even if a right holder can preliminarily prove the existence of the trade secret and the defendant's impugned infringement act, the defendant may still be able to be exempted

---

in the market, the customer in the trade secret claimed by the plaintiff has the right to freely choose the plaintiff or other market entities to conduct transactions. The value of the trade secret is mainly reflected in providing conditions and convenience for the formation of transactions with the customer. The existence of the trade secret does not necessarily lead to transactions. The trade secret can bring weak competitive advantage and low economic value to the plaintiff."

from the liability under special circumstances (that is, immunities). Common grounds for immunities include independent research and development, reverse engineering, the information involved in the case being different from the relevant trade secrets, no access to trade secrets, and lawful acquisition.

The first immunity is independent development. Independent development means that although the defendant's relevant information is identical or substantially identical to the right holder's trade secrets, the defendant can prove that the relevant information does not come from the right holder but from their own research and development. Compared with copyright infringement cases, in which it is almost impossible for two original works to be identical, it is not entirely impossible for different people to develop the same technical secret (such as a mechanical device). The defendant needs to provide evidence to prove their original creation and submit information on research and development. Based on this research and development evidence, the history of contact with the trade secret involved in the case, the timeline of independent development claimed by the defendant, and the characteristics of the trade secrets involved in the case, the courts may comprehensively judge whether the defendant's independent development is established.[35]

Independent development immunity is essentially the defendant's claim that they are not infringing, because the information they use is independently developed, not a theft of other people's achievement. The judicial interpretation and judicial cases from the Supreme Court on technical secret cases in 2020 show that independent development is an immunity of infringement.[36] This is tantamount to saying that the law protects trade secrets but also allows others to use and sell the same or similar information that is independently developed.

The second immunity is reverse engineering. According to the Supreme Court's judicial interpretation of trade secrets in 2020, reverse engineering refers to obtaining relevant technical information about a product by disassembling, measuring, and analyzing the

35 Zhuhai Qianyou Technology Co., Ltd. and Xu Hao, et al., Civil Judgment of Guangdong Provincial People's High Court (2019) Yue Zhi Min Zhong No. 457. The court held that "in this case, from the establishment time of Strategy Company and Nanpai Company and the online operation time of the accused game, the development time of the accused game can be calculated, which is obviously shorter than the industry experience. Therefore, the rationality of its independent development is doubtful."

36 The first paragraphs of Article 14 of the Provisions of the Supreme People's Court on Several Issues Concerning the Application of Law in the Trial of Civil Cases of Infringement of Trade Secrets (Judicial Interpretation [2020] No. 7) stipulate that if the alleged infringing information is obtained through self-development or reverse engineering, the people's court shall determine that it is not an infringement of trade secrets as stipulated in Article 9 of the Anti-Unfair Competition Law. Ningbo Wandai Punch Technology Co., Ltd. v. Kunshan Yamada Punch Co., Ltd. and other disputes over infringement of technical secrets, Zhejiang Provincial People's High Court Civil Judgment (2014) Zhe Zhi Zhong Zi No. 60. The court held that "Longyou Wandai Company and Hu Haoxiang could not prove that their acquisition of the same technical information as Yamada Company was the result of independent development, that he obtained the above technical information through reverse engineering, or that there are other legitimate sources. In addition, in light of the facts that Hu Haoxiang is the investor and legal representative of Longyou Wandai Company and Ningbo Wandai Company, Hu Haoxiang and Wang Guangbing are the inventors of the utility model patents of 'a cooling system for connecting rods of high-speed precision punches' and 'a locking device for high-speed precision punches' owned by Ningbo Wandai Company, and that Longyou Wandai Company and Ningbo Wandai Company in a short time after their establishment produced the punch products, being against the common sense. We found that Hu Haoxiang and Wang Guangbing disclosed the technical secrets of 'connecting rod cooling system' and 'mold locking device' in Yamada's punch products involved in the case to Longyou Bandai Company and Ningbo Bandai Company in violation of the agreement with Yamada Company or the requirement of Yamada Company to keep trade secrets. Longyou Bandai Company and Ningbo Bandai company illegally used the above technical secrets of Yamada company."

product acquired from public channels through technical means.[37] At present, judicial decisions on reverse engineering related to trade secrets published in China are very rare, and there is still a lack of systematic legislative and judicial interpretation of the important factors such as "personnel in the field" and "obtain by observation" that reflect the difficulty of acquisition of technical information.[38]

The essence of the immunity of reverse engineering is that the defendant claims that the right holder of the trade secret has not taken confidentiality measures, such as technical protection measures, to prevent product buyers from obtaining trade secret information through normal technical means, such as observation or disassembly. This renders the trade secret unestablished due to the absence of the element of "having taken confidentiality measures." For example, in the case of Jinan Sike Testing Technology Co., Ltd. in 2020, the Supreme Court held that the products produced and sold by the plaintiff in the market could be simply disassembled to obtain the confidentiality points of the trade secrets involved, and the plaintiff did not take measures against reverse engineering, so the information involved did not meet the legal condition of taking confidentiality measures, and the trade secret was not established.[39] However, if the defendant first illegally infringes on a trade secret and later resorts to immunity of reverse engineering, they are not free from tort liability.[40]

To prevent the first defense of independent development and the second defense of reverse engineering, the right holder of trade secrets may consider registering trade secrets for protection, such as through the registration of trade secrets as patents. Under the patent

37 The second paragraphs of Article 14 of the Provisions of the Supreme People's Court on Several Issues Concerning the Application of Law in the Trial of Civil Cases of Infringement of Trade Secrets (Judicial Interpretation [2020] No. 7). Jinan Sike Testing Technology Co., Ltd. v. Jinan Languang Electromechanical Technology Co., Ltd. Civil Judgment of the Supreme People's Court of the People's Republic of China (2020) SFZMZ No. 538. The court pointed out that "reverse engineering refers to obtaining the relevant technical information of the product by disassembling, mapping, and analyzing the product obtained from open channels through technical means."

38 Nanfang Zhongjin Environment Co., Ltd. v. Zhejiang Nanyuan Pump Industry Co., Ltd., the Hangzhou Intermediate People's Court, Zhejiang Province, (2020) Zhe 01 Min Chu No. 287. The court held that "it is necessary to distinguish whether the defendant's defence is easy availability or non-infringement according to the degree of difficulty of reverse engineering. Specifically, simple reverse engineering can be regarded as a defence of easy availability, a denial of secrecy; Article 9 of the Interpretation of Unfair Competition Cases should be applied to judge whether the technical information involved is easy to obtain; the more difficult reverse engineering should be regarded as a defence of non-infringement, a denial of infringement; the provisions of Article 12 of the Interpretation of Unfair Competition Cases should be applied to make decision, taking account into whether the defendant can prove that he actually carried out the dismantling, mapping, analysis and other facts."

39 Jinan Sike Testing Technology Co., Ltd. and Jinan Languang Electromechanical Technology Co., Ltd. Civil Judgment (2020) No. 538 of the Supreme People's Court of the People's Republic of China on the Dispute over Infringement of Technical Secrets. The court held that "in view of the fact that the carrier of technical secrets involved in the case is a market circulation product, it belongs to an external carrier. Therefore, the confidentiality measures taken by Sike Company to achieve the purpose of confidentiality should be able to resist the acquisition of its technical secrets by an unspecified third party through reverse engineering. This resistance can be achieved in at least two ways: one is that according to the nature of the technical secret itself, even if others disassemble the product containing the technical secret, they cannot know the technical secret through analysis; the other is to take physical security measures to resist the reverse engineering of others, such as adopting an integrated structure, disassembly will destroy the technical secrets."

40 Paragraph 3 of Article 14 of the Provisions of the Supreme People's Court on Several Issues Concerning the Application of Law in the Trial of Civil Cases of Infringement of Trade Secrets (Judicial Interpretation [2020] No. 7). This provision seems to imply that trade secrets can still be protected due to unjustified acts of the defendant even if the conditions of "taking confidentiality measures" are flawed in the resistance against reverse engineering.

legal system, as long as the patentee has submitted a patent application, they have the right to pursue others using the same technology even if it is independently developed and completed after the application date. This is different from trade secrets protection exempting others for independent development of the same information.[41] Of course, the disadvantage of this method is that the technical secret must be disclosed under the patent system. In addition, under the patent system, the tortfeasor's reverse engineering does not constitute an immunity.

The third exemption is that the information is different from the trade secret. As the master of the defendant's information, if the defendant can prove the difference between the key technical points of the defendant's information and the confidentiality points of the plaintiff's trade secret, so as to prove that the information of the defendant is different from or not substantially identical to the plaintiff's trade secret, of course, there is no trade secret infringement.

The fourth immunity is lawful acquisition. Lawful acquisition means that the defendant legally acquired the trade secret of the right holder, or that the defendant's impugned information has a legitimate source, such as through a legitimate technology transfer agreement. At present, laws or judicial interpretations have not included it as one immunity, and it is only a judicial practice.[42]

The fifth exemption is that there is no access to the trade secret. If the defendant can prove that it has no access to the trade secret, then, of course, the defendant had no chance to obtain the plaintiff's trade secret by unlawful means, and the infringement of trade secrets cannot be established.

192. Who are right holders and tortfeasors in trade secret infringement cases?

Answer: In judicial practice, the right holders in trade secret infringement cases are usually the owners of trade secrets, but other right holders, such as the licensees of trade secrets, may also become the right holders of trade secrets. The persons who are liable for infringements of trade secrets are not necessarily limited to the direct tortfeasor (such as the employee who acquires the trade secret), and a third party who accepts and uses the trade secret disclosed by the direct tortfeasor may also be liable.

Understanding these issues is very important for readers to learn who has the standing to claim damages against the tortfeasor and against whom the right holder may raise claims.

The right holder who has the right to safeguard the rights and interests of a trade secret and the plaintiff who has the right to file a trade secret lawsuit include the following

41 Article 75 of the Patent Law of the People's Republic of China. "The following circumstances shall not be deemed as an infringement of the patent right: (2) where the same product has been manufactured, the same process has been used, or the necessary preparations for manufacture or use have been made before the date of application for the patent, and the manufacture or use continues only within the original scope."

42 Mdcare (Tianjin) Technology Co., Ltd. v. Hua A Xing Technology (Tianjin) Group Co., Ltd., Civil Judgment of the Supreme People's Court of the People's Republic of China (2019) Zui Gao Fa Min Zai No. 268. The court held that "in summary, Wang Chenggang, Liu Fang and Zhang Hongxing violated the legal and agreed confidentiality of Huayang Company, disclosed the trade secret business information in its possession, and allowed Mdcare Company to use the above customer list; Mdcare Company knowingly used the above customer list without the permission of Huayang Company. According to the method of 'identical (substantial identical) + contact-legal source' for judging the infringement of trade secrets, it was not improper for the court of the first instance to find that Mdcare Company, Wang Chenggang, Liu Fang and Zhang Hongxing jointly committed the infringement of the trade secret of Huayang Company."

persons: trade secret proprietor, exclusive licensee (only the licensee can use it), non-exclusive licensee (only the licensee and the proprietor can use it) and trade secret proprietor as co-plaintiffs (or the non-exclusive licensee alone as plaintiff if the proprietor explicitly relinquishes the rights of the lawsuit), the ordinary licensee (the proprietor may license others in addition to the ordinary licensee to use it) and the proprietor of the trade secret as the co-plaintiffs (or the ordinary licensee as the sole plaintiff if authorized by the proprietor).[43]

The difference between an exclusive license and a non-exclusive license is that the licensee of an exclusive license is the only one who can use the relevant trade secret; even the proprietor themselves cannot use it. In a non-exclusive license, both the licensee and the proprietor may use the trade secret, but the proprietor must not license any other person to use it.

The persons who may bear civil, administrative, and criminal liabilities for infringement of trade secrets are as follows: the tortfeasor (including under the type of acquisition, disclosure, and use infringements) and the third party who knows or should have known that the tortfeasor's behavior is infringement but still commits the above three types of infringement.[44] Examples of such illegal acts include theft, bribery, fraud, coercion, electronic intrusion, breach of confidentiality obligations, and the use, and permitting to use, of unauthorized trade secrets. It also includes abetting, enticing, and aiding others to commit acts of infringing trade secrets.

193. What civil liabilities are trade secret infringers subject to?

Answer: The legal liabilities for trade secret infringement encompass civil liability, administrative liability (see "194. What administrative liabilities are trade secret infringers subject to?"), and criminal liability (see "195. What criminal liabilities are trade secret infringers subject to?").

The civil liability for trade secret infringement includes five types: cessation of infringement, compensating for losses, apologizing, bearing the cost of safeguarding rights, and special means.

The first type of liability is cessation of infringement, which is the most direct way to stop infringement of trade secrets. For the technical information type of trade secret, the law and practice of cessation of infringement are clear: the tortfeasor should immediately cease infringement until the trade secret is no longer valid (e.g., if it becomes public information) or the right holder permits it.

However, for business information, the cessation of infringement until the publicity of the information may unfairly restrict the free competition rights of third parties and free employment rights of the employees, so it is necessary to stipulate an appropriate period of cessation of infringement. This is the provision of the Supreme Court on the judicial

43 Article 26 of the Provisions of the Supreme People's Court on Several Issues Concerning the Application of Law in the Trial of Civil Cases of Infringement of Trade Secrets (Judicial Interpretation [2020] No. 7). "Where the licensee of the exclusive license contract for the use of trade secrets brings a lawsuit against the infringement of trade secrets, the people's court shall accept it according to law. Where the licensee and the right holder of the non-exclusive license contract jointly file a lawsuit, or file a lawsuit on their own if the right holder does not file a lawsuit, the people's court shall accept it according to law. Where the licensee and the right holder of a general license contract file a lawsuit jointly or the licensee files a lawsuit separately with the written authorization of the right holder, the people's court shall accept the lawsuit according to law."

44 Article 9 of the 2019 Anti-Unfair Competition Law.

interpretation of trade secrets[45] and also the practice of judicial practice. For example, in the case of Beijing Huasheng Yingjie Information Technology Co., Ltd. in 2007, the First Intermediate People's Court of Beijing considered business competition employment rights and ordered that the time limit for the employee's use of the customer information secrets of their former employer was one year.[46] There are also court decisions limiting the use of a former employer's client information secrets for two years.[47]

Cessation of infringement has an ancillary form of liability: destruction of the alleged infringing information. However, a special case is that if the tortfeasor has creatively improved or upgraded the trade secrets of the right holder, the court may allow the tortfeasor to continue to use the improved or upgraded information for the purpose of protecting the increased intellectual property rights of the infringer, but order the infringer to pay damages in the form of license fees.[48]

When the protection of trade secrets is urgent, the right holder can apply to the court for an injunction order, and the court should judge whether to grant it according to an overall assessment of the likelihood of the right holder winning the lawsuit, comparison of damages between granting and not granting the injunction, and the public interest.[49]

The second type of liability is loss compensation. This is the most common form of liability. The second paragraph of Article 20 of the Supreme Court's Judicial Interpretation of Trade Secrets stipulates: "When the people's court determines the amount of compensation in accordance with the fourth paragraph of Article 17 of the Anti-Unfair Competition Law, it may take into account the nature, commercial value, research and development costs, degree of innovation, competitive advantages that can be brought about by trade

45 Article 17 of the Provisions of the Supreme People's Court on Several Issues Concerning the Application of Law in the Trial of Civil Cases of Infringement of Trade Secrets (Judicial Interpretation [2020] No. 7). "When the people's court decides a civil liability of cessation of infringement of trade secrets, the duration for the cessation shall generally last until the trade secrets are known to the public. If the time to stop the infringement is obviously unreasonable in accordance with the provisions of the preceding paragraph, the people's court may judge the tortfeasor to stop using the trade secret within a certain period or scope under the condition of protecting the competitive advantage of the right holder's trade secret according to law."

46 Beijing Huasheng Yingjie Information Technology Co., Ltd. v. Beijing Boruisida Digital Technology Co., Ltd. and Others (Dispute over Infringement of Trade Secrets and Other Unfair Competition) Civil Judgment of the First Intermediate People's Court of Beijing (2007) YZMCZ No. 10042. "Business information, especially the list of customers, is unlikely to have the situation where information is legally and naturally known to the relevant public due to technological progress ... permanently ceasing to use the relevant business information on the customer list will unduly restrict ... the right to legitimate commercial competition and will also unduly reduce employment opportunities. Therefore, that is obviously unreasonable."

47 Hebi City Reflective Materials Co., Ltd. and Song Junchao, Li Jianfa, Hebi Ruimingte Technology Co., Ltd. Case of Infringement of Trade Secrets Civil Judgment of Hebi Intermediate People's Court of Henan Province (2015) H.M.C.Z. No. 96.

48 Guangzhou Tianzhi High-tech Materials Co., Ltd. v. Wu Danjin's appeal against disputes over infringement of technical secrets, the Supreme People's Court of the People's Republic of China Civil Judgment (2019) No. 562. In the case, the employee mastered the technical secret formula of the employer and disclosed it to a third party for use, and the third party produced products after renovation and renewal. The appraisal could not identify that the two formulations were substantially identical. The court ordered the third party to compensate for the loss, did not support the destruction of the formula of the third party company, ordered the employee jointly and severally liable for part of the loss, and did not support the apology for the loss of goodwill.

49 *People's Court Daily*, November 28, 2013, page 6: case guide, (2013) Hu Yi Zhong Min Wu (Zhi) Chu Zi No. 119, Shanghai the First intermediate People's Court ruled in the case of Eli Lilly and others suing Huang Mengwei for infringement of technical secrets. The court held that "under normal circumstances, the applicant must prove the follows: the substantial possibility of winning the lawsuit; irreparable losses that will be suffered if the injunction is not granted; plaintiff's possible injury being greater than any potential injury to defendant; public interest being not violated by the issuance of the injunction."

secrets, as well as the subjective fault of the tortfeasor, the nature, circumstances, and consequences of the infringement."

The determination of the amount of loss generally is to first consider whether the actual loss of the right holder can be measured. If the actual loss cannot be measured, the infringement income of the tortfeasor can then be used. For serious infringements, the Anti-Unfair Competition Law stipulates punitive damages of one to five times the actual losses. The court may also order a discretionary compensation below RMB 5 million according to the specific factors mentioned above.[50]

The third form of liability is making an apology or eliminating the influence and restoring reputation, which is the form of civil liability stipulated in Article 179 of the Civil Code. The liability form of apology is applicable to the situation where the tortfeasor's behavior infringes on the personality rights of citizens or legal persons and causes damage to the goodwill and reputation of the victim. The vast majority of judgments in trade secret infringement cases do not support such a claim, because the courts found that the goodwill and reputation of the right holder were not damaged.[51] However, if the tortfeasor's act of counterfeiting does cause confusion among customers or damages to the right holder's goodwill and reputation, the court may order the elimination of influence, the restoration of reputation, and an apology.[52]

---

50 Article 17 of the Anti-Unfair Competition Law of 2019 stipulates that "operators who violate the provisions of this Law and cause damage to others shall bear civil liability according to law. A business operator whose lawful rights and interests are impaired by an act of unfair competition may institute a proceeding in a people's court. The amount of compensation to be paid to the operator who suffers losses due to unfair competition shall be determined according to the actual losses caused by the infringement. If the actual losses are difficult to calculate, the amount of compensation shall be determined according to the profits that the tortfeasor has gained from the infringement. If an operator maliciously commits an act of infringing upon trade secrets and the circumstances are serious, the amount of compensation may be determined by more than one time and less than five times the amount determined by the above method. Where an operator violates the provisions of Articles 6 and 9 of this Law, and it is difficult to determine the actual losses suffered by the right holder as a result of the infringement or the profits obtained by the tortfeasor as a result of the infringement, the people's court shall, according to the circumstances of the infringement, judge that the right holder shall be compensated not more than RMB 5 million." Langfang Baiyue Commerce and Trade Co., Ltd. and Langfang Ruoke Glass Co., Ltd. Civil Ruling on Retrial Review and Trial Supervision of Infringement of Trade Secrets Disputes of the Supreme People's Court of the People's Republic of China (2020) No. 4074. The court held that "the infringement of Ruoke Company to a certain extent led to the loss of some customers of Baiyue Company and caused the economic losses of Baiyue Company. Although the evidence submitted by Baiyue Company proved the actual transaction volume between Ruoke Company and its customers to a certain extent, it is not inappropriate for the court of first instance to consider that Baiyue Company and its customers were not exclusive suppliers and that there were many factors affecting price changes and to conclude that the loss of market price fluctuations could not be attributed to the unfair competition of Ruoke Company. It is not improper for the court of second instance to apply statutory compensation and increase the amount of compensation awarded by the court of first instance as its discretion, taking into account the factors such as the nature of infringement, circumstances, subjective fault, transaction volume, number of transactions, and the impact of the disclosure of customer list on the market competitive advantage of Baiyue Company."

51 Civil Judgment of the Supreme People's Court of the People's Republic of China (2019) No. 7 of the Supreme People's Court on the Appeal Case of Technical Secret Infringement Dispute between Youkai (Shanghai) Machinery Co., Ltd. and Cao, et al. The court held that "[a]s a way of assuming civil liability, eliminating influence is generally applicable to the case of damage to commercial reputation and commodity reputation caused by infringement."

52 Maotuo Automation Control System (Shanghai) Co., Ltd., Pan Shirong and Magnatik Control System (Shanghai) Co., Ltd. Civil Ruling of Shanghai High Court (2018) Hu Min Shen No. 318. CAO Lei v. NANJING HUANZHENG ENTERPRISE MANAGEMENT CONSULTING CO., LTD. Trade Secret Infringement Dispute Case Civil Judgment of Jiangsu Provincial People's High Court (2010) S.Z.M.Z.Z. No. 0154.

Although the Civil Code divides apology and elimination of influence and restoration of reputation into two forms of liability, the courts do not appear to make a substantive distinction in cases involving infringement of trade secrets, and some cases appear to use them jointly.[53]

The fourth type of liability is the cost of safeguarding rights.[54] In most other types of civil cases, costs of safeguarding rights (or costs in proceedings) are not a supportable item; this form of liability is a unique form of liability in intellectual property cases. The People's Court of Yinzhou District, Ningbo City, Zhejiang Province held in the case of Zhejiang Holistic Health Industry Development Co., Ltd. in 2019 that the Anti-Unfair Competition Law does not explicitly support reasonable expenses for stopping infringement as the judicial interpretation of the Trademark Law does, so the right holder's reasonable expenses for trade secret infringement cases can refer to the treatment of reasonable expenses of trademark infringement cases, including reasonable costs for investigation, evidence collection, and legal fees.[55]

The courts may discretionarily determine the costs of safeguarding rights, which can be ordered separately or together with damages.[56] The liability of acquisition infringement is generally the reasonable costs for safeguarding rights, including legal fees, which may also refer to the fee standard of the legal industry, not necessarily strictly based on the actual lawyer fees.[57]

The fifth type of liability is the special means of the court vesting ownership of intellectual property stemming from the infringed trade secret to the right owner. This form of liability is not a statutory one. For example, a patent that an infringer registered by infringing a trade secret is deemed to be the property of the owner of the trade secret, so the owner is entitled to add up a claim against the defendant to transfer the patent involved back to themselves.[58]

53 Liyang Laijiang Environmental Protection Engineering Co., Ltd. and Liyang Wuhuan Environmental Protection Engineering Co., Ltd. et al. Trade Secret Infringement Dispute Case Civil Judgment of Jiangsu Provincial People's High Court (2003) S.M.S.Z.Z. No. 010.

54 Article 17 of the Anti-Unfair Competition Law of 2019. "The amount of compensation shall also include the reasonable expenses paid by the operator to stop the infringement."

55 Zhejiang Holistic Health Industry Development Co., Ltd. and Yang Qixi, Ningbo Yun Hospital Co., Ltd. Civil Judgment of First Instance on Infringement of Trade Secrets Civil Judgment of Yinzhou District People's Court of Ningbo City, Zhejiang Province (2019) Zhe 0212 Minchu No. 4855. "This court considers that infringement of trade secrets and infringement of the exclusive right to use trademarks are both infringements of intellectual property rights of others. Under the circumstances that the Anti-Unfair Competition Law and its judicial interpretation have not explained in detail the 'reasonable expenses paid by operators to stop infringement', it can be identified as a reasonable cost for the right holder or the entrusted agent to investigate and collect evidence of the infringement by referring to the judicial interpretation of the Trademark Law."

56 Civil Judgment of the Second Instance of Li Lili and Bian Rongjun's Trade Secret Infringement Dispute Civil Judgment of Guangdong Provincial People's High Court (2018) Yue Min Zhong No. 1574.

57 Sun Zhiyu and Ingersoll Rand Industries USA Civil Judgment of the Second Instance of the Dispute over Infringement of Technical Secrets Civil Judgment of the Supreme People's Court of the People's Republic of China (2020) ZFZMZ No. 1276. In this case, an employee downloaded the company's technical secret drawings to other memories without permission, which constituted theft of technical secrets. The court ordered the employee not to disclose and use the secret, to return the carrier immediately, and to compensate RMB 300,000 of reasonable rights protection costs.

58 VMI Netherlands and Sachi Intelligent Equipment Co., Ltd. Civil Judgment of the Second Instance of the Civil Dispute over the Ownership of Patent Rights Civil Judgment of the Supreme People's Court of the People's Republic of China (2020) Supreme Fa Zhi Min Zhong No. 902. The court held that "[a]ccordingly, according to the evidence of both parties and the court's investigation of the facts, it can be determined that Sachi Company obtained the prior confidential technology of VMI Company by unjustified means and then

194. What administrative liabilities are trade secret infringers subject to?

Answer: A trade secret infringer may be simultaneously liable for civil liability (please refer to "193. What civil liabilities are trade secret infringers subject to?"), criminal liability (please refer to "195. What criminal liabilities are trade secret infringers subject to?"), and administrative liability.

Administrative liability refers to the administrative penalties imposed by administrative authorities on infringers. Article 21 of the 2019 Anti-Unfair Competition Law stipulates that supervisory and inspection authorities can order infringers who violate trade secrets to cease infringement, confiscate illegal gains, and impose fines ranging from RMB 100,000 to RMB 5 million. Administrative fines are deposited into the national treasury.

A particular scenario arises when the infringer's assets are insufficient to cover both civil compensation and administrative penalties. In such a case, should the infringer prioritize paying civil compensation or administrative penalties? Currently, the law does not provide specific regulations on this matter. However, based on the provisions of the Company Law and a judicial decision in the Securities Law, the current judicial system tends to prioritize civil compensation.

Article 263 of the 2023 Company Law stipulates that the civil compensation liability of company promoters and shareholders should take precedence over administrative penalty liability. Additionally, in the third case of the "Top Ten Financial Commercial Cases of 2022" released by the Shanghai High People's Court, an investor's lawsuit dispute against Xian for manipulating the securities trading market, the court ruled that since the assets of the securities manipulator were insufficient to simultaneously pay administrative penalties, criminal fines, and civil compensation, they should first be used for civil compensation liability.[59]

195. What criminal liabilities are trade secret infringers subject to?

Answer: When an infringement of trade secrets reaches a certain severe level, it may constitute a criminal offense. Criminal liability for infringement of trade secrets is the most severe form of liability and the most powerful means for the right holder of trade secrets to stop infringement. Minor trade secret infringements, of course, only attract civil liability (please refer to "193. What civil liabilities are trade secret infringers subject to?") and/or administrative liability (please refer to "194. What administrative liabilities are trade secret infringers subject to?").

applied for the patent involved and was granted the same. Therefore, the patent involved should be owned by VMI."

59 The Shanghai High People's Court released the third case of the "Top Ten Financial Commercial Cases of 2022": Investor Lawsuit against Xian for Market Manipulation of Securities Trading—Determination of Liability Dispute Involving Various Methods of Securities Manipulation in the Main Board Market.

According to the provisions of Article 219 of the Criminal Law of 2023[60] and the Supreme Court's judicial interpretation of intellectual property criminal cases in 2020,[61] the acts of criminal suspects that meet the following three conditions constitute a crime.

First, the suspect's behavior constitutes the infringement of trade secrets, including acquisition, disclosure, and use infringement. These three types of trade secret infringement under the 2023 Criminal Law are completely consistent with the trade secret infringements under the 2019 Anti-Unfair Competition Law.

Of course, civil and criminal cases are distinct in the standard of evidence. The former are subject to the standard of balance of probability and the latter to the principle of being beyond reasonable doubt, rendering the establishment of criminal infringement acts having a much higher threshold than the civil one.

Second, the infringement has caused certain consequences, including causing illegal income of the infringer or damages to the right holder at more than RMB 300,000 (around US$ 40,000), or directly resulting in the bankruptcy of, or other major damages to, the right holder.

Third, the criminal consciousness of the criminal suspect is "being knowing." This is different from the state of "being knowing or should have known" of civil infringement of trade secrets stipulated in the Anti-Unfair Competition Law, which reflects the higher standard of illegality identification in criminal law than in civil law. In fact, in the previous version of the Criminal Act 2017, the criminal consciousness stipulated for the crime of infringing trade secrets was still "being knowing or should have known" as for civil infringement.

If all the above criteria are met, the criminal suspect shall be found to have committed a crime and shall be sentenced to fixed-term imprisonment of not more than three years. The criminal suspect's infringement of trade secrets causing losses to the right holder, or resulting in illegal gains of more than RMB 2,500,000, shall be deemed as "causing particularly serious consequences," and the criminal suspect shall be sentenced to three to ten years' imprisonment.

60 Article 219 of the Criminal Law. "Whoever commits any of the following acts of infringing upon trade secrets, if the circumstances are serious, shall be sentenced to fixed-term imprisonment of not more than three years and shall also, or shall only, be fined; If the circumstances are especially serious, the person shall be sentenced to fixed-term imprisonment of not less than three years but not more than 10 years and shall also be fined: (1) obtaining the right holder's trade secrets by theft, bribery, fraud, coercion, electronic intrusion, or other unjustified means; (2) disclosing, using, or allowing others to use the right holder's trade secrets obtained by the means mentioned in the preceding paragraph; (3) disclosing, using, or allowing others to use the trade secrets in violation of the obligation of confidentiality or the requirements of the right holder to keep the trade secrets. Whoever, knowing the acts listed in the preceding paragraph, obtains, discloses, uses or allows others to use the trade secrets shall be regarded as infringing upon the trade secrets. 'Right holders' as mentioned in this Article refers to the owner of trade secrets and the person who is permitted by the owner to use the trade secrets."

61 Article 4 of the Interpretation of the Supreme People's Procuratorate of the Supreme People's Court on Several Questions Concerning the Specific Application of Law in Handling Criminal Cases of Infringement of Intellectual Property Rights (III) (Judicial Interpretation [2020] No. 10). "Any of the following circumstances in committing the acts specified in Article 219 of the Criminal Law shall be deemed as 'causing great losses to the right holder of the trade secret': (1) having caused losses to the right holder of the trade secret, or having obtained illegal gains, of more than RMB 300,000 due to infringement of trade secrets; (2) having directly caused the right holder to go bankrupt or close down due to major operational difficulties; (3) having caused other great losses to the obligor of the trade secrets. If the amount of loss caused to the right holder of trade secrets or the amount of illegal gains from infringement of trade secrets is more than RMB 2,500,000, it shall be recognized as 'having caused especially serious consequences' as stipulated in Article 219 of the Criminal Law."

6.2 Non-Competition

196. What is the difference between non-competition and trade secret?

Answer: Non-competition is a restriction stipulated by an employer, prohibiting its employees from engaging in specific competitive work (including by self-employment or employment) either during or after their employment. The employee's access to the employer's trade secrets is the first prerequisite for both parties to agree that the employee undertakes the obligation of non-competition. Employees who have no access to trade secrets do not need to undertake the obligation of non-competition. However, the obligation of employees to protect trade secrets is different from the obligation of employees' non-competition.

First of all, the duration of trade secret protection is the period of existence of the trade secret; that is to say, as long as a trade secret does not become public information and lose its confidentiality, employees or anyone else are obligated not to infringe upon the rights of the employer. The period of non-competition for employees shall not exceed the statutory length of two years. That is to say, after two years, employees are no longer bound by the obligation of non-competition and are free to work in competitive industries, but as long as the trade secret still exists, employees are still obligated not to infringe on the trade secret.

Second, trade secret right is a kind of property right, like other property rights of the employer, such as their machinery and equipment. Irrespective of whether the employer pays a confidentiality fee to the employee or not, the employee bears the obligation not to infringe upon the right. On the contrary, the obligation of non-competition must be based on the employer's payment of non-competition allowance. If the employer unilaterally requires the employee not to engage in the competitive industry without paying the non-competition allowance, the employee may cancel the restriction. For details, please refer to "200. The non-competition agreement lacks a non-competition allowance clause. What should I do?" It should be noted that even if the employee cancels the restriction, they are still subject to the obligation of protecting the employer's trade.

The right holder of a trade secret may, of course, grant a paid license to others to use the trade secret. An interesting case related to a dispute after a trade secret license agreement expired is the case of Shijiazhuang Zexing Amino Acid Co., Ltd in 2020. In the case, both parties agreed upon a paid license of a trade secret without providing the licensee's rights after the contract expires. The Supreme Court held that although the licensee stopped the license fee payment after the expiration, it might continue to use the trade secret, while having no right to permit others to use it.[62] The Supreme Court probably interpreted both parties' contractual purpose, finding that the parties intended a long-term permission after the contract expiration. It was unlikely to recognize the licensee's right of infringement after the contract expiration.

197. What are non-competition and liability for breach of non-competition?

Answer: Articles 23 and 24 of the Employment Contract Law stipulate that non-competition is a measure taken by an employer to legally restrict employees who leave their jobs from working in competitive industries, so as to protect their trade secrets preventively.

62 Shijiazhuang Zexing Amino Acid Co., Ltd., Hebei Daxiao Biotechnology Co., Ltd. v. Beijing Junde Tongchuang Biotechnology Co., Ltd. in the case of disputes over infringement of technical secrets—the confidentiality obligation after the expiration of the agreed confidentiality period. Civil Judgment of the Supreme People's Court of the People's Republic of China (2020) ZuigaoFaZhiMinZhong No. 621.

Non-competition specifically means that the employer may sign an agreement with senior managers, senior technicians, and other persons who have the obligation to keep confidential the trade secrets of the employer, stipulating that after the termination or dissolution of the employee's employment relationship, the employee shall not be employed by other employers who engage in the same or similar business, such as the production or operation of the same or similar products or services, and shall not start their own business engaging in the same or similar business.

Only those employees who bear confidentiality responsibility are obligated to sign a non-competition agreement and be forbidden from engaging in competitive industry after leaving their jobs. Please refer to "198. Is it legal for an employer to sign a non-competition agreement with all its employees?"

Although there are no statutory provisions, current employees should not engage in a competitive industry while abiding by their obligation of employee's loyalty. Both parties can agree upon on-the-job non-competition obligation and contractual damages. Please refer to "199. The non-competition contract between an employer and an employee includes an on-the-job non-competition obligation. Is such an agreement valid?"

A non-competition agreement should stipulate the amount of non-competition allowance paid to the employee after employment termination. If, however, the non-competition agreement provides that the employee's wages consist of non-competition allowance, courts around the country have two practices on this matter. Please refer to "201. My employment contract stipulates that my wages include non-competition allowance. Is such provision legal?"

If a non-competition agreement only stipulates non-competition obligations in the absence of a non-competition allowance, it raises complex legal issues regarding the binding nature of the agreement on the employee and the amount of non-competition allowance that should be paid to the employee who has fulfilled the obligation. Please refer to "200. The non-competition agreement lacks a non-competition allowance clause. What should I do?"

Employees who violate the obligation of non-competition shall be liable for contractual damages and/or refunding the non-competition allowance in accordance with the non-competition agreement between the two parties.[63] Overly high contractual liquidated damages in a non-competition agreement may not be binding. Please see "203. The non-competition penalty stipulated in my non-competition agreement is RMB 5 million. Is this provision binding?" If the employee has paid the contractual damages to the employer, they may still assume the obligation to continue to perform the non-competition agreement unless the employer cancels the agreement or exempts the employee from the non-competition obligation. Please refer to "202. Can employers or employees cancel the non-competition agreement?"

It should be noted that even if there is no non-competition agreement between the employer and the employee, or both parties have terminated the non-competition agreement, the employee still bears the absolute legal obligation to protect the employer's trade secrets, and the employee who violates this obligation may bear the legal liability for infringement of trade secrets.

63 Article 19 of the 2023 Consultation Draft on the Interpretation of the Supreme People's Court on the Application of Law in the Trial of Labor Dispute Cases (II).

198. Is it legal for an employer to sign a non-competition agreement with all its employees?

Answer: This question is essentially whether the scope of employees permitted by law to undertake the obligation of non-competition includes ordinary employees.

Article 24 of the Employment Contract Law stipulates that non-competition personnel are limited to senior managers, senior technicians, and other personnel with confidentiality obligations to the employer. Non-competition agreements signed by persons who do not have access to trade secrets and stipulating the obligation of confidentiality are, of course, invalid because they conflict with the law.

Whether employees bear the obligation of confidentiality depends on whether they have access to trade secrets. Generally speaking, general managers, chief engineers, technical directors, department technical directors, financial managers of the company, and personnel who have access to the important business information and technical information of the company involved in these positions should be the only personnel who have access to trade secrets, so these are all the personnel with whom the employer can agree on a non-competition agreement. Ordinary employees who have no access to trade secrets are normally not personnel subject to a non-competition obligation.

For example, in the 2023 case of Yang in Beijing High Court, Judge Han Jungui pointed out: "When an employee is not a senior management personnel or a senior technical personnel, and they clearly assert that they are not 'other personnel with confidentiality obligations,' the mere existence of a non-competition agreement between the parties cannot directly lead to the presumption that the employer possesses trade secrets, nor can it naturally presume that the employee is aware of the employer's trade secrets and confidentiality matters related to intellectual property, or that they fall under the category of 'other personnel with confidentiality obligations.' Instead, a 'substantive review' should be conducted to determine whether the employer possesses trade secrets and whether the employee belongs to 'other personnel with confidentiality obligations,' and the employer should bear the burden of proof for the aforementioned matters to be proved."[64]

Therefore, whether a non-competition agreement signed by an employer and an ordinary employee is binding on the employee depends, in principle, on whether the employee belongs to "other personnel with confidentiality obligations." It is necessary to examine whether the employer has access to trade secrets and whether the related confidential information constitutes real trade secrets.

However, it is worth noting that in judicial practice of employment law, courts around the country adopt a formality assessment in a significant number of cases to determine whether the information that employees are in contact with constitutes trade secrets, instead of adopting a strict, substantial way to examine the three characteristics of trade secrets, namely, non-publicity, commercial value, and confidentiality measures. This is different from the strict control of the general protection of trade secrets by the courts in judicial practice. For example, in the case of Ge Jinhua before Sichuan Provincial High Court in 2015, the court held that the employee, as a front desk assistant of a plastic surgery hospital, had access to customer information, so she belonged to other personnel

64 A company v. Yang Beijing High People's Court Retrial Review and Trial Supervision of labor dispute Civil Ruling (2023) Jing Min Shen No. 4807.

with confidentiality obligations. The court did not proceed to a detailed analysis of the complex issues of whether customer information constitutes trade secrets.[65]

Some courts even presume that an employee on a confidentiality agreement belongs to the personnel bearing the obligations of confidentiality and non-competition, and require the employee to prove the opposite. For example, in the case of Tan Jianguang before Guangzhou Haizhu District Court in 2021, the court held that since the employee had signed confidentiality and non-competition agreements, and he did not provide sufficient evidence to prove that he was not non-competition-related personnel, the court therefore rejected the employee's claim.[66]

In determining whether an employee belongs to "other personnel with confidentiality obligations" or the validity of a non-competition agreement signed between an employer and a regular employee, there are contradictions and conflicts in both law and practice, which requires clarification in future legislation or case law.

199. The non-competition contract between an employer and an employee includes an on-the-job non-competition obligation. Is such an agreement valid?

Answer: The law does not specify during an employment relationship whether employees have the obligation of non-competition, whether the obligation requires their employers to pay non-competition allowance, and whether agreed contractual damages are binding.

At present, the judicial decisions of courts around the country tend to hold that employees have the duty of loyalty to their employers. If both parties agree in the agreement that they shall not engage in competitive industries during their tenure, the violator shall pay contractual damages, and the contractual damages clause shall be valid even if the employer has not paid non-competition allowance during the employment tenure.

For example, in the case of Zhai Haiyang before Guangdong Provincial High Court in 2020, the court held that the non-competition contractual damages during the employment tenure did not need non-competition allowance as a consideration, because employees had a duty of loyalty to the employer.[67] Sichuan High Court and Shanghai High Court all have similar decisions.[68]

65 Sichuan Xichan Plastic and Cosmetic Hospital Co., Ltd. v. Ge Jinhua Labor Dispute Case Sichuan Provincial People's High Court Civil Judgment (2015) CMTZ No. 408. The exceptional case is the labor dispute case of Duan Xuyang and others suing Xinjiang Meike Chemical Co., Ltd., the High Court of Xinjiang Uygur Autonomous Region, (2017) Xin Min Shen No. 1888, in which the court held that whether employees as technicians were exposed to trade secrets needed to be identified by specialized agencies and that the case was remitted for retrial.

66 Qin Jianguang, Guangzhou Jianzhong Enterprise Management Consulting Co., Ltd. Labor Dispute Civil Judgment of First Instance Civil Judgment of Haizhu District People's Court, Guangzhou City, Guangdong Province (2021) Yue 0105 Minchu Nos. 20406 and 20414. In the case, the employee claimed that he was not non-competition personnel, and the court held that he had signed a confidentiality and non-competition agreement but failed to provide evidence to prove the claim. Therefore, the court rejected the claim.

67 Zhai Haiyang, Foshan Sanmu Lighting Electrical Appliances Co., Ltd. Civil Ruling on Labor Dispute Retrial Review and Trial Supervision Civil Ruling of Guangdong Provincial People's High Court (2020) Yue Min Shen No. 6056.

68 The labor dispute application case between Li Lun and Sichuan Xingdeli Membrane Structure Technology Co., Ltd., Civil Ruling of Sichuan High Court (2013) C.M.S.Z. No. 2572. In the case, the court held that the non-competition clause of the Employment Contract Law included two non-competition obligations, namely, on-the-job and post-resignation, and that the agreed contractual damages were legal. The court, however, reduced the on-the-job contractual damages from RMB 300,000 to RMB 150,000. Civil Ruling on Labor Dispute Retrial Review and Trial Supervision of Tian Weixing and Guangzhou Hilali Cosmetics Co., Ltd. Civil Ruling of Guangdong Provincial People's High Court (2018) Yue Min Shen No. 1825. In the case, the

Therefore, if the agreement between the two parties stipulates the contractual damages for on-the-job non-competition obligation, the employee shall bear the obligation to compensate for the contractual damages if they violate the non-competition obligations. This liability is not conditional on the payment of a non-competition allowance. This is also the provision of Article 18 of the 2023 Consultation Draft on the Interpretation of the Supreme Court on the Application of Law in the Trial of Labor Dispute Cases (II). Of course, for whether this kind of contractual damages is established or not, we also need to consider whether the contractual damages constitute a fine imposed by the employer on the employee. If it constitutes a fine, the employer must also meet the monthly wage deduction limit on the employee. Please see "123. Can an employer impose a fine on an employee and deduct their wages?"

An interesting question arises when both parties' employment contract only stipulates that the employee is not allowed to engage in moonlighting, without explicitly prohibiting on-the-job non-competition, and the employee does engage in moonlighting of a competitive nature. Can the employer demand compensation from the employee? Judicial decisions suggest that the employer may have the right to claim the damages.

In the 2020 case of Longchuan Hengxin Dental Hospital v. Cui Xiulan, the employee worked as a dentist in the hospital, and the employment contract stipulated that the employee was not allowed to work moonlighting in other medical institutions. However, the employee violated the agreement by opening a private clinic. Consequently, the hospital terminated the employee's contract and filed a labor arbitration claim for compensation for losses. The court held that the employee's breach of the contract, which prohibited moonlighting, caused losses to the hospital. Therefore, considering the income standards in the healthcare industry, 30% of the employee's illegal income, totaling RMB 100,000, was determined as compensation for the hospital's losses caused by the employee.[69]

200. The non-competition agreement lacks a non-competition allowance clause. What should I do?

Answer: If a non-competition agreement does not stipulate a non-competition allowance, the employer and the employee usually face two problems: the first is, if the employee abides by the non-competition obligation, should the employer pay them the allowance, and if yes, at what standard? The second is whether the non-competition agreement is binding on the employee; that is, if the employee engages in the competitive industry, are they liable for the contractual damages stipulated in the agreement?

The 2020 Supreme Court's Judicial Interpretation stipulates that if a non-competition agreement only stipulates the obligation of non-competition but does not stipulate the non-competition allowance, and the employee fulfills the obligation of non-competition,

contractually agreed-upon on-the-job non-competition damages are five times the amount of wages, and the court confirms that the agreement is valid. Li Zhiyang and Shanghai Huige Technology Development Co., Ltd. Civil Ruling on Trial and Supervision of Other Labor Disputes Civil Ruling of Shanghai High Court (2017) Hu Min Shen No. 2217. Labor Dispute Case of Gao Zeyan v. Shenzhen Henglida Electronic Weighing Instrument Co., Ltd. Civil Ruling of Guangdong High Court (2014) Yue Gao Fa Min Shen Zi No. 1740.

69 Longchuan Hengxin Dental Hospital v. Cui Xiulan Labor Dispute Civil Second Instance Civil Judgment, Guangdong Heyuan Intermediate People's Court Civil Judgment (2020) Yue 16 Min Zhong Zi No. 935.

the employer shall pay the non-competition allowance at 30% of the average wages of the employee from the 12 months before their termination.[70]

Therefore, the answer to the first question is: in the case that the non-competition agreement does not stipulate the non-competition allowance, and the employee fulfills the obligation of non-competition, according to the aforementioned judicial interpretation of the Supreme Court, the employee can claim the non-competition allowance according to the standard of 30% of their average wage from the 12 months before their termination. The average wage from the 12 months here refers to all wage items, including overtime wages, bonuses, allowances, and so on.[71] Moreover, the amount of non-competition allowance shall not be lower than the local minimum wage standard.

An exceptional situation is that there is a higher local non-competition allowance standard in terms of percentage of average wages in some provinces and cities with legislative authority, different from the 30% stipulated by the Supreme Court's judicial interpretation. For example, in the case of Wu Zhisheng before the Guangdong Provincial High Court in 2016, the court pointed out that Shenzhen Special Economic Zone, based on its legislative power, stipulated a different proportion of non-competition allowance not less than 50% of the average wage from the previous 12 months, and that the calculation of the non-competition allowance standard should be applied to this special economic zone standard.[72]

For the second question, the judicial interpretation of the Supreme Court does not specify whether the non-competition obligation in the absence of non-competition allowance is binding on employees if the employee is unwilling to fulfill their non-competition obligations.

At present, the vast majority of courts hold that even if there is no provision on non-competition allowance, the non-competition agreement is still binding on both parties. If the employee engages in a competitive industry without cancelling the non-competition agreement, they shall be liable for the stipulated contractual damages. There are unequivocal cases in the high courts of Hebei and Zhejiang Provinces.[73]

---

70 Article 36 of the Interpretation of the Supreme People's Court on the Application of Law in the Trial of Labor Dispute Cases (I) (Judicial Interpretation [2020] No. 26). "If both parties have agreed on non-competition in the employment contract or confidentiality agreement, but have not agreed to provide non-competition allowance to the employee after the termination or dissolution of the employment contract, the employee has fulfilled the non-competition obligation, and now requires the employer to pay monthly economic compensation at 30% of the average wage of the worker from the 12 months before the termination or dissolution of the employment contract, the people's court shall support it. If 30% of the average monthly wage stipulated in the preceding paragraph is lower than the minimum wage standard at the place where the employment contract is performed, it shall be paid according to the minimum wage standard."

71 Beijing Lepu Diagnostics Co., Ltd. Civil Judgment of Second Instance of Labor Dispute Civil Judgment of Beijing the First Intermediate People's Court (2022) Jing 01 Min Zhong No. 4663.

72 Wu Zhisheng and Shenzhen Kangdaxin Real Estate Management Consulting Co., Ltd., Labor Dispute Retrial Civil Judgment No. 177 of Guangdong Provincial People's High Court (2016). The court held that if the parties did not stipulate non-competition allowance, but the employee fulfilled the non-competition obligation, the average wage standard shall apply 50% wages from the 12 months before their termination in Shenzhen Special Economic Zone (rather than 30% according to the 2020 judicial interpretation of the Supreme Court).

73 Civil Ruling on Labor Dispute Retrial Review and Trial Supervision of Zhang Xinjun and Chengde Pute Intelligent Electronics Co., Ltd. Civil Ruling of Hebei High Court (2018) Ji Min Shen No. 2681. Application for Labor Dispute between Chen Xiaotuan and Zhejiang Crystal Photoelectric Technology Co., Ltd. Civil Ruling of Zhejiang High Court (2013) Zhe Min Shen Zi No. 658. Judgment of Second Instance of Labor Dispute between Mo Jianzhe and Guohong Liquefied Gas Machinery Engineering (Dalian) Co., Ltd. Civil Judgment of Intermediate People's Court of Dalian City, Liaoning Province (2023) Liao 02 Min Zhong No. 1360.

Exceptionally, in the case of Li Guangming in 2014, the Guangzhou Intermediate Court held that the non-competition agreement for the employee, a university lecturer, was not binding due to lack of non-competition allowance provision. However, the real reason might be that the employee was not a person with confidentiality obligations.[74] Another special case is that if there is neither non-competition allowance nor non-competition contractual damages in the non-competition agreement, the court may find that there is no non-competition agreement between the two parties, so the employee is not bound by the non-competition obligation.[75]

Therefore, although the non-competition agreement does not stipulate non-competition allowance, if the employee fulfills the obligation of non-competition, the employer cannot refuse to pay the employee the non-competition allowance under the pretext of a lack of provision in the agreement. And conversely, even if the employee is not willing to fulfill the obligation of non-competition, the agreement is still binding on the employee. If the employee violates the obligation of non-competition, the employer may require the employee to bear the contractual damages and to continue to perform the obligation of non-competition.

Of course, if the employee wants to get rid of the restriction of the non-competition agreement, they can cancel the agreement through legal procedures. Please see "202. Can employers or employees cancel the non-competition agreement?"

201. My employment contract stipulates that my wages include non-competition allowance. Is such provision legal?

Answer: Article 23 of Employment Contract Law provides that "[e]mployees who are subject to a confidentiality obligation may agree to a non-competition clause with their employer in their employment contract or confidentiality agreement. The employer may also agree to provide the employee with monthly allowance during the non-competition period after the employment contract is terminated or dissolved." As to whether the employer can agree with the employee that the wages include the non-competition allowance, there are two approaches in the courts around the country at present.

The first approach is that this is the realm of autonomy between the employer and the employee; as long as the employment contract or payroll clearly distinguishes the wage and non-competition allowance in the employee's income, such an agreement is valid.[76]

74 Guangzhou University and Li Guangming Labor Dispute Appeal Case Guangzhou Intermediate People's Court of Guangdong Province Civil Judgment (2014) Sui Zhong Fa Min Yi Zhong Zi No. 5498. In the case, the employee, a university lecturer who was not involved with trade secrets, signed a non-competition agreement without agreed allowance. When the employee resigned from his job, he paid RMB 50,000 as the non-competition liquidated damages to the employer. The employee later sued for refund of the RMB 50,000. The court found that the employee was not obligated to pay the contractual damages and ordered the repayment.

75 Xi'an Qiyuan Consulting and Design Co., Ltd. of China Machinery Engineering and Xiao Yuanwen's Labor Dispute Appeal and Application for Retrial Civil Ruling No. 1829 of Shaanxi Provincial People's High Court (2019). In the case, both parties' non-competition provision was only a clause of the confidentiality agreement, and there was no provision about non-competition contractual damages. The court found that there was no non-competition agreement.

76 Yang Xiangang and Shenyang Intercontinental Advertising Co., Ltd. Civil Ruling on Civil Application for Retrial of Labor Dispute Civil Ruling of Liaoning Provincial People's High Court (2021) Liao Min Shen No. 310. The court held that the non-competition allowance contained in the wages during the period of employment is a valid payment. Wu Zhisheng and Shenzhen Kangdaxin Real Estate Management Consulting Co., Ltd. Labor Dispute Retrial Civil Judgment No. 177 of Guangdong Provincial People's High Court (2016). "This Court holds that this clause does not specify the specific amount of allowance for confidentiality and

At present, the high courts of Liaoning Province, Guangdong Province, and Beijing have judicial decisions supporting this view, and Jiangsu Province Nanjing Intermediate Court and the First Intermediate Court of Shanghai have made similar decisions.

The second approach is that since the law unequivocally stipulates that non-competition allowance is paid monthly after termination of employment, the non-competition allowance being included in employees' wages does not conform to the law and is invalid.[77] Courts holding this view include the First Intermediate Court of Beijing (but there are also cases in the court holding the first view), the Third Intermediate Court of Beijing, the Shenzhen Intermediate Court, and the Jinan Intermediate Court of Shandong Province.

Therefore, whether it is legal for your employment contract to stipulate that your wages include non-competition allowance depends on the place where you are and the specific practice of the regional court.

202. Can employers or employees cancel the non-competition agreement?

Answer: Employers have the unilateral right to cancel their non-competition agreements. The 2020 Supreme Court's Judicial Interpretation stipulates that an employer can pay three months of non-competition allowance to relieve the employee's non-competition obligation.[78]

---

non-competition. Moreover, Kangdaxin Real Estate Company has not submitted valid evidence to prove that its wage payment has included confidentiality and non-competition allowance." Wang Zhesan and Beijing Xinnongyuan Real Estate Development Co., Ltd. Labor Dispute Retrial Civil Judgment Beijing High Court Civil Judgment (2018) Jing Min Zai No. 81. The court held that although the agreement stipulated that the wages included non-competition allowance, the employee's payroll did not show the specific amount of compensation, so it was determined that it was not paid. Tang v. Nanjing Gao A Gear Group Co., Ltd., Civil Judgment (2020) Su 01 Min Zhong No. 6913 of Nanjing Intermediate People's Court of Jiangsu Province. Shanghai Qiongming Network Technology Co., Ltd. v. Tao Zhenqiu, Labor Dispute Case of Second Instance Civil Judgment of Shanghai the First Intermediate People's Court Civil Judgment (2021) Hu 01 Min Zhong No. 271.

77 Civil Judgment of the Second Instance of the Labor Dispute between Feijiu Medical Technology (Beijing) Co., Ltd. and Lu Liang Civil Judgment of the First Intermediate People's Court of Beijing (2021) Jing 01 Min Zhong No. 10919. The court held that "[a]lthough both parties agree that the labor remuneration includes the allowance during the period of non-competition, the above agreement does not conform to the payment method of non-competition allowance stipulated by law." However, in a later case, Beijing Lepu Diagnostic Technology Co., Ltd. and other labor disputes (2022) Jing 01 Min Zhong No. 4663, the First Intermediate People's Court of Beijing overturned the first instance's determination that the wage including non-competition allowance was illegal, holding that only because it was not clear that the agreed wages included the non-competition allowance, the court could not find that the the wages included the non-competition allowance. Qiu Xiao v. Shenzhen Mofang New Material Technology Co., Ltd. Labor Dispute Civil Judgment of Second Instance Civil Judgment of Shenzhen Intermediate People's Court of Guangdong Province (2021) Yue 03 Min Zhong No. 8533. The court held that "[j]ust as economic compensation for termination of employment contract cannot be included in the wages, the non-competition allowance cannot be included in the wages ... it should be recognized that the agreement on wages including non-competition allowance in the non-competition agreement has no legal effect." Beijing Xinnongyuan Real Estate Development Co., Ltd. and other civil judgments of the second instance of labor disputes, Beijing the Third Intermediate People's Court Civil Judgment (2018) No. 389. The court held that "the agreement that the non-competition allowance shall be paid together with wages is inconsistent with the form of payment prescribed by law." Shenzhen Qianhai Hongjing Information Service Co., Ltd., Hong Junyang Labor Dispute Civil Judgment of Second Instance Civil Judgment of Shenzhen Intermediate People's Court of Guangdong Province (2020) Yue 03 Min Zhong No. 4998. Labor Dispute Appeal Case between Shandong Dazhi Tiancheng Enterprise Management Consulting Group Co., Ltd. and Han Shujuan Civil Judgment of Jinan Intermediate People's Court of Shandong Province (2016) Lu 01 Min Zhong No. 3092.

78 Article 39 of the Interpretation of the Supreme People's Court on the Application of Law in the Trial of Labor Dispute Cases (I) (Judicial Interpretation [2020] No. 26). "If the employer requests to terminate the non-competition agreement within the period of non-competition, the people's court shall support it. When

Employees only have a conditional, limited termination right. According to Article 38 of the judicial interpretation, an employee can only notify the employer to terminate the non-competition agreement when the employer has not paid the non-competition allowance for three months.

The standard of non-competition allowance for the aforesaid three months shall be first determined in accordance with the non-competition allowance agreement between both parties. For example, in the 2022 case of Huang Pujiang v. Sciencetop Analytical Instruments (Beijing) Co., Ltd., the Beijing High Court held: "The employment contract between the two parties stipulated that the non-competition allowance for the two-year non-competition obligation is 8 months' salary. However, the salary clause in the employment contract only involves the fixed monthly salary amount, and does not include bonuses. Huang Pujiang's argument that the average monthly actual payment amount, including year-end bonuses and other items should be considered as the base for calculating the non-competition allowance is untenable."[79]

If both parties do not provide for a non-competition allowance, the allowance shall be determined in accordance with 30% of the average wages of the employee from the 12 months prior to the employment termination as stipulated by the 2020 Supreme Court's Judicial Interpretation. If the jurisdiction where the case occurs has a local standard higher than the aforesaid standard, then the non-competition allowance can be calculated according to that local standard. For example, in the 2016 case of Wu Zhisheng v. Shenzhen Kangdaxin Real Estate Management Consulting Co., Ltd, the Guangdong High Court held that the calculation ratio of the non-competition allowance should prioritize the standard of the Shenzhen Special Economic Zone.[80] Under no circumstances shall the non-competition allowance be lower than the local minimum wage standard.

Employees being exempted from the obligation of non-competition means that they are free to engage in competitive industries. However, this does not mean that employees can use the trade secrets of the former employer at will. The protection of trade secrets is similar to the protection of property rights; property rights exist, the protection remains. The right to trade secrets is a statutory rather than an agreed right, so employees are still obligated to keep the trade secrets of the employer after their termination, even if the obligation of non-competition is lifted. Otherwise, they may be liable for tort compensation.

203. The non-competition penalty stipulated in my non-competition agreement is RMB 5 million. Is this provision binding?

Answer: Above all, an employee who bears the obligation of non-competition but violated the obligation ought to assume the liability of breach of contract. Second, if the employee's non-competition agreement stipulates a high amount of liquidated damages, whether the liquidated damages are binding depends on the following factors: the amount of the employee's non-competition allowance, the income before the termination, the employee's length of service for the employer, the degree of the employee's fault, the loss caused to the

---

terminating the non-competition agreement, the people's court shall support the employee's request for the employer to pay the employee an additional three-month allowance for non-competition."

79 Huang Pujiang v. Sciencetop Analytical Instruments (Beijing) Co., Ltd., Beijing Higher People's Court Civil Ruling Document (2022) Jing Min Shen No. 6576.

80 Wu Zhisheng and Shenzhen Kangdaxin Real Estate Management Consulting Co., Ltd., Labor Dispute Retrial Civil Judgment No. 177 of Guangdong Provincial People's High Court (2016).

employer by the breach of contract, and the record of past payments of non-competition allowance by the employer.

In judicial practice, it is a common phenomenon that the courts alter excessive non-competition liquidated damages. The courts change the liquidated damages not only by considering individual factors, but also by considering comprehensive factors. For example, in the case of Yu Shoukai before the Xinjiang High Court in 2019 and the case of Ge Jinhua before the Sichuan High Court in 2015, the contractual damages were altered according to the multiple of the total amount of non-competition allowance.[81]

In the case of He Xianli before Kunshan City Court of Jiangsu Province in 2017, the court calculated the damages according to a certain proportion of the total wages paid by the employer to the employees.[82] In the case of Zhang Jiamei before Beijing Haidian District Courtin 2021, the court decided the damages according to the comprehensive consideration of income, length of service, degree of fault, agreed contractual damages, and payment history.[83] The most common practice by courts is to consider all kinds of factors to decide the contractual damages at their discretion.

Therefore, whether the RMB 5 million of liquidated damages stipulated in your non-competition agreement is binding depends on whether the defendant (the employee) requests adjustment of excessive liquidated damages in the dispute and how the court considers the aforementioned factors.[84]

6.3 Personal Information Protection

204. What are the impacts on employers of the newly implemented Personal Information Protection Act in China?

Answer: The first article of China's Information Protection Law specifies that the purpose of the Act is to safeguard the rights and interests of personal information, regulate personal information processing activities, and promote the reasonable utilization of personal information. It fills the legislative gap in China's personal information protection.

---

81 Sichuan Xichan Plastic and Cosmetic Hospital Co., Ltd. v. Ge Jinhua Labor Dispute Case Sichuan Provincial People's High Court Civil Judgment (2015) C.M.T.Z. No. 408. In the case, the non-competition allowance is the minimum wage standard, but the liquidated damages are set at RMB 5 million, and the court adjusted the standard to 12-month non-competition allowance as liquidated damages. Civil Ruling on Labor Dispute Retrial Review and Trial Supervision between Yu Shoukai and Xinte Energy Co., Ltd. Civil Ruling of the High Court of Xinjiang Uygur Autonomous Region (2019) Xin Min Shen No. 1719. In the case, the liquidated damages agreed to was 30 times the wages from the 12 months before resignation, and the court changed it to 3 times the total amount of non-competition allowance.

82 Kunshan Qingyan Ziguang Testing Technology Co., Ltd. and He Xianli Labor Dispute First Instance Civil Judgment Jiangsu Kunshan People's Court Civil Judgment (2017) Su 0583 Minchu No. 19267. In the case, the parties agreed on a liquidated damages of RMB 100,000, and the court adjusted the liquidated damages to 50% of the total wages received by the defendant during his tenure at the plaintiff's office.

83 Zhang Jiamei and Tencent Technology (Beijing) Co., Ltd. Labor Dispute First Instance Civil Judgment Beijing Haidian District People's Court Civil Judgment (2021) Jing 0108 Minchu No. 15930. In the case, the employee worked in Tencent for nearly three years, the last year's salary was RMB 504,000 with a year-end bonus of RMB 144,000, and the agreed contractual damages were twice the last year's salary income. Two months after her resignation, she joined a competitor. Therefore, the court comprehensively considered Zhang Jiamei's length of service in Tencent, salary level, degree of fault, non-competition period, payment of non-competition allowance, and other factors, and determined the contractual damages of RMB 600,000 (equivalent to half of the total salary or agreed contractual damages of the year before her resignation).

84 Under the contract law in China, a party to a contract who asserts excessive contractual damages must raise the claim of adjustment of the damages to the court.

A comparable legislation enacted in the European Union in 2018 is the General Data Protection Regulation, aiming to protect personal information security, privacy, and dignity.

According to Article 4 of the Act on the Protection of Personal Information, personal information refers to all kinds of information relating to an identified or identifiable natural person, recorded electronically or by other means, excluding information after anonymization. In other words, all information relating to identifying a specific natural person (including Chinese and foreigners, whether or not located in China), such as identity, contact information, qualifications, occupation, personal characteristics, property information, credit information, health and physical information, and things done, is personal information.

The basic principles of personal information protection are the consent of the individual and to the extent necessary. In principle, the use of personal information requires the consent of the individual, especially in the case of sensitive personal information, transferring personal information outbound from China, etc. The use of another person's personal information should be limited to what is necessary and should not exceed this limit. Among other reasons, sensitive information is personal information that if leaked or used illegally, could easily lead to the violation of a natural person's human dignity or endanger the safety of his or her person or property, including biometric, religious beliefs, specific identity, medical care and healthcare, financial accounts, whereabouts and trajectories, and other information, as well as the personal information of minors under 14 years of age (Article 28 of the Act).

As a result, all businesses as well as individuals currently in China may be affected by the Act.

The employment management by companies may be affected. Although, as Article 13 of the Personal Information Protection Law stipulates: "When it is necessary for the conclusion and performance of contracts in which an individual acts as one party, or when it is necessary for the implementation of human resource management based on legally formulated company rules and regulations and collectively signed employment contracts," so the employer may process employees' personal information, from a strict compliance perspective, the collection and storage of personal information such as the name, date of birth, and curriculum vitae of employees should be included in the employment process management. Any employment contract and company policies should stipulate that the company has the right to collect and store personal information about the employee and report it to affiliate companies for the purpose of staff management.

The Act is particularly relevant to businesses that provide products or services to, or analyze and assess the behavior of, natural persons in China, typically including businesses and individuals that have products or services for sale to natural persons in China (e.g., car companies such as Tesla) and any business or individual that provides registration or subscription for natural-person users in China (e.g., WeChat, mobile application software companies, website platforms, etc.).

205. How does a company operating in China handle cross-border provision of personal information?

Answer: Many businesses now have close communication with offshore customers, suppliers, or parent companies. The manager of a business may talk to the parent company about an employee who is ill and calls in sick, or he may report a client's personal issue. This potentially involves the cross-border provision of personal information. The Personal Information Protection Act requires that companies in China should follow one of the three pathways when providing personal information outside of China.

The first pathway of data outbound transfer is the security assessment pathway. This is the route for large personal information processors. According to the Measure on Data Outbound Transferring Security Assessment, this approach applies to information processors that provide important data (data related to national security) abroad,[85] operators of critical information infrastructures, information processors that process more than 1 million pieces of personal information, or information processors that have cumulatively provided more than 100,000 pieces of personal information or more than 10,000 pieces of sensitive personal information abroad from 2021 to date.[86] These information processors must file an information security assessment with a Chinese cybersecurity department. The specific application methods and review criteria are set out in the Measure on Data Outbound Transferring Security Assessment.

Compliance with this pathway must be completed by the end of February 2023 in accordance with Article 20 of the Measure on Data Outbound Transferring Security Assessment.

The second pathway is the standard information standard contract pathway. This is the route suitable for the vast majority of small and medium-sized enterprises (SMEs). The Measures on Standard Contracts for Outbound-transfer of Personal Information, the State Internet Information Office Decree No. 13 of 2022, applies to the vast majority of foreign companies in China as well as domestic companies. These companies are all processors of personal information other than those in the first security assessment route. They are all processors of information that provide non-critical data outside of China, non-critical information infrastructure operators, processors of information that handle fewer than 1 million pieces of personal information, and processors of information that have provided fewer than 100,000 pieces of personal information or fewer than 10,000 pieces of sensitive personal information outside of China in aggregate from 2021 to date.

Article 3 of the Measures on Standard Contracts for Outbound-transfer of Personal Information states that "the principle of combining independent contracting and record management shall be adhered to," but Article 6 clearly states that "the outbound transfer of personal information shall not be carried out until after the standard contract has entered into force." Therefore, it appears that all companies, including foreign companies, that need to provide personal information outside of China must enter into a standard form contract provided by the Chinese government with overseas data recipients or a contract

85 2022 State Internet Information Office Decree No. 11, the Measure on Data Outbound Transferring Security Assessment, Article 19: "The important data referred to in these measures refers to data that may endanger national security, economic operation, social stability, public health and safety once it is tampered with, destroyed, leaked or illegally accessed or illegally used."

86 Article 4 of the Measure on Data Outbound Transferring Security Assessment stipulates that if a data processor provides data to overseas entities and falls under any of the following circumstances, they shall apply for a data outbound transfer security assessment to the provincial-level cyberspace administration and report it to the national cyberspace administration: (1) The data processor provides significant data to overseas entities. (2) Operators of critical information infrastructure and data processors handling personal information of more than 1 million individuals provide personal information to overseas entities. (3) Data processors have provided personal information on 100,000 individuals or sensitive personal information on 10,000 individuals to overseas entities since January 1 of the previous year. (4) Other circumstances specified by the national cyberspace administration that require applications for a data outbound transfer security assessment.

modified from that standard contract. For details, see "206. How does our company enter into and conduct registration for a personal information standard contract?"

The third pathway is the personal information protection certification pathway. According to the Implementation Rules for Personal Information Protection Certification attached to the Announcement on the Implementation of Personal Information Protection Certification issued by the State Administration of Market Supervision and Administration and the State Internet Information Office No. 37 of 2022, the government encourages all personal information processors (i.e., all foreign and domestic enterprises) to apply for personal information protection certification. This certification management model includes technical verification, on-site audits, and post-issuance monitoring. This pathway is clearly voluntary in nature.

At the moment, the Act is just starting to be implemented, and there are still some questions that need to be clarified through further rule making or concrete implementation. For example, it is unclear whether this third pathway can replace the second pathway. Article 38 of the Personal Information Protection Act apparently considers that there is an optional parallel pathway between this pathway and the first and second pathways, but the second pathway, the Measures on Standard Contracts for Outbound-transfer of Personal Information, provides that the conclusion of an outbound-transfer standard contract is mandatory. This requires a follow-up observation.[87]

206. How does our company enter into and conduct registration for a personal information standard contract?

Answer: Currently, the signing and filing of personal information standard contracts should be the channel for personal information outbound transferring compliance that the vast majority of companies, including domestic and foreign-invested enterprises, must follow.

The signing and filing process of personal information standard contracts is governed by the Measures on Standard Contracts for Outbound-transfer of Personal Information. Generally, we recommend that companies allocate at least three to four months for preparation to adequately arrange and complete the following tasks:

> Preliminary Assessment: Before providing personal information to overseas entities, the data processor should conduct a personal information protection impact assessment. The assessment report is a necessary document for filing with the cyberspace administration.
>
> Autonomous Contracting: Data processors can autonomously enter into personal information outbound transfer contracts based on the standard contract templates provided by the cyberspace administration.
>
> Post-filing: Data processors should file with the provincial-level cyberspace administration within ten working days from the effective date of the standard contract. The filing should include the signed standard contract and the personal information protection impact assessment report.

87 Zhang Jinping, "On the Relationship between Outbound Certification of Personal Information and Security Assessment and Standard Contracts,",*China Information Security Magazine*, Issue 12, 2022. "The relationship between the security certification of cross-border processing activities of personal information ('outbound certification'), security assessment, and standard contracts needs to be clarified urgently to facilitate the promotion and implementation of the outbound certification system."

Re-assessment, Contracting, and Filing: In cases where re-assessment is required during the validity period of the standard contract, the data processor should conduct a new personal information protection impact assessment, supplement or renegotiate the standard contract, and complete the necessary filing procedures.

The Personal Information Outbound Standard Contract is a contract signed between the data processor (such as a foreign-funded enterprise in China) and the overseas recipient of personal information (such as the parent company), regulating the outbound transfer of personal information from China. This contract stipulates that personal information should only be transferred with the consent of the data subject, and the overseas recipient should fulfill corresponding obligations (such as not exceeding the agreed-upon scope of use of the personal information and cooperating with inquiries and investigations by the Chinese network information security management department). Both parties should provide a copy of the contract to the data subject, outlining their rights (including the right to complain or file a lawsuit), and the parties can agree to resolve disputes related to the contract through Chinese courts or international arbitration institutions. Additional clauses can be added to the contract, provided they do not conflict with the standard contract. The data processor should register the contract with the provincial-level cyberspace administration within ten days after signing.

It's important to note that according to Article 13 of the Measures on Standard Contracts for Outbound-transfer of Personal Information, the compliance transition period for signing standard contracts for the outbound transfer of personal information should be completed before December 31, 2023. This means that as of now, if you share an employee's performance data with your overseas headquarters without having signed a personal information standard contract, it would be considered a violation of the regulation on the outbound transfer of personal information.

However, from the current situation of signing and filing standard contracts for outbound transfer of personal information, it seems that only some companies have completed this, and there is still a considerable number of companies that have not yet done so. The follow-up compliance of companies and government regulatory measures still need further observation.

207. Will our company's registration of outbound transfer of personal information cause trade secrets to be leaked?

Answer: Companies in China, including foreign representative offices and foreign-funded enterprises, may have concerns that proceeding with compliant procedures for personal information outbound transferring, such as signing standard contracts and filing registrations, may potentially disclose customer information and other trade secrets. This a reasonably understandable concern.

However, Article 38 of the Personal Information Protection Act explicitly regulates that any company, including foreign-funded enterprises, is indeed required to conduct registration or approval through the three pathways under the article for personal information outbound transferring (please refer to "205. How does a company operating in China handle cross-border provision of personal information?"), while according to the procedural requirements in this registration or approval, these companies do have to disclose their affiliated companies, suppliers, or customers abroad to the Chinese government.

Laws and regulations about personal information protection provide some restrictive clauses. For example, Article 1 of the Personal Information Protection Act stipulates that the purpose of this Act is to protect the rights and interests of personal information, regulate the processing activities of personal information, and promote the reasonable utilization of personal data. Article 9 of the Measures on Standard Contracts for Outbound-transfer of Personal Information also stipulates that "network information departments and their staff members shall keep confidential any personal privacy, personal information, trade secrets, or confidential business information they become aware of in the performance of their duties, and shall not disclose, illegally provide to others, or illegally use such information."

Furthermore, the personal information standard contracts also specify that when trade secrets are involved, companies are allowed to appropriately edit the text before providing contract copies to the personal information subject in order to protect trade secrets. Such editing may involve deleting or redacting key information related to trade secrets.

208. Is my company liable for civil damages for violating the Personal Information Protection Act?

Answer: The purpose of the Personal Information Protection Act is to protect the security of personal information and individual privacy, and therefore, the subject of personal information is entitled to seek civil liability in tort from the perpetrator of a breach of the Act.

First, the subject of personal information has the right of access and reproduction. In the case of 2022 Guangzhou Vipshop in the Guangzhou Intermediate Court of Guangdong Province, where Vipshop refused a member's request to access and reproduce information collected by Vipshop about himself, the court held that the subject of personal information has the right of access to and reproduction of his own information, without taking the premise that personal information is at risk of disclosure.[88]

Second, infringements of personal information protection may be liable for public apologies and civil damages, depending on the nature and impact of the act. In the 2021 case of Li Bolun at the Zigong City Intermediate Court in Sichuan Province, the defendant lured customers with gifts to provide personal information, which he used to purchase mobile phone sim cards and then sold them. The court found that not only did the conduct constitute a criminal offense, but the illegal proceeds of over RMB 16,000 should be awarded as public interest damages, and ordered the perpetrator to make a public apology.[89]

Processing of personal information may be exempted from civil liability if it meets the conditions for statutory exemption. The Civil Code provides that the following circumstances are statutory exemptions from liability for handling personal information: consent of the subject of personal information, use of information that has been lawfully disclosed (unless the natural person expressly refuses or the information infringes on his or her

88 Guangzhou Vipshop E-commerce Co., Ltd. and Zhou Yancong Personal Information Protection Dispute Civil Judgment (2022) Guangdong Guangzhou Intermediate People's Court Yue 01MinZhong No. 3937.

89 Sichuan Zigong City People's Procuratorate, Li Bolun and other personal information protection disputes civil first instance civil judgment Sichuan Zigong City Intermediate People's Court Civil Judgment (2021) Chuan 03 Civil No. 102.

vital interests), and reasonable use in the public interest or in the interest of the subject of personal information.[90]

For example, in the 2021 case of Tencent at the Shenzhen Intermediate Court in Guangdong Province, the court held that the information used by Tencent's WeChat App was the plaintiff's public information in WeChat, and that such use of personal information was a use of information that had been made public within the original scope, and therefore, it did not constitute an infringement.[91]

209. What are the administrative penalties for violating the Personal Information Protection Act?

Answer: Violations of the Personal Information Protection Act may be subject to administrative penalties. At present, the legal database of PKU Law does not publish any administrative litigation cases involving administrative penalties under the Act.

Article 66 of the Act sets out the administrative penalties that companies or individuals who fail to comply with the handling of personal information may be subject to by the Chinese government, including an order to make corrections (i.e., a formal notice requiring corrections to achieve compliance), a warning (i.e., a formal warning of the violation), confiscation of the proceeds of the violation (i.e., the revenue obtained from the violation of personal information protection, most typically the revenue obtained from the operation of the network by software app companies in violation of the regulations), an order to suspend the use of the application (i.e., a formal notice to stop using the software application), an order to cease operations (i.e., a formal notice requiring the cessation of the company's production or operations), a fine of up to RMB 1 million (i.e., a fine imposed by a government department depending on the seriousness of the nature of the violation and the consequences arising from it), and a possible fine of between RMB 10,000 and RMB 100,000 for the individual responsible (i.e., the company personnel responsible for handling personal information are subject to a personal fine).

China has never had a Personal Information Protection Act in the past, so the awareness of personal information protection, from individuals to enterprises to the government, is very low. After the implementation of the Personal Information Protection Act, it is likely that the government will take a gradual approach to the enforcement of the Act, with

---

90 Article 1036 of the Civil Code: "The perpetrator shall not be held civilly liable for handling personal information under any of the following circumstances: (1) Acts reasonably carried out within the scope of the consent of the natural person or his or her guardian; (2) Acts reasonably carried out to handle information that the natural person has disclosed on his or her own initiative or has otherwise lawfully disclosed, except where the natural person has expressly refused or where the handling of such information infringes upon his or her vital interests; (3) Other acts reasonably carried out to safeguard the public interest or the lawful rights and interests of the natural person."

91 Article 69 of the Personal Information Protection Act: "Where the handling of personal information infringes upon the rights and interests of personal information and causes damage, and the personal information processor cannot prove that it is not at fault, it shall bear tort liability such as compensation for damage. The liability for damages under the preceding paragraph shall be determined in accordance with the losses suffered by the individual or the benefits obtained by the personal information processor as a result; if the losses suffered by the individual or the benefits obtained by the personal information processor as a result are difficult to determine, the amount of compensation shall be determined in accordance with the actual situation." Wang v. Shenzhen Tencent Computer System Co., Ltd. Personal Information Protection Dispute Civil Judgment of Second Instance Shenzhen Intermediate People's Court of Guangdong Province Civil Judgment (2021) Yue03 Min Zhong No. 9583.

warnings and orders for correction for first-time violators. However, it is important to note that a second violation after an administrative penalty may constitute a criminal offense.

During the transitional period until December 31, 2023, there should be no risk of a violation of the Act for foreign-invested companies communicating with an overseas personal information recipient. If a contract is still not in place by January 1, 2024, this may constitute a violation. As the level of compliance and enforcement of the Act increases, some government agencies or public utilities should also become more aware of the need to protect personal information. For example, it would now be illegal for some regional government departments to publish the personal photos and ID card information of old scoundrels in places such as bus or train stations, or for post offices not to take measures to conceal personal addresses and contact details on individual delivery notes.

210. Can a breach of the Personal Information Protection Act constitute a criminal offense?

Answer: Yes. While generally, a violation of the Personal Information Law leads to civil infringement and administrative penalties, under certain conditions and to a certain extent, it may also constitute a crime as per Article 253 of the Criminal Law. This crime involves infringing upon the personal information of citizens, and the legal consequences include potential imprisonment for up to three years, or criminal detention along with a fine, or a single fine. In cases where the circumstances are particularly severe, the perpetrator may face a prison sentence ranging from three to seven years in addition to a fine.[92]

According to the article of the Criminal Law and its relevant judicial interpretations, for an act to constitute the crime of infringing upon citizens' personal information, it must satisfy all of the following three necessary conditions.

The first condition is that the act falls into one of three categories: the first category is the provision type, which includes providing and selling personal information to others; the second category is the collection type, which involves stealing, using one's position or providing services to collect personal information; and the third category is the acquisition type, which includes buying, exchanging, and receiving personal information.

The second condition is that the aforementioned provision, collection, and acquisition of personal information violates relevant state regulations, including the Personal Information Protection Act, the Measures on Standard Contracts for Outbound-transfer of Personal Information, the Measure on Data Outbound Transferring Security Assessment, the Regulations on the Protection of Personal Information of Telecommunications and Internet Users, the Regulations on the Network Protection of Personal Information of Children, the Guidelines for the Protection of Personal Information Security on the Internet, and other state-level laws and regulations, departmental regulations, etc.

92 Article 253A of the Criminal Law (Crime of Infringement of Citizens' Personal Information): "Whoever violates relevant state regulations by selling or providing personal information of citizens to others, and the circumstances are serious, shall be sentenced to fixed-term imprisonment of not more than three years or criminal detention, and shall also be fined or solely fined; if the circumstances are especially serious, they shall be sentenced to fixed-term imprisonment of more than three years but less than seven years, and shall also be fined." Article 2 of the Interpretation by the Supreme People's Court and the Supreme People's Procuratorate on Several Issues Concerning the Application of Law in Handling Criminal Cases of Infringement of Citizens' Personal Information issued in 2017: "Violations of the provisions on the protection of citizens' personal information in laws, administrative regulations, and departmental rules shall be deemed as 'violating relevant state regulations' as stipulated in Article 253A of the Criminal Law."

The third condition is that the aforementioned violation of the relevant state regulations constitutes "serious circumstances." The seriousness of the circumstances includes one of the following situations: (1) the person has previously been criminally or administratively punished for infringing on the personal information of citizens and has again committed the aforementioned illegal act of providing collection and acquisition; (2) the person has provided personal information to another person whose whereabouts and trajectories have been used to commit a crime or knows that another person has used personal information to commit a crime; (3) the person has illegally acquired or provided more than 50 pieces of information on whereabouts and trajectories, communication contents, credibility information, or property information; (4) the person has illegally acquired or provided more than 500 pieces of information on accommodation, communication records, health and physiological information, transaction information, and other personal information of citizens that may affect personal or property safety; (5) the person has illegally acquired or provided more than 5,000 pieces of other kinds of personal information; or (6) the person has made a profit of more than RMB 5,000 in violation of the relevant state regulations on personal information. If the criminal suspect commits the acts described in items (3) to (6) above in order to perform duties or provide services, the standard for constituting a crime is half of the aforementioned thresholds for the number of personal information violations or the amount of profits. Additionally, the number of personal information violations involved in the illegal acts described in items (3) to (5) can be proportionally accumulated to determine whether the criminal threshold has been met by the summation.[93]

Therefore, an employee or manager of a foreign company in China may commit a crime if he or she provides other people's property information or 25 text message contents to the parent company abroad without registering outbound transferring of personal information. As long as the foreign company registers as soon as possible, however, it should be able to achieve compliance, and there will be no question of violating the Personal Information Protection Act or even incurring criminal liability for serious circumstances.

Private detective work in China is likely to be a crime, as it usually provides information on the whereabouts and trajectories of the person being followed. Commercial investigation practices, including lawyers acquiring information on the property of the natural person being enforced in the enforcement procedure of court judgments, are also likely to be criminal, as their access to relevant bank account and property information may have reached 25 pieces of personal information, the threshold of the crime. However, in the case of general website platforms and service software apps, if they clearly commit to not illegally using personal information during the collection process of registered members, and if members voluntarily provide their personal information, this usually does not constitute a crime.

93 Article 5 of the Interpretation by the Supreme People's Court and the Supreme People's Procuratorate on Several Issues Concerning the Application of Law in Handling Criminal Cases of Infringement of Citizens' Personal Information issued in 2017.

CHAPTER 7

Summary and Practical Guidelines

Introduction

This chapter will focus on "What are my rights and what should I do?" from the perspective of the employer or the employee. We will summarize and conclude specific employment law practice issues from the previous six chapters and, based on our practical experience, help employers and employees understand their rights and obligations, providing them with practical guides on how to prevent risks or take action to handle employment disputes before, during, and after the employment relationship.

To improve readability, we will only reference the serial numbers of the Q&A articles from the previous six chapters in this chapter, rather than their questions.

7.1 Principles of Conduct in Employment Relationships

The Employment Contract Law explicitly states that the purpose of the law is to protect the legitimate rights and interests of employees and to build and develop harmonious employment relationships. Therefore, both parties should treat each other with good faith, honesty, and fairness, avoiding unnecessary disputes and litigation, helping each other, and developing together, as this is in the fundamental interests of both parties.

Employees should comply with the employer's rules and regulations and with professional ethics, and protect the employer's interests. The employer should understand and accommodate difficulties faced by their employees and strictly guarantee the rights of employees as prescribed by law (please refer to Q&A article 1).

7.2 Collective Contracts and Individual Contracts

A collective contract is an employment contract signed between the employer and the collective of employees or the company trade union or industry trade union. Compared with the well-established collective bargaining–based collective contracts in developed countries, collective contracts in China have lower coverage and relatively limited impact. China's collective contracts must be filed with the labor administrative authority and take effect only after no objections have been raised (please refer to Q&A articles 3 and 4).

An employee may choose to join a trade union, seek the union's assistance, and sign a collective contract. Employees should actively urge the employer to file the collective contract with the labor administrative authority to make it effective, thereby obtaining the basic protections stipulated in the collective contract. Employees can also negotiate a more favorable individual contract with the employer based on the collective contract.

DOI: 10.4324/9781003583301-7

The employer must not obstruct employees from joining a trade union or organizing collective bargaining with the employer and should promptly file the collective contract with the labor administrative authority for it to take effect. Employers should particularly note that in most local court practices, the signing of a collective contract is not considered as fulfilling the employer's obligation to sign a written employment contract with employees. Therefore, the employer must sign individual contracts with employees in addition to the collective contract, or they may be liable for double-wage damages.

7.3 Distinguishing between Employment Relations and Contractor Relations

A working relationship where an individual works for another person or organization is not necessarily an employment relationship under Chinese employment law. The establishment of an employment relationship requires both parties being qualified subjects under employment law (for example, an individual cannot be a legal employer), the substantive nature of their relationship being one where the worker is subordinate to the employer rather than operating independently, and when the nature of the relationship is vague, the agreement and understanding of both parties, which may also influence the identification.

Common contractor relationships include any work relationship where the employer is an individual (including domestic services, rural individual contracting, personal assistants or apprentices, and hired hands for rural contractors), employment of persons over the statutory retirement age who receive pension insurance benefits, foreign company representative offices directly hiring employees, foreigners working in China without a work permit, and services provided by independently operated individual businesses, welders, electricians, plumbers, scaffolders, movie projectionists paid by the show, workers under 16 years old, and other temporary workers paid on a task basis (see Q&A articles 17, 19, 20, and 24).

Both employees and employers should understand the definitions of employment relationship and contractor relationship under Chinese employment law, as this is the basis for their respective rights and obligations. The former is a relationship in which the worker is subordinate to the employer, and the worker is entitled to the mandatory protection of employment law; the latter is an equal civil relationship, and service providers are not entitled to protections under employment, such as minimum wage and rest and vacation. However, it should be noted that in certain contractor relationships, such as those involving workers under 16 years old or over retirement age, or those directly hired by representative offices, if a work-related injury occurs, the worker should be entitled to work injury treatment as if they were an employee (see Q&A articles 7, 8, 12, and 15).

In addition, volunteer work does not constitute either an employment relationship or a contractor relationship. However, it should be noted that the use of workers in the name of volunteers but actually providing remuneration or employment law benefits may constitute an employment relationship (see Q&A article 11). The relationship between civil servants and government agencies constitutes a civil servant relationship, which is a legal relationship similar to employment relationship in Chinese employment law practice but is subject to government control in practice and is rarely disputed (see Q&A article 25). The employment of close family members (such as spouses) and on-campus student interns generally does not constitute an employment relationship or even a contractor relationship (see Q&A articles 18 and 41).

7.4 Selecting Different Types of Employment Contracts During Recruitment

A fixed-term employment contract is a contract with a fixed expiration date (typically a one-year term). The employer can legally dissolve the contract upon its expiration. This type of contract is advantageous for employers, as they can legally terminate employees who despite passing the probation period, are later found unsuitable on the ground of the contract's expiration (see Q&A article 5).

A permanent employment contract is, of course, the most ideal contract for employees, as it provides the best job security due to the absence of a set expiration date. If possible, employees may request to sign a permanent employment contract during recruitment.

An assignment contract is a type of employment contract for implementing a specific task, terminating upon the completion of that task. It can be considered a fixed-term employment contract with an uncertain expiration date. The difference between an assignment contract and a part-time employment contract is that the former typically involves full-time work aimed at completing temporary projects. Employees under assignment contracts are also entitled to rights such as social insurance coverage, signing a written contract, paid annual leave, sick leave, bereavement leave, maternity leave, special protections for female employees, work-related injury benefits, and economic compensation upon contract termination. Assignment contracts may not stipulate a probation period (please see Q&A article 16).

A general work hours or irregular work hours contract is a type of employment contract used when standard work hours cannot be implemented due to industry characteristics, work requirements, natural conditions, or seasonal factors. Its features include concentrated work periods, concentrated rest periods, rotating shifts and time-off in lieu, and flexible work hours, meaning non-standard and highly flexible work hours. The former is common in seasonal work (e.g., fisheries), while the latter is common in night shift work (e.g., security night shifts) (please see Q&A article 6).

A part-time employment contract is a flexible employment relationship in which the employee works no more than 24 hours per week and no more than 4 hours per day. Its main characteristic is the short working hours, allowing employees to work for multiple employers (please see Q&A article 9).

Labor dispatch is a tripartite employment contract relationship, where the dispatch employer (a human resources company) dispatches employees to the host employer (the employer actually using the employee) to engage in temporary, alternative, and auxiliary ("three characteristics") work. Foreign enterprise representative offices must use labor dispatch to employ staff, and other employers meeting the aforementioned characteristics may also use labor dispatch (please see Q&A article 22).

7.5 Rights and Obligations under General Work Hours or Irregular Work Hours Employment Contracts

A common issue of dispute between the parties is whether the agreed-upon general work hours or irregular work hours employment contract is valid. The validity of such contracts depends on the job position or industry characteristics, the nature of the contract agreed upon by both parties, and whether the contract has been approved by a labor administrative authority (see Q&A article 6). If the general work hours or irregular work hours employment contract is invalid, it will be deemed to be a standard work hours system.

Employees under a general work hours or irregular work hours system are entitled to rights such as social insurance coverage, signing a written contract, paid annual leave, sick leave, bereavement leave, maternity leave, special protections for female employees, work-related injury benefits, and economic compensation upon contract termination.

Employees should pay attention to whether their job position or industry characteristics align with the seasonal nature of a general work hours system (e.g., seasonal work) or the non-standard working hours characteristic of an irregular work hours system (e.g., night shifts) to determine if these contracts are valid. If these characteristics are not present, employees may request a change to a standard work hours contract.

Employers, in addition to considering the job position or industry characteristics, need to specify in the contract the general work hours system or irregular work hours system and decide, based on local employment law practices, whether to submit the contract for approval by the labor administrative authority. Failure by the employer to review these three requirements may lead to the invalidation of the employment contract and the risk of having to pay substantial overtime wages.

7.6 Rights and Obligations under Part-Time Employment Contracts

In part-time employment, employers and employees are not required to sign a written employment contract, and both parties can terminate the relationship at any time without the employer being obligated to pay economic compensation. A common area of dispute is how to define a part-time employment relationship. Judicial practice in China indicates that the most important reference factors are the weekly working hours not exceeding 24 hours, the mutual agreement and understanding of the relationship, and the method of remuneration calculation (see Q&A article 9).

Employees generally do not have the right to claim overtime wages for work done within the agreed working hours, but in most regions of China, it is recognized that employees are entitled to triple overtime pay for work done on public holidays, or that such overtime pay should be determined according to the local holiday wage standard for part-time employees. Aside from special protections for female employees and work-related injury benefits, employees are not entitled to other rights such as paid annual leave, sick leave, bereavement leave, or maternity leave.

Employees can use part-time employment relationships to provide services to multiple employers and receive remuneration. Employees also have the right to request that the employer pay wages at least once every 15 days. Employers may sign a written employment contract with employees to clarify rights and obligations and to establish the nature of the part-time employment relationship. Employers also have the right to manage employees' work and to impose penalties on those who violate company rules and regulations. Employers are required to purchase work-related injury insurance for employees, but employees should purchase other types of social insurance, such as medical insurance or pension insurance, on their own.

7.7 Rights and Obligations under Labor Dispatch Contracts

A labor dispatch contract is a tripartite employment contract signed by the employee, the dispatch employer, and the host employer. The host employer exercises management rights (such as daily attendance or work arrangements), while the management of the employment relationship (such as signing the employment contract or purchasing social insurance) is handled by the dispatch employer. This type of contract is typically used for hiring employees in foreign company representative offices or for general employers hiring employees for temporary, alternative, and auxiliary ("three characteristics") positions.

Employees under labor dispatch are entitled to rights such as social insurance coverage, signing a written contract, paid annual leave, sick leave, bereavement leave, maternity leave, special protections for female employees, and work-related injury benefits. However, it should be noted that the contract signed between a dispatch employer and its employees must be a fixed-term employment contract of at least two years. Most courts currently do not support employees' requests for permanent employment contracts (see Q&A article 23). If the employee is not dispatched, the dispatch employer unit must pay the employee wages at no less than the minimum wage standard.

If the host employer has a legitimate reason (such as economic redundancy or employee's serious violation of company rules and regulations), it can return the employee to the dispatch employer, who then decides, according to legal grounds for termination and dismissal, whether to terminate the employee's employment relationship. An employee may claim economic compensation or punitive damages if dismissed by the dispatch employer; however, they are not entitled to the same only because the host employer returns them to the dispatch employer.

An important issue with labor dispatch contracts is their validity. Current judicial practice identifies three situations where labor dispatch contracts may be invalid: false labor dispatch (including illegal labor outsourcing), the dispatch employer lacking legal qualifications, and the dispatched position not meeting the three characteristics. Courts have two opposing approaches to whether the latter two situations lead to the invalidation of labor dispatch (see Q&A articles 66 and 67). Employers or employees should understand local practices to determine whether the labor dispatch is invalid. The legal consequence of an invalid labor dispatch is that the employee and the host employer directly establish an employment relationship.

In the event of an employment dispute, the party to whom the employee should assert their rights (or sue) depends on the nature of the employment dispute. If the dispute involves employment relationship management (e.g., social insurance coverage, wage payments, etc.), the employee should usually address it to the dispatch employer. However, if the issue relates to specific employment management, such as disciplinary action by the host employer, the employee should address it to the host employer. If the employment dispute involves both the host employer and the dispatch employer (e.g., the host employer imposes disciplinary action, and the dispatch employer fines the employee based on this), the employee may hold both parties jointly liable.

7.8 Judicial Procedures for Employment Disputes

When an employment dispute arises between the employer and the employee, both parties should first attempt to resolve it amicably through negotiation. If this is unsuccessful, the employee may file a complaint with the labor administrative authority and seek resolution through government administrative processes.

However, the most common approach to resolving employment disputes is through the judiciary. The parties may submit a labor arbitration application to the labor dispute arbitration committee located in the area where the employer is based or where the employment contract is performed. If either party is dissatisfied with the arbitration award, they may file a lawsuit in the district court or county court where the arbitration committee is located; it is important to note that the employer has limited rights to appeal to the court. After the first-instance court's judgment, both parties have the right to appeal to the intermediate court. This is known as the "one arbitration, two trials" procedure in the Chinese judicial process for employment disputes (see Q&A articles 26, 32, and 33).

There is a time limit for parties to submit a labor arbitration application for specific employment dispute matters, known as the statute of limitations for labor arbitration. If this time limit is exceeded, the arbitration application may be struck out. The general statute of limitations for labor arbitration is one year, starting from the date the party knew or should have known about the matter (see Q&A articles 27, 28, and 29).

However, the application of the statute of limitations in judicial procedures is complex. Labor remuneration is generally regarded as a continuous claim without a specific time period limit and should be filed within one year after the employment relationship is terminated. The application for recognizing an employment relationship is subject to different interpretations in judicial practice regarding whether it falls under the one-year arbitration limitation. Other labor arbitration claims should generally be filed within one year from the date the right arises or the termination of the employment relationship.

Typically, labor dispute arbitration committees or courts will not proactively examine the statute of limitations unless the respondent (or defendant) raises a statute of limitations defense (i.e., requesting rejection of the applicant's or plaintiff's labor arbitration claim based on the time limit). The one-year statute of limitations for labor arbitration is not absolute; it can be interrupted, meaning the one-year period starts anew under certain circumstances, such as when the employee files a complaint with the labor administrative authority, and the limitation period can also be suspended, meaning the countdown is paused, and resumes after the suspension event ends; for example, if an employee is hospitalized due to illness and cannot exercise their rights, the limitation period is suspended during the hospitalization and resumes once the employee recovers, rather than starting over.

7.9 Matters Related to Recruitment and Employee Onboarding

The terms of the employment contract agreed upon between an employer and an employee during the recruitment process (such as the salary amount) are binding. The employer must fulfill these commitments in good faith and cannot renege on them. If the employer fails to honor these commitments, it may be liable for compensating the employee for any resulting losses (see Q&A articles 35).

The employer is also prohibited from withholding employee deposits or personal documents, although the lawfulness of the handling of employee equity investments and vehicle deposits in the taxi industry may depend on specific circumstances and the judicial practices of different regions. The employer cannot require job applicants to perform unpaid trial work. Whether the employer is required to pay wages to student interns depends on whether the intern has established an employment relationship with the employer (see Q&A articles 39, 40, and 41).

After an employee starts working, the employer should establish a personnel file, including the employment contract, wage payment records, performance evaluations, disciplinary action records, and termination record documents. The employee's personnel file should be kept for at least two years (see Q&A article 37).

The start date of the employment relationship after onboarding should be determined by considering the terms of the contract, the employee's actual start date, and the employer's incorporation date (see Q&A article 36).

7.10 Purchase of Social Insurance

Chinese employees' social insurance includes "Five Insurances and One Fund," namely, pension, basic medical, unemployment, work injury, maternity insurance, and the housing provident fund. Employers are required to purchase the "Five Insurances and One Fund" for most types of employees (e.g., employees with fixed-term, permanent, and other types of employment contracts) (see Q&A article 35). Employers are only required to purchase work injury insurance for part-time employees and are not obligated to purchase the housing provident fund for employees of foreign nationality. Enterprise annuities are a voluntary, non-mandatory supplementary pension insurance.

The contribution base for the five insurances is the employee's salary from the previous month or the average monthly salary of the previous year, subject to upper and lower limits, or the average monthly social salary of the previous year in the locality. Pension, basic medical, and unemployment insurance contributions are jointly paid by the employer and the employee, while work injury and maternity insurance are entirely covered by the employer. The contribution rates for these social insurance programs vary across different provinces and cities. The contribution base for the housing provident fund is the employee's average monthly salary from the previous year, with both the employer and the employee each contributing no less than 5%.

Currently, compliance with the payment of "Five Insurances and One Fund" nationwide is relatively low. The most typical non-compliance issue is that the calculation of the contribution base is not based on the employee's actual monthly salary or the average monthly social salary of the previous year but rather, on the minimum wage standard. There are even instances where both parties agree not to pay the "Five Insurances and One Fund."

Employees are entitled to claim damages resulting from inadequate social insurance contributions, such as insufficient compensation for work injuries or maternity-related benefits, as well as economic compensation for forced resignation due to non-compliance with social insurance requirements. Employers should endeavor to ensure compliance in the purchase of social insurance.

7.11 Signing Written Employment Contracts

Other than for part-time employment, employers are legally required to sign written employment contracts with their employees. Employers who fail to fulfill this obligation will be liable for double-wage damages as stipulated by law. A written employment contract refers to an agreement that complies with legal requirements; documents such as employee entry registration forms, employment registration forms for government records, and equity incentive agreements do not qualify as written employment contracts (refer to Q&A article 42).

Specifically, there are three situations in which employers are obligated to sign written employment contracts: when a new employee joins the company, when an existing employee meets the conditions for a permanent employment contract, and when the fixed-term contract of an existing employee expires and a new contract needs to be signed (refer to Q&A articles 43, 55, and 56). For the first and third situations, employers must sign a written employment contract with the employee within one month of the new employee's start date or within one month of the expiration of the fixed-term contract. For the second situation, employers must sign a written employment contract as soon as the conditions for a permanent employment contract are met.

However, there are possible exemptions for the employer's liability for double-wage damages if they fail to sign a written employment contract as required by law. These exemptions include situations where the employment contract is signed retroactively or subsequently, labor dispatch is invalid but the dispatch employer has already signed a contract with the employee, both parties continue to perform the original employment contract after fixed-term contract expires, the employee intentionally arranges for someone else to sign the contract on their behalf, both parties have signed a contract amendment agreement, and other cases where the employer is not at fault or the employee is at fault (refer to Q&A article 44).

It is important to note that if an employee refuses to sign an employment contract after starting work, the employer should immediately terminate the employment relationship with that employee (please refer to Q&A article 38).

Regarding the signing of employment contracts, employers should actively and promptly prepare versions of employment contracts that comply with legal requirements, provide them to employees, and request that employees sign them. Employees, in turn, should cooperate in signing the contract and raise any questions or requests for amendments with the employer in a timely manner. Employees should not maliciously delay signing the contract through deceitful means in order to claim double-wage damages from the employer.

The calculation of double-wage damages involves complex rules related to limitation of arbitration and determination of wage standards. For more details, please refer to Chapter 2, Section 3, "Calculation of Double-Wage Damages."

7.12 Probationary Period for Employees

A probationary period is a time period for employers to assess new employees' work abilities and suitability. During this period, employers have the right to terminate new employees immediately without paying economic compensation if they are deemed unsuitable for the position (please refer to Q&A articles 59 and 60).

The duration of the probationary period varies based on the term of the employment contract. For full-time employees, the probationary period cannot exceed one month for contracts of three months or more but less than one year; it cannot exceed two months for contracts of one year or more but less than three years; and it cannot exceed six months for fixed-term or open-ended contracts of three years or more. Probationary periods cannot be stipulated for fixed-term contracts of less than three months, assignment contracts, or part-time contracts.

Employers cannot impose a new probationary period on existing employees when their positions change or after mergers or divisions. However, there are differing opinions among courts in different regions regarding whether employers can impose a probationary period on rehired employees who have previously been employed (please refer to Q&A articles 60 and 62). Extending an agreed-upon probationary period requires the employee's consent and cannot exceed the aforementioned statutory maximum. Even so, some courts still consider such extensions to be illegal (please refer to Q&A article 61).

During the probationary period, employees are still entitled to statutory employment rights such as social insurances, written employment contracts, rest and leave, and punitive damages for unlawful termination. To terminate an employee's employment relationship during the probationary period, the employer must meet the legal requirements of not meeting hiring requirements. Therefore, when both parties have disputes over termination during the probationary period, they should carefully review the agreed-upon hiring requirements in the employment contract and the provisions of the contract or company rules and regulations regarding how to determine whether an employee meets the hiring requirements.

During the probationary period, an employee's wages cannot be less than 80% of the wages for the regular contract period. Violation of this regulation may result in the obligation to supplement the probationary period wages (please refer to Q&A article 61).

Employers can immediately terminate new employees who don't meet the hiring requirements during the probationary period without prior notice, but new employees must give three days' notice to the employer if they wish to resign during the probationary period. Employers can also notify employees of the termination within a reasonable period after the end of the probationary period (please refer to Q&A article 63).

7.13 Invalidation of Employment Contract

If an employer or an employee engages in fraudulent or coercive behavior, or takes advantage of vulnerability, when negotiating their employment contract, causing the other party to sign the contract against their true will, the other party may claim that the employment contract is invalid. If the employment contract is invalid, the party at fault may be liable for damages, while the party not at fault is not required to bear the statutory compensation for the termination of the employment contract (please refer to Q&A article 64).

In practice, the most typical scenario of an invalid employment contract is when the employee provides a false academic qualification or resume to establish an employment relationship with the employer, and the employer claims the contract is invalid and requests to legally terminate the employment contract. This issue is complex in judicial practice, and we summarize that whether the employment contract is invalid depends on the following three factors: the severity of the impact of the employee's false academic or professional qualification or resume on the employment relationship, the length of time the employee has worked at the company after fraudulent entry, and whether the company's rules and regulations clearly stipulate the situation.

If the employee uses another person's identification documents to establish an employment relationship with the employer, this also constitutes an invalid employment contract, and the employer can terminate the employment relationship based on this. It should be noted that regardless of the reason leading to the invalidation of the employment contract, the employer is still obligated to pay the employee's remuneration for actual work performed, including wages, overtime wages, etc.

Additionally, clauses in the employment contract provided by the employer that exempt the employer from statutory responsibilities, exclude the employee's rights, or violate laws and administrative regulations are also invalid. The invalidity of certain clauses does not affect the validity of other clauses in the employment contract.

7.14 Paid Annual Leave

Chinese employment law stipulates that employees who have worked continuously for one year are entitled to paid annual leave. In theory, the mentioned "continuous work for one year" includes the time the employee worked for their previous employer, but in practice, it is most common to refer to one year of work with the current employer. Depending on the employee's cumulative service years and service years for current employer, the number of days of paid annual leave ranges from 5 to 15 days (please refer to Q&A article 73).

Certain special types of employees are not entitled to paid annual leave, including employees who enjoy paid winter and summer vacations or employees who have taken a considerable amount of paid personal leave or sick leave during the year. There are currently two views in courts in the country regarding whether employees under the general work hours or irregular work hours systems are entitled to paid annual leave.

If paid annual leave overlaps with public holidays, weekend days, sick leave, bereavement leave, maternity leave, etc., the paid annual leave is considered unused. Employers have the right to reasonably schedule employees' paid annual leave based on production and business needs. However, they must consider employees' opinions and requests before making a final decision.

Paid annual leave days accrued from the work in the previous year can be used in the current year, and if not used within the current year, they can be carried over to the next year. If the days are still not used in the next year, the employer should pay the employee unused annual leave pay for the unused days (please refer to Q&A article 74).

If accumulated unused annual leave days over several years have not been converted into unused annual leave pay for the employee, the employee may face an issue of whether the claim is beyond the limitation of labor arbitration, which involves complex time limit calculations. However, Article 5 of 2023 Consultation Draft on the Interpretation of the Supreme People's Court on the Application of Law in the Trial of Labor Dispute Cases (II) simplifies this calculation by treating unused annual leave pay as wages. Regardless of how many years of unused annual leave days the employee accrues during their employment, the employee can claim it as a whole within one year after the termination of the employment relationship without losing the right due to the expiration of the limitation of arbitration (please refer to Q&A article 75).

7.15 Bereavement Leave

Bereavement leave refers to the paid leave granted to an employee when their immediate family members, including the employee's parents, current spouse, or children, pass away. Employees are entitled to three days or more of paid bereavement leave. In some regions, employees who travel to another region for the funeral may also be granted additional travel leave (please refer to Q&A article 76).

Bereavement leave is based on the existence of an employment relationship and does not require the employee to have worked for a certain period (such as the one-year continuous work requirement for annual leave). The right to bereavement leave is contingent upon the death of an immediate family member; employees are not entitled to bereavement leave for the death of non-immediate family members (e.g., parents-in-law).

The specific number of paid bereavement leave days and whether an employee traveling to another region for the funeral is entitled to travel leave depends on the relevant local regulations, and part-time employees are not entitled to bereavement leave.

7.16 Special Protection for Female Employees

Pregnant female employees are entitled to paid prenatal examination leave and after childbirth, to a basic 98 days of paid maternity leave. The number of days of maternity leave may be increased in cases of dystocia or multiple births (please refer to Q&A articles 88 and 89).

Employers are not allowed to reduce the wages of or terminate the employment relationship with female employees due to pregnancy, childbirth, or breastfeeding. If a fixed-term employment contract expires during the employee's pregnancy, childbirth, or breastfeeding period ("three periods"), the employment contract should automatically extend until the end of the three periods. Employers are not permitted to arrange overtime work for female employees who are more than seven months pregnant.

If a female employee has a miscarriage before reaching 4 months of pregnancy, she is entitled to 15 days of paid maternity leave; if the miscarriage occurs after 4 months of pregnancy, she is entitled to 42 days of paid maternity leave. The wage standard for the aforementioned paid maternity leave is the employee's average wage from the 12 months preceding the maternity leave, and it should be paid by the maternity insurance fund or the employer. Prenatal examination fees and medical expenses related to childbirth should also be covered by the maternity insurance fund or borne by the employer.

For female employees breastfeeding a child under one year old, their employers must provide one hour of breastfeeding time per day (with an additional hour for each additional child in the case of multiple births); the employer is not allowed to arrange overtime or night shift work for these employees.

In principle, female employees have the right to equal pay for equal work as male employees. However, judicial cases show that courts may not support claims for equal pay by female employees on the grounds of differences in job nature, qualifications, experience, or the distinction between positions within or outside the staffing of state-owned enterprises (please refer to Q&A article 90).

7.17 Maternity Leave and Paternity Leave

Female employees are entitled to 98 days of paid maternity leave for childbirth, including up to 15 days available before the due date. In cases of dystocia or multiple births, female employees are entitled to additional days of paid maternity leave. The wage standard for paid maternity leave is based on the employee's wage before taking maternity leave.

Paternity leave is the paid leave that male employees are entitled to when their wives give birth. Different provinces and cities have different regulations on the number of days of paternity leave. For example, in Guangdong Province and Shandong Province, paternity leave is 15 days, while in Hunan Province and Sichuan Province, it is 20 days (please refer to Q&A article No. 77).

Whether employees should receive unused paternity leave pay for days not taken (similar to unused annual leave pay) is a matter with different views in judicial practice. In regions that upheld unused paternity leave pay, the amount is generally equivalent to the employee's regular daily wages.

7.18 High-Temperature Allowance

The high-temperature allowance is an additional allowance that employers are required to pay to employees working in prescribed high-temperature environments during the high-temperature season under employment law.

In some regions, whether employers must pay the high-temperature allowance is determined by whether the working temperature (both indoor and outdoor) meets the prescribed standards, but most regions require employers to pay the allowance during specific months (usually in the summer) when the working temperature meets the standard (please refer to Q&A article 78).

If the employer has installed air conditioning equipment in the workplace, employees generally do not have the right to claim the high-temperature allowance. Employees working night shifts outdoors during the high-temperature season are also unable to receive the allowance if the temperature does not meet the standard. Employers are not allowed to replace the high-temperature allowance with heatstroke prevention beverages, and the employees' wages, after deducting the high-temperature allowance, must not fall below the local minimum wage standard.

Employees' claims for the high-temperature allowance are typically subject to a strict one-year arbitration time limit. For example, a claim for the high-temperature allowance for July of a given year must be made before July of the following year; otherwise, the employee's claim may not be upheld by the labor arbitration committee due to the expiration of the arbitration time limit.

7.19 Matters Related to Sick Leave

The entitled period of sick leave or leave for non-work-related injury is called medical care leave under Chinese employment law.

Employees who fall ill should promptly apply for leave from their employers. An unreasonable delay may result in the employee violating company rules and regulations and being subject to disciplinary action; even if the employee is suffering from a long-term illness and is engaged in legal proceedings with the employer, they are still required either to apply for leave or to attend work as usual (please refer to Q&A articles 80 and 87).

The number of days of paid sick leave an employee is entitled to depend on their cumulative service years and service years for the current employer. Within a computation duration (not a calendar year), the total number of sick leave days (i.e., medical care leave period) an employee is entitled to ranges from 3 to 24 months. Whether an employee suffering from cancer or other serious illnesses is directly entitled to the maximum 24-month medical care leave period or whether this must be strictly based on the aforementioned cumulative service years and service years for the current employer to determine the medical care leave period depends on the judicial practices of the court where the employment is performed (please refer to Q&A article 84).

The wage standard during an employee's medical care leave varies according to local regulations, generally ranging from 40% to 100% of the employee's own wage, but this standard must not be lower than 80% of the local minimum wage standard (please refer to Q&A article 82). If an employee's medical care leave has not expired but a fixed-term contract expires, the employer is not allowed to terminate the employment contract with that employee until the medical care leave expires (please refer to Q&A article 172).

In practice, a particularly confusing issue is how the employer should handle a situation where the employee's medical care leave period has expired, but the employee has not yet recovered. In principle, if the matter does not involve the employee's labor capacity appraisal, the employee should resume work; if the employee is unable to perform their original job, the employer should first transfer the employee to a different position that suits the employee. If the employee still cannot perform the job, the employer may terminate the employment relationship.

If the situation involves the employee's labor capacity appraisal, the employer must not terminate the employment relationship before the appraisal conclusion is made. After the conclusion is issued, the employer should handle the situation according to the level of labor capacity determined by the appraisal (please refer to Q&A articles 85 and 86). If the employee's labor capacity appraisal concludes that the employee's labor capacity level is between Class 5 and 10, and the employer terminates the employment relationship, the employer should pay medical treatment allowance to the employee (please refer to Q&A article 153).

7.20 Recognition and Handling of Work Injuries

In Chinese employment law, work-related injuries and occupational diseases are collectively referred to as "work injuries." The employer's liability for work injuries is a no-fault liability. An employee's injury or illness may either be recognized as work-related or classified as non-work-related.

Determining whether an employee's injury is recognized as a work-related injury is a complex issue that can be categorized into the following four scenarios: first, typical work-related injury, which is an injury occurring in the workplace, during working hours, and due to work-related reasons (e.g., a finger injury while operating factory machinery); second, injuries sustained during work-related travel, which includes injuries related to commuting (e.g., a traffic accident on the way to or from work); third, injury in an accident related to the workplace (e.g., slipping and falling in the company cafeteria); fourth, special circumstances deemed to be a work-related injury, which is sustained in accidents during emergency rescue operations or a recurrence of a previous work-related injury (please refer to Q&A article 91).

Occupational diseases are specific illnesses contracted by employees due to their work. The diagnosis and assessment of occupational diseases are conducted by specialized medical institutions, which evaluate the employee's occupational history, their exposure to occupational hazards, and the environment of the workplace in terms of occupational hazards. Identification of an occupational disease requires two conditions: the illness must be caused by occupational activities, and the disease must be within the scope specified in the Classification and Catalogue of Occupational Diseases (please refer to Q&A articles 92 and 93).

Work injury recurrence refers to cases where an employee who previously sustained a work-related injury or contracted an occupational disease experiences a recurrence after recovery or stabilization. Work injury recurrence also includes the recurrence of old military injuries in demobilized soldiers. Employees suffering from a work injury recurrence are entitled to the same benefits as for the original injury, including the paid work injury leave and medical benefits. There are two special situations concerning work injury recurrence. The first is retired employees. If a retired employee experiences a work injury recurrence, prevailing judicial practice in regions suggests that the former employer is no longer responsible for the injury. The second is if the recurrence occurs at a new employer after an employee sustained a work injury at the former employer. Judicial precedents generally indicate that the new employer should bear the responsibility for the work injury recurrence (please refer to Q&A article 94).

There are two challenging issues in practice concerning occupational diseases. The first is the former employer's liability if an employee is diagnosed with an occupational disease after employment termination. According to judicial practice, it depends on whether the employee's previous position involved occupational hazards related to the disease and whether the employee underwent an off-role occupational health examination (please refer to Q&A article 102). The second is which employer is liable for the employee's work injury if an employee worked for two employers, both of which had occupational hazards, and is diagnosed with an occupational disease while employed by the latter employer. This depends on the off-role and pre-role occupational health examinations conducted and the conditions of occupational hazards at each employer (please refer to Q&A article 103).

A difficult issue in judicial practice is how an employer should handle a situation where an employee's paid work injury leave expires, but the employee has not yet recovered. Our summary of cases and practices suggests that multiple factors will influence the employer's course of action, including the employee's own feelings, medical opinions from healthcare institutions, requests for an extension of the paid work injury leave, and the conclusion of the employee's labor capacity appraisal (please refer to Q&A articles 95, 96, 97, and 98).

7.21 Work Injury Entitlements

Employees who are injured at work or suffer from occupational diseases are entitled to five types of entitlements (please refer to Q&A Article 99):

1. Wages in Paid Work Injury Leave: Paid work injury leave is the period for employees to recover from a work-related injury or occupational disease, during which they receive the same benefits as before the injury. The duration of this period is determined by the local labor capacity appraisal committee or the employer based on medical evidence or the local classification directory for paid work injury leave.

A practical issue arises when an employee continues to work during the paid work injury leave instead of resting. The question is whether the employee is entitled to both their wages for working and the wages during the paid work injury leave. Courts in different regions have conflicting practices, with some allowing the accumulation of both wages and others not (please refer to Q&A article 100).

2. Medical Expenses for Work Injuries: Medical expenses related to work injuries should be covered by the Work Injury Insurance Fund. However, if the employer has not purchased work injury insurance for the employee, the employer is responsible for these costs. Courts differ on whether the employer should cover medical expenses that exceed the scope of the Work Injury Insurance Fund.
3. Hospitalization Meal Allowance: The cost of meal allowances during the hospitalization of employees who suffer work injury should be borne by the employer, with the amount determined by local regulations.
4. Nursing Fees During the Paid Work Injury Leave: The employer should arrange for care or pay nursing fees to employees who are unable to care for themselves during the paid work injury leave.
5. Nursing Fees after Disability Determination: If an employee is determined to be disabled, these fees should be paid monthly by the Work Injury Insurance Fund, or by the employer if no work injury insurance was purchased.

A practical issue arises when a work injury involves third party infringement liability. If an employee has already received infringement compensation from a third party, the question is whether they can still claim the aforementioned work injury entitlements. Current judicial practice generally allows employees to claim rights against both the third party tortfeasor and the entities, the Work Injury Insurance Fund and the employer, responsible for work injury benefits, but the employer or the Work Injury Insurance Fund may deduct certain overlapping items, such as medical expenses, from its payment (please refer to Q&A article 101).

Another practical issue is whether the employer can offset work injury compensation with commercial accident insurance payments if the employer purchased such insurance for the employee. The prevailing court rulings across the country suggest that employees are entitled to both types of compensation (meaning that the employer cannot reduce its work injury compensation obligations because of the commercial insurance payment), unless there is a clear agreement that the commercial insurance payment can offset the employer's work injury compensation or that the payment belongs to the employer (please refer to Q&A article 104).

7.22 Employee Wages

Employee wages are the remuneration paid by employers to their employees (please refer to Q&A article 107). In practice under employment law, the employee's received wage equals the due wage plus overtime pay plus unused annual leave pay minus allowable deductions (such as social insurance contributions, personal income tax, and mutually agreed deductions).

Employee wages are protected by the minimum wage standard. This means that the due wage paid by the employer to the employee must not be lower than the minimum wage standard in the location where the employment contract is performed. Some regions have separate minimum wage standards for part-time employees. Whether it is legal for the employer to pay only the minimum wage standard to employees under general work hours or irregular work hours during rest periods depends on the difference between the employee's wage level and the minimum wage standard; if this difference is significant, the employer may be acting illegally (please refer to Q&A article 111).

When an employer suspends operations (e.g., due to a market downturn or lockdown during a pandemic), the wages paid to employees during the first month of suspension should be based on the employees' wage standard before the suspension. Starting from the second month, the employer should pay employees who provided normal service a wage not lower than the local minimum wage standard, while providing employees who did not provide normal service with a local standard living expenses, which is typically 70%–80% of the minimum wage standard depending on local regulations (please refer to Q&A articles 109 and 110).

In the piecework wage system, wages are calculated based on the number of completed work units by the employee, reflecting the principle of more pay for more work done. The calculation of piecework wages includes wages under the piecework quota and wages for work completed beyond the piecework quota during overtime (please refer to Q&A article 112). A key factor in calculating piecework wages is that the employer should set a reasonable piecework quota and piecework unit price, taking into account the local minimum wage standard and industry practices (please refer to Q&A article 113).

The package wage system is a work hour system with a fixed monthly wage that includes a certain number of overtime hours. When an employee's overtime exceeds the stipulated amount in the contract, both parties need to retroactively calculate the employee's normal hourly wage based on the contracted monthly package wages and the included overtime hours, so as to calculate overtime wages for the overtime hours (please refer to Q&A article 114).

There are two special scenarios related to wage payment in employment law practice. The first is whether night shifts in which employees may sleep should be paid at the minimum wage. This issue hinges on whether a night shift during which the employee is allowed to sleep constitutes work (night shifts where sleeping is not allowed are obviously considered work). Judicial practice shows that whether such night shifts constitute work depends on factors such as the employee's work responsibilities during the shift and the extent to which the employee's freedom of movement is restricted (please refer to Q&A article 115).

The second special scenario is whether employees who are on call at home awaiting work assignments should be paid at the minimum wage. Whether on-call time is protected under employment law, similarly to whether night shifts constitute "work," depends on factors such as the demands placed on the employee during the standby period, the responsibilities they assume, and whether they can freely engage in personal activities. If, after considering these factors, it is determined that the employee is working for the employer, they should be paid a wage not lower than the minimum wage standard (please refer to Q&A article 14).

The employer, in principle, may not reduce an employee's wage without the employee's consent. However, there are two exceptional situations in employment dispute judicial practice where wage reduction is considered legal. The first is if the employee does not object to a wage reduction after it has been implemented for some time (which is considered implicit consent to the reduction); for example, if the wage paid at the start of the employment contract is lower than the agreed wage standard, and the employee does not raise an objection within a month. The second is if the employer reasonably reduces the employee's wage following a lawful position transfer (please refer to Q&A article 117).

Commissions or bonuses promised by the employer are also considered part of the employee's wage. Therefore, even after the employee leaves, the employer is still obligated to pay these commissions or bonuses to the employee (please refer to Q&A article 116).

7.23 Employee Overtime Pay

Under Chinese employment law, working hours beyond the standard working hours are considered overtime, and employers are required to pay overtime wages for such hours. Overtime is classified into three categories: weekday overtime, weekend overtime, and public holiday overtime (please refer to Q&A article 70).

The calculation method for an employee's overtime wage involves multiplying the employee's normal hourly wage by the number of overtime hours (after deducting time-off in lieu) and then multiplying the appropriate overtime rate (150% for weekday overtime, 200% for weekend overtime, and 300% for public holiday overtime). The employee's normal hourly wage must not be lower than the local minimum wage standard's hourly rate (otherwise, the local minimum wage standard's hourly rate should apply). Regarding time-off in lieu, public holiday overtime hours cannot be used for time-off in lieu, while weekend overtime hours can be, and the prevailing judicial practice across the country recognizes time-off in lieu for weekday overtime (please refer to Q&A article 72).

Regarding whether part-time employees should be paid overtime wages, most courts across the country currently uphold claims for overtime wages for public holidays but not for overtime wages for weekday and weekend overtime.

For overtime wages under the general work hours system, it is necessary first to determine whether the employee's total working hours during the accounting cycle exceeded the standard working hours. Any excess hours are considered overtime and should be compensated as overtime wages. As for overtime wages under the irregular work hours system, the prevailing opinion among courts nationwide is not to support the right of employees under the irregular work hours system to claim overtime wages (please refer to Q&A article 71).

7.24 Workplace Rights and Mental Damages

In addition to basic employee rights such as wages, rest, and vacation, employees are also entitled to workplace rights to be free from discrimination and harassment, and to receive equal pay for equal work (please refer to Q&A article 118).

The Employment Contract Law and related laws stipulate rules against wage discrimination, gender discrimination, job discrimination, and harassment. However, it is important to note that these rules are not frequently applied in practice, and there are real-life situations such as discriminatory differences in retirement ages between female workers and female cadres, and discriminatory wage disparities between employees within and outside of the system of state-owned enterprises or public institutions.

Employers are generally expected to respect employees' private time outside of work. However, based on principles of professional ethics and good faith, employees are expected to allow contact from the employer during non-working hours in special circumstances (e.g., in case of emergencies at the employer or during the employee's sick leave) (please refer to Q&A article 119).

Some companies that prioritize workplace rights, such as foreign-invested companies, may include provisions in employment contracts or company rules and regulations prohibiting employees from discriminating against or harassing colleagues and take disciplinary actions, including termination of the employment relationship, against employees who violate these provisions. If an employee experiences discrimination or harassment from a colleague or superior, they can file a complaint with the company management or labor administration authorities. However, if an employee proceeds a forced resignation on the ground of such issues and seeks economic compensation from the employer, such claims, as can be seen from judicial precedents, are unlikely to succeed, given the Chinese cultural and judicial reality.

Mental damages, also known as emotional distress, is a concept under China's civil tort law and is generally not applicable in labor dispute cases. However, there are five exceptional circumstances in labor dispute judicial practice, usually characterized by two features: the employee has suffered severe personal injury, and there is a causal relationship between this injury and the employer's actions (see Q&A article 105).

The first category is when an employer loses an employee's personal file. The second category involves recruitment discrimination. The third category arises when the employer's poor workplace pollution causes serious consequences. The fourth category is related to severe consequences resulting from work-related injuries or occupational diseases (see Q&A article 106). The fifth category involves administrative actions by the Social Security Bureau causing emotional distress to the employee.

7.25 Lawful Disciplinary Actions

Disciplinary actions are a tool used by employers to maintain workplace order and facilitate business production, and they an aspect of an employer's management autonomy (see Q&A article 121). Disciplinary actions include dismissal, but we will discuss lawful dismissal later.

First, lawful disciplinary actions require employers to comply with legally binding institutional rules under Chinese employment law. Employers must not subjectively, arbitrarily, or capriciously impose disciplinary actions on their employees, and any disciplinary actions must have legitimate institutional rules as their basis, including the employer's company rules and regulations, provisions in the employment contract, and basic professional ethics (please refer to Q&A article 120).

The company rules and regulations must have legal content and be formulated through a legal process to be binding on employees. Legal content means that company rules and regulations must explicitly stipulate the scope of misconduct that attracts disciplinary actions, and that the content of the employment contract cannot exempt the employer from legal obligations or exclude employees' legal rights. In addition, company rules and regulations must take effect through lawful means, which include employees signing on the text of the company rules or on the minutes of training or a meeting about the rules, and the employer sending or notifying the rules via company-wide emails or management software, holding staff meetings to study or discuss the rules, and referencing the rules in the signed employment contracts.

The provisions regarding labor discipline in employment contracts, if lawful, also constitute binding institutional rules, as they are agreed upon by both parties. Generally accepted basic professional ethics also form valid institutional rules. Even if company rules and regulations or the employment contract do not stipulate them, an employer may impose disciplinary actions for violations of these basic ethics. For example, if a driver for a passenger transportation company consumes alcohol while driving, the company has the right to impose disciplinary actions even if this is not explicitly stated in the company rules and regulations or the employment contract.

Second, legal disciplinary actions must also follow fair and reasonable procedures. Although the Employment Contract Law does not prescribe that disciplinary action must follow a specific procedure, other than that employers must notify the trade union or labor administrative authority, we recommend that employers follow fair and reasonable procedures in disciplining employees in order to strengthen the legitimacy of the disciplinary actions. This requires employers to conduct an objective investigation, inform the employees, provide the employees with a reasonable opportunity to explain, and genuinely consider the employees' opinion. Judicial precedents demonstrate that lawful disciplinary actions also require that employers follow the principles of objectivity, non-repetitive punishment, and timely punishment. The employer may also consider the cumulative effect of multiple instances of employee misconduct, meaning that a series of minor infractions may justify disciplinary action that a single infraction might not.

When conducting a suspension investigation as part of the disciplinary process, the employer must also adhere to the principles of fairness and reasonableness. First, initiating a suspension investigation must be based on reasonable, objective facts rather than subjective speculation. Second, any wage deduction during the suspension must have a basis in company rules and regulations. Finally, the suspension investigation must be completed within a reasonable time frame (refer to Q&A article 122).

Therefore, employers should establish a systematic, tiered set of rules and regulations, defining actions ranging from warnings to termination, and cumulative disciplinary measures (e.g., multiple warnings leading to lawful termination due to serious rule violations), along with reasonable procedural rules for disciplinary actions. Employees, in turn, should be aware of their legal rights during the disciplinary process and promptly raise questions on the substantive and procedural issues in disciplinary actions to protect their legal rights.

7.26 Employee-related Financial Compensation

Employee-related financial compensation includes compensations by employees to employers for financial losses, financial penalties imposed by employers on employees, and compensation for losses caused by employees to others. The first item refers to a situation where an employee causes a direct financial loss to the employer due to fault and must legally compensate the employer. The second item refers to the fine an employee must bear for violating labor discipline or company rules and regulations, which does not cause direct financial loss. The last item is the compensation an employee must make for causing losses to a third party.

For the first item, employee compensation to the employer must meet four conditions (please refer to Q&A article 124). First, the employee's behavior must have violated the employment contract or company rules and regulations. Second, the employee's fault must be intentional or constitute gross negligence. Third, there must be a causal relationship between the employee's fault and the loss. Fourth, the employer must have suffered actual direct losses. Additionally, even if the employee must compensate the employer, the deduction from the employee's monthly wage must not exceed 20% (although in some places, such as Shenzhen, Guangdong Province, the limit is set at 30%).

Another special circumstance where an employee must compensate the employer for losses is when the employee resigns without giving proper notice, causing losses to the employer. According to the Employment Contract Law, the employee must give 30 days' notice in the regular employment contract period or 3 days' notice during the probationary period when resigning. If the employee violates this rule, and the two conditions (the employer suffering direct losses and a causal relationship between the unlawful resignation and the losses) are met, the employee must compensate the employer for the losses (please refer to Q&A article 177).

If an employee resigns early in violation of a training service agreement signed with the employer, they must pay contractual damages to the employer as agreed in the contract. However, when determining the amount of contractual damages, factors such as a strict examination of the nature of the training, the actual training costs incurred, and a reasonable service period and limits to contractual damages should be taken into account (please refer to Q&A article 179).

Employees are still obligated to compensate the employer for any losses caused during their employment even after they leave (please refer to Q&A article 178).

For the second item, whether an employer imposing a fine on an employee for misconduct is legal is a controversial issue in Chinese employment law judicial practice, depending on the location of the employment dispute (please refer to Q&A article 123). In some regions, such as Shanghai, courts consider that as long as the employer has established rules and regulations, it can impose financial penalties on employees. However, in other places, such as Beijing, courts hold that since the Regulations on Rewards and Punishments for Enterprises' Employees has been repealed, employers have no right to impose fines on employees for their violations of company rules.

The last item, compensation for losses caused by an employee to a third party while working, is a relatively complex issue. The general principle is: if the employee's work is not recognized as performing the employer's duty (i.e., not a work-related act), or if the employee's behavior, even if seemingly work-related, has no inherent connection to the performance of their tasks, the employee should be personally liable for compensating the third party. Otherwise, if the employee's behavior is related to the performance of a work task or has an inherent connection to the task, the employer must bear the responsibility. Whether the third party can demand that the employee jointly bears personal responsibility depends on whether the employee's behavior was intentional or constituted gross negligence. Even if the employee does not need to bear personal responsibility to the third party, they may still need to compensate the employer according to company rules and regulations (please refer to Q&A article 127).

7.27 Multiple Employers' Use of an Employee

The use of an employee by multiple employers includes two situations: position transfer of the employee between two employers and simultaneous use of the employee by multiple employers.

Position transfer of an employee between two employers usually refers to a transfer controlled by the two employers rather than caused by the employee. The usual legal consequence of this type of transfer is that the employer to which the employee is transferred should recognize the employee's service years at the previous employer and when the employee is terminated, pay economic compensation or punitive damages based on the employee's total service years with both employers. However, if the employee claims for double-wage damages due to not signing an employment contract, courts shall consider whether the employers constitute mixed employment when using the employee (please refer to Q&A article 125).

The simultaneous use of an employee by multiple employers may constitute mixed employment. Whether a mixed employment exists should be comprehensively judged by considering factors such as the signing of the employment contract, the factual characteristics of the work content and location, the entity responsible for wage payment, the entity responsible for social insurance, and the relationship between the multiple employers. The legal consequence of mixed employment is that the multiple employers jointly assume the obligations and liabilities of the employer toward the employee (please refer to Q&A article 126).

7.28 Employee Position Transfer

An employer and an employee can, of course, legally transfer the employee's position (and corresponding wages) through mutual agreement. However, a common dispute in labor law practice is whether the transfer of the employee's position is legal when the employee disagrees with the employer's unilateral decision.

Under Chinese employment law, there are six situations where an employer can legally and unilaterally transfer an employee's position (please refer to Q&A article 128).

The first situation is when the employee is medically incompetent for the position. This refers to cases where the employee, after the expiration of the medical care leave for illness or non-work-related injury or after the paid work injury leave for a work injury, is no longer capable of performing the current position. The employer can reasonably transfer the position based on the employee's health condition. This requires a comprehensive assessment of the employee's health and their inability to perform the job due to health reasons.

The second situation is when the employee is not competent for the position due to lack of personal capability. The employer needs to provide evidence of the job requirements and the employee's work performance to determine whether the employee is competent for the job.

The third situation is a position transfer due to major change in objective condition. If the objective conditions under which the employment contract was concluded have undergone major changes, making it impossible to perform the original employment contract, the employer may terminate the employment relationship, but before that, it must negotiate with the employee to modify the employment contract, including transferring the position. The vital issue regarding the validity of this type of position transfer is whether the major change in objective condition is established (please refer to Q&A article 157).

The fourth situation is a position transfer due to major changes in objective condition under economic redundancy. When an employer faces major changes in operational difficulties, it can reduce staff or, as we reasonably infer, can take a less harsh approach, transferring employees' positions to cope with these difficulties (for conditions related to economic redundancy, please refer to Q&A article 155).

The fifth situation is a position transfer agreed upon in the employment contract or specified in company rules and regulations. This is a position transfer within a range of positions that the employee has consented to in advance.

The sixth situation is the employer's reasonable discretionary position transfer, not specified in the contract or by law. The basis for this transfer is reasonable needs for business operation or management. The legality of this type of transfer depends on the reasonableness of the needs for business operation and management, whether the transfer is insulting or punitive, the degree of negative impact on the employee, whether the employee's personal situation was considered, and whether the transfer has already been practically implemented without objection from the employee (please refer to Q&A article 129).

Employers should strictly implement position transfer in accordance with legal requirements, the employment contract, or company rules to reduce legal risk in this dispute-susceptible matter. Employees also have the right to express opinions on position transfer that is substantively or procedurally illegal and may even proceed a forced resignation on the ground of illegal position transfer, thereby demanding economic compensation from the employer.

7.29 Employee Collective Strike

Collective strike or strike by employees is a politically sensitive issue in China. Currently, Chinese statutory rules and judicial practice do not recognize the legality of employee strikes, and such actions are generally regarded as absenteeism.

Judicial precedents show that courts typically take into account the severity of the employees' collective work stoppage, the legitimacy of their demands, and the validity of company rules and regulations in determining the legality of disciplinary actions (including termination of the employment relationship) taken by the employer against employees who strike (please refer to Q&A articles 130 and 131).

Employers can explicitly state in their company rules and regulations that they encourage employees to actively communicate with the company's management regarding labor conditions and other issues, and that strike is deemed to be absenteeism. At the same time, employers should also actively address reasonable and lawful concerns raised by employees to prevent a dispute from escalating into a strike that could impact social stability, which might lead to government intervention that could result in unfavorable outcomes for the employer. Employees, on the other hand, should be cautious about or avoid using collective strikes as a means of negotiation, as this often results in the employer legally terminating employment contracts, particularly in light of current employment law in China.

7.30 Equity Incentive

An equity incentive agreement is an agreement between an employer and/or its affiliate and an employee in which the former conditionally rewards the employee with a certain amount of company equity, aiming to encourage the employee to make a long-term contribution to achieve a win-win situation for both the employer and the employee (please refer to Q&A article 132).

In principle, a dispute arising from an equity incentive agreement falls under the category of employment disputes, unless this equity incentive transforms the employee into a shareholder with substantial equity and management rights (please refer to Q&A article 133).

If the party granting the equity in the equity incentive agreement is not the employer but its affiliated company, the court typically treats this affiliated company as a co-defendant along with the employer and makes a substantive ruling on whether the two companies share the responsibility for the equity incentive obligations. An exception to this is when the affiliated company is an overseas foreign company, in which case the court or labor arbitration committee may decide not to docket the case (please refer to Q&A article 134).

For employees' claims for rights or benefits under equity incentives, which is the most common, labor arbitration committees or courts usually treat these claims as part of remuneration under the employment relationship. The labor arbitration committee or court typically reviews the conditions for the granting of rights or benefits under the equity incentive agreement and decides whether the employee meets these conditions before making a judgment regarding whether the benefits and rights should be awarded (please refer to Q&A article 135).

Therefore, employers should, in line with the company's business vision, clearly and reasonably stipulate the steps, conditions, and amounts related to the equity incentive and adhere to the terms of the equity incentive. If an employer cancels an employee's equity incentive rights, it must follow rules similar to disciplinary actions, handling the matter reasonably in both substance and procedure according to lawful and effective company rules and regulations or relevant contracts. Additionally, unlawful termination of an employee's employment contract by the employer does not necessarily result in the dissolution of the employee's equity incentive rights and benefits. Correspondingly, employees should carefully read the equity incentive agreement, seek legal advice, clarify or modify relevant clauses, and strictly adhere to the obligations under the equity incentive, loyally and diligently fulfilling their duties to achieve a win-win situation with the employer.

7.31 Unjustified Wage Deduction and Arrear

Unjustified wage deduction refers to an employer deducting an employee's wages without a legitimate reason, while unjustified wage arrear refers to the employer failing to pay wages at the designated time, resulting in wage arrear. The legal consequences of unjustified wage deductions or arrears are that the employer must pay the deducted or delayed wages and the corresponding supplementary damages, as well as economic compensation for the employee if they are forced to resign as a result (please refer to Q&A article 136).

In judicial practice under employment law, two conditions must be met for unjustified wage deductions or arrears that cause forced resignation: first, the employer must have acted with subjective malice in wage deduction or arrear; second, the amount of unjustified wage deduction or arrear must be relatively significant as a proportion of the total wages.

There are two conflicting views in judicial practice on whether an unjustified wage deduction that forces an employee to resign includes deduction of overtime wages. One viewpoint is that unjustified wage deductions for overtime pay are the same as wage deductions, and there is no need for the employer's refusal to pay to be a prerequisite for the employee's legitimate forced resignation; this is the mainstream view among courts in various regions. Another viewpoint argues that a legitimate forced resignation by the employee must be conditional upon the employer's refusal to pay (please refer to Q&A article 138).

Additionally, unjustified wage arrear is subject to a special limitation of arbitration of more than one year, meaning that no matter how long wages have been in arrear, an employee can claim payment within one year after the termination of the employment relationship. However, whether unjustified wage deductions are subject to this special limitation period or to the ordinary one-year limitation period—meaning the employee must claim payment within one year of the unjustified deduction, otherwise the limitation of arbitration expires—remains in question in judicial practice (please refer to Q&A article 137 for details).

Employers should ensure that wages are paid in full and on time to avoid paying supplementary damages or even economic compensation. Employees should be mindful of the limitation of arbitration and promptly make claims for wages or compensation within the limitation.

7.32 Administrative and Criminal Penalties for Employers Violating Employment Law

If an employer violates regulations regarding overtime limits (employees work more than 36 hours of overtime per month), fails to comply with rules about labor safety facilities and labor environment conditions, employs child labor or illegally employs minor workers, violates special protections for female employees, or uses violence, threats, or unlawful restrictions on personal liberty to force labor, insults, assaults, illegally searches, and detains employees, intentionally fails to sign employment contracts, unreasonably fails to pay social insurance, obstructs or resists labor inspections, refuses to correct violations after being ordered to do so, refuses to report, conceals facts, destroys evidence, or refuses to comply with labor administrative decisions, the employer or responsible persons may be subject to administrative penalties. These penalties include warnings, orders to correct, orders to pay, fines, orders to suspend operations for rectification, revocation of business licenses, and detention (please refer to Q&A article 139).

The employer or responsible persons may also face criminal liability for actions that violate employment law, including crimes such as causing a major labor safety accident or a major liability accident, compelling risky operations, forced labor, employing child labor in hazardous work, refusal to pay labor remuneration, illegal detention, intentional injury, and other crimes related to safety responsibilities (please refer to Q&A article 140).

Needless to say, owners or shareholders of employers should be aware of these legal liabilities and remain compliant.

7.33 Resignation and Forced Resignation of Employees

The Employment Contract Law grants employees the right to resign with advance notice. Employees are required to provide 30 days' notice for resignation during the regular period of the employment contract, and they are entitled to resign with 3 days' notice during the probationary period; otherwise, they may be liable to compensate the employer for any losses caused. If an employee resigns voluntarily for personal reasons, the employer is not required to pay economic compensation.

Employers cannot restrict an employee's right to resign by claiming that "company approval is required." Once an employer receives a resignation letter, the employee does not have the right to retract it unless the employer permits it (please refer to Q&A article 142). In practice, when both parties dispute on the reasons for termination, courts typically treat it as a termination of the employment contract by mutual agreement for which the employer should pay economic compensation to the employee. Therefore, employees should request a written termination notice from the employer when being dismissed to retain the opportunity of a punitive damages claim, and employers should require a written resignation letter from employees upon resignation to avoid possible liability of economic compensation (please refer to Q&A article 145).

If an employee is forced to resign on legally valid grounds, the employer must pay economic compensation to the employee (please refer to Q&A article 143). The valid grounds include the following: the employer commits unjustifiable wage (or overtime wage) deductions or arrears, fails to legally purchase social insurance, or violates labor protection or labor conditions stipulated by law or company rules and regulations; the labor contract is invalid; or the employer uses violence or illegal means to restrict the employee's personal freedom or endangers the employee's safety. Whether an employer's relocation constitutes a legally valid reason for forced resignation depends on whether the new address is covered by the work location specified in the employment contract, the negative impact of the relocation on the employee, and whether the employer has taken reasonable mitigatory measures (please refer to Q&A article 144).

Employers should comply with employment law when signing employment contracts, formulating company rules and regulations, and performing the employment contract. They can also include multiple work addresses in the employment contract or specify details of company relocation and the rights and obligations of both parties to prevent employees from having valid reasons for forced resignation. When an employee decides to resign due to legally valid ground(s) for forced resignation, they should clearly state the legal grounds for forced resignation in the resignation letter to obtain recognition of forced resignation and the right to economic compensation from the employer.

7.34 Employee Retirement

In China, the statutory retirement age is 60 years for male employees, 50 years for female workers, and 55 years for female cadres. However, for those engaged in special occupations, such as heavy physical labor or underground, high-temperature, high-altitude work, the retirement age is lower (please refer to Q&A article 146). Starting from 2025, the statutory retirement age shall be gradually (over 15 years) extended to 63 years for male employees, 55 years for female workers, and 58 years for female cadres.

Distinguishing between female workers and female cadres involves complex rules that vary by region (please refer to Q&A article 147). This distinction may depend on whether the female employee is engaged in management or technical positions at the retirement age of 50 or above, the length of time they have held such a position by that age, or their status as recorded in social insurance registration.

Whether an employer can terminate the employment relationship with an employee who has reached the retirement age is a complicated issue. If an employee has reached retirement age and is already receiving basic pension insurance benefits, the employer may dissolve the employment relationship without paying economic compensation. However, the issue of whether an employer can terminate the employment relationship with an employee who has reached retirement age but is not receiving basic pension insurance benefits varies in different regions' judicial practices (please refer to Q&A article 148).

Judicial practices vary: (1) allowing the employment relationship to automatically terminate; (2) prohibiting the employer from terminating the relationship; (3) determining whether the employer can terminate the relationship based on whether the employer is at fault for the employee not receiving basic pension insurance benefits; or (4) giving the employer the right to choose whether to terminate. In practice, if an employee is on paid work injury leave due to a work injury or on medical care leave due to illness or non-work-related injury, there are two different approaches to whether the employer can terminate the employment relationship of such an employee when they reach retirement age (please refer to Q&A article 149).

Therefore, employers and employees need to understand the local rules for determining the retirement age of female employees and the local judicial practices regarding whether employers can terminate the employment relationship with employees who have reached retirement age but are not receiving basic pension insurance benefits. This understanding will help determine whether to continue or terminate the employment contract. Employers should also be particularly cautious when handling the employment relationship with employees who reach retirement age while on work injury leave or medical care leave, given the uncertain practice in different regions.

7.35 Employee Death and Employer Demise

The death of an employee due to illness or non-work-related injury will lead to dissolution of the employment relationship between the employee and the employer. The employee's family members are not entitled to claim economic compensation from the employer but may receive funeral subsidies and survivor's benefits. In cases where the employee dies due to a work injury, the family members are also not entitled to economic compensation but can receive benefits according to the standards for one-off work death allowance.

The issues of funeral and condolence allowances involve whether the 2020 Interim Measures for Survivor Benefits of Enterprise Employees' Basic Pension is applicable in different regional labor law practices, whether the employer or the social security fund is responsible for these payments, the scope of applicants eligible for funeral and condolence allowances, the calculation standards, and the method of payment. For specific details, please refer to Q&A article 150.

When an employer undergoes bankruptcy, company dissolution, or is ordered to close, its employment relationships with the employees are dissolved, and the employer is obligated to pay economic compensation to the employees. In the event of bankruptcy, the employers' unpaid wages and compensations owed to the employees should be paid from the bankruptcy estate prior to ordinary creditors (such as suppliers) being paid (please refer to Q&A article 151).

Whether the owner (e.g., shareholders) of the employer is personally liable for the unpaid wages or compensations owed to the employees depends on the type of employer. In general partnerships, the owners are typically personally liable, except for limited partners in a limited partnership. Owners of sole proprietorship enterprises and sole traders are also personally liable (please refer to Q&A article 174). In principle, owners of a limited liability company are not personally liable, except in the following cases: commingling of company and personal assets, illegal contributions by owners at the time of the company's establishment, illegal actions by owners that harm creditors during the company's operation, or when owners have provided guarantees or commitments for the company's debts (please refer to Q&A article 175).

Shareholders or owners of a limited liability company must strictly adhere to legal requirements in the management of the company, clearly distinguish between company actions and personal actions, and avoid abusing their powers in ways that harm the interests of creditors, to prevent personal liability. When employees seek unpaid wages or compensations and find that company assets are insufficient to meet these obligations, they should seek assistance from a lawyer familiar with company law to potentially hold the company's shareholders or owners personally liable.

7.36 Lawful Dismissal

In principle, lawful terminations on different grounds normally involve two main requirements: the first is that the termination must be accordance with substantive legal requirements, such as legitimate grounds, factual basis, statutory or regulatory rules, or legally binding company institutional rules (see Q&A article 120); the second is that the termination must meet procedural legal requirements. This may involve the employer fulfilling certain statutory or regulatory procedural obligations or reasonable procedural obligations, such as notifying the trade union or the labor administrative authority (see Q&A articles 121 and 152).

In mutual agreement termination, both parties typically sign an agreement of employment termination, arranging matters such as economic compensation. In terminating a fixed-term employment contract on the ground of expiration, the employer only needs to notify the employee of the intention not to renew the contract. Judicial precedents show that employers are not required to notify trade unions for these two types of terminations.

When terminating an employee during the probationary period on the ground of the employee not meeting hiring requirements, the employer can immediately terminate the relationship if it can prove the employee does not meet the requirements; therefore, it is crucial for the employer to clearly define the hiring requirements in the employment contract and outline the methods for assessing whether the employee meets the standard. The employer must notify the trade union.

When terminating an employee on the ground of health incompetence or ability incompetence, the employer must arrange a position transfer for the employee; if the employee is still incompetent, the employer should notify the trade union and notify the employee of the termination with 30 days' notice (or a payment in lieu of notice) (see Q&A articles 85 and 158).

When terminating an employee on the ground of the employee's serious violation of company rules and regulations, the employer must confirm two issues. The first is that the employee must have seriously violated the employer's legally binding institutional rules (including company rules and regulations, provisions of contractual agreements, and basic professional ethics). The employer must prove that the employee has committed the misconduct, that the company has established legally binding institutional rules, and that the employee's misconduct reached the threshold for dismissal as stipulated by these rules. The second is that the termination procedure must comply with statutory procedural requirements. The employer must prove that they have fulfilled the obligation in notifying the trade union when terminating the employee (unless the company has not established a trade union and the local court does not require an alternative notification of the local trade union). Additionally, the employer should adhere to the fair and reasonable procedures outlined in the company rules and regulations or the employment contract when handling the termination. We recommended that the employer reasonably consider and implement procedures such as advance notice, objective investigation of the incident, and careful consideration of the employee's explanation to strengthen the legality of the termination of the employment relationship.

When terminating employees who are criminally liable, employees on the ground of gross negligence or corruption, and employees on the ground of the employee making the employment contract invalid, employers must notify the trade union before they terminate the employment. When terminating an employee on the ground of major change in objective condition, the employer must first negotiate with the employee for position transfer. If this fails, the employers then may notify the trade union and terminate the employee with a 30-day notice (or a payment in lieu of notice). In economic redundancy, the employer must notify the trade union or the employee congress and then the labor administrative authority before it terminates the employees.

The aforesaid procedural requirement for notifying the trade union is a complex legal issue. First, the employer must inform the trade union in writing of the reasons and factual basis for terminating the employee's employment and consider the union's opinions. Chinese employment law allows the employer to correct the absence of this before the case reaches court (i.e., to notify the trade union after the dismissal as a remedial measure) and considers it as having legally notified the union. Second, if the employer has not established a trade union, most courts in China do not require the employer to notify a union. However, a few regions, such as Jiangsu and Zhejiang Provinces, require the employer to notify the local trade union instead (please refer to Q&A article 152).

It is important to note that for dismissals on the ground of health incompetence or ability incompetence, major change in objective condition, or economic redundancy, certain types of employees are afforded special protection and cannot be dismissed. These include: 1) female employees in the "three protected periods" (pregnancy, maternity, and lactation periods); 2) employees who have served for 15 years or more and are less than 5 years away from retirement; 3) employees who have fully or partially lost their labor capacity due to occupational disease or work-related injury; 4) employees who are on medical care leave due to illnesses or non-work-related injuries or on paid work injury leave due to work injury; 5) employees engaged in work that exposes them to occupational hazards who have not undergone a off-role occupational health examination; 6) employees suspected of having occupational diseases who are under diagnosis or medical observation (please refer to Q&A article 160).

7.37 Economic Redundancy

Economic redundancy refers to a situation where an employer legally reduces the number of employees (20 people or 10% or more) due to severe difficulties in production and operation (see Q&A article 155).

There are three situations applicable for economic redundancy: bankruptcy reorganization (bankruptcy courts ruling on reorganization), operational hardship (at least consecutive losses for the latest two or three years), and business transfer (including productional transfer, major technological innovation, operational adjustment, and other major change in objective condition).

Employers must follow legal procedures when implementing economic redundancy. Employers must notify trade unions or employee congresses, seek their opinions, and report to the labor administration authority. The employers must notify employees of the decision to terminate the employment relationship one month in advance (or pay one month's payment in lieu of notice) before the termination, and pay economic compensation.

Employers need to pay special attention to whether the situation falls under the three situations of economic redundancy, whether the statutory number of layoffs is met, and whether layoffs strictly follow relevant procedural regulations. Employees should ensure that the redundancy falls under the said statutory situations and that the employer has adhered to the procedures, and they are entitled to economic compensation and one month's notice (or a payment in lieu of notice). Employers are also prohibited from dismissing employees who are under special employment relationship protection (e.g., female employees during the three protection periods, etc.).

7.38 Termination for Major Change in Objective Condition

An employer has the right to terminate an employee's employment relationship on the ground of major change in objective condition as stipulated in Article 40 of the Employment Contract Law. The distinction between applying this legal provision and economic redundancy lies in that the latter must meet the requirement of meeting the conditions for the number of layoffs and occurrence of operational hardship (please refer to Q&A article 159).

Judicial practice under Chinese employment law generally holds that major change in objective condition is limited to a major change in the external environment of the enterprise that the enterprise cannot alter or control (e.g., changes in government policies), and not to general poor business conditions or organizational adjustments aimed at improving operations.

A contentious issue in judicial practice is whether major strategic adjustments by a company qualify as major change in objective condition. Some regional courts, such as the Hangzhou Intermediate Court, believe that major strategic adjustments themselves prove the existence of major change in objective condition, while others, such as the Beijing Third Intermediate Court, hold the opposite view.

When an employer terminates an employee's employment relationship on the ground of major change in objective condition, it must follow legal procedures. The employer must first negotiate with the employee to amend the terms of the employment contract (e.g., position transfer). If the negotiation fails, the employer must give the employee one month's notice of the termination decision (or a payment in lieu of notice) and notify the trade union (unless the company has not established a trade union and local judicial practice does not require an alternative notification of the local trade union) before terminating the employment relationship, and pay economic compensation to the employee.

7.39 Termination of Employment for Employee's Incompetence

Under the Employment Contract Law, there are two situations where an employer may terminate an employment relationship due to an employee's incompetence: health incompetence and ability incompetence.

Health incompetence involves two scenarios: when an employee is unable to perform their original work after their medical care leave for an illness or non-work-related injury, or after the end of their paid work injury leave. In either case, the employer must first assign the employee to another suitable role. If the employee is still incompetent, the employer may terminate the employment relationship after giving 30 days' notice or a payment in lieu of notice.

However, if the employee's health condition results in a loss of labor capacity, the employer must maintain the employment relationship during the period of the employee's labor capacity appraisal and handle the situation according to the legal requirements based on the conclusions of the labor capacity appraisal. (For cases involving illness or non-work-related injury, please refer to Q&A articles 85 and 86; for cases involving work injury, please refer to Q&A articles 95, 96, 97, and 98.)

Ability incompetence refers to an employee's inability to perform work for reasons unrelated to health. The employer should first arrange training or a position transfer for the incompetent employee. If the employee still cannot perform the work, the employer may terminate the employment relationship after giving 30 days' notice or payment in lieu of notice.

Regardless of whether the incompetence is due to ability or health, the employer must provide evidence proving the employee's incompetence, including providing the employee's job description (or work requirements) and evidence of the employee's actual work performance. Additionally, the employer must fulfill the requirement to notify the trade union (unless the company has not established a trade union and local judicial practice does not require an alternative notification of the local trade union).

7.40 Termination of Employment Due to Employee's Gross Misconduct

An employer may terminate an employment contract with an employee due to gross misconduct in the following situations: serious violation of the employer's company rules and regulations, gross negligence or corruption resulting in significant loss to the employer, the existence of concurrent employment relationships with other employers, the employee being held criminally liable, and the employee being the cause of an invalid employment contract. In such cases, the employer is not required to pay economic compensation or punitive damages.

The employer may terminate the employment contract of an employee involved in criminal liability. Situations of criminal liability include being sentenced to fixed-term imprisonment (including those on suspension) by the courts, under criminal detention, being discharged of conviction by a court, and being discharged of prosecution by a procuratorate. If an employee is under investigation by the police or procuratorate authorities, and their personal freedom is restricted due to suspected criminal activities, the employer may suspend the performance of the employment contract, cease wage payments, and simultaneously suspend social insurance contributions. If the employee is found not guilty, the employer should restore the employment relationship unless it is objectively impossible to do so (refer to Q&A article 161).

The employer may also terminate the employment of an employee who, through gross negligence or corruption, causes significant loss to the employer. However, this type of termination is rare in employment law practice, and employers are often unsuccessful in terminating employees on these grounds. Generally, employers specify the specific acts of gross negligence or corruption as serious violations of company rules and regulations or terminate their employees on the ground that these acts severely violate basic professional ethics (refer to Q&A article 162).

If an employee has a concurrent employment relationship with another employer that seriously affects their work with the current employer, or if the employee refuses to correct the situation after being informed by the employer, the employer may terminate the employment relationship. The most common scenario in employment law practice in China is when an employee establishes or participates in establishing a company that competes with their employer. Courts usually do not consider the aforesaid statutory condition, "seriously affect," and directly recognize the legality of the employer's termination. This type of termination applies only to full-time employees engaged in regular work (refer to Q&A article 163).

The employer may incorporate all these situations into the serious misconduct behaviors outlined in the company's rules and regulations. When terminating the employment relationship, the employer must follow reasonable and lawful procedures, such as notifying the trade union (unless the company has not established a trade union and local judicial practice does not require an alternative notification of the local trade union), informing the employee of the ground(s) of the termination, and allowing the employee to present their explanations (please refer to Q&A article 154).

Please refer to Q&A articles 164 to 171 and article 173 for conditions of and calculation methods for economic compensation, punitive damages, payment in lieu of notice, employee losses, unemployment insurance benefits, and supplementary damages resulting from termination of employment, as well as for whether an employee can request reinstatement after being unlawfully dismissed.

7.41 Protection of Trade Secrets

A trade secret is a type of information that requires protection. To establish that an employee's actions constitute an infringement of trade secrets, two conditions must be met: first, the information held by the company must qualify as a trade secret, meaning it is non-public, has commercial value, and the company has taken measures to keep it confidential (please refer to Q&A article 182); second, the employee must have engaged in improper conduct that infringes upon the company's related information. We consider that these behaviors can be categorized as theft, disclosure, or use (including assisting others in using) of another's trade secrets (refer to Q&A articles 186 and 187).

To hold an employee liable for compensation for infringing trade secrets, the employer must also make sure that the employee does not have any justifiable defenses, such as the impugned information not being identical to the company's trade secret, reverse engineering, lack of access to trade secrets, independent development, or lawful sources (please refer to Q&A article 191).

Under Chinese civil and criminal law, courts can order current or former employees who have infringed trade secrets to cease the infringement, compensate for losses, and return or destroy materials containing the trade secrets, and in some cases, even impose criminal liability on the employee. Relevant government agencies may also impose administrative penalties on the infringer (refer to Q&A articles 193, 194, and 195).

At present, Chinese law is not very clear on whether an action of customer poaching constitutes infringement of trade secrets, and judicial practice varies with different rulings. However, most courts generally take into account the justification of the accused employee's actions, the legitimacy and importance of the trade secret holder's rights, as well as the interests of third parties and the public. They ultimately determine whether it is fair and reasonable to decide that "the employee's action of poaching customers should not be penalized" when assessing whether the poaching behavior constitutes infringement.

Protecting trade secrets involving employee infringement spans both employment law and intellectual property law and involves many complex technical and legal issues (please refer to Q&A articles 181 to 192). Employers should seek the assistance of professional lawyers. At the very least, employers should clearly understand the definition of trade secrets, take appropriate confidentiality measures, and enter into confidentiality agreements with employees to protect the trade secrets they hold. Employees, in turn, should uphold their duties of honesty, integrity, and loyalty by not infringing on the trade secrets that belong to their employer.

7.42 Non-Competition Agreement

A non-competition agreement restricts an employee from engaging in work within industries (or businesses) that compete with the employer for a certain period (not exceeding two years), under the condition that the employee has contacted the employer's trade secrets. As opposed to behavior restriction and the limited protection period of non-competition obligation, protection of trade secrets is a form of property rights protection and is valid for as long as the trade secrets exist (please refer to Q&A articles 196 and 197).

Only employees who have undertaken confidentiality obligations are required to sign non-competition agreements and are prohibited from engaging in competing industries after leaving their job (please refer to Q&A article 198). Current employees are also prohibited from engaging in competing industries based on their duty of loyalty. Both parties can agree on on-the-job non-competition obligations and contractual damages in the non-competition agreement (please refer to Q&A article 199).

A non-competition agreement should specify the amount of non-competition allowance that the employee will receive after leaving the job. However, if the agreement states that the employee's salary includes pre-paid non-competition allowance, courts across different regions in China have varied in their rulings, with some finding this practice lawful and others not (please refer to Q&A article 201).

If a non-competition agreement only specifies the non-competition obligation without specifying the allowance, the general view of Chinese courts is that the agreement is still binding on the employee. If the employee violates the non-competition obligation, they should be held liable for contractual damages. On the other hand, if the employee fulfills the non-competition obligation, they are entitled to claim monthly non-competition allowance from the employer, calculated at 30% of the employee's average wage from the 12 months before leaving the job (or a higher local standard, such as 50% in Shenzhen) (please refer to Q&A article 200).

If an employee breaches the non-competition obligation, they are liable for contractual damages and must return the non-competition allowance if stipulated in the agreement. Excessively high liquidated damages in the non-competition agreement may not be enforceable and may be reduced by court ruling (please refer to Q&A article 203). Even if the employee pays contractual damages, they may still be required to continue fulfilling the non-competition obligation unless the employer terminates the agreement or waives the employee's non-competition obligation (please refer to Q&A article 202).

Therefore, employers can include in the employment contract or non-competition agreement a provision for the employee's on-the-job non-competition obligation. In regions where it is legally recognized, employers may also consider including a clause that the employee's wages include pre-paid non-competition allowance.

Employees should be aware of the following issues. First, if the employee is not a senior management or senior technical personnel or another person with confidentiality obligations, the non-competition agreement signed by the employee is not binding. Second, even if the employer and the employee have not agreed on a non-competition agreement, or if the agreement has been terminated, the employee still has an absolute legal obligation to protect the employer's trade secrets. Employees who violate this obligation may face legal liabilities for infringing trade secrets. Finally, if the non-competition agreement signed by the employee does not specify the amount of non-competition allowance, the employee is still obligated to fulfill the non-competition obligation but has the right to request non-competition allowance.

7.43 Personal Information Protection

China's Personal Information Protection Law, enacted in 2021, impacts all companies operating in China (please refer to Q&A article 204).

Employers may need to communicate with customers, suppliers, or parent companies outside China and may need to provide personal information to them. Therefore, they should comply with the law through one of three compliance pathways: the security assessment pathway, the personal information standard contract pathway, and the personal information protection certification pathway (please refer to Q&A article 205). The personal information standard contract pathway is applicable to most companies. According to the Standard Contracts for Outbound-transfer of Personal Information, companies operating in China that need to transfer personal information abroad should complete the signing and filing of the standard contract by the end of 2023; however, the Chinese government's enforcement of this compliance requirement remains to be seen (please refer to Q&A article 206).

Companies or individuals operating in China who violate the Personal Information Protection Law may face civil liabilities (including damages for infringement), administrative liabilities (including orders to correct, warnings, fines, confiscation of illegal gains, orders to suspend the use of applications, and orders to cease operations), and criminal liabilities (please refer to Q&A articles 208 to 210).

Employers can refer to the Q&A articles in this book to understand their obligations to protect personal information, how to comply with personal information protection regulations, and how to avoid related legal liabilities.

7.44 Company Rules and Regulations and Contracts Management

This is a guide specifically for employers. Employment contracts and related agreements, along with company rules, are the core documents for managing employment relationships. These documents typically comprehensively define the rights and obligations between the employer and the employee. Chinese employment law allows employers to establish various contracts and company rules and regulations based on their business autonomy and to require employees to sign or adhere to them. Contracts or company rules and regulations that have been signed by employees are binding, and company rules and regulations can also become effective through public notification or informing the employees.

First, the employment contract is the most important employment management document. Employers should select the appropriate type of employment contracts based on the nature of the work and sign written contracts with employees in a timely manner to avoid the liability for double-wage damages. Employment contracts can also include clauses in which employees undertake that they have no existing unsettled employment relationship or have not violated non-competition agreements when joining the company, thereby reducing the risk of the employer being held accountable by the employees' former employer.

The employment contract should clearly state the contract terms and work locations. In employment law practice, it is common for employers to sign fixed-term contracts of about one year with new employees; if an employer plans to relocate the company, it can also specify in the employment contract that the work locations include both the current address and the new address to which the company will move. This transparency can reduce the risk of employees claiming forced resignation due to the company's relocation and demanding economic compensation.

Employee wage-related clauses are, of course, the most important clauses in the employment contract. Employers can negotiate a reasonable wage structure with employees, designing a remuneration system that includes monthly, quarterly, and annual wages (such as a year-end bonus) that balances immediate appeal with deferred rewards for employees. If necessary, employers should also design a legal and effective monthly package wage system or piecework wage system to achieve a win-win situation for both parties.

AFTERWORD

Employment law is one of the areas of Chinese law most influenced by the past planned economy system in China. Besides the National People's Congress and the Supreme People's Court, various government departments have also taken part in the creation of numerous regulations and rules. Due to the rapid economic transition over the past three or four decades and the administrative departments' shortcomings in legislative techniques, the field of employment law has witnessed a proliferation of conflicting legal rules, gaps, inconsistencies between judicial practice and legal rules, and a lack of uniformity in court rulings across different regions.

This highly complex situation, characterized by legal rule conflicts and practical discrepancies, presents a significant challenge to providing clear and concise answers to readers' questions on the topic of "What are my rights and what should I do?"

We have attempted to explain complex legal issues using a unique tree-like and web-like structure. As mentioned in the Preface, some practical issues involve multiple variables that require separate, detailed explanations. Thus, some Q&A sections in this book offer general answers that encompass sub-issues. This structure allows readers to quickly obtain information by reading the general Q&A or to delve into the details by reading the sub-issues. Furthermore, different Q&A sections are interconnected through tags, creating a web-like network of links. Compared with the traditional method of explaining complex legal issues in lengthy passages, this approach better aligns with how the human brain processes and acquires knowledge. In today's information-overloaded world, learning is more about the selection and filtering of information rather than mere collection and aggregation.

We recognize that this Q&A short-article and tree-like knowledge block structure represents the linguistic framework needed for future legal artificial intelligence (AI). With the rapid advancement of natural language processing AI, significant breakthroughs in legal analysis by AI may be on the horizon. Our experience in legal practice has shown that judgments on many complex legal issues, such as determining whether someone should be held liable for tort, often result from an aggregated weight of multiple legal factors. Therefore, the preconditions for AI to analyze and solve legal problems include defining specific legal factors for particular legal issues, assigning values to these factors, and determining how to apply specific legal logic and connections to use and measure these values. The logical deduction of specific legal issues thus requires a tree-like and web-like knowledge block structure and logic, which legal AI may have to learn.

Hence, the way legal issues are presented in this book may represent the future direction of legal information dissemination, transforming complex and obscure legal rules into clear and concise guidance. It is our sincere vision that this will make legal knowledge and problem-solving more accessible and less costly for ordinary people. Law should be a bridge to fairness and justice instead of a barrier.

Our next step is to draft practical guides on Chinese family law, as well as Chinese business law, using this approach. While the creation process is demanding, summarizing past experiences, conducting case law research and analysis, and refining our thoughts is also a rewarding experience.

This is the first book authored by both of us. Over 40 years ago, Dong Wang saw a book on foundry technology on a bookshelf at home—a book that his father had written based on practical experience in a factory. Father was quite proud of it. Dong Wang is grateful for his father's love and influence and wishes his parents good health and long life. Peng Zhao's wife selflessly gave up her profession to support his busy legal work and writing, taking on household responsibilities and caring for their children. Peng Zhao is grateful for her contributions to the family and her support for his career. Our firm's legal assistant, Yinjie Wang, contributed significantly to the case research, analysis, and text compilation for this book, making him an indispensable contributor to its creation.

We hope this book will be helpful to our readers and sincerely welcome your feedback and suggestions.

Dong Wang wangdong@royalaw.com
Peng Zhao zhaopeng@royalaw.com
April 27, 2024

INDEX

ability incompetence 185, 207, 247, 252, 346, 349
absence of signed employment contract, double-wage damages for 51–53
accidental injuries 129–130, 148–150
accrued annual leave, management of 107–109
accumulative service years 104, 116, **117**, 119, 121
acquisition infringement of trade secret 282, 284, 285, 299
actionable period, for double-wage damages 62–67
administrative penalties 202–204; for employers violating employment law 343; for violation of Personal Information Protection Act 317–318
age of retirement 24–25; during medical treatment, termination and 223–225; national and local regulations for 217–219; statutory 215–217; and termination 219–223
allowance: condolence 225–227, 345; funeral 141, 225–227, 345; high-temperature 111–114, **113**, 331; hospitalization meal 133, **142–143**, 146, 334; medical treatment 124, 230–231, 258, 332; night 164–165; non-competition *see* non-competition allowance; one-off disability 140, **142–143**
appraisal, labor capacity *see* labor capacity appraisal
assignment contract 1, 3, 15, 16, 82, 91–92, **98–99**, 209, 322; and employment relationship, distinguished 21–22

bankruptcy 227–228
bereavement leave 109, 329–330
bonus 48, 165–166, 336; equity incentive 196; quarterly 81; year-end 81, 201, 247
burden of proof 18, 275, 304; legal existence of trade secrets 276; non-publicity of trade secrets 277–281; right holders of trade secrets 284–287
business closure: and termination 227–228; wage payment during 159–160

cancer, medical care leave for 119–121
causal contract 3; and employment relationship, distinguished 21–22
causal employees: and full-time employees, distinguished 13–14; request to permanent employment 14–16
child labor 22, 202, 205, 343
chronic illness 124–125
civil law: double-wage damages 59; equity incentive agreement 196; infringement acts of trade secrets 284; labor dispatch contract 93; limitation of labor arbitration 34, 37; mental damages 154, 155; procedure for resignation 209; trade secrets 273; wage commitment 45
civil servant disputes 29–30
civil servant relationship 29, 321
collective contracts 3–4, 320–321; legal effect of signing 4–5
collective strike 341; employees, legality of dismissing 189–191; employees' entitlement to 188–189
commercial accident insurance 152–153
commissions 165–166
company deregistration 227–228
company rules and regulations 169–171, 353
compensation agreement, labor arbitration after reaching 270–271
computer software source codes 281–282
condolence allowance 225–227, 345
contract: assignment 1, 3, 15, 16, 21–22, 82, 91–92, **98–99**, 209, 322; causal 3, 21–22; collective 3–5, 320–321; employment *see* employment contract; individual 3–5, 26–27, 320–321; labor dispatch *see* labor dispatch contract; management 353; *see also individual entries*
contractor relationship 9, 10, 28, 48, 50, 221; common, in daily life 12–13; and employment relationship, distinguished 17–19, 21–22, 24, 25, 321; legal consequences of 20–21; minimum wage 158; termination of 223, 224

corruption, termination for 245–246
court: company's appeal to, after losing in labor arbitration 41–42; limitation of labor arbitration, review of 34–36; *see also* The Supreme Court's Judicial Interpretation (2020)
criminal law: trade secret protection 273, 351
criminal penalties, for employers violating employment law 343
customer poaching 272, 274, 275, 288–290, 351; infringement 290–292

damages: bearer of liability for 182–184; civil, for violation of Personal Information Protection Act 316–317; double-wage *see* double-wage damages; mental *see* mental damages; non-competition contractual 305, 308; probation period 38, 85; punitive 32, 124, 141, 248–249, 252, 253, 257, 259; supplementary 32, 257, 342, 343
death: of an employee 345–346; due to illness or non-work-related injury 225–227
demise of an employer 345–346
disciplinary action: chronic illness and 124; for collective strike 188, 341; definition of 172; and equity incentive 342; fairness and reasonableness of 172; in labor dispatch contract 324; lawful 337–338; legal permission for 172–173; for mental damages 337; professional ethics for 171; for sick leave 331
disclosure infringement of trade secret 281, 282, 284, 285
discrimination: gender region 168; job 168; recruitment 153–154, 169, 337; wage 168, 336
dismissal *see* termination
divisible arbitration limitation accounting 66–69
double-wage damages: for absence of signed employment contract 51–53; actionable period for 62–67; amendment agreement after expiration of fixed-term contract 60–61; calculation of 62–81; exemptions for 54–62; for invalid labor dispatch 58–59; liability for 4, 52–54, 56–57, 59, 62, 72, 91, 179, 235; for newly joined employee 65–66; for not signing a permanent employment contract 69–71, 77–79; retroactive signing of employment contract 56–58; wage standard for 79–81
due wages 79, 81, 157, 158, 197, 250, 334

economic compensation 2; calculation of 247, 249–252; circumstances of 262–263; for forced resignation 210–214, 251, 326, 343; limitation of arbitration for 39, 40
economic loss: compensation for 265–268; fault and 176–178; and resignation 263–265
economic redundancy 185, 207, 348; and termination 233–236, 241–243
employee: on call at home 19–20; causal *vs* full-time 13–14; death due to illness or non-work-related injury 225–227; employment arbitration application, time limitation for filing 31–34; employment relations 1–2; entitlements *see* employee entitlements; female *see* female employees; legal effect of signing collective contract 4–5; multiple employers' use of 340; onboarding 325–326; refused to sign an employment contract 47; resignation 208; retaining employees' certificates 47–49; special status of 9–10; start of work 45–46; volunteers as 16–17; wages 334–336; *see also individual entries*
employee entitlements: accidental injuries 129–130, 148–150; accrued annual leave, management of 107–109; basic leave rights 96–97; bereavement leave 109; chronic illness 124–125; commercial accident insurance 152–153; female employees, special protections for 127; high-temperature allowance 111–114, **113**, 331; maternity leave 125–126; medical care leave *see* medical care leave; mental damages in employment disputes 153–155; occupational disease *see* occupational disease; overtime pay *see* overtime pay; of paid annual leave 104–106; paternity leave rights 110–111; pneumoconiosis 150–151; public holidays 97–98; sick leave *see* sick leave; time-off in lieu offsetting overtime hours 103–104; types of **98–99**; work-break entitlement 114–115; work injury *see* work injuries
employee-related financial compensation 338–339
employer: contact employees outside work hours 169; demise of 345–346; deposit collection 47–49; employment arbitration application, time limitation for filing 31–34; employment relations 1–2; legal effect of signing collective contract 4–5; probation period damages, claiming 38; refusal to pay overtime wage 201–202; reneges on wage commitment to an employee candidate 45; set up and maintain employees' employment files 46–47; subject qualification of 8–9; *see also individual entries*
employment: arbitration *see* employment arbitration; commencement *see* employment commencement; contract *see* employment contract; disputes *see* labor disputes;

mixed 180–182; relations *see* employment relations; rights 3, 11, 20, 24, 25, 32, 50, 169, 256, 296, 297, 328; special type of 10–11; termination *see* termination
employment arbitration 11, 67, 107, 166, 200, 257, 267; application, time limitation for filing 31–34; committee 108, 228; limitation of *see* limitation of arbitration
employment commencement: assignment contract 91–92; double-wage damages *see* double-wage damages; invalid employment contract 88–91; no-pay trial work 49; probation period *see* probation period; social insurance 43–45; student intern workers 49–51; termination *see* termination
employment contract: absence of signed, double-wage damages for 51–53; amendment agreement of 60–61; circumstances to sign 53–54; collective 3–4; fixed-term *see* fixed-term employment contract; individual 3–4; invalid 88–91; invalidation of 328–329; performance of *see* performance of employment contract; permanent *see* permanent employment contract; retroactive signing of 56–58; someone else to sign on behalf of the employee 59–60; time specification in 45–46; types of 322; *see also individual entries*
Employment Dispute Arbitration Committee 20
employment relations: civil servants 29–30; common, in daily life 8–11; and contractor relations, distinguished 17–19, 21–22, 24, 25, 321; family member of the boss 22–23; hired by human resource companies 26–28; legal consequences of 20–21; limitation of arbitration *see* limitation of arbitration; principles of 1–2; principles of conduct in 320; representative office of a foreign company 28–29; retirement age and 24–25; at the start of work 45–46; student intern workers 49–51; types of 2–3
epidemic lockdown, wage payment during 160
equal pay for equal work 4, 5n10, 81, 127–128, 168, 330, 336
equity incentive agreement 342; definition 191–192; equity benefits in 195–197; labor dispute and 193–195

family member of the boss: employment relations 22–23
fault: and economic losses 176–178; and termination 215
female employees: earnings of 127–128; special protection for 127, 330; statutory retirement age for 216–217
fine: administrative 47, 202, 203, 317; for contractual damages 306; for criminal offences 318; for misconduct 339; right to impose 174–176; *see also* penalty
fixed-term employment contract 2; amendment agreement of 60–61; circumstances to sign 53–54, 71, 72; double-wage damages for not signing 69–70, 77–79; exemptions after expiration of 55; exemptions from obligation to pay double-wage damages 55; expires before medical care leave 258; legal effect of signing 5–6; permanent employment contract be signed after two consecutive 72–76, 91
forced labor, crime of 204–205
forced resignation 208, 344; business closure and 159; economic compensation for 210–214, 251, 326, 343; equity incentive and 196; mental damages and 337; position transfer and 187; refusal to pay overtime wage and 201–202; wage deduction and 168, 197, 199, 342–343
foreigners 10
full-time employees and causal employees, distinguished 13–14
funeral allowance 141, 225–227, 345

gender region discrimination 168
general work hours 3, 6–8, 16, 82, 87, **98–99**, 101; bereavement leave and 109; for female employees 127; long-term unpaid leave and 247; minimum wage for 161, 165, 334; overtime wages for 336; paid annual leave and 104–106, 329; paternity leave and 111; for pregnant employees 125; rights and obligations of employment contract 322–323; sick leave and 118–119; work injury entitlements 141, 144
gross misconduct, termination for 349–350
gross negligence 177, 245–246, 266, 267, 339, 347, 349, 350

harassment 337; sexual 169
hazardous operations, in violation of regulations 204
health incompetence 208, 233, 346–347
high-temperature allowance 111–114, 331; rules **113**
hospitalization meal allowance 133, **142–143**, 146, 334

host employer 3, 26–28; double-wage damages for invalid labor dispatch 58–59; labor dispatch contract 92–95, 322–324; obligation to pay double-wage damages 54, 55; permanent employment contracts 29; probation period 82, 83
housing provident fund 44–45, 211, 326

identification of work injury 11n35, 130
illegal termination 244; economic losses and 264, 267; equity inventive and 196; procedure for notifying 228, 240; punitive damages for 32, 124, 141, 248–249, 252, 253, 257, 259; supplementary damages and 257; wage loss after 253–255
immunities, for trade secret infringement 292–295
imprisonment, for crime 244–245
incompetence: ability 185, 207, 247, 252, 346, 349; health 208, 233, 346–347; medical 340; termination for 240
independent development immunity 293
individual contracts 3–4, 26–27, 320–321; wage growth ratio of 5
indivisible arbitration limitation accounting 66–69
infringement: acquisition 282, 284, 285, 299; customer poaching 290–292; disclosure 281, 282, 284, 285; trade secret *see* trade secret infringement; use-based 276, 279, 280
in-school student worker. 10
insurance: maternity 44, 126, 326, 330; pension *see* pension insurance; social *see* social insurance; unemployment 44, 207, 225, 255–256; work injury *see* work injury insurance
internal retirement 11n33, 247n87
interruption of limitation of arbitration 39
invalidation of employment contract 328–329
invalid employment contract 88–91, 211
invalid labor dispatch 54–55; contract 92–94; current judicial rule for 94–95; double-wage damages for 58–59
irregular work hours 3, 6–8, 82, 87, **98–99**; bereavement leave and 109; for female employees 127; long-term unpaid leave and 247; minimum wage for 161, 165, 334; overtime wages for 336; paid annual leave and 104–106, 329; paternity leave and 111; for pregnant employees 125; rights and obligations of employment contract 322–323; sick leave and 118–119; work injury entitlements 141, 144

job discrimination 168
judicial procedures, for labor disputes 324–325
juvenile workers 203

labor administrative authority 4, 206; collective contracts 320, 321; employer–employee disputes, handling 30; employment termination 233, 235, 236, 242, 257; fine to collect deposits or retain employees' certificates 47; judicial procedures for employment disputes 324, 325; lawful disciplinary actions by 338; lawful dismissal by 346, 347; newly hired employee's probation period, extending 119n52; penalties to employment law violation 202, 203; unjustified wage correction by 199; validation of employment contract 6, 7, 322, 323
labor arbitration committee: authority to handle labor dispute cases 40–41; limitation of labor arbitration, review of 34–36
labor capacity appraisal 96, 258, 332, 333, 349; after employee suffers a work-related injury or occupational disease 140–141; after expiration of medical care leave 121–124; after expiration of paid work injury 134–138; disability identified by 144–146; extension of paid work injury leave 138–140; work injury recurrence 132, 133
labor capacity appraisal committee 119n53, 124, 132, 133, 138, 139, 141, 144, 333
labor discipline 170, 171, 176, 246, 338
labor dispatch 3, 9, 25–27; of causal employees 82; contract *see* labor dispatch contract; invalid *see* invalid labor dispatch; mandatory requirements for 29; procedure 30–42
labor dispatch contract 3, 16, 27, 92–95, 322; exemptions from obligation to pay double-wage damages 54–55; invalid 92–94; permanent 28; reverse 93; rights and obligations under 323–324
labor disputes: claim for mental damages in 153–155; equity incentive agreement 193–195; handling 30–31; judicial procedures for 324–325; labor arbitration committee's authority to handle 40–41; mental damages in 153–155; *see also individual entries*
labor outsourcing agreement 25–26
labor safety accidents 204
lawful disciplinary actions 337–338
lawful dismissal 187, 233, 235, 246, 346–348
layoff *see* termination
leave: annual *see* annual leave; basic rights 96–97; bereavement 109, 329–330; long-term unpaid 10, 55, 61, 62, 247, 249; maternity *see* maternity leave; medical care *see* medical care leave; paid annual 104–107, 329; paternity 110–111, 330–331; sick *see* sick leave

legal existence of trade secrets 276
liability: administrative 296, 300; for breach on non-competition 302–303; civil 183, 265, 296–300, 316; contractual negligence 45; criminal 157, 245, 296, 300–301, 319, 343, 350, 351; for damages, bearer of 182–184; for double-wage damages 4, 52–54, 56–57, 59, 62, 72, 91, 179, 235; joint 183, 184; of mental damages 155; personal 183, 184, 207, 259–261, 346; of punitive damages 124, 131; for remuneration 259–260; reneges on wage commitment to an employee candidate 45; tort 182, 183; for work-related injury 9, 22, 130, 132–134, 144, 146, 150
limitation of arbitration: accrued annual leave 107–108; commissions or bonuses 166; compensation agreement 270; double-wage damages 65, 69, 70, 327; employment arbitration application, filing 34–36; general 32; high-temperature allowance 112, 114; interruption of 39; one-year 34, 36–39, 53, 56, 63, 66, 67, 79, 180; paid annual leave 329; paternity leave rights 111; proactive review by labor arbitration committee and court 34–36; special 32; suspension of 39, 40; between unjustified wage deduction and unjustified wage arrear 199–201, 343
limited liability company: outstanding wages of 260–262
long-term unpaid leave 10, 55, 61, 62, 247, 249

major change in objective situation 185, 195, 236–239, 241–243, 252
maternity insurance 44, 126, 326, 330–331
maternity leave 11, 61, 125, 126, 203, 330–331; employees' entitlement for 125–126
medical care leave 96, 135, 138–140, 331–332, 345; for cancer 119–121; employee not recovered after expiration of 121–123; employees' pay during 116–118, **117**; fixed-term employee expires before 258; health incompetence for work after 208, 230; labor capacity appraisal after expiration of 121–124; for non-work-related injury 123, 124, 131, 135, 223, 224, 244, 331, 340, 347, 349; position transfer after expiration of 184; retirement age during 223, 224
medical incompetence 340
medical treatment allowance 124, 230–231, 258, 332
mental damages 96; in employment disputes, claim for 153–155; occupational diseases/work-related injuries and 155–156; workplace rights and 169, 336–337
mental harm 154, 155
minimum wage standard: business closure and 159–160; for causal employees 158; double-wage damages and 81; economic loss and 178; for employees' received wages 157; employee wages and 334–335; epidemic lockdown and 160; fines and 175; forced resignation and 210; high-temperature allowance and 114, 331; illegal termination and 254, 255; medical care leave and 332; night allowance 164–165; non-competition allowance and 307, 310; overtime wage and 101, 336; for paid work injury leave 137; piecework system and 161–163; poor performance and 240; during probation period 83; punitive damages and 250; purchase of social insurance and 326; right to appeal 41; sick leave wage and 117, 118; social insurance and 44
mixed employment 180–182
multiple employment relationships, termination for 208, 246–247
mutual agreement, termination by 208, 346

night allowance 164–165
non-competition: agreement *see* non-competition agreement; allowance *see* non-competition allowance; contractual damages 305, 308; definition of 302–303; liability for breach on 302–303; on-the-job obligation 305–306; penalty 310–311; and trade secrets, distinguished 302
non-competition agreement 351–352; cancellation of 309–310; lacking of non-competition allowance clause 306–308; legality of signing 304–305
non-competition allowance 272; clause in non-competition agreement 306–310, 351, 352; employer's payment of 302, 303; labor dispatch contracts and 324; legality of 308–309; obligations of 305, 306; penalty and 311; standard of 310
non-publicity of trade secrets 277–281
non-work-related injury: circumstances of 128; death due to 225–227, 345; medical care leave for 123, 124, 131, 135, 223, 224, 244, 331, 340, 347, 349; medical treatment allowance for 230; retirement for 258
no-pay trial work 49
nursing fees: after disability determination 334; during paid work injury leave 334

occupational diseases 22, 125, 128; classification of 131–132; definition 130; diagnosis of 130–131; employees' entitlement for 144–147, 154, 333; handling

of 332–333; hazard and 150–151; judicial practices for wage standards 136; labor capacity appraisal for 135, 140–141; liability for 96; and mental damages 155–156; recurrence 132, 134
occupational hazard 130–131; diseases and 151–152; injuries and 333; non-termination protection 244; pneumoconiosis-related 150–151
one-off disability allowance 140, **142–143**
on-the-job misconduct 263
operational adjustment, and economic redundancy 236
overtime pay 107, 157, 161, 164, 165, 336; calculation of 100–101, 158; on public holidays 323; under special work hour systems, calculation of 101–102; in wage standard for double-wage damages 79–81
overtime wage 20, 336; calculation of 100–101, 111, 158, 335; deductions of 199, 200, 210, 257, 343; medical treatment allowance under 231; night allowance under 164, 165; for package system 164; for piecework 162; on public holidays 97; refusal to pay 201–202; right to claim 323; under special work hour systems, calculation of 101, 102; time-off in lieu offsetting 103, 104

package wage system 164
paid annual leave 329; employees' entitlement for 104–106; management of 106–107
paid sick leave 116, 118–119, 329, 331
paid work injury leave 132, **142–143**, 149, 184, 187, 239, 244, 333; application for extension of 138–140; continues working after 147–148; employee not recovered after expiration of 134–136; labor capacity appraisal after expiration of 136–138; length of 144; nursing fees during 147, 334; retirement age during 223, 224; wages in 333–334
part-time employment contract 322; rights and obligations under 323
paternity leave 330–331; rights 110–111
payment in lieu of notice 233, 240, 241, 247, 258, 347–349; calculation of 252–253
penalty: administrative 202–204, 317–318, 343; criminal 343; non-competition 310–311; *see also* fine
pension insurance 21, 45, 218, 224, 226, 255, 321, 326; basic 24, 25, 219–223, 225, 227, 345; rural 24; social 24, 44, 222; for volunteers 16
performance of employment contract: administrative penalties 202–204; collective strike 188–191; commissions and bonuses 165–166; disciplinary action *see* disciplinary action; equity incentive agreement 191–197; minimum wage standard *see* minimum wage standard; mixed employment 180–182; night allowance 164–165; package wage system 164; piecework 161–163; received wages 157–158; suspension investigation 173–174; unjustified wage arrear *see* unjustified wage arrear; unjustified wage deduction *see* unjustified wage deduction; wage reduction *see* wage reduction
permanent employment contract 2, 6, 15, 54, 64, 82, 91, 92, 118, 322; circumstances to sign 71–72; double-wage damages for not signing 69–71; labor dispatch company 28; signed after two consecutive fixed-term employment contracts 72–76, 91
personal disputes *see* civil servant disputes
personal information: administrative penalties for violation of 317–318; civil damages for violating 316–317; criminal offense in 318–319; cross-border provision of 312–314; impact of 311–312; outbound transfer of 315–316; outbound transferring 314, 315; protection 311–319, 352–353; protection certification pathway 314; standard contract, registration for 314–315
personal liberty 202–204, 212, 244
piecework: quota and unit price 162–163; wage system 161–162, 190, 335
poaching *see* customer poaching
poor performance, termination for 239–241
poor working environment 154
position transfer: based on company rules and regulations 341; for change in objective condition 340–341; circumstances of 184–186; discretionary 341; legal consequences of 178–180, 186–188; for medical incompetence 340; resignation for 187, 213–214; and wage reduction 167–168
probation period 322, 327–328; damages 38, 85; double-wag damages 61; illegal 41; legal consequences of 84–85; length of 81–82; reneges on wage commitment 45; resignation in 209; rights and obligations of 82–84; second 85–87; termination in 262–264; termination of employment after 87–88; trial work 49
productional transfer, and economic redundancy 236
professional ethics 84, 177, 272, 320, 337, 347; basic 171, 338; special 171; violation of 124, 171, 173, 178, 246, 265, 267, 350
public holidays 97

punitive damages, for illegal termination 32, 124, 141, 248–249, 252, 253, 257, 259
purchase of social insurance 326

received wages 79, 250, 334; calculation of 157–158
recruitment: discrimination 153–154, 169, 337; employee 344–345; fraud, termination for 89–90
regular work schedule 19
reinstatement 131, 196, 207, 244, 248, 253, 254, 258–259, 350
relocation *see* position transfer
remuneration 16, 49, 321, 323, 325, 329, 334; accrued annual leave and 108; arrears 199, 200; bankruptcy and 227; equal civil relationship with company 27; equal pay for equal work 127; equity incentive and 192–195, 342; interruption and suspension of limitation of arbitration 39; for labor outsourcing 26; legal consequences for 20; liability for 259–260; period 14; probation period damages and 38; refusal to sign in contract after joining the company 47; refusing to pay 205; for student intern workers 49–51; unjustified labor 32; for volunteers 16, 17
representative office of a foreign company 28–29
resignation 344; employee 208; forced *see* forced resignation; inadequate notice of, employer's losses and 263–265; procedure for 209–210; for relocation 213–214
responsibility accidents 204
retirement: age of *see* age of retirement; internal 11n33, 247n87; statutory age for 24–25, 215–217
retroactive signing of employment contract: exemptions from double-wage damages 56–57; judicial decisions on 57–58
reverse engineering immunity 293–295
right holders: burden of proof 284–287; and legal existence of trade secrets 276–277; and non-publicity of trade secrets 277–281; proving infringement acts of trade secrets 284–285; in trade secret infringement cases 295–296

safeguarding rights, cost of 299
salary *see* wage
security assessment pathway 313
segmented treatment rule 251, 252
self-employed individuals 12
service years for current employer 116, **117**, 329
sexual harassment 169
Shenzhen work injury entitlements **142–143**
sick leave 331–332; apply for 115; communication of 124–125; employees' entitlement for 104–105, 116; employees' pay during 116–118; legal consequences of 20; paid 116, 118–119, 329, 331
social insurance 16, 18, 46, 345, 350; agencies 128, 203; authority 152; deduction of 18, 20, 27; for fixed-term employment contracts 72; fund 133, 225–227; imprisonment for crime and 244–245; institutions 149, 150; irregular and general work hours entitled to paid sick leave 118; non-compliance in 251; payment registration 216; premiums 203; purchase of 19, 46, 179, 181, 211, 326; registration status 217, 219; retirement age and 223; types of 43–45, 323; for volunteers 16
Social Insurance Bureau 126, 151, 154
special non-termination protection, in employers' layoffs 243–244
special protection, for female employees 127, 330
standard information standard contract pathway 313–314
standard work hours 3, 6, 8, 97, 101, 102, 161–165, 322, 323
student intern workers 49–51
supplementary damages 32, 257, 342, 343
The Supreme Court's Judicial Interpretation (2020): after two consecutive fixed-term contracts 74, 76, 77; compensation of losses after termination 266; contractor relationship in daily life 13; criminal liabilities 301; criminal offence in Personal Information Protection Act 318; economic compensation for employees' forced resignation 210; immunities for trade secret infringement 293–294; interruption and suspension of the limitation of arbitration 39; labor arbitration after reaching compensation agreement 271; multiple employment relationships 247; non-competition agreement, cancellation of 309–310; obligation to pay double-wage damages 55; position transfer 179; procedure of notifying termination to trade union 228; refusal to pay overtime wages 199, 201; wage reduction 167suspension investigation 173–174, 338
suspension of limitation of arbitration 39, 40

technological innovation, and economic redundancy 236
termination: for ability incompetence 233; after probation period 87–88; age of retirement

and 219–223; certificate of 46, 256; with clear evidence 214; for commiting a crime 208; company deregistration and 227–228; of contractor relationship 223, 224; definition 207; for economic redundancy 209; economic redundancy and 233–236, 241–243; employees refusal to sign an employment contract and 47; for employment contract expiration 209; of employment for employee's incompetence 349; fault and 215; for gross misconduct 349–350; for health incompetence 208, 233, 346–347; illegal *see* illegal termination; for invalid employment contracts 208; lawful 346–348; for major change in objective situation 236–239, 241–243, 348–349; for materiality of false qualifications 89; for multiple employment relationships 208, 246–247; by mutual agreement 208, 214, 346; payment in lieu of notice 252–253; poor performance and 239–241; during probationary period 232; procedure for notifying the trade union 228–230; processes for 208–209; for recruitment fraud 89–90; reinstatement and 207, 244, 248, 253, 254, 258–259; repeated disputes and 215; requirements for 231–233; retirement age during their medical treatment 223–225; right to terminate second fixed-term contract 75–76; unemployment insurance benefit after 255–256; unequivocal 214; for violation of company rules and regulations 208, 232
three protected periods 127, 204, 207, 243, 347
time-off in lieu 96, 97, 100, 157, 322, 336; offsetting overtime hours 103–104
tortfeasors, in trade secret infringement cases 295–296
trade secret infringement 272–275, 279, 282, 285, 288, 290; acquisition infringement 282, 284, 285, 299; administrative liabilities for 300; cases, right holders and tortfeasors in 295–296; civil liability for 296–299; criminal liability for 300–301; customer poaching infringement 290–292; disclosure infringement 281, 282, 284, 285; immunities for 292–295; types of 282–284; use infringement 283
trade secrets: information, types of 281–282; infringement *see* trade secret infringement; legal criteria for 274–275; legal existence of 276–277; and non-competition, distinguished 302; non-publicity of 277–281; protection of 272–301, 350–351; right holders of 284–287
training service agreement 32, 262, 268–270, 339
transfer *see* position transfer
trial period *see* probation period
unemployment insurance 44, 207, 225, 255–256
unjustified wage arrear 342–343; by employer 197–199; limitation of arbitration 199–201; overtime wage and 201, 210; supplementary damage and 257
unjustified wage deduction 168, 342–343; by employer 197–199; limitation of arbitration 199–201; overtime wage and 201, 210
unused annual leave pay 96, 105–108, 110, 157, 181, 329, 331, 334
use infringement 283

volunteers, as employees 16–17

wage: arrear, unjustified *see* unjustified wage arrear; causal employment 14; deduction, unjustified *see* unjustified wage deduction; due 79, 81, 157, 158, 197, 250, 334; employee 334–336; employees on call at home 19–20; full-time employment 14; loss, after illegal termination 253–255; minimum standard *see* minimum wage standard; overtime *see* overtime wage; piecework 161–163, 190, 335; received 79, 157–158, 250, 334; reduction *see* wage reduction; standard, for double-wage damages 79–81; *see also individual entries*
wage discrimination 168, 336
wage reduction 335–336; acceptance of 167; legality of 166–168; position transfer and 167–168
waiting-for-work 61, 159, 200, 215, 234
work-break entitlement 114–115
work hours system: general *see* general work hours; irregular *see* irregular work hours
work injuries: circumstances of 128–130; entitlements *see* work injury entitlement; identification of 11n35, 130; insurance *see* work injury insurance; medical expenses for 334; recognition and handling of 332–333; recurrence 130, 132–134, 147n121, 333; *see also* work-related injuries
work injury entitlements 96, 130, 131, 140, 141, 144–156, 333–334; disability identified by labor capacity appraisal 144–146; hospitalization meal allowance 146; nursing fees during paid work injury leave 147; nursing fees for post disability identification 147; Shenzhen **142–143**; treatment of medical expenses 146
Work Injury Insurance Fund 134, 136, 140–142, 146–151, 334
work injury insurance occupational diseases and 146; absence of 150; commercial 152;

contribution rations for 44; irregular and general work hours entitled to paid sick leave 118; nursing fees for post disability identification 147; for pregnant employees 126; purchase of 22, 43, 133, 141, 326
work injury leave pay, continues working after 147–148
workplace rights 336–337
work-related injuries: circumstances of 129–130; completion of labor capacity appraisal for 140–141; employee entitlements for 144–147; handling of 332; judicial practices for wage standards 136; labor capacity appraisal for 123; legal consequences of 20; liability for 9, 22, 130; and mental damages 154–156; recurrence of 130, 132; retirement age and 21; rights to stop work due to 188; *see also* work injuries
written employment contracts, signing 326–327

FSC
www.fsc.org
MIX
Papier | Fördert gute Waldnutzung
FSC® C083411

Kolibri 360 GmbH
Ferdinand-Jühlke-Straße 7
99095 Erfurt, Deutschland
produktsicherheit@kolibri360.de